The Coaches' Handbook

MW00817197

This comprehensive practitioner guide provides an accessible evidenced based approach aimed at those new to coaching and who may be undertaking coach training for a certificate in coaching or professional credentials or accreditation with the AC, ICF, EMCC, CMI or ILM. The book will also be useful for those who want to enhance their coaching skills.

The Coaches' Handbook is edited by Jonathan Passmore, an internationally respected expert and executive coach, with chapters from leading coaching practitioners from across the world. The book is divided into seven sections. Section one examines the nature of coaching, its boundaries, the business case for coaching and how organisations can build a coaching culture. Section two focuses on deepening our self-understanding and understanding our clients, the non-violent communications mindset and the coaching relationship. Section three focuses on the key skills needed for coaching including goal-setting, powerful questions, active listening, using direct communications and the role of silence, emotions and challenge in coaching. Section four offers a range of coaching approaches including behavioural, person-centred, solution-focused, psychodynamic, neuroscience, narrative, positive psychology, out-door eco-coaching, team coaching, careers coaching and integrated coaching. Section five focuses on fundamental issues in coaching such as ethics and contracting and evaluation. Section six explores continuous professional development, reflection and the role of supervision, as well as how to establish your coaching business. The final section contains a host of coaching tools which practitioners can use to broaden their practice.

Unique in its scope, this key text will be essential reading for coaches, academics and students of coaching. It is an important text for anyone seeking to understand the best practice approaches that can be applied to their coaching practice, including human resources, learning and development and management professionals, and executives in a coaching role.

Jonathan Passmore is Director of the Henley Centre for Coaching. He has also held a number of executive and non-executive board roles and worked for global consulting firms, including PwC and IBM. He has also edited and written 30 books and over 100 scientific articles.

"This thought-provoking book provides an accessible pathway from current academic thinking to practical advice. Recommended reading for all coaches wishing to deepen their knowledge and sharpen their practice".

Dr Gill Stevens, Programme director – Coaching, University of Cambridge, UK

"Coaching is the personnel development instrument of the future. This handbook provides an excellent practical and scientifically sound foundation for preparing for this future as a coach."

Professor Dr Carsten C. Schermuly, Vice President of Research at SRH Berlin University of Applied Sciences, Germany

"This is the go-to book for novice coaches through to seasoned practitioners".

Jeannette Marshall, Director of Accreditation, Association for Coaching (Global)

"A must-read handbook for students, novice and experienced coaches and academics. With the right balance of cutting-edge theory and practice, this is by far the most thought-provoking and comprehensive book on coaching currently available."

Dr Andrea Giraldez-Hayes, Programme Director – Coaching and Positive Psychology, University of East London, UK

"What a fantastic, science-based practitioners handbook! Great value for all those who want to become dedicated professional coaches helping to unlock peoples' full potential in an increasingly challenging world. An absolute must have for any coaching student!"

Dr Robert Wegener, Co-Responsible of the Coaching Studies FHNW (University of Applied Sciences North Western Switzerland), Initiator of the International Coaching Conference, author and editor, and Business Coach

"As professional coaching begins to reach a stage of maturity, it is crucial we have a credible resource supported by thoughtful and evidence-based reflection. This handbook offers the pathway for sustainable practice and decision-making either for those interested in their development as coaches or for those looking for a reference book in coaching services."

Alexandra Barosa Pereira, Programme Director – Professional Certificate in Executive Coaching, Nova Business School, Lisbon, Portugal

"I love the way this book is like being able to knock on the doors of the individual expert practitioners, and have a chat with each of them, all in one place."

Dr Patricia Bossons, Leadership Development and Coaching Lead, Massey Business School, New Zealand

"The scope and substance of this book make it ideal as a text for coach education and as a resource on every coach's bookshelf."

Francine Campone, Ed.D., MCC, Coaching & Coach Development

The Coaches' Handbook

The Complete Practitioner Guide for
Professional Coaches

Edited by Jonathan Passmore

Routledge
Taylor & Francis Group

LONDON AND NEW YORK

First published 2021
by Routledge
2 Park Square, Milton Park, Abingdon, Oxon OX14 4RN

and by Routledge

52 Vanderbilt Avenue, New York, NY 10017

Routledge is an imprint of the Taylor & Francis Group, an informa business

© 2021 selection and editorial matter, Jonathan Passmore; individual chapters, the contributors

The right of Jonathan Passmore to be identified as the author of the editorial material, and of the authors for their individual chapters, has been asserted in accordance with sections 77 and 78 of the Copyright, Designs and Patents Act 1988.

All rights reserved. No part of this book may be reprinted or reproduced or utilised in any form or by any electronic, mechanical, or other means, now known or hereafter invented, including photocopying and recording, or in any information storage or retrieval system, without permission in writing from the publishers.

Trademark notice: Product or corporate names may be trademarks or registered trademarks, and are used only for identification and explanation without intent to infringe.

British Library Cataloguing-in-Publication Data
A catalogue record for this book is available from the British Library

Library of Congress Cataloging-in-Publication Data
Names: Passmore, Jonathan, editor.
Title: The coaches' handbook: the complete practitioner guide for professional coaches/edited by Jonathan Passmore.
Description: First Edition. | New York: Routledge, 2020. |
Includes bibliographical references and index. | Identifiers: LCCN 2020020167 (print) | LCCN 2020020168 (ebook) | ISBN 9780367539207 (hardback) | ISBN 9780367546199 (paperback) | ISBN 9781003089889 (ebook)
Subjects: LCSH: Executives–Training of. | Mentoring in business. | Leadership–Study and teaching.
Classification: LCC HD30.4 .C6263 2020 (print) | LCC HD30.4 (ebook) | DDC 658.3/124–dc23
LC record available at https://lccn.loc.gov/2020020167
LC ebook record available at https://lccn.loc.gov/2020020168

ISBN: 978-0-367-53920-7 (hbk)
ISBN: 978-0-367-54619-9 (pbk)
ISBN: 978-1-003-08988-9 (ebk)

Typeset in Bembo
by Deanta Global Publishing Services, Chennai, India

Contents

Editor's bio

Jonathan Passmore

Jonathan is an executive coach, author and researcher based at Henley Centre for Coaching, Business School, University of Reading and University of Evora. He was ranked in the Global Gurus Top 30 (2020) and Top 8 coach in the Thinkers 50 coaching list (2019). He has worked in consulting for IBM, PWC and Embrion over the past two decades. He is now professor of coaching and behavioural change at Henley, UK, and professor of psychology at Evora, Portugal. He has published widely with over 30 books and 100 scientific papers and book chapters on themes of coaching, change and leadership. Recent books including: *Mindfulness at Work*, *Top Business Psychology Models*, *Becoming a Coach* and *Excellence in Coaching* which have been translated into more than a dozen languages. He maintains an active coaching and supervision practice supporting leaders and coaches in their development journeys.

Contributors' bios

Tim Anstiss

Tim is a medical doctor specialising in behaviour change and wellbeing improvement. He is a member of the BPS and has been involved in several national and international behaviour change initiatives. He has written widely on the development of third wave cognitive-behavioural approaches and their adaptation to workplace coaching.

Tatiana Bachkirova

Tatiana is Professor of Coaching Psychology and Director of the International Centre for Coaching and Mentoring Studies at Oxford Brookes University, UK. She is a recognised author, international speaker and an active researcher.

Paul J. Barbour

Paul is an executive and team coach. He is also a writer and speaker with strong interests in team coaching and conflict resolution. He has co-authored with Lucy Widdowson *Building Top Performing Teams* (2021). Paul is also a Lead Tutor on team coaching at the Henley Centre for Coaching, Henley Business School (University of Reading, UK).

Michael Beale

Michael is a Goldsmith Certified coach who works worldwide. He offers stakeholder coaching to corporates and personal mastery programmes to individuals to help them develop themselves and their businesses.

Robert Biswas-Diener

Robert is a positive psychologist, author and academic at Portland State University. He has published widely, including *Positive Psychology Coaching* (2007), *Happiness: Unlocking the mysteries of psychological wealth* (2008) and *Practicing Positive Psychology Coaching* (2010).

Richard Bryant-Jefferies

Richard is the author of over 20 books on counselling themes, including two novels. He worked as a primary care and specialist alcohol counsellor and manager of substance misuse services, and Head of Equality and Diversity at an NHS Trust in London. He is married and lives in Surrey. He can be contacted via: www.richardbj.co.uk.

Alex Burn

Alexandra is an independent business coach and L&D professional, working with individuals, teams and organisations. Alex's passion for coaching and nature has led to her research into the benefits of outdoor coaching at the Henley Centre for Coaching, Henley Business School (University of Reading, UK).

Stephen Burt

Stephen is a leadership coach for whom high-quality listening is the core of both coaching and leadership. He has written on the theme of listening: 'The Art of Listening in Coaching and Mentoring' (2019). He hones his own listening skills through performing jazz and improvised comedy.

David Clutterbuck

David is one of the original founders of the EMCC, and has written widely on coaching, mentoring and leadership, including *Coaching the Team at Work* (2007, 2020) and '*The Practitioner's Handbook of Team Coaching*' (2019). He is a Visiting Professor at the Henley Centre for Coaching, Henley Business School (University of Reading, UK).

Edith Coron

Edith is an executive coach (PCC-ICF) and coach supervisor who previously worked as a journalist. Her career spans four continents. She chairs the ICF-France Committee on Digital/Artificial Intelligence and Coaching.

Kristina Crabbe

Kristina is an accredited coach, coaching super-visor, Time to Think teacher and Human Resources consultant. She holds an MSc in Coaching and Behavioural Change and is a Doctoral student researching 'The value and impact of coaching super-vision for coach development and the wider system'.

Ian Day

Ian is the co-author of '*Challenging Coaching: Going Beyond Traditional Coaching to Face the FACTS*' (www.challengingcoaching.co.uk), an executive coach with over 20 years' experience of working internationally at c-suite level and course director for the coaching qualifications delivered at the University of Warwick in the UK. Ian has presented at international coaching conferences and is a highly respected coach.

David Drake

David is the CEO of The Moment Institute in California, the founder of Narrative Coaching and Integrative Development, a Thought Leader for Institute of Coaching at Harvard, and author of over 60 publications.

Julie Flower

Julie is a leadership and team development coach, consultant and facilitator, specialising in versatility to address meaningful challenges within complex systems. Her eclectic approach includes techniques from improvised comedy.

Karen Foy

Karen is an experienced accredited coach with an MSc in coaching psychology. She runs an independent coaching practice and is also a lecturer in coaching at the Henley Centre for Coaching, Henley Business School (University of Reading, UK).

Alison Hardingham

Alison is a psychologist, accredited executive coach and coaching supervisor. In 2004 she wrote *The Coach's Coach*, which is still widely read today. She was one of the founding members of the Henley Centre for Coaching, Henley Business School (University of Reading, UK) and its coach training programmes.

Rachel Hawley

Rachel is a Leadership Associate at the NHS Leadership Academy and co-author of *Values and Ethics in Coaching* (2017). Her doctoral study at Sheffield Hallam University explores influences on leadership for public engagement.

Ioanna Iordanou

Ioanna is a Reader in Human Resource Management (Coaching and Mentoring) at Oxford Brookes Business School, co-author of *Values and Ethics in Coaching* (2017) and co-editor of *The Practitioner's Handbook of Team Coaching* (2019).

Karen Izod

Karen is a consultant, researcher and academic specialising in group and organisational dynamics. She is Course Lead for the Doctorate in Consulting to Organisations at the Tavistock and Portman NHS Trust.

Ann James

Ann is an Executive Fellow at the Henley Centre for Coaching, Henley Business School (University of Reading, UK), where she tutors on coaching programmes and provides supervision. She brings the principles of reflective practice into the everyday for herself and her clients.

Rebecca J. Jones

Rebecca is an Associate Professor in Coaching at the Henley Centre for Coaching, Henley Business School (University of Reading, UK), Programme Director for Henley's MSc in Coaching and Behavioural Change and a Chartered Psychologist. Her research interests lie in examining the factors that influence coaching effectiveness, a topic on which she has published widely.

Sarah Leach

Sarah is an experienced Life and Career Coach (ICF PCC). She is the owner of Stride Coaching and Consulting. Sarah works with senior executives and teams to enable personal and professional growth. Sarah is also a lecturer in coaching at the Henley Centre for Coaching, Henley Business School (University of Reading, UK).

Suzanne Lines

Suzanne is a Master Certified Coach (ICF, 2012), experienced supervisor, mediator and a member of faculty at the Henley Centre for Coaching, Henley Business School (University of Reading, UK) and runs her own private practice. She is co-founder of abamentis ltd and focusses on leadership and top team performance. She has over 25 years of global business development experience working to board level with FTSE 50 and entrepreneurial companies with Ernst & Young, DeAgostini-Rand McNally and the BBC.

Ruth E. Price

Ruth is a chartered psychologist, certified coach and psychometric practitioner. An experienced consultant who has assessed, recruited and developed individuals internationally at senior levels including c-suite, she is now the director of an executive development and coaching practice. She holds a Psychology PhD and is a lecturer in coaching at Henley Centre for Coaching, Henley Business School (University of Reading).

Patricia Riddell

Patricia is Professor of Applied Neuroscience in the School of Psychology and Clinical Language Sciences at the University of Reading. She has published widely, including *The Neuroscience of Leadership Coaching*. She is also a member of faculty at the Henley Centre for Coaching, Henley Business School (University of Reading, UK).

Jenny Rogers

Jenny is one of the UK's most experienced executive coaches, with 26 years' of successful experience. Her clients include Chief Executives and Directors of some of the UK's best-known organisations. She is a popular speaker and writer, with titles including *Coaching with careers* and *Coaching with Personality Types*.

Aboodi Shabi

Aboodi is currently a lecturer in Coaching and Behavioural Change at the Henley Centre for Coaching, Henley Business School (University of Reading, UK). He has worked in executive coaching and coach training since the mid-1990s. He was founding Co-President of the UK ICF Chapter.

Charlotte Sills

Charlotte is a coach, coach supervisor and also a psychotherapist. She is Professor of Coaching at Ashridge Business School and teaches on their Masters in Executive Coaching and Diploma in Organisational Supervision programmes.

David Tee

David is an independent coaching psychologist and researcher. He is the editor of *The Coaching Psychologist*, published by the British Psychological Society, and co-editor of *Coaching Researched* (2020).

Arthur F. Turner

Arthur is a practising coaching scholar and development facilitator who has taken a particular interest in the creative side of the topic of executive coaching. His interests include walking, use of finger puppets, art and pictures, metaphors and, in a current phase of investigation, he is exploring silence, laughter and humour in the coaching relationship.

Christian van Nieuwerburgh

Christian is executive director of Growth Coaching International, and Professor of Coaching and Positive Psychology at the University of East London. He has written widely, with several books and research articles including *Introduction to Coaching Skills, Advanced Coaching Practice* and *Coaching in Education*.

Anna-Marie Watson

Anna-Marie is an executive coach, coach supervisor and expedition leader with a serious passion for the outdoors. She's on a mission to encourage fellow coaches work with their clients in the natural environment and move more. She co-leads the Global ICF Executive and Leadership Community of Practice.

Lucy Widdowson

Lucy is an accredited executive and team coach. A thought leader and the UK ICF lead on team coaching and is the co-author of *Building Top Performing Teams* (2021). Lucy is also a lead tutor on team coaching at the Henley Centre for Coaching, Henley Business School (University of Reading, UK).

Rob Willson

Rob is a cognitive-behaviour therapist, trainer, researcher and author based in London, UK. He has a keen interest in the relationship between therapy and coaching and teaches on the MSc Coaching and Behavioural Change at the Henley Centre for Coaching, Henley Business School (University of Reading, UK).

Julia Yates

Julia is a chartered occupational psychologist and career coach. She is a senior lecturer in psychology at City, University of London, researching and teaching career development and coaching psychology and has published several books including: *The Careers Coaching Handbook* (2013) and *The Careers Coaching Toolkit* (2018).

Section 1

Coaching context

1 Coaching defined and explored

Jonathan Passmore

Introduction

Before we can start to coach, we need to understand what coaching is, and what it is not. However, one challenge coaching practitioners face is that there is no universally agreed-upon definition of coaching. In this chapter, we argue that while understanding the origins of coaching and a variety of its different definitions, most coaches need to think for themselves and discern what coaching is in their context, organisation or culture. First, we explore a range of commonly used definitions and consider the roots of coaching. Then we will compare coaching with other popular organisation interventions such as mentoring, performance management, appraisals and 1–1's as well as discussing counselling and occupational health, before closing by encouraging coaches to develop their own elevator pitch to describe what they do and how they do it.

What is coaching?

Answering this question is both simple and complex. Coaching has been around for three or more decades and most people have an idea of what coaching is. This has been helped by the fact that most writers have broadly similar views. While there has been broad agreement over these years, different writers, professional bodies and practitioners have emphasised different aspects of coaching in their definitions.

But why should we be interested in discussing a definition? There are several good reasons why starting with a definition is a very good place to start. Firstly, if you are providing a service to clients, individuals or organisations, the coach needs to be able to explain what they are offering. Having a clear elevator pitch to articulate what you do is vital for all coaches. A second reason is that if you are learning about a topic, knowing what is or is not enables you to establish boundaries for what you need to learn and what knowledge is not part of the topic. A third reason is for research; we need to define what we are doing, to ensure what we are doing is X, rather than Y, and thus establish that it is X, rather than Y that leads to positive outcome. The following analogy illustrates this point. Both French fries and bananas are yellow and oblong. However, if we eat too much of one of these, we are likely to put on weight and, over time, increase our chances of coronary heart disease. Understanding the difference between the two can help us to make better choices based on their likely effect on the human body.

The roots of coaching?

In her review of the history of coaching, Leni Wildflower notes that the roots of coaching have spread far and wide (2010). Wildflower highlights several important strands that have shaped and influenced coaches for good, as well as ill. One strand is the human potential movement. This arose out of the counterculture movements in the USA during the 1960s. At its heart was a belief that the development of human potential was far greater than we had recognised and humans had within them a capacity for self-development which can unleash greater happiness, creativity and fulfilment. These ideas were picked up by Michael Murphy, the founder of Esalen Institute in the 1960s, who provided a physical space for thinkers and practitioners to come together. This in turn influenced the work of John Whitmore and Tim Gallwey, as well as Thomas Leonard and Laura Whitworth (Brock, 2009; Brock, 2012).

A second strand was sports coaching, which emerged from the use of coaching in debating societies within universities at the turn of the century. The earliest records date back to the 1910s and 1920s with the work of Trueblood (1911) and Huston (1924), who report the use of coaching as a tool to improve debating performance. These ideas were picked up by university sports teams who started applying the ideas to baseball and American football (Griffiths, 1926).

A third strand identified by Wildflower is the work of the therapists, Sigmund Freud, Carl Jung Fritz and Laura Perls, who argued that development or change could be realised through exploratory conversations to develop greater self-awareness.

A fourth, often-ignored strand is the small but growing development of coaching in the workplace, which dates back to the 1930s. In a short article, the Detroit-based editor of *Factory Management and Maintenance* examined the role of worker development (through training and coaching) to improve factory processes (Gordy, 1937). The article noted how coaching could be used to reduce waste in manufacturing. Other articles followed describing the potential of coaching (Bigelow, 1938). While neither Gordy or Bigelow offered a formal definition of coaching, the use of the term suggests that coaching was being used in the workplace before the start of World War II. However, the arrival of the war meant the term seemed to disappear until the 1960s, when it appeared again in a host of different guises.

How does coaching compare with other interventions?

As we saw in the last section, coaching has drawn from a variety of sources, and different cultures have placed different priorities on these different traditions; for example, in Germany the influence from counselling is stronger than in the US, where the human potential movement has been a significant driver in defining and shaping coaching as we know it today. These different traditions have also influenced professional bodies; for example, the ICF, which has grown out of the US tradition, focuses more on ideas drawn from the human potential movement, while the German Coaching federations such as DBVC have been more influenced by ideas from counselling and psychology.

One way of thinking about coaching is to consider it alongside other widely used organisational interventions, such as appraisals, 1–1 and training. A range of similar interventions is illustrated in Figure 1.1.

We think there are both similarities and differences between each of these. By thinking about the similarities and differences we can better understand what coaching is, and what it is not.

Figure 1.1 Coaching boundaries

One common area of confusion is between coaching, counselling and therapy. Clearly all three types of intervention are usually 1–1 conversations, which are interested in exploring how things might be different from how they are now. However, how they do this is one of the ways they differ. For example, we would suggest that counselling is generally a one-to-one conversation which involves a significant amount of time exploring issues in the past and present. In contrast, coaching, while acknowledging the past and present, encourages a stronger focus on the present and future. In a similar way, therapy often involves a significant focus on the past, with some consideration of the present and future. The types of themes they deal with also differ. One way of thinking about this is what I call the three D's framework (dream, distress and damage). As coaches we can see these three interventions as traffic lights, as illustrated in Figure 1.2. Coaching focuses a client's attention towards their dreams: "What do you imagine being different tomorrow and how can you make this a reality?" In these cases, the coach is green to go ahead with coaching. Counselling recognises that we all experience problems in our lives from managing bereavement, relationship breakdown or anxiety at work. In counselling, the focus is on helping clients manage this distress. These types of issues may be coded as amber. In these cases, the coach may proceed with caution. However, in doing so they need to

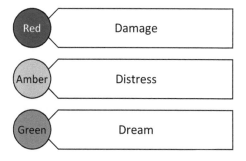

Figure 1.2 Three D's model

answer three questions: Is the issue within the boundaries of the contract agreed with the client? Am I qualified or trained to help the client with this issue? Do I have sufficient experience of working with this type of issue? In the cases where the coach is not qualified, or the experience or issue is outside of the boundary of coaching, the coach should stop and refer the client to another helping professional. Where the scope of the work is within the experience and training of the coach, and has been contracted for, such as relationship coaching, the coach may proceed. Finally, a few people need more sustained and specialist help to manage deeply traumatic events in their life; mental health issues or habituated behaviours, such as drug or alcohol dependency. Therapy is there to manage the damage that these events or mental health conditions present. In these cases, the coach should always stop and refer to a suitably qualified helping professional.

As you think about other interventions used in the workplace, you might start to think about training, mentoring, annual appraisals, performance management, 1–1 meetings, careers counselling, action learning sets and OD consulting. All of these have some similarities with coaching. Most of these are concerned with supporting or enabling learning and change. Most involve setting goals or objectives. Most use conversations as a means to bring about learning or change. However, there are also differences between coaching and each of these. For example, in training there is usually a predetermined syllabus or agenda that the training is required to follow. The activity is also often undertaken in a group, and may involve some form of assessment to evaluate the learning or change which has happened. In mentoring the relationship is likely to be less formal, more long-term and more focused on career and personal development, while in coaching the line manager or sponsor may be involved at the start, and a formal contract and short time-frame may be established for the delivery of the agreed-upon goals between the three parties. We have summarized the similarities and differences between coaching and mentoring in Table 1.1.

Table 1.1 Coaching and mentoring

Criteria	Coaching	Mentoring
Level of formality	More formal: Typically involving a written contract or agreement.	Less formal: Typically, word of mouth agreement.
Who's involved in contracting	Two or three parties: Can often involve a sponsor or line manager in an initial tripartite meeting at the start and at the end.	Two parties: Mentor and mentee.
Length of contract	Shorter: Typically, 4–12 meetings agreed over 12 months or less.	Longer: Typically, unspecified number of meetings, often runs over 3–5 years (and beyond).
Focus	More performance focus: Typically concerned with development of skills for current role and performance.	More career-focused: Typically concerned with the long-term career development.
Level of sector knowledge	More generalist: Typically, coaches have limited sector knowledge.	More sector knowledge: Typically, mentors are a respected person in the organisation or sector.
Training	More training: Typically, coaches are trained and accredited.	Less training: Typically, are untrained or may have a single day's worth of training, but bring formal qualifications in the role of sector.

Table 1.2 Coaching and other interventions

Comparison	Similarities	Differences
Coaching and counselling		
Coaching and training		
Coaching and OD consulting		
Coaching and mentoring		
Coaching and performance management		
Coaching and carers counselling		
Coaching and annual appraisals		

As you reflect on these similarities and differences between coaching and mentoring, other similarities and differences may come to mind in relation to the other interventions we described above, such as training and performance management. Of course, our individual experiences and how that intervention (such as appraisals) is undertaken in our organisation will make a big difference, but just reflecting on each of these can help us start to narrow down what it is that is distinctive about coaching. We have set out a table (Table 1.2) to encourage your personal reflections based on your own experiences in your organisation or culture.

In the next section, we start to move towards a definition of coaching, or maybe we should more accurately say definitions of coaching. We use the plural as we don't hold the view that one definition trumps all. We recognise that coaching is not one single thing but that its application needs to reflect the systemic and cultural context in which it is situated and the unique needs of the individual and organisation. What is important is that each coach should be explicit about what they mean by the term coaching, and that they make this clear to clients in their advertising, contracting and in the delivery of their coaching services.

Defining coaching

In the previous section we discussed a range of other interventions, which have similarities with, but are not, coaching. In fact, coaches can often slip into these ways of working, thus understanding more about coaching's brothers and sisters (such as appraisals or mentoring) can help us better understand what true coaching is. In this section we discuss some of the most popular definitions. Our aim is to offer a variety of perspectives, or flavours. Each one, while still being "ice cream", reflects the context in which it was developed and the purpose and audience for which it was intended, and thus come in many flavours.

Possibly the most widely cited definition is John Whitmore's. Whitmore is widely recognised as one of the founding fathers of coaching. He suggested that coaching was about: "unlocking a person's potential to maximise their own performance. It is helping them to learn rather than teaching them – a facilitation approach" (Whitmore, 1992, p. 8).

Whitmore drew heavily on Timothy Gallwey's inner game model. Gallwey had noted that, in sport performance, the internal state of a player was a significant factor. He went further, arguing that it was even more significant than the opponent in individual sports like tennis and golf. If the individual could control their self-talk, sizable performance gains could be made (Gallwey, 1986). John Whitmore built on this idea. He argued that the purpose of coaching was helping individuals develop greater self-awareness and personal responsibility: "Performance coaching is based on awareness and responsibility" (Whitmore, 1992, p. 173).

Other founding writers offered alternative definitions. Laura Whitworth (Kimsee-House et al., 2011), one of the pioneers in the US, along with Thomas Leonard (Brook, 2009), developed co-active coaching which defined coaching as "a relationship of possibilities … based on trust, confidentiality". These perspectives highlighted the nature of the coaching process and its dependency on people, interpersonal interactions and collaboration. This relational aspect distinguishes coaching from training interventions where, arguably, knowledge exchange is at the heart of the process. This perspective has led to one stream of coaching research focusing on interpersonal and relational aspects in the belief that, if the relationship is sound, effective outcomes will result.

In an academic article, Jonathan Passmore and Anette Fillery-Travis (2011) offered a more process-based definition in an attempt to differentiate coaching from mentoring, counselling and other conversation-based approaches to change. They suggested coaching involved "a Socratic-based dialogue between a facilitator (coach) and a participant (client) where the majority of interventions used by the facilitator are open questions which are aimed at stimulating the self-awareness and personal responsibility of the participant".

Tatiana Bachkirova, also writing from an academic perspective, suggested that coaching is "a human development process that involves structured, focused interaction and the use of appropriate strategies, tools and techniques to promote desirable and sustainable change for the benefit of the coachee" (Bachkirova, Cox and Clutterbuck, 2010, p. 1), while Yi-Ling Lai (2014) draws our attention to the reflective processes involved in the process. Coaching is defined as a "reflective process between coaches and coachees which helps or facilitates coachees to experience positive behavioural changes through continuous dialogue and negotiations". Again, positive behavioural changes are pointed out as the main purpose of coaching, with a recognition that a structured process is involved. Moreover, "negotiation" is put forward in Lai's re-interpretation of coaching, suggesting that coaching is a relationship-based learning and development process.

Specialist approaches to coaching

While these writers have focused on generic applications of coaching, coaching has been adopted and adapted to fit specific applications, from executive coaching to health and life coaching; safety coaching to learner driver coaching; and from relationship coaching to prison coaching. Each requires a distinctive approach, to meet the needs of the individual client and their context and in many cases as seen specific definitions offered by writers ion these fields.

Executive coaching

The application of coaching in the workplace, and specifically with senior managers, has led to the development of what has been labelled "executive coaching". At its simplest, executive coaching could be defined as coaching for senior, or c-suite, managers. Richard Kilburg, a US-based psychologist, went further and suggested that executive coaching was distinctive in being:

a helping relationship formed between a client who has managerial authority and responsibility in an organization and a consultant who uses a wide variety of behavioural techniques and methods to help the client achieve a mutually identified set of goals to improve his or her professional performance and personal satisfaction and, consequently, to improve the effectiveness of the client's organization within a formally defined coaching agreement.

(Kilburg, 1996, p. 142)

Similarly, Erik de Haan, (2013), echoing earlier relational definitions, suggested that executive coaching is a relationship-focused development intervention. Both argued that executive coaching was a form of leadership development that took place through a series of contracted, one-to-one conversations with a qualified "coach", and maintained that the process itself was tailored to individuals to enable them to learn through a reflective conversation, but such learning could only occur because of the unique relationship created by the coach based on trust, safety and support.

Both definitions of executive coaching highlight the professional working relationship in the coaching process and the importance of contracting. However, the definition by de Haan and colleagues (de Hann et al., 2013) notes that the process is one delivered by a "qualified coach". This raises the awareness of a "standard" of formal coaching qualifications held by the coach. Given de Haan's own background as a facilitator and coach trainer, this is not surprising, but his definition opens up the discussion about qualifications and standards.

Health coaching

A further strand that has emerged and is continuing to grow in popularity is health coaching. The approach has grown in both the UK, within the National Health Service (NHS) (Evidence Centre, 2014), and in the US, through private health providers. A literature review identified 275 published studies, with the approach now widely used by nurses, doctors and allied health professionals such as physiotherapists and health advisors (Evidence Centre, 2014).

The study defined health coaching as:

a patient-centred process that is based upon behaviour change theory and is delivered by health professionals with diverse backgrounds. The actual health coaching process entails goal setting determined by the patient, encourages self-discovery in addition to content education and incorporates mechanisms for developing accountability in health behaviours.

(Evidence Centre, 2014, p. 3)

A similar definition was offered by Stephen Palmer and colleagues, who defined health coaching as "the practice of health education and health promotion within a coaching context, to enhance the wellbeing of individuals and to facilitate the achievement of their health-related goals" (Palmer, Stubbs and Whybrow, 2003, p. 91). The distinction being the focus on self-discovery, which echoes Whitmore's primary aims of coaching as a process that focus on two goals: Self-awareness and personal responsibility.

However, what is less clear from these definitions is where health coaching starts and finishes. If coaching is employed to help individuals with chronic conditions and to improve health outcomes, does coaching include approaches such as Motivational Interviewing, which is widely used for drug and alcohol treatment, or brief solution-focused therapy and cognitive behavioural therapy, which might be considered for inclusion within the definitions above but which the practitioner delivering it might label their intervention as counselling or therapy? Again, definitions often reflect the context in which they are developed. In this case, Stephen Palmer has a background as a UK psychologist with extensive experience in counselling and health psychology.

Life and wellbeing coaching

A parallel sub-domain to health coaching is "life coaching". Like health coaching, life coaching has become a popular means of helping non-clinical populations in setting and reaching goals and enhancing their wellbeing (Green, Oades and Grant, 2006).

Life coaching can be broadly defined as a collaborative, solution-focused, result-orientated and systematic process in which the coach facilitates the enhancement of life experience and goal attainment in the personal and/or professional life of normal, non-clinical clients (Grant, 2014). In simple terms, life coaching has been often considered to be coaching outside of the work arena; for example, in education (Green, Grant and Rynsaardt, 2007) or coaching for wellbeing (Green, Oades and Grant, 2006).

One possible distinction between life coaching and health coaching is based on who provides the service. "Health coaching" is delivered by health professionals, while "life or wellbeing coaching" is delivered by those outside of the health sector. In the UK and Australia, the term 'life coaching' itself has slipped in popularity being replaced by the term 'wellbeing coaching'.

The continued growth and adaptation of coaching

Coaching continues to grow and spread to new areas beyond business and sports. Coaching is now being applied to support driving development (Passmore and Rehman, 2012; Wilmott and Wilmott, 2018), to improve safety outcomes in safety-critical environments such as offshore oil and gas (Passmore Krauesslar and Avery, 2015), as well as in construction and the military. Coaching is also being applied to maternity and childcare (Golawski, Bamford and Gersch, 2013), to support couples in marital relationships (Williams and Williams, 2011; Ives and Cox, 2015), in prisons (McGregor, 2015) and in sexual relationships (Britton, 2011).

In each case, the definition of what coaching is changes to reflect the context, clients and issues that are at the heart of the conversation. As you reflect on the variety and diversity of both the definitions and the applications of coaching, you may be wondering whether a single definition would make life easier. While we are sure it would, a single one-size-fits-all definition would ignore the complexity of how and with whom coaches work. As Palmer and Whybrow note, "definitions seldom stay static, unless the area has stagnated" (2007, p. 3). In this sense, we hope coaching definitions will continue to change and adapt as coaching moves forward.

Developing your definition

So where does this leave us? Let's refocus on three of the most popular definitions, which we have titled practical, practitioner and academic in Table 1.3.

Table 1.3 Three definitions

Practical definition	Coaching is unlocking a person's potential to maximise their own performance. It is helping them to learn rather than teaching them (Whitmore, 2017).
Practitioner's definition	ICF defines coaching as partnering with clients in a thought-provoking and creative process that inspires them to maximise their personal and professional potential (International Coaching Federation, 2019).
Academic definition	A Socratic-based future-focused dialogue between a facilitator (coach) and a participant (coachee/client), where the facilitator uses open questions, active listening, summaries and reflections which are aimed at stimulating the self-awareness and personal responsibility of the participant (Passmore and Fillery-Travis, 2011).

This, however, is not the end of the story. As you reflect on the context and clients who you work with, what is your definition of coaching? In thinking about this question we would encourage you to take into account the essence of coaching being a collaborative, future-orientated, Socratic conversation. Imagine if you had to explain to a client, in 60 seconds or less, a description of what you do: What is your definition of coaching?

Conclusion

In this chapter we have set the scene, exploring the development of coaching and the debate around coaching definitions. We have offered a variety of definitions, but ultimately we invite each coach to consider their clients, organisation and cultural context to define their own personal approach to coaching within the spirit of the endeavour of developing greater self-awareness and personal responsibility.

References

Bachkirova, T., Cox, E. and Clutterbuck, D. (2010). *The complete handbook of coaching*. London: Sage.

Britton, P. (2011). *The art of sex coaching: expanding your practice*. New York: W. W. Norton and Company.

Brock, V. (2009). 'Coaching pioneers: Laura Whitworth and Thomas Leonard'. *International Journal of Coaching in Organisations*, 1(1), pp. 54–64.

Brock, V. (2012). *The sourcebook of coaching history*, 2nd edition. Self-published.

de Haan, E., Duckworth, A., Birch, D. and Jones, C. (2013). 'Executive coaching outcome research: The contribution of common factors such as relationship, personality match, and self-efficacy'. *Consulting Psychology Journal: Practice and Research*, 65(1), pp. 40–57.

Evidence Centre. (2014). 'Does health coaching work?' Retrieved on 10 January 2019 from https://eoeleadership.hee.nhs.uk/sites/default/files/Does%20health%20coaching%20work%20-%20summary.pdf.

Gallwey, T. (1986). *The inner game of tennis*. London: Pan.

Golawski, A., Bamford, A. and Gersch, I. (2013). *Swings and roundabouts: A self-coaching workbook for parents and those considering becoming parents*. Abingdon: Karnac Books.

Gordy, C. (1937). 'Everyone gets a share of the profits'. *Factory Management and Maintenance*, 95, pp. 82–83.

Green, L.S., Oades, L.G. and Grant, A.M. (2006). 'Cognitive-behavioral, solution-focused life coaching: Enhancing goal striving, well-being, and hope'. *The Journal of Positive Psychology*, 1(3), pp. 142–149.

Green, S. Anthony, Grant, A.M. and Rynsaardt, J. (2007). 'Evidence-based life coaching for senior high school students: Building hardiness and hope'. *International Coaching Psychology Review*, 2(1), pp. 24–32.

Griffith, C.R. (1926). *Psychology of coaching: A study of coaching methods from the point of view of psychology.* New York: Charles Scribner's and Sons.

Huston, R.E. (1924). 'Debate coaching in high school'. *The Quarterly Journal of Speech Education*, 10, pp. 127–143.

ICF. (2019) 'ICF coaching definition'. Retrieved on 2 April 2020 from https://coachfederation.org/about.

Ives, Y. and Cox, E. (2015). *Relationship coaching: The theory and practice of coaching with singles, couples, and parents.* Hove: Routledge.

Kilburg, R.R. (1996). 'Toward a conceptual understanding and definition of executive coaching'. *Consulting Psychology Journal: Practice and Research*, 48(2), pp. 134–144.

Kimsey-House, H., Kimsey-House, K., Sandahl, P. and Whitworth, L. (2011). *Co-active coaching: Changing business, transforming lives*, 3rd ed. Boston: Nicholas Brealey.

Lai, Y-L. (2014). *Enhancing evidence-based coaching through the development of a coaching psychology competency framework: Focus on the coaching relationship.* Guildford, UK: School of Psychology, University of Surrey.

McGregor, C. (2015) *Coaching behind bars: Facing challenges and creating hope in a women's prison.* Maidenhead: OUP-McGraw-Hill.

Palmer, S., Stubbs, I. and Whybrow, A. (2005). 'Health coaching to facilitate the promotion of healthy behaviour and achievement of health-related goals'. *International Journal of Health Promotion*, 14(3), 91–93.

Passmore, J. and Fillery-Travis, A. (2011). 'A critical review of executive coaching research: A decade of progress and what's to come'. *Coaching: An International Journal of Theory, Practice and Research*, 4(2), pp. 70–88.

Passmore, J. and Rehman, H. (2012). 'Coaching as a learning methodology – A mixed methods study in driver development using a randomized controlled trial and thematic analysis'. *International Coaching Psychology Review*, 7(2), pp. 166–184.

Passmore, J. Krauesslar, V. and Avery, R. (2015). 'Safety coaching: A critical literature review of coaching in high hazard industries'. *Industrial and Commercial Training*, 47(4), pp. 195–200. doi: 10.1108/ICT-12-2014-0080.

Trueblood, T.C. (1911). 'Coaching a debating team'. *Public Speaking Review*, 1, pp. 84–85.

Whitmore, J. (1992). *Coaching for performance.* London: Nicholas Brealey.

Wildflower, L. (2010). *The hidden history of coaching.* Maidenhead: Open University Press-McGraw-Hill.

Williams, J. and Williams, J. (2011). *Marriage coaching.* Springfield: GTRC.

Wilmott, G. and Wilmott, C. (2018). *Who's in the driving seat: The driving instructor's guide to client-centred learning.* Oldham: Active Driving Solutions.

2 The business case for coaching

Rebecca J. Jones

Introduction

Does coaching work? What is the return on investment of coaching? Will coaching improve performance? Why should I choose coaching over other forms of development? Questions such as these have dominated conversations in both the coaching literature and amongst organisations using coaching as a development tool. This is not surprising given the demand for organisations to evidence a return on their investment in human capital. In this chapter, I will attempt to address some of these questions by reviewing the evidence-base in relation to coaching effectiveness, with the overall aim of building a business case for coaching.

The growth of coaching

In order to establish a business case for coaching, it is first important to understand why coaching has benefitted from increasing popularity as a learning and development tool, addressing the question: Why has coaching become so popular?

Over the last 30 years, coaching has risen to an industry of over 50,000 professional coaches worldwide, with an annual spend of over \$2 billion (ICF, 2016). The CIPD stated that just over eight out of ten respondents in their 2010 Learning and Development survey reported that they use coaching in their organisations (CIPD, 2010). There is no indication that, since these industry reports, the growth of coaching has slowed, therefore it is likely that the current size of the coaching industry far exceeds these estimates. What explanation is there for the increasing demand from individuals and organisations for coaching?

It is largely agreed that the current business environment is dynamic, volatile, uncertain, complex and ambiguous. Businesses compete on a global scale and competitive advantage now relies much less on the uniqueness of the product or service: Instead, the role of employee talent has become increasingly important. Factors of organisational competitiveness are consequently linked to the knowledge, skills and abilities of the organisations' human resources. Furthermore, if the business environment is dynamic and volatile, in order to retain any competitive advantage, the employee talent must also adapt in-line with the environmental demands. The challenge for individuals to adapt to an ever-changing environment is evident in the woeful change management statistics that indicate that as many as 70 per cent of change management initiatives are unsuccessful (Ashkenas, 2013). Therefore, if we accept the following two assumptions to be true: Human capital is more important than ever for organisational competitive advantage, and human capital needs to be able to effectively adapt to an ever-changing, uncertain business environment, we can start to understand why coaching has increased in popularity.

The role of training, learning and development is to equip employees with the requisite knowledge, skills and abilities to meet dynamic and adapting organisational objectives. Many decades of scholarly research on the impact of training in the workplace has established that it works at improving organisational performance; therefore, organisations have the tools necessary to provide effective training to develop employee talent. In previous decades, training in the workplace was often focused on imparting knowledge and information to the workforce in order to educate them as to how to perform their job roles more effectively. However, in today's organisations, when you couple the provision of instructional training with a web-enabled working environment, the challenge for employees is no longer how to access the information they need to improve and perform their job more effectively (the traditional function of training in the workplace); instead, the challenge for employees is how to make sense of the wealth of information that is readily available at their fingertips – this is where the case for coaching is made. These factors offer a potential explanation for the rise in popularity of coaching. Swart and Harcup (2013) propose that coaching helps managers to expand their insight and develop their sense-making abilities. If the biggest challenge to employees in today's organisations is not how to access information but instead how to filter this information into what is relevant, and understand how to apply this to an ever-changing work environment, then coaching may provide a solution to this challenge.

Coaching is a learning and development approach that places the learner at the centre of the learning experience. Coaching provides the employee with the time, mental space, support and guidance they may need to make sense of the information available to them and explore how to apply it most effectively in their unique situation. One-to-one coaching provides a tailored approach to help understand and apply work-based learning, ensuring that the employee has the capabilities to move with and adapt to a dynamic working environment. Therefore, in this challenging, volatile business environment, coaching provides an adaptable learning and development solution to facilitate sense-making from work experiences and other more instructional forms of training. This context helps to explain why the use of coaching has seen such a meteoric increase in recent years. Evidence suggests that most people believe that coaching is beneficial for them and good for their business (Law, Ireland and Hussain, 2007). Coaching is also viewed favourably by the learners as it provides them with one-to-one support from a respected individual; it can be done on-site so it is convenient; it fits in with the leaner's timeframe and schedule; and often its results can be seen relatively quickly.

Now that we have established why coaching continues to be increasingly popular in organisations, the next step in building a business case for coaching is to establish what "effective" coaching looks like in the context of the following question: Is coaching effective? To do this, I will now review the literature that examines the types of issues that tend to be addressed in coaching.

Common coaching goals

One of the key advantages of coaching is that it is a tailored, bespoke approach to learning and development. Coaching is also lead by the client. This means that the types of issues, problems, challenges and goals of coaching tend to vary widely depending on the needs of the client and their organisation. As coaching is inherently goal-bound, with goals generally forming the starting point of any coaching session, in order to understand what effective coaching looks like, a good starting point is to understand what are the typical goals that clients tend to focus on in coaching. In order to build the business case for coaching, we need to understand what clients tend to focus on in coaching before we can move on to establishing whether coaching actually makes a difference to these issues.

In order to get a clear picture on the types of goals clients tend to address, it is helpful to use a framework of coaching outcomes in order to group data from the evidence-base. Jones, Woods and Guillaume (2016) propose a framework of coaching outcomes which classifies the types of outcomes that can be expected from coaching as affective outcomes (i.e. how the client feels); cognitive outcomes (i.e. how the client thinks); skill-based outcomes (i.e. what the client does) and results outcomes (i.e. what the client achieves). Interestingly, when reviewing the coaching literature, a surprisingly small number of studies provide specific details regarding the types of goals that clients tend to set during coaching. However, a handful of studies were located, and the following section provides an overview of the research that investigates the types of goals and issues that clients tend to focus on, using the framework of coaching outcomes.

Affective outcomes as the focus in coaching

Affective outcomes describe outcomes that we would understand as being outcomes felt by the client or experienced internally by the client; therefore, how does the client feel? These include outcomes such as changes in attitudes, motivation, satisfaction, confidence, resilience or stress. Jones, Woods and Zhou (2019) describe the types of goals set by participants in their field experiment to examine the effectiveness of coaching. In their study, 4 1-hour long sessions were provided to 53 working adults. Clients set between one and four goals each. In terms of the types of goals clients set, 38 per cent of goals were focused on addressing an affective outcome, for example, "to become more emotionally resilient and avoid taking on others' problems".

Drilling down into the specific types of affective outcomes that tend to form the focus of coaching, in the studies reviewed, these fall within three categories: Well-being, work attitudes and self-confidence. In relation to well-being, Bowles et al. (2007) describe how goals aimed at improving quality-of-life, such as mental well-being, were the most frequently set in their sample of 59 participants involved in US Army recruiting who were participating in a 12-month coaching programme. Similarly, in a large-scale survey of coaching practices, Passmore, Brown and Csigas (2017) surveyed 2,791 participants from a total of 45 European countries. From this sample of coaches, 21 per cent specified that they support clients wishing to tackle mental health issues and 41 per cent specified that they support clients wishing to tackle life style issues, both of which are likely to fall within the affective outcome category. Also, Wasylyshyn (2003) reports research on 87 executives that she coached between 1985 and 2001, where reducing stress was identified as a theme in the focus of coaching across her participants. In relation to work attitudes, in a sample of 30 participants who had received coaching, Smith and Brummel (2013) described how each executive in their study identified between 1 and 3 competencies that were the target of their coaching engagement, and improving motivation was listed as a focus of coaching in this sample. Wasylyshyn (2003) reported that managing perceptions of "ambition" was a theme in the focus of coaching in her research. In the final group of affective outcomes, Wasylyshyn (2003) reported that her participants sought to develop self-confidence and, in particular, reduce harsh self-criticism.

Cognitive outcomes as the focus in coaching

Cognitive outcomes are a group of outcomes that we can also describe as knowledge and understanding, or the client's mental process or mental actions. In other words, how does the client think? Examples of cognitive outcomes from coaching can include gaining new declarative knowledge (facts and pieces of information), procedural knowledge (knowing how to do something) and cognitive strategies (such as problem-solving, decision-making or reflective thinking). In their experimental study of the effectiveness of coaching with 53 participants, Jones et al. (2019) report that 11 per cent of participants focused on a cognitive outcome, for example, "to gain more subject specific knowledge in communications".

In terms of the specific types of cognitive outcomes that tend to form the focus of coaching, in the studies reviewed, cognitive outcomes fall within two categories: Cognitive strategies and knowledge. In relation to cognitive strategies, In Smith and Brummel's (2013) study, they described how clients sought to develop strategic thinking and decision-making in coaching. Wasylyshyn (2003) also details shifting from tactical to strategic thinking as a desired outcome in her study of 87 executives who had received coaching. Finally, Yu et al. (2008) explored the effectiveness of coaching with a sample of 105 participants. Yu et al. describe the cognitive outcome of gaining career-direction clarity as one of the reasons why participants sought coaching, with 21.8 per cent of their sample listing this as a desired outcome. In relation to knowledge, Smith and Brummel (2013) described the focus of coaching for some of their participants as aimed at increasing business acumen.

Skill-based outcomes as the focus in coaching

Skill-based outcomes are a group of outcomes that we can also describe as our expertise or abilities to complete certain tasks, so what does the client do? Compared to affective and cognitive outcomes, skill-based outcomes are more easily detected by others. Skill-based outcomes are often the focus of client goals and may include the development of skills such as leadership skills, assertiveness, communication, delegation or time-management skills. In their experimental study, Jones et al. (2019) report that 37 per cent focused on a skill-based outcome, for example, "to develop informal networking skills".

In the studies reviewed, the specific types of skill-based outcomes that tend to form the focus of coaching fall within two categories: Leadership and interpersonal skills. In relation to the former, Bowles et al. (2007), Smith and Brummel (2013) and Wasylyshyn (2003) all specifically name leadership skills as the focus of coaching for many of their participants. In addition, Smith and Brummel (2013) name coaching skills, which can be considered a specific type of leadership skill, as a focus of coaching. In relation to interpersonal skills, Smith and Brummel (2013) identified that their participants sought to address communication skills specifically, as well as interpersonal skills generally. For Wasylyshyn (2003), skill-based outcomes were the type of outcome most frequently listed in this sample and include interpersonal skills such as listening skills, tact/diplomacy, collaboration, persuasion, influence and fostering stronger relationships.

Results outcomes as the focus of coaching

The final group of outcomes we can expect from coaching is results, so what does the client achieve? We can further differentiate results into individual level results, team level results and organisational level results. Results is a broad group of outcomes that include any type of outcome where the client's behavioural change has had an impact. Therefore, examples at the individual level might include performance at work or financial indicators such as increased sales. By aligning individual goal-setting to team or organisational-level goals and objectives, achieving results outcomes at the individual level may also impact the performance of the team and the organisation. Jones et al. (2019) report that 11 per cent of participant coaching goals focused on a results outcome, for example, "to create a business case for the organisation to fund an external qualification".

Interestingly, in the studies reviewed, the types of results outcomes that tended to form the focus of coaching were all individual level (rather than team or organisational level) goals. For example, Bowles et al. (2007) report that their participants set recruitment/sales objective-related goals and Passmore et al. (2017) reported that 76 per cent of the 2,791 coaches surveyed specified that they help clients with their work performance.

Now that we have established the types of outcomes that clients tend to focus on during coaching, the final stage in building a business case for coaching is to review the evidence to indicate where coaching actually makes a difference to these outcomes.

Does coaching work? Assessing the coaching effectiveness evidence

The final stage in establishing the business case for coaching is to explore the evidence-base that directly tests the effectiveness of coaching. As with the section above, exploring the types of goals that tend to form the focus of coaching, in order to group together the research on coaching effectiveness, I will discuss the studies related to coaching effectiveness using the framework of coaching outcomes: Affective, cognitive, skill-based and results.

Evidence that coaching can produce change at the affective outcome level

As explained earlier, affective outcomes describe outcomes that we would understand as being outcomes felt by the client or experienced internally by the client; therefore, how does the client feel? In the context of the existing coaching literature, Bozer and Jones (2018) report a systematic literature review summarising the theoretical determinants of coaching. In this review, Bozer and Jones (2018) report that affective outcomes are the most frequently assessed outcome, with 93 out of 117 studies exploring affective outcomes (although some studies reported multiple outcomes). Examples of affective outcomes from the coaching literature once again can be grouped into three categories: Well-being, work attitudes and self-confidence.

Studies investigating well-being include Jones, Woods and Zhou (2018) who found that, in a sample of 161 clients, coaching had a positive effect on work well-being and that this effect was strongest when coaching was provided by external coaches and used a blended format (i.e. face-to-face coaching was combined with telephone or videophone coaching). Grant (2014) found that a cognitive-behavioural coaching programme consisting of 4 90-minute sessions with 31 executives and managers resulted in a decrease in depression. In a similar study, where 4 1-to-1 cognitive-behavioural coaching sessions were provided to 41 executives, Grant, Curtayne and Burton (2009) found that following the coaching, participants demonstrated a significant decrease in anxiety. Finally, Bright and Crockett (2012) conducted a test of telephone coaching to support a classroom-based workshop with a sample of 115 working participants, specifically designed at decreasing stress. They found a significant decrease in stress for participants when compared to a control group.

Studies investigating work attitudes include research by Bozer, Sarros and Santora (2014) who found that in a study of 72 executives who received between 10 to 12 weekly cognitive-behavioural, solution-focused coaching sessions over a period of 4 months, participants experienced a significant increase in career satisfaction following coaching. In addition to identifying that coaching resulted in a decrease in depression, Grant's (2014) study of 31 executives and managers who received coaching also found an increase in resilience. Finally, Luthans and Peterson (2003) explored the impact of coaching when coupled with 360-degree feedback in a sample of 20 managers and found that, following coaching, participants experienced higher levels of organisational commitment.

Studies investigating confidence have often operationalised confidence as self-efficacy. Research indicates that individuals higher in self-efficacy have strong beliefs in their task-related capabilities and set more challenging goals than those with lower self-efficacy (Bandura, 1986). A number of studies have investigated self-efficacy as an outcome for coaching. For example, Baron and Morin (2009) investigated the impact of an 8-month coaching programme with 73 managers and found significant increases in the clients' self-efficacy following coaching, where they also found evidence to indicate that the impact of coaching on client self-efficacy was explained by the quality of the coach–client relationship (i.e. improvement in self-efficacy for clients was higher when the relationship was stronger). In a sample of 23 leaders, Finn, Mason and Bradley (2007) explored the effectiveness of coaching when coupled with a year-long training programme and found that participants experienced improvements in self-efficacy when compared to a control group that did not receive coaching. Grant et al. (2017) examined the effectiveness of 6 1-hour coaching sessions with 31 participants working in public health and found that, following coaching, participants experienced a significant increase in their leadership self-efficacy. Leadership self-efficacy also increased in a sample of 20 executives who received a combination of group and individual coaching over a 1-year duration (Moen and Federici, 2012).

Evidence that coaching can produce change at the cognitive outcome level

Cognitive outcomes are a group of outcomes that we can also describe as knowledge and understanding, or the client's mental process or mental actions. In other words, how does the client think? Bozer and Jones (2018) demonstrated that cognitive outcomes are the least frequently evaluated outcome from coaching, with only 13 of the 117 studies testing cognitive outcomes. This could be partially due to the challenging nature of accurately capturing the development of new mental models and problem-solving strategies following coaching. Examples of cognitive outcomes from the coaching literature once again can be grouped into two categories: Cognitive strategies and knowledge.

Studies investigating cognitive strategies include Grant et al.'s (2017) study of 31 public health professionals discussed earlier, who, in addition to demonstrating increases in leadership self-efficacy following coaching, also found that participants experienced an increase in solution-focused thinking, which indicates a participant's ability to focus on finding solutions in complex systems. Gyllensten and Palmer (2006) interviewed nine participants who had received coaching in order to understand their perceptions of the impact of coaching. A theme across the participants was that coaching supported problem-solving, which indirectly contributed to the reduction of stress at work. In their study of 72 executives who received cognitive-behavioural, solution-focused coaching, in addition to an increase in career satisfaction, Bozer et al. (2014) found that coaching resulted in an increase in client self-awareness when coaching was provided by coaches with an academic background in psychology.

Knowledge as an outcome of coaching has been explored less extensively; however, examples include a study by Taie (2011) who investigated the effectiveness of training and coaching of nurses in life support skills. Taie found that compared to those who did not receive coaching, participants in the coaching group demonstrated higher scores in a knowledge assessment four months after an initial assessment. Additionally, Ammentorp, Jensen and Uhrenfeldt (2013) found an increase in self-reported learning following coaching, which Ammentorp et al. call "progressive insight". Their study involved interviewing five health professionals who had received between two and four coaching sessions over a period of ten months. Participants indicated that coaching enabled them to picture their job and duties from a new perspective.

Evidence that coaching can produce change at the skill-based outcome level

Skill-based outcomes are a group of outcomes that we can also describe as our expertise or abilities to complete certain tasks, so what does the client do? Following affective outcomes, skill-based outcomes are the next most popular group of outcomes assessed in the coaching literature with 57 of the 117 studies exploring outcomes of this type (although some studies reported multiple outcomes) (Bozer and Jones, 2018). Examples of skill-based outcomes from the coaching literature once again can be grouped into two categories: Leadership and interpersonal skills.

Examples of leadership skills from the coaching literature include a study by Williams and Lowman (2018) who examined the impact of 4 1-hour goal-focused coaching sessions with a sample of 64 senior executives. Williams and Lowman (2018) found that there was an increase in leadership competencies and behaviours for the coaching group, but not the control group. Bowles et al. (2007) reported that coaching resulted in an increase in leadership competencies in their sample of 59 participants involved in US Army recruiting who participating in a 12-month coaching programme. Specifically, Bowles et al. (2007) found that the increase in leadership competencies was highest when participants' buy-in to coaching was high. Boyce, Jackson and Neal (2010) collected data from 74 clients who were participating in a leadership coaching program at a military service academy. Boyce et al. (2010) found that an increase in leadership performance following coaching was explained by the clients' perceptions of the coaches' commitment to their development. Goff et al. (2014) explored the effectiveness of coaching with a sample of 26 high-school principals who received between 2 to 4 coaching sessions and 360-degree feedback and compared them to a control group of the same size (who received 360 feedback without coaching). Goff et al. found that coaching resulted in an increase in leadership competencies and, in particular, that coaching and 360-degree feedback together facilitated self-reflection which lead to changes in leadership skills.

Examples of studies reporting interpersonal skills as an outcome include two studies in a construction context that found that coaching improved communication skills. These were a quantitative study of 51 site foremen by Kines et al. (2010), and a qualitative study of 6 site managers who received coaching by Styhre and Josephson (2007). Improved communication skills following coaching were also found by Kombarakaran et al. (2008) in their survey of 114 executives who had received coaching. Other interpersonal skills that appear to be positively developed via coaching include soliciting ideas for improvement from managers. In their large-scale coaching effectiveness study, Smither et al. (2003) found that there was a significant increase in feedback-seeking skills in their sample of 404 executives who worked with a coach. Kochanowski, Seifert and Yukl (2010) found that coaching coupled with a feedback workshop to a sample of store managers of a supermarket chain resulted in a significant increase in collaboration skills. Finally, in a mixed-methods study, Dippenaar and Schaap (2017) explored the effectiveness of 9 coaching sessions over a period of 9 to 12 months with a sample of 30 financial services leaders and compared this to a control group of the same size who did not receive coaching. Dippenaar and Schaap (2017) found that coaching resulted in an increase in interpersonal skills, including empathy for others and relationship-building skills.

Evidence that coaching can produce change at the results outcome level

The final group of outcomes we can expect from coaching is results, so what does the client achieve? We can further differentiate results into individual level results, team level results and organisational level results. Whilst outcomes at the results level are arguably most important from an organisational perspective, these are 1 of the least frequently explored in the coaching literature, with only 17 out of 117 studies investigating outcomes within the results group (Bozer and Jones, 2018). This is likely because assessing results level outcomes is highly complex. It is often very difficult, if not impossible, to isolate the impact of coaching on results outcomes, as a vast range of factors such as the economic context and the behaviour of the wider team often influence outcomes at this level.

Examples of results outcomes explored in the literature include a study by Gardiner, Kearns and Tiggermann (2013) who investigated the impact of a nine-hour cognitive-behavioural coaching program with rural GPs in South Australia. Gardiner et al. (2013) found that coaching had a significant effect on retention. Specifically, they reported that over a 3-year period, 94 per cent of the coaching group remained in general practice, compared with 80 per cent of the control group. Olivero, Bane and Kopelman (1997) found that a managerial training program coupled with 8 weeks of 1-to-1 coaching with 31 managers in the public sector had a 22.4 per cent increase in productivity following training, compared to an 88 per cent increase in productivity after training plus coaching. Libri and Kemp (2006) report a case study where cognitive-behavioural coaching was provided to a single participant working in finance sales and found that coaching resulted in an increase in sales performance. In their study of the effectiveness of coaching with the sample of 51 site foremen discussed earlier, in addition to enhanced communication skills, Kines et al. (2010) also reported that coaching resulted in increased safety performance. Feggetter (2007) reported job promotion as a results outcome in a sample of ten Ministry of Defence employees who received coaching, and Andrews and Jones (2020) reported that business students who received coaching were more likely to successfully secure work placements than students who did not receive coaching.

An important point to note in relation to the research on coaching effectiveness at the results level is that, whilst theoretically we can argue that coaching can produce results at the team and organisational level, there is as yet no research that explores outcomes at this level. The existing literature on the impact of coaching on results focuses exclusively on individual level results. This is likely due to the complexity of gathering data at the team and organisational level; however, it clearly signals a gap in the coaching effectiveness literature that needs to urgently be addressed.

Conclusion

In this chapter, I have sought to create a business case for coaching. I have argued that the growth in the practice of coaching can be explained by an increasing demand for employees to be able to make sense of the information available to them and understand how to effectively apply this to an ever-changing work environment. The tailored, one-to-one approach to coaching provides the ideal developmental format to meet this need. The literature indicates that clients tend to focus on a wide range of goals in coaching, and the evidence gathered to date indicates that coaching is an effective intervention for the achievement of outcomes such as improved well-being, work attitudes, self-confidence; the development of new cognitive strategies and knowledge; enhanced leadership, interpersonal skills and the targeting of a range of individual level results such as retention, sales and promotion.

References

Ammentorp, J., Jensen, H.I. and Uhrenfeldt, L. (2013). 'Danish health professionals' experiences of being coached: a pilot study'. *Journal of Continuing Education in the Health Professions*, 33, pp. 41–47.

Andrews, H. and Jones, R.J. (2020). 'Can one-to-one coaching improve selection success and who benefits most? The role of candidate generalized self-efficacy'. *Unpublished manuscript in preparation*.

Ashkenas, R. (2013). 'Change management needs to change'. *Harvard Business Review*. Retrieved from https://hbr.org/2013/04/change-management-needs-to-cha.

Bandura, A. (1986). *Social foundations of thought and action: A social cognitive theory*. Upper Saddle River, NJ: Prentice-Hall, Inc.

Baron, L. and Morin, L. (2009) 'The coach–coachee relationship in executive coaching: a field study'. *Human Resource Development Quarterly*, 20, pp. 85–106.

Bowles, S., Cunningham, C.J.L., De La Rosa, G.M. and Picano, J. (2007). 'Coaching leaders in middle and executive management: Goals, performance, buy-in'. *Leadership & Organization Development*, 28(5), pp. 388–408.

Boyce, L.A., Jackson, J.R. and Neal, L.J. (2010). 'Building successful leadership coaching relationships: Examining impact of matching criteria in a leadership coaching program'. *Journal of Management Development*, 29(10), pp. 914–931.

Bozer, G., Sarros, J.C. and Santora, J.C. (2014). 'Academic background and credibility in executive coaching effectiveness'. *Personnel Review*, 43(6), pp. 881–897.

Bozer, G. and Jones, R.J. (2018). 'Understanding the factors that determine workplace coaching effectiveness: A systematic literature review'. *European Journal of Work and Organizational Psychology*, 27(3), pp. 342–361.

Bright, D. and Crockett, A. (2012). 'Training combined with coaching can make a significant difference in job performance and satisfaction'. *Coaching: An International Journal of Theory, Research and Practice*, 5(1), pp. 4–21.

CIPD (2010). 'Coaching and mentoring'. Retrieved from www.cipd.co.uk/subjects/lrnanddev/coachmntor/coaching.htm. [Accessed 2 April, 2020].

Dippenaar, M. and Schaap, P. (2017). 'The impact of coaching on the emotional and social intelligence competencies of leaders'. *South African Journal of Economic and Management Sciences* 20(1), pp. 1015–8812.

Feggetter, A.J.W. (2007). 'A preliminary evaluation of executive coaching: Does executive coaching work for candidates on a high potential development scheme?' *International Coaching Psychology Review*, 2(2), pp. 129–142.

Finn, F.A., Mason, C.M. and Bradley, L.M. (2007). 'Doing well with executive coaching: Psychological and behavioral impacts'. *Paper presented at the Academy of Management Annual Meeting Proceedings*, Philadelphia, United States.

Gardiner, M., Kearns, H. and Tiggemann, M. (2013). 'Effectiveness of cognitive behavioural coaching in improving the well-being and retention of rural general practitioners'. *Australian Journal of Rural Health*, 21(3), pp. 183–189.

Goff, P.J., Guthrie, E., Goldring, E. and Bickman, L. (2014). 'Changing principals' leadership through feedback and coaching'. *Journal of Educational Administration*, 52(5), pp. 682–704.

Grant, A.M., Curtayne, L. and Burton, G. (2009). 'Executive coaching enhances goal attainment, resilience and workplace well-being: A randomised controlled study'. *The Journal of Positive Psychology*, 4(5), pp. 396–407.

Grant, A.M. (2014). 'The efficacy of executive coaching in times of organisational change'. *Journal of Change Management*, 14(2), pp. 258–280.

Grant, A.M., Studholme, I., Verma, R., Kirkwood, L., Paton, B. and O'Connor, S. (2017). 'The impact of leadership coaching in an Australian healthcare setting'. *Journal of Health Organization and Management*, 31(2), pp. 237–252.

Gyllensten, K., and Palmer, S. (2006). 'Experiences of coaching and stress in the workplace: An Interpretative Phenomenological Analysis'. *International Coaching Psychology Review*, 1(1), pp. 86–98.

International Coaching Federation. (2016). *2016 ICF Global Coaching Study: Executive Summary*. Retrieved 5 March 2018 from https://coachfederation.org/research/global-coaching-study.

Jones, R.J., Woods, S.A. and Guillaume, Y.R.F. (2016). 'The effectiveness of workplace coaching: A meta-analysis of learning and performance outcomes from coaching'. *Journal of Occupational and Organizational Psychology*, 89, pp. 249–227.

Jones, R.J., Woods, S.A. and Zhou, Y. (2018). 'Boundary conditions of workplace coaching outcomes'. *Journal of Managerial Psychology*, 33(7/8), pp. 475–496.

Jones, R.J., Woods, S.A. and Zhou, Y. (2019). 'The effects of coachee personality and goal orientation on performance improvement following coaching: A controlled field experiment'. *Applied Psychology: An International Review*.

Kines, P., Andersen, L.P.S., Spangenberg, S., Mikkelsen, K.L., Dyreborg, J., and Zohar D. (2010). 'Improving construction site safety through leader-based verbal safety communication'. *Journal of Safety Research*, 41(5), pp. 399–406.

Kochanowski, S., Seifert, C.F. and Yukl, G.A. (2010). 'Using coaching to enhance the effects of behavioral feedback to managers'. *Journal of Leadership & Organizational Studies*, 17(4), pp. 363–369.

Kombarakaran, F.A., Yang, J.A., Baker, M.N. and Fernandes, P.B. (2008). 'Executive coaching: It works!' *Consulting Psychology Journal: Practice and Research*, 60(1), pp. 78–90.

Law, H., Ireland, S. and Hussain, Z. (2007). *The psychology of coaching, mentoring and learning*. Chichester, England: John Wiley & Sons Ltd.

Libri, V. and Kemp, T. (2006). 'Assessing the efficacy of a cognitive behavioural executive coaching programme'. *International Coaching Psychology Review*, 1(2), pp. 9–18.

Luthans, F. and Peterson, S.J. (2003). '360-degree feedback with systematic coaching: empirical analysis suggests a winning combination'. *Human Resource Management*, 42(3), pp. 243–256.

Moen, F. and Federici, R.A. (2012). 'The effect from external executive coaching'. *Coaching: An International Journal of Theory, Research and Practice*, 5(2), pp. 113–131.

Olivero, G., Bane, K.D. and Kopelman, R.E. (1997). 'Executive coaching as a transfer of training tool: Effects on productivity in a public agency'. *Public Personnel Management*, 26, pp. 461–469.

Passmore, J., Brown, H. and Csigas, Z. (2017). *The state of play in European coaching & mentoring*. United Kingdom: Henley Centre for Coaching at Henley Business School. Accessed from: https://assets.henley.ac.uk/defaultUploads/The-State-of-Play-in-European-Coaching-Mentoring-Executive-Report-2017.pdf?mtime=20171204192802.

Smith, I.M. and Brummel, B.J. (2013). 'Investigating the role of the active ingredients in executive coaching'. *Coaching: An International Journal of Theory, Research and Practice*, 6(1), pp. 57–71.

Smither, J.W., London, M., Flautt, R., Vargas, Y. and Kucine, I. (2003). 'Can working with an executive coach improve multisource feedback ratings over time? A quasi-experimental field study'. *Personnel Psychology*, 56, pp. 23–42.

Styhre, A. and Josephson, P.E. (2007). 'Coaching the site manager: Effects on learning and managerial practice'. *Construction Management and Economics*, 25(12), pp. 1295–1304.

Swart, J. and Harcup, J. (2013). 'If I learn do we learn?': The link between executive coaching and organizational learning'. *Management Learning*, 44, pp. 337–354.

Taie, E.S. (2011). 'Coaching as an approach to enhance performance'. *Journal for Quality and Participation*, 34, pp. 34–38.

Wasylyshyn, K.M. (2003). 'Executive coaching: An outcome study'. *Consulting Psychology Journal: Practice and Research*, 55(2), pp. 94–106.

Williams, J.S. and Lowman, R.L. (2018). 'The efficacy of executive coaching: An empirical investigation of two approaches using random assignment and a switching-replications design'. *Consulting Psychology Journal: Practice and Research*, 70(3), pp. 227–249.

Yu, N., Collins, C.G., Cavanagh, M., White, K. and Fairbrother, G. (2008). 'Positive coaching with frontline managers: Enhancing their effectiveness and understanding why'. *International Coaching Psychology Review*, 3(2), pp. 110–122.

3 Developing a coaching culture in your organisation

Jonathan Passmore and Kristina Crabbe

Introduction

There has been much discussion over the past decade about the development of coaching cultures in organisations. However, in reviewing the papers, books, reports and conference presentations, while most highlight the value of building such cultures, few offer practical steps on how organisations can move from where they are towards a more efficient and effective use of coaching. In this chapter we aim to explore what we mean by the word 'culture', and how this might translate into a coaching culture. We will then offer a model, LEAD, as one way of conceptualising a coaching culture and offer a route map that would help leaders audit their own organisational practices to enhance the way they use coaching at all levels of their organisation.

What do we mean by 'organisational culture'?

The term culture is widely used but, like coaching, it has a wide variety of definitions that are applied by different leaders, organisations and sectors. One of the clearest and shortest definitions is by Terrence Deal and Allan Kennedy: "the way things get done around here" (Deal and Kennedy, 1983:501). A more academic definition was offered by Ed Schein:

> a pattern of shared basic assumptions that was a learned by a group as it solved its problems of external adoption and internal integration, that has worked well enough to be considered valid and, therefore, to be taught to new members as the correct way you perceive, think and feel in relation to those problems.
>
> (Schein, 2004:8)

More recently others have adapted Schein's original work to provide a more dynamic definition of culture:

> the culture of a group can be defined as the accumulated shared learning of that group as is solves its problems of external adaption and internal integration; which has worked well to perceive, think, feel and behave in relation to those problems. This accumulated learning is a pattern or system of beliefs, values and behavioural norms that come to be taken for granted as basic assumptions and eventually drop out of awareness
>
> (Schein and Schein, 2017:6)

Drawing on this thinking about organisational culture, we have defined a coaching culture as:

an organisation that aims to maximise the potential of all who work with it, through its use of coaching as the default style of leadership and employee engagement, and where its people are supported and challenged to become more self-aware, with increased autonomy to deliver their workplace goals. This way of being becomes and is integral to the behaviours, values, development and strategy of the organisation [and in time, the distributed network].

To bring a new culture alive, the organisation requires a planned approach: One way of delivering coaching culture is through the three C's approach; common mindset, champions and campaign.

Common mindset: This involves the development of a shared view about the role of coaching within the organisation which flows from the senior team to frontline employees, partners and suppliers.

Champions: This requires a cadre of leaders from across the organisation who see bringing coaching alive as their personal project. This cadre needs to be cross-functional as well as diagonal across the multiple levels of leadership in the organisation, from board to team supervisors.

Campaign: This requires an effective campaign to communicate to each and every employee what coaching is, what role it plays as part of the business strategy, how they are expected to use the approach with partners, colleagues and team members and how they can access coaching within the organisation.

The old-style approach to coaching

Coaching has been actively used by managers since the 1980's. In many organisations it has remained a personal benefit, almost like a reserved parking space, disconnected from the wider organisation's strategy. This old-style approach to coaching is typified by a number of common features:

Firstly, the why of coaching. Organisational leaders understand that coaching is valuable to its leadership. However, these leaders have yet to integrate coaching into the wider HR or business strategy. Leaders in the organisation understand how coaching can help individuals, but less how it serves the wider business strategy.

Secondly, the issue of appointments. The selection of the coach is undertaken by the individual manager, often without due process and frequently based on personal relationships or recommendations. Such processes differ from the way employees and external consultants are appointed.

Thirdly, the assignment focus. The focus of the assignment is decided by the individual manager with little or no reference to the wider organisational agenda or business objectives.

Fourthly, the coach is seen as an external contractor, responsible for their own personal development and standards, rather than part of the organisation's wider network of key suppliers, who need to understand and be part of the wider organisational change agenda.

Finally, evaluation. The evaluation of the coach's work is based on the perceptions of the individual manager as to how they felt the coach performed, with limited input from the wider system of peers, colleagues or a sponsor.

It is clear that, whilst personal coaching may benefit the individual manager, it offers little to the organisation. Greater value can be gained by linking the coaching process more closely to the organisation's objectives through developing a coaching culture.

The benefits of building a coaching culture

Building a culture of coaching offers a range of potential benefits for individuals, teams, the organisation and its wider network. By the very nature of coaching, everyone may benefit.

A wide number of authors have outlined the benefits of building a coaching culture (Bresser, 2013; Forman, Joyce and McMahon, 2013; Clutterbuck et al., 2016; Jones and Gorell, 2014; Hawkins, 2012). The broad consensus from these writers is that they believe that everyone can achieve their potential if they are given the time and opportunity to develop personal awareness and generate their own solutions. In building a coaching culture, the potential value increases through the dimensions of team, group, organisational and distributed networks.

Organisational snapshot – JK Organisation, India

Building on a legacy excellence: Facilitating a coaching culture

JK is one of India's largest industrial groups and employs more than 22,000 individuals across India and the globe. JK defined a coaching culture as: "When we describe a coaching cultures, we're describing a learning culture that is respectful and that values people's potential and promotes innovation".

The decision-makers at JK chose to adopt coaching as a strategy for talent development, leadership enhancement and change management, breaking the mould where senior employees have all grown up in the culture of expecting instruction from their bosses.

The aim was to overcome the perception that coaching was seen as a remedial intervention. This was helped by explaining "what coaching was" and "was not".

A trickle-down strategy was used, starting with 124 senior and high-potential leaders engaging in executive coaching relationships where they participated in 360-degree feedback prior to the process. The process asked participating executives to identify two to three goals for the coaching engagement with an eye towards the transformations they believe would most impact themselves, their team and the business, and also one goal that may not be explicitly related to their professional lives. The coaching engagements lasted between 8–12 months and included mid-term and end-of-engagement with the coach, executive and HR team. The coach also checked in with the key stakeholders throughout the process to monitor the effectiveness of the coaching. At the end of the coaching engagement the coach, executive and executive line manager all submitted written feedback about the process and outcomes to the HR team to continue the development of the learning process.

JK then took the next step of engaging professionally certified coaches to provide a course in coach-specific training to leaders interested in becoming internal coach practitioners. The mix of leaders involved in the training were senior executives, vice presidents and functional heads.

The outcomes of the programme were as follows: Revenues grew by 105%, employee satisfaction increased by 16% and attrition of high-potential employees decreased by 2%. Leaders reported positive impacts on: Stress management, management skills, role transitions, self-confidence and enhanced teamwork. The improvements were also felt outside of work, with leaders reporting a higher quality of life at home and with their extended families.

The impact is a shift from a top-down management style to a collegial style, with stronger collaborative relationships between senior and mid-level managers, peers and direct reporters. The focus of employees has shifted from age and tenure to creativity, solutions and a more active engagement in the decision-making process. As a result, the working environment now has a greater sense of belonging, is less hierarchical and has a stronger team focus.

Benefits at the individual coaching dimension:

- Improved performance and outcome focus;
- Increased motivation, commitment and engagement;
- Effective self-management and management to change, transition and transformation;
- Time effective mastery of role transition, technologies and tools;
- Increased self-awareness, reflection into action and relationships with others;
- Leadership skills, personal and professional growth and development leading to an engaged and committed workforce;
- Resilience, agility, sustainability and wellbeing (balance);
- Communications and clarity of strategy, goals and process.

Benefits at the team and group coaching dimensions:

- Synergy and increased value as a team (not merely the sum of the parts or less);
- Enhanced value from teams of teams all working and connecting within this dimension;
- Deeper level of understanding of team and group dynamics leading to effective performance, alignment of goals, working relationships and conflict, growth and development;
- Team agility and resilience;
- Access to divergent and different thinking from groups;
- Creating group connections and developing diagonal networks across organisational structures and hierarchies.

Benefits at the organisational coaching dimension:

- Reduce turnover by increasing retention;
- The coaching approach attracting new talent to the organisation;
- Developing and motivating all employees, driving efficiency, quality and customer service;
- Enabler for change;
- Boosting financial performance;
- Improving overall business performance;
- Bedding in and practice of organisational behaviours, values and success factors;
- Effective processes, structures and systems to deliver strategy;
- Loudspeaker for learning and continuous professional development;
- Environment for learning, generation of ideas and innovation;
- Wellbeing and resilience for employees – 'healthy organisation';
- Builds a networked web of connections across the whole organisation;
- Organisational capacity for complexity and change on change.

Benefits of coaching beyond the organisation and into the distributed networks:

- Effective use of resources across the organisational network and partners;
- More effective use of natural resources;
- Positive perception and greater impact of the business' products and services in the market place;
- Maturity of processes across network and partners for sustainability;
- Shared learning and development, knowledge and wisdom for win–win;
- Stakeholder intelligence and collaboration;
- Positive impact on society, wider systems and potentially ecosystems.

In crafting the coaching aspects of the organisational strategy, each organisation needs to consider its own distinctive challenges, from organisational culture, to operating environment to competition. Underhill (2018) echoes this view, suggesting an evolutionary approach in the journey towards the implementation of coaching. The LEAD framework follows this, providing zones of development through a step-by-step approach within each zone to realise the benefits from all of the dimensions outlined above. The acronym 'MODEL' associated with the LEAD framework provides further components to mobilise and evaluate the LEAD framework. These components add clarity and transparency to the benefits of the coaching culture. Ideally these benefits form the basis of organisational stories which underpin the momentum to take up and understand the value of the coaching approach throughout the organisation, as well as concurrently building sustainability.

The LEAD coaching framework

LEAD offers a framework that can help organisations to move away from an old-style personal coaching approach towards a more integrated, strategic approach. By doing so, organisations are best placed to maximise the true value that coaching can offer as a tool for employee management, development and engagement.

To develop a coaching culture, we have suggested four broad zones. Each zone contains a checklist that the organisation can apply to evaluate its progress towards full implementation of the coaching culture. See Figure 3.1.

Zone 1 – Leaders – Managing access to external coaches

Some key starting questions that the HR Leader and Practitioner need to ask at this stage are:

I. Who owns 'culture' on the board? What culture do we have, what type of coaching do we want?
II. Why? What contribution will coaching make? Are we ready as a business to take this forward?
III. What do we already have in place in terms of values and competencies working towards our current business strategy that are relevant and can be built on?
IV. What existing systems, processes and technology can support us and what is the additional need to be put in place?

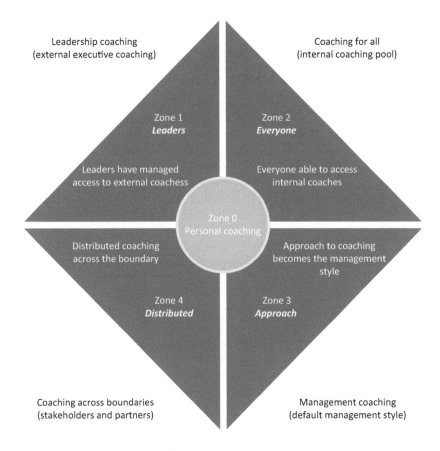

Figure 3.1 The LEAD framework

These first three questions form the fundamentals in taking the first step of integrating coaching into HR strategy, taking realities and current relationships forward to build initiatives that support the integration of coaching, the business and HR.

The next step drives the commission, management and supervision of external coaches to facilitate, co-ordinate and orchestrate the buying in of the coaching capability whilst keeping control of developing and maintaining measurement and feedback.

Step three of this zone is where coaching is positively acknowledged, identified and actively managed with a dedicated line in the budget. Coaching is understood and valued by senior managers and then, in time, coaching is also understood and valued by all employees. Discussions and leadership decisions start to consider more and more the impact, standards and outputs linked to strategy.

Zone 2: Everyone – Access to internal coaches

In this zone the focus is on how coaching can be extended from the top team to all managers, supervisors and employees. Using external coaches is an expensive option and thus one which most organisations preserve for senior leaders. While it may be cost-prohibitive to extend the use of external coaches to all managers, the organisation can develop its own in-house pool of coaches. Zone 2 focuses on how organisations can select, train, manage, support and evaluate internal coaches.

Organisational snapshot – CareSource, Ohio, USA

An initiative started with a six-month programme to enable new leaders to address the challenges of their roles. The programme was extended and expanded to training managers and leaders in using coaching skills.

The programme has been credited with retaining high-potential employees and leaders, with an estimated saving of $396,600 USD. Additional estimated savings in leader and employee efficiency ($201,972 USD), overtime reduction ($91,023 USD) and avoidance of contracting/consulting fees ($55,036 USD). Overall, CareSource estimates savings of $744,632 and a return on investment (ROI) of 211% over 5 years from its development of a coaching culture.

The key starting questions that the HR Leader and Practitioner need to ask at this stage are:

I. What are the principles underlying the development of our internal professional coaching capability?
II. How do we ensure confidentiality and create psychological safety?
III. What can we do to support our internal coaches to carry out their role professionally?
IV. What systems and technology that we currently use can support us and what do we need to put in place?

The first step in this zone is to build an internal coaching pool by building and developing the internal coaching capability structure. This can be achieved by engaging with professional bodies like the ICF (2020) or Asssociation for Coaching, as well as providers of accredited coach training. This provides the recognition necessary for business value and impact. An alternative approach is to develop and deliver bespoke programmes for internal coach development. Each organisation needs to determine its own approach taking into account its size and the estimated scale of its internal demand and required outcomes.

The role of internal coach comes with a number of complexities not experienced by external coaches, and these are best considered at the initial phase and issues planned for through the commissioning and contracting process. Support is an important element. Coaching supervision should form part of this process as a way to both keep coaching quality in place, and also to manage ethical and practice issues which are likely to emerge.

The next step of the Everyone Zone is for managers and leaders to select their coach from the internal coaching pool. Success of the internal coaching pool is when there is a clear link between expectations in terms of both personal and professional growth and alignment to personal development plans and business initiatives. This is key for alignment of the coaching provision and business performance.

The final step of this zone is to provide access to internal coaches, such that the coaching pool reflects the organisation in terms of its diversity, facilitating the opportunity of divergent and different thinking, the range of functional capabilities, development opportunities, growth of organisational capacity through knowledge and wisdom across the generations and beyond; ultimately representing all communities within the organisation.

Zone 3: Approach – Coaching is the default leadership style

In this zone the focus is on how organisations can develop a coaching style of management. By this we mean how can they enable managers to use coaching as their default leadership style. This requires coaching skills to be an integral part of leadership, management and supervisor training programmes, managers need to understand what management coaching is, when to use it and how to use it best within the line management role. They also need to understand how it fits alongside other styles of managing from directive (giving clear, explicit instructions) to a democratic employee consultation style and objectives setting. Each has a place, but we would advocate that for most businesses and for most employees, the coaching style can be a dominate style to be used for 50% or more of conversations with team members, encouraging self-reflection and personal autonomy.

One danger of a default style is that it becomes seen as the silver bullet: The solution to all employee problems and for use in all situations. We are not advocating that. Coaching is not a silver bullet for managers, any more than it's a silver bullet for employee performance management or development. While it's highly effective, it's just one tool that managers need to use alongside other styles of engagement. Our argument is that it's the 'go-to tool', the default setting, before the manager evaluates and decides if to switch to directing, consulting, empathising or goal-setting interventions.

These key questions take us through the Approach Zone to continue to build the coaching culture:

   V. What is our route map to train all managers in coaching skills and to give them the confidence that they can coach?
   VI. How do we use our employee lifecycle to develop coaching as a default management style?
   VII. Which other coaching modalities can we use and do we have the expertise internally to use team and group coaching to develop business performance?
   VIII. What are the existing systems and technology that can support this or need to be put in place?

We believe it is important that the coaching approach continues to be managed by the HR department, ensuring that coaching strategy is embedded in the broader HR strategy. HR strategies and initiatives will need to flex and evolve with the changing and dynamic organisational strategy. As the managers and leaders themselves are recognised as competent coaches, the business outcomes will enable further steps to be taken towards full alignment and sustainability. Coaching becomes the capstone within the HR strategy.

The accumulated learning and development evolving from coaching, and forming the default management style, ensure that these approaches become embedded in the system of beliefs, values and behaviours. Over time the philosophy which underpins coaching, of empowering others, becomes part of the way the organisation works, part of the organisation's unconscious.

Zone 4: Distributed – Coaching across organisational boundaries

In this zone the focus is on extending coaching beyond the organisation's boundaries. A century ago most organisations purchased the raw materials and built their product. Today, most organisations now work with multiple partners: contractors, suppliers, agents to manufacture or deliver their products or service. The modern organisation's 'boundary' has become blurred, as a result of these multiple relations. No longer do organisations simply employ workers as employees on a weekly or monthly contract. They have added to this core through zero-hours employees, day rate contractors, agents, subcontractors and customers, all of whom may contribute to the co-creation of content or assemble of parts. Many of these relationships are critical to organisational success, as for all intents and purposes these partner's act as if they were employed. If organisations are aspiring to create a coaching culture, this culture must flow seamlessly across these fluid boundaries.

In the public sector, relationships may be equally complex, with agencies working together to deliver public goods or social impact. In terms of a coaching culture this may mean creating cross-organisational pools, where health workers, police, fire, government and social housing collaborate. In the commercial sectors it may mean moving away from win–lose arrangements, with a model which instead focuses on win–win outcomes.

Organisational snapshot – Rentokil Initial, UK

The appetite for group coaching has been both surprising and exciting. Managers have deeply appreciated the high levels of trust they have developed with their peers and the resulting relationships have been sustained beyond the life of the programme. The managers really value working in this way and have taken the learning back into their teams. (Brigid Garvey, Group Director of Talent, Rentokil Initial)

Developing talent

Rentokil's initial approach to talent development was based on 5 principles:

1. Learning is transferable to the workplace and learning opportunities are created from work situations;
2. Adults learn best through experience, and reflecting on experience, rather than being taught or told;
3. Great leadership starts with emotional maturity and increased self-awareness;
4. Personal change has to begin with oneself and flow outward;
5. Sustainable change comes from working on several levels, including behaviour, mindset, emotions and purpose.

Developing a coaching culture – Living Leadership

Rentokil committed itself to an innovative and substantive approach to learning and development and designed its signature 'Living Leadership' programme in 2009 with group coaching at its heart. The programme is still running.

The programme involves four group coaching sessions over six months of the programme. The experience deepens delegates' emotional and psychological development and builds their coaching capability through working with fellow group members on real practical business challenges.

The group coaching is designed to create a sense of a management community and a forum for managers to network, share experiences and ways of working with each other, as well as driving the development of a culture based on a coaching style of leadership.

Feedback and learning from the group coaching

- "Feedback is positive from both managers and employees";
- "Being part of a coaching group was a life changing experience";
- "The group coaching work ... has given me a chance to reflect inwards and really identify my strengths".

The programme's impact on the organisation

- Delegates reported increased confidence, enhanced leadership capability and knowledge and report being more equipped to respond to challenging situations;
- Improved work relationships;
- Improved business results – increasing sales, improving employee engagement and retaining customers and employees;
- Sustainable changes in leadership style.

Here are some suggested questions to start to build the landscape of the organisation's distributed network and determine possible value linked to organisational strategy:

- Which of our coaching modalities and practices can we share within our distributed network?
- What coaching initiatives have the potential to add-value across the distribution to create win–win?
- How can we measure the impact of this coaching approach across organisational boundaries? See Figure 3.2 and Table 3.1.

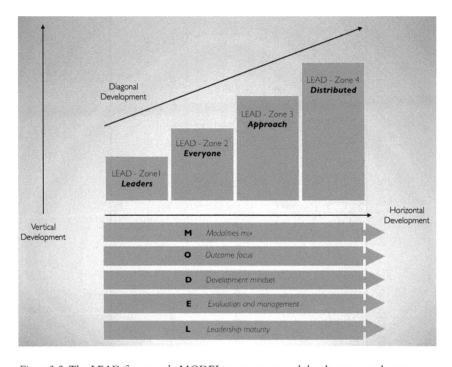

Figure 3.2 The LEAD framework, MODEL components and development pathways

Table 3.1 The LEAD Framework Zones Mapped to MODEL Components

MODEL Component	Pre-LEAD Framework	LEAD – Zone 1 Leaders	LEAD – Zone 2 Everyone	LEAD – Zone 3 Approach	LEAD – Zone 4 Distributed
M Modalities mix	Ad hoc individual exec coaching.	HR commissions and manages external coaches.	HR builds internal coach practitioner pool.	HR expands team, group and coaching supervision capability.	HR partners with peers in the distributed network to share expertise.
O Outcome focus	Led by individual.	Steps 1–3 of the 12-step plan (see steps below).	Steps 4–7 of the 12-step plan (see steps below).	Steps 8–11 of the 12-step plan (see steps below).	Step 12 of the 12-step plan (see steps below).
D Development mindset	Led by external coach–coachee relationship.	Aligned to personal objectives and competence (horizontal).	Aligned to personal and organisational capability (vertical).	Aligned to personal and organisational capacity (diagonal).	Extending, sharing and harnessing development across the distributed network.
E Evaluation and management	Based on individual satisfaction.	E.g., Individual personal development – impact, standards, strategy and values.	E.g., Interpersonal development – impact, standards, strategy and values.	E.g., Team and group outputs – impact, standards, strategy and values.	E.g., Additional benefits across the distributed network – impact, sustainability.
L Leadership maturity	Not evaluated.	Building self-awareness and of others.	Building experience through perspective and practice.	Leaders as coach and building knowledge of 'The Deeper work'.	Extending the coaching approach through the distribution.

Twelve steps to developing a coaching culture

At a practical level, what can organisations do to move forward towards a coaching culture? The LEAD frameworks and its associated audit tool offer multiple actions at each level for organisations to review their practices. Here are 12 steps that organisations can consider to help them move forward with their own approach to coaching:

1 Integrate coaching as part of the HR strategy;
2 Commission, manage and supervise individual external coaches, not firms;
3 Coaching is acknowledged as a dedicated line in the budget;
4 Build an internal coaching pool;
5 Managers should select their own coaches from the pool;
6 Pool mirrors the make-up of the organisation;
7 Internal coaches are outside the line management relationship;
8 Train all managers in coaching skills;
9 Encourage coaching as the organisation's default management style;
10 Use team coaching to develop team performance;
11 Maintain development, wellbeing and ethical approach to the coaching provision using coaching supervision;
12 Developing a coaching style of the organisation with partners and suppliers focusing on a win–win business model.

Conclusion

Coaching is a key tool for organisations that can help them deliver change, as well as more effectively engage, develop and lead their workforce. However, to achieve maximum value from coaching, organisations need to adopt a strategic approach, integrating coaching into every part of their business. The LEAD framework offers a practical, hands-on tool for organisations to review their existing practices, from their employment of external coaches to building internal coaching pools, developing coaching skills in their managers and extending coaching beyond the boundaries of their organisation to contractors, partners and supplier relationships with a focus on win–win outcomes.

References

Bresser, F. (2013). *The global business guide for the successful use of coaching in organisations*. Cologne: Bresser.
Clutterbuck, D., Megginson, D. and Bajer, A. (2016). *Building and sustaining a coaching culture*. London: CIPD.
Deal, T.E. and Kennedy, A.A. (1983). 'Culture: A new look through old lenses'. *The Journal of Applied Behavioural Science*, *19*(4), 498–505. doi: 10.1177/002188638301900411.
Forman, D. Joyce, M. & McMahon, G. (2013). *Creating a Coaching Culture for Managers in Your Organisation*. Abingdon: Routledge
Hawkins, P. (2012). *Creating a coaching culture*. Maidenhead: Open University Press.
ICF. (2020). 'Prism awards'. Retrieved on 27 March 2020 from https://coachfederation.org/prism-award.
Jones, G., and Gorell, R. (2014). *How to create a coaching culture*. London: Kogan Page.
Mann, C. (2016) *Ridler Report 2016*. London: Ridler & Co.
Schein, E. (2004). *Organisational culture and leadership*, 3rd edition. San Francisco, CA: John Wiley & Sons.
Schein, E. and Schein, P. (2017). *Organisational culture and leadership*, 5th edition. Hoboken, NJ: Wiley.
Underhill, B.O. (2018). 'Centralizing coaching provision'. In J. Passmore, B.O. Underhill and M. Goldsmith, eds., *Mastering executive coaching*. Abingdon: Routledge, pp. 178–193.

Section 2

Understanding yourself and your clients

4   Understanding yourself as a coach

Tatiana Bachkirova

Introduction

The motivation to become a coach often comes because of an individual's interest in people and a desire to help them to reach their potential (Anderson, 2016). Quite often this interest originates from an interest in oneself. Coaches are usually curious about their drives, values and qualities that allow them to be productive and happy. They are also curious about qualities that make it more difficult for them to achieve what they want and create obstacles to their success and wellbeing.

This chapter is about how this desire to understand oneself is an important prerequisite for being a good professional coach. I will make a case for three levels of self-understanding that a professional coach benefits from developing: self-inventory, self as an instrument and a fully professional self. Starting with a brief discussion of what the self actually is, in each of the following sections I will introduce one of these three levels of self-understanding and suggest ways to develop them.

The nature of self in a nutshell: A precursor for self-understanding

On a very basic level, understanding oneself often means knowing one's strengths and weaknesses. However, there could be much more to this process than that. In order to expand this picture, it is probably useful to start by asking how the 'self' is defined. This is not an easy question to answer in spite of the many disciplines of knowledge dealing with it: philosophy, psychology, neuroscience, phenomenology and education, to name just a few. The actual fact that the puzzle of the self attracts so many disciplines indicates that this is a very complex matter. It is also a plausible explanation for why it is not easy to arrive at some consensus as to the notion of the self (Gallagher and Shear, 1999).

The discussion about what the self is can be highly theoretical and this is not the purpose of this chapter. However, in recognising the effort of many approaches to exploring this topic and trying to arrive at something that can be useful for practitioners, I offer three ways of looking at the self (Bachkirova, 2011). When we think about the self, we usually mean one of these three ways:

- How we experience things – A very unique first-person perspective, like a personal window on the world;
- How we act – What allows us to respond to challenges, make decisions and engage with things, supporting our sense of agency;
- How we describe ourselves – A narrative about oneself, the description of who we think we are, creating a sense of identity.

From these descriptions, we can see how difficult it is to arrive at one definition of the self. Different disciplines tend to concentrate on one of the ways described above. Phenomenology studies the way we experience things; biology and neuroscience look at how we function and act; and social psychology explores our identity and narratives.

In my book (Bachkirova, 2011), while exploring the nature of the self for coaching practice, I suggest that we should accept the fact that these three ways of conceptualising the self are quite legitimate. None of them can be reduced to another. Accordingly, the self can be seen as a combination of three centres:

- Centre of awareness;
- Executive centre;
- Centre of identity.

Centre of awareness is the most basic pre-reflective sense of self, a subjective perspective on the world. Even animals have it, as it allows an organism to locate itself in space and time and recognise experiences as 'mine' (Claxton, 1994). This centre is crucially important for our functioning but very difficult to study, as it can be described only from the first-person perspective and is by definition subjective.

Executive centre represents a perspective that can be more objective. It means that there are various properties and areas of the brain that are associated with the actions of the organism. To put it simply, the executive centre is a neurological network responsible for the coherent behaviour and functioning of the individual in the world (Gazzaniga, 2012; Kurzban, 2010).

Centre of identity could be seen as a narrative construction; a linguistically based aspect of human nature that enables us to make sense of our engagement with the world by creating various stories of who we are and what we are like. This is also a subjective and very fluid view on the way we see ourselves in certain contexts and certain periods of life.

It is important to notice that I label these notions of self as 'centres' only for uniformity and simplicity. Neither of them implies a specific place in the mind/brain which can be clearly identified. For example, what I name the 'executive centre' can be seen as a neurological network of multiple mini-selves. Each mini-self is a particular pattern of links between different areas of the brain that becomes activated or inhibited when the organism is involved in an act (Bachkirova, 2011). The centre of identity should be understood as a combination of fluid stories that we construct about ourselves depending on the circumstances. Only the first of these notions may actually *feel* like a centre, but the first-person perspective nature of it means that a physical centre for it is unlikely to be discovered.

There are some obvious implications of this view on the self for coaches. The first suggests that the nature of self is not as simple as we might assume. It would be difficult, for example to make some typically blunt and forceful recommendations to discover "your true self", to be "true to yourself", etc., as each of them would imply a further question: "Which self?". We need to recognise that our own nature is complex, that it may be as complex as the nature of organisations, events and anything else that is described by the complexity and systems theories. In light of this, as coaches, we need to be much more thoughtful and appropriately tentative about how we understand our clients' selves and avoid imposing on them strong expectations for an 'objective and accurate' evaluation of oneself (e.g., Hullinger, et al., 2019).

It would be wise to adopt the same attitude when we think about the nature of our own self. If we recognise the complexity of our own selves, we need to continue learning, observing ourselves in action, gathering feedback and questioning our perceptions that depend on many interrelated factors in complex contexts. I would also argue that for us this is not a choice – it is a requirement of being a professional coach. To discuss further the role of such learning for professional coaches, we shall explore three different ways, or processes, for understanding oneself as a coach in the next sections. These processes are not just discrete and random activities that we might be involved with when we wish to understand ourselves. I refer to them as levels because they, arguably, indicate the degree of complexity involved for each process and represent a typical sequence of a coach's professional development path.

Level 1: Self-inventory

This first level can be called self-inventory in the context of being a coach because, firstly, it involves undertaking an honest assessment of one's professional capabilities. It requires that we identify our basic strengths and weaknesses and what we need to do to fill in the gaps. This level starts from some very important conditions, such as understanding that you need to have the sufficient knowledge and skills required to do the job. It includes consideration of the level of experience needed for particular assignments and a monitoring of how the changes in your experience with time influence your practice. For example, this monitoring should help you to establish how you deal with the complexity of the different contexts in which you work. These three aspects (knowledge, skills and experience) have to be regularly reviewed and improved with the use of coaching supervision and through the process of continuing professional development (CPD).

There is another category of knowledge about oneself that goes beyond this basic professional assessment. The self-inventory level of self-understanding can include extra information about oneself that could help to identify an important professional niche or specialisation in the wider field of coaching. For example, if coaches are trained within a particular school of practice, such as cognitive-behavioural, gestalt or existential, they may clearly associate their professional identity accordingly. Similarly, their growing level of expertise in a particular context or modality may allow them to identify specifically as, e.g., business coaches, maternity coaches or team coaches, etc.

Sometimes this level of self-inventory can help in building a more nuanced professional identity in addition to one's training or context of practice. For example, during the training to become a coach, and later through one's CPD, coaches may become engaged with many tools and exercises that are aimed at gauging their psychological preferences, traits, values and attitudes that have relevance to their practice. Coaches could experiment on themselves with these procedures or various psychometric instruments. This might assist them in enhancing their self-inventory by developing extra knowledge of their own psychological traits. With enhanced awareness of these traits, coaches might decide that some elements of their professional identity would benefit from 'fine-tuning' and make the necessary adjustments.

There are specific examples as to how this extra multifaceted information about oneself as a coach can be used in a more formal way. For example, Walker (2004) has developed a model about different styles of working in the business of people development using three bipolar dimensions of capabilities which he identifies as logic, empathy and control.

Using this model, coaches who know their characteristics and preferences in terms of these dimensions can identify their own 'coaching signature', which could help them to become more congruent with their approaches to practice.

To summarise, self-inventory as a level of self-understanding as a coach is important because it is necessary simply in order to identify oneself as a professional coach. It would be unprofessional, for example, not to have an appropriate qualification and commitment to further development. This level of self-understanding is a prerequisite for starting your practice. It implies importance of the focus on oneself as a coach. This focus is pursued not in the session, where attention is fully on the client, but in any other professional activities that are undertaken. However, with further experience, reflection on one's practice and focused professional development enable coaches to reach more advanced levels of self-understanding, and it is to this that we now turn.

Level 2: Self as an instrument

This level of self-understanding usually emerges when coaches become more experienced. They begin realising that they are much more than just a 'bag of tools', however useful and productive these tools may be. Their observations, confirmed by research (e.g., de Haan and Gannon, 2017), show how important the role of relationships is in the process of coaching. Simple logic suggests that effective relationships require the coach to be trustworthy in the eyes of the client. It is not surprising, then, that connecting with clients on a personal level and building relationships that are based on trust cannot be created only by the coach's skills and knowledge. It requires more than that.

Clients often bring to a coaching session issues that affect their whole lives. They need to feel that, by engaging with topics of such personal importance, the coach is not just playing a role, however professionally. They want to connect with a person. Coaches also know that when they are at their best, what they offer comes from personally resonating with the client in the moment and, therefore, from the coach as a person. Such interventions are perceived as genuine because they are the expression of the coach's life experiences, current worldview and feelings that came to fruition 'right now' and not only a recollection of the "right thing to say". I call this level of coach self-understanding as 'coach as a main instrument of coaching' (Bachkirova, 2016).

When a coach comes to the realisation that they are the main instrument of coaching, this entails a new level of self-understanding. The difference at this point is that, in the session, they begin to pay a great deal of attention not only to the content of the client's story, or what is happening to the client in the process of coaching, but also to their own internal states: their feelings, thoughts and intuitions. This level of self-understanding requires a much higher degree of self-awareness because it implies a double focus during the session, including both the client and the coach.

In terms of the actions which usually follow from this level of self-understanding, it is possible to notice several specific features. For example, coaches feel more confident in bringing to the process an appropriate level of self-disclosure (Jourard, 1971). This is no longer a compulsive 'sharing' of their experiences, nor a timid holding back of any information in fear of deviating from the client's agenda. The ability to do this confidently and effectively is determined by the coach's sufficient and non-judgmental attention to the impulse to share something personal with the client. This impulse is then checked in light of other observed nuances; e.g., the client's receptivity, timing or the importance of the implied message, before being regulated in terms of the length and the form of sharing.

Another important change that comes with this level of self-understanding is a different relationship with one's own intuition (Sheldon, 2018), which is referred to as 'immediacy' in other fields of practice (Egan, 2017). A practitioner who develops this ability can notice their own emotions, hunches and subtle messages from their body as they occur, and utilise them in the session. Such information becomes additional data that can be used to influence the course of the conversation. This can be done explicitly by including this data in the conversation, or implicitly – by informing the immediate or future interventions. Research by Sheldon (2018) has provided some interesting ideas that illustrate this level of work. She discusses the differences in the effectiveness of these type of interventions as attempted by novices and by more experienced coaches. This finding, in my view, confirms that the second level of self-understanding is qualitatively different from the self-inventory level as it requires further developmental work from coaches.

My assumption is that this level of self-understanding is also a foundation for the ellusive quality of 'presence' that is now highly promoted in the professional coaching milieu. Noon (2018) has argued, on the basis of the results of his study, that presence is a way of being that is developed through the practice and experience of the coach. He advocates a more contextual and tacit understanding of this quality which, in my view, would clearly require a higher level of self-understanding than provided by self-inventory.

Capacity for self-disclosure, immediacy and presence are undoubtedly the benefits that this level of self-understanding brings to the quality of a coach's service to their clients. I would also argue that there are additional benefits to coaches themselves when they reach this level of self-awareness. Seeing their whole selves as instruments of coaching enables them to act in ways congruent to their current thoughts, beliefs and feelings. Their work becomes part of their natural self-expression. As they do not feel that they need to play a role in their professional encounters, this becomes more liberating, involving less emotional labour and is therefore less tiring.

All the above suggest that enhancing the quality of self-understanding to the level of the self as an instrument is a worthwhile endeavour. Educational literature on coach development suggests what can be done in this regard. It is noted, for example, that this process usually starts with a genuine curiosity about oneself, not just strengths and weakness, but emotions, physical states and fleeting thoughts. This focus of attention could be practised in more 'easy' contexts than coaching sessions, and recorded and reflected on after you noticed them at a more convenient time and environment. There are many useful exercises in the Gestalt tradition, and I can particularly recommend the book by John O. Stevens (2007), *Awareness: Exploring, Experimenting, Experiencing*, which is full of interesting activities designed to facilitate this process.

When it comes to coaching practice, supervision can play important role in developing this level of self-understanding as all its functions involve explicit work with the self-awareness of the coach. Although the experiences of this level are discussed in supervision 'after the event', an opportunity to explore them in a detailed and focused way enhances learning that can be derived from them. This helps to promote the sensitivity and readiness of the coach to 'catch' them in time and in the midst of new events.

Level 3: Fully professional self

This level of self-understanding implies a wider focus of attention, expanding further from the self-inventory level and even the self as an instrument. At this new level, coaches see themselves not only as an instrument that is part of a complex dynamic system with a client, but also as being part of a much wider set of social relationships that are at play when they coach. The focus of the coach's attention includes not only the client's story and its unfolding in the session, and not only the coach's internal states and processes, but also a complex interplay of the many different relationships in the interdependent environment of which both the client and the coach are part (Stacey, 2003). It could be said that, in the coaching session, this level involves a triple focus of attention.

Coaches who reach this level of self-understanding come to see coaching engagements as a self-organizing process of continuously active living systems (Thelen and Smith, 1994) and understand themselves as an integral part of such systems. Haämaälaäinen and Saarinen (2008) argue that practitioners operating at this level have 'system intelligence', as they are aware of the influence of the whole on them, as well as of their own influence on the whole. It is important, of course, to consider what abilities such system intelligence involves in the context of coaching. The following are the constituents of system intelligence that I have adapted for coaching from Martela and Saarinen (2013). They include a broad set of skills or abilities that are required of the coach a), in the session and b), outside of it:

(a)
- Awareness of the changing situation in the session that includes variation in states and actions of both the coach and the client, and the dynamics of the session;
- Tuning into this dynamic by sharing emotions and observations in order to facilitate intersubjective perception of the process;
- Agency as ability to adapt and act in different situations in the session.

(b)
- Reflexivity as the ability to reflect on one's motives, behaviours, ways of thinking and values that influence practice;
- Perspective-taking as the ability for adopting new perspectives and interpretations of practice;
- Long-term systemic orientation as an ability to recognise and attend to the cumulative and long-term effects of changes in the profession.

All of these abilities also need to be seen in the context of wider influences that coaches are subjected to. For example, coaches at this level of self-understanding are aware that they are affected by two dominant worldviews that co-exist at the moment: modernism and postmodernism. Being influenced by the modernist science-centred worldview, they may aspire for their coaching interventions to be evidence-based and supported by knowledge and theories provided by the core disciplines such as psychology. Being influenced by the postmodernist view that emphasises the world as socially constructed, these coaches aim for their intervention to be focused on the meaning-making conversations. Coaches with this level of self-understanding can recognise that modernist and postmodernist influences work at the same time and create various incompatible beliefs about our practice. For example, we, as coaches, believe in the unique self-expression of individuals, but create uniform competences frameworks. We may hate hierarchies but develop categories of professionalism, e.g., master-coach (Bachkirova, 2017).

Some of these coaches recognise being influenced by another worldview - pragmatism. Bachkirova and Borrington (2019) advocate philosophical pragmatism as the most appropriate philosophy of coaching. This position can be differentiated from both modernism and postmodernism because it avoids reducing strategic action to a single model, and

Table 4.1 Comparison Between Competent, Dialogic and Pragmatic Selves

Aspects Worldview	Competent Self Modernist	Dialogic Self Postmodernist	Pragmatic Self Pragmatist
Role of the coach	Expert at least in the process of coaching	Partner in a dialogue	Co-experimenter
Skills and tools	Are the main assets of the coach	Are secondary in comparison to a meaningful conversation	Are means for experimenting
Concerned with	Good practice, effectiveness, impact	Joined meaning-making in the session	New ideas for responding to client's situation
Coaching relationship	Is a means for successful work (development of trust)	Is a purpose in itself: A model of meaningful dialogue	A product of working collaboratively
Aiming for	Resolutions and action points	Often does not lead to closure and/or appreciate the value of issues remaining unresolved.	Extended ability to cope with issues and to act
Potential problems	Excessive structures and frameworks may stultify the process and reduce creativity	Coaching process without structures could become circular without benchmarks for progress	The criteria for success might not be explicit

Adapted from Bachkirova, 2016 and Bachkirova and Borrington, 2019.

allows greater flexibility for the role of the coach relevant to context and the task in hand. This attitude is compatible with complexity theories and with an understanding of self as a network of different mini-selves described above (Bachkirova, 2011). In this way, pragmatism allows the coach to act strategically in different ways according to changing situations.

Table 4.1 shows the differences between three mini-selves that are in tune with the three worldviews just described. The coach can recognise their dominant worldview, as modernism/postmodernism/pragmatism and a corresponding mini-self, as competent/dialogic/pragmatic, which may capture most appropriately their predominant style of coaching. At the same time, coaches can develop a capacity to act as any of them depending on the requirements of the situation. For example, the focus of attention by coaches on good practice and impact (competent self) may be highly appropriate at the point of contracting but then can shift to mainly meaning-making in a conversation (dialogic self) and, gradually, to experimenting and generating new ideas for the client's actions (pragmatic self).

What is important for the level of self-understanding as fully professional self is that coaches are able to take a look at who they are in relation to their practice and explore the ways they function in light of various important influences rather than being blindly led by them. This does not mean that they become fully independent from the ideas and discourses that affect them. This is not possible – we are part of our professional world as another complex and dynamic social system, and as such we are constantly being 're-made' by this system. However, awareness of such influences allows a little more flexibility and space to manoeuver in how we act, which also makes a contribution to this system and has some influence in the longer term.

Another feature that differentiates coaches at this third level of self-understanding is their ability to create a rationale of their approach to practise – their individual model of coaching as a unique professional offer to their clients. This ability requires a sophisticated analysis of their knowledge, skills and their own values and principles, examined through the lens of good number of theories and perspectives that have been influencing their view on human nature, change and development. Building such a model has been described as the 'Three Ps': philosophy, purpose and process (Bachkirova, et al, 2017; Jackson and Bachkirova, 2019), which can be simply presented as answering three questions: 'why, what and how' in relation to the approach to coaching.

'Why' refers to examining values and theoretical frameworks, a philosophy of practice, something that could be called a 'mission' on a wider scale, something that explains the 'what', which is what you as a coach are trying to achieve in your work. 'How' is about the process – what you do as a coach, what actually happens in your coaching sessions. What is important is that these three Ps are well aligned. For example, it would be a misaligned model if your 'why' includes allegiance to a pure person-centred perspective, but your 'what' is about helping a client to fit with specific demands of the organisation and your 'how' includes extensive use of psychometrics and other instruments. The model altogether should also be congruent to who you are as a person. It is in this way that this level of self-understanding builds on the previous level of the self as an instrument.

In order to develop this level of self-understanding of a fully professional self, coaches may need to invest in further education or re-visit a wide range of theories and conceptual perspectives. They need to develop a good level of criticality in relation to various influences, particularly to the flood of popular ideas that might be otherwise taken on board without any discernment (Bachkirova and Borrington, 2020). In terms of more specific skills, coaches would benefit from learning to observe themselves in their practice and actions in the same way that they observe others. This could help in taking a detached perspective to how we are in the midst of the complex dynamics of various systems. Finally, this level of self-understanding depends almost entirely on our reflexivity as a unique human capacity of paying attention to our own actions, thoughts, feelings and their effect in the interplay with the events in our environment. Good supervision for this work is simply invaluable.

Conclusion

Each level of self-understanding that I have explored in this chapter corresponds to the three centres that represent the notion of self on a theoretical level, which were introduced earlier. The level of self-inventory responds to the needs described in the centre of identity – this is how coaches build their professional identity. The level of the self as an instrument responds to the needs of the centre of awareness – bringing more of your self-observation for the needs of practice. Finally, the level of a fully professional self is about coaches in action, having a coherent rationale and taking responsibility for the interventions that they offer to their clients. These parallels show that theories of selfhood are not that far from our self-understanding and self-realisation in coaching practice – a fascinating union that we can and should promote.

References

Anderson, N. (2016). *Becoming a coach. MA in coaching and mentoring practice dissertation.* Oxford: Oxford Brookes University.

Bachkirova, T. (2011). *Developmental coaching: Working with the self.* Maidenhead: Open University Press.

Bachkirova, T. (2016). 'The self of the coach: Conceptualization, issues, and opportunities for practitioner development'. *Consulting Psychology Journal: Practice and Research*, 68(2), pp. 143–156.

Bachkirova, T. (2017). 'Developing a knowledge base of coaching: Questions to explore'. In T. Bachkirova, G. Spence and D. Drake, eds., *The SAGE handbook of coaching*, London: Sage, pp. 23–41.

Bachkirova, T., Jackson, P., Gannon, J., Iordanou, I. and Myers, A. (2017). 'Re-conceptualizing coach education from the perspectives of pragmatism and constructivism'. *Philosophy of Coaching: An International Journal*, 2(2), pp. 29–50.

Bachkirova, T. and Borrington, S. (2019). 'Old wine in new bottles: Exploring pragmatism as a philosophical framework for the discipline of coaching'. *Academy of Management Learning and Education*, 18(3), pp. 337–360.

Bachkirova, T. and Borrington, S. (2020). Beautiful ideas that can make us ill: implications for coaching. *Philosophy of Coaching: An International Journal*, 5(1), pp. 9–30.

Claxton, G. (1994). *Noises from the darkroom*. London: Aquarian.

De Haan, E. and Gannon, J. (2017). 'The coaching relationship'. In T. Bachkirova, G. Spence and D. Drake, eds., *The SAGE handbook of coaching*. London: Sage, pp. 195–217.

Egan, G. (2017). *The skilled helper: A problem-management and opportunity-development approach to helping*, 9th ed. Belmont, CA: Brooks/Cole.

Gallagher S. and Shear, J. (eds.). (1999). *Models of the self*. Thorverton: Imprint Academic.

Gazzaniga, M. (2012). *Who's in charge? Free will and the science of the brain*. London: Constable and Robinson.

Hämäläinen, R.P. and Saarinen, E. (2008). 'Systems intelligence – The way forward? A note on Ackoff's' why few organizations adopt systems thinking'. *Systems Research and Behavioral Science*, 25(6), pp. 821–825.

Hullinger, A., DiGirolamo, J. and Tkach, T. (2019). 'Reflective practice for coaches and clients: An integrated model for learning'. *Philosophy of Coaching: An International Journal*, 4(2), pp. 5–34.

Jackson, P. and Bachkirova, T. (2019). 'Three Ps of supervision and coaching: philosophy, purpose and process'. In E. Turner and S. Palmer, eds., *The heart of supervision*. London: Routledge, pp. 20–40.

Jourard, S. (1971). *The transparent self*. New York: Van Nostrand Reinhold Inc.

Kurzban, R. (2010). *Why everyone (else) is a hypocrite: Evolution and the modular mind*, Princeton, NJ: Princeton University Press.

Martela, F. and Saarinen, E. (2013). 'The systems metaphor in therapy discourse: Introducing systems intelligence'. *Psychoanalytic Dialogues: The International Journal of Relational Perspectives*, 23(1), pp. 80–101.

Noon, R. (2018). 'Presence in executive coaching conversations – The C2 model'. *International Journal of Evidence Based Coaching and Mentoring*, S12, pp. 4–20.

Sheldon, C. (2018). 'Trust your gut, listen to reason: How experienced coaches work with intuition in their practice'. *International Coaching Psychology Review*, 13(1), pp. 6–20.

Stacey, R.D. (2003). *Complexity and group processes: A radically social understanding of individuals*. Hove, UK: Brunner-Routledge.

Stevens, J.O. (2007). *Awareness: Exploring, experimenting, experiencing*. Gouldsboro, ME: The Gestalt Journal Press.

Thelen, E. and Smith, L.B. (1994). *A dynamic systems approach to the development of cognition and action*. Cambridge, MA: MIT Press.

Walker, S. (2004). 'The evolution of coaching; patterns, icons and freedom'. *International Journal of Evidence Based Coaching and Mentoring*, 2(2), pp. 16–28.

5 Understanding your clients

Alison Hardingham

Introduction

This chapter is about the most important person in the coaching encounter. Where most of social life is about trades and trade-offs, coaching is one of those special asymmetric relationships where one side's needs trump all. That side is the side of the client. In this chapter, I aim to give you frameworks for thinking as well as practical tools that will enable you to understand, accept and demonstrate respect for your clients. You may find that your coaching increases many times in effectiveness as a consequence.

Starting out

It is never too early to begin to imagine what life may look like through your client's eyes. From the first moment of contact with the industry, the organisation, the sponsor or refer-ring individual and, of course, the clients themselves, we can use every bit of information gained, every experience we have had and every spark of our own imagination, to begin to generate hypotheses about how the clients themselves might see their worlds. We will need to be seen as prepared and knowledgeable when we meet with our clients and their organisations for the first time.

Having done this diligent work of preparation, we will then need to set it all aside. For what we most need to offer our clients is openness, a willingness to learn about them and collaborate with them on a project of change of their choosing.

How can we walk this tightrope, between being prepared and yet unprepared, demon-strating that we are interested in our prospective clients and yet infinitely open to their truth, willing to learn what only they know? How can we, to borrow an expression from O'Connell's (1998, p. 42) description of solution-focused therapy, "develop a respectful collaborative stance which is oriented towards client goals"?

You will have noticed that I used the phrase "generate hypotheses" in the first para-graph. That is because this is the best way to think about all "knowledge" that we might infer about a client. A focus on generating hypotheses ensures we think about our clients, but keeps our thinking tentative. It is a way of thinking that demands of us that we listen and look for evidence to prove or disprove our hypotheses. It is a way of thinking that encourages us always to proceed slowly and, in proceeding slowly, we allow our client to teach us. We don't "know" anything about how the client perceives his world until he tells us, and even then we must always be prepared for developments, surprises and unfathom-able depths. How often has your understanding of a person fundamentally changed fol-lowing a sudden revelation of some fact about their life?

What is important in our wish to understand our clients is to know that, in truth, we never can fully know them. That ability to be comfortable with not knowing is of profound significance in all human endeavours. It is so important that Keats gave it a name, and saw it as at the heart of all creativity. He called it "negative capability": "the capability to be in the midst of mysteries, wonders and miracles, without irritable reaching after fact or reason" (1899). As coaches, we need to develop that negative capability in ourselves. We need to recognise that when we label, or decide on how, what, who and where a person is, we are "irritably reach[ing]" after a model or fact that gives us the certainty that we crave. Instead we would do better to follow Jung's advice, as quoted in Sedgwick (2001, p. 8): "Learn your theories as well as you can, but put them aside when you touch the miracle of a living soul". Or, as Bob Thomson (2009) captured for coaches in the title to his book, "don't just do something, sit there".

Thinking about our clients in this way helps us also to address our primary task, which interestingly enough is not "understanding", but rather acceptance. We need to accept who and what our client is. As Jung is reputed to have said, we cannot change anything until we accept it, and of course as coaches we are in the business of change. This deep acceptance of another's way of being in the world – even though we can never hope to understand it completely – is what we mean by "respect". It is the basis of rapport, and the foundation of trust. Interestingly, it is when, and only when, the client feels wholeheartedly accepted in this way that he begins to create his agenda for change (O'Connell, 1998).

A word of caution

Some readers may expect a psychologist (which is what I am) to provide them with a model for understanding their clients. Many abound, (see Passmore, 2012 for a review of psychometric models). Coaches may use these tools to stimulate discussion, raise awareness and identify strengths and weaknesses in their clients, and they can be very useful if properly introduced and handled.

But I am talking in this chapter about understanding, not diagnosis. I am talking about the sort of understanding which builds and sustains the coaching endeavour, and which is the foundation of the safe and trusting relationship on which most coaches would agree all effective coaching depends. Sometimes psychological models are useful here, but more often than not they can lead to pigeonholing and to assumptions about who and what the client is. More dangerously, they can encourage the coach to take an expert position in relation to the client, a position in which the coach imagines that they know the client better than the client knows him or herself.

Carl Rogers contrasted the attitude of many psychologists with that of a truly person-centred practitioner: "there are … many whose concept of the individual is that of an object to be dissected, diagnosed, manipulated" (1951, p. 21). How far that is from the coach, who seeks to develop with his clients a "partnership of equals" (Rogers, 2012, p. 9).

Developing our ability to understand: A golden opportunity

There is one thing we can do that will open our eyes to what our client may be thinking and feeling about the coaching in the first session and beyond. It is to be coached ourselves. So much can be learned from literally sitting in the client's chair! Every would-be coach should have plenty of opportunities to be coached and to reflect on that experience.

This experience can be a rich one, to engage in a full coaching experience for yourself quite independently of any coach training you may do. Indeed, people who have had one or several experiences of coaching are very aware of the vulnerability of being the client, the time it takes to reassure oneself about confidentiality, the difficulty of providing honest feedback to their coach and many more aspects of the coaching encounter. All these things they might have known about, indeed been taught about, but their true significance is only apparent when you have an experience of them at an emotional level.

Let me give you an example. Many novice coaches remain sceptical about the need for coaches to put aside advice giving. How can it not be helpful, they say, when you can see the problem clearly and know exactly what the client should do? And, of course, we may present all the rational arguments against advice, and they grudgingly begin to accept them, with their minds.

But they don't become convinced until they have the experience. Then they notice, for example, how annoyed they are when their coach gives them a solution. They notice how delighted they are when their coach gives them enough respectful space to work things out for themselves. They notice how joyful it is, and how challenging, when their coach asks them a question which they hadn't thought of that creates new lines of thinking in their mind. They become convinced, a conviction of the heart which can only be born from experience.

In order to learn from the golden opportunity being a client gives you, you need to keep four questions in your mind. Reflect on them before, during and after every coaching experience and you will grow inestimably in awareness of what can influence your client. These are the questions:

- What does my coach say and do which makes me feel confident in his ability to coach me?
- What does my coach say and do which makes me feel I can rely on them?
- What does my coach say and do which makes me feel comfortable with them?
- What does my coach say and do which makes me feel that they really care about me and my future (and care about that more than their own self-interest)?

(*after* Maister, Green and Galford, 2002)

The answers to these questions will develop your ability to understand your clients more than any psychological model I could give you. The opposites are at least as informative: "What does she say and do which makes me doubt her competence, her reliability, her genuine care of me?"; "What does she say and do which makes me feel less safe?" Mistakes and ruptures in the relationship can be as informative as good moments (de Haan, 2008, 2019).

Understanding how your client feels about you

People are generally ambivalent about meeting a coach. On the one hand, they may have feelings of pleasurable anticipation; on the other, they are likely to have some apprehension. How this mix of hope and fear (Hardingham, 2004) plays out in a particular individual will largely depend on how we have been introduced into their world, what their previous experience of "people like us" is, and the context of their life at the moment. I shall look more closely at each of these three factors in turn.

How we have been introduced into the client's world, and how they perceive us to have been, are very important to understand. When they have chosen us they are likely to have much more hope; when we have been forced upon them, more fear. I remember a client who I believed had a choice: I was recommended to him by a colleague who had become his boss. I accepted his ensuing 'choice' of me as his coach at face value, no doubt because it suited me, and also because I had enjoyed working with his boss. (I was expecting another enjoyable assignment!) Eventually, after two or three sessions in which he was very guarded with me, I realised that the relationship had always felt to the client like much more of a forced than a free choice. He had elements of hope, but he felt that if he did not go along with his boss's recommendation he would be unlikely to a have a future in the organisation. I had not spent enough time exploring his point of view; I had not spent enough time establishing a relationship in which he felt safe and accepted, a relationship of our own.

A client's previous experiences of coaching will also be key. If they have had a good relationship with a coach before, the client will generally expect good things from us. If the client has had a coach who failed, they will generally be more wary. These are things which are worth exploring in early conversations. You want to hear about their previous experiences because they may provide you with invaluable information about how you should proceed.

Similarly, the context of the coaching is very relevant. For example, are we seen as a "remedial coach", a last chance before redundancy? Or as someone who is a "tick in the box" before becoming eligible for promotion?

Throughout a coaching assignment, we can return to simple questions which, when asked in a calm and unthreatening way, will enable both coach and client to understand the client's starting point and current attitude better. Here are just a few.

- How did you come to this coaching relationship?
- How do you feel about it?
- What hopes do you have of our work together?
- And what fears?
- Have you had coaching in the past?
- What was your coach like?
- How is coaching seen in your organisation?
- How do you feel about coaching in your organisation?
- Do you know anyone who has been coached by me? What kind of relationship do you have with them?
- If our work together is successful, what will be different for you?

The intention is not to deliver a battery of questions at the start, but rather to have them in mind. Perhaps the question which drives all of these is: What do I represent to this client? And how does that serve them? And how does that change over time? Because the answers to these questions will in large part determine the balance of hope and fear in them, and therefore how much they are willing to disclose and therefore able to achieve.

If you are genuinely interested in this, you will notice many signals apart from their answers to direct questions. You will notice when they look away and when they engage with you directly; you will notice when they become comfortable with silence; you will notice when their tone is sharp, when neutral, when animated; all these things and many more will interest you and cause you to have hypotheses about what is going on for your client. Some of them you may gently enquire about: "I notice how you dropped your voice then". Some of the "noticings" you make you will hold in mind and wait to see if a pattern emerges before you enquire. Some you will simply hold lightly for a while and then you will turn your attention to other things.

You can see that one of the keys to understanding your client is to be interested in him, always and perhaps some would say obsessively so. And another key is your noticing, what is sometimes called "sensory acuity". Without sensory acuity, I believe we have no chance of understanding anyone.

I don't think curiosity serves us well here. Curiosity can too easily slip into wanting information for its own sake. We should only want information for our client's sake. We are interested in what he wants to tell us, and we are interested in "glimpses of brilliance" and "glimpses of resistance" – that is, things which will help them achieve their goals and things which will impede them. This is why we need to understand them as a unique individual.

For example, I have coached many people who do fascinating jobs about which I am intensely curious. But when I am in the role of coach, that curiosity is replaced by interest in the person in front of me, and in what they need to achieve and in how they believe I can be of use to them. Similarly of course I, like most other people, prefer others to like me and trust me. But that is not why I am so attentive to signs in my client that they do or don't. I know that I can only be useful to them if I am constantly building and maintaining a warm, safe relationship, removing at every opportunity obstacles to the work. And it is important that I don't take it personally when I uncover that the client is ambivalent about me. The question is, do they have enough hope to bring about change? And do they feel safe enough to use me and our relationship to do that? I remember one client who told me at the end of the work that she had initially engaged me to "get her boss off her back". (She knew that I came recommended by a consultant who had the ear of her boss.) Over time she felt safe enough to work on some quite sensitive issues that were important to her, with considerable success. I had noticed her reserve initially and, having understood that she was wary of me, I was able to allow time, and her experience of me, to enable the growth of hope. How differently that relationship might have worked out if I had been in a hurry to persuade her of my potential value as a coach, or if I had taken her reserve as a personal affront!

How can you communicate your interest and openness?

The messages a person hears about us are primarily determined by our intent, not by what we say. For example, when I say, "how are you?" you know whether I am truly interested or whether I am in a hurry to get to my agenda. I can even say, "I am interested in whatever you want to tell me", and be heard as merely going through the motions of interest. It will be my intent in that moment which gives me away.

We need to be sure that our intent is to understand as much of our client's world as they wish to share. The answer is to make that our conscious intent, especially at the start of the coaching relationship.

I have two thoughts that I take very consciously with me into every coaching encounter. One is from Flaherty (1999, p. 12): "Clients are always and already in the middle of their lives". The other is: "There is always pain in the room" (a comment attributed to Peter Frost, author of Toxic Emotions at Work). These two thoughts ensure that I begin every encounter with interest in and sensitivity to the world of the other, the world I am about to enter.

I also find it useful to remember that "in every consulting room there ought to be two rather frightened people. If there are not one wonders why they are bothering to find out what everyone knows" (Bion, 2014, pp. 9–10). That simple statement reminds me of my purpose in coaching: To find out something that is not common knowledge, something that perhaps neither I nor my client knows, something that will change things. This saying also reminds me that it can be a frightening space I am about to enter and enables me to bear my anxiety.

John Whittington, a systemic coach and author, recommends that all coaches hold a picture in their mind as they begin every coaching encounter: Imagine a peacock's tail fanning out behind your client, each feather representing a system with which the individual is connected. The feather's barbs and barbules represent the vast and complex array of interconnections which are at play. His recommendation ensures that we begin with respect for the total system of which the client is part, and awareness of the resources they have to draw on and the complexity they have to navigate.

These are all ways of drawing the coach's attention to the difficulty and excitement of the endeavour, and to the importance of working in that space of not knowing, the space of "negative capability".

You may have your own way of accessing your interest in and openness to another human being, and so communicating to them that you are a prepared and well-intentioned person. The important thing is to have a way.

Understanding their "model of change"

You need to understand what "model of change" your clients have. This will not generally be a fully worked out schema of how they believe change happens (although it can be!); it is more likely an amalgam of experiences of change that has worked and change that hasn't, a few general beliefs about change, things that they have noticed and have stuck with them and some views about how much change is desirable and what the risks are. If you can understand how they see change as happening in their lives, and in doing so enable them to understand it, then they can begin to explore what they already have which will help them.

The most straightforward route to understanding this is simply to ask, with interest, "When have you brought about a change?" You may need to prompt them, with questions like "In your professional life? What about your personal life?" You may need to stay close to the matter at hand, "When have you had this reaction to someone before? How did things develop from there?" You may need to go quite far away in your "fishing expedition": "Have you ever at any time been aware of anything changing in you?" The questions are infinite, but what you are doing is following your interest in their change process and helping them to become interested in it themselves. Patience, ingenuity and confidence are key here. Patience because your client may need a lot of time to think: They may be thinking about this for the first time so it could be difficult for them. Ingenuity because you need to be able to generate a path for them to follow, you need to think of different lines of questioning when one doesn't yield fruit and you need to be able to spot when your client is onto something. And the confidence which goes with knowing that, however hidden from view and however difficult to access they are, the client does have relevant experiences of change.

You do not have to proceed in this straightforward way. You should in any event always have your antennae out for mention of change, explicit or implicit. For example, a client of mine once told me about a habit he had established of six-monthly silent retreats.

These were times, he described, when he could recover from the stresses of his job. My antennae were very active at this point! By the end of our coaching relationship, he was able to identify much more fluidly and responsively when he needed a retreat, and took to scheduling them at times when he was beginning to lose patience with people around him. This enabled him to regain perspective and ultimately played a significant part in his being seen differently at work and being promoted to Finance Director.

If you are attuned in this way, you will pick up on many things in your client's conversation which will give you clues on how he sees change. A casual comment, when repeated enquiringly by you, becomes something to explore and yields initially unexpected dividends. I remember a client who remarked about her issue "I know what it's all about: I saw a psychiatrist when I was younger. What I need is something I can do about it!" In that moment I abandoned all thoughts of insight-driven methods and opted to work in a much more immediately practical way.

Using their words

I have already discussed how being a client increases our understanding of what clients feel by giving us an experience of it. Using the client's unique words can sometimes have a similar power. Language is the medium through which we understand the world. The words we use are not random; they carry enormous amounts of meaning about the world as we see it. As coaches, we may choose to use the client's exact words to capture the unique aspect about the situation or circumstances. But in doing so we need to be careful to avoid becoming a parrot, our aim is to reflect back our deep understanding of what the client is communicating.

When we repeat a word or phrase that our client has used, we find our emotional state changing to match that of our client. Let me give an example. Working with a client on his relationship with his boss, he used the phrase "pocket rocket" to describe her. When I reflected back "pocket rocket?" he laughed. He eventually realised he gave that nickname to women whom he found intimidating, and that opened up a whole new line of thinking. But I noticed how it changed my perception of her, too, and I was able to appreciate how he had been feeling about her constant change initiatives and "Duracell bunny energy" (to quote my client further).

Using the client's own words (but never parroting!) can be a powerful way to understand their world. Of course, the insights we gain can only be hypotheses until our clients confirm them, but they are hypotheses well worth having. In contrast, conventional summarising with our words may reassure us we have understood what they have said, but rarely provides new emotional insight. At worst, it will sound to the client as if their words weren't good enough and needed rephrasing, and so fail to build equality in the relationship. Nancy Kline (1999, p. 165) is particularly vehement on this point: "the best wording is the thinker's own … Those words mean something to the thinker. They come from somewhere and are rich with the thinker's history, culture, experience and any number of associations in the thinker's life".

Understanding their "resistance"

The word "resistance" belongs to the battlefield model of the helping relationship. In this model, the helper is on one side, fighting the good fight against the client's dark side, which is trying to drag him back into his "old ways". In this model, resistance has to be "overcome" if the client is to truly move forward.

I think there is another way to understand "resistance". It is the part of our client that protects what they are, the part of our client that is not yet ready to risk change. As a part of our client it also must be understood, accepted and respected. In fact, its appearance can be welcomed as a sign that the client is seriously contemplating making a change.

If we can embrace our client's resistance when we experience its push-back, then our client will be reassured at a deep level that we are safe and mean them no harm. If we can be as interested in their resistance as in their cooperation, they may well themselves become interested and so learn something of great value to them.

Here is an example. A client of mine brought a very difficult work situation to the table. The representative of HR and a consultant who had been engaged to work alongside this client said in the three-way meeting that the organisation needed her to learn new skills. The reason why the consultant had been engaged was that he had those skills, and my client could learn them from him. Once she had learned them, she would be ready to move fully into the role which she was currently sharing with the consultant.

Once these two people had left the meeting, my client asked for confirmation of the confidentiality of our meetings, and then promptly broke down in tears. She couldn't get on with this consultant, and her tears prevented her examining why. You could say that the tears were her "resistance" to change. But I was patient and waited to see what happened. I thought (but of course didn't know) that the tearful part of her might have some information that neither the calm part of her nor I had, and that information was what the tears were about. Eventually, after about three sessions of profound distress, she found that she had evidence that the consultant was planning to take her place in the organisation with the full support of her boss. She became able to face that painful and in some ways humiliating truth, check that it was real and ultimately plan a way out of that dead-end situation. Ultimately, she found a way to continue to develop her career in the organisation.

This brings us back to the central point of this chapter. We need to be endlessly interested in every aspect of our client that they choose to reveal to us. Because that is who they are, and they will find a way to use everything that they have, including their resistance, to achieve what they want. Whether they are hopeless, helpless, angry, complacent, hostile, manipulative or any number of other things that might irritate us, the challenge is for us to find a way to stay patient and interested. The more of themselves they show us, the more there is to work with.

Staying close: Little questions and feedback forms

We cannot understand our clients when we make assumptions about any aspect of their lives. To borrow and plunder a popular phrase: The price of understanding is eternal vigilance!

I know of no better way of practising the art of eternal vigilance in coaching than by the regular use of what I would call "little questions". These are questions that ensure we remain close to, and in touch with, our client's experience as we do the work together. I give some examples below:

- How is it going?
- What has helped you so far?

- Are you closer to your goal?
- How are we working together?
- How are you feeling about our work together?
- How helpful is this?

In every case, the little question can lead to an exploration of the client's perspective. It is important that we ask these questions with intentionality (even though they are small, they may well open up large issues). We also need to be ready to move on if the client is happy with the work and can see value in what we are doing. We are asking them so that we can know how the coaching process, for which we are responsible, is working for the client. It may not be until we articulate the questions that the client begins to see themselves as having not only responsibility for the work but also for making ongoing evaluations of the process of working with us.

Whenever we feel the need to take an even more considered look at the client's perception of our work and indeed of the relationship between us, a feedback form will open up the areas we need to explore. The feedback form below is a suggestion, to be used certainly when we have had our first meeting and then at other times as we feel the need. See Table 5.1.

Questionnaires like this one are simply tools to assist reflection and discussion. Some clients find it hard to say how things are going; they fear offending us. But when they have the opportunity to give these ratings, they may indicate their dissatisfactions with perhaps a 9 or an 8. It is worth exploring any rating which is below 10, and the ensuing

Table 5.1 Questionnaire to help a coach and client to assess their working alliance

To what extent did I feel comfortable in the session?

Very uncomfortable	1	2	3	4	5	6	7	8	9	10	Completely comfortable

To what extent does the coach clarify the coaching process?

I am still very confused	1	2	3	4	5	6	7	8	9	10	I now feel very clear

To what extent do I feel I am heard and understood?

Coach didn't seem to listen	1	2	3	4	5	6	7	8	9	10	Coach heard and understood me perfectly

To what extent do I feel I am making progress towards my goals?

Not at all	1	2	3	4	5	6	7	8	9	10	Extremely

How open am I able to be?

Not very	1	2	3	4	5	6	7	8	9	10	Completely

How supported do I feel?

Rather unsupported	1	2	3	4	5	6	7	8	9	10	Very supported

How much new thinking am I doing?

None	1	2	3	4	5	6	7	8	9	10	A huge amount

To what extent do I believe we can continue to work well together to achieve my goals?

Not at all	1	2	3	4	5	6	7	8	9	10	Strongly

conversation will provide you with a great deal of information about your client that might otherwise remain hidden. Not only that, it will provide you both with opportunities to understand the relationship which is developing between you, to communicate at the "meta level", which is so profoundly important in enabling dynamic shifts and breakthroughs (de Haan, 2008).

Conclusion

Hopefully I have achieved what I set out to in this chapter: To demonstrate and provide frameworks that help you to understand your client in ways which will support your coaching of them. That will not be a static understanding (such as a diagnosis) but a dynamic understanding, always changing and shifting along with the client's understanding of themselves. For as O'Connell (1998, p. 15) put it, "the purpose of [your] dialogue is to negotiate jointly a meaning to the client's situation which will create the possibility of change for him".

References

Bion, W.R. (1974). *Bion's Brazilian lectures: 1.* In C. Mawson, ed., *The complete works of W.R. Bion* pp. 3–10 (2014). London: Karnac.

de Haan, E. (2008). *Relational coaching: Journeys towards mastering one-to-one learning.* Chichester: John Wiley and Sons.

de Haan, E. (2019). *Critical moments in executive coaching: Understanding the coaching process through research and evidence-based theory.* Abingdon: Routledge.

Flaherty, J. (1999). *Coaching: Evoking excellence in others.* New York: Butterworth-Heinemann.

Frost, P.J. (2003). *Toxic emotions at work: How compassionate managers handle pain and conflict.* Boston, MA: Harvard Business School Press.

Hardingham, A. (2004). *The coach's coach: Personal development for personal developers.* London: CIPD.

Jung, C.G. (1928). *Contributions to analytical psychology.* London: Kegan Paul.

Jung, C.G. (1933). *Modern man in search of a soul.* Abingdon: Routledge Classics.

Keats, J. (1899). *The complete poetical works and letters of John Keats.* London: Houghton, Miffin and Company.

Kline, N. (1999). *Time to think: Listening to ignite the human mind.* London: Ward Lock.

Maister, D., Green, C. and Galford, R. (2002). *The trusted advisor.* London: Simon and Schuster.

O'Connell, B. (1998). *Solution-focused therapy.* London: SAGE.

Passmore, J. (2012). *Psychometrics in coaching. Using psychological model and psychometrics for development.* London: Kogan Page.

Rogers, C.R. (1951). *Client-centered therapy.* London: Constable and Company.

Rogers, J. (2004). *Coaching skills: A handbook.* Maidenhead: Open University Press.

Sedgwick, D. (2001). *Introduction to Jungian psychotherapy: The therapeutic relationship.* New York: Brunner-Routledge.

Thomson, R. (2009). *Don't just do something, sit there: An introduction to non-directive coaching.* Oxford: Chandos.

Whittington, J. (2012). *Systemic coaching & constellations: An introduction to the principles, practices and application.* London: Kogan Page.

6   Non-violent communication

Alison Hardingham

Introduction

Non-violent communication sounds a strange title for a style of communication for a coach, but this model of communication sits at the very heart of good coaching practice. In this chapter, I shall be applying various principles of non-violent communication to our work as coaches. I shall illustrate how they help us to coach effectively, and also give suggestions as to how we can develop our non-violent communication skills.

A brief overview of non-violent communication

Marshall Rosenberg invented the term "non-violent communication" in the 1960s (Rosenberg, 1999). Since that time, it has grown and diversified its appeal and become an international movement which seeks to replace the more manipulative and coercive forms of communication with communication based on understanding, compassion and peace. It has been used in conflict-torn environments of all kinds, often to great effect, enabling communication between, for example, Israelis and Palestinians, and police and revolutionaries. Its influence has also spread to parents and children, doctors and patients, the rich and the poor, the mentally unwell and society as a whole; indeed, to any groupings which were originally based on a dynamic of power. In this sense, it is a perfect foundation for thinking about our communications in coaching.

Marshall Rosenberg was a psychologist by education and profession, who acknowledged Carl Rogers as a key influence. Much of his theory is based on Rogers' humanistic practice.

Non-violent communication requires attention to be focused on four aspects of a communication: Observations, feelings, needs and making and receiving requests with empathy.

An observation is an honest and specific description of something which needs to be addressed in the speaker's mind. For example, "I notice you roll your eyes when I speak". So as not to cloud the communication with emotion (a tactic often used by people in "violent" communication) the observation is made calmly, and the words are chosen with care.

Then attention is paid to the feelings of the speaker. He might say, "I feel undermined when you do that". You can only describe your own feelings and not those of another person. (You can already see how different this exchange is from normal, "violent", communication, which would probably have already combined observation and feelings with some comment like "You are always raising your eyes to the ceiling as if I was stupid!!")

Then comes the identification of what need in the speaker is or isn't met and has given rise to that feeling of being undermined. Again, it is his own needs that the speaker is focusing on. He might say "I see how I need more respect than I am currently receiving". He is still speaking calmly.

Finally, he makes a request, which he believes will satisfy that need. "Would you be willing to tell me what you are thinking when you roll your eyes?"

In non-violent communication the listener first listens empathically. Then he responds with attention to his own observations, feelings, needs and requests, and the original speaker listens empathically. And so the process continues. As it does, it builds an atmosphere of mutual respect, interest, compassion and concern for the other's unmet needs.

Non-violent communication requires us to differentiate between what is observable (and hence a matter of objective fact) and our feelings about it (which result from our own needs, values, culture and are in essence a judgement). Not only that, it requires us to begin to understand ourselves and others at a deeper level and see the unmet needs behind the feelings and actions. That is why it is a practice of compassion.

It also requires of us that we can speak truthfully about what we need, and put requests to others which may of course be denied but are at least clearly understood. That is why it is a practice of collaboration.

I am sure you can see how much self-discipline is present in non-violent communication. We have to discipline ourselves to hold back and ultimately set aside our judgements for they will hamper our understanding and block the path to collaborative enterprise. Non-violent communication is at heart a spiritual practice, something which Rosenberg readily acknowledged. But the lessons it teaches are relevant to us all, and particularly relevant to coaches, whether or not we choose to practise at a spiritual level.

First principle: Separating our observations from our responses

When we coach, of course we are responding all the time. Many of our responses will be judgements about our clients, about the gravity of their situations, about what they should do next and so on. We cannot become a *tabula rasa* on which the client can write his own story, nor should we. For it is our experiences of being human which make us uniquely valuable to our clients and give to us the foundations of empathy. In short, it is who we are that has the potential to build a relationship, and who we are is the sum of all our experiences.

But we need to hold our judgements at arm's length, because they are not necessarily going to be helpful to our clients. In fact, they will probably be positively unhelpful, for they introduce an element of evaluation into the conversation which is likely to make the coaching space feel less safe for the client. Evaluations also discourage independence of thought and personal responsibility in the client, both of which are necessary for a successful coaching relationship.

One of the most useful tools here is the ability to separate our observations from our responses. This is in fact exactly what Rosenberg writes about in the third chapter of his book, and he sees it as the foundation of non-violent communication. It is also the foundation of effective coaching.

One way to support novice and experienced coaches to enhance their ability to separate observations from responses, is the "The Henley Eight". This consists of eight questions which a coach can ask herself in order to understand a response she has to something the client said or did. In understanding it, she can achieve more distance from it. It runs as follows:

Box 6.1: Worked example of the Henley Eight

Imagine a client starts a session saying "I don't really have a goal today". That is what the coach observed: It is factual, can be observed by anyone present and could be recorded if so desired. So the answer to the first question the coach asks herself is: "What did I observe?"

The coach may respond in a number of ways. She may, for example, feel anxious about what she will do in the session, or critical of the client for not doing enough preparation, or concerned to help the client "get a goal". (I have heard all these responses to a comment like the one we are considering here, and many more, reported by coaches.)

To draw her attention to that response, she simply asks the second question: "How did I respond?"

It can take time and practice for us all to disentangle our responses from our observations. The response follows the observation within microseconds, and often one has the impression that the response came first, that it is actually what happened. For example, a coach may report in a frustrated tone: "My client came without a goal!" We all need to learn how to put distance between our observations and responses, and we all will find it particularly difficult when our responses to certain behaviour are ingrained, or imbued with our deepest held values. Imagine a coach, for example, who places a high value on preparation. Her sense of being disrespected by this client who says "I don't really have a goal today" might be immediate and strong.

The next question in the Henley Eight is therefore essential, if a coach is to be encouraged in drawing this difficult distinction. That question is: "What does the relationship between my observation and my response tell me about me?" That is when the coach sees that in separating the observation from the response there is the opportunity to build self-awareness. She becomes interested in her responses rather than being captivated by them. She asks herself, what does it say about me that I responded to that innocent statement "I don't have a goal" with a feeling of being disrespected?

There is even more for the coach to get out of exploring this relationship between observation and response. The remaining questions in the Henley Eight point the way: What does that characteristic of mine (which I have just discovered/re-discovered) tell me about me as a coach? What does it tell me about my strengths? And what does it tell me about my potential pitfalls? So what do I need to learn to do right now, to capitalise further on my strengths and to mitigate the risk of my pitfalls? How will I know how effective that learning has been? What will I observe?

My client talked for the first ten minutes without pausing.

How did I respond?

I felt like there was something I should have been doing to stop him, but I didn't feel I could interrupt. I felt pretty useless.

What does that response tell me about me?

I am not used to being out of control. I like to help others by getting involved.

What does that tell me about me as a coach?

I might find it difficult just to listen.

What does it tell me about my strengths as a coach?

I suppose I really care about my clients and want to help them. I am really keen to learn and do the right things.

And what does it tell me about my potential pitfalls?

I might not be patient. And I might do something just to get less anxious, and it might not be helpful.

What do I need to learn?

The first thing is probably to check with more experienced coaches what they do.

How will I know how effective that learning has been?

My anxiety will come down. And I won't feel so useless.

Box 6.1 takes you through a complete worked example, from a novice coach who was just learning to separate her observations from her responses.

You can practise separating observations from responses in all areas of your life. Once you have learned this technique, you may well find it opens up to you the possibility of becoming more self-aware in many respects.

There is another, related technique for developing this capability. It is the left-hand column (see Senge et al., 1994, pp. 246–252). Next time you are in a meeting, divide your note paper into two columns. On the right, you record things that people do or say (observations). On the left, you jot down any reactions you are having (for example, *bored, what is he repeating himself for?, don't believe him*). Senge suggests many uses of the "left-hand column approach", from improving team work to problem solving. But you can use it as a way of simply understanding yourself better, as with the Henley Eight.

The practice of reflection, which is an essential part of being an effective coach, starts with the ability to separate what happened (observations) from how we responded at the time. So any self-reflective tool is helping us to develop this core capability.

But be warned. As Daniel Kahneman notes "What can be done about biases? How can we improve judgments and decisions … ? The short answer is that little can be achieved without a considerable investment of effort" (Kahneman, 2012, p. 417).

Second principle: Identifying and expressing feelings

Just as it is vital for a coach to enable their client to express their feelings so it is also vital that they, the coach, can identify and express their own feelings. And this is the second capability which non-violent communication develops.

The coach quite naturally has all sorts of feelings about the client. These can either be put to good use, or they can get in the way of effective coaching. Let me give an example of each.

I worked with a client who I really admired. She was an HR Director and before I coached her I had worked alongside her on a number of projects. I had always found her to be impressively smart and knowledgeable, extraordinarily diplomatic, hard-working, well connected, egalitarian and humble. After an amazing career she felt burnt out, and asked me to be her coach. Session after session came and went; she was in despair at the prospect of "abandoning" her colleagues, the "impossibility" of finding consultancy work as an independent practitioner, and the general pervasive misery of the way she felt. The one thing I held onto, for her as much as myself, was my certainty that should she find it possible to take the step, she could succeed in any way she chose. Even when she was at her most distressed (and I too) I admired her. Had it not been for those feelings of admiration, which I did not speak about explicitly, I doubt I could have resisted being dragged down with her. Suffice to say, she did leave her organisation and she crafted a great second career for herself. She has always said that my coaching had enabled her to see this through.

I saw another client who made me nervous. I never overcame the sense of fear with which I approached every meeting, and I know that fear led me to avoid saying what needed to be said. I was unable to talk about it in our coaching. Had I been able to do this, it could have been transformational, as I picked up enough about this client from interviews which she had asked me to conduct on her behalf to know that I was not the only one she intimidated. At the time, I was not in regular supervision and so had no one to whom I could talk about my nervousness.

In non-violent communication, it is an essential part of the dialogue for both parties to be able to identify and express how they feel. Not only that, it is essential for the speaker also to be able to step away from the feeling – which can of course be overwhelming in the moment – and say calmly what it is. In that moment the speaker masters herself sufficiently to be able to speak about a possibly intense emotion calmly.

This is an ancient idea. Lao Tzu, the ancient Chinese philosopher and founder of Taoism, said: "He who controls others may be powerful, but he who masters himself is mightier still" (Lao–Tzu, 2000).

As coaches, and as non-violent communicators, we do not need absolute self-mastery as advocated by Lao-Tzu, but we do need to be able to become calm about some of our strongest feelings, so that we can reflect on what they might mean, and judge whether or not it could be helpful to communicate them to others. In both my examples of the power of my emotion in enhancing or interfering with my coaching, that calmness (and its absence) were key. In the first example, I was able to acknowledge my deep admiration of that HR Director, and calmly judge that it would not be appropriate to voice it. In the second example, I was never able to articulate my nervousness calmly, but continued to suffer from it throughout.

How can we build this capability in ourselves, to be able to put the intensity of feeling to one side and reflect calmly on what it tells us and what it would be best to do about it?

First, the simple act of noticing that we are feeling something intensely can be calming. In that moment of noticing, we have begun to separate, to become an observer of ourselves.

Then again, the simple act of putting a name to what we are feeling continues this process of separation. We might like to keep a diary of feelings that we have at different moments in our lives, to practise this art. We might like to watch films, and identify the feelings of the characters. There are all sorts of everyday activities which build our ability to identify our feelings (for example, see "The EQ Edge", Stein and Book pp. 53–65).

To build a vocabulary of emotional language, you could begin with the lists of emotions in chapter 4 of Rosenberg's book. Practise using these words in your diary or when you are watching films; that way you will become more able to identify your own feelings.

Finally we need to develop the capability to articulate calmly to our client what we are feeling. At the moment of speaking about our emotion, there is a risk that we become emotional. It is so important to avoid this in non-violent communication, because otherwise we will start a chain of emotionally charged and hence "violent" communication with our first utterance. It is also important in coaching if and when we decide to articulate our feelings. If I had said in a nervous manner to the second client I described above, for example, "When you speak like that about your colleagues, I feel intimidated", he would no doubt have felt something in his turn, and gone on to reassure me, intimidate me more, deny angrily, or communicate in some other emotional way; our coaching would have been derailed. If I had been able to speak and act calmly, saying, for example, "I am wondering about why it is that I feel intimidated when you talk about your colleagues in that way, and I am wondering whether we could explore this together, whether it might be a reaction that others feel too", then the path to useful coaching would have remained clear.

Sustaining an attitude of purposeful reflection is the key to this calmness. If we enter any communication with an attitude of curiosity rather than with a feeling, we can remain in this state of calmness even when we are talking about our feelings. We are inviting our client to become curious with us: What could this emotion, experienced by my coach, mean? Have I ever elicited it before? Or is it about her, to do with how she is prone to feel? How did I notice it? What am I learning about myself here? Reflective conversation about emotions that are strongly felt is the bread and butter of effective coaching.

Principle Three: Seeing needs behind behaviours and communications

This principle is where non-violent communication teaches us as coaches a practical method of developing our compassion, both our compassion for ourselves and our compassion for our clients. We develop this compassionate stance by looking beyond the behaviours to the needs which gave rise to those behaviours. It is a compassion which results from the effort we put into understanding why a client might be behaving in the way that he is. It is not compassion that simply is or is not in you, it is not emotional empathy; it is intelligent compassion, cognitive empathy, (Bloom, 2016), which requires work and time to bring forth, and which is therefore available to everyone.

I shall illustrate this too with an example drawn from a coaching encounter. A coach whom I was supervising came to our session very upset. He had met his client for the first time the week before, and had been offended and hurt by what the client had said in that first meeting. The coach had introduced himself, and had mentioned his background (he had been a teacher for many years, then held a post in a local government authority and was now starting to develop his coaching abilities). The client was a business woman. When the coach had finished his personal introduction, his client leant back in his chair, and what the coach described as a "smirk" crossed her face. Then she said, with a laugh: "Ha! No experience of the real world then".

The coach had struggled on with the coaching and managed to regain a temporary composure. But he brought this story to supervision because he recognised that his own feelings of hurt were interfering with the relationship. He couldn't get back that calm concern for his client with which he had started the coaching. His own strong feelings meant he wasn't able to listen to his client as attentively (Stone, Patton and Heen, 2000, pp. 89–90).

It is at this point that the hard work of compassion begins. The coach needed to reflect on the many possible reasons for the hurtful comments by their client. At the start he felt that the client didn't value him as a coach and didn't respect him. That may have been true; but the coach needed to think further. What other possible explanations could there be?

I am sure you, as an objective and distanced observer, can already think of many. For example, perhaps the client felt uncomfortable, being the vulnerable one in this encounter. She needed to identify the coach's vulnerability as a way of avoiding hers. Perhaps she was just clumsily making a joke: She needed to reduce her own anxiety in that way. Or perhaps she needed to assert the "reality" of the situations she faced, because she was fearful of not being taken seriously by this coach who had not experienced them.

I do not, and neither will I ever, know what the true explanation is. More importantly, neither will the coach. What is important is that he brought the issue to supervision and did some hard thinking about what needs of his client may have given rise to that comment. In that thinking, he regained both his calm and his compassion. He was then well-placed to engage in the next coaching conversation holding all these possibilities lightly in mind, having compassion for all the possible circumstances of the client's life and calmly interested once more in whatever his client wished to focus on.

There is one question which unlocks this kind of thinking more than any other. Assume first that the client is smart and well-intentioned. (This would be a good starting point for most coaching conversations!) Then ask yourself: Why might he have said or done this thing? Generate at least three possible hypotheses, applying each time your criteria of assuming his intelligence and positive intention. That simple but disciplined approach will in all likelihood elicit your compassion. In many cases, it can do so very quickly, if it is a practised habit, as it needs to become for a coach.

Principle Four: Making and receiving requests with empathy

The next principle takes the application of empathy further. It is worth making the distinction here explicit, between emotional and cognitive empathy. It is the latter we need and not the former.

Emotional empathy is the shared feelings which ultimately arise from the identification of one human being with another. It means "your suffering makes me suffer, ... I feel what you feel" (Bloom, 2016, p. 17). It is without doubt powerful, it is largely unconscious and instinctive, and is the basis of much good in the world, including our enjoyment of literature and films. It is also why emotions are contagious and can be overwhelming in their effects. Emotional empathy is not a choice. It cannot be switched on or off at will.

Cognitive empathy is quite different. It is a conscious choice, to imagine the life of another person. It lacks the immediacy of emotional empathy, and requires us to make the effort to understand another fully. The fourth principle of non-violent communication is to use cognitive empathy to make and receive requests.

In a sense, the coach is making requests of their client all the way through their coaching encounter. In fact, you could say, coaching *is* making requests of your client! From the first question, which is requesting a focus from your client (What do you want to achieve in this session? What do you want to think about? What's going on in your world?), to the last, which is requesting a commitment (What do you want to do? How will you know? When would you like to meet again?), we are asking the client to think and marshal their thoughts in a particular way. That is no doubt why people often comment on how much hard work it is to be coached. That is almost certainly one of the reasons why some people avoid it.

One of the most important things here is knowing and making the distinction between requests and demands (Rosenberg, 1999, pp. 79–81). The coach is entitled, expected, to make requests. But she is not entitled to make demands. Any request, however phrased, however spoken, can be heard as a demand. The only way to be sure we as coaches have made a request is to notice how it lands, and to be responsive to that.

A simple example will perhaps clarify things. It can be found in Box 6.2.

In this exchange, the client knows that the coach has made a request of them rather than a demand because of the way the dialogue develops. The paraphrasing that the coach uses demonstrates that they are open to any response to their request for a focus, including a statement that appears to deny the request. That is how the client knows that it was indeed a request and not a demand. The tone throughout from the coach is calm and accepting, indicating neither impatience nor urgency.

Box 6.2 An example of making and receiving requests

Coach: Well what do you want to think about today?

Client: I'm not sure.

Coach: You're not sure what you want to think about today.

Client: I'm so tired.

Coach: Is it possible for you to say if you need anything from me right now?

Client: Some space to gather my thoughts, I guess.

Coach: Some space to gather your thoughts. What does that space to gather your thoughts look like?

Client: I think it's quiet, and up to me, and I will let you know when I've had enough.

Coach: OK. I can be quiet and you will let me know when you've had enough. We have 30 minutes today for our coaching.

Client: I'm not sure that's long enough.

Coach: You're not sure that will be long enough for you to gather your thoughts?

Client: Uh, no.

Coach: I will need to be elsewhere after our 30 minutes. What will you need from me, if you haven't had long enough after 30 minutes?

Client: We can schedule some more time next week.

Coach: OK. Let's agree that if we get to the end of this 30 minutes and you haven't had enough time to gather your thoughts, we will schedule some more time next week.

What is also going on in this example is the establishing of empathy by the coach. This is one of the reasons why it appears to be such a painstaking piece of communication. It is indeed an effortful process, to engage in truly empathic communication. Empathy requires we listen, not just to the words, but also to the feelings and needs behind the words. As Peter Drucker, is said to have quipped, "the most important thing in communication, is hearing what isn't said". The kind of painstaking paraphrasing shown in Box 6.2 is where we feel and demonstrate empathy with our client. As we speak their words, we gain insight into what it is like to be them. As we speak his words, he feels understood in a way he is generally not used to. Carl Rogers (1964, quoted in Rosenberg, 1999, p. 113) put this very powerfully:

> When someone really hears you without passing judgement on you, without trying to take responsibility for you, without trying to mould you, it feels damn good. When I have been listened to and when I have been heard, I am able to re-perceive my world in a new way and go on. It is astonishing how elements that seem insoluble become soluble when someone listens. How confusions that seem irremediable turn into relatively clear flowing streams when one is heard.

Non-violent communication is the essence of coaching communication, which enables our clients to make soluble what seemed insoluble before. Practising the disciplines of non-violent communication is the key to deep listening, listening which enables our clients to replace confusion with a clear flowing stream.

There is a final point to be made about empathetic communication of the kind which is recommended in non-violent principles. Because it is based on hard work, on an act of will and discipline to listen and speak from a place of cognitive empathy, it guarantees the coach's presence. Presence stops being a mysterious quality which a coach must strive for at all times. It becomes instead a consequence of disciplines applied painstakingly throughout a coaching conversation. When we are seeking to understand the points our client is making, seeking so hard that we repeat their words, reframe our misunderstood requests, enquire for clarity until our client feels understood and check that they do at all times, then we are present with them. When we make assumptions about what our clients mean, make careless demands on them, let ambiguities and generalisations pass without enquiring further and rarely check whether they feel understood, then we are not present with them. When we are listening for the feelings and needs behind our client's speech, we are present with them. When we are taking what he says at face value, we are not.

Appreciation

Compliments have no place in non-violent communication. They imply a judgement, albeit a positive one. They imply a hierarchy between the two people, one who has the authority to offer the other a compliment. It is too in coaching. If I as a coach say to my client: "Well done!" or "Good solution!" or even "Fantastic that you delivered on all your commitments", it undermines the safety and the equality of our coaching relationship.

Appreciations are different. If I notice something that you have done that has met a need of mine, and also notice how I felt in consequence, and then tell you about it, then we are both affirmed. There is no question of judgement and so no risk of inequality. That atmosphere of affirmation is a good and informative thing, entirely at one with the coaching endeavour.

Just to give one example of this from my own practice, I had been coaching a Finance Director for some time. I recognised that he had allowed himself to be vulnerable in my presence. At the end of our coaching session, I said: "When you spoke of your sadness, I felt trusted and that reminded me of why I do the work I do. I thank you for enabling me to appreciate it anew".

Similarly, do not take pleasure in compliments that your clients pay you. If they say you are great, ask them what you have said or done that they valued, how it made them feel and what they were able to do in consequence. Enabling your clients to follow the non-violent principle of appreciation will enable you to grow in confidence and skill as a coach.

Conclusion

Non-violent principles are at the heart of the coaching encounter, and have power to achieve some of the most important goals of our enterprise: Deep listening, presence, rational compassion, collaboration and a non-judgmental stance. As you move forward you may like to reflect on how you can build non-violent capabilities in yourself and develop as a coach. I will end with a quote which underlines the spiritual nature of non-violent communication wherever it is practised.

> The more you become a connoisseur of gratitude, the less you are a victim of resentment, depression, and despair. Gratitude will act as an elixir that will gradually dissolve the hard shell of your ego – your need to possess and control – and transform you into a generous being. The sense of gratitude produces true spiritual alchemy, makes us magnanimous, large souled.
>
> (Rosenberg, 1999, p. 184)

References

Bloom, P. (2016). *Against empathy: The case for rational compassion*. London: Bodley Head.

Kahneman, D. (2012). *Thinking, fast and slow*. London: Penguin.

Lao-Tzu (2000). *Tao-Te-Ching* (Book of the way). London: Kyle Cathie.

Rosenberg, M.B. (1999). *Nonviolent communication: A language of life*. Encinitas, CA: PuddleDancer Press.

Senge, P.M., Kleiner, A., Roberts, C., Ross, R.B. and Smith, B.J. (1994). *The fifth discipline fieldbook: Strategies and tools for building a learning organisation*. London: Nicholas Brealey.

Stein, S.J. and Book, H.E. (2003). *The EQ edge: Emotional intelligence and your success*. Toronto: MHS.

Stone, D., Patton, B. and Heen, S. (2000). *Difficult conversations*. London: Penguin.

7 Understanding the coaching relationship

Charlotte Sills

Introduction

The 21st century has seen a significant shift in the philosophical, theoretical and methodological focus in coaching. It is a shift that has mirrored similar movements in many walks of life, from philosophy, organizational theory and psychotherapy, to art and architecture. It has become known as "the relational turn" and it acknowledges, in coaching and psychotherapy in particular, that the human personality is largely formed in a relationship and therefore is likely to change in a relationship. It involves a shift in emphasis from the individual to the social, and from the intrapsychic to the interpersonal. It moves from focusing on the development of individual insight and skills to engagement with patterns of relating. It places the relationship – to self, to colleagues, to coach – at the heart of the work.

In this chapter, I start by describing what is known about the importance of the relationship in coaching and then go on to describe the impact of the relational turn on the work.

Why has the relationship become so figural?

Many factors have influenced the increasing recognition of the coaching relationship's importance. They include discoveries in neuroscience, sociology and child psychology, which come together to highlight relationships as being key to the development of human beings: to the quality of their well-being; to the formation of their ways of living and behaving; and – most importantly for coaching – to change and growth.

Most convincing evidence is the information that emerged from the now well-known psychotherapy outcome research. Coaching shares many features with counselling and psychotherapy (for example, two people in a relationship, both committed to the growth and development of one party who is willing to share and explore their situation in order to discover more effective ways of living). Coaches can therefore learn important lessons from some of the research into successful psychotherapy outcomes, the data from which has been gathered over the last 70 or 80 years. This research has identified the "common factors" that contribute to positive change and studied their relative importance. In the last 25 years, new research and several meta-studies have been carried out (e.g. Asay and Lambert 1999; Wampold 2001; Norcross and Lambert 2011, 2019; Norcross and Wampold 2019; Flückiger et al. 2019) which have confirmed again and again that a significant contribution to a successful outcome is the existence, from the client's point of view, of a positive therapeutic relationship. That means a relationship in which the client feels themselves to have been met and understood, with empathy and acceptance, even after they have begun to show aspects of themselves that they are anxious about or ashamed of. There are other factors of course, but many of them are, in any case, a part of establishing this relationship – in particular, the making of clear agreements about the broad goals of the engagement and how therapist and client are going to work together. With that core foundation of the secure relationship, all manner of different theoretical approaches and methods can be effective, provided they pay attention to the establishing and sustaining of a working relationship.

Interestingly, it seems also that the therapist needs to be both confident and committed to his approach and, at the same time, flexible about responding to the client "where he or she is" so that they can work in a way that suits the individual client. Norcross and Wampold (2019, p. 2) quote Osler (1906) whom they describe as the "father" of modern medicine, as saying "It is much more important to know what sort of a patient has a disease than what sort of disease a patient has"!

As coaching is a much newer profession, the research is necessarily less extensive, but initial findings into coaching outcomes support the same conclusion (see, for example, Baron and Morin 2009; De Haan and Duckworth 2013, De Haan, Grant, Burger and Eriksson 2016). Having a relationship in which the client feels understood and accepted is significant to a good outcome. Interestingly, De Haan et al. (2016) suggest that, in terms of outcome, the agreement about goals and tasks (in other words, the contract) is as, or even more, important an aspect of the relationship than the bonds of warmth and respect. This points to a need for further research.

In a way, however, we have no need of research to tell us that people learn best in supportive relationships. If people are asked to recall a relationship or conversation they have had which has been generative, productive and even transformative, they will consistently report that they were in the presence of someone who gave them space to think and speak their own thoughts and feelings, did not judge them and, on the contrary, seemed to really understand and empathise. The reader is invited to do this exercise themselves. Leading psychotherapists and neuroscientists put it even more strongly: Fosha (2000, p. 60) says 'The roots of resilience and the capacity to withstand emotionally aversive situations without resorting to defensive exclusion are to be found in the sense of being understood by and *existing in the mind and heart* of a loving, attuned, and self-possessed other'; Schore (2019) emphasises the importance of "positive affect interactions" and non-verbal affective connection between right hemispheres of brains – what he calls the "right brain to right brain connection". Of course, they are echoing the ideas of Carl Rogers, who wrote about the six "necessary and sufficient" conditions for growth as long ago as the late 1950s (Rogers 1957). They are summarised in Table 7.1.

The implications for practice are clear. The coach needs to consciously pay attention to building a strong working alliance, including a bond of warmth, empathy and non-judgement. The coach does that by listening attentively, both verbally and non-verbally, offering back summaries of what they have heard in terms of content, values and perhaps unspoken feelings. They are empathic and engaged, with a spirit of open inquiry. They also attend to such boundary issues as confidentiality, clarity and a contract about broad goals and how to meet them. There is a skill to agreeing a clear enough direction or goal to create a safe container, without tying the work down so tightly that it restricts the possibility of new issues emerging. Clients (and their organisations) may well feel safer making measurable, behavioural-outcome goals at the beginning of the work, but coaches need to be ready to talk about perhaps deeper, more complex or more distressing issues later if clients feel warmth and acceptance from the coach.

Table 7.1 Rogers' "necessary and sufficient" conditions

---

1. Two people (in this case coach and client) in "psychological contact" with each other – in other words, a meaningful encounter.
2. The client experiences what Rogers described as "incongruence". They are at odds with themselves and feeling some distress for which they are seeking help.
3. The coach experiences congruence, which means they are as fully self-aware as possible, authentic and true to themselves.
4. The coach demonstrates "unconditional positive regard" – in other words, warmth, acceptance and respect for their client, even in their less likeable aspects.
5. Empathic understanding for "the client's private world as if it were your own, but without ever losing the 'as if' quality" (Rogers 1957, p. 829) – without becoming merged with the client.
6. These core attitudes of the coach are at least somewhat successfully communicated to the client. Interestingly, this involves, to a certain extent, the client being open and empathic to the coach and enters the domain of the relational approach (see below).

Of course, all this does not mean that the coach needs to be nurturing, agreeing, offering support and never confronting the client. It is by joining the client in a bond of trust and then bringing their separate mind to bear on an issue that the coach will offer a valuable experience. It is the complex balance of sameness and difference that makes the nature of the encounter between coach and client so rich.

Carl Roger's "sixth condition" for change is an important one here. The other five involve two people in relationship, one (the client) sharing their difficulties and the other offering empathy, congruence and unconditional respect. However, the sixth condition states that the client must genuinely experience the coach's warmth and acceptance, and this might be easier said than done. It is not OK if the coach "knows" they are empathic but the client feels missed or misunderstood. In order for the trust to be real, they will have to explore differences and expectations, projections and perhaps historical biases. Differences of gender, race, nationality, age and sexuality can all be experienced as potential barriers to the establishment of the bond and the coach needs to find a way that these things can be spoken about.

Box 7.1: Story

Jo was one of a team of coaches involved in a consulting intervention into Sam's organisation. Jo was assigned randomly to Sam for six sessions of coaching. Jo was a white working-class woman from the north of England. Sam was a black African American from a professional family in Philadelphia, who had relocated with her husband to London.

They spent the first session identifying what Sam wanted to work on, setting goals thinking about a three-way meeting with Sam's manager and finding out what impact the consulting intervention was having on Sam. Jo noticed that they were being rather polite and formal with each other.

After a pause, she said

I am aware that we have quite a lot in common – we are the same sort of age and gender, we are both married … And I am also aware that we are very different as well. I am wondering how that is going to be for us – and what we can do to make our differences a source of something interesting and helpful – not an obstacle. I imagine that you will have some experiences of being you in DL [Design Life – the organisation] that I might not understand – and I really hope that won't stop you bringing them so we can both engage with them.

Looking relieved, Sam agreed. They spent some time talking about their very different experiences (both positive and negative) of being "other" in DL and in London, and gradually a feeling of warmth and trust began to build.

Relational coaching

In many fields, including coaching, the focus on relationships has gone beyond recognising the importance of a trusted, empathic bond. This extended focus is founded on the premise that the relationship – including the coaching relationship – is the central vehicle for change (see, for example, Sills, Critchley and Smith 2002; de Haan 2008; Denham-Vaughan and Chidiac 2008, 2010; Critchley 2010; de Haan and Sills 2012; Critchley and Sills 2017, Cavicchia and Gilbert 2018). *Relational coaching*, as it is known, emerges from a particular view of people and organisations.

First and foremost, human beings are "hard-wired" to connect. Relatedness is an organising principle of life and we develop our sense of ourselves in relationship with others. In other words, we are born in relationship, shape and are shaped by others in relationship and develop relational patterns which tend to endure. Sometimes these relational patterns become unconscious and habitual and, as the world changes, the person fails to adapt to the new reality. Change comes about, again in relationship, as we experiment and co-create potentially new ways of relating. Our sense of reality and the world is constructed socially. The meaning we make of our experience is therefore an inter-subjective process. This worldview extends to organisations, seeing them not as fixed entities but as complex social processes, which are constantly moving between flux and stability, ever-changing.

This way of thinking means that coaches – in addition to the usual tasks of helping clients develop the skills and insight they need for their jobs – are always interested in the processes of relating: the client to themselves, the client to their organisation, their colleagues, the world and also to the coach. They will be aiming to use here and now data from the coaching encounter to help the client recognise the way the client is in the world – out of choice or out of habit – and question whether it is still appropriate. This means that the coach cannot simply be a supportive sounding board. They must bring themselves to the encounter – a "two-way street" which has the possibility for both repetition of old patterns and novelty.

The relationship will have its stumbles and moments of misunderstanding. If they are to be used as information about the client's (and, no doubt, the coach's) way of being in the world, they must be welcomed and explored. It is important to keep attending to the relationship – checking with the client about how it is going, repairing any ruptures that emerge, exploring. Another way of thinking about this, is Stark's (1999) now famous model of "one-, one-and-a-half- and two-person" approaches to helping relationships. In a one-person approach, the client brings their problems and the coach helps them finds answers. The coach aims to be a skilful instrument. In one-and-a-half-person approaches, the coach becomes more of a supportive guide or mentor. In other words, the person of the coach is important, but largely in a helping role. In two-person approaches, there are two full human beings in the room together, both bringing themselves, their habits and their experiences and mutually shaping each other. The coach as person is completely relevant although always, of course, in the service of the client.

Relational coaching in practice

Relational coaching, therefore, has some particular biases when it comes to practice. Neuroscience tells us that change comes from re-experiencing an old pattern, feeling or reaction *in the present* at the same time as observing it and reflecting on it. The coach will be paying attention to the dynamic that is created between themselves and the client and be ready to raise the client's awareness of it in collaborative inquiry. When making the contract about their work together, they will have explained a little about how people can often get in their own way by using old patterns of relating – sometimes learned way back in childhood – and that their way of working is to invite noticing and inquiry about how the client is relating in the here and now – to themselves, to the coach and also to others in the client's life. Getting an agreement about that way of working engages the client in collaborative curiosity and awareness.

As part of exploring the relational dynamic between them, the coach will take seriously all of her own here and now responses in the room, be they thoughts, intuitions, images, feelings, pieces of music – anything. She will use it not as truth but as data about what might be happening, and she will be willing also to share some of it. This can be valuable feedback for the client to learn that at least one person in the world experiences him a particular way – and the hypothesis is, of course, that it might be a response the client commonly evokes in others. Alternatively, the coach may be resonating with a feeling or experience that the client has not allowed himself to connect with. In this case, offering it in a spirit of inquiry can help the person to know himself more deeply.

Box 7.2: Story

Eddie's client, Robert, was a large man, muscular and assertive. His small engineering firm had been taken over by a big global operation, and he had been made COO. The HR Director recommended him for coaching as his "people management skills" were not thought to be strong. Eddie sensed that his client felt somewhat humiliated by being "sent" to coaching and was therefore quite empathic about Robert's frequent rather dismissive and scornful comments to him. Eddie often felt quite attacked, but (having read all the research about successful helping relationships!) felt that it was his job to stay empathic and understanding.

One day the attack was particularly vicious – with Robert brusquely asserting that coaching was a waste of time and that he didn't want to listen to someone "talking about feelings all the time". In that moment, Eddie felt as if a bucket of water had been thrown over him. Frozen, he simply agreed to Robert's demands, empathising with his need to take charge of the process and merely suggesting that they give each other feedback more regularly.

In supervision, Eddie reflected on what had happened. He knew that he wanted to be seen as the robust, understanding coach. But he realised that he had actually felt hurt, frightened and humiliated in the session and he recalled his school-day experiences of having to show that he was tough in order to avoid being bullied. As Robert had taken the bully role, Eddie had avoided feeling vulnerable by being understanding and interested in Robert's thoughts.

In the following session, he said,

> I was thinking about last session and what was happening between you and me. It made me feel a bit like how I felt at school. And it brought to mind something you told me about your father. I wondered if your father made you feel scared and ashamed when you were little.

Robert looked shocked and then began to talk about his experience with his bullying father and his decision never to let anyone see him as vulnerable. The growing closeness in the coaching relationship began to "open the edges" of his rigidity.

Both of them had been trapped in an old relational dynamic. Bringing it to awareness, they could regain their capacity for mentalising and contribute to the development of meaning and thought. Robert gradually realised that he had been using the same self-protective measures in his role at work.

The vignette points to a valuable area for relational coaching concerning the phenomenon known as *parallel process*. This was first described by Harold Searles (1955) and refers to a relational dynamic in one place being repeated in another. What this means for a coach is that they need to be aware not only of the client in their organisation – their patterns, strengths and weaknesses – but also of the organisation in the client and the organisational dynamic in the consulting room. The relational dynamics of an organisation can be very significant; frequently they have been unconsciously practised and emphasised for years and this can be a very powerful shaper of the individual's experience and way of being. Certain ways of relating are amplified and repeated while others are "disappeared". If the coach notices those in the coaching sessions, it can be extremely useful for a client to begin to understand the "sea" in which he is swimming (see Chidiac 2018).

Box 7.3: Story

Sarah was a recently promoted senior manager in a consulting organisation and came for coaching to help her develop into her role. Harriet was disconcerted at how well the coaching seemed to be going! Normally she ended each session receiving glowing praise from Sarah and she felt very happy with the good job they were doing together. She began to wonder, however, when after three sessions, they paused for review and Sarah had absolutely no "developmental" feedback for Harriet. She had nothing but rather generalised positives to say. More tellingly, Harriet found herself reluctant to say anything but warm appreciation for Sarah. She also noticed that she did not seem able even to comment on their mutual appreciation. The expression "spitting in the soup" drifted unbidden across her mind.

She plucked up courage and said "Have you noticed, we seem both to be having trouble giving each other any negative feedback at all?" Sarah said she hadn't particularly noticed. However, as she reflected, she realised that her own organisation – psychologically sophisticated as it was – never seemed to exchange any robust feedback internally. They were excellent at supporting each other and rather poor at helping each other develop. As they talked, Sarah wondered whether it was because they felt united in "dealing with" the demands of clients and couldn't bear any criticism from colleagues. She saw that the effect was not only that she did not get much clear guidance from her superior or her colleagues. She also realised that she did not quite trust the good and appreciative feedback she received.

They began to talk about how she might make a difference in her organisation, starting with her own team and also identifying some colleagues with whom she might be able to "change the conversation".

Caveat: Relational yet flexible

Coaching approaches are not "one size fits all". Relational coaching means focusing on the person in the room. As was described above, the research shows that, paradoxically, while the coach needs to whole-heartedly believe in their approach, she also needs to be willing to flexibly respond to the client where the client is and in the way they find most useful. For the coach, this means being alert to what makes sense and seems helpful to the client. Are they someone who works best with clear behavioural objectives, do they prefer to think things carefully through a situation before doing anything else, are they someone who needs to be met in their feelings and invited to pay attention? The coach needs to be aware of their own proclivities in these matters and consciously adapt to the client's preference, meeting them in the way that makes sense and perhaps later inviting them to explore other aspects or ways of working.

In other words, a relational approach is an attitude – even a philosophy – not a model or theory, so it can be used in many ways. Box 7.4 lists a number of core skills that the relational coach can employ, whatever their approach.

Box 7.4 Relational skills

- Paying full attention (holding the paradox of intention without investment in particular outcome);
- Reflecting back/paraphrasing;
- Offering summaries;
- Asking open questions (inquiry);
- Noticing own feelings and responses;
- Noticing relational dynamics;
- Self-disclosing as appropriate;
- Noticing language, pattern and metaphor;
- Offering feedback;
- Allowing intuition to work on the unfolding story;
- Offering hypotheses;
- Suggesting options.

(Adapted from Critchley 2002)

Relational style

In recognising the need to be flexible in approach, it can be useful to think about *attachment styles* – a way of understanding a person's life-long patterns of relating, developed by Mary Ainsworth and colleagues (2015) from the work of John Bowlby (see, e.g. 1975). Their ground-breaking research into children's reaction to separation from and reunion with an attachment figure, their response to strangers and their capacity to engage with their world, identified four patterns of relating that seem to endure over time and form the basis of the adults' attachment styles. The first style is *secure* – a person who relates easily and comfortably to people, who trusts the constancy of their attachment figures (e.g. spouse, partner, friends, colleagues) and who engages confidently in the world and the challenges of their professional role. These "securely attached" individuals are likely to respond well to the intimacy of a relational approach and be interested in learning about themselves in the immediacy of the here and now. Then there are three styles of less confident or "insecure" relating: *avoidant/dismissive*, *preoccupied* and *disorganised*. The avoidant style is a person who has learned to relate only minimally to their own experiences and feelings. They find it difficult to get close to colleagues and can appear rather aloof and dismissive. It is important that coaches regulate their own style so that the avoidant person does not feel intruded upon but experiences the coach's interest and attention. She needs to be active, but not too active, as they build the alliance, probably meeting the client in their thinking about the task. The "preoccupied" person is preoccupied with relationships and making sure to avoid aloneness. Clients with a more preoccupied style can give the impression of engaging well with coaching, but they can get dependent and invite the coach to do the thinking for them. In their professional roles, they have a tendency to sacrifice creative thinking and rigour in favour of the relationship and they get uncomfortable with disagreement. The coach's task is to meet them in their emotional experience and then invite them to think and plan for action.

Disorganised attachment styles are hugely emotional and changeable – quick to anger, usually controlling and scared by what they experience as an unpredictable and dangerous world. They are unlikely to come to coaching and would probably be better off with psychotherapy. However, if the client does seem to have this style, the coach's job will be to provide a safe calm space in which the client can learn to think about their feelings and begin to mentalise about themselves and the people around them. (Mentalising, in brief, is being able to notice, think about and make sense of one's own motivations, thoughts, beliefs, feelings and behaviour, and also experience another's behaviour and think about what feelings and thoughts might underlie it).

The two styles of preoccupied and dismissive – or flavours of them – are not uncommon in coaching clients. It is important to think about the emotional distance – getting too close or standing too far back? – taking into account the likely effect of their own attachment proclivities. The original attachment theory was developed before the relational turn had its impact on the therapeutic world. As a result, although it emphasised that attachment styles are a direct result of early relationship, the adult's attachment style was seen to be something of a fixed pattern. A relational coach on the other hand will be fully aware of their impact as they co-create relational opportunities for repetition as well as for experiment, change and growth.

Conclusion

The core work of coaching of course remains the same – raising awareness, identifying unhelpful patterns, supporting clients in learning new skills and behaviour and so on. However, research, as well as developments in our understanding about the importance of relationships, have provided a new context for the work of coaching. The implication is that coaches need to recognise that they in their "personhood" are their most important "active ingredient" in the coaching. They need to get to know themselves, their attachment styles, their biases and preferences and notice how they shape the coaching encounter. They need to pay attention to building a steadfast working alliance and then invite the client to "play" and explore as they engage with new strategies and new ways of being in their organisations.

References

Ainsworth, M., Blehar, M., Waters, E. and Wall, S. (2015). *Patterns of attachment*. New York: Routledge.
Baron, L. and Morin, L. (2009). 'The coach–coachee relationship in executive coaching. A field study'. *Human Resource Development Quarterly*, 20(1), pp. 85–106.
Bowlby, J. (1975). 'Attachment theory, separation, anxiety and mourning'. In Silvano Arieti, ed., *American handbook of psychiatry*, 2nd ed, Vol. 6. New York: Basic Books, pp. 290–308.

Cavicchia, S. & Gilbert, M. (2018) *The Theory and Practice of Relational Coaching*. London: Routledge.

Chidiac, A.-M. (2018). *Relational organisational gestalt*. Oxon: Routledge.

Critchley, B. and Sills, C. (2017). 'A relational approach to coaching'. *Coaching Perspectives*, 12, pp. 40–45.

De Haan, E. and Sills, C. (2012). *Coaching relationships*. London: Libri.

De Haan, E. and Duckworth, A. (2013). 'Signalling a new trend in coaching outcome research'. *International Coaching Psychology Review*, 8(1), pp. 6–19.

De Haan, E., Grant, A., Burger, Y. and Eriksson, P.-O. (2016). 'A large scale study of executive and workplace coaching: The relative contributions of relationship, personality match, and self-efficacy'. *Consulting Psychology Journal: Practice and Research American Psychological Association*, 68(3), pp. 189–207.

Denham-Vaughan, S. and Chidiac, M. (2008). 'Dialogue goes to work – Relational organisational gestalt'. Paper presented at International Association for Advancement in Gestalt Therapy, (AAGT) Conference, Manchester, UK (July 2008).

Denham-Vaughan, S. and Chidiac, M.-A. (2010). 'Dialogue goes to work: Relational organisational gestalt'. In R. Hycner and L. Jacobs, eds., *Relational approaches in gestalt therapy*. Cambridge, MA: Gestalt Press.

Flückiger, C., Del Re, A. C., Wampold, B. and Horvath, A.. (2018). The Alliance in Adult Psychotherapy: A Meta-Analytic Synthesis. *Psychotherapy*, 55. 10.1037/pst0000172.

Fosha, D. (2000). *The transforming power of affect: A model for accelerating change*. New York: Basic Books.

Norcross, J. C., & Lambert, M. J. (2011). Psychotherapy relationships that work II. *Psychotherapy*, 48(1), 4–8.

Norcross, J. and Lambert, M.J., eds. (2019). *Psychotherapy relationships that work. Volume 1: Evidence based therapist contributions*, 3rd edition. Oxford: OUP.

Norcross, J. and Wampold, B., eds. (2019). *Psychotherapy relationships that work. Volume 2: evidence based responsiveness*, 3rd edition. Oxford: OUP.

Rogers, C. (1957). 'The necessary and sufficient conditions of therapeutic personality change'. *Journal of Counseling Psychology*, 21, pp. 95–103.

Schore, A. (2019). *Right brain therapy*. New York: W.W. Norton.

Searles, H.F. (1955). 'The informational value of the supervisor's emotional experiences'. *Psychiatry*, 18, pp. 135–46.

Section 3

Core coaching skills

8 Goal-setting in coaching

Ruth E. Price

Introduction

Goal-setting is a key component of many coaching conversations. In recent years widely accepted best practice has been challenged through new research findings, and new thinking is encouraging the testing of what has previously been held as unquestionably true. The coach lore that we as coaches have practised has largely been based on theories and research drawn from organisations, and specifically from management models for controlling performance. How generalisable is this to the messy and multifaceted world of coaching?

This chapter assumes no prior knowledge of coaching theory or practice. It takes the reader on a journey in four parts. First, the presentation of the traditional guidance for goal-setting, namely the use of SMART goals and the need to situate these early on in the coaching process. Second, a summary of how understanding and acceptance of goal-setting has started to move away from the traditional approach. Third, an identification and description of the salient factors at play – the goal, the client, the coach, the organisational sponsor and the environment – in order to raise awareness of the nuances of goal-setting in the coaching context. Fourth, a broadening of the two concepts of traditional goal-setting to encourage flexibility, sophistication and thoughtfulness in coaching practice.

Traditional goal-setting practice

Start with a goal

A popular type of coaching practice begins with the early articulation of a goal. Typically this means setting a goal at the start of a single session, determining what result the client would like to achieve. Here, the coach's role is to distil the client's presenting topic into a "bite-sized chunk that is achievable in the timeframe" through questioning and probing (Alexander, 2010, p. 84). For greater coaching success, ownership for the goal lies with the client and not the coach (Gessnitzer and Kauffeld, 2015).

The setting of the goal becomes the catalyst that drives the remainder of the coaching conversation. This is demonstrated in the linear application of a coaching model, such as GROW (Alexander, 2010; Whitmore, 2017), where:

- Goal – The desired outcome for coaching is determined;
- Reality – The distance between the current situation and the desired outcome is established;

- Options – The ways of closing this gap are identified and evaluated;
- Will/Way Forward/Wrap-Up – The client decides and commits to action that will help them achieve their goal.

In the traditional practice, the aim of goal-setting is to create the direction and motivation for the individual to attain the goal set. How, therefore, can goals be framed to ensure goal success?

SMART goals

The pervasive SMART framework, originally published as a method for setting objectives within organisations, states that a goal must fulfil five specific criteria, which results in the SMART acronym (Doran, 1981). The original framework, and variations of it, are shown in Table 8.1.

This framework probably originates from the work of Edwin Locke, who in the late 1960s conducted a review of existing research to create a theory explaining the link between setting conscious goals and successful task performance (Locke, 1968). Amongst his conclusions were that difficult goals produce a higher level of performance output than easy-to-achieve goals, specific hard goals produce a higher level of output than "do your best" goals and working towards a goal is a strong form of motivation in itself. This prompted Gary Latham to put the theory to the test in a workplace setting, providing empirical evidence for the link between goal-setting and performance. Their combined work resulted in five principles of goal-setting (Locke and Latham, 1990):

- Clarity. To be motivating a goal needs to be clear. It is not open to interpretation and it is obvious when it has been achieved;
- Challenge. Ensure that the goal is stretching, but achievable. Setting a goal that is too easy or too hard to achieve will not be motivating;
- Commitment. Individuals have to understand and buy-in to the goal from the outset;
- Feedback. To keep motivation levels high, provide regular feedback throughout the whole process. This also ensures progress is kept on-track;

Table 8.1 SMART framework and its variations

		Variations
S	Specific – Target a specific area for improvement	Simple Single
M	Measurable – Quantify or at least suggest an indicator of progress	Meaningful
A	Assignable – Specify who will do it	Agreed Actionable Achievable Attainable Attractive
R	Realistic – State what results can realistically be achieved, given available resources	Relevant
T	Time Related – Specify when the results can be achieved	Time-phased Time-bound

- Task complexity. For a goal to motivate, it must be kept relatively simple. Highly complicated goals can be overwhelming and should be broken down into sub-goals.

Use of the traditional approach in coaching

Given the wealth of supporting evidence for traditional goal-setting, it makes sense that coaches are keen to adopt these principles and models in their practice: In order for the client to achieve their desired outcome, a goal is first set and this goal is framed as SMART. There is also evidence that coaching clients want to set goals that are specific and measurable (Wastian and Poetschki, 2016).

There are certain coaching issues and coaching contexts that are likely to benefit from this approach. Research in the 21st century, albeit outside of the coaching context, has shown that this type of goal-setting has positive effects where the task is straightforward, the task is routine, the person believes they have the competence and self-efficacy to achieve the task and they are looking to improve their performance. Grant (2013a) studied solution-focused, cognitive-behavioural coaching over a four-session coaching engagement, at the start of which clients described a goal they would like to achieve. He concluded that a goal-focused relationship, where the coach facilitated the setting of stretching yet attainable goals and achievable action plans, along with asking about progress and blockers, was the strongest predictor of coaching success (i.e. goal attainment).

But coaching encompasses a much wider range of contexts and issues than this; what does that mean for goal-setting?

A challenge to traditional goal-setting

Thought leaders have been articulating, documenting and debating the realities of the multifaceted ways of approaching goal-setting in coaching (see, for example, David, Clutterbuck and Megginson, 2013). Interview studies with coaches found that they utilise different forms of goal-setting in their practice, and do not stick solely to the SMART approach (Kotte, Müller, Diermann and Möller, 2018, cited in Müller and Kotte, 2020).

Coaching research is overturning and clarifying earlier findings on which practice is based (e.g. Braunstein and Grant, 2016 study on approach vs avoidance goals). There is a call for more testing of what we hold to be true, where no evidence in either direction exists.

Professional bodies are revising competencies for coaching practitioners; for example, replacing the competency of Planning and Goal-Setting, including explicit reference to setting SMART goals, with Facilitating Client Growth (ICF, 2019). From this, there is an expectation that coach training and practice will similarly follow suit and realign to new ways of thinking and doing. This chapter hopes also to play a part in this change.

Other writers have provided a wide-ranging critique of classic goal-setting theory, criticising the over-prescribing of goal-setting within organisations and arguing that goal-setting can be more damaging than beneficial (see, for example, Ordoñez, Schweitzer, Galinsky and Bazerman, 2009).

Factors that impact goal-setting in coaching

What is it about coaching that means the traditional model of goal-setting is not always a good fit? I set out five salient factors, which are not intended to be exhaustive, but rather serve to illustrate the point about the complexity of goal-setting in coaching.

The goal

SMART goals are just one type of goal, even if popular use of the term leads us to consider them as synonymous. Goals are much more multi-dimensional in nature than this narrow definition suggests. In order to encompass this multi-dimensionality, I am adopting a broader definition of goals, which also captures the purpose of goal-setting in coaching as a mechanism for change: Goals are "internal representations of desired states, where states are broadly defined as outcomes, events or processes" (Austin and Vancouver, 1996, p. 338).

The SMART framework was designed nearly 40 years ago, as guidance for creating objectives in a steady, top-down organisational context. How can the more recent, alternative and broader literature inform our approach to goal-setting in a coaching context? At present, there remains a call for a single perspective to draw together all of the theories and research findings related to goals (Clutterbuck and Spence, 2017). Table 8.2 summarises a selection of the various dimensions of goals, based on theory and research, in relation to their practical application for goal-setting in coaching.

The client

Clients are all individuals with their own idiosyncratic preferences and characteristics. We can expect that they will differ in their preference for working with goals. A study on SMART goals found that 25% of people are motivated by them, 25% preferred to work with the image of a desired state, 25% preferred to focus on incremental steps towards the goal (rather than the goal itself) and 25% preferred not to explicitly plan at all (McKee, 1991, unpublished PhD dissertation, cited in Clutterbuck and Spence, 2017). Where SMART goals were not preferred (all in the latter three groups), people reported greater stress and reduced motivation. Observation has also been made that some clients have become down-hearted by past attempts to reach their goals and so are not energised by the idea of setting specific goals (Drake, 2015).

Clients will also differ in their readiness to change and move to action. Part of the coach's role is to identify where their client is, as rushing a client who is not ready to set a goal is likely to lower coaching success. A helpful distinction can be made between clients in a *contemplation stage*, where they are considering making a change but have not taken any steps to do so, and those who are in the *preparation stage*, where commitment to change has increased and the client intends to make changes in the near future. These are two of the six stages from the Transtheoretical Model of Change (Prochaska, Norcross and DiClemente, 1994).

This may play out in the purpose behind why the client has sought coaching – what are their reasons for engaging with a coach? If a client is looking for broader life coaching and deeper growth and development (cf. incremental improvement in workplace performance coaching), they may be in the contemplation stage. Here, more time for learning, insight, exploration and self-reflection will best serve them rather than goal-setting (at least, goal-setting in the traditional sense).

A client's current (adult) developmental stage will also influence their goal selection (Kegan, Congleton and David, 2013). To apply the five stages of Kegan's (1994) theory, the majority of adults are considered to be at stage 3 – the "socialised mind", where what matters most are the ideas, norms and beliefs of the people and systems around them. We would therefore expect to encounter clients who wish to set goals that satisfy how they appear in the eyes of others, driven by the "should" or "ought" self (a controlled goal).

Table 8.2 Goal dimensions and their practical application to goal-setting in coaching

	Goal dimension	Summary	Practical application to goal-setting in coaching
1	Approach or avoidance goals	Approach goals are a state the client wishes to move towards (what they want); conversely, avoidance goals are a state the client wishes to move away from (what they do not want).	Approach goals have been advocated as more beneficial as they are more concrete and attainable and evoke positive possibilities. However, it may be that what matters most is not the type of goal set, but that the exploration of the goal is solution-focused rather than problem-focused (Braunstein and Grant, 2016).
2	Proximal or distal goals	Goals vary in their time horizons, from the short-term proximal goal (i.e. what will be done today) to the long-term distal goal (i.e. what will be done by the end of this year).	Proximal and distal goals are both important, as proximal goals encourage detailed action planning that help to achieve the distal goals. Distal goals also serve as the "dream goal" (Whitmore, 2017) and inspiration to carry out the proximal goals. Combining both leads to an increase in long-term performance (Weldon and Yun, 2000).
3	Concrete or abstract goals	A concrete goal is one that is highly specific, whereas an abstract goal is one that is highly expansive (i.e. vague or fuzzy).	Coaching clients may typically be around the middle of this concrete–abstract continuum – they have a general striving or intention for a consistent desired future state (Clutterbuck and Spence, 2017). An abstract goal may be sufficient to create motivation and change. For others, facilitating more concrete goals may be best.
4	Autonomous or controlled goals	Autonomous goals are those that have been chosen freely, based on an intrinsic desire, interest or value. Controlled goals are those that are chosen either because of an external inducement or an internal sense that they "should" or "ought" to (Deci and Ryan, 2000).	Goals are more effective when they are aligned with an individual's intrinsic interests, motivations and values – the autonomous goal. This alignment is known as self-concordance (Sheldon and Elliot, 1999). "Should" or "ought" goals may appear in the coaching engagement, and be mistaken by the client as an autonomous goal. Client goal-setting may also be "controlled" by their organisational sponsor. Coaches can assist their clients in increasing the self-concordance of their goals.
5	Reactive or adapted goals	A reactive goal is one that a client may present with early in the coaching engagement. An adapted goal is the changed or new goal that results following opportunity to reflect on the original reactive goal (Clutterbuck and David, 2013).	The goal that the client initially wishes to set in coaching may not be the "best" one to serve their needs. Taking time to explore and reflect on the goal will help the client to confirm whether a new goal needs to be set or not.

(Continued)

Table 8.2 (Continued) Goal dimensions and their practical application to goal-setting in coaching

	Goal dimension	Summary	Practical application to goal-setting in coaching
6	Vertically congruent or incongruent goals	Vertically congruent goals are those where higher-order, more abstract goals (i.e. values) are aligned with lower-order, more specific goals (actions to be taken). Vertically incongruent goals are those where the lower-order goals (actions) do not support the higher-order goals.	Vertical congruence is preferential for two reasons. The first is that the lower-order actions need to be kept on track in order to achieve the higher-order goals. Highlighting any disconnect can provide useful insights to the client here. Second is that the higher-order goals provide the motivation to carry out the lower-order actions, which can themselves feel unrewarding and unenjoyable. When a client over-focuses on the lower-order actions and "forgets" their higher-order goal, this is known as "goal neglect". Taking the client back to their higher-order goal helps them to avoid or overcome any feelings of dissatisfaction and disengagement which comes from goal neglect.
7	Performance and learning goals	Performance goals are focused on task execution – performing well or winning positive judgements about competence. Learning goals are focused on task mastery.	Performance goals can be highly motivating, especially if a client has a "quick win". They may be less effective when the task is too complex, too challenging or the individual feels they do not have the resources (internal or external) to achieve it. Learning goals can better support task performance. Complex tasks are seen as a challenge and not as a threat, there is greater immersion in a task and higher levels of intrinsic motivation.
8	Public and private goals	Private goals are those that are shared only between the coach and their client, compared with public goals, which would be known by the organisational sponsor also (Downey, 2002).	If an organisational sponsor is involved, and it becomes clear through exploration that the coaching offered does not fit with the client's own interests, then there may be opportunity to set private goals, separate to the public goal(s). The contracting stage will have determined whether this was within the remit, including whether any private goals need to contribute in some way to organisational performance.
9	Horizontally congruent or incongruent goals	Horizontally congruent goals are those that complement each other (i.e. the client has multiple goals that are in harmony). Horizontally incongruent goals are those that compete with each other in some way.	Horizontal congruence is preferential. Highlighting any conflict between goals, facilitating alignment of goals and developing complementary goals supports client goal-setting.

(Continued)

Table 8.2 (Continued) Goal dimensions and their practical application to goal-setting in coaching

	Goal dimension	Summary	Practical application to goal-setting in coaching
10	Stretch or shift goals	Stretch goals "exist on the fringes of possibility" (Clutterbuck and Spence, 2017, p. 225); shift goals encourage an increase, but with less distance to cover.	Shift goals, which are both challenging and realistic, are seen as preferable for greater engagement and success to extreme stretch goals. As coach, understanding the accuracy of a person's self-awareness about an appropriate level of challenge is important. Top performers do not set high goals, rather they set goals just slightly above their current performance levels. Conversely low performers do not set low goals, rather they set goals that are far beyond their competence level, resulting in failure (Latham, 2000). A reality check could be in order, to either encourage clients to have a sense of what more is possible for them, or to test the reality of their goal (whilst being careful not to place your own limitations on their ambitions!).
11	Understood or assumed goals	A goal that is understood means the coach and the client share an accurate representation of the goal. A goal that is assumed means the coach has their own interpretation of the client's goal (e.g. a "better work–life balance" means different things to the coach and the client).	There is a risk that coaches (particularly new coaches) who are keen to set a goal with their client may attempt to force what the client is saying into their own mental model (Cavanagh and Spence, 2013). This assumed goal can be avoided through exploration with the client, increasing understanding and goal clarity.
12	Deep or shallow goals	Deep and shallow goals are terms I have adopted to refer to the strength of connection the client has with the goal, where a deeper goal means a greater sense of connection.	The greater the sense of connection, the greater the desire and likelihood of achieving the goal (Downey, 2002; Starr, 2016). Strengthening the connection could come through linking goals to values, exploring how the goal will positively impact the client's life, and through visualisation techniques (what can you see, hear, feel?)
13	Power to influence or no power to influence goals	A goal can either be within or outside of the control of a person. A goal can only be reached when it is within the control of the individual who wants it.	Check the client's power to influence the goal set (Starr, 2016; Whitmore, 2017). Changing the behaviour of someone else (e.g. a line manager's leadership style) is not feasible, but changing the client's response and feelings about this is. An end goal, such as securing a particular job, is not within absolute control, but identifying the performance level required can give you a good chance of achieving it – reframe goals to give the control and influence back to the client.

(Continued)

Table 8.2 (Continued) Goal dimensions and their practical application to goal-setting in coaching

	Goal dimension	Summary	Practical application to goal-setting in coaching
14	Overt or hidden goals	An overt goal is one that is known and shared between the parties involved in the coaching relationship. A hidden goal is not shared. It may be known by one of the parties (e.g. that the coaching intervention has been requested in the hope of moving someone on from the organisation) or it may be unconscious and unknown to all.	Being aware of and surfacing any hidden goals is suggested as a critical skill when working with goals (Clutterbuck, 2013). His recommended technique is "painful goal honesty" where "each party is encouraged to reflect on the motivations for the relationship and to push the boundaries of their openness" (p. 318).
15	Conscious or unconscious goals	A conscious goal is one that has been set wilfully and knowingly; it is the prompt for any following action or behaviour. An unconscious goal is one that the person is unaware of, but has prompted them to behave or act in a certain way.	Coaching can perhaps help to uncover the unconscious goals (reasons) that sit behind undesirable behaviours and actions, re-setting these goals and better facilitating change (Custers and Aarts, 2010; Grant, 2013b).

Equally, we may work with clients who are at stage 4 – the "self-authoring mind", where the individual defines who they are, rather than being defined by others. Goals set by these clients will be driven by their intrinsic values and interests (an autonomous goal).

Whether a client comes with a fixed or growth mind set is likely to impact whether they set a goal that prioritises task attainment over task mastery. A fixed growth mind set is one where people believe their qualities are set and cannot change; they focus on demonstrating their current qualities rather than working to develop or improve them (a performance goal-orientation). Conversely, those with a growth mind set have an underlying belief that they can change and develop over time with experience (a learning goal-orientation).

Client self-awareness of their competence is likely to play a part in the level of stretch that they set. Those who are highly self-aware set goals that are just ahead of their current performance, leading to more success in achieving them. Those with lower self-awareness set goals that are beyond their bounds of competence and are unrealistic to the point of not being achievable (Latham, 2000).

The coach

Just as clients are all individuals, so are coaches, and their approach to goal-setting will not be homogenous. They come to coaching with a particular preference (or not) for goal-setting, based on the experiences they have had in their own personal and working lives.

As well as individual differences, a preference for goal-setting has been found to differ based on the location of the coach, length of training they have undertaken and duration of their coaching experience (David, Clutterbuck and Megginson, 2014). This study with 194 coaches from across the US and Europe found that coaches from the US were more goal-oriented than their European peers, perhaps due to the differences in how coaching developed in each region. Regardless of location, coaches who received more training (five weeks or longer), when compared with those who undertook shorter training or no training, were found to be the most goal-oriented in their practice. There was some evidence to suggest that the more experienced a coach is, the less goal-oriented they are. However, this finding held only for European coaches, and not for coaches from the US. The authors commented that this lessening of goal-orientation may be due to coaches feeling more confident to "let go" of the traditional models, or it may reflect that new coaches in the field are being trained to be more goal-oriented in their practice than their predecessors ever were.

Ultimately each coach will have adopted and developed their own approach to coaching, which will vary in the emphasis placed on the importance and centrality of goal-setting.

The organisational sponsor

Along with the client and the coach, there may be a third stakeholder in the coaching relationship: The organisational sponsor, typically the client's line manager or HR representative. Given that they have made a financial investment and have a legitimate stake in the coaching outcome, we can expect them in some way to influence the goal set (which may be particularly relevant for Autonomous vs Controlled goals). This third party may have requested the coaching on behalf of the client, perhaps to address a performance gap identified through 360-degree feedback. The coaching may form part of a wider development program for future leaders, focusing on the development of key competencies. In these scenarios, the goals set by the organisational sponsor may or may not align with what the client sees as important or relevant to them.

Even when the organisational sponsor has agreed to the coaching at the request of the client, say to support them in career progression or promotion opportunities, and has stepped away from goal-setting per se, there will be an expectation that the goals of the client are aligned in some way to benefit the organisation. Another situation may be where the client sets goals because they feel it is what they "should" or "ought" to do within their organisational context.

The environment

Goal-setting does not live in a vacuum, free from context and environment. Rather it exists within a system – the outside world, which can sometimes be linear, predictable and slow moving, and can sometimes be messy, complex and fast-paced. In a linear, predictable and slow-changing environment, it is possible to know how cause and effect are related to each other and that this connection will remain stable for a period of time. In other words, when a goal is set (the effect), the ways to achieve it (the cause) can be articulated and actioned, and the goal ultimately achieved. Feedback is used to adapt behaviours to keep on track for achieving the goal. The traditional approach of SMART goals and the linear application of a coach process model (e.g. GROW) appear to be suited to this context.

Where a person is not operating within this kind of system, this form of traditional goal-setting is unlikely to be effective. When things are changing, particularly at a fast pace, a specific goal may quickly become redundant or it may not always be clear what actions need to be taken to achieve the goal. Drake (2015) observed that clients sometimes do not know what actions will lead to the outcome they want. In this environment, feedback is used to adapt the goal itself, rather than keeping the goal in-place and adapting the behaviour to reach it. In the coaching world, it is suggested that clients may be best served by goals that are evolving (Cavanagh, 2006).

Broadening goal-setting in coaching

Now is a good point to take stock. The above is not intended to lead to the conclusion that the traditional view of goal-setting has no value, or that goal-setting should be abandoned altogether! Indeed, goals and moving towards a new future state – whether defined as a vague vision or a specific objective – are a feature of the coaching conversation that distinguishes it from both an everyday conversation and a therapeutic conversation (Grant, 2013a). Even the new wave of thinking acknowledges that it is "a misnomer to suggest that coaching can be conducted 'goal free'" (Clutterbuck and Spence, 2017 p. 229). Instead, the conclusions drawn so far are to:

- Rethink and reconceptualise what we mean when we refer to goal-setting in coaching, and not limit ourselves to only the classic tradition;
- Appreciate and understand the wide variety of factors at play in the coaching context;
- Approach goal-setting in a more flexible way, considering how we work best in the service of each individual client.

This final section revisits the classic approach to goal-setting in this new light. The proposition "Start with a Goal" is recast as "Goals Evolve and Emerge"; and "SMART Goals" are recast as "The Skilled and Mindful Art of Goal-Setting".

Goals evolve and emerge

Early stages of coaching

A coaching conversation may start with a goal early on; although, unlike the traditional approach, this goal may not necessarily be concrete, but more of an abstract vision. Indeed, as captured in Table 8.2, it is asserted that the more likely starting point for clients is the middle of this concrete–abstract continuum; clients present with general intentions for a desired future state (Clutterbuck and Spence, 2017).

During coaching

Whilst it is conceivable that an initial goal may remain the same throughout the coaching engagement, it is more likely that the goal will change in some way. Research with 140 coaches found that for all but 8 coaches, the focus of the coaching sessions did change during the course of the engagement, and the greatest reason cited for this was a move to "deeper goals" (Kauffman and Contu, 2009, p. 8).

It may help to think of goals changing in two ways: First, the original goal adapts or evolves in some way; second, the original goal is discarded and makes way for a new emergent goal.

In the first way, a goal that was initially articulated as a general intention may increase in its specificity over time. This echoes the traditional approach presented at the start of this chapter, where a general topic is distilled into a specific goal. The difference here is that it is not intended as a strict imperative to move from an abstract to a specific goal, nor does this need to be achieved as a starting point for the remainder of the coaching conversation. Rather, this may naturally be the course that the conversation takes in service of the client, and it could occur at a later stage of the coaching process. This is captured in various process models (e.g. Grant's (2011) REGROW model). Remember that for some clients, however, learning and motivation may not be contingent on setting specific goals.

In the second way, there is more dramatic movement in goal-setting. As captured in Table 8.2, clients may enter coaching with a reactive goal, an initial presenting goal that may not be the "best" one to serve their underlying needs. If the coach fixes too early on the "wrong" goal, blindly accepting this goal without exploration, coaching is devalued and motivation is likely to be limited. With time for thinking and reflection, the client acquires greater understanding of self, questions their original goal and a new goal emerges, known as the adapted goal (Clutterbuck and David, 2013).

The skilled and mindful art of goal-setting

Rather than present you with a new framework or an extended acronym, I invite you focus on developing your skill set and mind set around the use of goal-setting in coaching.

Skill set

Familiarise yourself with all the nuances and factors that play a part in goal-setting to enable you to work in a more tailored and bespoke way with goal-setting, based on the salient factors laid out earlier (goal dimensions; client characteristics; your own position; the organisational sponsor; the environment).

Develop your questioning and listening skills so you gain a comprehensive understanding of your client at the contracting stage and continue to update your understanding of them throughout the coaching engagement. Clutterbuck and Spence (2017) identified three areas for understanding:

- The client's preference for using goals, and their mind set and readiness for learning and personal growth;
- The client's development status – are they operating from a more socialised or more self-authored stage? (Kegan, 1994);
- The contexts, such as home or work, in which the client functions.

Be an educator – part of the coaching conversation can be to share with your client how goals are more multi-dimensional and dynamic in nature than the SMART definition. This will help you and your client find what approach has greatest value for them (Clutterbuck and Spence, 2017).

Mind set

Having a goal gives a sense of direction and, as such, provides a sense of security about what you, as coach, "need to do in the conversation" (Starr, 2016, p. 172). To help you let go of the need to set a goal, think of coaching as a learning conversation rather than a goal based conversation

Increase your own self-awareness. How comfortable are you working with or without goals (in the traditional sense)?

Keep your practice client-centred. How can you take what you know about goal-setting and work with goals that best serve their needs?

Expect the unexpected. Goals may shift, change and emerge. Become comfortable with being flexible and open. Trust the coaching process – even when there is no fixed process!

Conclusion

The traditional approach to goal-setting is just one of a range of options in the context of coaching. Coaching is more multi-faceted than the contexts within which these frameworks were developed and applied. Time has also marched on, and the environment we and our clients operate in has changed. Rather than feeling obliged to apply and stick rigidly to a particular framework in your practice, think instead about how you can remain flexible and tailor the use of goal-setting to best serve your individual client in supporting them to achieve their desired outcome. Expect twists and turns along the way as the coaching relationship, exploration and client's insights deepen.

References

Alexander, G. (2010). 'Behavioural coaching – The GROW model'. In J. Passmore, ed., *Excellence in coaching – The industry guide,* pp. 83-93. London: Kogan Page.

Austin, J.T. and Vancouver, J.B. (1996). 'Goal constructs in psychology: Structure, process, and content'. *Psychological Bulletin,* 120(3), pp. 338–375.

Braunstein, K. and Grant, A. (2016). 'Approaching solutions or avoiding problems? The differential effects of approach and avoidance goals with solution-focused and problem-focused coaching questions'. *Coaching: An International Journal of Theory, Research and Practice,* 9(2), pp. 1–17.

Cavanagh, M.J. (2006). 'Coaching from a systemic perspective: A complex adaptive conversation'. In D.R. Stober and A.M. Grant, eds., *Evidence-based coaching handbook: putting best practices to work for your clients,* pp. 313-354. Hoboken, NJ: Wiley & Sons.

Cavanagh, M.J. and Spence, G.B. (2013). 'Mindfulness in Coaching: Philosophy, Psychology or Just a Useful Skill?' In J. Passmore, D.B. Peterson and T. Friere, eds., *The Wiley-Blackwell handbook of the psychology of coaching & mentoring,* pp. 112-134. Chichester: Wiley Blackwell.

Clutterbuck, D. (2013). 'Working with emergent goals: A pragmatic approach'. In S. David, D. Clutterbuck and D. Megginson, eds., *Beyond goals: Effective strategies for coaching and mentoring,* pp. 311-325. Surrey, England: Gower.

Clutterbuck, D. and David, S.A. (2013). 'Goals in coaching and mentoring: The current state of play'. In S. David, D. Clutterbuck and D. Megginson, eds., *Beyond goals: Effective strategies for coaching and mentoring,* pp. 21-35. Surrey, England: Gower.

Clutterbuck, D. and Spence, G. (2017). 'Working with goals in coaching'. In T. Bachkirova, G. Spence and D. Drake, eds., *The SAGE handbook of coaching,* pp. 218-237. London: Sage.

Custers, R. and Aarts, H. (2010). 'The unconscious will: How the pursuit of goals operates outside of conscious awareness'. *Science,* 329, pp. 47–50.

David, S., Clutterbuck, D. and Megginson, D. (2013). *Beyond goals: Effective strategies for coaching and mentoring*. Surrey, England: Gower.

David, S., Clutterbuck, D. and Megginson, D. (2014). 'Goal orientation in coaching differs according to region, experience, and education'. *International Journal of Evidence Based Coaching and Mentoring*, 12(2), pp. 134–145.

Deci, E.L. and Ryan, R.M. (2000). 'The "what" and "why" of goal pursuits: Human needs and self-determination behaviour'. *Psychological Inquiry*, 11, pp. 227–268.

Doran, G.T. (1981). 'There's a S.M.A.R.T. way to write management's goals and objectives'. *Management Review*, 70, pp. 35–36.

Downey, M. (2002). *Effective coaching*. London: Texere.

Drake, D.B. (2015). *Narrative coaching: Bringing our new stories to life*. Petaluma, PA: CNC Press.

Gessnitzer, S. and Kauffeld, S. (2015). 'The working alliance in coaching: Why behavior is the key to success'. *Journal of Applied Behavioral Science*, 51(2), pp. 177–197.

Grant, A. (2011). 'Is it time to REGROW the GROW model? Issues related to teaching coaching session structures'. *The Coaching Psychologist*, 7, pp. 118–126.

Grant, A. (2013a). 'Autonomy support, relationship satisfaction and goal focus in the coach-coachee relationship: Which best predicts coaching success?' *Coaching: An International Journal of Theory, Research and Practice*, 7, pp. 18–38.

Grant, A. (2013b). 'New perspectives on goal setting in coaching practice: An integrated model of goal-focused coaching'. In S. David, D. Clutterbuck and D. Megginson, eds., *Beyond goals: Effective strategies for coaching and mentoring,* pp. 55-83. Surrey, England: Gower.

ICF. (2019). https://coachfederation.org/core-competencies. Accessed 25th March 2020.

Kauffman, C. and Conntu, D. (2009). 'The realities of executive coaching'. *Harvard Business Review: HBR Research Report*, January, pp. 1–25.

Kegan, R. (1994). *In over our heads: The mental demands of modern life*. Cambridge, MA: Harvard University Press.

Kegan, R., Congleton, C. and David, S.A. (2013). 'The goals behind the goals: Pursuing adult development in the coaching enterprise'. In S. David, D. Clutterbuck and D. Megginson, eds., *Beyond goals: Effective strategies for coaching and mentoring,* pp. 229-243. Surrey, England: Gower.

Latham, G. (2000). 'Motivating employee performance through goal setting'. In E.A. Locke, ed., *Handbook of principles of organizational behaviour,* pp. 107-109. San Francisco, CA: Blackwell.

Locke, E.A. (1968). 'Toward a theory of task motivation and incentives'. *Organizational Behavior & Human Performance*, 3(2), pp. 157–189.

Locke, E.A. and Latham, G. P. (1990). *A theory of goal setting & task performance*. Englewood Cliff, NJ: Prentice-Hall, Inc.

Müller, A.A. and Kotte, S. (2020). Of SMART, GROW and goals gone wild: A systematic literature review on the relevance of goal activities in workplace coaching. *International Coaching Psychology Review*, 15(2), pp. 69–97.

Ordoñez, L.D., Schweitzer, M.E., Galinsky, A.D. and Bazerman, M.H. (2009). 'Goals gone wild: The systematic side effects of overprescribing goal setting'. *Academy of Management Perspectives*, 23(1), pp. 6–16.

Prochaska, J.O., Norcross, J.C. and DiClemente, C.C. (1994). *Changing for good*. New York: Avon Books.

Sheldon, K. M. and Elliot, A. J. (1999). 'Goal striving, need satisfaction, and longitudinal well-being: The self-concordance model'. *Journal of Personality and Social Psychology*, 76, pp. 482–497.

Starr, J. (2016). *The coaching manual*, 4th edition. London: Pearson.

Wastian, M. and Poetschki, J. (2016). 'Goal setting and goal attainment in coaching'. *Coaching Theorie & Praxis*, 2, pp. 21–31.

Weldon, E. and Yun, S. (2000). 'The effects of proximal and distal goals on goal level, strategy development and group performance'. *Journal of Applied Behavioral Science*, 36, pp. 336–344.

Whitmore, J. (2017). *Coaching for performance*, 5th edition. London: Nicholas Brealey.

9 Questions in coaching

David Clutterbuck

Introduction

One of the common myths about coaching is that it is about helping clients find solutions. But, as one CEO expressed it to me: "I have an abundance of potential solutions. Before I can decide which one to go for, I need to find the right question". If we define coaching in line with its origins in the mentoring dialogues of Athena, the Greek Goddess of Wisdom, as "helping another person with the quality of their thinking about issues that are important to them", then the role of a coach is to help the client find the questions that will enable them to think more clearly. This does not mean that the coach necessarily has to provide those questions. Highly skilled coaches do ask powerful questions, but they also create the environment where clients can generate questions of their own that stimulate insight. In this chapter, we explore the nature of questions as the fundamental underpinning of effective coaching from six perspectives: How questions work; choosing the type of question; what makes a powerful question; helping the client build their skills of self-questioning; common errors in questioning; and avoiding the "tyranny of the question".

How questions work

The purpose of questions in coaching is to support the client's thinking in greater width and depth. In particular, they:

- Enable a constructive challenge to the client's assumptions;
- Promote reflection;
- Support paraphrasing and summarising;
- Enable creativity;
- Bring structure to the coaching conversation without imposing control.

Studies of goal achievement suggest that, if you want to get something done during the day, instead of telling yourself "I will do X today", you should ask instead "Will I achieve this today?" The reason for this counterintuitive conclusion is that, in the first case, our mind envisions the future with the assumption that we have done what we set out to. We are this vulnerable to distractions that prioritise other things that happen during the course of the day. And we go home with our good resolution unfulfilled. If we pose the goal as a question, on the other hand, the issue remains in our consciousness and we are more likely to give it priority.

Choosing the type of question

There are many types of question. A useful way of categorising is by *structure, purpose and perspective*.

Question structure

Among the most commonly cited are:

Open v closed questions. Closed questions elicit a yes/no answer. Open questions encourage the client to think and are therefore much more aligned with the coaching mind-frame. However, closed questions do have their place – for example, in challenging a statement:

- Do you really believe that?
- Is that always true?
- Is it your opinion I am hearing, or that of your boss?

It is relatively easy, with thought, to reframe closed questions. For example, "Do you expect to be here in 12 months' time?" can become "What are your thoughts about how long you want to stay in this role?"

Closed questions can also be highly leading. So, for example, "Are you annoyed about this?" not only leads to a yes/no answer but may stimulate an emotion that was not strongly present before, while "What are you feeling when you look back at this?" generates a much wider range of emotional recognition.

Choice questions. The question just above is also an example of these. Other examples might be:

- Which of these two (or more) options do you feel most intuitively drawn to?
- Which of these job options gives you more career choices in the future?

The danger with choice questions is that we focus the client's mind only on the options presented. Before we use them, therefore, it is important to ensure that a full range of options is considered.

Rhetorical questions. Often a subset of closed questions, these are not intended to produce answers but rather to gain permission or approval to carry on with a line of thinking. For example, "So, we are agreed that your key objective is to lead the culture change working group?" A problem with rhetorical questions is that, in our own heads, we have already decided what the answer is, so we may ignore the nuances of the client's response. I recently observed a client responding to a rhetorical question with a hesitant "Yeeessss …", only for the coach to continue without pause. A more observant, less process-focused coach would have picked up on the hesitation and explored what lay behind it. As it was, the coach ended up steering the client towards a solution that seemed good to the coach but clashed with one of the client's personal values.

Simple v complicated questions. As we shall see later, in general, the simpler a question is, the more impact it is likely to have. Consider this choice question: "Would you prefer, X, or Y or Z?" It requires a substantial mental effort from the client. We can make it easier with a simple reframe: "So, we have three choices here – X, Y and Z. What is it that stands out about each of these for you?"

Who, where, what, when, which … And why? Although we have many ways to ask a question without using a question format (for example, a statement with a question implied, as in "So, that's it then?"), most questions rely on one of these interrogative openers. Some sources suggest that coaches avoid using *why* questions because they can appear confrontational. Yet the *5 whys* technique, derived from quality management in Toyota, is one of the most useful available to a coach. When someone answers a *why* question, you can drill down into their reasoning by asking *why* again and again, until they have reached the foundations of their thinking and emotions. Used appropriately and sparingly, *why* can be very effective in signalling to someone that they are not being logical or honest with themselves.

Question purpose

Coaches use four main types of questions for different purposes:

- Challenging questions are particularly used to help people unfreeze existing assumptions, values and beliefs, which may be self-limiting or preventing them from taking alternative perspectives;
- Probing questions are aimed at opening horizons and creating insights by building on the new perspectives;
- Testing questions are aimed at drawing ideas together, setting boundaries and creating self-confidence (for example, that different outcomes are achievable);
- Confirming questions help people to focus on their inner values and beliefs and explore their motivation to bring about change.

Challenging other people can be confrontational, but then they are unlikely to really listen and may respond by defending rather than thinking about what has been said. Challenging is much more effective when it is done in a learning manner. Here are some useful guidelines and phrases that can be adapted to make challenging easier and more acceptable in most cultures, even in those where there is a high level of concern about losing face or causing another person to lose face.

- When challenging logic: *Help me to understand …* This makes the other person work through their logic, often leading them to see gaps they had not noticed;
- When challenging behaviour: *Can you please explain to me what you were intending to achieve there?* This takes away the sense of being judgemental;
- When challenging assumptions: *What factors were you taking into account here? What assumptions were you making?* This prevents the other person feeling that we are questioning their intellect;
- When challenging perceptions: *Can you explain to me the context in which you were looking at this?* – so we don't appear to be questioning their judgement;
- When questioning values: *What are the personal/organisational values you are trying to apply here? What's important to you in this situation?*

Some questions can achieve additional importance as a touchstone for difficult decisions. We call these benchmark questions because they have a long duration and can be applied time and again. They fade in impact over time, as people become older and wiser and adopt different priorities in their lives. They are especially important in helping clients become more authentic. Be prepared, however, for clients to ask you about your own benchmark question(s)!

For example:

- Will each of these choices make you respect yourself more or less?
- Is this truly taking you where you want to go?
- Where does this support or conflict with your deepest values?
- What would your hero do now?

Perspectives of questioning

There are several frameworks to categorise questions. One that has emerged from my own observations as particularly relevant to coaching and mentoring is as follows:

- *Questioning to demonstrate superiority or to undermine.* For example: "Who do you think you are?" "Do you really expect that to work?" These questions are all about the ego of the questioner.
- *Questioning to elicit specific information.* This is a transactional mode of questioning. In general, it requires no depth of relationship with the person receiving the question. For example: "Do you have a pair of these in size 11?" In coaching, however, a reasonable level of trust may be needed to address questions, such as: "What's the purpose of this team?"
- *Questioning for self-curiosity.* At an extreme, this is voyeurism. When the client says "And then I made the mistake of getting drunk with one of my team and sleeping with him" (real case), it tends to arouse in the coach an instinct to explore all the salacious detail. Well-grounded coaches deftly avoid this trap but may still fall into more subtle distractions when the client's story invokes strong associations from their own experience – going into more detail when it is not needed. An important question for the coach is "How will exploring this help the client better understand their issue?"
- *Questioning for other-curiosity.* This is the bread and butter of effective coaching. We are curious not only on our own behalf, but to understand how the client makes sense of his or her circumstances. It is curiosity on behalf of the client, and the question for coaches is "How will delving this help the client understand their world and their place in that world?" This other curiosity in turn has several levels. At the first level, the coach is focused simply on the client's process of sense-making. At the second level, the focus is on multiple perspectives – how both the client and their stakeholders interpret events. At the third level, the focus becomes holistic and systemic – what is going on in the client's systems that is shaping both their sense-making and that of the systems?
- *Seeking the right question.* Frequently when I give a demonstration of coaching, I am asked how I structured the sequence of questions that resulted in a shift of the client's thinking. There is always some disappointment when I say that there is no planned structure or sequence, that each question is an experiment based on what the client has just said. The "right" question – the one that will unlock the door to insight – emerges from this experimentation, not from any piece of cleverness on the part of the coach. Rather than make it happen, the coach *allows* it to happen.

The importance of shifting perspectives

Observation of coaches and mentors in a variety of settings revealed that one of the secrets to keeping the conversation purposeful and moving forward was to frequently shift perspective (Lancer, Clutterbuck and Megginson, 2016). The stepping in/stepping out model has two axes: Rational v emotional; stepping in (exploring the client's perspective) v stepping out (exploring the perspectives of other players or stakeholders). A client presenting in the stepping in/emotional quadrant may be stuck in this perspective, unable to think rationally about their issue or understand that other people may have a different and legitimate perspective on it. The coach helps them gradually to move into other quadrants, deepening their understand of the context until they are ready to seek a more productive way forward. The same principles apply wherever the client's starting point.

Some examples of questions for each quadrant are:

Stepping in/emotional

- How do you feel?
- What values are you applying?
- What would that mean for you?

Stepping in/rational

- What (really) happened?
- What do you want to achieve?
- What's the impact on your job?
- What choices do you have?

Stepping out/emotional

- How do you think the other person felt?
- How might your colleague feel if you handled it this way?
- What could you do to reduce their fears?

Stepping out/rational

- Who might mediate to help you have the conversation you need with this person?
- How would you advise someone else?
- What resources can you draw upon?

These (and similar) approaches are simple ways to access the wider client system. At root, all coaching other than basic skills coaching uses questions to help the client understand both their inner world (for example, their identity, values, aspirations, fears, assumptions, biases and self-limiting beliefs) and their external world (for example, the threats and opportunities, their champions and rivals, how the technology and the context of their role is changing). Coaching and mentoring create conversations that link understanding of the internal and external worlds to achieve clarity and better decisions.

Circular questioning (Brown, 1997; Athanasiades, 2008) is a technique developed from the work of Gregory Bateson (1979) used in family therapy that has practical application in group and team coaching. It encourages people within a system to identify connections that would not otherwise have been obvious to them. It has three key elements. In the first, each person in the system is asked about relationships or interactions between other people in the system – not as usual in therapy about their own emotions and reactions. For example, "How does your team leader show his resentment towards Peter's insubordination?"

The second element, neutrality, is expressed by the therapist (or coach) taking the side of the family (or team) as a whole, rather than individuals within it.

The third element, hypothesizing, encourages the family or team to make connections amongst aspects of the stories other members tell and the behaviours within those stories. The therapist or coach may also offer additional, different hypotheses, with different patterns of connection, and ask the team to determine the relevance of these.

Another useful model of changing perspectives is the Reflective Space Curve (Clutterbuck, 2013), based on a theory of how people think through Significant Unresolved Issues (SUIs). The pivotal point in this reflective process, whether done alone or with the help of a coach or mentor, is the achievement of insight – either a breakthrough in clarity or the reaching of an understanding that the issue is not the same as initial assumptions may have suggested. Where the client is on the curve may be pre-insight (where they are trying to work out what the issue is and how to put it into context) or post-insight (where they want to figure out what to do now they see the issue differently). Each position requires a different style and focus of questions. For example, pre-insight questions may be more probing and clarifying; post-insight questions aim more at releasing creative thinking.

The process of achieving insight is unpredictable. Neither the coach nor the client knows when it will happen. Carson (2011) describes it thus: "During moments of insight, cognitive filters relax momentarily and allow ideas on the brain's back burner to leap forward into conscious awareness". Researchers at Northwest University (Salvi et al., 2016) observed brain behaviour as participants reached the "Aha! Moment". First there is a period of alpha wave activity (which they suggest turns attention inwards), then a sudden burst of alpha waves as a solution bursts into conscious awareness. Insight typically occurs involuntarily, rather than as a product of structured thinking and tends to lead to better solutions. So, questions that explore context rather than focus on a defined goal may lead to more rapid resolution of issues.

Similarly, the phase of the coaching relationship also influences the format and nature of questioning. Once the relationship is established, questioning is most effective when it is unplanned and emergent. (If you know where the conversation is going, it isn't coaching!) At the beginning, however, having a structured approach to learning about the client and their circumstances is justified by the need to establish as complete a picture as possible. A checklist helps to provide consistency and can be the foundation for a much wider enquiry.

Powerful questions

The art of coaching is fundamentally posing the right question at the right time, taking the client's attention and imagination to places that they may not have explored on their own. Powerful questions cannot be manufactured – they are the "in the moment" product of deep intuition and attentiveness on the part of the coach. The power of the question is not exerted by the coach but in how the client chooses to internalise it.

The power of questions can be illustrated with a simple experiment. Set out at the beginning of the day with the intention to tackle a task you have been avoiding. You might say to yourself "Today I will get this done". But the likelihood of achieving the task is greater if you ask yourself the question "How am I going to get this done today?" With the first statement, you may mentally tick the action off in your mental "to-do" list as if it were done – and find at the end of the day that other things have got in the way. With the question, this is much less likely to happen, because the probability of success remains open.

However, rote use of questions can be counterproductive and may deeply frustrate a client. While questions such as "On a scale of 1 to 10 …"; "If you could wave a magic wand …"; or "If you did have the answer, what would it be?" can be effective in the right circumstances, they rapidly lose impact if used frequently with the same client. Worse, such clients report that they feel manipulated and that the trust essential between coach and client has been undermined.

The phrase "Socratic questioning", after the ancient Greek philosopher, Socrates, is often loosely associated with coaching, but with little concept of what specifically is involved. In its "purist" form, Socratic dialogue involves asking a logical series of questions that test assumptions until they reach the point of *reductio ad absurdum* – no longer tenable because they are patently ridiculous.[1] Using this approach in therapy has been criticised (Padesky, 1993) as emphasising the therapist's superiority. Equally, it is not the role of the coach to expose the absurdity of his or her client's thinking or assumptions.

A more person-centred adaptation of Socratic questioning, says Padesky, involves asking the client questions that:

a) The client has the knowledge to answer;
b) Draw the client's attention to information which is relevant to the issue being discussed but which may be outside the client's current focus;
c) Generally, move from the concrete to the more abstract;
d) Allow the client to apply the new information to either re-evaluate a previous conclusion or construct a new idea.

In Padesky's model, the therapist (or coach) has no idea where the conversation is going but trusts the conversation to create its own logic. She explains: "Sometimes if you are too confident of where you are going, you only look ahead and miss detours that can lead you to a better place". The difference is between trying to change the client's mind and helping them to understand their own thinking.

Creating powerful questions

Context is all! A question that stimulates a significant response in a client at one time might not have any noticeable effect on another client at another time.

In my analyses of hundreds of powerful questions – most of them used by coaches in observed "real plays" – a clear pattern emerged. All of the questions that made clients stop and think had most or all of the following characteristics, summarised in the acronym PRAIRIE:

These questions were *Personal* – even if the coach had used them before, they felt as if they were crafted specifically for this client at this time. The vast majority used the word "you".

They were also *Resonant* – they had immediate and sometimes very strong emotional impact. For example, "When did you last feel truly listened to?" can frequently lead to tears.

They were *Acute and Incisive* – getting straight to the point or "cutting to the quick". They were succinct, precise and delivered with quiet confidence.

They were *Reverberant* – so full of meaning for the client that they cannot be fully answered in the moment. Many highly experienced coaches can recall cases where clients have referred back to a question asked months (and sometimes years) ago. Both consciously and unconsciously, such questions stimulate long-term reflection. For example, to an executive who had no time for any activities outside work, the question "How do you reward yourself?" led them to tell me weeks later: "I've been constantly trying to answer that question and I am still working on it". Several months later, she quit her high paid job in a bank and took a role in a charity at a much lower salary but with much greater job satisfaction and an opportunity to rediscover life outside work.

They were *Innocent* – as free as possible of the coach's agenda and focused on the client's agenda. This includes letting go of the need to find a solution during the coaching conversation, which tends to be more about the coach's desire to show they have been effective.

They were *Explicit* – leaving little room for avoidance, yet not leading to yes/no answers.

Recommended good practice for coaches is to keep a record of questions that appear to have had an impact. (The client's view of this may be different from yours – often the questions which have struck home deepest for them may be ones you regard as obvious or routine.) Review these questions against the PRAIRIE elements and consider how you might sharpen them should a future opportunity to use them arise.

Another point at which a structured approach to questions may be useful is in summarising at the end of a coaching session. The "Four Is" are a useful framework here:

- What *Issues* did we explore?
- What *Ideas* emerged?
- What *Insights* were generated? (What did you learn about the situation and about yourself?)
- What *Intentions* do you now have as a result?

Helping the client build their skills of self-questioning

One of the ways in which coaches assist clients in developing their competence and identity is to role model the crafting of questions. When students are taught self-questioning skills, their learning agility increases (King, 1995). A pragmatic approach initially is to end each coaching session with one or more questions that the client can reflect upon before the next session, but with the eventual aim that they will create the reflective space to generate their own insight-provoking questions.

Creating questions with the client can also help to build competence in self-questioning. Among many techniques here are:

- Giving the client half the question and asking them to complete it;
- When the client jumps to a solution, asking: "If that's the answer, what is the question?"

In the context of teams, team coaches encourage team members to pose positively challenging questions to each other and for the team as a whole. This promotes both co-learning and psychological safety. It also helps the team reduce the volume of "elephants in the room" (issues that need to be discussed but which the team avoids addressing) and hence makes it easier to maintain a pace of change better aligned with what is happening in the team's external environment.

It is common for coaches to use questionnaires as a substitute for conversations with their clients, or to give clients one or more standard questionnaires at the beginning of assignments. While this can be helpful in getting to know the client, there are some downsides. In particular:

- Questionnaires only produce information on a limited range of issues. Conversations can open up much wider issues, making it less likely that the assignment may focus on the wrong things;
- Senior executives and leaders in particular may feel "questionnaired out" – resistant to completing other, more issue-specific questionnaires and diagnostics later;
- Unreliability – many diagnostics, such as the Meyers–Briggs Type Indicator, have low test–retest validity, in spite of the marketing hype (Grant, 2013).

Common errors in questioning

Novice coaches, in particular, tend to fall into a number of frequently observed traps, including the following:

- *Asking too many closed questions.* While closed questions can be very useful, particularly when challenging (for example, "Are you asking me to make the decision for you?"), they tend to close down the conversation and may lead to yes/no answers.
- *Queggestions.* Questions that suggest the "right" answer tend to prevent people from working things out for themselves and can steer them towards solutions that might be right for you, but not for them. For example:
  - *Wouldn't it be a good idea if …*
  - *Have you thought of …*
  - *Why don't you …*
- *Multiple questions in one.* The coach asks several questions, leaving the client confused as to which to answer. The cause of this is that the coach is doing their thinking out loud, trying out different questions until they find the right one. The cure is to do that thinking silently.
- *Rote questions.* As noted above, rote questions can undermine the quality of the relationship. If you find yourself using the same questions all the time that may be a sign that your coaching is getting lazy – a routine process rather than a genuine, curious exploration.
- *Being distracted by the need to have a question ready.* If you are thinking about the next question, you are not attending fully to the client. Develop the habit of allowing a short silence whenever the client pauses. If a question doesn't naturally occur, encourage the client to continue and have confidence that one will be there when you need it!
- *Not allowing the client time to reflect on the question.* Sometimes inexperienced coaches ask a really potent question, then spoil the effect by jumping in with another question too quickly. Like any powerful medicine, small doses tend to be most beneficial!
- *Doing their thinking out loud.* The process of crafting a question taxes the reasoning circuits in our brains. In supervision, when we review the audio tape of a coaching session, it is common to hear the coach start to ask a question, then modify it and repeat this until finally they hatch a fully formed question. Thinking out loud, may help the coach, but by the time the question is asked, the poor client is utterly confused. One

of the benefits of listening to yourself asking questions is that you learn habits, such as taking all of this emergent thinking back internally, while the client waits. If all else fails, ask the client "Give me a moment, please, to find the right words for what I'm thinking".

Avoiding the "tyranny of the question"

Novice coaches tend to be overly conscious of the need to have a question ready for when the client stops talking. As a result, their attention can turn inwards, towards "what am I going to say next?" rather than outward, towards the client. With greater confidence, coaches can let go of this instinct, which is more about the coach's need to appear competent than about the client's need to be stimulated to think.

Observation of coaches at various levels of coach maturity, in coach assessment centres, indicates that less experienced and less confident coaches ask significantly more questions than more mature coaches. Moreover, these questions tend to be less impactful.

A technique I find helpful starts from the premise that the time we spend thinking about the next question to ask is time we are not spending attending to the client. Novice coaches often become anxious about what they are going to do, if they don't have a question ready, when the client stops talking. This is one of the factors that drives them towards rote questions – had they been listening completely, a more powerful question would probably have emerged on its own! If a question occurs to them, a better approach is to park it at the back of the mind and turn attention back to the client. Then, when the client pauses, say nothing. Deliberately create space, where the client (and the coach) can reflect on what has been said.

During this reflective period, the question may come back. Ask yourself these four questions:

- How might I make this question more impactful?
- Will it interrupt or enhance the flow of the client's thinking?
- Does it need to be voiced right now, or is it OK to hang on to it for a while?
- What else might the client have to say, before it is the right time to ask this question?

A simple nod and sound of encouragement – "Mmhm" – is usually enough for the client to resume talking. If not, ask "What else?"

When you have done this twice, give yourself permission to ask your question *if it is still relevant*. Most of the time, you will find that one of four things happens:

- The client asks the same or a similar question of themselves;
- The client asks a better question of themselves;
- The question is reshaped in your unconscious, so that it emerges in a much more powerful form;
- The question is no longer needed.

Alternatives to questions

When we observe highly experienced and effective coaches, they tend to ask far fewer and far more insightful questions than novice coaches do. It's almost as if they save up their questions for when they will have greatest impact. They also typically understand that when we ask a question, we are exerting a level of control over the conversation – there is no such thing as a non-directive question!

Instead of overwhelming the client with questions, they use a wide repertoire of methods to enable the client to "have the conversation they need to have with themselves". For example:

- "I'm curious about …";
- "And …" / "Therefore …" / "So …";
- "Tell me about this from the perspective of …?"
- "I'm noticing …"/ "I'm feeling …" / "I'm wondering …";
- "Tell me what you are noticing about this …";
- "Let's pause and reflect …";
- "Remind me …";
- "Assume that the opposite is true …".

So, when they do ask a question, it is a signal to the client that a new train of thought may be required – and this learned response in the client enlarges the depth and scope of their reflection.

Conclusion

Questions are at the very heart of coaching, not least because they help to prevent us slipping into a telling mode. With practice, they can be constructed to help a client radically reframe their assumptions and consider alternatives that might never have occurred to them; to reconnect with their values; make better decisions; and otherwise step outside their normal modes of thinking. However, overused questions, questions that pursue the coach's assumptions about what is important, rather than honour the client's, and badly constructed questions can all stunt the client's self-enquiry.

Note

1   This made Socrates so unpopular that he was forced to commit suicide by drinking hemlock!

References

Athanasiades, C. (2008). 'Systemic thinking and circular questioning in therapy with individuals'. *Counselling Psychology Review*.

Bateson, G. (1979). *Mind and nature: A necessary unity* (Vol. 255). New York: Bantam Books.

Brown, J. (1997). 'Circular questioning: An introductory guide'. *Australian and New Zealand Journal of Family Therapy*, 18(2), pp. 109–114.

Carson, S. (2011). 'The unleashed mind'. *Scientific American MIND*, April.

Clutterbuck, D. (2013). *Everyone needs a mentor*, 5th edition. London: CIPD.

Clutterbuck, D. (2013). *Powerful questions for coaches and mentors*. European Mentoring and Coaching Council, ISBN: 978-0-9576945-1-4.

Grant, A. (2013). 'Goodbye to MBTI, the fad that won't die'. *Psychology Today* Blog posted, September 18.

King, A. (1995). 'Inquiring minds really do want to know: Using questioning to teach critical thinking'. *Teaching of Psychology*, 22(1), pp. 13–17.

Lancer, N., Clutterbuck, D. and Megginson, D. (2016). *Techniques in Coaching and Mentoring*, 2nd edition. London: Routledge.

Padesky, C.A. (1993). 'Socratic questioning: Changing minds or guiding discovery?'. Keynote address delivered at the European Congress of Behavioural and Cognitive Therapies, London, September 24.

Salvi, C., Bricolo, E., Kounios, J., Bowden, E. and Beeman, M. (2016). 'Aha is right: Insight solutions are more often correct than analytic solutions'. *The Quarterly Journal of Experimental Psychology*, 69(6), pp. 1064–1072. doi:10.1080/13546783.2016.1141798.

10 Listening in coaching

Stephen Burt

Introduction

One of the first challenges when you start out as a coach is to become a better listener. Without listening well, it is impossible to discover what concerns a client and why. It's not that new coaches can't listen or that they are uniformly poor listeners, it's more that we all have accumulated habits, preferences and blind-spots that limit the quality of our listening. So it is a priority for each aspirant coach to get to know themselves as a listener and begin to build on their strengths, fill the gaps and tackle their weaknesses.

This chapter explores what happens when someone listens well, particularly the impact on the client when he or she feels they are being heard. It describes what might get in the way of good listening. It then sets out how – systematically – to listen well and what to listen for. But first we need to be clear what we mean by listening and what is involved if we do it well.

What is good listening?

Wolvin and Coakley (1996) claim that in communications theory there are over 50 different definitions of listening. The coaching literature similarly abounds with descriptions of what coaches do when they listen and what they attend to. Many of these accounts suggest a progression through various levels of competence. They start with describing the everyday behaviours associated with poor listening, progress through "quiet attending" to active listening, and on to high levels of listening which often include noticing non-verbal clues and the listener using their intuition.

This mapping of listening has led me to suggest a definition of listening with coaching in mind:

> Listening encompasses all the ways in which a listener becomes aware of what a speaker is experiencing and expressing in a given moment. It is therefore, over time, how the listener gets to know who the speaker is."
>
> (Burt, 2019, p. 3)

In the presence of a good listener, the skills and behaviours involved are integrated, fluid, responsive and elegantly demonstrated. But if we are to reach those heady heights, we need to understand the component parts in a way that enables us to focus and improve. With that in mind, I have offered a model of listening which includes four modes, each of which captures an area of expertise that contributes to good listening. The four modes are:

- **Attention** – The quality of concentration, focused on the speaker and what they are saying, fully engaged without distraction or presumption;
- **Inquiry** – The skill to respond and explore the speaker's account, being curious in a way that deepens both the coach's understanding and the client's awareness;
- **Observation** – The ability to notice non-verbal clues and use them to lay bare further levels of meaning in what the client is recounting;
- **Resonance** – The sensitivity and awareness that allows the coach to notice how they are impacted emotionally and somatically by the client and their issue; and make what they notice available to the client.

In practice, these four modes are rarely discrete. Indeed, there is evidence that good listeners engage in "multi-modal listening" (Wolvin and Coakley, 1996) in which good attention is the foundation for all other modes: Observation and resonance feed inquiry, and inquiry gives rise to what the listener sees and feels. But for the purposes of development, a coach can use the four modes to bench-mark their listening, identify their learning edge as a listener and prioritise where they intend to improve. Before we get more deeply into the four modes I would like to expand on why listening matters in coaching and highlight what can get in the way.

Why does listening matter in coaching?

Coaching is a dialogue in which the topic, the direction of exploration, the judgements about what is significant and ideas about action and resolution all come from the client. In order to be a partner in this activity the coach needs to listen well to what the client is saying. Without listening well, the coach will struggle to follow the interest of their client. In that sense, listening is a fundamental and foundational practice in coaching.

However, listening has its own impact. Although many coaching approaches and techniques build on listening, it is not simply a basic skill on which more refined, elegant and impactful skills will build. As a coach listens and as a client feels heard, positive changes happen in the client, in the coach and in the relationship between them.

Being heard impacts the client emotionally, cognitively, physically and spiritually. The emotional impact partly reflects the rarity, the novelty, for many people, of receiving non-judgemental attention (Myers, 2000). What they experience is beautifully captured by David Augsberger: "Being heard is so close to being loved that for the average person they are almost indistinguishable" (1982). This poetic formulation is increasingly supported by neuroscience because "love alters the structure of the brain" (Lewis, Amini and Lannon, 2000, p. 123) and clients are affected by the compassion inherent in good listening.

This emotional impact often goes hand in hand with a cognitive impact. Quietening emotional turmoil, leaving the amygdala unstimulated and generating a positive emotion can release the cognitive brain so that the client starts to think more clearly (Brann, 2014; Kline, 1997). Further, the coach's interest, their encouragement, their pertinent questions and other interventions that are part and parcel of good listening enable the client to explore, expand and refine their thinking. Or, as Nancy Kline puts it, this is listening to "ignite the human mind" (1997, p. 37).

The idea of listening having a physical and spiritual benefit may surprise you. But a few observations suggest that this can happen. The emotional and the physical are inextricably linked. We carry and express our emotions physically – whether it is tension, despair, excitement or love. And as those emotions change or are released, we change physically. That means that a client's felt sense of themselves can shift as they explore an issue and feel heard. And the observant coach can see that happen.

Where these emotional and physical changes are strong, they can have a bearing on a client's sense of purpose, their search for meaning and their sense of hope. Although we may each have a different understanding of "the spiritual", affecting purpose, meaning and hope takes us into the spiritual realm.

With these deep and important impacts and benefits, it is not surprising that listening well and feeling heard also contribute significantly to the development of the relationship between coach and client. The coach gets to know the client and what concerns them. That supports the quality and usefulness of their responses and interventions. It generates empathy and compassion. It requires the client to trust their coach and encourages them to do so. Overall, listening and being heard create the conditions in which the client feels able to speak. To play their part in this, the coach needs to quieten both their mind and their body, and they benefit from doing so (Kohlrieser, 2006).

Listening well and the experience of being heard contribute significantly to many of the benefits from coaching that clients report. In coaching, listening well is powerful, it is necessary and, in my experience, it is sometimes sufficient. This means that all coaches could benefit from investing in their listening not only when they start out, but also throughout their professional development.

What gets in the way of good listening?

Listening well is as much about unlearning and unleashing as it is about acquiring and adding. It is a natural ability which is affected both positively and negatively by life experience. It is useful for a coach to know their listening strengths so that they can make sure to value them and build further. Their strengths may well provide a central pillar of their listening as they grow. Equally, each coach will have accumulated habits and behaviours that may be inimical to listening well and they need to be aware of them in order to overcome them.

Some habits will simply be poor listening; for example, listening for the gap so you can respond (Downey, 2003). Other behaviours might hitherto have served a coach well in their personal or professional life. Quick analysis and conclusion, agreeing and amplifying, challenging and correcting can all be useful in a work context. But they need to be unlearnt if a coach is to listen and coach well.

What gets in a listener's way will vary from person to person. But it is helpful to think about listeners encountering barriers that fall into three over-lapping categories:

1. Distractions and internal "noise" that attract or muffle a listener's attention;
2. Unhelpful intentions reflected in habitual responses and behaviours;
3. Beliefs about the speaker, themselves as a listener or the situation or relationship.

In the first category come all the everyday distractions – both internal and external – that can make it hard to listen. Listening is hard if we are emotionally agitated, perhaps by a recent or anticipated "difficult" conversation or feeling a pressure to perform. We can be unfocused, with part of our attention still solving an earlier problem, or starting to wrestle with tomorrow's. Or we can be physically distracted by hunger, discomfort and injury, or simply affected by an environment that is not conducive to listening.

Barriers in the second category, unhelpful intentions, are often about meeting the needs of the coach rather than the client. The resultant behaviours include listening to judge the person, their views or arguments; listening for the meaning to you rather than the speaker; or listening to respond, argue, refute or give your view (Clutterbuck, 2017; See Burt, 2019, p. 13 for a fuller list).

For a coach, these habitual behaviours can turn up as a desire or need to "solve" the client's issue, or reveal that they like being an expert or source of wisdom. These intentions can drive an urge to give advice. They go hand in hand with an assumption that the client's reality is similar to the coach's (and therefore prompt an inference about what action the client should take) but, as Downey (2003) points out, each client has a unique map of reality.

Finally, unhelpful beliefs seem particularly to turn up when someone starts to focus on "doing coaching". As coaches, we all want to help our clients. We feel we have done a good job if their issue is resolved. We want to support and validate them and help them get perspective. But these values can become introjects — i.e. "shoulds" or "musts" that drive our behaviour. We then push for ideas and resolution rather than being patient and continuing to listen to the emerging story. We rescue and move away from pain in order to protect the client and, perhaps, ourselves. If we do these things, then we listen poorly and fail in our primary purpose to serve our clients as well as we can.

This range of barriers, of distractions, habits, behaviours and beliefs may be daunting. And there is no magic bullet for overcoming them. But they are all forms of "interference" (Downey, 2003), and coaches can progressively minimise the interference and support their listening by honing and maintaining their attention.

Mode 1: Attention

A clear intention and sustained attention are two of the foundations for good listening, and they need to be initiated, monitored and supported.

The **first phase** is to set an intention to pay good attention. This may seem obvious, but much can get in the way or seem more important. Particularly if you are a new coach, you may be carrying a range of conscious and unconscious intentions: to ask "good" questions, to help the client find an outcome or action, to apply techniques that you have learnt, to perform, to be a good coach, not to get lost or stumble and not to show yourself up. These and many other intentions can overwhelm your listening. A simple intention to listen can help you keep it in mind.

The **second phase** is about focusing your attention and preparing to listen. Each coach needs to find what works for them by experimenting and learning from more experienced coaches. My approach is simple: Focus my attention outward, leaving my concerns behind and check in with myself that I am ready to listen. The first part I do by consciously noticing what is around me, both as I walk to a session and while I am in the coaching room. The second part involves me noticing my posture, energy and breathing: After many years of coaching, I know what this feels like if I am ready. But I got there by using a simple mnemonic that I learned when I trained as a coach: FOE, checking that my Focus is strong and outward, that I am Open and free of assumptions and baggage, and that my Energy is high but calm. You can give each FOE a score out of 10 and often the awareness that comes from a score of less than an "8" is sufficient to make the change required.

The **third phase** involves ensuring that you sustain your attention. The bad news is that your attention will almost inevitably weaken, waver and wander. The good news is that you can simply notice this and return your attention to the client (Downey, 2003). That does however require you to be aware of what is happening to your attention in the moment. This takes practice. And it is supported by your knowledge and understanding of when and how your attention can drop. And that takes reflection, supported by supervision.

The **fourth phase** is about developing your power of attention so that you are "resourced" when you need to be. Each mode of listening – attention, inquiry, observation and resonance – is like a muscle: It needs to be used, stretched and given a work-out if it is to be strong. I shall come back to how you can do such "work-outs" at the end of the chapter.

Mode 2: Inquiry

The skills and mind-set of inquiry are at the heart of good listening. How to find powerful questions, follow the client's interest and summarise well are covered in other chapters. All these are part of listening well. Along with the quality of the coach's attention, they generate the benefits and impacts described earlier. In particular, the benefits of inquiry are to:

- "Encourage the speaker to speak and facilitate their freedom of expression;
- Build a relationship based upon trust;
- Support the speaker's thinking and reflection;
- Deepen the speaker's awareness of their issue and themselves."

(Burt, 2019, p. 62)

So inquiry is about helping the client find out what they mean by what they say. The coach's questions are fuelled by their curiosity, but their purpose is to raise the client's awareness. The coach will come to understand more about the client's issue and about them as a person, but they neither need a "complete" understanding of the issue nor is it their role to analyse the person.

The problem with words

Helping the client become clearer is, however, not straightforward. There is a problem with how we all use words. When someone expresses themselves in words, particularly if the topic is complex, personal and emotional, how they express what they are feeling or have experienced can be incomplete, filtered and oblique. Similarly, the coach's understanding is based on their own sense-making. This dual process is fraught with risks of misunderstanding. As Laquercia explains, "Language is a double-edged sword. It can foster communication and yet can also limit our experience of what the (speaker) is conveying" (2005, p. 62). That is why coaches ask questions and check their understanding.

This prompts two practical questions:

- What can I most usefully inquire and be curious about?
- How do I inquire into what the client means?

About what, and how, do I inquire?

When a client describes an issue or event they are often finding their way to communicate it as they speak. Their first attempt may be imprecise and generalised, so precision can be a useful outcome from a coaching conversation. And the tools of precision are the familiar clarifying questions that begin with: When, who, where, how much and how often, etc.

It is also worth looking out for "lazy" words; words that are close to becoming clichés. I have in mind nouns and verbs like "teamwork", "communicate or communication", "support", "vision", that occur frequently in a business context. It's important to be alive to such words – the more common they are, the more curious you can usefully be – and simply explore what they mean to the client, particularly what, in their view, good teamwork, etc., looks like.

But, as well as finding out precisely what a client means, or how they are using a familiar word, it is useful to explore what, for them, lies behind the words. When we speak, whether consciously or unconsciously, we choose the words we use. What lies behind that choice? As Treasure (2017) points out, what a word means is not simply a matter of "denotation", i.e. what it refers to; meaning also involves connotation, i.e. its significance to the speaker. My "alerts" to what might be significant, and how I might respond, include the following:

- Unusual words, words out of their usual context – "tell me more about …";
- Repeated words that feel weighty – "I notice that you have said … a number of times";
- Metaphors – "Tell me more about how it feels to be …";
- Emphasised words – simply repeat the word with a questioning inflection;
- Words with a different energy and / or emotion – simply reflect back the difference I noticed.

This may sound straightforward but it is very easy to miss the client's choice of words, particularly if you are intent on completing the story or moving onto possible action. So to listen well and notice the words, slow down, allow yourself time to notice and be curious.

Listening for the person and the narrative beneath the words

If you listen carefully to the words that the client uses, you not only get a sense of what their issue or story means to them, you also begin to notice patterns of behaviour and thinking, how they regard themselves (their self-identity) and who they are.

A good start on getting into this deeper territory is to notice a client's generalisations, the comparisons they make and the imperatives to which they subscribe. On hearing a generalisation, the coach's simplest response is to ask for evidence, to probe for counterfactuals, to ask for an example. This can help the client become aware that their perspective is skewed or out of balance and enable them to feel more positive or resourceful.

Sometimes however the truth of a generalisation may be emotional rather than evidential. If, for example, someone claims that a colleague or their boss never listens to them, it may be factually untrue (because they do sometimes listen) but nevertheless be an accurate reflection of how they are feeling – unheard. The coach can then help their client to explore that feeling, its significance for them and how it impacts them.

In comparisons the reference point may be hidden or unexpressed. "I want to be a better leader" sounds clear and a coach might assume that the client wants to improve and build their leadership skills. As a minimum the coach can tease out what being "a better leader" might look like for their client. But more than that, they can probe the comparison that gave rise to that goal. Better than they have usually been? Better than they were in a recent situation? Better than the norm in their organisation? As good as the best? The answers to such questions make the implicit explicit, enable the client to be more aware and guide the coach.

Imperatives often speak with voices from the past. "I should do this" or "I must do that" reflect a client's personal history, the culture that has shaped them and the authority figures who still whisper in their ear. Imperatives drive and constrain behaviour so they may be at the heart of patterns of behaviour that don't serve the client and limit their options. So when you hear an imperative you can ask "who says that you should/must …" and "what might happen if you didn't?"

The feel of inquiry

Good inquiry is skilled, but it is not just a technical activity. Good inquiry involves inviting the client to explore their issue in a way that creates clarity and helps them with their goal. As well as asking good questions, two things can help the coach inquire well: Using a broad and developing range of invitations; and aligning their presence and mind-set with that intention.

Often a summary acts like an invitation to say more or to emphasise something. Other invitations include gentle requests like "tell me more about …"; reflecting back what has been heard, perhaps adding an inference or connection to something else (see Miller, 2018); or simply holding an attentive and respectful silence (see Burt, 2019, pp. 57–59). This variety not only expands the coach's armoury, it also helps make the dialogue more natural.

The presence and mind-set of the coach reflect the work they have done to become ready to listen and the intention they have set to do so. They matter because the client will not only respond to the coach's invitations, they will also be affected by the coach's non-verbal communication, their focus and what it feels like sitting with them. If the coach truly slows down and gets curious, the client will notice and be encouraged to speak.

Mode 3: Observation and non-verbal communication

People communicate non-verbally as well as through the words they use. Non-verbal clues "complement, contradict, replace, repeat or accent the verbal messages (Wolvin and Coakley, 1996 p. 106). So coaches can listen with their eyes as well as their ears. All they need to do is notice when and how their client expresses themselves non-verbally (in a way that might be significant), draw attention to what they have noticed and invite the client to explore what it might mean.

Like much of listening this sounds simple but, in practice, it can be far from easy. Observation is another element of listening in which any coach can encounter barriers or blockages and needs to know themselves well. In my experience, this is principally a product of habits and fears. Habits might include focusing mainly on the words and little on the non-verbal signs, ignoring emotions that are expressed physically or not noticing fleeting non-verbal clues. Fears might include the fear of being wrong or of damaging the relationship by drawing attention to something physical (see Burt, 2019, pp. 35 and 87–89).

Once again, intention matters and helps with habit-breaking. Intending to notice and reflect back the non-verbal acts as a mental reminder to do so. Coaches can support themselves in this by explicitly contracting with their client to act as a mirror in this way. They can be instinctive – simply noticing something and reflecting it back immediately, or more deliberate: Occasionally taking a moment to pause and reflect on what they are noticing about their client. They can also use focused observation to notice specific bits of non-verbal communication or use a "soft gaze" to notice and reflect back a broader impression.

The art of reflecting back

Once you begin to notice and get curious about non-verbal communication the challenge is to use it well. Here are some ideas that can guide you:

- Treat what you notice as a clue;
- Look for clusters of clues to support your perception that your client is communicating something significant. For example, if a client appears tense in their upper body, is that tension also evident in their facial expression and their hands?
- Notice whether the physical clues are congruent or not with what the voice and words are saying. The client's words might be animated but their body still and their voice flat. You can then draw attention to either the similarity or the difference;
- Be aware of culture and start by understanding your own. Different cultures have norms that involve different levels of expressiveness. Beware of your own culturally determined assumptions;
- Focus on what you saw not what you think it means. If you have an interpretation, hold it lightly, offer it if you think it might help. Be prepared to let it go if it does not "land" with the client;
- Compare people with themselves. Get to know their "normal" physical state and their expressive range;
- Notice when and how they shift across that range;
- Keep your reflecting back simple – "I notice that …";
- Be courageous – simply "blurt" out what you notice and be OK with it being "wrong".

Many people speak in way that is rich with non-verbal clues. But this does not mean that you need to reflect back what you see at every opportunity. Listen with your eyes to notice and draw attention to when and how your client is different to usual or how they change as they explore an issue. You can offer both specific observations and a more general impression that comes from observing with a "soft gaze". And combine your observations with your inquiry – use what you notice to fuel and inspire your questions so that your listening is "multi-modal".

Mode 4: Resonance: Using yourself as a listener

Most people can recall when and how an emotional story impacted them physically: A surge of joy, a stab of fear, a wash of sadness. These are the signals of empathy and compassion.

These reactions are potential sources of understanding for the coach and awareness for the client. But they pose two problems for the coach: How to be empathetic without being swamped by the resultant emotion; and how to know whether what is being triggered in them is empathy for the client or "stuff" from their own experience.

Meeting these challenges requires the coach to work hard to develop their own self-knowledge and resilience and points to ways of sharing their responses. Both self-knowledge and resilience are deep and long-term areas of development. However, you can do well by adopting two key practices:

- Noticing what triggers your "stuff", particularly any "unfinished business" (see Clarkson, 2004, pp. 51–53) from your own life. Then use supervision to explore and understand;
- Regularly step outside your comfort zone. Learn what it feels like to be on the edge. Get more familiar with not knowing what to do.

Courage and humility are at the heart of using yourself as a listener: Courage because you will be entering emotional territory that might be hard for you, the client or both; and humility because what you notice might not "land" with the client.

This may sound tough but the potential benefits are huge. If you try to keep your own responses at bay then you close down a part of your humanity. Your physical-emotional self is both a receiver and, as discussed earlier, a transmitter that impacts the client. It is a potentially a powerful source of awareness and validation for the client. Using this facility can be hard to balance with staying focused on the client, prioritising their needs and following their lead. But, like sharing an observation, it is something to do occasionally, when the impact on you is strong and could be significant. And always in the service of the client – not to show how empathetic a coach you are.

In practice, using yourself is simply a matter of noticing how you are affected and sharing it. I'll say more on how you get better at noticing below but committing to share what you notice is a sound intention. Share even though you are not sure what you are feeling. Just "blurt". Just have a go. Embrace the risk of being unclear or incoherent. Your client will forgive you for being inarticulate and will value your effort and commitment to them. And the more you do it, the easier it gets.

Developing as a listener

In many ways, the whole of this chapter has been about how you can develop as a listener. An essential part of developing is to get to know yourself as a listener – your strengths, habits, gaps or weaknesses and what can get in your way. Finding your learning edge as a listener enables you to use the four modes of listening to focus your development. All this takes place within a framework of reflective practice and experimentation.

As you practise, you learn to integrate the four modes of listening, using one to support another, responding to what the client offers and always looking to enable the client to speak and become more self-aware. You also learn to integrate your learning with who you are as a listener – finding and developing your signature listening style.

There are techniques to try out and learn. But all aspects of listening build on, harness or release natural abilities. And we can all practise these outside of the coaching room and build familiarity, skill and resourcefulness.

- Practising **attention** is about getting used to being still, silent and outwardly focused. Mindful meditation helps many coaches do this. But many other practices and activities that require stillness and silence – like running or fishing – can help too;
- Practising **inquiry** involves parking assumptions and being curious about the familiar. You can flex your curiosity by writing down the open questions you would like to ask a current politician, celebrity or historical figure, particularly if you don't instinctively warm to them;
- You can practise **observation** by listening without the words. Follow a drama on TV with the sound turned down or observe others in a public place and guess at their relationship or notice the energy of their dialogue;

- Practising **resonance** means using your "interoceptive awareness" – getting used to noticing what you're feeling. You can do that by listening to music, through art, theatre, sport or opera – anything that hits you first somewhere in your body without your cognitive-self becoming involved.

You may now feel that the road to being a good listener seems long and arduous. But simple steps matter: Set a positive intention, get to know yourself as a listener, find your learning edge, work at it and enjoy your progress. And remember: Being heard is so precious and impactful that simply listening to someone, giving them your full attention, is a generous and valuable act; and it might be enough.

References

Aubsberger, D. (1982). *Caring enough to hear and be heard.* Ventura, CA: Regal Books.

Brann, A. (2014). *Neuroscience for coaches.* London: Kogan Page.

Burt, S. (2019). *The art of listening in coaching and mentoring.* London: Routledge.

Clarkson, P. (2004). *Gestalt counselling in action*, 3rd edition. London: Sage.

Clutterbuck, D. (2017). *Powerful questions for coaches and mentors.* Brussels, Belgium: European Mentoring and Coaching Council.

Downey, M. (2003). *Effective coaching*, 2nd edition. Boston, MA: Centage Learning.

Kline, N. (1997). *Time to think.* London: Cassell.

Kohlrieser, G. (2006). *The hostage at the table.* San Francisco, CA: Jossey-Bass.

Laquercia, T. (2005). 'Listening with the intuitive ear'. *Modern Psychoanalysis*, 30(1), pp. 60–72.

Lewis, T., Amini, F. and Lannon, R. (2000). *A general theory of love.* New York: Vantage.

Miller, S. (2018). *Listening well. The art of empathetic listening.* Eugene, OR: Wipf & Stock.

Myers, S. (2000). 'Reports on the experience of being heard'. *Journal of Humanistic Psychology*, 40(2), pp. 148–173.

Treasure, J. (2017). *How to be heard.* Coral Gables, FL: Mango Publishing.

Wolvin, A.D. and Coakley, C.G. (1996). *Listening.* Madison, WI: Brown and Benchmark.

11 Affirmations, reflections and summaries in coaching

Tim Anstiss

Introduction

Coaches need to be skilful questioners and good listeners. They need to pay particular attention to developing and strengthening the relationship factors which evidence shows strongly influences outcomes regardless of the approach used – factors like empathy, alliance, congruence, positive regard and warmth. Three conversational skills help coaches get better outcomes, but have been almost universally ignored in the coaching literature: Affirmations, reflections and summaries. In this chapter I will look at each of the three skills in turn and consider how coaches can enhance their use of these skills in their coaching conversations.

Affirmations

Affirmation are statements made by the coach about something positive about the person. Things which the coach might affirm include the client's:

- Values;
- Achievements;
- Character Strengths – like caring, persistence, flexibility, creativity;
- Effort;
- Progress;
- Determination;
- Intentions.

To offer clients affirmations the coach first may have to get better at spotting what is right with their client; what is strong about them, not what is wrong with them, and what matters to them, not what is the matter with them.

Affirmations can be quite brief and commonly take the form of clear words of recognition and appreciation. They may sound something like:

- "You are the kind of person who cares a lot for other people ...";
- "You're someone who can build a good team";
- "You didn't want to come in today, but you did anyway, I appreciate the effort that took";
- "You are really trying with your public speaking, even though you find it a struggle";
- "Being the best mum you can be is really important to you";

- "Managing your frustration with certain other people is something you're really try-ing to do ...";
- "Fairness is important to you";
- "Putting up with all this, you sound like quite a resiliente person";
- "You are the kind of person who cares a lot for other people ...";
- "You're quite a determined person";
- "You're someone who can stop smoking – you managed to quit for three weeks";
- "You've been working hard";
- "You've been successful in the past";
- "You are really trying with your weight, even though you find it a struggle";
- "Your technique has really improved since you've started coming regularly".

Affirmations may help to build a client's feeling of personal agency and control, strength, confidence, self-efficacy and hope. They can also significantly strengthen the relationship and sense of alliance. They help to show the client that they have many of the resources and strengths within them to improve and make progress, and they can also induce a mild positive emotional experience which can be important for openness and personal growth (Fredrickson, 2004).

It's worth noting at this stage that affirmations are not the same as complements or praise. They do not take the form "well done" or "that's great" or "excellent". They are more precise, more specific, pointing to something about the client – an observation if you will – and are based on specific evidence or information the client has shared with the coach.

Two other things about making good affirmations – they should be genuine and used sparingly. If the client thinks the coach is just trotting out some complement or technique, this is less likely to "land" and have the impact the coach wishes. And, similarly, if the coach uses them every few minutes, they will have diminishing and potentially negative returns. I might try and offer a client three or four affirmations in a typical session.

Making affirmations are one of the ways in which the coach can express positive regard – one of three critically important interpersonal qualities Carl Rogers (1965) thought essential for therapeutic success (the others being genuineness/congruence and empathy). In research studies, positive regard is sometimes measured using the "level of regard" scale of the Barrett-Lennard Relationship Inventory (Wampler and Powell, 1982), which seeks to operationalise the ideas of Carl Rogers. If we change the word counsellor for coach, some of the items in this scale would read:

- "My coach respects me as a person";
- "My coach is friendly and warm towards me";
- "I feel appreciated by my coach";
- "I feel that my coach disapproves of me" (reverse scored);
- "My coach is impatient with me" (reverse scored);
- "At times my coach feels contempt for me" (reverse scored).

In one meta-analysis, involving 64 studies and 3,528 subjects, the strength of the link between positive regard and outcomes was found to perhaps be as high as 0.36 – indicat-ing that better outcomes are to be expected when practitioners affirm their clients and convey unconditional warmth and liking (Farber et al., 2018). Extrapolating from the data, the reviewers made the following recommendations for practice:

- Practitioners should embody and express positive regard for their clients. At a minimum, it "sets the stage" for other active ingredients in client progress and, at least in some cases, may be sufficient to effect positive change;
- Affirming clients seems to serve many valuable functions. It may strengthen the client's sense of self or agency and belief in their capacity to be engaged in an effective relationship, reinforce engagement in the therapeutic process and facilitate psychological growth and resilience;
- Practitioners should ensure they communicate a caring, respectful and positive attitude that affirms a client's sense of worth. This does not mean a stream of compliments or a gushing of positive sentiment which may overwhelm or even terrify some clients;
- Positive regard is best conveyed through multiple channels, including offering reassuring, caring words, creating positive narratives, active listening, flexibility in scheduling, speaking in a gentle tone of voice, establishing responsive eye contact and maintaining positive body language;
- Practitioners are advised to monitor their expressions of positive regard and adjust these as a function of particular client and specific situations. Practitioners vary in the extent to which they convey positive regard and clients vary in the extent to which they need, elicit and benefit from it. It seems likely that the inevitable ruptures in alliance result not only from a practitioner's technical errors, but also from their occasional inability to demonstrate minimal levels of positive regard.

Box 11.1: Affirmation example

Barry came for coaching as he was struggling with a wayward son, whom he shared custody with his ex-wife. He was trying to get work whilst trying to maintain a good relationship with his teenage son who had been excluded from school for fighting. After talking about the situation and the effort Barry was making, the coach said "you're juggling many things right now, trying to build a better life for you and your family. You son's future is obviously really important to you, and you're being the best dad you can be".

Reflections

Offering a client a reflection, or making reflective listening statements, is a key skill for strengthening key aspects of the relationship, whilst encouraging clients to talk and expand, helping them learn about themselves and helping them get unstuck and grow.

Reflective listening involves saying back to the person something of what they have said. Many coaches believe that the coach should use the exact words or phrase the client has used and should not "put words in the client's mouth". But this is not what Carl Rogers or the research evidence on empathic listening recommends, nor the research evidence on empathic listening. Just repeating or mirroring what the client says can sometimes be irritating to the client ("I just said that") and does not demonstrate deep listening, going "under" that the client has said to connect with what they might mean. It's paying attention to the words, but not the music. Empathetic reflections aim to accurately capture the meaning of what the client has said, and also to let them know you are really (and deeply) listening and are trying to understand them. This doesn't happen with pure mirroring or repeating types of reflections.

Here are some of the things reflecting listening can do:

- Express empathy and help build the alliance;
- Check for correct understanding;
- Move the conversation along without asking a question;
- Help the client get a better understanding of themselves;
- Encourage exploration;
- Build confidence and self-efficacy;
- Create momentum;
- Structure the conversation;
- Gently guide the session in more productive directions;
- Convey warmth and non-judgement;
- Keep the session on track for the benefit of the client.

Reflections come in different shapes and levels of depth. These include simple and complex reflections.

Simple reflections

Simple reflections don't add anything to what the client has said, and typically involve making a few word changes while staying as close as possible to the client's intended meaning.

For instance:

Client: "I wasn't really sure about coaching, but I thought I'd give it a go".
Coach: "You're willing to give it a try".

Complex reflections

Complex reflections "go underneath the surface" of what the person has said, to what the coach senses or imagines the client may be feeling or meaning. Sometimes they use a "metaphor" to convey this "guess".

For instance, using the same client statement:

Client: "I wasn't really sure about coaching, but I thought I'd give it a go".
Coach: "You had mixed feelings, but you are open-minded".

Other ways of reflecting can be to:

Say what was said back, changing one or two words. For instance:

Client: "I used to really enjoy exercise, but don't have the time these days".
Coach: "You used to enjoy being active, but you're too busy at the moment".

Rephrase the sentence. For instance:

Client: "I used to really enjoy exercise, but don't have the time these days".
Coach: "You're missing something which was important to you".

Capture the imagined feeling:

Client: "I used to really enjoy exercise, but don't have the time these days".
Coach: "Which must be frustrating for you".

Finish the sentence:

Client: "I used to really enjoy exercise, but don't have the time these days".
Coach: "And you're looking forward to getting back into it".

Use a metaphor:

Client: "I used to really enjoy exercise, but don't have the time these days".
Coach: "All the other things you're doing has squeezed out time for yourself".

All of these reflections are acceptable and each might have a slightly different impact on the client. All, hopefully, will encourage the client to keep talking and exploring the idea or the topic. The coach uses these to guide the conversation and focus on specific aspects of what the client is saying.

And, depending on how the client reacts, the coach might continue to offer reflections, or make an affirmation if the opportunity arises:

"Staying healthy is important to you".

Or ask a question:

"When do you see this changing?" or
"What kind of exercise did you used to enjoy?".

The reflection can be question-like, in that the client might respond with a yes or a no, depending on whether or not the reflection is accurate. Sometimes this leads to a client response of: "Exactly!" or a "definitely", if you've really nailed it.

One of the ways you make a reflection more like a statement is to pay attention to the intonation at the end of the reflection. For example, compare the impact of the coaches response spoken with different intonations:

Client: "Since I've moved back in with my parents, I've started to get angry with my mum".
Coach: "You're getting angry with your mother" (spoken/read with voice going up at the end).
Coach: "You're getting angry with your mother" (spoken/read with voice staying flat or going down at the end).

It might be helpful when trying to understand what reflections are by exploring what they are not. Thomas Gordon (1970) describes 12 "roadblocks" which get in the way of reflective listening. They are "roadblocks" in that they often "divert" the client away from the continued exploration and elaboration of their train of thought and can stop forward

Table 11.1 Roadblocks to coaching conversation

1. Ordering, directing, or commanding;
2. Warning or threatening;
3. Giving advice, making suggestions, providing solutions;
4. Persuading with logic, arguing or lecturing;
5. Moralising, preaching or telling clients their duty;
6. Judging, criticising, disagreeing or blaming;
7. Agreeing, approving or praising;
8. Shaming, ridiculing or name calling;
9. Interpreting or analysing;
10. Reassuring, sympathising or consoling;
11. Questioning or probing;
12. Withdrawing, distracting, humouring or changing the subject.

(Adapted from Gordon, 1970)

momentum. This doesn't mean to say they are wrong, or course. Just that they are not reflective listening. These roadblocks are summarised in Table 11.1.

Reflective listening can be hard to do, and even harder to do well. But the good news is coaches can get better at offering reflections with practice. It is also helpful to cultivate the right mindset and attitude. This includes:

* Having a genuine interest in what the client has to say;
* Having respect for the client's knowledge and opinion (they know a lot more about themselves than you do!);
* A willingness to "stay close" to what the client is talking about rather than rush ahead;
* The humility to check that what you think the client means is actually what they mean.

Because our minds often go straight to questions when coaching, it can be helpful to have some "starter" words or phrases to help get into the reflection habit. Here is a selection (obviously, the one you use will be tailored to what the client has just or recently said). It's worth keeping in mind that with a reflection you are not questioning or gather facts, but trying to understand them and communicate your attempt to understand them.

So, it's important to you that …
You're finding that …
You really care about …
You're learning that …
You're hoping …
You want too …
You need …
Part of you realises that …
You're realising …
You've put a lot of thought into …
Sometimes it feels like …
You're tired of the same thing…

It seems like ...
You've been really thinking about ...
You're the kind of person who ...
And that shows a lot of ...
On the one hand ... on the other ... (a double-sided reflection)
In some ways ... in other ways ... (another double-sided reflection).

Skilful, accurate, empathic listening is one the key ways in which the coach conveys empathy. The American Psychological Association (Elliot et al., 2018) evaluated the links between how empathic a practitioner seems to be (in their own eyes, their client's eyes or those of a trained observer) and outcomes. Their findings are of importance to coaches. Two of the modes of therapeutic empathy they described were:

- "Empathy as the establishment of empathic rapport and support, in which the practitioner exhibits a benevolent, compassionate attitude toward the client and tries to demonstrate that they understand their experience";
- "Empathy as an active effort to stay attuned on a moment-to-moment basis with the client's communications and unfolding experience during a session, an effort most commonly showing itself in empathic responses".

Analysing 82 studies, they found a mean correlation between empathy and outcomes of 0.28, equating to an effect size of 0.58 − a statistically significant, medium-strength relationship, which explains about 8% of the difference in client outcomes, similar to the difference accounted for by the quality of the therapeutic alliance and greater than that explained by the specific therapeutic method used. Thus, the more the practitioner communicates their understanding of (and compassion for) the client, the better the outcomes tend to be. One way in which empathy (as perceived by the client) is measured is the empathy scale of the Barrett-Lennard Relationship Inventory mentioned above. Here are some further examples of statements which have been adapted from the Inventory:

"My coach usually senses or realises what I am feeling".
"My coach looks at what I do from his/her own point of view" (reverse scored).
"My coach may understand my words but he/she does not see the way I feel." (reverse scored).
"My coach wants to understand how I see things".
"My coach nearly always knows exactly what I mean".

Over 80 studies and multiple meta-analyses indicate that empathy is a robust, medium-sized predictor of outcomes in counselling and psychotherapy and there is very reason to assume these benefits would transfer across the parallel world of coaching. The effect of empathy shows itself across different theoretical orientations, formats and client problems. In summaries we can conclude from these studies the following:

- Coaches should continuously try to understand their clients and to demonstrate this understanding through responses that address their client's perceived needs;
- Coaches should avoid parroting clients' words back and aim to reflect back meaning;
- Coaches seek to understand overall goals and tasks, moment-to-moment experiences and unspoken nuances and implications;

- Empathy should be valued as both an "ingredient" in a healthy relationship and a specific, effective response which strengthens the client's sense of self and promotes deeper exploration;
- Coaches continually adjust their assumptions and understandings, attending to the "leading edge" of client experience to facilitate awareness of emerging feelings and perspectives;
- Coaches should not assume that their clients are mind readers, nor that their experience of understanding the client will be matched by the client themselves feeling understood;
- Empathy is shown as much in how well the coach receives, listens, respects and attends to the client as in what they do or say;
- Empathy should always be offered with humility and held lightly, ready to be corrected;
- Empathy entails tailoring the response to the client. For example, some clients may find the usual expressions of empathy intrusive, while hostile clients may find empathy too directive, and others may find any empathic focus on feeling alien;
- Coaches should seek to offer empathy in the context of positive regard and genuineness. Empathy will probably not be effective unless it is grounded in authentic caring for the client.

Summaries

Summaries bring together some of the things the person has said or has been talking about in a longer statement, checking you have understood things correctly and helping them develop an overview or see the patterns which are emerging in the conversation. In this way, the summary is like the final paragraph in a chapter, drawing one part of a conversation to a close, and acting as a signal to the client that the opportunity to move to the next part of the conversation is there, if they are ready to do so.

Jonathan Passmore has compared the reflection to a rose, which the coach hands to the client. It is a beautiful thing, which makes the client feel special, while the summary is akin to handing the client a bouquet, which draws together many flowers and arranging them in such a way as to help the client see them anew and be able to move forward.

Bill Miller and Steve Rollnick consider the summary as a "special application" of reflective listening (Miller and Rollnick, 2013) that can be used at different times during the session.

Start of a session

They can be used at the start of a session, if you've seen the client before:

> Last time we met, we spent some time talking about X and Y. As I recall, you said you were thinking of doing A and perhaps B, and I said I would look into Z. Is that your understanding?

Periodically

They can be offered periodically throughout the session, perhaps after, for instance, using the decisional balance strategy:

So, can I just summarise … the good things for you about changing jobs are A and B and also possibly C. The downside is that H might happen, and also J. The advantages of you as staying as you are are P and Q, but if you don't change jobs you are worried that X and also that Y. Is that about right?

Change direction

And they can be used to help change direction, or before gently bringing the session to a close:

So, just to check where things are … we talked about X and you were strongly of the opinion that A and B and C, and we also spent some time exploring what that would be like if it did happen, and you felt X and Y and Z.
   We've got about 15 minutes left, and I know you said you also wanted a quick chat about Z. Shall we do that now?

We often ask permission to offer a summary:

Can I check my understanding ….
Is it OK if I check I've heard you correctly.

Or use a starter such as:

So, what you seem to be saying is that X and Y and Z, and also A and B and C … is that correct?.

Summaries by their very nature are shorter than what the person said, and involve selection by the coach. The elements of the conversation which the coach chooses to include in the summary will in part be influenced by the approach and theoretical orientation of the coach. For instance, coaches using a motivational interviewing style (Miller and Rollnick, 2013) might include both sides of the argument for and against change when summarising, but perhaps finish on the "change talk" (client arguments in favour of change) rather than the "sustain talk" (client arguments against change), depending on the context.
   Different types of summaries have been described (Milner and Rollnick, 2013), including:

- Collecting;
- Linking;
- Integrating;
- Transitional.

Whilst they overlap, they serve slightly different purposes.
   Collecting summaries gathers information together, presents it back to the client and helps to keep the conversation moving forward.
   The aim of linking summaries is to contrast ideas heard recently in the conversation with information picked up earlier – literally linking things together. This can help the client become more aware of any conflict or contradiction between different parts of themselves, as well as further explore their ambivalence or mixed feelings about an issue:

> Can I just summarise … you seem to be saying that X and Y and also Z. And earlier in the conversation you said you felt A was important to you, and also B …
>   What do you make of this?.

Integrating summaries can bring together, or integrate, information from outside or collateral information:

> You've said you feel unappreciated by the organisation, and that many of your ideas are ignored or not taken forward. You also feel your boss undermines you. And yet you've shown me your performance reviews, which are glowing, they are paying for you to have this coaching with me and you won that internal award last year.
>   How do you make sense of this?

Transitional summaries are used to choose or change the direction in the session. They may be slightly longer summaries and come before an open-ended question that leads in a new direction or can be used to close a session. They can also be used as a prelude to the "key question" – about whether or not the client is going to change, e.g. after exploring two possible futures with them:

> So can I summarise …? If you did leave you partner, in 12 months' time you think that you would be A and B, doing more C and D, and hope also to be E. But you are worried that F. And if you stay in the relationship for another year, you feel in one year's time that P and Q would be the case, and also that perhaps W.
>   Is that about right?
>   So, what do you think you will do? (the "key question").

Generally speaking, succinct summaries are best. The coach should try not to talk until they see the client's eyes glaze over! The aim is to get to the heart of the message conveyed. Before attempting to provide a summary the coach needs to think about the reason for offering the summary and focus on their client's needs. Too much talking will mean the summary loses its power or impact. Keeping the summary to 3–4 sentences means this is more likely to be achieved.

Conclusion

Affirming, reflecting and summarising are key skills for coaches to use, practise and develop. They significantly impact those all-important relationship factors like empathy, warmth, congruence, alliance and positive regard. Like any skill, they can be improved with practice, but deliberate practice of the right things will lead to more rapid skill development than letting things improve by chance. I hope this chapter helps to deepen your appreciation of these important conversational elements, and guides you towards being a more skilful, engaging and effective coach.

References

Elliott, R., Bohart, A.C., Watson, J.C., et al. (2018). 'Therapist empathy and client outcome: An updated meta-analysis'. *Psychotherapy*, 55(4), pp. 399–410.

Farber, B.A., Suzuki, J.Y. and Lynch, D.A. (2018). 'Positive regard and psychotherapy outcome: a meta-analytic review'. *Psychotherapy*, 55(4), pp. 411–423.

Fredrickson, B (2004). 'The broaden-and-build theory of positive emotions'. *Philosophical Transactions of the Royal Society London B*, 359, pp. 1367–1377.

Gordon, T. (1970). *Parent effectiveness training*. London: McKay/Random House.

Miller, W. and Rollnick, S. (2013). *Motivational interviewing*. New York: Guildford Press.

Rogers, C. (1965). *Client-centred therapy*. New York: Houghton Mifflin.

Wampler, K.S. and Powell, G.S. (1982). 'The Barrett-Lennard Relationship Inventory as a Measure of Marital Satisfaction'. *Family Relations*, 31(1), pp. 139–145.

12 Tools and techniques in coaching

Sarah Leach and Jonathan Passmore

Introduction

Exploring new tools and techniques is one aspect which many new coaches get excited about. New coaches are often fascinated about what new tools they can add to their repertoire, and how such tools can provide a fast or even magic solution to a client's problems. We believe that tools and techniques can be really helpful, and having a diverse range of tools in one's kitbag is a strength. Some techniques may fit within a specific approach or model we are using. Or we might develop a particular skill in using a technique. Whatever the reason, coaching tools and techniques are like a doctor's stethoscope or a farrier's irons, in that they can support the coach in their task. But we also recognise tools are not the solution in themselves. In fact, tools can be a distinct disadvantage on some occasions. They can stop the coach forging a genuine relationship with their clients, or can end up driving the direction of the coaching as the coach falls back on their old favourite technique or tool, rather than working with each client as a unique individual. In this chapter we look at what we mean by coaching tools and techniques, when they might be helpful and what some of the risks might be if we start to rely on them too much. Finally, we will offer some guidelines to help coaches decide what tool or technique to use and when.

What are coaching tools and techniques?

Coaching tools and techniques are in one way a mechanism to introduce a creative process for clients which has a well tried and tested process, a little like a recipe.

Similarly, they can also be an effective means of communication by way of complementing a client's preferences and understanding of the presenting issue. John Whitmore (2009, p. 9) suggests that "coaching delivers results in large measure because of the supportive relationship between the coach and the client, and the means and style of communication used". Therefore, it is reasonable to assume that the use of coaching tools and techniques are important resources to support the means and style of communication that enables your client to do their best thinking.

Coaching tools and techniques are practical and often very tangible interventions that you can use whilst coaching, to complement powerful dialogue and active listening, the basics of any great coaching conversation. Some are universally relevant and others, as suggested by Bossons, Kourdi and Sartain (2012), work best when addressing a specific issue; for example, decision-making or dealing with difficult relationships. Depending on your style and approach to coaching, tools and techniques can be used in different ways. Some coaches prefer to use models or techniques in isolation from others, in their most pure form, and perhaps concentrate on ones related to their individual specialism or coaching perspective. Whereas, others adapt and develop individual techniques or may blend them with another tool. This group are more likely to create and flex their coaching style in the moment depending on a client's needs. Hardingham (2004) describes this approach as a more eclectic style of coaching, which often comes with more confidence and experience in coaching. Neither approach is right or wrong, just representative of the individual and personal nature of coaching both from a practitioner and client's perspective.

The language we use to describe these interventions, such as tools, techniques, models and approaches, gets used interchangeably; however, you might like to consider the following to help distinguish one from the other.

Perspective – A coaching perspective may be described as the theory or source upon which a coaching tool or technique is based such as behavioural psychology, cognitive behavioural psychology or positive psychology. In other words, a particular field or domain on which a certain style of coaching is developed. For example, the person-centred, previously named client-centred, approach to coaching is based on the perspective that people are their own best experts. This approach, aligned to humanist psychology, was originally developed by Carl Rogers during the 1950s and was seen as a response to other perspectives such as behaviourism (Cox, Bachkirova and Clutterbuck, 2011)

Approach or method – This terminology is often used interchangeably with techniques but is more concerned with the application of a perspective, such as cognitive-behavioural theory (CBT), a method informed by the cognitive-behavioural perspective, or positive psychology coaching, which is the application of positive psychology perspective in coaching;

Model – This is a structure to enable clients or the coach to logically structure the conversation. The GROW model is one example of this. The model is based within the behavioural coaching approach and is informed by the behavioural psychology perspective. The model offers four stages to guide the conversation and thus provides a logical structure that is easy to remember and use;

Framework – The word is often used interchangeably with model;

Toolkit – This is a collection of tools which the coach has at their disposal. The coach understands the tool, its origins, when it may be most useful to a client, how to use it and how to integrate it with their other tools, models and methods. The tools may be clustered or grouped in some way such as in PERFECT (physical, environmental, relational, feelings, effective thinking, continuity, transcendence) as described by Scoular (2011). This toolkit is a way of helping coaches to guide them on "what to do and in what order";

Tools – These are individual exercises that form part of a coach's toolkit. For example, the ABC client sheet used to capture clients' thinking, having applied the ABCDE framework, could be considered a coaching tool. Another example might be FLOW, a positive psychology tool that enables clients to define what optimum performance might look like for them (Scoular, 2011) or "Three Good Things", a very simple but effective exercise for increasing feelings of positivity (Passmore and Oades, 2016). In addition to exercises we would also include psychometric tools such as 16Personalities, VIA or Strengthscope in this category;

Technique – While similar to a tool, a technique may be considered to be less formal. It might include ways of reflection; for example, using amplified reflection rather than a simple reflection (Passmore, 2011), mirroring or matching a client's language or behaviour in our communications.

For the purposes of the rest of this chapter, we will use the term tools and techniques.

How can tools and techniques help in coaching?

If used correctly within the context of the overall coaching relationship, tools and techniques can be sources of creativity, enhancing clarity and promoting change (Hardingham, 2004). They can help clients to think out of the box, away from their normal thought patterns, and to take a different or new perspective on a familiar situation or challenge. They become an integral part of the coaching practice and, when used well, are almost as unobserved as any specific coaching tool or technique by the client.

For the coach, tools and techniques can help expand the range of interventions that the coach can use while working with a client. This can help the coach to feel more confident in the way in which they coach, but also help them to be more resourceful in terms of what they bring, and how they apply themselves, to the role of coach.

Tools and techniques can also bring a degree of rigour to the coaching relationship, providing a useful frame of reference, as well as encouraging a degree of discipline and professionalism in the way in which the coach fulfils his/her role. They can be used by the coach as a way to remain objective, detached from the issue and provide a process which is tried and tested for clients, thus increasing the prospects of a successful outcome.

When clients are particularly challenging, or presenting with multiple or complex issues, tools and techniques can help both the coach and client to maintain a degree of focus (Scoular, 2011). This is also useful when working at speed or under pressure as the tool can help to structure the client's thinking, encourage a more specific outcome and, consequently, help the client move towards action.

When a client is caught up in the presenting issue, it can be difficult for them to see the connections and/or implications for other areas of their life. A coaching tool can be helpful in prompting additional thinking, insights and observations regarding related topics that might not have otherwise come up. In other words, it helps the client, and often the coach, to see beyond the obvious, and get beyond the limiting belief or barrier to change that might be keeping them "stuck" in a perspective. For example, the miracle question is a technique originating from the solution-focused therapy perspective, which enables clients to imagine what could be different and how to make it happen. This technique is demonstrated beautifully in a case study of a fiercely independent client whose need to do things her own way was causing significant team issues and had left her employer questioning her organisational fit (Watts and Morgan, 2015, see chapter 4). In asking the miracle question, the client was able to see beyond her current situation and consider a range of future options she'd not been able to see before.

As coaches we are continuously looking for ways to enable the client to learn more about themselves and the topic they are trying to address, to enable forward momentum. Models, often pictorial diagrams, can be used to support further learning (Bird and Gornall, 2016) by simplifying a complex situation or making the learning more accessible. Depending on the success or otherwise of the technique introduced, a positive knock-on impact may occur. The client learns how to apply this technique for themselves, enhancing their personal responsibility for the future.

Tools and techniques may also appeal to clients who like to follow a more structured approach to analysing and reflecting on a given situation or challenge. Some tools and techniques can help clients interpret events differently, reframe negative interpretations and change their behaviour accordingly. They can be used to stretch a client's thinking and help them to see a new and different perspective that might not otherwise be available to them.

In a very practical way, tools and techniques can help a coach to build credibility with a client. They can be used specifically as a marketing tool, highlighting a specialism or set of skills that might appeal to a certain client group. Examples might include cognitive-behavioural coaches or career coaches who might attract clients by describing a defined approach and an associated set of techniques that are used in supporting clients in a given situation. Being able to describe a niche in this way can really help coaches to focus on and target their ideal client.

What are the risks of using tools and techniques?

However, there are always two sides to a story! Jenny Rogers (2016) suggests that "you have to know all the techniques yet restrain yourself from using them except when they are totally appropriate". Rogers makes the distinction between "doing coaching" and "being a coach" where you can get stuck in and work too hard on using the tools and techniques, forgetting that being a coach is easier and more fluid when you "trust the process" (2016, p. 287). In other words, if you're constantly searching for a tool to use, you have probably stopped listening. Rogers suggests that "the point about coaching is to ask wise, not clever questions, and to keep out of the client's way" (2016, p. 287). Using too many tools and techniques has the potential to interfere with this easy and natural process of coaching and inadvertently you find yourself stuck in the client's way.

The danger is the coach focuses on the process of using the tool or method instead of paying attention to the client. Hardingham (2004, p. 93), for instance, talks about that moment when "they sensed my absolute attention to them had been disrupted by my interest in the application of some technique". Tools can easily detract from your authentic approach to coaching and ability to be totally and completely present. Hardingham (2004) goes on to suggest that the use of a technique does not imply coaching effectiveness and by relying too much on a technique the coach will remain a "craftsperson", causing the relationship with the client to become superficial.

When the coach becomes focused on the technique, the client may follow suit! The client may become focused on following the coach's instructions and become too concerned about using the tool in the right way. The client may feel like the model becomes a test or a hurdle, rather than an enabler to their learning and progress. This could result, at an extreme, in a degree of performance anxiety over using the tool rather than dealing with the issue itself.

It is inevitable that overuse of tools and techniques can lead to more of a "painting by numbers" approach to coaching, where the coach has not fully integrated the technique into his/her own way of being. This might inhibit the coach's creativity and spontaneity, as the coach becomes too formulaic in their approach and their coaching becomes clunky and doesn't necessarily follow a natural flow.

The other risk associated with a more formulaic approach is that it can limit the client's thinking in one direction and, at an extreme, force a particular outcome. They can appear to manipulate the client's thinking with the coach finding themselves drawn into a more directive style of coaching. This happens as a result of guiding the client through the tool and, at an extreme, the coach starts giving advice and providing solutions on behalf of the client.

Over time, it is inevitable that the coach may get trapped into using the same tools and techniques because that is all they know or because it's a tool they enjoy using. Consequently, there is a risk that the coach attempts to "fit" the tool to the presenting issue regardless of its appropriateness or match to the client's need. In addition, the tool may not appeal to the client or indeed match their preferences. Being able to choose a tool fit for purpose assumes a level of knowledge and understanding about the client, or a willingness to be open about trying something different with a risk that it may not work out. It is possible that the introduction of a tool, if not applied and interpreted in an appropriate way, may simplify the client's issue and fail to address the root cause.

Guidelines for using tools and techniques in coaching

Powerful dialogue and active listening are at the heart of any great coaching conversation; however, tools and techniques can be used very effectively to draw out specific learning and actions.

The experienced coach will be able to decide, in the moment, when it is appropriate to introduce a new tool into the coaching conversation and, perhaps most importantly, which tool or technique to use to address the particular client's need, matching the client's preferences as appropriate.

The only way, as with most things in life, to become skilled in the use of coaching tools and techniques is to practise! Depending on your style of coaching there will be some that you find more or less useful, and depending on the type of client you attract, you will find that you naturally reach for a core set of techniques that you know will work in a particular situation.

However, keep it fresh! Continue to keep your practice up to date with new and different approaches, experimenting with coaching peers, friends or even clients! Some clients love the idea of learning something new; be open and honest with them about your level of skill in a technique and ask them openly if they're prepared to experiment. This collaborative partnering with your client can lead to greater levels of rapport and trust. It might be useful for the coach to discuss, in the contracting phase of the relationship, the idea of using a selection of coaching tools and techniques, including the possibility of "experimentation". Contracting also provides an initial opportunity to explore the client's preferences, which would be useful in determining whether tools and techniques will be helpful or disruptive for the work the client wishes to undertake. However, it is important for the coach to continue to test their assumptions with regard to the client's needs throughout the relationship and avoid "forcing" the client in any way.

Tools and techniques can be adjusted and adapted to suit the situation. Don't feel like you must always stick to the rules. Be prepared to bend and flex as appropriate. This confidence will come with more experience of using your tried and trusted techniques; however, don't be afraid to stretch the boundaries of the technique to suit the situation you find yourself in. For example, an adaptation of the Gestalt Empty Chair technique (Pugh, 2017), is aimed at helping individuals to shift their perspective on a particular issue and to allow for greater empathy when it comes to relationship building. However, it could easily be adapted for team environments that help teams explore relational dynamics.

Similarly, adapting organisational business change techniques to individual challenges can also help. For example, communication plans or stakeholder engagement matrices might be useful in a one-to-one coaching session when thinking about developing

Table 12.1 Five top tips for using tools and techniques in coaching

5 Top Tips	Description
Ensure fit for purpose	Use tools and techniques that are aligned and appropriate to the presenting client issue. Be mindful of "forcing" clients through an unnecessary or inappropriate process.
Build a core set	Build and develop a core set of tools and techniques that you are skilled at using and know will work in a given situation. However, try not to become more attached to the tool than the need to address the client's issue.
Practise and experiment	Keep it fresh, keep practising and don't be afraid to introduce something new to your repertoire. This will enable more choice, creativity and resourcefulness in your coaching.
Push the boundaries	Be prepared to adapt, blend or even deconstruct tools and techniques to suit the situation at hand, bringing your wider experience to bear in a way that is useful and complementary to the way in which you coach.
Contract for their use	Be open with your client about the use of tools and techniques from the start of your relationship, including the possibility of experimenting with new or adapted approaches.

influencing and negotiation strengths. Experienced coaches bring what they know from their coaching and business backgrounds and apply it in a way that is of service to their clients.

Not every technique or approach is suitable for every coach. Learn and spend time on those techniques that you find comfortable, useful and complementary to the way in which you coach and the types of clients you tend to work with. In fact, John Whitmore, in talking about his very structured approach to coaching with the GROW model suggested that, as confidence builds and the framework becomes more and more familiar, the coach will "destructure the concept" (2009, p. 19) as it becomes their own.

We would encourage coaches to take the same approach to tools and techniques to master a dozen or three dozen tools and techniques and, through practice, deconstruct the tool and be able to adapt and apply it appropriately to each individual client and situation, which enables the client to focus on their issue and not the tool or technique, thereby finding the process that enables them to make a positive step forward. See Table 12.1.

Conclusion

In conclusion, feeling enabled, being inspired and getting creative with the tools of the trade, so to speak, rather than being constrained by their structure or perceived boundaries, is essential in building your coaching practice.

Tools and techniques can prove valuable to clients, helping them to think in new and fresh ways about their issue.

Finding a set of tools that you feel able and confident in using, but are not wedded or attached to in a way that forces your client through an unnecessary or inappropriate process, can enrich and enable the most effective coach.

Finally: Practice, practice, practice!

References

Bird, J. and Gornall, S. (2016). *The art of coaching: A handbook of tips and tools*. Oxford: Routledge.

Bossons, P., Kourdi, J. and Sartain, D. (2012). *Coaching essentials: Practical proves techniques for world-class executive coaching*, 2nd ed. London: Bloomsbury.

Cox, E., Bachkirova, T. and Clutterbuck, D. (2011). *The complete handbook of coaching*. London: Sage publications Ltd.

Hardingham, A. (2004). *The coach's coach: Personal development for personal developers*. London: CIPD.

Passmore, J. (2011). 'MI techniques – reflective listening'. *The Coaching Psychologist*, 7(1), pp. 49–52.

Passmore, J. and Oades, L.G. (2016). 'Positive psychology coaching techniques: Three good things'. *The Coaching Psychologist*, 12(2), pp. 33–34.

Pugh, M. (2017). 'Pull up a chair'. *The Psychologist*, 30, pp. 42–47.

Rogers, J. (2016). *Coaching skills: The definitive guide to being a coach*, 4th ed. Maidenhead: Open University Press.

Scoular, A. (2011). *Business coaching*. Harlow: Pearson Education Ltd.

Whitmore, J. (2009). *Coaching for Performance: GROWing Human Potential and Purpose: The Principles and Practice of Coaching and Leadership*, 4th ed. London: Nicholas Brealey Publications.

Watts, G. and Morgan, K. (2015) *The Coach's Casebook: Mastering the 12 Traits That Trap Us*, Cheltenham, UK: Inspect & Adapt Ltd.

13 Silence in coaching

Arthur F. Turner

Introduction

In this chapter I will be exploring the role of silence in coaching and explicitly the role of silence in executive coaching. I will draw from a broad range of human activities, including music, computer sciences and theatre, before looking at those experiencing coaching or learning how to coach and their views of silence within their practice. It is hoped that this exploration will encourage coaches of all persuasions to work with silence in a much more incisive and deliberate manner. It could be argued that silence itself is an act of communication, although it may spell reflectiveness (taking time to consider inwardly) or, in a more negative sense, withholding or not communicating (Stevenson, 2016). In this chapter we are holding onto silence as a skill to be learn and a technique to be utilised.

How is silence treated outside of coaching?

Literature, art and science understand silence in different ways and their reflections on silence are helpful before reviewing silence in the field of coaching. In order to explore silence in this context of executive coaching, I have looked at silence in three other very different fields: Computer science, music and the use of silence in writing scripts for plays and within literature. Computer science allows us a glimpse into the importance of silence and, in its balance with energy (in terms of an electronic pulse) (see, for example, Dhulipala, Fragouli and Orlitsky, 2010), it reminds us that the gaps between these pulses are as important as the pulses themselves.

Music, too, has a long history of using silence to emphasis difference in tempo and melody. One example is John Cabe's piano musical piece "4 minutes, 33 seconds". Experiencing this silent concerto will be explored further on in the chapter through a vignette explaining the reaction of a group that is listening to it. The Cabe concerto is, throughout, a musical entity, a period of time where no notes are struck and, in the silence, as well as in the minds of the listeners, potential music is formed (Kania, 2010). The lyrics of a famous Bossa nova song, 'Silencia', (Buena Vista Social Club, 2010) also hint towards the role of positive silence has, as a reflective space between two people.

These examples of music remind us of the ways in which the silences are affectively turning the listeners thoughts back inside their brains, inducing a state of reflection (whether or not that reflection is viewed in a negative or positive way). The creation of a suitable rapport between the coach and the client leads towards a much more positive view of the reflective silence, one could argue.

Cain (2013) and Maitland (2009) from their different perspectives of introversion and solitude, respectively, have both extoled the virtues of silence in everyday life. Cain tried to find the voice of introverts within business life by identifying silence as "a tool of contemplation". While Maitland wrote about the pleasures and powers of silence and how, in her very auto-ethnographic research, she noticed silence causes "the dissolving of barriers" and "the presence of something that is not sound" (2009, p. 29).

In forms of artistic impression, silence is identified as being similarly important. For example, Qi and Wang (2010) write extensively about the role of silence in theatrical expression and communication. Here, they write about Harold Pinter's plays and his rational for the use of silence:

> The speech we hear is an indication of that we don't hear. It is a necessary avoidance, a violent, sly, anguished or mocking smoke-screen which keeps the other in its place. When true silences fall we are still left with echo but never nakedness. One way of looking at speech is to say it is a constant stratagem to cover nakedness.
>
> (p. 30)

This stance can also be seen in the films of Francis Ford Coppola (such as Apocalypse Now), which juxtaposes eerie scenes set in silence with music from Wagner.

In order to understand the phenomenon of silence within coaching I will take a social constructionist approach (Burr, 2015) in which the coach and their client are critical of any taken-for-granted notions of truth. This means that both the coach and their client extract from the questions, feedback and reflections their own type of meaning from a conversation. Therefore, carefully held and constructed silences, within a coaching conversation, act as portals into the mind of the client. Beyond these portals lie the different landscapes of challenge that can be described, re-defined and articulated. Many of these new portal-reached terrains look and feel different and unusual (like walking into an unknown or unfamiliar land or country) (Lee, 2010). A balance between the exploration of ideas and inner knowledge is key. Peering through new portals, wandering, metaphysically, in new terrains and articulating the differences is potentiated by the silence controlled and enhanced by an ego-free coach intent on providing space for the client to hear their own truth (Watson, 2018). This uncomfortable yet supportive liminal space (Zaeemdar, 2017) holds the coaching relationship and shapes the very contours of trust and interest that are so vital in a coaching dynamic and a productive coaching relationship (Mocci and Penna, 2009).

A wide review of the role of silence in coaching and other leadership development topics reveals a patchy and sometimes disinterested passing interest in the topic, but one that can be related to the traps and challenges involved in coaching practice. Turning my gaze to organisational literature, Vakola and Bouradas (2005) have suggested that supervisors and managers who are used to and more tolerant of silence create more trust and have a more positive effect on members of staff, breeding greater input into decision-making and a positive employee attitude.

These can be partially explained by looking into the work of Myles-Downey (Hill, 2004), who articulated the ideas of a spectrum of interventions between telling and listening to understand often referred to as the push-pull model. Of course, these tensions exist elsewhere in organisations at all levels (Morrison and Milliken, 2003) and at all times when employees make the decision to say something or not more strongly identified, for example, with the role of "whistle-blowers".

As Hilary Armstrong suggested:

> Trusting the dialogue to do its work can mean at times feeling apprehensive about the turbulence and discomfort that is always possible in an open, undirected and unfettered space. It can also mean a charged atmosphere of anticipation and expectation.
>
> (Armstrong, 2012, p. 34)

When I looked at the definitions of silence I used at the start of my journey (Turner, 2019), I was surprised by how many of the words were so negative in sound and yet seemed to have a positive root; words such as muzzle, censor, stifle, dumbness, muteness, taciturnity, reticence, uncommunicativeness and unresponsiveness.

However, in the context of the coaching process and what has been covered so far, the more helpful and appropriate synonyms for the coaching context include words such as still, stillness, tranquillity, peacefulness, quiescence and "peace and quiet". These positive synonyms relate very strongly to reflective and mindful/liminal spaces that the successful coach hopes to take their clients to.

Listening and the use of silence can be easily linked in the dynamics of a coaching conversation. As has been recently identified by Myles Downey himself (Downey, 2015), people are surprised how much listening (and therefore, elements of silence) are involved in good practice. However, this has been covered by several key writers (see for example, Megginson and Clutterbuck, 2004). Yet remarkably this topic remains hidden from view within coach training. Even further back in time, authors (Nicholls and Stevens, 1957) were recognising how silence can be a very effective tool in providing space and room for thinking and reflection. The research of Ralph Nichols found expression, many years later, in coaching practice (see Gillingham, 2014).

> Let the person answer the question. Silence can be difficult, especially around challenging issues, but resist the temptation to give advice or answer the question yourself. Your silence is a gift to others—it allows them to express emotions that need to be expressed in a safe atmosphere.
>
> (Gilllingham, 2014, p. 50)

Lee, in 2010, outlined the ways in which those working in one-to-one work need to relish the:

> particular appreciation of the role of restraint and silence in one-to-one work. Viewed as a space for thinking more than doing, reflecting more than solving, coachees come to experience the coach's restraint as an invitation to go deeper into oneself, to ask the question "why", to sit with the discomfort of not knowing, to tolerate distressing feelings, and to discover the transformative potential of awareness.
>
> (Lee, 2010, p. 34)

This quotation from Graham Lee may point to one possible function of silence within coaching. Silence seems to be one of the least understood of the skills needed to be a good coach (cf. Passmore, 2010). However, the coach is often in control of the place in which coaching occurs by setting the space and pace of the interactions (Heneberry and Turner, 2016). The gaps between speaking are important – not that the environment could or must be quiet; I am not talking about environmental noises and intrusions but the gaps between the questions and answers. These silent gaps provide a space for reflection, thought, quiet inquiry and the emergence of ideas, views and slants on a topic or an issue.

Having scanned many articles, papers and periodicals it is clear that silence is not as commonly covered as the usual skills of questioning, listening and giving feedback are (Stanier, 2016, Hill, 2004, Whitmore, 2010). More recently, Starr (2016) has mentioned, in passing, the topic of silence. She identifies some of the ways in which skilful use of silence can be used as an important ally in the coaching process by helping to produce reflective moments, constructive pauses in the flow of thought and quiet insights into resolving the need for new action and changes in purpose.

Although the topic of silence in coaching remains ill-researched, some writers have made claims about silence and its profound value within coaching interactions. Papatriantafillou (2014) suggests that silence is a way of communication:

> It has many faces, can mean different things to different people, can communicate different things and its meaning depends on the context. Even though there are times that the use of silence can block communication, there is also the constructive use of silence, which enhances and strengthens it.
>
> (p. 1)

Olga Papatriantafillou goes on to identify a number of different ways of using silence. Amongst the categories she identifies are caring, busy, mindful, magical and being centred. In practice, of course, the use or value of silence cannot be programmed or stipulated, as it is an organic and often spontaneous factor in any session. Indeed, it may be that what we are talking about is not just one thing but, as Inuit people would attest to in their description of snow, something which has many different facets; for example, the silence that descends on the thoughtful moment, the silence that is used as the coach thinks of the next question or the silence that hangs heavily on a turning-point in understanding or pivotal moment in the coaching (Day et al., 2008).

However, since 2010, researchers have started to look in more detail at the empirical data offered in the understanding of silence in coaching. For example, Passmore (2010) suggests that silence is a powerful tool:

> which participants in this study recognised as useful in helping them reflect in a way they had not previously done about the issue.
>
> (p. 54)

In a model in which Fillery-Travis and Cox (2014) coined the term "linguistically poor", they have suggested that silence, whilst not linguistically rich (the other end of the spectrum), is rich in meaning and impact. Being termed as linguistically poor may sound like an anathema to a practising coach. Indeed, intolerance of silence may lead to one of the traps of coaching practice: that of interruption, or the coach being drawn into suggestions and advice. A micro-analysis of any coaching conversation would always reveal, I suggest, silences, both large and small; brief betrayals of thought, perhaps, as well as gaps between streams of co-produced words, narratives and ideas. What, for me, is emerging is a view of silence can and should be an active "thing", another tool to use for the coach and client, not a mere marker along the passage and flow of a conversation. Fillery-Travis and Cox's plea was that silence was one of many factors in the dyad relationship need further forensic investigation and analysis.

Two examples from practice

A creative coaching session

During the last coaching session with a coaching client, "Joe", we had been working together to look at elements of confidence. "Joe" manages mental health services in a "halfway" house and had been having challenges with his own confidence as he worked with managerial and leadership issues mainly linked to staffing problems. We had agreed a creative focus for the session.

"Joe" and I had already experienced silence in the previous five sessions. These included various types of silence. One was the usual silence between my questions/explanations and "Joe's" response – these had a variety of lengths and "tones". There were elements of silence in our co-delivery of our words and sentences. These silences felt normal, in the sense that they were familiar to us in terms of other types of silence that inhabit our spoken and listening world.

I have been working with mediating objects in my coaching practice following Material Engagement Theory (See Ihde and Malafouris, 2019), and often bring random collections of objects to my coaching sessions. The use of these objects is often very reflective, and induces much more silence than might normally be the case when following a more traditional question-and-answer type of coaching format framed by a coaching model such as GROW (Whitmore, 2017).

The coaching "task" that I set out was three-fold. I had casually bought with me three sets of six similar objects (similar to each of the six versions of three types of object: Patterned coasters, fridge magnets and illustrated strengths cards). Firstly, to choose a patterned coaster out of six and reflect upon its relevance to the topic brought out of previous discussions – that of confidence (or lack of it). This brought about several minutes of quiet (silent) contemplation or reflection from us both, but mostly "Joe", who had not expected this new approach (although he was quite open to trying a new technique as identified in our original contracting meeting). Secondly, a set of a dozen fridge magnets depicting Arabic/Moroccan doorways were offered to "Joe" and he again was asked to pick one door that was, to him, the most "confident". The one he chose "carried" with it the descriptive words of solid, colourful and simple (as in non-ornate). The supposed room behind it he described as being empty and bland. Finally, the client chose one card from a randomly offered set of strengths cards. First, he chose the picture of a small child engaged in active play. The card on the back of the picture read: "Conscientious". This again led to a long period of silence (punctuated with some quiet and slow mutterings and murmurings under his breath).

Although this exercise only took about 20 minutes, in total, it was characterised by both the coach and the client sitting in silence. This was not truly silent; there was a lot of soft ambient noise around (it was a quiet corner in a hotel lounge), such as the murmuring of voices, the slow hum of a nearby motorway and the soft roar of the distant wood fire. Offering these mediating objects (Malafouris, 2014) to induce reflection produced more silence than a set of direct questions would, fitting in well with the psychodynamic idea of coaching as expressed by Graham Lee (2010).

One further element of this exercise was that, as my client drew out his card from the offered six cards, the grandfather clock situated behind us chimed 6 o'clock. Both coach and client burst into gentle laughter. Humour, established through contracting, built rapport and the development of a productive relationship and, mediated by an enforced period of reflective silent space, spilt out into the coaching session in a way that was light-hearted but also part of a deeply warm moment of coaching.

The feedback from this session was stated in a text message – "Out of all the sessions we have had I found this one to be the most interesting and helpful as it got me looking at things in a totally different way … and I didn't feel awkward at all".

A silent vignette from a facilitated session with a master's group studying coaching

As part of a coaching module held at a British university, I was working with ten students. As part of the third-day session, we were working on higher level skills and this included the exploration of silence. As described in this chapter's second section, I asked the participants to listen, in silence, to the John Cabe musical piece "4 minutes, 33 seconds" without any explanation, other than to listen to the music and then write a short response to what they had thought of as they listened to the track. The participants listened to the recording as a YouTube clip on the internet. Eight of the participants reflected on how they responded to the silence with random thoughts and matters of daily concerns such as washing, children's homework, work, boredom and frustration (even thought this musical "clip" was only less than five minutes). However, two of the delegates produced some interesting feedback.

Firstly, one wrote:

> The longer the silence went on the more curious I became.

The second delegate wrote at greater length:

> It made me think how everything in life is such a rush. How expectations are for the instant. It made me realise how impatient I am, the temptation to tap the screen and see how long was left of the performance was strong, but I didn't and was proud that I didn't!
> It made me think how much we underestimate the power of silence; the space of silence.
> It made me think what are my fears of silence, why does it make me feel uncomfortable?

Discussion

Over the past four or five years I have had a long look at the topic of silence in the context of coaching. By looking at the ways in which other forms of human communication (such as literature, computer science and music) use silence I have tried to shed light on the ways in which silence can be used in coaching practice, not just as a peculiar adjunct to the practice of questioning, listening and feedback (arguably three of the keys skills in coaching), but also to focus the attention of the practitioner on the subtleties and possibilities of being more cognisant of silence in their own practice. For some, particularly those at the beginning of their coaching experience (either as being coached or coaching as a new skilled behaviour), silence can be a feared occurrence that quickly has to be filled in with words, actions or advice. For others, it can be a constituent of a toolkit that can be used in ever-more subtle ways, crafting the coaching session and interactions between the coach and client in ever-more fascinating ways.

I return to work that I had undertaken a few years previously with my colleague (see Heneberry and Turner, 2016) where, amongst other ideas, we explored the triad of notions, namely space, place and pace as part of our action learning model. This model can provide a framework for understanding silence in a coaching session:

Space: This is where the coach and client utilise the notion of liminality – the creation of a space that has within it the notion or possibility of change. Within that specific liminal space lies the potential for elements of silence between, and silence around, the coaching relationship. This potential for a silent space can be set to provide the right set of circumstances for the client and the coach (see co-coaching in Garvey, Garvey, Stokes and Megginson, 2017) to consider options and plan actions for change.

Place: This can be a check to where the coaching takes place as a consideration to the noise and impact of the "outside" intruding into the space allocated. With this consideration checking the backdrop of the conversation so that it is "quiet enough" for a space to be made, for what Stelter, in 2009, described as the "space for the unfolding narratives". This is the optimal place for the emergence of a co-constructed coaching narrative

Pace: This is also primarily under the control of the coach, so that the gaps between the words spoken and the questions raised provide a thoughtful use of silence as a powerful adjunct to the words, emerging narrative and sense of reflection.

Conclusions

In this chapter I have looked at the role of silence (and possibly listening and being quiet too) in coaching practice, using samples and ideas from a broad range of human activity, while also including examples from my own teaching and continued practice as an executive coach. Silence captures many things and must be seen in the lived experiences of both the coach and client (Walker-Frazer, 2011). Silence is not, I believe, a topic to be taught per se, but an awareness to be held by both the coach and their clients.

It was in the writings of Parker J. Palmer that I found the way to end this chapter (Palmer, 2018).

He spoke, in a recent podcast, these words:

> The impact of silence is not only solace, but disturbance. Silence forces you to look at your life in some very challenging ways. I think in our culture that's one of the reasons silence is not popular. It's one of the reasons we fill the air with noise, and we fill our minds with noise, because we avoid having to take that deep dive into ourselves.

I urge all coaches, whatever their specialist field, whatever their experience, to begin to consider the role of silence in their coaching relationships and take to their peer support groups and one-to-one supervision reflective moments and insights from silence that will continue to nurture and develop their practice.

References

Armstrong, H. (2012). 'Coaching as dialogue: Creating spaces for (mis) understandings'. *International Journal of Evidence Based Coaching and Mentoring*, 10(1), pp. 33–47.

Burr, V. (2015). *Social constructionism*. London: Routledge

Buena Vista Social Club (2010). 'Silencia' Accessed 19 June 2020 from https://www.youtube.com/watch?v=0mStndtGGOE

Cain, S. (2013). *Quiet: The power of introverts in a world that can't stop talking*. London: Penguin.

Day, A., De Haan, E., Sills, C., Bertie, C., & Blass, E. (2008). Coaches' experience of critical moments in the coaching. *International Coaching Psychology Review*, 3(3), 207–218.

Dhulipala, A.K., Fragouli, C. and Orlitsky, A. (2010). 'Silence-based communication'. *IEEE Transactions on Information Theory*, 56(1), pp. 350–366.

Downey, M. (2015). *Effective modern coaching*. London, LID Editorial.

Fillery-Travis, A. and Cox, E. (2014). 'Researching coaching'. In Cox, E., Bachkirova, T., & Clutterbuck, D. A. (Eds.). (2014). *The complete handbook of coaching*. Sage. *The complete handbook of coaching*, pp. 445–459.

Garvey, R., Garvey, B., Stokes, P. and Megginson, D. (2017). *Coaching and mentoring: Theory and practice*. London, Sage.

Gillingham, D.K. (2014). 'Spirit house/life coach women winter 2014'. awomanshealth.com. Accessed on the 24 January 2020 from www.dkgcoaching.com/wp-content/uploads/2016/06/1-Spirit-Hous e-Winter-2014.pdf.

Heneberry, P. and Turner, A. (2016). 'Critical action learning-rituals and reflective spaces'. *Action Learning: Research and Practice*, 13(1), pp. 60–68.

Hill, P. (2004). *Concepts of coaching: A guide for managers*. Oxford: Chandos Publishing Limited.

Ihde, D. and Malafouris, L. (2019). 'Homo faber revisited: Postphenomenology and material engagement theory'. *Philosophy & Technology*, 32(2), pp. 195–214.

Jobin, A.C., and Lees, G. (1960). 'Quiet nights of quiet stars (Corcovado)'. Accessed 27 February 2020 from http://keyboardimprov.com/the-jazz-pianists-ultimate-guide-to-the-real-book-table-of-conte nts/quiet-nights-of-quiet-stars-corcovado-from-the-jazz-pianists-ultimate-guide-to-the-real-book/.

Kania, A. (2010). 'Silent music'. *The Journal of Aesthetics and Art Criticism*, 68(4), pp. 343–353.

Lee, G. (2010). 'The psychodynamic approach to coaching'. In E. Cox, T. Bachkirova, and D. Clutterbuck. *The complete handbook of coaching*. London: Sage, pp. 23–36.

Maitland, S. (2009). *A book of silence*. London: Granta Books.

Malafouris, L. (2014). 'Creative thinging: The feeling of and for clay'. *Pragmatics snd Cognition*, 22(1), pp. 140–158.

Megginson, D. and Clutterbuck, D. (2004). *Techniques for coaching and mentoring*. Oxford: Routledge.

Mocci, S., and Penna, M.P. (2009). 'The systematic approach to communicative silence'. *Sixth Congress European Congress for Systemic Science*. Accessed on 5 January 17 from www.afscet.asso.fr/resSystemic a/Paris05/penna.pdf.

Morrison, E.W. and Milliken, F.J. (2003). 'Speaking up, remaining silent: The dynamics of voice and silence in organizations'. *Journal of Management Studies*, 40(6), pp. 1353–1358.

Nichols, R.G. and Stevens, L.A. (1957). *Are you listening?* (pp. 4–6). New York: McGraw-Hill.

Palmer, Parker J. (2018). 'On the brink of silence'. Accessed on the 22 March 2020 from https://encount eringsilence.com/parker-j-palmer-part-1-on-the-brink-of-silence-episode-33/.

Paptriantafillou, O. (2014). 'Silent coaching'. Accessed on 10 August 2018 from https://coachfederation .org/blog/silent-coaching.

Passmore, J. (2010). 'A grounded theory study of the coachee experience: The implications for training and practice in coaching psychology'. *International Coaching Psychology Review*, 5(1), pp. 48–62.

Qi, X. and Wang, Z.X. (2010). 'Silence: True communication'. *Canadian Social Science*, 3(4), pp. 30–32.

Stanier, M.B. (2016). *The coaching habit: Say less, ask more & change the way you lead forever*. Toronto: Box of Crayons Press.

Starr, J. (2016). *The coaching manual: The definitive guide to the process, principles and skills of personal coaching*, 4th ed. London, United Kingdom: Pearson Education.

Stelter, R. (2009). 'Coaching as a reflective space in a society of growing diversity-towards a narrative, postmodern paradigm'. *International Coaching Psychology Review*, 4(2), pp. 207–217.

Stevenson, H. (2016). 'Coaching at the point of contact: A gestalt approach'. *Gestalt Review*, 20(3), pp. 260–278.

Turner, A.F. (2019). 'Silence and its role in coaching'. *The Coaching Psychologist*, 15(1) 56–58.

Vakola, M. and Bouradas, D. (2005). 'Antecedents and consequences of organisational silence: An empirical investigation'. *Employee Relations*, 27(5), pp. 441–458.

Walker-Fraser, A. (2011). 'An HR perspective on executive coaching for organisational learning'. *International Journal of Evidence Based Coaching & Mentoring*, 9(2) 67–79.

Watson, A.M. (2018). 'Coaching confidence'. Accessed 19 June 2020 from www.coachingconfidence.co .uk/tag/silence/

Whitmore, J. (2010). *Coaching for performance: Growing human potential and purpose-the principles and practice of coaching and leadership*. London: Nicholas Brealey.

Zaeemdar, S. (2017). 'Coaching as a liminal space: Exploring the use of theatre in management training and development'. In Black, K., Warhurst, R., and Corlett, S. *Identity as a foundation for human resource development*. Oxford: Routledge, pp. 179–192.

14 Using emotions in coaching

Aboodi Shabi

Introduction

Although it is now widely accepted that emotions are a legitimate and important part of coaching, the field of emotions remains one of the more challenging areas for both new and seasoned coaches.

In this chapter, we will consider some of the background to these challenges, before exploring some approaches.

It is important to bear in mind from the outset, however, that working with emotions in coaching is not so much about using tools and techniques as it is about the coach's capacity to show up in the coaching relationship in such a way that emotions can be acknowledged, expressed and worked with.

History

The importance of emotions has not always been recognised in coaching. It was a common claim in the early days of the coaching profession that coaching was about the future rather than the past, more about action and less about emotions, and that there were clear differences between coaching and counselling. Hart and colleagues, in a study of the differences between therapy and coaching, revealed that practitioners "relate to coaching and therapy coachees differently and described coaching as more goal directed, action based, and outwardly defined. By contrast, there is an assumption that in therapy the client is often 'damaged', lower functioning, or in crisis" (Hart, Blattner and Leipsic, 2001, p. 235).

That view has been changing as the coaching profession has matured over the past two decades. There has been a turnaround in coaching research from seeking to distinguish and effectively polarise coaching from therapy to seeing virtue in drawing from research in counselling, recognising that they share much in common (Kilburg, 2004; O'Broin and Palmer, 2007; McKenna and Davis, 2009; Smither, 2011).

Given the limited research within coaching, this chapter seeks to fully acknowledge the contributions of counselling and therapy, and thus most of the referenced literature is from those professions.

Emotions are now seen as an important territory to cover in our work with clients. The International Coaching Federation's core competency model now contains multiple references to emotions:

- Develops and maintains the ability to regulate one's emotions;
- Mentally and emotionally prepares for sessions;

- Acknowledges and supports the client's expression of feelings, perceptions, concerns, beliefs and suggestions;
- Manages one's emotions to stay present with the client;
- Demonstrates confidence in working with strong client emotions during the coaching process.

(ICF, 2019)

As an essential part of human life, emotions play a crucial role in coaching and behavioural change. They are not just about how we feel but are also a pre-disposition to action. "Emotions condition not only our experience, but also our actions. They define the range of possible behaviours. Just as a calm mind is well suited for relaxing or taking photos, an alarmed mind is efficient at self-defence or flight" (Kofman, 2006, p. 242).

If all that human beings needed in order to make behavioural change was information or instruction about which behaviours to adopt, then there would be no need for any of the talking professions, coaching included: A simple manual for living would be sufficient. But "self-help books are like car repair manuals: you can read them all day, but doing so doesn't fix a thing" (Lewis, Amini and Lannon, 2000, p177). It is emotions that shape our actions and our capacity for change, and which make context and relationship at least *as* important as content in coaching. And, as Daniel Kahneman notes, drawing on the work of Slovic and Damasio, emotions, even so-called 'negative' emotions play a central role in decision-making: "people who do not display the appropriate emotions before they decide … also have an impaired ability to make good decisions. An inability to be guided by a "healthy fear" of bad consequences is a disastrous flaw" (Kahneman, 2011, p. 139).

The challenge

Emotions are not just something that we have or are born with – emotions are also something that we learn. From very early life, we are learning how to relate to others, and about which emotions are acceptable and which are not. Attachment theory highlights the importance of a baby's first relationships in shaping their emotions into adulthood. "Mary Ainsworth … found that the kind of mother a baby has, predicts his emotional traits in later life" (Lewis, Amini and Lannon, 2000, p. 73). "Securely attached children … learn that they can play an active role when faced with difficult situations … children with histories of abuse and neglect … are being conditioned to give up when they face challenges later in life" (van der Kolk, 2015, p. 113).

It's not only psychologists who have recognised this. Charles Dickens in *Great Expectations* (Dickens, 1861) created two characters who were emotionally scarred as a result of past experiences. One, Estella, is brought up to mistrust others, by a mother, Miss Havisham, who hated men after she had been jilted at the altar by her lover. Boarding school children often learn to shut off their emotions – they will often tell themselves, for example, that they don't need affection in order to cope with being separated from their parents and their affection (Duffel, 2000). In the early days of the kibbutz movement in Israel, there were idealistic experiments with communal child raising. Noam Shpancer (2011) noted that children "were socialised to be strong and sunny, simple and similar. Emotional expression was demeaned as weak and self-involved. We learned to numb ourselves. I haven't cried since I was 10. I'd like to, but I can't".

In coaching, we will be seeing people with these kinds of emotional backgrounds – the leader who gives up easily when she is faced with challenges, or the client who finds it hard to express his sadness, etc.

The narratives of the world we live in continue to impact emotional learning throughout adulthood. Organisations with their drive for efficiency and focus on the bottom line reinforce the still-common belief that emotions are not always compatible with working life. The over-riding emphasis on the bottom line means that compassion is not always valued in the workplace, and that employees can feel that they are disposable for the sake of profit (Hardingham, 2003). In the US, the time off from work allowed for bereavement has shrunk to just 72 hours (Levine, 1997). In fact, ideally, we wouldn't even show our grief at all – mourning is often seen as self-indulgent; we almost admire those who can conceal their feelings and carry on as if nothing had ever happened (Didion, 2012). It's not just so-called "negative" emotions that are problematic – Calvinism, with its emphasis on the virtues of hard work, saw enjoyment and fun as a "non-productive" use of time (Ehrenreich, 2007).

Even the word "emotional" itself can be used as a criticism when talking about someone's behaviour, especially when talking about women. Madeleine Albright, the first female US Secretary of State, is just one example of women feeling that they have to behave "rationally" and "unemotionally" in order to succeed socially and professionally (Brescoll and Uhlmann, 2007).

We also learn that that some emotions are "better" than others, that some emotions are positive while others are negative. It's not just kibbutzim that want people to be "strong and sunny" – this drive for positivity is a part of modern life, with significant impact on much of life. The pervasiveness of the fetishisation of positive thinking is neatly summed up by Barbara Ehrenreich:

> Optimism wasn't just a psycho-spiritual lifestyle option; by the mid-'00s it had become increasingly mandatory. Positive psychologists, inspired by a totally overoptimistic reading of the data, proclaimed that optimism lengthens the life span, ameliorates ageing and cures cancer. In the past few years, some breast-cancer support groups have expelled members whose tumors metastasized, lest they bring the other members down. In the workplace, employers culled "negative" people, like those in the finance industry who had the temerity to suggest that their company's subprime exposure might be too high.
>
> (Ehrenreich, 2009)

This is especially relevant for coaching, which has drawn much from the field of positive psychology; coaches often fall into the temptation to look for the positive when clients present with so-called "negative thinking", which only reinforces the cultural narratives about emotions.

As we consider these examples, we can reflect on what narratives might have shaped our clients in their emotional lives, but also (and perhaps even more importantly for us as practitioners) how *we* have been shaped.

We have *all* been steeped in narratives where emotions are relegated in favour of efficiency, rationalism or ideology, and where some emotions are seen as negative. With this background, none of us can be said to be *neutral* about emotions, and it's not surprising that it is hard for clients to express some emotions, and for us as coaches to be comfortable with emotions when they show up in coaching. We all have conscious and unconscious biases about both negative and positive emotions, and about whether (and which) emotions are a legitimate area of professional and personal life.

Emotions

Despite all this, however rational or efficient we might want to be or think we are, we are still primarily *emotional* beings. We don't stop grieving just because the official mourning period is over, childhood trauma and attachment difficulties affect us well into adulthood, and children separated from their parents in kibbutzim would try to get back to their parents' room every night and beg to be let in (Shpancer, 2011).

Awareness of this is growing, even in organisations. A Google study of 180 of its teams revealed that "the best indicator of a team's success or effectiveness was how well the team worked together or communicated, and that the most important factor was 'psychological safety'" (Hall, 2019, p. 34).

Whether explicit or implicit, emotions are always present in coaching. The coachee who sits in front of us has been shaped by narratives which impact their behaviour, worldview and choices as they contemplate their coaching issues.

Sometimes emotions are at the heart of the stated objectives. An individual may ask us to help them improve their relationships with colleagues, or to be more influential in the boardroom, for example. Or a coaching sponsor may contract with us to help an otherwise talented and promising leader to stop flying off the handle at their direct reports. (Hall, 2013, p. 177)

At other times, the clues might be in the client's language or in the way they show up, and the coach can be curious about the underlying emotions. When a client says, for example, "there's nothing I can do about my workload", or "I don't know how to get my manager to listen to me", there will be emotions behind those statements, which careful listening and questioning from the coach can elicit. Or the client's body might reveal emotions – the client's voice shakes when they talk about a difficult relationship at work, or they may fidget when they are talking about the deadlines they are struggling to meet.

Emotions are not just about our feelings – they pre-dispose us to action. Emotions shape both how we act, and what actions are available to us. When I am happy, I will see different options available to me than when I am sad; when I am resentful, I will perform the same tasks differently than I might if I were feeling grateful or content. Another way of putting this is that emotions tell a story – sadness tells us that we have lost something we care about; anger tells us that a boundary has been violated or an injustice perpetrated; boredom tells us that there is nothing to engage us; a client who is feeling hopeless will experience coaching itself very differently from one who is enthusiastic.

This last example is especially relevant; if a client is resigned and doesn't believe they can change, then no coaching goal or idea for action is going to mean much until we address the underlying emotions. Whilst it is true that coaching is about helping people choose different futures, the coach has to be able to be with a client who feels that she has no choices. A coach who is not prepared to say, 'I just can't see a way forward for you on this one' … and share the coachee's sense of frustration and impotence, is likely to seem out of touch with the coachee's world. (Hardingham, 2003, p. 30)

The path for the coach

It would be so much easier for coaches if there were specific tools and techniques for working with emotions in coaching.

Those new to coaching (and also experienced coaches at times) will often ask for lists of powerful coaching questions, or ask what to do when a coachee is sad, tearful or angry, but that's like asking for effective chat up lines; it ignores that chat up lines and coaching questions and interventions are useless out of context – what makes both effective is the connection. It requires leaving the "script" behind and being fully present with the other person.

It's not so much what the coach *does* that matters in coaching as how the coach *is* – the coach's presence in the coaching relationship: "When we meet the other, it is our presence that helps them more than our words" (Murdoch, 2011). Or, as Jung advised his students, "learn your theories as well as you can, but put them aside when you touch the miracle of the living soul" (Jung, Baynes and Baynes, 1928).

The importance of the relationship in coaching cannot be overstated.

When we are really in tune with someone else, we know a lot about what they are feeling. As Lewis and colleagues noted, the attuned therapist "doesn't just hear about a [client's] emotional life – the two of them *live* it" (Lewis, Amini and Lannon, 2000, p. 178). Stephen Burt observes that "when my children were young they often knew how I was feeling before I did. From another room, they could hear how I put my keys and bag down when I arrived home and sometimes ask, 'What's the matter, daddy?'" (Burt, 2019, p. 4).

That kind of listening is not something we can develop a technique for – it's something that can only come from working on ourselves. "What makes the difference between a good coach and a great coach is on-going work on yourself" (Whitmore, 2006).

Sometimes techniques can even get in the way. Coaches can be drawn to questions like "What would you do if you weren't afraid?", and, whilst such questions *might* get the client to think beyond their fear and consider different actions – if they don't push them away completely – they are likely to close down curiosity about the client's fear and prevent a deeper enquiry. When the coach listens more deeply, they also feel, and express, empathy and compassion. They not only get insights and understand the nub of a coachee's issue, they are also affected by how a coachee experiences what they are describing. They learn to feel who the coachee is and how they are. (Burt, 2019, p. 21)

The big question for coaches is how to meet the client where she or he is, without needing to get away from the moment.

In order for coaches to be able to work comfortably with coaches' emotions, the first – and on-going – priority is for the coach to do her or his own work. If we find a client's emotions difficult then, as John Whitmore observed, we will be more concerned with managing our own discomfort than being present with the client (Whitmore, 2006).

Moreover, we also need to think about what it is that makes us label an emotion as difficult:

> We want to define difficult emotional situations as those that give the coach a 'bad feeling', i.e. those that tend make the *coach* feel uncomfortable in some way, and to acknowledge that what is termed a difficult emotion may vary from coach to coach.
> (Cox and Bachkirova, 2007, p. 180; my emphasis)

The therapist's "every preconception about how a person should feel risks misleading him as to how that person does feel". (Lewis, Amini and Lannon, 2000, p. 183) Instead of jumping away from an emotion that we as the coach find difficult, how can we meet it, honour it, legitimise it, so that we can connect with the client?

What has shaped our own learning about emotions? We can see from the examples in the first part of this chapter that coaches are just as immersed in narratives about emotions as our clients; and that is the first place for our work: We need to explore our own narratives. "Nietzsche claimed that a philosopher's system of thought always arises from his autobiography, and I believe that to be true for all therapists" (Yalom, 2013, pp. 31–32). As coaches, how has our autobiography, our emotional history, shaped our own systems of thought and our approaches to coaching?

The more work we do on ourselves, exploring our own uncomfortable emotions, etc., and the more we understand that it is not the truth that sadness is "bad" or "negative", that it is not the truth that being emotional is a sign of weakness, the more we can be present and simply listen and encourage a coachee who is sad, or stuck, or unable to feel joyful or optimistic without having to "fix" anything or reassure them. Simply put, doing our own work enhances our capacity to be of service to our clients – this is not an intellectual or theoretical journey, but a lived experience. Hassidic wisdom tells us that,

> if you want to raise a man from mud and filth, do not think it is enough to stay on top and reaching a helping hand down to him. You must go all the way down yourself, down into mud and filth. Then take hold of him with strong hands and pull him and yourself out into the light.
>
> (Buber, 2002, p. 85)

In a very real sense, the coach can be said to be taking a lead in opening up the emotional space. As we've seen, clients might not legitimise, nor even acknowledge, some of their emotions. If the coach isn't able to acknowledge and legitimise those emotions in themselves first, then there is no space for those emotions to be expressed and worked with in coaching. If a client is telling themselves to "get over" their sadness, or that their anger is not OK, and the coach goes along with that, then no useful work can be done. If the coach is comfortable with their anger or sadness, then they open a door for the client to acknowledge it and be present with it.

As John Whitmore observed, this work is an on-going process, a lifetime's work; it can take many forms – the most obvious of which is supervision – a place where we can start to explore any emotions that come up in coaching (either our own or the client's) which we find challenging, or cause us to react. Whilst supervision is a great professional resource, sometimes we need to do more personal work; for example, by exploring our emotional selves in individual therapy, or by looking at how who we are impacts others and at how we are impacted by the feelings of others in group therapy. All of these will help us to develop our own emotional intelligence, which "for the purpose of coaching … can be understood as the ability to understand our own feelings, notice the emotions of others, and, importantly, change our behaviour based on this information" (Van Nieuwerburgh, 2017, p. 128).

A coach is not just a neutral or distant observer of the client. We also need to be *intimately* involved in the coaching conversation, immersed in the connection and, if we are, then we will be impacted on many levels by the client, by what she or he is saying, and not saying, and by *how* they are being. It's this intimate relationship that forms the heart of working with emotions in coaching, and it requires, as we have seen, deep and on-going personal work on the part of the coach.

Approaches to working with emotions

Whilst the importance of our own work in this area cannot be overstated, there are things we can do in our coaching work that, while they wouldn't really be called techniques, are helpful approaches in opening up the world of emotions in coaching.

Firstly, we can be curious about the coachee's emotions.

What do we notice in the client, as they are speaking about their issue or goal? What emotions do they show or consciously speak about? What might we notice in their bodies or language that might be a cue for an unexpressed emotion? For example, a client might say, "I don't see a way out of this", or "I should keep going" or "I have to do everything". Or the client might sit forward and become animated when speaking about some aspect of their coaching topic, or tense up their shoulders as they speak about their boss. We can be curious about what we *notice*, bringing our client's attention to what we see, and we can ask questions about what emotions that language or somatic behaviour might be conveying.

Of course, we need to approach all of this with care and with the client's permission, but the primary preparation lies in developing our own comfort with emotions and sensitivity to them, and in sharpening our curiosity about what we observe.

Box 14.1

Yitzhak comes to coaching, talking about his difficulties in managing his team. Initially, he speaks in a matter-of-fact way, and talks about his frustration with the pressures he and they are facing, and how hard it is for people to perform their workload. As he continues, he starts to tear up, and apologises. I let him know that his tears are fine, and ask him if we might explore further. He agrees, and he starts to speak about how what he really cares about is the well-being of his team, and how he feels frustrated with the organisation because he feels pressured to push people hard when they are already too busy. As we explore, he talks about the kind of manager he wants to be – someone whom people can talk openly to, especially when things are hard, and how he might bring more of that into his current work situation. He talks about what that might do for his team.

Secondly, we can be curious about our own emotions. What do we notice in *ourselves* as the coachee is speaking? What is happening to us as the client speaks? We as coaches can look at our own emotional state, and notice and be curious about any changes that occur during the coaching conversation. We might notice, for example, that we feel sad when a client talks about not achieving her goals, or angry when a client tells us about how his boss is treating him. While it is true that our attention needs to be on the client, we can also be aware of what might be happening to us emotionally when we are present with our coachee as a whole person. Our reactions might serve the coaching, by surfacing things that are not explicit in the client's words, or just open up an avenue for exploration (or rejection) by the client. If my emotional state changes when a client is speaking, then I can at least be curious (without being attached to being right) about what might be happening with the client that could be causing that change in me. Or we might notice that we are closing down or resisting a particular emotion the client is exhibiting, or an aspect of what the client is saying, which we might then take to supervision to reflect on what stops us from being open to that.

Whilst it may seem as if this is "all about the coach", this curiosity about *our own* emotions is a function of being present with a client. That closeness "evokes genuine emotional responses in the therapist – he finds parts of himself stirring in response to the particular magnetism of the emotional mind across from him" (Lewis, Amini and Lannon, 2000, p. 178). It helps us to become more aware of our own instrumentality and to acknowledge "the use of self as our prime asset in achieving the helping relationship. It is not an option but the cornerstone of our work" (Cheung-Judge, 2001, p. 12).

Box 14.2

Conchita comes to coaching talking about quitting her job as a teacher. Initially she says that her mind is made up, that she has stopped caring about education and that she would be "only too glad to see the back of those kids". As we spoke, she talked about "not caring" being her "go-to place" when things got difficult ever since she was young. The more she talked about her past, and about how she had "learned not to care", the sadder I was feeling, even though she remained impassive and her tone wasn't changing. Eventually, I told her that listening to her I wanted to sob my eyes out. At that, she softened slightly, and began to talk about the pain she had been feeling that she hadn't wanted to admit. It was a strong and intense moment between us, and the coaching began to shift. She acknowledged that underneath the not caring lay a profound sadness. We started to explore how she might listen to her sadness and her care for her work, and how she might address the challenges of the work.

We can also be curious about what emotions the client has *learned*. As we saw earlier in this chapter, we are shaped by the narratives we have been immersed in, and these narratives shape our actions. James Flaherty calls this process the "structure of interpretation", an interpretation that will persist across time, across events, across circumstances. Our job as coaches will be to understand the coachee's structure of interpretation, then in partnership alter this structure so that the actions that follow bring about the intended outcome. (Flaherty, 1999, p. 9) This builds on the notion of structural determinism, developed by the Chilean neuro-physiologist, Humberto Maturana (Leyland, 1988, p. 360). "Structural determinism is the idea that things operate according to how they are made. Just as mechanical objects operate according to their structure, so we human beings act according to how we have been shaped" (Shabi and Whybrow, 2019, p. 220).

Clients might have grown up learning that it isn't OK to be angry, or to be told that "boys don't cry", or to always look for the positive. There might have been family or cultural pressures in favour of certain emotions and against others. Exploration of these might help a client to understand more about why some emotions are difficult for them (and to consider what value there might be in feeling a previously less-expressed emotion). Crucially for coaching, if we come to see that at least some of our emotionality is a function of learning, then we can "learn" new emotions.

We cannot teach a new emotion by instruction, but we can learn a new emotion by immersion. Because limbic states can leap between minds, feelings are contagious, while notions are not. If one person germinates an ingenious idea, it's no surprise that those in the vicinity fail to develop the same concept spontaneously. But the limbic activity of those around us draws our emotions into almost immediate congruence. (Lewis, Amini and Lannon, 2000, p. 64)

We might enquire of a client about the emotions of the groups they live and work in, and we can help them to think about the impact of those and whether they might choose to engage with groups where different emotions might be more available. While there are many determinants of happiness, whether an individual is happy also depends on whether others in the individual's social network are happy. Happy people tend to be located in the centre of their local social networks and in large clusters of other happy people. (Fowler and Christakis, 2008)

Box 14.3

Daphna comes to coaching wanting to explore how to better handle the pressures of her new role. As we talk, she talks about how serious and important her work is, and as we continue to explore, she acknowledges that she has always been rather serious. As a young girl, she had to take care of her younger siblings while her parents were working, and there was little time for play or joy in her early life. We spoke about how she had learned to prioritise work over pleasure, and that she found it "very hard to just let go and be light". We explored where she might go to experience playfulness and she agreed to try out comedy improv. Although she found it very uncomfortable at first, she began to enjoy the improv sessions and reported that she was being more playful in her social life and enjoying her friends' lightness rather than withdrawing from it as previously; she was starting to feel less pressure at work as she progressed in her new position.

Finally, an important part of the work we can do in this field is to help clients legitimise their emotions and learn from them, rather than focusing solely on solutions.

When we as coaches can listen, we create a space for our clients to acknowledge their own emotions and to become more curious about them. This requires patience on the part of the client, resisting the temptation to move quickly towards a solution. It is common for clients to report that they can speak about things in coaching that they can't speak about elsewhere. In a real sense, a large part of the value of coaching is the relationship and the *space* we give our clients to reflect more deeply on the issues they are facing and their underlying causes and emotions. It's a space that we miss in our everyday very busy lives. "People don't often have the chance to tell their stories in this unhurried way" (Hardingham, 2003, p. 112).

Box 14.4

Anja turns up to a coaching session, wanting to "talk about relationships". At first the conversation is abstract and impersonal, but, with gentle enquiry, she begins to open up and eventually admits that her marriage is failing and that she is scared of acknowledging her sadness because she might "not be able to stop crying". What she wants is a "solution". I ask her to consider that there might not be an immediate solution, and ask her what support she might need as she navigates the difficult journey ahead. She acknowledges this, and identifies a few close friends who can be there for her to support her in her sadness and "hold" her as she figures out the path ahead. A few months later, she reflected on the role that our coaching had played, not so much in providing a solution as allowing her to feel the emotions as her marriage unravelled and to be able to share those with her friends and receive support from them at a very painful time.

Finally, a note of caution. Sometimes coaching isn't enough. A client who has severe attachment issues might, as we saw above, give up at the first obstacle. Coaching might help the client to understand that they have been shaped by this early learning, but therapy might be what they need to help them work with this at the appropriate level. A coach needs to know when to make this distinction.

Conclusion

There is much to be gained from working with emotions in coaching, for the client, but also for the coach. The more comfortable we are with our own emotions, the more present we can be with our clients. The on-going challenge for us as practitioners is to do what we can to open our hearts. "But it requires an open heart to really feel how another feels. An open heart gives us the empathic capacity to connect directly with another person from within" (Scharmer, 2013).

References

Brescoll, B. and Uhlmann, E. (2007). 'Can an angry woman get ahead? Status conferral, gender, and expression of emotion in the workplace'. *Psychological Science*, 19(3), pp. 268–275.

Buber, M. (2002). *Ten rungs: collected hasidic sayings*. London: Routledge.

Burt, S. (2019). *The art of listening in coaching and mentoring*. London: Routledge.

Cheung-Judge, M.-Y. (2001). 'The self as an instrument'. *OD Practitioners*, 33(3), pp. 11–16.

Cox, E. and Bachkirova, T. (2007). 'Coaching with emotion: How coaches deal with difficult emotional situations'. *International Coaching Psychology Review*, 2(2), pp. 178–189.

Dickens, C. (1861). *Great expectations*. London: Chapman and Hall.

Didion, J. (2012). *The year of magical thinking*. London: Fourth Estate.

Duffel, N. (2000). *The making of them*. London: Lone Arrow Press.

Ehrenreich, B. (2007). *Dancing in the streets: A history of collective joy*. London: Granta Publications.

Ehrenreich, B. (2009). 'Overrated optimism: The peril of positive thinking'. *Time Magazine*, 10 October 2009. Retrieved on 23 March 2020 from http://content.time.com/time/health/article/0,8599,1929155,00.html.

Flaherty, M. (1999). *Coaching: Evoking excellence in others*. London: Routledge.

Fowler, J., and Christakis, N. (2008). 'Dynamic spread of happiness in a large social network: Longitudinal analysis over 20 years in the Framingham Heart Study'. *British Medical Journal*, 337. Retrieved on 18 June 2020 from https://www.bmj.com/content/337/bmj.a2338

Hall, L. (2013). *Mindfulness in coaching*. London: Kogan Page.

Hall, L. (2019). *Coach your team*. London: Penguin.

Hardingham, A. (2003). *The coach's coach*. London: CIPD.

Hart, V., Blattner, J. and Leipsic, S. (2001). 'Coaching versus therapy – A perspective'. *Consulting Psychology Journal: Practice and Research*, 53(4), pp. 229–237.

ICF. (2019). 'Core competencies'. Retrieved on 16 March 2020 from https://coachfederation.org/core-competencies.

Jung, C.G., Baynes, H.G. and Baynes, C.F. (1928). *Contributions to analytical psychology*. London: Routledge.

Kahneman, D. (2011). *Thinking, fast and slow*. London: Penguin.

Kilburg, R. (2004). 'When shadows fall: Using psychodynamic approaches in executive coaching'. *Consulting Psychology Journal: Practice and Research*, 56, pp. 246–268.

Kofman, F. (2006). *Conscious business: How to build value through values*. Boulder: Sounds True.

Levine, R. (1997). *A geography of time*. New York: Basic Books.

Lewis, T., Amini, F. and Lannon, R. (2000). *A general theory of love*. New York: Random House.

Leyland, M. (1988). 'An introduction to some of the ideas of Humberto Maturana'. *Journal of Family Therapy*, 10, pp. 357–374.

McKenna, D.D. and Davis, S.L. (2009). 'Hidden in plain sight: The active ingredients of executive coaching'. *Industrial and Organizational Psychology*, 2, pp. 244–260.

Murdoch, E. (2011). International Coaching Federation, UK Conference, London.

O'Broin, A. and Palmer, S. (2007). 'Reappraising the coach–client relationship: The unassuming change agent in coaching'. In S. Palmer and A. Whybrow, eds., *Handbook of coaching psychology: A guide for practitioners*. London, UK: Routledge, pp. 471-486.

Scharmer, O. (2013). 'Uncovering the blind spot of leadership'. *Blog Post*. Retrieved on 23 March 2020 from www.dailygood.org/story/450/uncovering-the-blind-spot-of-leadership-c-otto-scharmer/.

Shabi, A. and Whybrow, A. (2019). 'Ontological coaching'. In S. Palmer and A. Whybrow, eds., *Handbook of coaching psychology: A practitioners guide*. London: Routledge, pp. 219–228.

Shpancer, N. (2011). 'Child of the collective'. *The Guardian*, 19 February 2011. Retrieved on 23 March 2020 from www.theguardian.com/lifeandstyle/2011/feb/19/kibbutz-child-noam-shpancer.

Smither, J.W. (2011). 'Can psychotherapy research serve as a guide for research about executive coaching? An agenda for the next decade'. *Journal of Business Psychology*, 26, pp. 135–145. doi: 10.1007/s10869-011-9216-7.

van der Kolk, B. (2015). *The body keeps the score: Brain, mind, and body in the healing of trauma*. New York: Random House.

van Nieuwerburgh, C. (2017). *An Introduction to Coaching Skills: A Practical Guide*. London: Sage.

Whitmore, J. (2006). Association for Coaching Conference, London, May 2006.

Yalom, I. (2013). *Love's executioner*. London: Penguin.

15 Balancing challenge and support in coaching

Ian Day

Introduction

When reading a counselling textbook about the use of challenge in therapy, the words used to describe challenge included "manipulation", "confrontation", "aggression", "control" and "abusive". All of these words are shocking and a long way from what I understand by "challenge". However, for many people these words are valid, and show how loaded the word "challenge" can be. Words carry an emotional weight which is greater than the mass of the letters which make up the word itself. This emotional weight is based on the experience of the reader and the associations made between words and experience. In this chapter I wish to move beyond the emotionally loaded words, and explore challenge, explain what challenge is and how challenge can be used to have a very positive impact on coaching outcomes. To do this, I will discuss the origins and principles of coaching, and will introduce challenge as a positive coaching intervention, exploring the support / challenge matrix as a model for finding the right balance in a coaching relationship. I will introduce the concept of the Zone of Uncomfortable Debate (ZOUD) and use this to explore how coaches can challenge effectively in their work. I will also consider the barriers to challenge in coaching and discuss how challenge can be used positively by coaches to move beyond the limitations of the accepted norm of non-directive person-centred coaching.

The value of challenge

Coaching is about helping the client develop awareness, and through awareness comes change. The coach can assist the development of awareness by holding up a mirror. This can provide a complete reflection of self, and by looking in the mirror the client can answer the question "is my perception reality?" Alternatively, if the coach tilts the mirror, then the client will see an image from a different angle, a new reflection and a new possible reality.

Coaching has the power to stretch and help people be as they want to be today and as they want to be in the future. Coaching has the ability to enable clients to be more at ease with themselves, be more accepting, more self-aware and to be more present. But coaching also has the power to create greatness for the future, to move clients out of their comfort zone to realise their latent potential, enabling sustained individual change. The "ripple" effect of this individual change can be felt in organisations and societies as a whole, in the short- and long-term. As Sir John Whitmore said, "coaching is bigger than coaching". But for this to happen, coaching must be more challenging and move away from the notion that non-directive person-centred coaching, which focuses on supporting the individual, is the only way to coach.

The evolution of coaching

Consider the evolution of the coaching profession and the influences on its early development. Coaching is a very young profession. Unlike other professions, such as medicine, engineering and accountancy, which have existed for hundreds of years, coaching is a young and immature profession. For example, Sir John Whitmore, Graham Alexander and Alan Fine pioneered coaching in the UK in the 1980s with the GROW model, the EMCC (European Mentoring and Coaching Council) was formed in 1989; Coaches Training Institute (CTI) was founded in 1992 by Laura Whitworth and Karen and Henry Kimsey-House; and the International Coaching Federation was formed in 1995 by Thomas Leonard.

However, even in this short span of time, the coaching profession has changed, developed and adapted. We have seen coaches specialise in approaches such as cognitive behavioural, solutions focused and somatic coaching, and we have experienced the influence of neuroscience and the growth of team coaching and mindful coaching. We have seen the development of coaching supervision as the means of supporting coaches in their practice. Most of all, coaching is now accepted as the most powerful mainstream personal development process.

This rapid progression has been aided by the associated profession of counselling. Coaching shares a significant proportion of its DNA with counselling. For example, there are significant similarities relating to the skills used by both a therapist and a coach. Both a therapist and coach will focus on the individual and try to support and accept the individual for who they are. The therapist's/coach's role is to build trust, to listen and ask the right questions, tackle difficulties and work on behavioural change. This relates to the subjective experience of the client, and the effectiveness of the intervention is correlated to the quality of the relationship between therapist/coach and client.

However, there are also significant differences in terms of the topics of discussion. For example, a therapist is likely to focus more on processing the past, helping a client manage periods of mental illness, trauma, abuse, addiction or stress, etc.

Through the connection with counselling, coaching has gained the sound theoretical underpinnings developed by Carl Rogers (1957 and 1967). Carl Rogers was one of the most influential thought leaders within the profession of counselling. In the 1940s he developed the person-centred therapeutic approach, which suggested the therapist could be of most help to clients by allowing them to find their own solutions to their problems. This was a non-directive approach, with the therapist holding the belief that clients have within themselves vast resources for development and the capacity to grow. The therapist's role is to create the conditions where growth is encouraged. Carl Rogers' "core conditions" of empathy (ability to sense the client's world as if it were your own, through active listening, summarising, reflecting, paraphrasing, clarifying and acknowledging, etc.), congruence (the therapist is open to own feelings, without front or façade) and unconditional positive regard (non-judgmental acceptance that each person is worthy).

Since its origins, non-directive person-centred coaching has become the overriding accepted approach. The competency frameworks of the professional coaching bodies firmly place non-directive person-centred coaching at their centre. As a result, traditionally, coaching comes from a very supportive stance, helping an individual grow and develop. Most coaching literature and coach training programmes focus on the supportive skills which a coach needs to build trust and rapport:

- Understands and consistently applies coaching ethics and standards of coaching;
- Develops and maintains a mindset that is open, curious, flexible and client-centred;
- Partners with the client and relevant stakeholders to create clear agreements about the coaching relationship, process, plans and goals. Establishes agreements for the overall coaching engagement as well as those for each coaching session;
- Partners with the client to create a safe, supportive environment that allows the client to share freely. Maintains a relationship of mutual respect and trust;
- Is fully conscious and present with the client, employing a style that is open, flexible, grounded and confident;
- Focuses on what the client is and is not saying to fully understand what is being communicated in the context of the client systems to support client self-expression;
- Facilitates client insight and learning by using tools and techniques such as powerful questioning, silence, metaphor or analogy;
- Partners with the client to transform learning and insight into action. Promotes client autonomy in the coaching process.

(Definitions from the updated ICF Core Competency
Model October 2019)

Take a moment to reflect on these behaviours and ask yourself if these skills dominate your understanding of coaching, and consider the proportion of time you have spent developing these skills while in coach training.

A great deal of the accepted coach rhetoric proposes that non-directive person-centred coaching is sacrosanct and is "*the*" way to coach. Breaking away from what coaches have read and have been taught seems like sacrilege. As a result, this traditional non-directive person-centred stance goes unquestioned. However, the reluctance to do this introduces the three risks of collusion, irrelevance and self-obsession (Blakey and Day 2012, Culley and Bond 2011).

- **Collusion** arises when the coach is only asking questions in a very supportive fashion, being non-directive and predominately taking a "clean" approach. Here, there is a risk that the coach might collude with the client and align 100% with their worldview, failing to challenge or provide feedback from an alternative perspective;
- **Irrelevance** occurs when the coach always holds to the client's agenda, regardless of the wider or alternative perspectives. In this situation it is possible that, by the end of the second coaching session, the coach will help improve the client's golf swing rather than address the 'real" issue which the client may be avoiding. Whilst this is a deliberately extreme example, in the midst of a coaching session, how many coaches reading this book have ever asked themselves the following question "How does this relate to my client's stated goal, and what are they avoiding?"
- **Self-obsession** is the risk of fuelling the "me, me, me" attitude which can lead to hedonism and detachment, focusing purely on the client's agenda, which exacerbates a myopia rather than developing a greater awareness of the wider context of the connected system in which we all live and operate.

These three risks have significant implications for non-directive person-centred coaching. But, as this is the accepted rhetoric, it cannot be questioned. Yet coaches should challenge

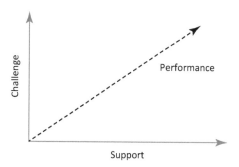

Figure 15.1 Balance between Support and Challenge

themselves harder to question the limitations of traditional approaches. To be constructively critical, to evaluate and to augment rather than destroy. This augmentation comes in the form of challenge. Through support *and* challenge, coaching becomes much more powerful.

Support and challenge

Nevitt Sanford (1967), and later Laurent Daloz (1986) found that, within a student environment, the optimum learning occurs when there is a balance between the levels of support and challenge. See Figure 15.1.

Support refers to acts which affirm the value of the client and reduce uncertainty and anxiety. Confidence is built by focusing on qualities and achievements. Through empathy, the client feels heard, understood and feels trust. The client is OK where they are and feels capable of moving on when they are ready. Support involves active listening, demonstrating empathy, acceptance and the coach having a positive expectation of outcome, providing confidence, affirmation and a sense of safety.

As mentioned earlier, there is an emphasis on these supportive skills in coach training and within the coach professional bodies. So, for the benefit of this chapter, I will focus on the less familiar but equally important aspects of challenge, with the aim of readdressing the balance.

What is challenge?

Challenge refers to interventions that compel the individual to face their current reality and to meet the changing expectations of their stakeholders and the wider world around them (Blakey and Day 2012). Within the 63 competency statements from the ICF, there is one that stands out:

> Challenges the client as a way to evoke awareness or insight.
> (from the Updated ICF Core Competency Model
> October 2019, from section 7. Evokes Awareness)

It is understandable that coaches don't use challenge. What does it say about the value of challenge when there is 1 out of the 63 ICF competency statements? Also, too often people actively avoid challenging interventions, fearing that these will cause disruption and create ill will. The limit of this approach is that the absence of challenge risks complacency and indulgence. At worst, the outcome is apathy and disinterest (Culley and Bond 2011).

When the stakes are high, a lack of challenge allows people to play safe and play small in an ever-demanding environment that is requiring us to "step up" and address big issues that call for a new way of thinking and being.

I propose a conscious, intelligent use of both support and challenge, so the coach can dynamically shift between the two, depending on the circumstances and environment. So, at this point, let me clarify what challenge is *not*.

Challenge is:

- *Not* directive;
- *Not* adversarial;
- *Not* aggressive;
- *Not* offensive;
- *Not* uncontrolled;
- *Not* based on the coach's personal agenda;
- *Not* rescuing the vulnerable;
- *Not* "fixing" the client;
- *Not* imposing a "right" way of doing things.

As coaching is about helping the client develop awareness, and so change (Culley and Bond 2011), the coach can assist the development of awareness by holding up a mirror, which may show a reflection of reality which the client does not wish to see. Despite the denial, the reflection *is* reality to be faced.

What challenge is:

- Holding up the mirror for the client to view an alternative reality;
- Encouraging the client to evaluate their actions, motives, thoughts and assumptions;
- Encouraging the client to think for themselves, rather than act based on historical experience or habits;
- Positively confronting the validity and implications of assumptions;
- Recognising that assumptions are personal and unique to every individual and not factual reality;
- Encouraging the client to consider alternative perspectives;
- Providing direct feedback on the impact of what the client has said, and how it has been said;
- Creating doubt and so stimulating thought and reflection;
- Creating awareness of inconsistencies and contradictions between intention and action, between differing assumptions, between feelings and actions; for example, between stated aim and action, or between body language and words spoken;
- Creating awareness of words used by the client such as "should", "ought" and "must";
- Developing awareness of, and overcoming, "blind spots";
- Exploring potentially self-defeating beliefs;
- Shifting the client beyond their self-perceived limitations;
- Creating change by stepping out of a comfort zone of habits, embedded through many years of reinforcement;
- Positively confronting and moving beyond inertia;

- Developing awareness and removing blockages to the client's achievement of their stated aim;
- Holding the client accountable for actions they have agreed to undertake;
- Naming avoidance of a topic or action and so developing awareness to address the real issues;
- Replacing vagueness with clarity;
- Accepting personal responsibility rather than deflecting and blaming others;
- Acknowledging and accepting behaviour that is inhibiting change;
- Exploring deeply to develop a greater level of self-awareness;
- Creating a sense of agency and self-empowerment;
- Exploring different self-images;
- Identifying patterns and "joining the dots" so that a picture, unseen until now, becomes obvious to the client;
- Identifying potential unintended consequences;
- Playing back unacknowledged feelings, such as "I'm sensing you're angry about what happened to you";
- Helping growth, development and sustainable change.

(Sanders, Frankland and Wilkins 2009; Culley and Bond 2011; Heron 2012; Hargie 2018)

The key to challenge is that it is a skill which can be developed by the coach. Like the supportive skills such as rapport, empathy and active listening, the capability to challenge can be learnt. Also, challenge is variable in level. The same coaching intervention (questions, reflection, silence, etc.) can be experienced differently by every person. Everyone's experience of challenge is unique, so a coach needs to be skilled and flexible to calibrate the optimal level of challenge appropriate for each client. Challenge may be in many different forms, and may be the opposite to the client's expectations or experience. For example, a person familiar with a noisy and energetic environment may find it challenging to deal with silence and reflection. Real and deep listening may be challenging when the person has experienced being ignored with superficial engagement. As Laurent Daloz (1986) said "for what is support for one person may be challenge to another". As a result, challenge is a difficult concept.

Challenge is deliberate and conscious. Challenge is not accidental, nor is it an uncontrolled emotional reaction or impulse. Challenge is always in service of the client (and sponsoring organisation, where appropriate). This is very different to a boss who is stressed out, demanding that a team member achieves an impossible objective, or a frustrated parent or teacher scolding a child. Challenge requires skill and practice.

Support and challenge

Now we understand what challenge is, let us explore further and expand on support and challenge by using the 2×2 matrix in Figure 15.2 (Blakey and Day 2012).

If we consider the low-challenge/low-support quadrant, there is inertia and apathy. If this is all the coach can offer, there will not be much interaction, no action, nothing. This environment is too dull, and the client becomes bored, disinterested and the "why bother?" question looms large, resulting in a lack of motivation to act. The low-support / high-challenge quadrant produces stress. This is a scary place in which we get frightened, defensive and hostile. This can be confrontational, stressful and may seem like an

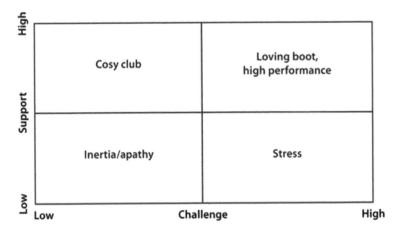

Figure 15.2 Challenge and Support Matrix

interrogation. However, this can also expose the client to new ways of thinking. Done skilfully, for short periods of time, this can help develop resilience and create dramatic shifts. The high-support / low-challenge quadrant is the "cosy club", this is far too comfortable and, in this zone, we don't reach our maximum potential. In this zone there is high empathy, active listening and questioning, but also the risks which we discussed earlier including collusion. Here there is acceptance, nurturing, but there is no moving on and possible dependency on the coach. The high-support / high-challenge area is where growth and development really takes place. This is the "loving boot" which can stimulate and "kick" or "nudge" a person to pursue a new direction or goal and to achieve their stated aim. This is where the client can really explore, through support *and* challenge awareness is raised, which can provoke the client into new ways of being. This is the optimum balance of support and challenge (Egan 2017).

The point of this 2×2 matrix is to encourage coaches to think about where they might be as the coaching sessions develop and deepen as the external circumstances change. Take the metaphor of a train on a track, it can only go forwards and backwards and on a limited gradient. Now compare this with a 4×4 all-terrain vehicle, which has the power and ability to go in any direction as the environment changes. If we switch back to coaching, often we have a preferred coaching style or a default position. Link this with the coach training focusing on a person-centred approach, which is viewed as sacrosanct, and the coach develops skills without knowing that they will be a train on a track, only able to go one way. As a coach, can you develop the skills to choose to operate effectively in any of the quadrants of the support challenge matrix? With the exception of low-support/low-challenge, growth can occur in any of these quadrants, as long as the coach has developed the skills to work in these areas.

Consider a client who appears "stuck". Coaching session four seems pretty much the same as sessions two and three. There is no change, the conversation seems to repeat itself and there is no progress. The client is stuck. Something is holding them in their current state of being. If we believe that there is a reason for every behaviour, then it is the duty of the coach to help the client to develop awareness of their "stuckness". This is done through challenge and holding up the mirror. For example:

- "The objective you identified in session one was … we're now in session four, how do you feel about that objective now?"
- "It seems that each session we're discussing the same things, and nothing has changed, how do you see this?"
- "What's holding you back?"
- "Why are you sabotaging yourself?"
- "Whose time are we wasting?"

These are progressively more challenging questions, not to be delivered like a machine gun. The coach should judge pace, so it is calm and reflective, allowing silence to take a role, but always serving the client to achieve their stated aim, even if this requires the exploration of uncomfortable topics.

The zone of uncomfortable debate

Let us consider how conversations and interactions take place and look at a model developed by Cliff Bowman (1995) (see Figure 15.3). The centre of the diagram represents the core of the issue which, once discussed, provides the key to making a breakthrough; moving understanding to the next level, or moving an idea forward, unblocking a problem or resolving an argument. Around this are two concentric layers, firstly the "zone of comfortable debate" and, secondly, the "zone of uncomfortable debate" (ZOUD). When two people interact, the conversation begins in the zone of comfortable debate, and then, depending on the situation, may or may not move into the ZOUD. How individuals respond when in this uncomfortable zone will determine if the issue at hand is resolved and the people involved in the conversation get to the heart of the matter, or whether they avoid the tension and move back into the comfortable zone. The model proposes that people in an interaction must work through the ZOUD, rather than avoid it, to make progress.

When an interaction begins between two or more people there is typically a period of small talk, rapport building and developing an understanding of common ground, etc. This is where the conversation is easy and nice, feels relaxed and there's no tension. The people are chatting about easy, obvious things – for example, catching up on news and gossip, what has happened since they last met, common interests such as sport and family and there is a simple exchange of information. These "watercooler" conversations are very straightforward and are firmly in the zone of comfortable debate.

If this conversation is to be more than a social chat, there is usually a matter at the heart of the discussion. The parties have come together for a purpose – to agree action, to decide, to resolve a problem, etc. To achieve this, a socially comfortable conversation is not sufficient and, to get to the heart of the issue, the conversation must move to a *zone of uncomfortable debate*. In this zone there is a feeling of increased tension. The pressure starts to build as the parties may disagree and may not see "eye to eye". What often happens is that the individuals feel the tension, find it uncomfortable and, fearing that the pressure will permanently damage the relationship, move the conversation back out to the zone of comfortable debate. The tension is diffused and the rapport is maintained, but the matter at hand has not been resolved. The core issue is still the same and no movement has taken place. To resolve the issue, the conversation must stay in the ZOUD and the parties work through it to uncover differences in understanding, assumptions and motives, etc. By

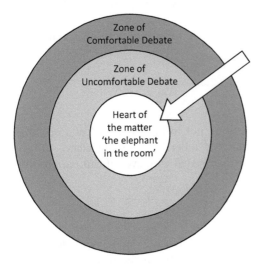

Figure 15.3 Zone of Uncomfortable Debate (ZOUD)

sustaining the ZOUD people can move to the heart of the issue, resolve it permanently and then move on to a new topic.

The heart of the issue is like having an "elephant in the room". Here is something enormous that is taking up significant space. However, the "elephant" is not dealt with directly as it is such a big and difficult animal. Perhaps we don't want to make the elephant angry in case it damages the whole house, or maybe we are too polite to comment on it. What happens is that people find innovative and creative ways to move around the "elephant", to manage it and live with it. Until they face up to the fact that there is actually an "elephant in the room" and try to remove it directly, the situation will remain unchanged. Facing up to this fact and dealing with it is going to be uncomfortable – there are risks involved, so this is like entering the ZOUD.

Coaches frequently work in difficult areas of personal development and must be prepared to go into the ZOUD and hold the tension until the "heart of the matter" is opened up and resolved.

There are risks associated with this; through the challenge and tension of the ZOUD, the coaching relationship could be irreparably damaged. The coach may feel that there is a risk of rapport being lost and so releases the tension, moving the conversation back to the benign zone of comfortable debate. So, there is an elaborate dance of dialogue that takes place around the core issue. There is one step into the ZOUD and then a step back into the zone of comfortable debate, and the dance continues without addressing the significant issues. A more constructive strategy is for the coach to stick with the tension and accept it as positive and constructive. This uncomfortable feeling is inevitable and essential to get to the heart of the matter, and so there needs to be the confidence to stay in the ZOUD and confront challenging issues.

Another risk is that the individual may lose resourcefulness, they may feel tense and stressed and lose the ability to draw on their natural cognitive abilities. In this state there can be a great deal of unguarded openness, and things may be said that are unchecked as the client expresses hidden issues which may be unknown to either party. This loss of resourcefulness is the place for support, so that the challenge and tension created in the

ZOUD is balanced by support, so that the client's resourcefulness is restored. At this point, the coach does not exit ZOUD but offers supportive statements or an observation, which enables the client to "regroup", take a breath and then move forward through the ZOUD. This is to balance support and challenge.

During this process the coach may also feel a loss of resourcefulness, the coach may be out of their comfort zone, with the natural inclination to reduce the challenge and move back to the zone of comfortable debate. Again, an authentic statement such as "I can feel real tension here!" helps connect the coach and the client, so the client knows that the coach feels as they do, and this breaks the tension for a moment before moving on.

Have you ever done something so difficult that you felt like giving up? For example, running a marathon for the first time. Runners describe "hitting the wall". In a physical sense, this is the same as the ZOUD. With determination, visualisation of the finish line, and maybe a pause for breath, the runner regains the physical and mental resources to continue the marathon. So, when a coachee or a coach "hits the wall", take a breath and then continue.

When I talk to coaches about challenge, some say that they are already doing it. However, I am not talking about powerful questions to make the coachee stop and think, or the use of silence, which may be uncomfortable, encouraging depth of thought. There is nothing new here. Real challenge moves a client outside of their comfort zone, they confront issues, take risks and work towards achieving their stated aim.

However, if a coach develops awareness of the value of having challenging behaviours in their repertoire and has the skills to deploy these frequently, then they will be more like the all-terrain vehicle. They will be able to serve both individuals, sponsoring organisations and society more effectively to create sustained renewal. This is about the ability and choice of the coach.

Barriers to challenge

Challenge may be rarely seen, as some coaches may have difficulty with this as a concept. As a coach you may believe that you are a nice person who is there to help serve your client. When I started coaching, I certainly wanted to help people as coaching had helped me. This addresses the self-image that the coach has of their role. With all the coach training and professional bodies emphasising the importance of rapport, being non-directive and holding the client in unconditional positive regard, challenge seems a long way away from this. But, it is how "*help*" is perceived by the coach and client and recognising the three risks identified earlier.

Barriers to challenge include:

- The coach is personally uncomfortable with challenge, based on previous experiences or personal preference (to explore this further, consider the Thomas Kilmann Inventory);
- The coach assumes that the client is not ready for challenge, thinks it's too soon and so delays until the time is right, which never comes;
- The coach feels that the client has some vulnerability and so cannot be challenged, believing that the client is too fragile and could not handle it;
- The coach believes that challenge would permanently damage the rapport of the coaching relationship.

These are all to do with the perceptions and assumptions of the coach, which may or may not be true. For example, these assumptions may be based on the coach's previous experience of working with another client. However, what if a coach held the following beliefs to be true about my client:

- Clients are whole and resourceful;
- Clients are capable of choice;
- Clients have freedom to act and change;
- Clients are inherently good and creative;
- Clients seek to fulfil their full potential, and are capable of greatness.

If I believe these assumptions were true about my client, then I can provide challenge. Clients are not *broken* or *vulnerable*, I do not need to rescue them or keep them safe and small. To challenge is to trust that the client can achieve their greatness.

How to challenge

As long as a coach can embrace the philosophical value of challenge, they can develop the skills through practice. For some, unpicking years of non-directive person-centred training and rhetoric can be very difficult.

The key to challenge is to diminish the impact of the coach's own ego. There is nothing to prove. Through adult-to-adult communication, which is calm, matter-of-fact and non-critical, the coach can challenge. A coach can share their perspective, thoughts and feelings as a question rather than a statement of fact, and then the client is able to answer the question.

This is a matter of congruence for the coach. Congruence has been described as a state of being, when the outward responses consistently match the inner feelings towards a client. When congruent, there is a match of thoughts, feelings to the words spoken and action taken. There is consistency. Carl Rogers wrote about congruence being the basis of trust, that being perceived as trustworthy requires the therapist to be "dependably real". Through congruence, "It is only in this way that the relationship can have reality" (Rogers 1967).

This is the same for the coaching profession, but, congruence does not seem to be as valued or discussed. In his seminal book *On Becoming a Person* (1967), Carl Rogers commented that

> The therapist "permits as little of his own personality to intrude as is humanly possible". The "therapist stresses personal anonymity in his activities, i.e., he must studiously avoid impressing the patient with his own (therapist's) individual personality characteristics". To me this seems the most likely clue to the failure of this approach.

Carl Rogers wrote this in 1967, but why are coaches still trying to be invisible and deny their own thoughts and feelings, fearing these would have a negative influence on the coaching space? Are coaches promoting incongruence and so denying one of Carl Rogers' three core conditions, preventing challenge in the process?

Conclusion

When I'm asked when a coach should challenge, I say "challenge sooner". I want to emphasise that the purpose of this chapter is to *balance* support and challenge. I'm not saying that one is good and the other is bad, I'm saying that there needs to be a balance. Support and challenge are necessary and sufficient to create sustained change for the client. But, with only one, either one, the possibility of big significant change is limited.

Challenge creates a gap between the client's perception and reality. The client seeks balance and equilibrium and is motivated to act, questioning assumptions, querying their worldview and considering alternative perspectives.

Non-directive person-centred coaching is the foundation on which a coaching relationship is built, but is not sufficient to create the change which the client is seeking. Non-directive person–centred coaching should not be the only building material that is used. Challenge is a skill that needs to be practised and implemented with great sensitivity and there is a fine line between helpful challenge and destructive challenge. Too many of us have experienced destructive challenge, and the word challenge has an added but negative weight. With the current coaching rhetoric, there is an under development of the skills to effectively challenge.

Coaching has learnt much from counselling, but maybe not enough. There is a richness of complexity and subtlety which provides greater understanding. Rather than simple acceptance, coaches need to question and explore further. To challenge *and* support.

References

Blakey, J. and Day, I. (2012). *Challenging coaching: Going beyond traditional coaching to face the FACTS*. London: Nicholas Brealey Publishing.

Bowman, C. (1995). 'Strategy workshops and top-team commitment to strategy change'. *Journal of Managerial Psychology*, 10(8), pp. 4–12.

Culley, S. and Bond, T. (2011). *Integrative counselling skills in action*. London: Sage.

Daloz, L. (1986). *Effective teaching and mentoring: Realizing the transformational power of adult learning experiences*. San Francisco: Jossey-Bass.

Egan, G. (2017). *The skilled helper: A client-centred approach*, 5th ed. Belmont: Cengage Learning EMEA.

Hargie, O. (editor). (2018). *The handbook of communication skills*, 4th ed. London: Routledge.

Heron, J. (2012). *Helping the client: A creative practical guide*, 5th ed. London: Sage.

Rogers, C.R. (1957). 'The necessary and sufficient conditions of therapeutic personality change'. *Journal of Consulting Psychology*, 21(2), pp. 95–103.

Rogers, C.R. (1967). *On becoming a person: A therapist's view of psychotherapy*. London: Robinson Publications.

Sanders, P., Frankland, A. and Wilkins, P. (2009). *Next steps in counselling practice: A students' companion for degrees, HE diplomas and vocational courses*. Ross-on-Wye: PCCS Books.

Sanford, N. (1967). *Where colleges fail: A study of student as person*. San Francisco: Jossey- Bass.

Whitmore, J. (2017). *Coaching for performance: The principles and practice of coaching and leadership*, 5th ed. London: Nicholas Brealey Publishing.

Section 4

Coaching approaches

16 The universal eclectic model of executive coaching

Alison Hardingham

Introduction

"The world is so full of a number of things, it's a wonder we aren't all bats!" quipped Ogden Nash. Faced with the number of tools and the diversity of technique available to coaches, we could be forgiven for appearing slightly batty to our clients. We know that they get benefit from choice and variety in working towards their goals (de Haan, 2012), but they need that choice and variety served up by a coach who is a master of their craft and can select and present a range of tools with confidence, wisdom and finesse. They need, in short, an eclectic approach. In this chapter we point the way to expanding and deepening your eclecticism whatever your stage of development as a coach.

The Universal Eclectic Model

People have long been interested in how human beings learn and grow. Over the centuries, a whole variety of theories have sprung up, each of which focuses on some aspects of how human beings learn and grow. There is, for example, Socratic dialogue (Clark and Egan, 2015), which emphasises the value of open questions in exposing assumptions and provoking changes of view; there is David Kolb's theory of experiential learning, which places thoughtful experimentation at the heart of change (Kolb, 1984); and many, many more.

The science of psychology embraced and furthered much of this thinking. It also, importantly, subjected the theories to test, seeking to establish an evidence base for them. An eclectic model recognises this rich diversity of theory and evidence. It orders it within a specific discipline and acknowledges what each contributing strand can offer. The Universal Eclectic Model of executive coaching is within that tradition of eclecticism.

The eclectic model covers eight major psychology-based sources of coaching tools: Person-centred, Gestalt, systems, psychodynamic, evolutionary, behavioural, cognitive-behavioural and biological.

The model identifies which aspects of human learning and growth each major source focuses on; in other words, what theory of change is being applied. Person-centred approaches assume that change is natural, providing the "fundamental conditions" are in place (warmth, genuineness and unconditional positive regard). Gestalt approaches assume that increases in awareness are key to change. Systems approaches recognise the centrality of context in determining the course of change, and indeed in determining whether or not change can occur: Unless the system changes, nothing changes. Psychodynamic approaches focus on the deep forces which operate out of awareness in our unconscious minds. They argue that change comes from revisiting the past and experiencing it differently. Evolutionary approaches prioritise the processes of natural selection and human development, and place emphasis on the need for change to reflect these; the insights available from neuroscientific research are examples here (Ellis and Solms, 2018). Behavioural approaches emphasise the importance of rewards and punishments in changing behaviour. Cognitive-behavioural approaches include many tools for helping people to think about things differently and pick the route to change they favour. Biological approaches include all the somatic work that many coaches know and find extremely useful, such as breathing exercises, relaxation and movement; these approaches draw attention to the physical nature of being a human and seek to enable change through using the body differently.

The eclectic model is intentionally inclusive. The list of approaches I have given above is not a definitive list; as the name implies, this model can be expanded to cover anything that can be used and is useful, and where there is at least the possibility of providing evidence of its efficacy. For example, within the Universal Eclectic Model lie tools and techniques which derive from organisational development and management theory. Examples are Peter Senge's work with his colleagues at MIT on systems thinking and the learning organisation (Senge et al., 1994) and also Cooperrider's method of appreciative enquiry (1995). Coaches also make frequent use of tools such as SWOT analysis (ten Have et al., 2003), Kurt Lewin's "force field analysis" for planning effective change (Lewin and Gold, 1999) and, of course, William Bridges' framework for managing transitions (Bridges, 2003).

Whilst we can in principle identify the roots of many of these tools in the eight categories I outlined, in practice, they have simply acquired their reputation through organisation development and management applications in which they have proved very effective.

Many of the most useful tools for a coach come from a hybrid mix of different schools of thought.

Sports psychology has given us the "inner game" approaches (Gallwey, 1975), for example. Indeed, the founders of management coaching in its modern form, including Sir John Whitmore (Whitmore, 2002), began as sports coaches. They learned many tools and techniques coaching sports people that turned out to be effective in the management context (Hardingham, 2004). Sports psychology takes whatever findings in psychology prove relevant and applies them in the sportsfield.

Neurolinguistic programming (NLP) is another well-known hybrid mix which, like a jay, has borrowed and stolen from a wide range of approaches. It is an interesting example of a school of thought that claims to be "theory free". It evolved through studying effective therapists who consistently enabled change and enabled it fast, and took the techniques that they used and built them into a repertoire of "excellence". Of course, the theoretical underpinnings are vast, if not generally acknowledged. In fact, Ian McDermott, a UK NLP practitioner, proposed four elements that represented the essence of an NLP approach in which we can clearly identify some of the contributing theories (McDermott, 2003). These elements are: The capacity to establish and maintain rapport (person-centred); an outcome orientation (behavioural); heightened sensory acuity (biological); and great behavioural flexibility (cognitive-behavioural).

Carole Kauffman's PERFECT coaching model represents yet another way of conceptualising the vast array of tools and techniques at the coach's disposal (Kauffman, 2010).

What makes an activity eligible for inclusion?

The next question is this: Are there boundaries round what the Universal Eclectic Model can and cannot incorporate? My view is that there are no absolute boundaries. Others certainly share this view. Philippe Rosinski writes, for example, "Coaching is the art of choosing an effective approach in a given situation, of creatively combining technical tools, models, and perspectives to address specific challenges, and of devising innovative processes to serve coachee needs" (Rosinski, 2003, p. 5). James Flaherty writes that "coaching is a principle-shaped ontological stance ... any activity [is] coaching when the ontological stance is [appropriate]"(Flaherty, 1999, p. 13). In fact, coaches are inventing new things to do with their clients every day, proposing new questions and new ways of being that may help their client make progress towards their goals.

Put simply, it is the intent of the coach and the context of the coaching which determine the eligibility of an activity. The intent must always be to support another in "reaching her goals" (Flaherty, 1999, p. 3) and in no way to manipulate or otherwise control. The context that must be taken into account includes: The expertise and characteristics of the coach, the culture of the client (and I am using "culture" in its broadest sense), the coaching relationship as a whole, and the organisational and/or societal context in which the coaching is taking place. If an activity is used with integrity, and with sensitivity to the client's context, the worst that can happen is that it will prove ineffective, and even then there will be learning from that, sometimes more than from a "successful" application of technique.

Megginson and Clutterbuck (2005, p. 9) present useful practical advice which reflects these principles. "[The] coach should use the technique openly and in consultation with the client; and ... the technique's intended effects should be discussed and agreed before embarking on it".

How does the coach select the right tool for the job?

Whilst the coaching literature abounds with descriptions of tools and techniques from all the sources we have identified and more, there is little guidance on how to choose one technique, or even one approach, over another in a given situation. The eclectic model implies "mix and match". But how to mix, and what to match?

The existing literature is rather silent on these points. Beyond general exhortations such as to "be aware of the underlying assumptions about learning [in the different methods]", (Zeus and Skiffington, 2002, p. 86) for example, and to "integrate cultural perspectives" in choosing how to work with a client (Rosinski, 2003, p. xix), the literature leaves it largely up to the coach to judge which approach to use in response to the specific work required for a specific client. Those books which present an eclectic range of techniques (such as Hardingham, 2004; Megginson and Clutterbuck, 2005; Bossons et al., 2012) tend to group techniques from all the different approaches together, choosing to categorise them by type of coaching work undertaken rather than by originating approach. So, for example, you will find as recommended techniques for "developing self-awareness" a contribution from the world of psychometric assessment, a technique from the psychodynamic approach, one from management theory, one from a creative thinking self-help book and a use of "parallel process" – a direct application of a method from psychodynamic thinking (Hardingham, 2004).

So whilst there are many frameworks for matching tools and techniques with the type of coaching activity to be undertaken, there do not appear to be frameworks for deciding on an approach. Why might a coach, for example, decide to use a technique which had its origins in cognitive psychology rather than a behaviourist one? Why would she ask at a particular time "What does success mean to you?" rather than "Can you describe how you will know when you have achieved your goal?" And the decision of which question to ask is not trivial: The first question leads to an exploration of belief systems which may change the whole orientation of coaching, the second to a behavioural specification which can be used immediately to focus on and measure progress.

I think there are two primary reasons for the paucity of advice on this point. Firstly, choice of approach must be a matter for the coach's judgement. To catalogue in a prescriptive way all the dimensions to which the coach must attend as he makes that judgement would be impossible. Many relevant dimensions are in any case totally situation specific. For example, perhaps my client has had a "bad experience" with a hypnotherapist. However apt an Ericksonian-style story (Rosen, 1982) might be to the issue that client is wrestling with, a wise coach is unlikely to go down that path, for such stories and the way they are told are firmly rooted in the practice and philosophy of hypnotherapy. To use such a method would show insufficient regard for my client's sensitivities.

The second reason why we will not find a great deal of guidance on which approach to use when is that the vast majority of coaching tools and techniques are themselves hybrids. For example, a coach may take a complete history of a client at the start of a coaching relationship. Superficially, this would seem to be heading down a psychodynamic path (Jacoby, 1984), as the client describes her family of origin, important childhood experiences and so on. But the coach may simply listen respectfully – a client-centred approach (Rogers, 1951) – or use the information from that history to identify the distinctive competencies the client brings to her current dilemma – a solution-focused approach (O'Connell, 1998), to name just a couple of alternative directions the coaching may take.

It seems to me that the important thing is for coaches to understand as much as they can about as many of the tools and techniques they use as possible. If they match that level of deep and broad understanding with a similar level of appreciation of their client and his context, they will be well placed to mix and match to good effect.

And here is a final and, it seems to me, significant benefit of the eclectic model: It encourages an exploration of all the different contributing fields, an exploration which, through comparison and contrast, educates developing coaches in what specific tools and techniques are for, where they come from and what assumptions they rest on. I only fully understand a hammer when I have also learned to use a mallet and a screw-driver.

What are the benefits of an eclectic approach?

I have already mentioned many benefits of the more creative, diverse and resourceful style of coaching which follows the eclectic model. In theory at least, an eclectic approach enables a technique to be selected which fits the client's requirements exactly, rather than requiring the client's issue to be framed to fit a particular approach. (In practice, of course, an eclectic approach in the hands of an unskilled coach may just mean that a different "wrong" technique is selected for every occasion. At least if the only tool you have is a hammer, it will work on nails when nails come along. If you have the complete toolkit but no idea how to use it, you will have trouble even with nails!)

Another important benefit of the eclectic approach is that it does not assume a high level of knowledge of different approaches and their consequences on the part of the client. The client and coach can work together to discover which techniques (and hence which approaches) work best in that particular coaching relationship. If the coach is skilled and flexible enough, the coaching may come to follow a single approach predominantly

– but that approach will have been chosen as a result of mutual exploration and experimentation by coach and client, not because the client "just happened" to choose a coach who was an expert in a particular approach.

Finally, the Universal Eclectic Model avoids imposing a particular philosophy of how human beings develop and change as a by-product of coaching. Each of the several approaches drawn on is likely to be based on a different philosophy, so the client is exposed to many philosophies as part of the eclectic coaching process and in all likelihood not over-influenced by one. As the "medium is the message", if a single approach is followed, the risk is that the most potent influence of coaching on the client is a covert one. If my coach is, for example, skilled only in "Inner Game" methods (Gallwey, 1975), I may come to believe as a by-product of being exposed exclusively to those methods that I can only change aspects of myself that I am aware of. Yet systems approaches tell us that change can also result from responding unconsciously to change in others, psychodynamic thinking tells us that change can result from re-experiencing the past and strict behaviourism tells us that awareness is an unnecessary construct!

What are the risks of an eclectic approach?

There is a risk that the eclectic model becomes in practice a collection of disparate techniques, none of which are understood by the coach nor experienced by the client in any depth. After all, most of us would agree that a person may have several "episodes" of coaching in his life. There is an opportunity to experience different approaches in full in distinct episodes, rather than have many approaches sampled in a single episode. Many approaches, such as solution-focused work, cognitive approaches and psychodynamic approaches benefit from one or more sessions entirely devoted to their use. Too much eclecticism could rob the client of some very useful experiences.

There is also a risk that the focus of coaching begins to be on "finding something that will work" rather than on supporting the client in a process of change and development which has its own pace and rhythm. Techniques must remain secondary to relationship, as so many authors and researchers in the field of coaching and other related fields have emphasised. Perhaps the renowned family therapist Salvador Minuchin put it most succinctly in his classic text "Family Therapy Techniques": "The goal is to transcend technique … Only a person who has mastered technique and then contrived to forget it can become an expert therapist"(Minuchin and Fishman, 1981, p. 1). Paradoxically, an adherence to one specific approach can enable the coach to be freer from attending to technique in the moment of coaching than does a commitment to eclecticism. The eclectic coach may have to divert too much of her attention away from the client and towards making choices about interventions, rather than be able to relax into a well-trodden path which by its very nature limits the field of choice.

Finally, there is a risk that techniques will be used without the client being clear where they come from and what their effects are likely to be. Whereas commitment to a single method usually begins with an explanation of the principles and disciplines behind that method, if a single technique from a general method is used, its origins may never be fully understood by the client. So she may be less in charge of the application of that technique, more in the position of having the technique "done to her" than of participating equally in exploring what it has to offer. This runs counter to the very essence of coaching: To enable another to act more, and with more creativity and self-direction.

How can we get the best from the Universal Eclectic Model?

My experience as a coach, and as a trainer and supervisor of coaches, suggests to me that to apply the eclectic model effectively requires quite a long period of professional development. It is important for coaches to be exposed to, and have the opportunity to practise, a number of different approaches in some depth. Many very skilled coaches who I know and have worked with began with a strong grounding in one particular approach that was often learned in a different context from coaching. They subsequently became curious about other approaches, and developed their understanding and skills in those, without of course losing comfort with their "first love". I can think of other skilful coaches who have always operated with a degree of eclecticism and have continued to develop their repertoire throughout their coaching practice. But they have studied and understood each approach from which they draw techniques in its own right: They do not just collect "techniques"; they explore methods and philosophies behind techniques.

This constant attention to one's own development means that the coach is moving in and out of "conscious" and "unconscious competence" all the time. If we believe with Flaherty (1999, pp. 11–12) that the coach needs to be learning herself to be effective for her client, then this is another advantage of following the eclectic model.

Developing coaches need to be aware of which approaches are most consistent with their own values, beliefs and style. That is one of the reasons why it is important to identify where a tool comes from, for only then can one tell whether the model of change on which it depends is a model of change which one can personally hang one's hat on. So another essential part of an eclectic coach's development is development in knowing himself. Minuchin (1981, p. 10) put it well in describing the developmental path for a family therapist: "Eventually a disconnected cluster of skills becomes an integrated style that fits with his person".

Finally, it seems to me that it is essential that the eclectic model is not itself applied in a purist way. The effectiveness of the coaching process should not be judged by how many different approaches the coach uses. There is some indication in the literature that clients find diversity of technique helpful (de Haan, 2012). But sometimes it will meet the needs of a specific client better to conduct a whole programme of coaching following one approach alone.

Of course, it should be an approach selected by the coach for that client, rather than the only one the coach knew.

From theory to practice: A short case study

Andy is an executive in an international bank. He began a programme of executive coaching as part of the standard development package for the "top 120" high potentials: Those individuals considered to have the potential to make it to the Executive Committee in five years or less. I was appointed his coach, and this case study draws on notes I took during and after each coaching session with him. Andy gave his permission for this material to be used.

What Andy wanted from his coach was "challenge and support to articulate and realise his career and leadership aspirations". He wanted to explore the difference between being a manager and being a leader, and felt he "could do better". More specifically, he wanted to articulate his distinctive characteristics as a leader and plan to use these more effectively in his current and future roles in the bank. His ultimate goal was to have a Managing Director or equivalent role in a corporate environment.

As his coach, I used elements of the solution-focused approach (O'Connell, 1998), both at the start of his coaching and whenever new goals and aspects of goals emerged, to enable Andy to focus on what precisely he wanted to change and to measure his progress towards his goal. Also, when Andy developed a tendency to ask me for advice, I chose the solution-focused approach to adjust the balance of responsibility-taking. Several times that approach put Andy "back in the driving seat".

In the first session with Andy, I took a complete biography from him, including information about his family relationships and his entire growing-up, education and career so far. This is a typical starting point for me, and it generally forms part of the explicit coaching contract up-front with a prospective client. So it was built into Andy's expectations and it was one of the reasons he chose to work with me as his coach. I identified with him, as I had said I would, some interesting themes and patterns from his formative years which seemed relevant to his situation today (Lee, 2003). For example, he found some aspects of himself as a child which he decided could represent the foundation of real areas of distinctive strength for him as a leader. He is the eldest of four children. He is close to all his siblings, and "made space" for them as they came along, one after another. Academically he is the most successful, but he is firmly grounded as a result of his family upbringing in the view that everyone is equal, that people have different talents, and that elitism and self-importance are inappropriate and unhelpful. I led him in an exploration of how he balances a drive to achieve with an equally strong drive to build and be part of his family, initially, and later, teams and groups. Again the parallels with his family position and dynamic were striking to him as he recounted his history, and the sense of his leadership style continued to emerge. I moved between a "client-centred" approach, simply listening and responding as he reflected on the personal and professional journey which had brought him to this point, and some interventions from a cognitive basis to expand his view of his own possibilities. For example, he had seen his "lack of extremes", his "balanced" approach to life, as a sign of moderated ambition and maybe lower leadership potential. Someone had sold him the idea of "leadership spikes" – extremes of character which make a leader known and unique – and he thought he didn't have any; I asked him questions which led to his questioning that view. Maybe he did have leadership "distinctions", even if he didn't have "extreme" behaviours, he began to think.

This "cognitive reframing" became a theme for several sessions. One of the reasons I used it was that Andy said from the start he liked to be challenged. And indeed, when he was challenged, it was noticeable that his energy levels and attentiveness increased.

I suggested using a psychometric questionnaire in the third session to help Andy further in his quest to differentiate himself, but he had taken such questionnaires before and did not want to do another at this time.

Whilst on this journey with his coach, a new problem emerged for Andy. He began to feel blocked and bored in his current role. Now the focus for coaching was to find a new role in the bank. He wanted to do some practical and business-focused work to get out of a situation which was threatening his motivation and his relationship with the bank. I sped up the pace of our work, and used some systems-thinking tools with him to help him develop his plan of action (mapping the roles and the relationships connected with different opportunities [Hardingham, 2004], understanding how difficult it would be for him to develop further personally while his scope for leading was so limited by his place in the system). I also used a Gestalt technique (Hardingham, 2004) to help him prepare for a difficult conversation with his current boss in which he needed to elicit that boss's support to move on. That technique was in itself challenging for Andy as he had never done anything like it before, and it increased his sense of urgency about making changes. The meta-messages in the use of that technique at that time were "Do something different", and "There is no time like the present".

Once he had found a new role, his opportunities to develop as a leader increased greatly. He now had profit and loss accountability for a unit of 60 staff. I used a couple of business-based tools – force-field analysis (Lewin, 1999), and the "Trust Equation" (Maister, Green and Galford, 2002, pp. 69–83) – as well as some visioning exercises (Megginson and Clutterbuck, 2005) to enable him to clarify what he needed to do to realise the potential of his business unit and his potential as a business leader. Again, there was a strong theme in the coaching of breaking new ground and moving on, in recognition of the business imperatives and the new level of role. Andy used coaching sessions to learn how to coach his own direct reports, and so the behavioural technique of "modelling" (his coach modelled with him the kinds of conversations he needed to be having with others) now came explicitly to the fore. The coaching relationship continued for a year, with sessions every month.

Conclusion

I hope that this case study elucidates some of the competencies required to implement effectively the Universal Eclectic Model. But as I reflected on this case and the write up, I thought with some dissatisfaction about what it said, and what it did not say.

The reason why this piece of coaching was successful is not to be found in the interweaving of tools and techniques according to the Universal Eclectic model. The reason is to be found, I believe, in the nature of the relationship between coach and client (Passmore, 2006). It is to be found in the degree and style of engagement, the quality of mutual respect, the points of striking similarity and profound difference of view. It is to be found in the everyday coaching conversation with all its jokes, arguments and dead-ends.

So the final point which needs to be made about the Universal Eclectic Model, or indeed any other model of coaching, is this: It is good to have an extensive and well-understood toolkit drawn from different approaches. But maybe what is most important about having such a toolkit is not the range of tools in itself, but the fact that having such a range takes away our anxiety that we might not be able to "think of something to do". The release from anxiety enables the coach to be authentic and fully present, and that is the essence of coaching.

References

Bossons, P., Kourdi, J. and Sartain, D. (2012). *Coaching essentials: practical proven techniques for world-class executive coaching.* London: Bloomsbury Academic.

Bridges, W. (2003). *Managing transitions: making the most of change.* London: Nicholas Brealey Publishing.

Clark, G.I. and Egan, S.J. (December 2015). 'The Socratic method in cognitive behavioural therapy: A narrative review'. *Cognitive Therapy and Research*, 39(6), pp. 863–879. doi: 10.1007/s10608-015-9707-3.

Cooperrider, D. (1995). 'Introduction to appreciative enquiry' In *Organization development*, 5th ed. Ed D L Anderson New York: Prentice Hall.

De Haan, E., Duckworth, A., Birch, D. and Jones, C. (2012). 'Executive coaching outcome research: The contribution of common factors such as relationship, personality match, and self-efficacy'. *Consulting Psychology Journal: Practice and Research*, 65(1), pp. 40–57. doi: 10.1037/a0031635.

Ellis, G. and Solm, S.M. (2018). *Beyond evolutionary psychology.* Cambridge: Cambridge University Press.

Flaherty, J. (1999). *Coaching: Evoking excellence in others.* Oxford: Butterworth Heinemann.

Gallwey, W.T. (1975). *The inner game of tennis*. London: Pan Macmillan.

Hardingham, A. (2004). *The coach's coach: Personal development for personal developers*. London: Chartered Institute of Personnel and Development.

Jacoby, M. (1984). *The analytic encounter: Transference and human relationship*. Toronto: Inner City Books.

Kauffman, C. (2010). 'The last word: How to move from good to great coaching by drawing on the full range of what you know'. *Coaching: An International Journal of Theory, Research and Practice*, 3(2), pp. 87–98.

Kolb, D. (1984). *Experiential learning as the science of learning and development*. Englewood Cliffs: Prentice Hall.

Lee, G. (2003). *Leadership coaching: From personal insight to organizational performance*. London: Chartered Institute of Personnel and Development.

Lewin, K. and Gold, M. (1999). *The complete social scientist: A Kurt Lewin reader*. New York: American Psychological Association.

Maister, D., Green, C. and Galford, R. (2002). *The trusted advisor*. London: Simon & Schuster.

McDermott, I. and Jago, W. (2003). *Your inner coach*. London: Piatkus.

Megginson, D. and Clutterbuck, D. (2005). *Techniques for coaching and mentoring*. Oxford: Elsevier Butterworth-Heinemann.

Minuchin, S. and Fishman, H.C. (1981). *Family therapy techniques*. Cambridge: Harvard University Press.

O'Connell, B. (1998). *Solution-focused therapy*. London: SAGE Publications.

Passmore, J. (2006). *Excellence in coaching: The industry guide*. London: Kogan Page.

Rogers, C. (1951). *Client-centered therapy*. London: Constable and Company.

Rosen, S. (1982). *My voice will go with you: The teaching tales of Milton H. Erickson*. New York: Norton.

Rosinski, P. (2003). *Coaching across cultures: New tools for leveraging national, corporate and professional differences*. London: Nicholas Brealey Publishing.

Senge, P.M., Kleiner, A., Roberts, C., Ross, R.B. and Smith, B.J. (1994). *The fifth discipline fieldbook: Strategies and tools for building a learning organization*. London: Nicholas Brealey Publishing.

ten Have, S., ten Have, W., Stevens, F. and van der Elst, M. (2003). *Key management models: The management tools and practices that will improve your business*. London: Pearson Education.

Whitmore, J. (2002). *Coaching for performance: Growing people, performance and purpose*. London: Nicholas Brealey Publishing.

Zeus, P., and Skiffington, S. (2002). *The coaching at work toolkit: A complete guide to techniques and practices*. Sydney: McGraw-Hill.

17 Behavioural coaching
The GROW model

Sarah Leach

Introduction

The GROW model is the most widely used coaching model in the world. On one hand it is incredibly simple, but on the other it allows coach and client to work at depth on topics with clarity and purpose. This chapter looks to explore the GROW model as a structure that supports and enables the process of change through behavioural coaching. In other words, the process in which a client is taught, trained and guided towards learning a new behaviour. In behavioural coaching, the role of the coach is to facilitate the development of new behaviours which help the client achieve their goal. With this in mind, the GROW model provides a clear and simple structure for any coach to use as the foundation of their coaching conversation, when trying to enable a behavioural shift that encourages the client to see new possibilities and new ways to overcome a challenge or barrier to change. This chapter explains what the GROW model is, how it is used in practice, offers tools and techniques for use within the GROW framework, explores when the framework works best and offers examples of commonly used GROW questions.

The GROW model explained

The GROW model was developed in the 1980s by John Whitmore, Graham Alexander and Alan Fine as a result of observing and reflecting on coaching conversations with senior executives, and noticing an underlying pattern in the structure of these conversations (Alexander and Renshaw, 2005). Alexander (2016) noticed that it wasn't always possible to predict how the conversation would develop, but that a clear structure occurred in most. To capture this structure in a simple and memorable format that other coaches could use and repeat, the GROW model was developed.

GROW is made up of four simple steps and stands for Goal, Reality, Options and Wrap-Up, (sometimes called Will or Willingness) (see Figure 17.1). In practice, there are actually five steps, as the model starts first with identifying a topic (known as T-GROW). Once a topic is defined by the client, the session starts with a goal being set and a measurable outcome agreed for the coaching conversation. This is followed by understanding and exploring the reality of the current situation, where the client may begin to uncover some potential issues and barriers to change. The next step is options, where possible solutions to the problem are explored and preferred solutions identified. At this point, the conversation enters the final wrap-up stage where the coach tests the client's will to enable the change. Here, options are discussed, implications reviewed, actions determined and a willingness to commit is tested. Finally, the coach checks in with the client to see if the goal of the coaching session has been achieved.

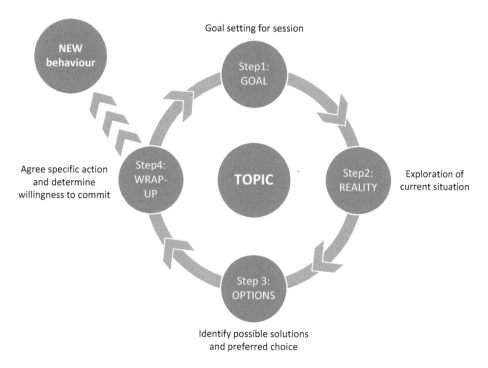

Figure 17.1 The GROW model

The great thing about the GROW model is that it easily allows the coach to use other tools and techniques at each stage of the process, a few examples of which we will explore later in the chapter. Scoular (2011) describes GROW as an accordion that expands in and out as much as you want depending on the time available and the nature of the topic being discussed. As with any other tool or technique, it is important not to become obsessed with the rigour of its application and to allow the coaching to remain fluid, natural and authentic within this framework (Alexander, 2016), responding in the moment to the presenting issue as appropriate (see Figure 17.1).

Behavioural coaching theory and research

The origins of the behavioural perspective lie in the work of Ivan Pavlov, B.F. Skinner, Edward Thorndike and John B. Watson, who identified through their research with animals that learning occurred through association (classical conditioning), through interventions (rewards or punishments) designed by the "instructor" (operant conditioning) and through social processes (social learning). While both classical and operant conditioning still unconsciously underpin much of our approach to human resources management in modern workplaces, the ideas of Albert Bandura and his social learning theory have been widely accepted as influencing human learning and have influenced the development of behavioural-based coaching approaches (Eldridge and Demkowski, 2013).

The popularity of the behavioural approach is closely related to the desires of managers and organisational coaching purchasers who wish to see tangible (behaviour change) outcomes from the coaching process.

In noting the behavioural influence, it is also important to acknowledge the role of the human potential movement in the development of the GROW model, specifically the work of Tim Galewey in his book the "Inner Game of Tennis" (1986).

While there has been substantial research into the development of behavioural psychology, this research has not been extended to assess the impact of behavioural coaching per se. The small number of studies which have taken place focus on measurement of goal attainment (Eldridge and Demkowski, 2013). One example is Anthony Grant's comparative study (2001). Grant sought to compare the effects of cognitive, behavioural and cognitive-behavioural coaching on academic performance, study skills, self-regulation, mental health, private self-consciousness and self-concept. The study had 3 cohorts of 20 students which each received coaching using one of the 3 approaches and also included a control group. Trainees in the cognitive-only cohort reported enhanced study skills and increases in their deep achieving approaches to learning, reduced anxiety and lower levels of depression. However, academic performance declined relative to the control group. In the behavioural-only group, students showed reduced study-related anxiety and improved academic performance. The final group which received cognitive behavioural coaching also demonstrated improved academic performance and reduced anxiety coupled with enhanced study skills, self-regulation and self-concept. Grant concluded that the combined cognitive and behavioural coaching program was the most effective means of enhancing both performance and well-being. Beyond this research, few studies have compared different approaches or explored the effectiveness of specific models such as GROW.

GROW in practice

The model starts with a topic, something identified by the client that they want to discuss. It is important to remember that the responsibility for the topic and the coaching goal remains firmly with the client (Bossons et al., 2012). Topics suggested by the client can often be quite vague as the client struggles to pin down exactly what they want to discuss. Hardingham (2004) points out that clients turn up to coaching conversations in the middle of busy lives and, consequently, it can take time for them to settle, park the background noise and day-to-day distractions in order to focus on the issue. It is important to spend time unravelling the component parts so that a specific topic becomes clear. Gaining this insight and focus often plays a large part in resolving the topic (Alexander, 2016). Once the client identifies a clear topic, the rest of the model follows as described below.

Step 1: Goal

Step 1 is to agree on the goals for the coaching session itself, i.e. determining a specific outcome from the conversation. At this stage the use of SMART goals, or other similar approaches (see Figure 17.2), can be helpful to establish measurable outcomes. It is perfectly normal for the goals of the sessions to change several times before the client commits to a final clear vision (Bossons et al., 2012). If multiple goals present themselves, which is often the case, a simple question such as asking the client, "Which of these do you want to work on today?", can help to bring focus to the session.

It can sometimes feel that a disproportionate amount of time is spent in the goal-setting stage; however, the greater the control and clarity the client has over setting the coaching

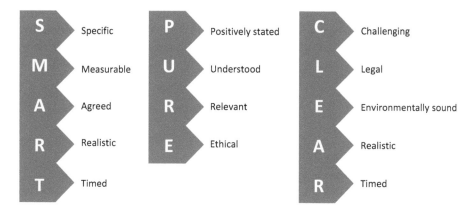

Figure 17.2 Goal-setting methods

goals, the more likely they are to achieve success (Bossons et al., 2012). It is also true that the greater the level of external influence and/or reliance on others outside of the coaching process is, the less likely the client will remain fully committed to the stated goals. It is important at this stage to differentiate between the ultimate objective of the client, the milestone goals that might take them towards the ultimate objective, and the objective for the coaching session itself. Therefore, spend enough time on setting the goal to allow for potential confusion and lack of clarity around the desired future state to be explored. Without a clearly defined goal, the conversation can meander, achieve little and become almost purposeless. Figure 17.2

Step 2: Reality

Whitmore (2017) argues that the most important reason to examine reality is to enable objectivity. Objectivity is influenced by the opinions of others, in addition to judgments, assumptions, hopes and fears, to name but a few! In being objective, you are able to raise awareness of things as they really are. In becoming more self-aware, you are more able to recognise those internal factors that also influence our perspective. Ultimately, the purpose of this stage is to bring the client as close to objectivity as possible in order to be able to see things the way they really are, and therefore take the appropriate action to address.

Clients can become stuck here! Clients often find it easy to describe the current context from their point of view and may find themselves caught up in their own stories. However, it is here that the coach can notice, reflect and observe things that might not necessarily be obvious for the client who is living this reality. For many clients so deeply entrenched in their own story, important things from the very practical to the very emotional can be buried in the subconscious mind or hidden from view somehow because of their particular perspective. The coach can notice habitual patterns of behaviour that might blinker the client (Scoular, 2011). In other words, deepen the client's awareness. Whitmore (2017) suggests we only have a measure of choice and control over what we are aware of and it is those things we are unaware of that control us. The role of the coach at this point is to bring everything, seen and unseen, into sharp focus for the client. To raise self-awareness, bringing new insights and clarity to an issue or need. Scoular (2011, p. 67) helpfully uses a military metaphor, referring to this stage as "reconnaissance", as in "time spent in reconnaissance is never wasted". It is in this stage that Alexander (Alexander, 2016) talks about the coach's intention being one of clarifying meaning, stripping away assumptions and judgments, using precise language and bringing real world examples as critical to this part of the model.

Step 3: Options

Having understood the reality of their current situation, in Step 3 the coach supports and encourages the client to identify some possible options to move forward. In many instances, the client may surprise themselves at how relatively easy it is to see a way through their current issues and identify possible solutions. As we see in lots of coaching conversations, having given the client the time and space to vocalise their issues and have someone listen intently to their internal dialogue, the solutions become "obvious". In complete shock and, sometimes, complete annoyance, I often hear clients say, "Why didn't I think of that before?"

Some clients may still find themselves a little bit stuck at this stage and so the coach may start by asking some open-ended questions. The coach's role is to hold the mirror up to the client and reflect back what they hear, in the client's words not their own, to encourage deeper thought and insight. By using the client's heightened sense of self-awareness, facilitating the learning associated with that and introducing new tools and techniques as required, the coach can challenge the appropriateness or otherwise of the solutions being presented. It is feasible that the client may ask for the coach's input at this stage to help generate some more ideas. Collaborative brainstorming techniques may generate a more comprehensive set of viable solutions. After all, two heads are better than one! However, the coach must ensure to offer his or her ideas with no attachment or intention of directing the client to one solution or another. The coach's suggestions may have little relevance for the client. In addition, if the conversation places more focus and energy on the thoughts of the coach, it may reduce the client's ability to access their own learning and wisdom (Starr, 2016).

Whilst the coach has supported the client in broadening the options, they also have a role to play in supporting the client in narrowing the options down again by evaluating the pros and cons of each. Again, the client must determine the criteria by which the options are evaluated (Scoular, 2011). With a comprehensive list of evaluated options, the client can now move on to Step 4 and determine the best way forward.

Step 4: Wrap-up or way forward

This stage is all about action and forward momentum, determining both what the client will do and how motivated they are to do it. Depending on the depth and rigour of the first three stages, actions may become obvious (Alexander, 2016, Passmore, 2019). However, clients often jump to immediate and obvious preferences with little understanding of why and how that may happen. It is important for the coach to ask direct and specific questions here, which enable a degree of granularity about what exactly the client will do and by when. The coach can bring a degree of toughness to the conversation without causing any bad feelings, but only in an attempt to activate the will of the client

(Whitmore, 2017).The client's level of confidence and certainty in making those choices must be tested and evaluated before making any final decisions.

Having made a decision, action planning can start in earnest by breaking the solution down into specific action steps. Alexander suggests the coach must support the client in evaluating the implications of each action, its practicality and any other obstacles that may arise as a result (Alexander, 2016). At this stage, it is useful to think about using simple, closed questions, such as what, when, who, how and where, to prompt a greater level of focus and commitment. It is often easy for the coach to inadvertently let the client off the hook at this point by being less challenging of the plan itself. It is also good practice for the coach to ask the client if there are additional resources or sources of support required to enable these actions. Asking for help doesn't always come naturally and may be something that clients overlook.

A final action plan is generated, with steps clearly articulated, deadlines and timelines defined, identification of who or what else might be involved and how and when the actions will be reviewed. In closing, asking the client "how will you feel when this is done?" and "on a scale of one to ten, how likely are you to take this action?" are powerful questions that help to assess the level of intent and willingness to change. Remember this isn't a rating of the certainty of the outcome happening, but the client's intention to carry out the action he or she has agreed. Experience would suggest that those who score less than an eight rarely see the action through to completion (Whitmore, 2017). If this is the case, the client may choose to go back to the original goal or re-assess the reality of the situation to see if they missed something. Alternatively, they may look to break down the size of the task or adjust the timeline for delivery, for example, so that they feel more able to complete the action and score eight or above. For those highly motivated clients, they may even look for ways in which they can move their score to a ten!

An alternative perspective

Another way to look at the GROW model is to compare it to completing a gap analysis (see Figure 17.3). Step 1 is to facilitate the client in articulating where they want to be; in other words, setting the goal (Point A). Step 2 looks to assess where they find themselves

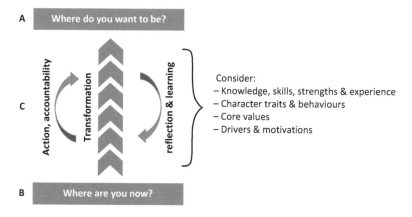

Figure 17.3 Gap analysis

currently in relation to that goal, i.e. the reality (Point B). Step 3 allows the client to explore the options for transitioning from A to B, the reality of "today" to the desired "future state". It is in examining this opportunity for transformation (Point C) where we can encourage our clients to be as creative as possible, to explore the opportunities from multiple perspectives and to stretch their strengths to find new and different approaches. It is often during this process of exploration and option generation, that some of the more personal and emotional barriers to change, as well as the practical barriers to change appear, building on from those you may have already identified in examining the reality of the current situation. A heightened self-awareness is key here in terms of acknowledging whether the barriers to change are coming from a value-based perspective, core drivers and motivations or previous experiences, for example. It is important to have spent some time understanding these dynamics, the client's strengths, skills and knowledge, as well as character traits and behavioural patterns, in order to understand the appropriateness and suitability of the possible options.

In theory, we are all capable of changing. The key is helping the client identify the actions they are committed to, no matter how small or large. As suggested previously, part of committing to the change might be in understanding the options for a phased step-by-step approach to the change, as depicted in Figure 17.3. This might, over time, create a more significant change or enable the client to reach their ultimate goal. As General Creighton Abrams is reported to have said, "When eating an elephant, take one bite at a time"!

It is important to note that there may be an extended and reiterative period of action, accountability, reflection and learning, in order to experiment with the different options before making a final choice. The "piloting" of a new idea may also encourage and motivate the client to commit to taking the required action, enabling a new type of behaviour. Therefore, whilst the GROW model appears linear, it is very much cyclical in nature. Consequently, over the course of one conversation, and over the course of a number of sessions, it is normal to find the coaching dialogue traversing backwards and forwards over each step in the process, with the coach expertly guiding the client through each necessary step, until there is clarity and the client is able to move forward.

Tools and techniques

The simplicity of the GROW model allows the coach to blend and integrate other tools and techniques into the process to encourage deeper insights and learning for the client. As we've discussed, getting clarity on the topic and therefore the coaching goal can be the first challenge for many clients. You may hear, for example, clients saying they don't feel fulfilled anymore and something's got to change, or they think they want a new job but don't know what they want to do or they need a better balance between work and home. These are vague and potentially enormous topics, so the first step is to get clarity on the topic and identify a specific goal that can be addressed in the session.

Tools such as the life wheel (see Figure 17.4), which encourages the client to see their life as a whole and identify the parts that may be more or less fulfilling, could be used to help the client focus in on the particular part of their life that is really causing them concern. Alternatively, an exercise where the client is asked to visualise their ideal day and share it in the present tense, from the moment they wake to the moment they go to bed at night (Rogers, 2012). This can help the client to spot the key issues they want to address and therefore focus on a more defined topic and coaching goal. These techniques are proactively used as part of the first stages of the Co-Active Coaching model, too (Kimsey-House et al., 2011), as a way to bring clarity to the coaching goals and deepen levels of self-awareness, both of which are common to the GROW model.

In exploring the reality of a situation in Step 2 and perhaps again in Step 4, when weighing up the possible solutions and deciding on a plan of action, it can be useful for the client to understand what is within their control. This may influence their decisions and/or the milestones within the plan. The CIA (control, influence, accept) model (see Figure 17.5) is a useful tool for this. The model encourages the client to look for the issues or elements of the situation that are within their control, to identify the elements that they can't control but might be able to influence in some way and, finally, accept the things that they can neither control nor influence. In understanding these different positions, the coach can help the client to put things into perspective and develop a greater sense of what they can achieve. Ultimately, this enables the client to focus their efforts on the things that might have the most impact in relation to their goal.

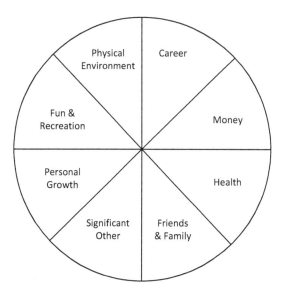

Figure 17.4 The Wheel of Life

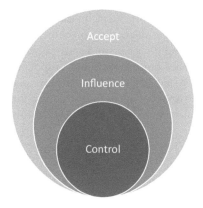

Figure 17.5 CIA Model

When does GROW work best?

GROW's simplicity means that it can underpin the majority of coaching conversations, from professional in-depth coaching to facilitating the relationship between line manager and employee in the workplace. As coaching becomes an essential skill and approach to the role of line management everywhere, so the GROW technique can easily be applied by most at one level or another. Unlike other approaches it does not require a background in psychotherapy to use it and its approach complements the organisational view of the world (Alexander, 2016), such as outlined in Figure 17.3, comparing GROW to an organisational gap-analysis approach. It can be used for personal development conversations to improve performance at the individual, team and organisational level, to empower employees to take responsibility for their actions and help to improve leadership and management effectiveness. Its origins in coaching sporting professionals show how useful it is in enhancing performance and demonstrate its applicability to most situations. For instance, Whitmore (2017) talks about using the GROW approach in one-to-one conversations between peers, between a manager and an employee, between a teacher and their student and a coach and a performer.

Ten useful questions for GROW coaches

There is no pre-defined list of perfect questions to ask clients when working with the GROW model. Rather than list ten questions, I have listed ten questions at each of the four stages of GROW in Table 17.1.

Like with all powerful questions, it is important to note that each question posed by the coach must be contextually appropriate and, by noticing how the question lands with the client, an effective coach should have the confidence to draw from a range of possible questions in the moment in order to invoke insight and learning for the client.

Conclusion

In conclusion, the GROW model presents a very effective basis for any coaching conversation. Used by novices and master coaches alike, as well as leaders and managers across different organisational settings, the GROW model can be used to enable behavioural change. Whilst it is very easy to use and effective in its simplest form, it can also be extended and adapted to allow for deeper learning and insight depending on the client's presenting topic. The coach can use this approach successfully with a simple set of powerful questions and an ability to hear and see what is being both spoken and unspoken. For more depth, the model allows room for the coach to integrate additional tools and techniques at each stage as required, using the GROW model as an overall structure for the coaching conversation. There is plenty of room to play your own "accordion" in this approach!

Table 17.1 Effective questions to use at each stage of the GROW model

Stage	Effective Questions
Topic	1. What would you like to talk about today? 2. Is there anything particular you want to work on today?
G – goal	1. What do you want to do? 2. What change are you looking to make? 3. What will be different as a result of this change? 4. Why is this change important now? 5. What might success look like for you? 6. How much control do you have over this goal? 7. How much of a stretch does it feel? 8. How much time will you give yourself to achieve this goal? 9. How will you know you are still heading in the right direction? 10. How will you know when you have achieved it?
R – Reality	1. What else is happening right now that has an impact on this goal? 2. Who else might be involved, directly or indirectly? 3. What are the consequences of your intended goal? 4. What have you done about this so far? 5. What is currently missing? 6. What is stopping you from making any more progress? 7. What might others say about the current situation? 8. What strengths/knowledge/skill/experience do you have that you might not be using right now? 9. What is happening as a result of keeping things the way they are? 10. What is not happening as a result of keeping things the way they are?
O – Options	1. What might you choose to do next? 2. What else? 3. If you had already made the change, what might you have done to make it happen? 4. How do you feel about it? 5. What might you like to do differently? 6. Would you like another suggestion? 7. If your child/parent/sibling/best friend/manager were here, what might they offer up as a suggestion? 8. What if anything was possible (no constraints)? 9. What are the pros and cons of each? 10. What are the pros and cons of not doing each?
W – Will	1. Which option(s) will you choose? 2. What steps do you need to take now? 3. What do you need to have in place to enable "X" to happen? 4. To what extent does this course of action meet your original objectives? 5. How motivated do you feel to do this? 6. On a scale of 1 to 10, how likely are you to take this action? 7. What kind of resistance are you feeling right now in contemplating this change? 8. When are you going to do this? 9. How will you feel when it's done? 10. What is your criteria and measurement for success?

References

Alexander, G. (2016). 'Behavioural coaching'. In J. Passmore, ed., *Excellence in coaching: The industry guide*, 3rd ed. London: Kogan Page, pp.99–111.2.

Alexander, G. and Renshaw, B. (2005) *Super Coaching: The missing ingredient for high performance*, London: Random House Business Books.

Bossons, P, Kourdi, J. and Sartain, D. (2012). *Coaching essentials: Practical proves techniques for world-class executive coaching*, 2nd ed. London: Bloomsbury.

Eldridge, F. and Demkowski, S. (2013). 'Behavioural coaching'. In J. Passmore, D. Peterson and T. Freire, eds., *The Wiley Blackwell handbook of the psychology of coaching and mentoring*. Chichester: Wiley, pp. 298–318.

Galewey, W.T. (1986). *The inner game of tennis*. London: Pan.

Grant, A.M. (2001). *Coaching for enhanced performance: comparing cognitive and behavioural coaching approaches*. Paper presented to the 3rd international spearman seminar, Sydney.

Hardingham, A. (2004). *The coach's coach: Personal development for personal developers*. London: Chartered Institute of Personnel and Development.

Kimsey-House, H., Kimsey-House, K., Sandahl, P. and Whitworth, L. (2011). *Co-Active Coaching: Changing Business, Transforming Lives*. Boston: Nicholas Brealey Publishing.

Passmore, J. (2019). 'Behavioural coaching'. In S. Palmer and A. Whybrow, eds., *The handbook of coaching psychology*. London: Brunner-Routledge, pp. 99–107.

Rogers, J. (2012) *Coaching Skills: A handbook*, 3rd ed. Maidenhead: Open University Press.

Scoular, A. (2011). *Business coaching*. Harlow: Pearson Education Limited.

Starr, J. (2016). *The coaching manual: The definitive guide to the process, principles and skills of personal coaching*, 4th ed. Harlow: Pearson Education Limited.

Whitmore, J. (2017). *Coaching for performance: The principles and practice of coaching and leadership*, 5th ed. London: Nicholas Brealey Publications.

18 Person-centred coaching

Richard Bryant-Jefferies

Introduction

The person-centred approach to coaching is grounded in the theoretical ideas of Carl Rogers. Through his own therapeutic work he formulated an approach to therapy that placed primacy upon the relationship between therapist and client as the key factor in achieving positive outcomes for the client. The approach is not based on a therapeutic theory that focuses on diagnosis and treatment. At the heart of the person-centred approach (PCA) lies a belief that the person has within their nature an actualising tendency which can be encouraged through the experience of a particular quality of relationship to direct the person towards more effective behaviours and fulfilling lifestyle choices. It is the nature of the relationship within the collaborative coaching alliance that is key for positive and constructive outcomes.

Person-centred coaching explained

Whereas therapy is often regarded as helping a person in the present to come to terms with how their past experiences have affected them, coaching is more concerned with looking forward. Yet in my experience as a person-centred counsellor working with people with addiction problems, I have noted how there is often movement from looking back to looking forward, and then back again. Counselling clients often oscillate between the two within the therapeutic journey, addressing the effects of past experience and bringing this to bear on their formulation of goals for the future. Throughout this process, the approach of the person-centred helper does not change. The focus remains on maintaining a facilitative relational environment within which a person can develop a way of being that reflects, or is expressive of, an increasingly authentic sense of self.

Rogers proposed that the presence of certain conditions within a therapeutic relationship would enable a person to develop what he referred to as "fuller functionality". Over the years, and based on clinical experience, he refined his ideas leading to the notion of "the necessary and sufficient conditions for constructive personality change". These he described as:

1. Two persons are in psychological contact;
2. The first, whom we shall term the client, is in a state of incongruence, being vulnerable or anxious;
3. The second person, whom we shall term the therapist, is congruent or integrated in the relationship;

4. The therapist experiences unconditional positive regard for the client;
5. The therapist experiences an empathic understanding of the client's internal frame of reference and endeavours to communicate this experience to the client;
6. The communication to the client of the therapist's empathic understanding and unconditional positive regard is to a minimal degree achieved.

(Rogers, 1957, p. 96)

These conditions lie at the core of person-centred coaching. Let us briefly elaborate on their meaning in the context of a coaching relationship.

1. Psychological contact. This means that the field of awareness of the client is affected by the presence of the coach. This does not require them to physically be in a room together, but is about the coach's level of engagement, being wholly and totally focused on the client in the present moment;
2. Incongruence. The client is troubled by something. Something is not right. An aspect of their life does not match their desires or wishes. They may be experiencing a disconnection, a lack of a sense of fulfilment or feel stuck in a pattern or situation that they are experiencing an urge to grow out of or develop beyond. The person they experience themselves as being is not reflected in the person they present to the world, or the person they want to be;
3. Congruence. This is a disciplined way of being in which the coach is "openly being the feelings and attitudes that are flowing within at the moment" (Rogers, 1980, p. 115). Realness, transparency, genuineness and authenticity have also been used to help appreciate the nature of this condition. However, it should be stated this does not mean endless self-disclosure. Congruent expression is most helpful where it is informed by the existence of an empathic understanding of the client's inner world, and is offered in a climate of genuine warmth and acceptance towards them;
4. Unconditional positive regard. This is not simply agreeing with everything the client says or plans to do, it is rather a warm acceptance of the fact that they are being how they need to be. You cannot make yourself have this attitude as a coach. It has to be genuinely present. To quote Rogers again, and placing his words in the context of coaching, when the coach "is experiencing a positive, acceptant attitude towards whatever the client *is* at that moment, therapeutic movement or change is more likely to occur" (Rogers, 1980, p. 116);
5. Empathy. For Rogers, this meant "entering the private perceptual world of the other ... being sensitive, moment by moment, to the changing felt meanings which flow in this other person ... It means sensing meanings of which he or she is scarcely aware, but not trying to uncover totally unconscious feelings" (Rogers, 1980, p. 142). This is so much more than letting the client know what you have heard them say. It is more "the actual *process* of listening to a client, of attending to what is being offered and communicated and received *at the time that the [client] is speaking, at the time that the [client] is experiencing what is present for them*" (Bryant-Jefferies, 2005a, p. 9);
6. Perception. Rogers tells us that "the final condition ... is that the client perceives, to a minimal degree, the acceptance and empathy which the therapist experiences for him. Unless some communication of these attitudes has been achieved, then such attitudes do not exist in the relationship as far as the client is concerned, and the therapeutic process could not, by our hypothesis, be initiated" (Rogers, 1957).

The relationship or bond between the coach and the client allows the client to explore who they are and what they want to achieve based on their own self-experience and self-evaluation. The quality of the experienced coaching relationship characterised by the above encourages and enables the client to

> deeply listen to their inner wisdom – what Rogers referred to as the Organismic Valuing Process. Thus, they become able to analyse their situations more objectively, understand their own needs better, become more trusting of themselves, and become able to find their self-direction.
>
> (Joseph and Bryant-Jefferies, 2019, p. 136)

One factor that needs emphasis is the impact of diversity and difference on the coaching relationship. This must always be taken account of when the coach is reflecting on his or her ability to offer the relational conditions outlined above. This is not just a consideration in terms of how the coach relates to the client; the diversity issues that may affect the client's perception of and relationship towards the coach must equally be considered. This is very likely to be a focus early on in supervision.

Later in this chapter we will consider how these conditions are applied within a coaching relationship.

Person–centred coaching theory and research

The person-centred approach is an established psychological tradition that is underpinned by over 60 years of research and theoretical development (see Barrett-Lennard, 1998). Its application to coaching is a natural progression because, as noted earlier, it contains a theoretical stance that regards human beings having within them a tendency towards growth, complexity and fuller functionality. More recently the developing field of positive psychology (e.g. Joseph, 2015) has added a further area within which PCA theory and practice finds a home.

In terms of coaching, research has shown that, for clients, what is particularly important is the relationship with the coach. McKenna and Davis (2009) identify this relationship or alliance as one of the four main active ingredients in effective executive coaching. Haan et al. (2009) found in a study focusing on the experience of executive coaching that clients valued the relationship with, and the qualities of, the coach. Less distinction was made with regard to the specific interventions of that same coach. The findings of the study supported "the idea that common factors are at work in executive coaching, so that helpfulness is much less predicted by technique or approach than by factors common to all coaching, such as the relationship, empathic understanding, positive expectations etc." The comment was also made that the study found "some support for Carl Rogers" (1957) idea that what they appreciate most in their coach is general support, encouragement, listening and understanding" (de Haan et al., 2009).

De Haan and Gannon (2016), in the context of understanding the bond that develops in the coaching relationship, highlight "the intellectual and empirical debt owed to the psychotherapeutic literature where the bond is one of the key constructs in the working alliance".

In a review of findings from a range of studies, Cooper (2004) indicates that "there is growing support for a relationship-orientated approach to therapeutic practice" (Cooper, p. 452). Although this refers to therapeutic practice, it has relevance for the PCA coaching practitioner because the same principles and processes govern the interactions that occur. Included within the evidence that he cites is a vast review of research on the therapeutic relationship commissioned in 1999 by the American Psychological Association Division of Psychotherapy Task Force, which, citing Norcross (2002), was the largest ever review of research on the therapeutic relationship, with its distillation of evidence coming to over 400 pages. Cooper writes: "Its main conclusion was that 'The therapy relationship … makes substantial and consistent contributions to psychotherapy outcome independent of the specific type of treatment'" (Steering Committee, 2002, pp. 441). (The "therapy relationship" is defined here as "the feelings and attitudes that therapist and client have towards one another, and the manner in which these are expressed" [Norcross, 2002, p. 7].)

Further conclusions cited by Cooper (2004) from this study include, "Practice and treatment guidelines should explicitly address therapist behaviours and qualities that promote a facilitative therapy relationship" and "Efforts to promulgate practice guidelines or evidence-based lists of effective psychotherapy without including the therapy relationship are seriously incomplete and potentially misleading on both clinical and empirical grounds" (Steering Committee, 2002, p. 441). In addition, the recommendation is made that practitioners should "make the creation and cultivation of a therapy relationship … a primary aim in the treatment of patients" (Steering Committee, 2002, p. 442).

Whether the helping relationship is strictly therapeutic, more coaching oriented, or moving dynamically between the two, the relationship that PCA coaches have with their clients and the attitude that they hold within that relationship are key factors in facilitating movement towards fuller functioning and greater effectiveness in the areas that the client wishes to develop.

Person-centred coaching practice

A crucial feature of movement towards constructive personality change within person-centred theory is the notion of the actualising tendency (Rogers, 1986). He wrote:

> the person–centred approach is built on a basic trust in the person … [It] depends on the actualizing tendency present in every living organism – the tendency to grow, to develop, to realize its full potential. This way of being trusts the constructive directional flow of the human being towards a more complex and complete development. It is this directional flow that we aim to release.
>
> (Rogers, 1986, p. 198)

Rogers' theory of the development of the self includes reference to the development of conditions of worth where we try to live to other people's hopes and expectations. Movement towards fuller functionality involves shifting towards a stronger internal locus of evaluation and away from the external one that may have been dominant. The client moves towards more authentic living and experiencing and is better able to perceive that which is best and right for them. In this process, changes in behaviour occur. Rogers formulated a set of propositional statements related to this:

> Behaviour is caused, and the psychological cause of behaviour is a certain perception or a way of perceiving;
>
> The client is the only one who has the potentiality of knowing fully the dynamics of his perceptions and his behaviour;

In order for behaviour to change, a change in perception must be *experienced*. Intellectual knowledge cannot substitute for this;

The constructive forces which bring about altered perception, reorganization of self, and relearning, reside primarily in the client, and probably cannot come from outside;

Therapy is basically the experiencing of the inadequacies in old ways of perceiving, the experiencing of new and more accurate and adequate perceptions, and the recognition of significant relationship between perceptions;

In a very meaningful and accurate sense, therapy *is* diagnosis, and this diagnosis is a process which goes on in the experience of the client, rather than in the intellect of the clinician.

(Rogers, 1951, pp. 221–223)

Later in his life Rogers also devised a seven-stage process of change model, which he summarised as follows:

"This process involves a loosening of feelings";
"This process involves a change in the manner of experiencing";
"The process involves a shift from incongruence to congruence";
"The process involves a change in the manner in which, and the extent to which the individual is able and willing to communicate himself in a receptive climate";
"The process involves a loosening of the cognitive maps of experience";
"There is a change in the individual's relationship to his problem";
"There is a change in the individual's manner of relating".

(Rogers, 1967, pp. 156–158)

The above has been usefully further summarised by Tudor and Worral (2004) as "a movement from fixity to fluidity, from closed to open, from tight to loose, and from afraid to accepting" (2004, p. 47). Psychological and behaviour change inter-relate. A re-balancing and integrating process occurs within the person which is then evidenced through changed behaviours (Bryant-Jefferies, 2005b). Satisfaction that is then experienced from change, from developing new skills and talents, feeds back into the motivation to maintain and build on what has been achieved.

The following dialogue[1] provides an example of person-centred coaching dialogue to illustrate the practice of applying the necessary and sufficient conditions for constructive personality change detailed earlier.

It was Diane's second session of coaching. She still wasn't sure what she wanted to do in the session, only that she had become increasingly unhappy about her weight and wanted to make changes. But it always came back down to "how?". She had tried diets in the past but they never lasted long. Something never felt quite right when she was on them. But she couldn't really put her finger on exactly what it was.

Diane's coach, Rose, sat opposite her. She had really listened to her in that opening session. It had felt good to feel that someone was there with her. It wasn't something she felt used to. It had allowed her to feel able to talk. Diane hoped the session would be the same today.

Rose had felt a natural warmth towards Diane. She had herself had issues with weight and had worked on them in the past, but she had been very mindful in that first session not to allow her own experience to get in the way of attending to what Diane was saying. She knew how easy it was to get trapped into thinking that being congruent was about self-disclosure. It wasn't. She had been able to put her momentary reminder of her own experience to one side. Had she not been able to then she would have taken that to supervision. (1)

"So", Rose began, "how would you like to use our session today?". She did not want to direct Diane towards any particular focus. This was crucial in her person-centred practice to try not to be directive. (2)

Diane took a deep breath. "It's really difficult. I really liked our conversation last week. It felt good, but I feel I need to move on, make changes. It felt like last week I kind of set the scene, as it were. And I was amazed how much I had to say. And since then, well, it's been a strange week".

"A strange week?" Rose did not attempt a lengthy reflection of what Diane had just said. That didn't feel appropriate. It felt much more important to communicate that she had heard her final comment. (3)

"It's hard to describe". Diane paused, wondering how to capture in words how her week had been. "It's like I'm more aware of my eating but in a different way. And when I am sitting around at home, there's something different".

"Something different?". Again Rose kept her response short and focused on where Diane's words had taken her.

Diane nodded slowly, reflectively. She didn't say anything for a moment and Rose allowed the silence to be. It was, she felt, a working silence. She respected it and wanted to allow Diane the space she needed to connect with and communicate what she was experiencing. (4)

"It's like I am watching myself, like I am sort of … I don't know, it's really hard to describe".

This time Rose responded, leaving the focus on Diane's first comment whilst embracing all that she had said. "Hard to describe but it is like you are watching yourself?".

Diane nodded. "Yes, like I want to understand what I am doing". As soon as she said it Diane wasn't sure if that was what she meant. "No, not understand but kind of get a hold of myself, get a grip, you know?".

"Something about feeling you want to get a grip on yourself".

"And make changes, different choices. I'm uncomfortable with what I am seeing, who I am. It's really hard to describe. I don't feel the same". (5)

"Something has changed, you don't feel the same". Rose was not thinking about what Diane was saying. That wasn't her role as a PCA coach. She was listening and holding her full attention on what she was experiencing emerging out of her empathy for what Diane was saying and how she was being. In the moment this was her only reality, a moment-to-moment connecting.

Diane was speaking more quickly now. "It's like I want to change, I've wanted to for a while, but it feels different now. It's like *I* want to make changes. I watch myself like I'm watching TV, I can't stop myself reaching for the chocolates but I am somehow not the person who is doing the reaching". Another pause. "Does this make any sense to you?".

Commentary

(1) The importance of congruence is highlighted here. One of the areas that a person-centred coach is most likely to explore consistently in supervision is whether they are able to maintain congruence, and if not, what is happening within the coach to make it difficult to maintain integration in the relationship.

(2) Non-directivity is a core feature of person-centred practice. The client is seen as the expert on their situation, the person who knows best what they need to focus on in the moment.

(3) So often empathy is thought of as reflecting back what a person has said. It is so much more than that. As the client speaks she is on a journey, and it has taken her to a point which the coach is then responding to. It allows the client, if they wish, to then journey on without being taken back over something that had been said before, even if it was only two sentences ago.

(4) The coach has to be able to stay with silence. The client is in effect communicating silence, and silence is an empathic and respectful response. But that does not mean activity, the coach will be still fully attending to the client and not allowing her thoughts to drift off. If they do, this may be a supervision issue.

(5) This is powerful insight that is emerging within the client's experience. She is more deeply connecting with, or perhaps we should say becoming, the person who wants change.

This is a small section of dialogue representing an early stage in the coaching experience. There is movement, a shift from fixity towards an expanded sense of self that encompasses greater psychological and emotional ownership of the need for change. From this behaviour change can occur, and because the behaviour change is rooted in this underlying psychological change, I would argue it is much more likely to be sustained.

Tools and techniques

The person-centred coach doesn't tend to think in terms of tools and techniques. The focus is more on respecting the individual as the expert on their own situation and allowing them to find their own way through whatever they are bringing to the coaching relationship. Goals are not set by the person-centred coach and no attempt is made to direct the client towards a particular outcome. A relational space is created within which the client is freed up to experience and think about themselves and their situation differently. The importance of this time to think, or perhaps we should say re-think, has also been highlighted in the context of executive coaching by Kline (1999).

It comes down to the way of being of the coach. Can they provide a non-directive, empathic, warmly accepting and genuine relational attitude towards the client as they explore what it is they are striving to achieve, change or develop in their lives? Can they stay beside them, and be experienced as a person who genuinely wants to understand what the client is experiencing and considering?

The following is another example of PCA coaching practice.

Mick was attending his third session of coaching. He had a gambling habit, particularly on-line, and he knew it was out of control. His wife had got on at him to stop, so had his parents. He knew they were right but he felt pushed and wanted to push back. He usually pushed back by gambling a bit more, sometimes a lot more.

Mick had got to a point of knowing things couldn't go on as they were. He'd arrived at the first session expecting someone to tell him what to do. That was not what he got from his coach, Sanjeev. It had been strange for Mick at first, and a bit frustrating. He wasn't sure that Sanjeev really understood him. How could he? He clearly had a totally different background. Yet he had found that, as the session had gone on, and in the one that followed, he had felt much more at ease with his coach. He was much more open to an increasing sense that his gambling lay much deeper. He had noticed that he was more aware of the choices he was making between the sessions, and, even though his gambling hadn't stopped, he felt that something was different.

"I have thought about just stopping all my access to on-line gambling. Get rid of my computer, go back to an old phone, and maybe that will work … Maybe". Mick paused. As he spoke the words he knew he wasn't convinced by what he was saying.

Sanjeev could hear the hesitancy in Mick's voice. Rather than empathising with the words, he empathised with the tone of what Mick was saying. "You don't sound too sure about that?". His response had a slight questioning tone, offering the opportunity for Mick to explore more without it coming across like a question that had to be answered. (1)

"I suppose it might help, but … I don't know. It will still be me, won't it?".

"Still be you?". Again a slight questioning tone in Sanjeev's response, this time reflecting the self-questioning tone of Mick's words. (2)

"I need to make changes, I know that. But it's me that needs to make those changes".

"'Me that needs to make those changes'". Sanjeev had dropped the questioning tone. This was a straight response to a very affirming statement from Mick. (3)

Mick looked at Sanjeev. He felt slightly strange. He looked away. A kind of tingling numbness and his heart had started thumping. Yes, he thought, me, I have to do it, I have to … His thoughts trailed off as a fresh insight burst upon him. He heard himself speaking the idea that had suddenly consumed him. "It's not about doing. It's more than doing". He looked up at Sanjeev again. "I have to *be* the change". (4)

Sanjeev felt the goosebumps as he listened to Mick, his tone of voice, what he had said, and watched the expression on his face. It was a big moment. He had learned from experience that in those moments you did not think about what to say, you allowed your response to come from the connection you were making with the client. He spoke slowly, slower than Mick had spoken. "I have to be the change". (5)

Mick heard Sanjeev responding and it felt both close and distant at the same time in some weird way. "And I have to be it for me". (6) He felt a deep silence within himself. He took a deep breath.

Commentary

(1) Empathy not for the words, but for the way they had been said. The response emerges out of Sanjeev's sense of connection with Mick.

(2) Sanjeev avoids his response sounding like an answer. It is not for him to affirm the truth about something that his client is considering. The slight questioning tone invites further exploration with pushing the client. There is a lightness in the tone of his response.

(3) From self-questioning Mick has moved towards something more self-affirming. Sanjeev reflects this in the tone of his response. The questioning tone, the lightness, has gone. It's a big moment. The effective PCA coach catches and responds to it.

(4) Mick has moved further in his self-affirming stance. He is on a journey, making connections within himself, seeing his position and his role in finding a solution to his problem more clearly.

(5) Sanjeev has entered into the moment with Mick. There is a deep connection. Sanjeev is experienced enough to know that these moments are full of creativity and insight, and that they have to be entered into carefully, gently. Often, what is emerging, whilst it can be affirming, can also be tenuous, as new perspectives or a new sense of self breaks into awareness for the first time. The coaching relationship is fostering a tendency for Mick to actualise fresh insight and understanding and sense of himself.

(6) A shift takes place in Mick's locus of evaluation. He knows what he needs to do has to be for him, not because of what others are saying, or how others are judging him.

The client hasn't even formulated much of a behaviour change, but he has now moved towards a place in himself where he can more realistically consider his options. These will emerge from his own understanding of his situation and what seems realistic to him. They will not be driven by the coach, whose role will continue to be providing the relational environment in which the client can explore and formulate the behaviour changes that he experiences as being right for him.

Ten useful person-centred coaching questions

The person-centred coach is less likely to be asking questions of the client. The PCA coach is much more likely to be asking questions of themselves, either after a session or within some form of supervision. As a result, the questions in this section are more for personal reflection by the coach. The focus for the questioning will be on areas where the coaching relationship and the responses and reactions of the coach need processing and understanding with a view to increasing the coach's effectiveness.

1. Do I have a sense of psychological connection with my client and how would I describe this?
2. Am I experiencing unconditional positive regard for my client, and, if not, what is it that is making this difficult?
3. Can I truly listen and attend to my client, or are there times when I lose this focus?
4. What am I experiencing within myself as I seek to connect with and hear what my client is communicating?
5. Am I feeling drawn into talking about myself and my experiences when I am with my client?
6. Do I feel any particular anxieties when I am working with my client or when I am reflecting on that work?
7. Are there any issues of diversity and difference that might be affecting my effectiveness in relating to my client with acceptance and non-judgementally?
8. What were the key moments within the coaching session(s)?
9. What thoughts and feelings am I left with after a coaching session with my client?
10. What do I need to explore more deeply in supervision so that I can be more effective and present in the next coaching session?

Conclusion

In this chapter I have sought to present a flavour of person-centred coaching practice, briefly describing key theoretical components and how they can be applied in the coaching relationship. The PCA perspective provides for working with a client who needs to not only look forward, but in the process of exploring and making changes needs to touch into the past and aspects of their sense of self that might otherwise get overlooked. I would argue that sustainable behaviour change has to be underpinned by constructive personality change.

Note

1   The use of fictitious dialogue to demonstrate the application of the person-centred approach has been extensively developed by the author in the *Living Therapy* series of titles now published by Routledge.

References

Barrett-Lennard, G.T. (1998). *Carl Rogers' helping system: Journey and substance.* London: Sage.

Bryant-Jefferies, R. (2005a). *Counselling for obesity: Person-centred dialogues.* Oxford: Radcliffe Publishing, now published by Routledge.

Bryant-Jefferies, R. (2005b). *Counselling for problem gambling: Person-centred dialogues.* Oxford: Radcliffe Publishing, now published by Routledge.

Cooper, M. (2004). 'Towards a relationally-orientated approach to therapy: Empirical support and analysis'. *British Journal of Guidance and Counselling*, 32, pp. 4. Brunner-Routledge.

de Haan, E. Culpin, V. and Curd, J. (2011). 'Executive coaching in practice: What determines helpfulness for clients of coaching?' *Personnel Review*, 40(1), pp. 24–44. Emerald Group Publishing.

de Haan, E. and Gannon, J. (2016). 'The coaching relationship'. In T. Bachkirova, G. Spence and D. Drake, eds., *The Sage handbook of coaching.* London: Sage, pp. 195-221.

Joseph, S. (2015). *Positive therapy: Building bridges between positive psychology and person-centred psychotherapy.* London: Routledge.

Joseph, S. and Bryant-Jefferies, R. (2019). 'Person-centred coaching psychology'. In S. Palmer and A. Whybrow, eds., *Handbook of coaching psychology: A guide for practitioners*, 2nd ed. London: Routledge, pp. 131–143.

Kline, N. (1999). *Time to think: Listening to ignite the human mind.* London: Cassell.

McKenna, D.D. and Davis, S.L. (2009). 'Hidden in plain sight: The active ingredients of executive coaching'. *Industrial and Organizational Psychology*, 2(3), pp. 244-260.

Norcross, J.C. (2002). 'Empirically supported therapy relationships'. In J.C. Norcross, ed., *Psychotherapy relationships that work: Therapist contributions and responsiveness to patients.* Oxford: Oxford University Press, pp. 3-16.

Rogers, C.R. (1951). *Client centred therapy.* London: Constable.

Rogers, C.R. (1957). 'The necessary and sufficient conditions of therapeutic personality change'. *Journal of Consulting Psychology*, 21, pp. 95–103.

Rogers, C.R. (1967). *On becoming a person.* London: Constable. (Originally published in 1961).

Rogers, C.R. (1980). *A way of being.* Boston: Houghton-Mifflin Company.

Rogers, C.R. (1986). 'A client-centered/person-centered approach to therapy'. In I. Kutash and A. Wolfe, eds., *Psychotherapists' casebook.* San Francisco, CA: Jossey Bass, pp. 197–208.

Steering Committee. (2002). 'Empirically supported therapy relationships: Conclusions and recommendations on the Division 29 task force'. In J.C. Norcross, ed., *Psychotherapy relationships that work: Therapist contributions and responsiveness to patients.* Oxford: Oxford University Press, pp. 441–443.

Tudor, K. and Worral, M. (2004). *Freedom to practice: Person-centred approaches to supervision.* Ross on Wye: PCCS Books.

19 Solution-focused coaching

Jonathan Passmore

Introduction

Solution-focused coaching is grounded in the work of the Brief Family Therapy Centre in Milwaukee, US, and specifically the work of Steve de Shazer and Insoo Kim Berg. As a result of their therapy work with families they recognised that the therapeutic process had typically been constructed as "moving away from the problem". In contrast, de Shazer argued that it could be more helpful if the focus was shifted to "moving towards a solution". de Shazer also noticed that most clients seemed to make the most progress in their early sessions, and that the returns then gradually diminished. This led to the second shift towards a brief intervention.

In this chapter we will look at solution-focused coaching, its background, the growing research agenda, how it is applied in practice and some useful tools and techniques which coaches can use to bring the approach to life in their practise.

Solution-focused coaching explained

The solution-focused approach encourages clients to think about what is possible by considering solutions rather than focusing their attention and energy on the problem. In this sense, solution-focused coaching may be defined as an outcome-orientated approach that works with the art of the possible, rather than the imagination of the desirable. It is goal-directed, client-centred and works from an approach of "let's get this done". For all of these reasons this approach, which emerged in therapy, is highly compatible with ideas within coaching: Goal-driven, future-focused and collaborative.

This forward focus within the solution-focused approach contrasts with many other therapeutic approaches. The traditional approach; for example, in psychodynamic or cognitive behavioural approaches, is to look back at the past: To focus on understanding the problem and to explore its cause through methods such as Psychodynamic analysis or Cognitive Behavioural's ABCDE. However, de Shazer (1988) argued that this problem-oriented thinking was more likely to lead to blame and result in resistance. In contrast, focusing energy towards a solution is much better suited for creating a collaborative environment where past problems are overcome by the will to reach a shared goal.

O'Connell and others have described a number of features which make the solution-focused approach different (O'Connell, 1998; Greene and Grant, 2003; Iverson et al., 2012):

Plain language

A solution-focused approach aims to avoid pathologising clients and their problems. It aims to avoid a language of dysfunction, replacing it with everyday language to create a collaborative relationship of equals between the client and coach.

Solution not problem

A focus on encouraging clients to construct solutions, as opposed to spending time describing and analysing past problems.

Client as expert

The client is recognised as the expert with regard to the issue they face and the solution which fits their context, rather than the therapist (coach) analysing and guiding towards a solution.

Growth mindset

Each session is seen as a learning experience for both the therapist (coach) and the client. Each holds a growth mindset in the session, seeking opportunities to learn and grow through the conversation.

Client's resources

The therapist (coach) helps the client identify and use their own resources, as opposed to the therapist (coach) offering advice or resources.

Action-expectation

There is an expectation by the therapist (coach) that the client will achieve positive change through their own actions.

Goals

Each conversation is structured around a clearly defined goal, which is realistic given the resources and time available to the client.

Short term

Small changes can be achieved quickly, in days or weeks and, overall, any plan does not require months or years to develop.

Personal

Each individual is different and thus each conversation, goal and plan are unique to that client and that situation.

Table 19.1 Comparing a solution-focused and problem-focused approach

Problem-focused	Solution-focused
• How can I help? • Could you tell me about the problem? • Is the problem a symptom of something deeper? • How are we to understand the problem in the light of the past? • What defence mechanisms are operating? • How many sessions will be needed?	• How will you know that the problem has been solved? • What would you like to change? • Have we clarified the central issue on which you want to concentrate? • Can we discover exceptions to the problem? • What will the future look like without the problem? • How can we use the skills and qualities of the client? • Have we achieved enough to end?

Future focus

Conversations are focused on the future, not the past or present.

Being and doing

The process is designed to change the way the client thinks, as well as acts. See Table 19.1.

Solution-focused coaching theory and research

While research into comparing different coaching practices has been limited, compared to the research in counselling, solution-focused therapy and solution-focused coaching are comparatively well researched.

One coaching study directly compared the relative effectiveness of solution-focused coaching with problem-focused coaching approaches (Grant and O'Connor, 2010). This found that both coaching approaches were effective at enhancing goal attainment. However, those in the solution-focused group had significantly greater increases in goal attainment compared with the problem-focused group. Secondly, the problem-focused group did not change the way they felt, whereas the solution-focused approach significantly increased positive effect, decreased negative effect, increased self-efficacy and generated more action steps to help the group members achieve their goals.

In a follow up 2012 study involving 74 participants, Anthony Grant compared the impact of problem-focused and solution-focused questions. He concluded that solution-focused coaching questions appeared to be more effective than problem-focused questions in this controlled study. Although he noted that in real-life coaching conversations coaches would be rarely able to solely use solution-focused questions, but instead using more solution-focused questions, on balance, appeared to be advantageous to clients.

In 2017, Grant argued that combining solution-focused and cognitive-behavioural coaching into what be labelled as SFCB coaching could enhance performance, reduce stress and help build resilience. Thus, SFCB may be the ultimate coaching approach for enhancing both performance and well-being, while also serving as a preventative mechanism that can reduce the probability of stress-related fatigue and burnout.

Finally, Grant and O'Connor (2018) added to their research around solution-focused questions, drawing on the work of positive effect (Fredrickson, 2004). The researchers randomly allocated 512 participants to compare: (1), Problem-focused coaching questions (2), Solution-focused coaching questions (3), Positive affect (4), Solution-focused plus positive affect. The broad findings of their research were that PF questions performed the worst on all measures, and that PA induction and SF coaching questions were equally effective at enhancing positive affect, increasing self-efficacy, enhancing goal approach and developing action steps. The best outcome, however, was to combine solution-focused and positive affect.

Other writers, too (Jordan and Kauffield, 2020), have compared solution-focused and problem-focused approaches. Their work using 23 coach–client dyads found that solution-focused questions were more likely to elicit solution statements and self-efficient statements from clients. Similar findings have also been found in therapy (Neipp et al., 2016).

Solution-focused coaching in practice

The research suggests that solution-focused coaching is an evidenced-based approach and, as such, it's an approach most coaches should have available within their tool kit. What does solution coaching look like? What do solution coaches do? How do they structure their sessions, and what tools and techniques do they use to help clients move towards their goals?

It may be helpful to start by thinking about the structure of a typical solution-focused session. Of course, no two sessions are identical and, in any coaching approach, I would argue that the coach needs to be led by the client's agenda. However, for the purposes of this chapter I have set out a typical pathway that a solution-focused coach might use in an "average session', if such a thing exists (see Table 19.2).

Like behavioural coaching, solution-focused coaching has a framework which can be used to guide the coach through the conversation: OSKAR (Jackson and McKergow, 2002). Like GROW, the letters provide a handrail for the coach in their solution-focused conversation, helping them stay on track. The model incorporates a number of the interventions in the structure described in Table 19.2, including goal setting, scaling, the miracle question and seeing the client as the expert.

Phases of the OSCAR model

Outcome:

- What is the objective of this coaching?
- What do you want to achieve today?
- What does success look like?

Scaling:

- On a scale of 0–10, with 0 representing the worst it has ever been and 10 the preferred future, where would you put the situation today?
- You are at N now; what did you do to get this far?
- How would you know you had got to N+1?

Table 19.2 Structure of a solution-focused session

Stage	Possible question/coach response
1. Issue	What do you want to focus on today?
2. Goal	What would you like to achieve as the outcome of this situation?
	What will you do differently in your real-life situation after having reached your goal? ... And what else?
3. Session goal	What would need to happen here in our meeting today so that you can say later that it was worth having this conversation? ... And what else?
4. Miracle question	Okay, now, just using total fantasy here ... tonight, while you sleep in bed, there was a miracle, the miracle is that the things that brought you here are solved ... just like that ... (but, since you are asleep, you do not know that the miracle has happened). How would you know that the miracle had happened, and that things are really solved? ... And what else will tell you that the miracle happened and there is now a perfect solution?
5. Consequences	How will you react to this miracle? ... What else will you be doing differently?
6. Change in perspective	Which people in your surroundings will first notice the differences in your actions? ... What will they notice? ... And how else has your perspective changed?
7. Exceptions	What examples in the recent past come to mind that have already had at least little pieces of this miracle ("perfect solution") showing up? ... And what else?
8. Resources	What did you do that contributed to the situation you described? ... And what else was helpful?
9. Scaling	Given what you have said, where do you stand on a scale from 1–10, where 10 is the morning after the miracle, and 1 is the opposite?
10. Next step	Suppose you are one step further on the scale. What would you have noticed that has resulted in moving one point up? ... And what else will you notice?
11. Change of perspective	How will others notice that you have reached the next point? ... And what else will they notice?
12. Confidence	Using a new scale (again 1–10), how confident are you that you will reach this next step? ... What is giving you hope that you will get one point higher on the scale? ... And what else?
13. Small signs	After our conversation today, what will be the first small signs that you have already started taking the next step? ... And what else?
14. Progress check	On a scale of 1–10, how useful has this conversation been for you so far?
15. Maintaining progress	What are the points that you are taking away? ... What could we do now to make things even more useful to you?
16. Accountability and support	Who could support you in putting things to action? ... How will you get them involved to act as your supporter? ... When will you do this?

Know-how and resources:

- What helps you perform at 'N' on the scale, rather than 0?
- When does the outcome happen for you?
- What did you do to make that happen? How did you do that?

Affirm and action:

- What is already going well?
- What is the next small step?
- You are at 'N' now; what would it take to get you to 'N+1'?
- What else could you do to move to 'N+1'?

Review:

- What is better?
- What did you do that made the change happen?
- What effects have the changes had?
- What do you think will change?

Tools and techniques

Solution-focused coaching is rich in tools and techniques which the coach can draw upon to help their client. In this section, we will explore half a dozen techniques including: The coaching agreement, structuring the session, oscillation, the miracle question, moving on from being stuck and seeking exceptions.

The coaching agreement

The first coaching session would probably start with a brief explanation of what coaching is, and what it is not. The coach will explain their role and clarify the collaborative relationship and that the client knows what is best in their life. This initial part of the coaching relationship is vital in setting expectations, and prevents the client looking to the coach for their advice. It also provides permission for the coach to challenge and be provocative.

The coach might say something like, "During our coaching, I will probably sometimes ask you questions that will be quite difficult or challenging. Is that OK with you?" Many professional coaches will have a printed client agreement. They may also share their code of ethics or make reference to it and outline how best to complain. Most of these aspects are common practice in most coaching relationships, although in solution-focused coaching the coach is likely to make both the 'collaborative relationship' and the 'client as expert' more explicit. The coach might then ask the client what they would like to get out of the coaching relationship and agree a goal of what the client wants to get from the individual session. Some clients can clearly describe what they want to achieve. Others turn straight to describing the problem. At this point, the coach will actively intervene to shift the conversation away from a retelling of events and the problem to focus on the desired future. This needs to be done in a way that does not alienate the client, so some degree of patience may be needed, and the coach's intervention may start with a reflection of what they have heard and some empathy about the feelings experienced before the solutions flip. The coach will continue to repeat this process through the sessions, redirecting energy from problem to solution if they are staying true to the solution approach.

Structuring the coaching session

A structured coaching session is one where there are clearly differentiated sections within a single coaching session. Each segment or part has a specific function. These may include contracting, goal setting, exploring the issue, developing alternative options and finalising a step-by-step plan. Such a detailed approach allows the conversation to be highly focused, with each part having a clear reason for its inclusion within the conversation. Experienced coaches are able to track the coaching process and know at any time which section they are in and what the next step for their client is in the journey towards an outcome. Solution-focused approaches use the OSKAR model as the route map to structure the conversation. Outcome, Scale, Know-how, Action and Review, which we have described in more detail above.

Oscillation

A typical process is for the client to start by talking about their problem. In the client's eyes, it's the problem which has brought them to coaching. In a solution-focused coaching session, the coach then seeks to flip the conversation towards a focus on solutions. However, it's not uncommon for the client to drift back to discussing the problem. This requires the coach to once again reflect back, empathise and flip the conversation to a solution mode. This can be repeated multiple times in the first session. This back and forth oscillation can become frustrating for the less experienced coach. It's important for the coach to recognise this returning to talking about the problem is normal, and that, in the clients eyes, it's why they are there: "It's usually the stone in our shoe which makes us take off our boots, not the dream of walking without pain". However, the coach needs to stay with the client, and allow some acknowledgement of the problem, to prevent the relationship being undermine, while not allowing the problem focus to dominate. It is this ability to sit with the uncertainty and ambiguity that differentiates the effective solution coach from the novice.

The miracle question

Of all the tools within the solution-focused approach, the miracle question best encapsulates the approach. The technique can be used when the client has signalled a shift from thinking about the issues, to thinking about what they can do about them. This happens when the client's oscillations back to the problem start to reduce and the client begins to engage in thinking about solutions.

If the coach asks the miracle question too early, before the client has moved away from focusing exclusively on the problem, the client may feel as if they have not been heard. This damages the relationship, and may result in slower progress later.

The coach also needs to take care when using the question. For example, in bereavement or health coaching, asking the question to a grieving person, such as someone with a relative who has been affected by cancer or someone dismissed from their job, may well elicit responses like:

> "Well, my husband would still be alive, wouldn't he?"; "The cancer would never would have happened"; "I would still have a job". This simply builds resentment rather than enables the client to move forward.

Finally, the aim is for the client to feel their answer to the miracle question, to emotionally experience it and not just to think about it. This helps to make the imagined future more real, and not just a theoretical construct. So, rather than getting someone to answer straight away, get them to step in the imagined future for a few moments and really "see and feel" the result of the miracle. Ask them to imagine the answer rather than tell you in

Table 19.3 Miracle question variations

Okay, now, just using total fantasy here … tonight, while you sleep in bed, there was a miracle, the miracle is that the things that brought you here are solved … just like that … (but, since you are asleep, you do not know that the miracle has happened). How would you know that the miracle had happened, and the things are really solved?
Suppose I could give you a prescription of a very special potion that would give you an almost supernatural power to do exactly the things you need to do in order to overcome your problem. What kind of almost supernatural power would you need to overcome your problem? And once you had that power, how would you handle the situation?
Picture in your mind two videos. One video shows the problem as it is; the other video shows how you wish things were. Describe to me the difference between the two.
Suppose I had some superhuman powers, and simply by snapping my fingers like this (*snaps fingers*), I could make your problem disappear (or I could give you the skill or ability you need). If this was possible, what would be the first opportunity for you to test if the snap works?
Suppose I meet you by chance in town next summer at a cafe. You'd be there sitting and having a coffee. I would notice that you look really happy and relaxed. I would come over to you and I would ask you how you are doing. You would say that you are doing really well; that you are happy with your life and how things were going. I would naturally become curious, and so I would ask you to give me some details about what happened over the past year. What would you tell me?

words. There are several variations of the question I have found to work well. These can be seen in Table 19.3.

It's important to recognise that the miracle question is not a single question, but the start of a chain of questions which help the client to first of all imagine a different outcome is possible. From there the coach can start to help the client make this imagined future more concrete. The coach may go on to ask questions such as:

- What will you notice around you that let you know that the miracle had happened?
- What will you see?
- What will you hear?
- What will you feel inside yourself?
- How would you be different?
- Now choose the smallest, least significant thing that you would be doing if your problem had gone, that you don't already do;
- I am going to invite you to act "as-if" your problem was gone for the rest of today and to experiment with this one small change;
- Now the next day, choose something else, some other small insignificant thing, to do as well. Add a new behaviour each day, acting as if a miracle had happened.

Using the miracle question is a wonderful way to bypass the usual worries about *how* things could change, the details of which can be tackled later. Instead, the miracle question switches to a motivational focus on *what* the client really wants to see change.

When stuck

Occasionally the coach reaches a dead-end with a client. They are unsure where to go next. There are have several questions which can help to restart the conversation, helping the coach reverse out of the dead-end road:

"Tell me more about this?" – The client feels as if what they have said is of interest and the question encourages the client to talk more about the topic. The word of caution is to avoid using this question when the client has been talking about a problem.

"What would be the most useful question I could ask you right now?" – This question can be really helpful in building the non-expert collaborative spirit of the relationship. It assumes that the client knows best, including what questions are best used to further explore their situation.

The aim with these questions is to get the client speaking, and if possible to get them speaking about solutions or their desired outcomes.

Seeking exceptions

The final technique we explore is seeking exceptions. In this approach the coach askes the client when the situation or problem does not occur. For example in 'public seaking', when do you not have a problem speaking in public. The client for example might identify that they don't have a problem when speaking to friends and family, for example at a pub, or at family gatherings at Christmas. The coach can then explore what they can draw from these successful public communications to apply to the problem situation.

When does solution-focused coaching work best?

Solution-focused coaching can, in some ways, be seen as a coaching approach for all seasons. It is highly consistent with the principles of coaching as a collaborative relationship, where the client is the expert in their life. This requests a specific coaching mindset, where the coach can step away from offering solutions or needing to act as the expert. It also requires the coach to manage the process, helping develop a mindset within the client which is more directed towards the solution than focusing on a problem. As we noted earlier, there may be some times of highly emotionally charged presenting issues, where a person-centred approach may be better suited, or where the issue is one of trauma or a mental health condition where other interventions may be preferable.

Unlike with the behavioural approach, the solution-focused coach needs to work at multiple levels with their client. The coach uses the full range of basic communication skills of questioning, reflection, paraphrasing and summarising to help raise the client's awareness of the facts of the issue and, in doing so, help them imagine and then plan possible solutions.

By working with the client's thoughts and emotions, the coach is able to amplify the client's motivation. This aspect of the coaching conversation is rarely discussed in the solution-focused literature, but has been explored within motivational interviewing, which has many similarities with solution-focused coaching, including a need to consider the client's changing language or talk and the desire to develop intrinsic motivation.

Finally, for the approach to be effective the coach needs a sophisticated set of process skills, effectively structuring the individual coaching sessions, helping the client to design action plans and take positive first steps towards their new imagined solution.

Ten useful questions for the solution-focused coach

In this section I will offer ten themes and a handful of questions that could be asked under this theme. See Table 19.4.

Table 19.4 Ten solution-focused questions

Theme	Useful questions
1. Set goals	If coaching were to prove really worthwhile for you, what would be happening that is not happening at present?
2. Problem deconstruction	Tell me exactly what happens first?
3. Seek competence	What is happening at the moment that makes you hopeful you can change the situation?
4. Refocusing	Let's just stop you there, rather than focus on the problem, what could you do to start making the situation better?
5. Seek exceptions	When don't you have this problem?
6. Scaling	On a scale of 1–10, where are you now?
7. Positive Action	What would need to change to move from where you are now to a higher number
8. Miracle question	Suppose … tonight, while you sleep in bed, there was a miracle, the miracle is that the things that brought you here are solved … just like that … (but, since you are asleep, you do not know that the miracle has happened). How would you know that the miracle had happened, and the things are really solved? … And what else will tell you that the miracle had happened and there is now a perfect solution?
9. Circular questions	What does he/she do? How do you react?
10. Accountability	Who could support you in putting things into action?

Conclusion

In this chapter we have explored the solution-focused approach. We have suggested that the solution-focused approach is highly compatible with coaching, as a forward-focused, goal-orientated collaborative process, which sees clients as the experts in their own lives. Given the research evidence, the solution-focused coach is well placed to enable their clients to make efficient progress towards improvements in their lives and do so in the knowledge that the steps they are taking reflect their own values and priorities.

References

de Shazer, S. (1988). *Clues: Investigating Solutions in Brief Therapy*. New York: W.W. Norton & Co.

Fredrickson, B.L. (2004). 'The broaden-and-build theory of positive emotions'. *Philosophical Transactions of the Royal Society of London. Series B: Biological Sciences*, 359(1449), pp. 1367–1377.

Grant, A.M. (2012). 'Making positive change: A randomized study comparing solution-focused vs. problem-focused coaching questions'. *Journal of Systemic Therapies*, 31(2), pp. 21–35. doi: 10.1521/jsyt.2012.31.2.21.

Grant, A.M. (2017). 'Solution-focused cognitive-behavioral coaching for sustainable high performance and circumventing stress, fatigue, and burnout'. *Consulting Psychology Journal Practice and Research*, 69(2), pp. 98–111.

Grant, A.M. and O'Connor, S.A. (2010). 'The differential effects of solution-focused and problem-focused coaching questions: A pilot study with implications for practice'. *Industrial and Commercial Training*, 42(2), pp. 102–111.

Grant, A.M. and O'Connor, S.A. (2018). 'Broadening and building solution-focused coaching: Feeling good is not enough'. *Coaching: An International Journal of Theory, Research and Practice*, 11(2), pp. 165–185. doi: 10.1080/17521882.2018.1489868.

Greene, J. and Grant, A.M. (2003). *Solution focused coaching*. Harlow: Pearson.

Iveson, C., George, E. and Ratner, H. (2012). *Brief coaching: A solution focused approach*. Hove: Routledge.

Jackson, P.Z. and McKergow, M. (2002). *The solution focus: Making coaching and change simply*. London: Nicholas Brealey.

Jordan, S. and Kauffeld, S. (2020). 'A mixed methods study of effects and antecedents of solution-focused questions in coaching'. *International Journal of Evidenced based Coaching and Mentoring*, 18(1), pp. 57–72. doi: 10.24384/w8ne-fx80.

Neipp, M.C., Beyebach, M., Nuñez, R.M. and Martínez-González, M.C. (2016). 'The effect of solution-focused versus problem-focused questions: A replication'. *Journal of Marital and Family Therapy*, 42(3), pp. 525–535. doi: 10.1111/jmft.12140.

O'Connell, B. (1998). *Solution focused therapy*. London: Sage.

20 Cognitive-behavioural coaching

Rob Willson

Introduction

If cognitive-behavioural coaching (CBC) is a branch of the cognitive-behavioural tradition, it benefits from being a branch of a very large, well-established tree, deeply rooted in empirical research. CBC is a focused, problem-solving, goal-directed approach. It aims to help clients to live and work more productively and achieve greater psychological and emotional well-being though change in thinking, mental activity and behaviour.

The CBC coaching relationship is collaborative and "empirical" – finding out how things work; especially how the client's mind and relationships work. The style is warm, understanding and pragmatic. Alongside their goals for coaching, the CBC coach is interested in getting to know the client as an individual, their strengths and what they want to be, in addition to finding out about the areas of their lives that are important to them.

The figures most strongly associated with the development of the cognitive-behavioural approach are Albert Ellis (1962) and Aaron Beck (1976). However, the approach (including Ellis and Beck) has been strongly influenced by behaviour therapy (e.g. Wolpe, 1958; Lang, 1963) and has philosophical roots in ancient Greek Stoicism. Since its initial development, the cognitive-behavioural approach has been extensively evaluated and developed (Beck and Haigh, 2014).

The cognitive-behavioural approach explained

Beck's version of CBT, cognitive therapy (CT), has been characterised as being "scientific" in its approach, compared to Ellis' rational emotive behaviour therapy (REBT) being more "philosophical" (Padesky and Beck, 2003). While these distinctions are overly simplistic, there is some truth in them: CT emphasises treating thoughts as hypotheses to be "tested out"; REBT has greater emphasis on people practising helpful attitudes of flexible preferences, high frustration tolerance and self-acceptance. In practice, the significant majority of practitioners are less concerned with a particular theory and more with the efficacy of CB strategies. To many, Beck's oft-given definition of CBT will appeal: "Anything that helps move the person from problem to goal!".

CBC is rightly associated with identifying, challenging and generating alternative thoughts, attitudes and beliefs. However, the term "cognition" encompasses a much wider range of mental events and activities. In recent years, many clinicians and researchers have included working with attention (e.g. Wells, 2011), worry (e.g. Papageorgiou and Wells, 2000), rumination (e.g. Watkins, 2018) and imagery (e.g. Holmes, Arntz and Smucker, 2007).

At the heart of CBC is building a working hypothesis of the maintenance of a client's difficulty, often referred to as a "formulation". A formulation can be very simple, such as sharing a theoretically underpinned hunch that "your avoidance of public speaking might be maintaining your fear of it, does that sound plausible?" Alternatively, a cognitive-behavioural formulation could be complex, including childhood experiences, core beliefs, assumptions, automatic thoughts and a range of avoidance and compensatory strategies. A good rule of thumb is to keep a formulation as simple as possible while keeping enough information to help the client feel understood, and for the formulation to be a good working theory of how the problem is maintained.

Two famous versions of cognitive-behavioural formulation are the "ABC" model (Ellis, 1962) and the "hot cross bun" model (Greenberger and Padesky, 1995). I shall look at both briefly. The main difference is the way that information is organised, and there is a greater emphasis placed upon thoughts and beliefs in the ABC model. It's my experience that the ABC model provides a strong framework to help keep meaning at the heart of CBC, whereas the hot cross bun model is more flexible and can be more accessible to people new to CBC.

The "ABC" model

ABC (with added D and E!) is potentially an entire coaching process, outlined below:

A. – **Activating event**. This is what the client feels their unhelpful emotion about. The "event" might be past, present or future. It might be "external", such as another person's action, or "internal", such as a bodily sensation;
B. – **Beliefs**. These are the unhelpful thoughts and beliefs that went through the client's mind at the time of feeling their unhelpful emotion about "A";
C. – **Consequences**. In CBC, these are emotional and behavioural results of "Beliefs" about "A". Given that CBC principally aims to help people change emotion and behaviour, "C" is often the best place to start;
D. – **Disputing**. The coach helps the client to step back and consider how helpful, logical and realistic their beliefs and thoughts at "B" are. To help keep things rooted in the pragmatic, the coach helps the client consider whether their thoughts and beliefs are conducive to achieving their goal. As the coach helps the client dispute their unhelpful thoughts, they help them to consider more helpful alternatives;
E. – **Effect**. The coach helps the client consider the emotional and behavioural effect of their new thinking derived from "D". Refer back to "C" and assess whether the new perspective changes (or would change, if the situation arose again) their emotions or behaviour. This may lead to a behavioural experiment or plan on how the client might act "as if" they believed their more helpful alternative, and thus strengthen their belief.

The hot cross bun model

The hot cross bun model illustrates how our cognitive processes (including, but not limited to, our thoughts and beliefs), emotional feelings (e.g. stress, anxiety, anger, low mood), behaviours (such as avoidance or over-working) and physiology (e.g. increased heart rate) all interact. Behaviours can include mental acts such as the excessive reviewing of a performance situation in one's mind. In CBC, all of these areas are potential targets for change.

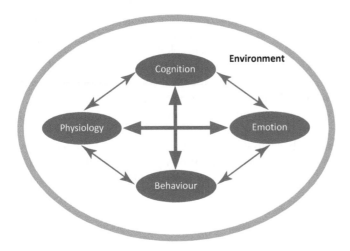

Figure 20.1 Click here to enter text.

Because each dimension will affect the others, it can give several potential points of intervention. See Figure 20.1.

As the model above shows, our thinking is driven by our emotions and vice-versa. This can be a vicious cycle of negative feelings maintaining negative thoughts, and negative thoughts maintaining negative feelings. Compounding the problem is the way that our behaviour (e.g. avoidance or safety-seeking behaviours) can prevent our thoughts from being disconfirmed. For example, someone who fears falling apart while engaged in public speaking might avoid giving presentations and never have their catastrophic thought that they will make a fool of themselves disproved. Furthermore, changes in behaviour may impact mood (e.g. rushing around from one meeting to the next boosts stress) or our physiology (e.g. eating junk food for lunch lowers mood and reduces energy).

Cognitive-behavioural coaching theory and research

Where it comes to research, CBC has a distinct advantage over other approaches; CBT is the most extensively researched model of psychotherapy by a considerable margin (Bennett-Levy et al., 2004). CBT dominates evidence-based practice in the psychological treatment of mental health problems because of the large amount of high-quality research supporting its efficacy. This gives a strong evidence-base from which CBC can draw.

Partly because it's a younger profession, by comparison the number of studies conducted on CBC seems small, but there is a growing body of research supporting the efficacy of CBC. Space here allows only for a few examples; for a more extensive review of the research and a discussion on CBC, see Palmer and Williams (2013).

There is evidence that CBC helps reduce stress: Gardiner, Kearns and Tiggemann (2013) found that CBC reduced GP stress levels and lowered their desire to escape from rural general practice; in a recent study, Ogba et al. (2019) evaluated the effectiveness of a 12-week 90-minute group CBC (SPACE) programme in a sample of 65 Nigerian school administrators. They found a significant decrease in their perceived stress and stress symptoms compared to wait-list controls.

There is also evidence that CBC helps improve well-being: In a randomised controlled trial, Grant, Curtayne and Burton (2009) found that executive coaching enhances goal attainment, resilience and workplace well-being; Green, Oades and Grant (2006) found that cognitive-behavioural, solution-focused life coaching enhanced goal striving, well-being and hope.

Additionally, there is a small body of evidence that CBC improves management skills. For example, in a pre-post test study of a CBC program for 23 mid-level managers, Ratiu David and Baban (2016) found an increase in coaching skills, assertive communication skills and motivation of subordinates.

What appears to still be needed in CBC is some large-scale, multi-centred, randomised controlled trials. The ultimate hope would be that these could then be subjected to systematic review or meta-analysis and substantially strengthen the empirical support.

Specific CBT treatment protocols for numerous mental and physical health conditions have been developed and tested (see Clark and Fairburn, 1997 for reviews of some of these). To an extent, this has widened the gap between CBT and CBC. The specific protocol for OCD or panic disorder, for example, does not have an obvious place in coaching. However, in more recent years the field has been moving towards identifying "transdiagnostic processes" in CBT; the psychological mechanisms that are important in the maintenance of a wide range of clinical problems. Such processes include:

- Cognitive biases, such as black-or-white thinking and personalising;
- Intolerance of uncertainty;
- Ruminating – literally meaning repeatedly "chewing things over" in our minds. Often meaning we "dwell" on past events or on the way we feel emotionally;
- Worrying – also a form of repetitive over-thinking but future-focused and often seems like an to attempt plan and prepare for possible difficulties;
- Mental reviewing of social interaction;
- Attentional bias towards threat (vigilance);
- Self-focused attention;
- Avoidance and safety-seeking behaviours.

(Frank and Davidson, 2014)

Importantly, transdiagnostic research supports the assertion that coaches should be at least as interested in the style of their clients' thinking as the content of their thoughts. Arguably, these processes occur across a wide range of clinical problems and can give coaches confidence that they are likely to be relevant in CBC. Evaluating the benefit of helping clients modify factors such as mental-reviewing, ruminating and where they focus their attention has the potential to be a fruitful area of future research.

Cognitive-behavioural coaching in practice

The ultimate aim of CBC is for the client to become their own cognitive-behavioural coach. This is not limited to learning a few "coping strategies" but instead involves helping the client develop a good understanding of how their mind works and how to work it more effectively.

CBC approaches coaching in a particular "spirit" known as "collaborative empiricism". This means that the coach and client team up together with a scientific approach to the world. The atmosphere the coach aims to create is one of enquiry as to how the world works. It's important to note that this is at least as much testing out whether a particular strategy is helpful as divining truth or facts. For example, in performance anxiety, it's not possible to know for sure the thoughts in someone else's mind, but a client can discover the effect of self-focused versus externally-focused attention.

Below is a list of some of the more common areas to which CBC is applied.

- Low mood and related low motivation;
- Stress and fatigue;
- Anxiety;
- Perfectionism;
- Lack of confidence;
- Interpersonal disputes/conflict;
- Risk-taking and decisiveness.;
- Procrastination;
- Stress management;
- Performance anxiety;
- Anger and aggression (including passive-aggression);
- Excessive worry about work and other life responsibilities;
- Building resilience;
- Problem-solving;
- Building persistence;
- Effective communication and assertion;
- Time management.

The following are some key steps to include in a CBC session.

1. **Defining problems and goals**

   To help keep coaching focused and heading in the right direction, clients are helped to define their problems and goals at the outset.

   To help frame the problem in a manner that makes it more accessible to CBC, the client should define the problem in terms of:
   - Feelings/emotions;
   - A situation or theme that triggered your emotion;
   - The way you tend to act in the situation when you feel your problem emotion.

   The coach can help the client define their goals. One model to do this is SPORT, a variation on SMART goals:
   - **S**pecific about where, when and/or with whom you want to feel or behave differently;
   - **P**ositive: Encouraging yourself to develop more, rather than less, of something. For example, you may want to gain more confidence (rather than become less anxious) or to hone a skill (rather than make fewer mistakes);
   - Ideally containing an **o**bservable description of a behavioural change that you can define. Despite the importance placed on changes in thought, attitude or meaning in CBC, these are best seen as a mechanism of change, not a goal in themselves;
   - **R**ealistic and achievable;
   - **T**ime-limited.

2. **Choose a problem to work on**

    If a client lists more than one problem, the coach can ask them to choose which problem they would like to work on first.

3. **Work with a specific example of the problem**

    Invite the client to describe a recent representative example of the problem. This provides an opportunity to collaborate on starting to deconstruct and identify key elements.

4. **Develop a formulation**

    As the client describes the problem, help them to fill out the emotion, cognition, behaviour and physical sections of the cognitive-behavioural model. Some of the key questions described below will help to do this. Invite the client to step back and look at the diagram. Ask "What do you make of this?" since helping to elicit their impression of the formulation may lead to productive discussion of their understanding of the problem and opportunities for change. Probe further on their view on how these different sections influence each other. Ask "What do you think is the effect of ... (one aspect on another)?"; e.g. "What do you think is the effect of feeling anxious on how strongly you believe people are judging you negatively?"

    When clients step back and look at the problem formulation for the first time, it's striking how many individuals will say something like: "I hadn't realised there was so much going on, it makes sense now why it hasn't been easy to just stop feeling this way".

5. **Identify targets for change and their alternatives**

    Next, agree upon a target for change from the formulation. This might be a thought (such as an unhelpful self-criticism), physical action (such as avoiding a difficult conversation with a colleague), mental act (such as mentally reviewing a meeting or comparing oneself or one's circumstances to others), an attention bias (such as becoming self-focused in a meeting) or a physical issue (such as a poor sleep pattern). It's not unusual for clients to quickly spot an unhelpful thought or behaviour and to spontaneously generate some ideas for change. If this happens, don't overwork the problem and move on to the next step. Ask "Where do you think we should start to help move from your problem to your goal?" (it's usually a good idea to re-state both of these).

    If the client is less sure where to start, work through the cognition and behaviour sections in more detail to help them consider how helpful certain thoughts or behaviours are and whether there might be more helpful ways of thinking or behaving. The tools, techniques and questions sections below offer further insights.

6. **Agree out-of-session practice (homework)**

    Completion of homework assignments can make a very significant difference to outcome (Burns and Spangler, 2000). It can be helpful to characterise the sessions as a being rather like seeing a physiotherapist or tennis coach – with practice outside the session being key to success. It might be reading some relevant material, filling out a thought record, or a behavioural experiment or other behaviour change.

    Naturally, the assignment needs to flow logically from the work the coach has done so far, and it's important for the coach to check with the client about what is being agreed to and whether the client sees sense in the task.

Tools and techniques

The cognitive-behavioural tradition is well known for its plethora of tools and techniques. Here I've introduced some of the more core, practical tried-and-tested strategies.

Psychoeducation

Psychoeducation has always been a key part of the cognitive-behavioural approach. In the first instance, the coach "socialises" the client into the CBC model, and very often this is most elegantly done by using the model as a structure to help understand the client's problem better. The coach can also use a story or metaphor to illustrate a key point. There are also numerous cognitive-behavioural self-help texts that a CBC coach can recommend to their client to help them understand a problem, or the principles of managing it better.

Socratic questioning

Socratic questioning is used to facilitate "guided discovery" and help the client uncover their unhelpful thoughts and beliefs. It is also used to help them reflect, consider their thought, generate alternatives and build strength of belief in them. The aim is to stimulate and support the client to work things out for themselves rather than tell them. However, it's important that we ask questions that the client can answer, and not leave them feeling interrogated or at a loss as to what it is that we are looking for. There are very definitely times when a short didactic explanation is more helpful. Below are some examples of Socratic questions:

To help a client elicit their thoughts, images and behaviour:

What's going through (or went through) your mind?
Did you see anything in your mind's eye?
What did X mean to you?
What did you do when X happened?

When helping the client re-consider an unhelpful thought:

What's the effect of thinking this way?
What's the evidence for …?
Could there be any alternatives (e.g. ways of interpreting an experience)?
What are the costs and benefits of this (thought or assumption)? How does that compare
     to the alternative?
How might someone else view the situation?

When considering evidence that may help disconfirm an unhelpful thought:

How does this fit with …?
How do you put _____ (thought) together with _____ (evidence)?
Now you have stepped back and looked at the situation, what do you make of your original conclusion?

Table 20.1 Functional analysis

Behaviour	Intended Consequence	Unintended Consequence	Alternative to try out
Avoidance of making a presentation.	I avoid the risk of making a fool of myself.	I never build my confidence or test my fears.	Volunteer for several presentations over the next few months.
Avoid giving critical feedback at appraisal.	I don't risk upsetting my colleague and creating bad feeling.	Problems are not dealt with and frustrations can build	Be direct while trying to remain warm.
"Taking control" at meetings.	I make sure we focus on what's important.	I end up feeling too responsible. No voice for others.	Deliberately sit back and use questions to prompt if needed.
Trying to do things perfectly.	Avoiding being criticised.	At *lot* of extra stress and finding myself distanced from my colleagues.	Focus more on being practical and expedient. Use time to connect.
Criticising a colleague's professionalism.	To show how competent I am.	I probably look insecure and do not show my best side.	Take pleasure in my own work. Highlight the strengths in others.

To move on to implementing change:

How could we find out more?
What do you think would happen if (you changed X behaviour)?
How could we put this (thought, theory, assumption) to the test?
How might you practise thinking or acting to help build on this?

Functional Analysis

Functional analysis has its roots in behaviour therapy but is part of contemporary CBC, focusing more on modifying the style of psychological response more than content. This is a highly flexible technique that can be used to help see beyond the intention of their strategy, through to the unintended consequence. I've provided simple illustrations of behaviours at work here, but it can also be used for mental acts like self-criticism, mental-reviewing of a performance, ruminating and self-focused attention. See Table 20.1.

Identifying "thinking errors"

Also referred to in the literature as "cognitive distortions"; various ways in which human beings are prone to bias in processing information. Thinking errors are explained in detail in numerous texts on CBT and CBC (e.g. Branch and Willson, 2019) and, for reasons of space, I will not go into great detail here.

Common thinking errors include:

- All-or-nothing thinking;
- Personalising;
- Catastrophising;

- Mind-reading;
- Making rigid demands (musts and shoulds);
- Labelling (oneself or others) e.g. as useless, worthless or a failure;
- Mental filtering and disqualifying the positive (focusing upon the negative and discounting the positive);
- Overgeneralising.

Giving clients a list of common thinking errors can help them step back, reconsider their interpretation or attitude or perhaps be more able to detach from their unhelpful thoughts.

Behavioural experiments

Actions speak louder than words, and few things have more impact on our thinking than a change in behaviour. Behavioural experiments are a core technique in CBC and can be used in several ways, such as:

- To test the validity of a thought or belief, to test the validity of an alternative thought or belief or to compare and contrast the two;
- To gain information on what happens following a change in behaviour;
- To discover the effect (increasing or decreasing) mental or behavioural activities have on emotional or physical response. A particularly important experiment is to help clients discover that their anxiety will subside of its own accord if they tolerate it rather than seek to avoid or control it.

The coach can take the client through the following steps to devise a behavioural experiment:

1. **Identify a target for experiment**
   Identify a problematic thought, belief, behaviour or mental activity that the coach and client think might be important to change or learn more about.
2. **Formulate a prediction or theory to be tested**
   Help the client formulate a specific theory or prediction that they can put to the test. Elicit what they think will happen if they try out a new way of behaving in real life. You can ask for a rating of the degree to which they believe a prediction will come true on a percentage between 0 and 100.
3. **Brainstorm some ideas on an experiment**
   Help the client to think of ways of putting a new belief or behaviour to the test in a real-life situation. Try to devise more than one way to experiment.
4. **Agree an experiment**
   The coach and client agree together on the experiment the client is going to try out. The coach should explore potential obstacles that might arise and how they might be overcome.
5. **Ask the client to carry out the experiment and to record exactly what they did, and what happened as a result**
   This will provide important information to discuss, usually at the next session. It's important to learn from the client what exactly they did as it's not unusual for people to modify (or avoid) the experiment in some way. Whatever happens, it's all good data and there's something to be learned.

6. **Consider the results of the experiment**

Invite the client to see whether their prediction came true. If it didn't, check out what they have learned from the results of the experiment. The coach could also share their perspective, with the agreement of the client, as to their own predictions. In light of the results of the experiment, the coach could invite the client to re-rate their conviction in the original prediction(s).

Attention training and switching the focus of attention

If an attention bias is identified as part of the formulation, or the person has a tendency to worry or ruminate, an attention intervention can be helpful. Working with attention is a natural fit for coaching as it has significant implications on how effectively we run our minds. Attentional focus is an important topic in sports psychology, and attention is hugely important in the way we think, feel, focus our minds and process information.

Self-focused attention (such as upon how we feel we look or sound) can be especially important in performance or social situations. It can overload our minds and make it harder to think or recall information. The resulting self-consciousness can also mean that we are far more likely to infer that others are thinking critically. When we ruminate, worry, or mentally review (over-think), our attention has moved from the present, external world. It can be helpful ask clients how helpful and productive these strategies are, including perhaps carrying out a functional analysis (above) or a cost-benefit analysis, so they are more inclined to work on changing them.

Clients can learn to "switch" their attention into the environment away from themselves (or out of their heads when over-thinking), or away from a particular threat, within a situation such as a meeting or presentation. To help with this and improve control over attention, we might teach specific attention training techniques such as deliberate daily ten-minute walks practising paying attention to the outside world. Clients who are familiar with mindfulness practice will often understand that the focus of their awareness (or attention) is something that can be deliberately and helpfully influenced.

When does cognitive-behavioural coaching work best?

Cognitive-behavioural coaching (CBC) is a problem-solving approach to coaching. Because of its roots in psychological therapy, CBC is often helpful when the client has a psychological problem. This might be an emotional response that is distressing or one that interferes in performance. Often the impact of an emotional problem can be through the strategies the person uses to avoid having an emotional response activated. For example, an individual might procrastinate on a task to try and avoid the uncomfortable feelings of anxiety that it triggers. So, in the area of common psychological problems such as stress, low mood, anger, low self-esteem, performance anxiety and the many behavioural problems associated with these issues, CBC is a logical and evidence-supported choice.

CBC is also a good fit when the client prefers a practical and problem-solving approach to difficulties. It also works well when the client is psychologically minded and is willing to experience a degree of discomfort to achieve growth. My experience is that people tend to hold fairly rigid ideas about the nature of personal development (including, bafflingly, some CBT therapist colleagues who seem to seek far less well-proven interventions for their own difficulties). So if a person believes that a "deep" psychodynamic or exclusively mindful path is the only route to psychological health, they may (of course) be less receptive to CBC. Individuals who hold their environment (such as a difficult boss or subordinate) wholly to blame for their distress can also at times be less receptive to the highly "internally" focused nature of CBC. As is shown in the CB model, CBC does give space to incorporate environmental contributions. In such situations, it can be important to offer extra time for the client to feel understood and have their feelings validated. The coach can emphasise optimising the person's coping through establishing the most helpful cognitive-behavioural response.

Ten useful questions for cognitive-behavioural coaches

1. *What's the problem you'd like to work on?*
   CBC is a pragmatic, problem-solving approach. Like any problem-solving technique, it's only as effective as the definition of the problem.
2. *How would you like to be different?*
   This is a question designed to elicit a goal, and the CBC coach will guide their client help them focus upon goals that within their influence. It can be helpful to anchor goals in a change of behaviour as this is more observable and measurable than thoughts and emotions.
3. *What went through your mind?*
   Notice here that the question is not "what thoughts went through your mind". This is because we are also interested in images, which can carry a considerable amount of meaning. This is because these also influence the way the individual processes an experience and hence their emotional and behavioural reaction.
4. *What (specifically) did you do?*
   Understanding how a person behaved is critical for both the coach and the client to make sense of a given problem. A contemporary CBC coach will pay as much attention to their client's mental activity as to their overt physical behaviour.
5. *Where did you focus your attention?*
   As noted above, there is a growing understanding of the role of attention in psychological problems. The client becoming more aware of the focus of their attention, and gaining more control over it, brings out an often-neglected opportunity for improved emotional health.
6. *What's the effect?*
   As we've seen above, the cognitive-behavioural coach may draw attention to the function of an individual's mental or behavioural strategy. They will help the client see beyond their intended consequence of a given behaviour through to any unintended result. This can be especially important in helping the client to choose to change since they are more able to see the sense in doing so.
7. *What's the evidence?*
   A key question for helping people to step back and evaluate the evidence for and against their thoughts and beliefs. It is also helpful for the client to consider the evidence that might support a more helpful thought, belief or theory. Part of the aim in CBC is to help clients weaken their strength of belief (SOB) in an unhelpful thought and strengthen it on their more helpful alternative.
8. *What's an alternative?*
   Understanding that a particular thought or belief is irrational or a behaviour is unhelpful is, of course, only the start. For coaching to help the client grow and develop and to have something new and more helpful to practise in the real-world, generating alternatives is essential.

9. *How could we find out more?*

A cornerstone of the cognitive-behavioural method is agreeing on a homework assignment for the client to carry on outside of the session. This might be a behavioural experiment to test out a prediction or to see how a change in approach works out.

10. *What do you think is it going to be like, if you try it out?*

It can be tempting for both coach and client to get a bit carried away and agree a change or homework that sounds good in session, but may be more difficult to carry out in the real world. The coach can help the client think through the agreed exercise, a check that it is realistic and that they are better prepared for any discomfort they are likely to experience.

Conclusion

CBC is a highly practical, active, here-and-now focused approach. It has considerable potential to help people achieve greater emotional health, improved well-being and to overcome mental and behavioural blocks to improved performance. CBC benefits greatly from its origin and ongoing relationship to CBT both in terms of research findings and the development of techniques.

25% of the population (in any context) will be suffering from a mental health problem. Furthermore, some individuals will seek coaching for an emotional problem rather than counselling or therapy due to the stigma, shame or preconception. Problems like low mood and excessive worry are going to be common in any workplace and CBC offers the skills to help manage these challenges. In what are increasingly uncertain times, an approach that promotes tolerance of doubt and guards against excessive worry would seem to have a particular value.

References

Beck, A.T. (1976). *Cognitive therapy and the emotional disorders*. New York: International Universities Press.

Beck, A.T. and Haigh, E.A. (2014). 'Advances in cognitive theory and therapy: The generic cognitive model'. *Annual Review of Clinical Psychology*, 10, pp. 1–24.

Bennett-Levy, J.E., Butler, G.E., Fennell, M.E., Hackman, A.E., Mueller, M.E. and Westbrook, D.E. (2004). *Oxford guide to behavioural experiments in cognitive therapy*. Oxford: Oxford University Press.

Branch, R. and Willson, R. (2019). *Cognitive behavioural therapy for dummies*. London: John Wiley & Sons.

Burns, D.D. and Spangler, D.L. (2000). 'Does psychotherapy homework lead to improvements in depression in cognitive–behavioral therapy or does improvement lead to increased homework compliance?' *Journal of Consulting and Clinical Psychology*, 68(1), pp. 46–56.

Clark, D.M., and Fairburn, C.G., eds. (1997). *Science and practice of cognitive behaviour therapy*. Oxford: Oxford University Press.

Ellis, A. (1962). *Reason and emotion in psychotherapy*. Secaucus: Citadel.

Frank, R.I. and Davidson, J. (2014). *The transdiagnostic road map to case formulation and treatment planning: Practical guidance for clinical decision making*. Oakland: New Harbinger Publications.

Gardiner, M., Kearns, H. and Tiggemann, M. (2013). 'Effectiveness of cognitive behavioural coaching in improving the well-being and retention of rural general practitioners'. *Australian Journal of Rural Health*, 21(3), pp. 183–189.

Grant, A.M., Curtayne, L. and Burton, G. (2009). 'Executive coaching enhances goal attainment, resilience and workplace well-being: A randomised controlled study'. *The Journal of Positive Psychology*, 4(5), pp. 396–407.

Green, L.S., Oades, L.G. and Grant, A.M. (2006). 'Cognitive-behavioral, solution-focused life coaching: Enhancing goal striving, well-being, and hope'. *The Journal of Positive Psychology*, 1(3), pp. 142–149.

Greenberger, D. and Padesky, C.A. (1995). *Mind over mood: Change how you feel by changing the way you think*. New York: Guilford Publications.

Holmes, E.A., Arntz, A. and Smucker, M.R. (2007). 'Imagery rescripting in cognitive behaviour therapy: Images, treatment techniques and outcomes'. *Journal of Behavior Therapy and Experimental Psychiatry*, 38(4), pp. 297–305.

Lang, P.J. and Lazovik, A.D. (1963). 'Experimental desensitization of phobia'. *The Journal of Abnormal and Social Psychology*, 66(6), pp. 519.

Ogba, F.N., Onyishi, C.N., Ede, M.O., Ugwuanyi, C., Nwokeoma, B.N., Victor-Aigbodion, V., … Ossai, O.V. (2019). 'Effectiveness of SPACE model of cognitive behavioral coaching in management of occupational stress in a sample of school administrators in South-East Nigeria'. *Journal of Rational-Emotive & Cognitive-Behavior Therapy*, 1–24.

Padesky, C.A. and Beck, A.T. (2003). 'Science and philosophy: Comparison of cognitive therapy and rational emotive behavior therapy'. *Journal of Cognitive Psychotherapy*, 17(3), pp. 211–224.

Palmer, S., and Williams, H. (2013). 'Cognitive behavioural coaching'. In J. Passmore, D.B. Peterson and T. Freire, eds., *The Wiley Blackwell handbook of the psychology of coaching and mentoring*. Chichester: Wiley-Blackwell, pp. 327–330.

Papageorgiou, C. and Wells, A. (2000). 'Treatment of recurrent major depression with attention training'. *Cognitive and Behavioral Practice*, 7(4), pp. 407–413.

Ratiu, L., David, O.A. and Baban, A. (2016). 'Developing managerial skills through coaching: Efficacy of a cognitive-behavioral coaching program'. *Journal of Rational-Emotive & Cognitive-Behavior Therapy*, 34(4), pp. 244–266.

Watkins, E.R. (2018). *Rumination-focused cognitive-behavioral therapy for depression*. New York: Guilford Publications.

Wolpe, J. (1958). *Psychotherapy by reciprocal inhibition*. Stanford: Stanford University Press.

21 Gestalt coaching

Ann James

Introduction

"If you cn raed and udnrtsand this setnence, you are expreincnig Gestalt at wrok". In short, Gestalt focuses on how humans look for patterns, how they see the whole, when presented with fragments. For coaches, Gestalt offers a set of principles which can be applied in their work that, while different to many other coaching approaches, can help clients to develop new insights about themselves and their situations. In this chapter we will review the Gestalt approach, consider the evidence and how it can be applied, before reviewing tools, techniques and questions which coaches can use in their practice.

Gestalt coaching explained

Gestalt emerged from field of psychology in the early 20th century through the work of Max Wertheimer (1880–1943), Wolfgang Kohler (1887–1967) and Kurt Koffka (1886–1941).

Their approach was developed further from the 1920s by Fritz Perls for application in the therapeutic domain. Perls, along with his wife, Laura Perls, went on to challenge the more established behavioural and psychoanalytical approaches to therapy, which Perls regarded as adopting a narrower view of human development.

Over three decades, Perls continued to advocate for the intrinsic value of Gestalt principles in therapy. Today, these continue to resonate in the context of coaching. See Table 21.1.

Working as a coach with Gestalt demands recognition and acceptance of the fact that we are all, at all times, living each moment in the context of changing circumstances. Our capacity to thrive and remain safe depends on our ability to adjust and adapt in the face of this ever-changing present and ever-present change.

Much of the time it is helpful to us – even necessary for our safety – that our brain has the capacity to simply get on and make meaning of the multiple sources of data, information and experience available to us. It's what allows us to make sense of the world.

Bringing that to coaching, it follows that the "meaning" we make of a perceived whole is limited to, and by, the scope of our awareness. We cannot be aware of everything, all of the time.

The Gestalt coach works in the here and now, encouraging the client to pay attention to a broad field of data and information by engaging holistically with the senses, noticing what emerges, then experimenting with new ideas and adopting different perspectives to generate insight, choice and possibilities.

Table 21.1 Gestalt principles

- Each of us has the capacity to grow in the face of constant change; we can adapt and learn, provided we foster awareness and remain attuned to our needs;
- We are equipped to make the best decisions we can for ourselves; we are informed by our unique experience of our reality, its perceived opportunities and constraints;
- Awareness is everything; our capacity to adapt and grow is determined by the extent to which we are attuned to our circumstances or "reality";
- "Unfinished business" or unresolved events create obstacles to growth; engaging with these afresh in the moment can mobilise motivation, hope and energy;
- Being present with "what is" frees us up from the illusion of what we think "should be"; it allows us to engage with what is real, now, through all our senses;
- This embodied felt experience gives access to an array of information and inherent wisdom.

Gestalt coaching theory and research

Drawing upon the principles of Existential philosophy, Gestalt requires us to adopt an open, holistic way of being, a receptiveness to what *is* rather than an inclination to analyse. It calls upon us to connect with and pay close attention to our senses, physiological responses and spontaneous thoughts and emotions. We notice the presence of any preconceptions or distractions not to eliminate them, but rather to be curious about their purpose in calling for our attention.

We have said that Gestalt works with the concept of "the whole"; that is, the meaning we attach to overall form that is taken to be represented by its constituent parts, in its context.

For example, when we see flower, bush, grass, wheelbarrow, bench, outdoors, they collectively become "garden". When we see those things framed on a wall, they become "picture". If we were to see them piled in a bathtub, we may be confused.

Similarly, the person is always impacted by their relationship to what is referred to as the "field" or context in which they are present. Nothing and no one can exist in isolation; all is interconnected and in a state of constant flux.

Field Theory

Field Theory in Gestalt comes from the work of Kurt Lewin. He asserted that we all have a tendency to interpret and act upon our interpretation of the field depending on what's important to us in the moment. We experience this, for example, when our current circumstances lead us to notice things we otherwise might not: Pet-friendly holiday venues (or a shortage thereof) when we have just acquired a dog; the high cost of the things we want when we are short of cash; feeling anxious about certain conversations when we have had one that went badly.

The terms "figure" and "ground" are used to describe this juxtaposition of what we are focused on (the figure) and the context in which it exists (the ground). Visualise a solid black circle painted onto a white page … or is it a large area of white painted onto a black page, leaving a circular space uncovered? Depending on which you identify as the figure, and which as the ground, either could be true. And so it is with all experiences, sensations, thought and feelings. What we feel, notice and think will be the product of the present focus of our attention.

Gestalt recognises that nothing and no one exists in a vacuum; "reality" will always be an entirely subjective and temporary reading of the present. Moreover, the person experiencing their own reality is not apart from it; rather, they are a part *of* it and, as such, are themselves impacting the context in which they exist. Through the lens of Gestalt, one cannot by definition view one's world from the sidelines.

It is largely because of this that Gestalt is a highly effective vehicle for exploring interpersonal dynamics.

Systems Theory

There is much in Gestalt that draws upon Systems Theory, acknowledging not only the relationship of one part to another, but the dynamic interplay between the parts.

Peter Senge described it thus:

> A system is a perceived whole whose elements 'hang together' because they continually affect each other over time and operate toward a common purpose.
>
> (Senge et al., 1994)

That common purpose may be a desirable one or not – all we can know is that a purpose will emerge from any system left to determine its own direction.

One of the strengths of Gestalt work – whether in therapy or coaching, with individuals or groups – is its capacity to harness awareness as an influencer of direction.

Self and other

Perls suggested that the only way to understand the self is in the context of the field, or the wider context that is "other" than that self. Put another way, nothing can be described and given meaning unless it is understood in the sense of everything it is not.

Given that the field, or context, is ever-changing, the way in which one perceives one's "self" is conditional upon that change.

The coach and client are themselves components in their individual and shared fields. The "field" is continuously on the move and so, therefore, is the environment in which the coaching is taking place. The coaching relationship is an arena within which both the coach and client(s) are mutually determining their shared reality.

It's vital that the coach recognise this so that they can be aware of their own imprint on the client's experience; there will be an imprint, intended or not.

Paradox Theory of change and resistance

The Gestalt approach accepts the inherent contradiction that accompanies change. Change is by definition a means of becoming something other than what already is. The desire for change is therefore at some level a dissatisfaction with or even rejection of what already is.

> Change occurs when one is fully in contact with what is, rather than trying to be different.
>
> (Bluckert, 2015 p. 7)

The paradox, then, is that until we fully accept what is and who we are, we cannot create the change we want. With raised awareness, the client will find their own new meaning emerging from their mixed or even paradoxical experiences.

Gestalt coaching in practice

Coaches who align their work with Gestalt principles support their clients in connecting holistically with themselves and their experiences in the moment. This happens at physical, emotional, cognitive and physiological levels, giving the client access to thoughts, feelings, bodily sensations and responses that give them information about what's going on. One could think of it as an inquisitive "field trip" into the client's world with the coach for company.

The coach is able to heighten the client's awareness of their field: the "figure", or the topic that has brought them to the coaching; and the "ground", which defines the wider context that gives that topic its definition.

The coach can guide the client through exercises, activities and questions in a spirit of creative experiment, being curious without judgment, acknowledging resistance and "trying on for size" a variety of strategies in the safety of the coaching environment.

Working in the here and now, with awareness

Awareness is the cornerstone of Gestalt: Self-awareness in coach and client, awareness of their individual and shared fields, awareness of the impact each of them individually and in relationship are having on that field, moment to moment.

The here and now is fleeting. The past and future are important only in terms of their imprint on this moment's reality. If the client had an upsetting experience last year, it matters only in terms of its residue in this moment. If they are anxious about a meeting coming up next week, that event belongs here only in the form of the anxiety they feel now in the anticipation. In such moments, the upset or anxiety become the "figure", given meaning in context of the "ground" of the past or anticipated event. The events themselves do not exist.

John Leary-Joyce (2014) identifies two types of awareness important for coaches.

Undirected awareness takes a wide-open view, suspending expectation and judgment so that information can be received in a spirit of discovery. Whatever emerges, emerges and is valid in its own right.

This can be challenging for the coach and client alike: Setting aside analysis, engaging mindfully with the present moment and all that it is making available, slowing down and waiting for whatever comes. The coach who engages with reflective practice will be familiar with these challenges; the client may find that they oppose all the practices they have been trained to become good at: Solving the problem, planning ahead, getting a result.

Coaching is expected to produce results, of course, and these are in part determined by the attention and actions of the coach.

Directed awareness has a more focused and deliberate quality, allowing the coach to observe with focus, identify clues and cues, notice details that can usefully inform their interventions and questions.

Both levels of awareness have their place in coaching, whatever approach the coach favours. The type and intensity of awareness called for in Gestalt work can be a stretch for the client; the coach can model such awareness in action.

Unique individual experience

Discourse around Gestalt often makes reference to Phenomenology, a branch of philosophy that is concerned with the study of experience. Each one of us experiences our reality, or "truth", in a unique way because we feel, perceive and behave uniquely.

From a Gestalt perspective, the coach's job is to help the client explore his reality, to make meaning of his discoveries and to experiment with how those discoveries can usefully serve him.

Whatever the client brings to the coaching as a concern will be his current truth, the "figure" at the forefront of his experience right now. It claims his attention and energy and is thrown into relief against the backdrop of everything else that has faded into the "ground", with all its events, beliefs, values, assumptions, habits, ways of seeing the world and unfinished business.

If the client's truth is that they are not smart enough to get the promotion, the coach's view is unimportant. The coach's job is to start from that current reality, enabling the client to do their own detective work with the evidence offered by the present moment.

It is in doing this that the shifts and insights come; the client turns the kaleidoscope of their world view in front of their own eyes to reveal a different configuration with fresh possibilities.

Relationship

The relationship between coach and client can be a rich source of information about the client's relationships elsewhere. By experiencing what plays out in the coaching relationship, the coach is able to draw upon their own experience of the interaction and put information into the field to enhance the client's awareness.

This is an example of the use of the self as an instrument, where Gestalt coaches share their own observations and responses to and with the client, in the moment, aware of their own place and impact in the interactive field. The skill is to do this collaboratively and with intention, in service of expanding the client's awareness of the field.

Creative experimentation

Much has been said already about the importance of experiment in Gestalt coaching. With an available and accessible field and a receptiveness to whatever data the field offers, both coach and client have the opportunity to try out a range of strategies and responses in service of the client's growth and desired outcomes.

Experimentation in Gestalt calls for action, for getting out of the head and the theoretical, into the body and the moment. This can be uncomfortable for the client, and the value is in the discomfort. By introducing this stretch, the client can experiment safely with what it might be like to have a go in a way that they would otherwise avoid. An experiment might be embodied in a simple but powerful question such as "What would it be like if you …?"

More challenging might be an "enactment" of a scenario where the client adopts the position of a character, metaphorical or real, stepping into their shoes as part of the experiment.

Gestalt work offers the opportunity to develop new ways of trying out, even rehearsing, options without risk of adverse consequences and with the advantage of feedback.

The paradoxical nature of change and resistance

"Coaching invites resistance – and that's a good thing … It's not resistance that creates a problem, it's our reaction to it that can get in the way" (Maurer, 2011, p. 91).

People generally come to coaching because there's something they want to be different. They know they want the change, they may even yearn for it, and yet it isn't happening. At some level, for some reason, there is resistance to the change.

In Gestalt work, both the desire – the "push" – and the holding back – the "pull" – are very real, present and useful factors. Neither is friend or foe, good or bad, attractive or not so. They simply *are*. The coach's job is to facilitate the client's awareness of and curiosity about *both* of them; it is not their job to somehow overcome the resistance and advocate the desire.

Tools and techniques

"It is in the nature of Gestalt to evolve, and so it continues to do so in a way that prohibits the exposition of 'the' Gestalt way" (Allan and Whybrow, 2019, p. 181). Gestalt is a set of principles that informs how a coach works.

The aim of Gestalt coaching is to embrace the subjective present in a way that invites new experiences and perspectives to form a revised reality. Some other approaches to coaching might deal with the presented issue (the client's "figure") at an essentially trans-actional, problem-solving level and the outcome may be satisfactory. Sometimes, however, the "figure" re-emerges in other contexts or different "ground", suggesting an underlying pattern in the client's circumstances where some resolution can be helpful.

This is where Gestalt work can be at its best, leading to transformational and endur-ing change in the client's "ground", addressing the unfinished business that settles the system.

There are some coaching approaches that embody Gestalt principles more overtly than others, and examples of these will be offered here.

Working with enactment, exaggeration, metaphor, dynamic expression and physical space all lend themselves to the spirit of creative experimentation that underpins Gestalt coaching.

Here are some examples of ways of working, illustrated with extracts from coaching sessions described by coaches in supervision.

Working with enactment

Some of the best-known Gestalt approaches allow the client to adopt different physical positions and perspectives by enacting challenging scenarios.

This is not the same as role playing; that would require speculation and pretence, nei-ther of which honours the Gestalt commitment to harnessing what is real in the here and now. Rather, it is an immersive, experimental and experiential approach that expands the client's awareness of the scenario he wishes to explore. It encourages him to pay attention to physical sensations, perceptions, feelings and behaviour, informed by his experience as it unfolds.

Enactment is effective for dealing with conflict, tricky relationships, difficult conversa-tions or ambiguity. Examples of coaching approaches are Perceptual Positions and Chair Work, such as Empty Chair.

Box 21.1: Gestalt in action: Empty Chair

The session is set up, typically using two chairs: One that will be occupied by the client, and the other to represent the second person in the conversation.

The coach begins by asking the client to talk about their topic, to describe the environment and conditions in which the future conversation will take place. The client sets the scene by arranging the chairs as they are likely to be set up for the actual conversation.

In **POSITION 1** the client sits in her chair and is invited to say what she wants to say to the Empty Chair, addressing the other person directly, honestly and in the present tense. Some questions might be:

"What do you want to say to him?"
"Now what do you *really* want to say to him?"

"How does it feel as you say that?"
"Where in your body do you experience that feeling?"

The client is then invited to stand, "shake off" **POSITION 1**, and move to **POSITION 2** – the other chair. There, she is encouraged to adopt the demeanour, tone and posture of the other person, as if present:

"How is he sitting?"
"What's his expression?"
"How does he sound … what's the pace and volume of his voice?"
"What does he have to say in response to what he has just heard?"

In this position, the client is not role playing, second-guessing or pretending to be the other person, just experiencing what it might be like to be on the receiving end of herself, and responding spontaneously with whatever emerges in the moment.

In **POSITIONS 1** and **2**, the coach stays close to the client, a little out of their direct line of sight, which can make it easier for the client to stay fully present in her conversation with the Empty Chair.

The coach then guides the client to **POSITION 3** – a point in the room where she can observe both chairs. From here, she is invited to reflect:

"What do you notice about the exchange that just took place?"
"What is going on between these two people?"

"How is that evident?"

This will give the client some distance, and a different vantage point from which to explore the scene.

POSITION 4 can be further away, or viewing the chairs from a different angle. From here the client can reflect on different, more useful way of approaching her challenge, which she offers to herself:

"What insights can you share with her from here?"

"How might she handle her situation more effectively?"
"What is clear now that was unclear before?"

This allows the client to draw upon a raised level of awareness, opening up possibilities for new and different ways forward.

The session ends with the client returning to **POSITION 1** and having the opportunity to re-visit the initial conversation in a different way.

The session ends with the client reviewing what she has learned and how she will apply that learning to her challenge.

Working with exaggeration

Coaches are well practised in noticing what is being communicated by their client beyond what is actually being said. Sometimes what the voice articulates appears at odds with what the face or body is expressing.

This is an example of the kind of "direct awareness" discussed earlier, a skill that equips the coach to attend to the demeanour, breathing, gestures, movements and expressions of the client in such a way that brings what is observed into full awareness for them both.

In Gestalt therapy, exaggeration exercises invite the client to acknowledge, repeat and exaggerate an observed behaviour so that he might better understand the emotions attached to that behaviour from a position of awareness.

At their most sophisticated, these exercises are likely to require skills beyond those of the coach. That said, drawing upon active observation in order to draw attention is powerful, and can be usefully and safely transferred into the coaching context.

Box 21.2: Gestalt in action: If your foot had a voice …

We are 20 minutes into the coaching session, my third session with this client. When we started working together, he had just been promoted and was experiencing what he described as "imposter syndrome". He was one of the youngest ever to reach Partner level in his firm and was "worried sick" that he would not be up to the job. He had considered walking away to avoid being exposed.

What kept him there was his desire to demonstrate to his family that he was capable and deserving of their pride in his success. He had dropped out of university "first time round" and had felt such shame that he had distanced himself from his family and, he believed, their disappointment in him.

Today, he is smiling, speaking slowly and calmly, lounging slightly in his chair and telling me how well everything is going, how "chilled" he is with life. Yet something doesn't stack up. His words tell a good story, but I notice that his laid back posture is at odds with his left foot, which is crossed over his right and agitating energetically under the table.

He notices me noticing, and it stills.
"If your foot had a voice, what would it have to say?", I ask.
"Everything I'm not saying", he replies quietly after a pause.
"What happens if it joins in the conversation again?"
He rests the foot on his opposite knee, holds on to it.
For the next 15 minutes, the "foot voice" speaks: "I'm feeling twitchy"; "let's get out of here"; "you can't run away again"; "you're making a mess of this"; "she (the coach) thinks you can't even get this right"; "I want to walk away"; "I'm full of energy".
"What's it like for you to hear those things?" I ask, and so the session continues.

Working with space and metaphor

We have discussed the concept of the field in Gestalt work – the wider context which contains, determines and defines how each of us experiences our current reality. The field is also a system, "a continuously changing mass of relationships, hierarchies, loyalties and motivations" (Whittington, 2016, p. 9).

Working actively with physical space lends itself to Gestalt work: As with the Empty Chair example, the client can move around, experiment with different perspectives and experience with all their senses what it's like to be in another person's place.

Constellations is another coaching approach that works with movement and space. The client is guided by the coach as they place objects – these could be blocks, markers, people or just about anything that's to hand – in a contained area such as a sheet of paper, a table top or a room. The client moves the objects, prompted by questions from the coach to generate insight and reflection. The moves and changes are significant: The client is asked to reflect on them in the moment, attuning to their sensory, emotional and cognitive responses, eliciting rich information from the field.

The constellation becomes a metaphor for the client's current reality.

Metaphor is a potent mechanism for acquiring insight and understanding through representation. It gives us a way of capturing and expressing something when simple description is lacking. It can be found at a casual, conversational level – for example, in phrases such as "It's an uphill struggle", "I'm over the moon", "I'm banging my head against a brick wall" or "The cat is out of the bag". At its more complex, metaphorical narrative can become a symbolic story for expressing something that is difficult to convey literally.

Just as Gestalt principles are drawn upon in Constellations work, so the concept of representation and the power of metaphor can be useful in Gestalt-based coaching.

Box 21.3: Gestalt in action: Walking the stage

Seven members of the sales team in a motor finance company are spending a day with their coach/facilitator to explore how they can better work with other parts of the business. Some shared and individual challenges include:

"The product development team don't talk to us enough"
"They expect us to bring in the business but they don't give us what we need"
"I don't feel supported and I'm stressed"
"We rarely celebrate our successes"
Using the metaphor of a play on stage, the facilitator invites each person in the room to represent one "key character in this drama", human or otherwise. The cast includes "Product Development Team"; "Us"; "They"; "Expectation"; "Need"; "Support"; "Successes".
Each character is, in turn, invited to take up a position on the stage (an area defined by the room) that feels right for them and to experience what happens there. Each then speaks, prompted by the coach's enquiries:
"What is Expectation noticing?"
"How does Successes feel, and where in the body does she feel it?"
"What is Support's take on this?"
"What does Need need?"
As information emerges from the field, the characters adjust their positions, angles and relationship to others, adapting moment-by-moment to their changing reality.

When does Gestalt work best?

As we have seen in the extracts offered here, Gestalt-based coaching can be used to great effect with individuals, groups, teams and organisations. It is particularly useful when clients need to adapt to change, or when they want to feel better equipped to communicate with others and improve relationships.

The core principles of raising awareness, removing blocks and working with subjective realities in the here and now are well-suited to addressing internal personal conflict, tensions in groups, difficult conversations, unhelpful patterns of behaviour.

There is no standard approach or off-the-shelf model for working in this way; rather, the coach draws upon the core principles to inform how they work in partnership with the client.

The shape and direction of the session emerges from what the client discovers and what is co-created in the moment between coach, client or clients and their evolving shared field.

Clients who are seeking a goal-defined outcome might be less inclined to engage with this level of exploratory attention to the present moment; it may have limited appeal for those who are driven by performance metrics, who might be more drawn to identifying gaps in their skillset and action-based results.

The Gestalt stance is likely to appeal to the coach who likes to work systemically and holistically, where they themselves inhabit the field of the coaching experience that they facilitate. The coach's very presence and how they use it is the catalyst for change.

Both coach and client are called upon to engage with their own sensations, emotions and thoughts, bringing their whole "selves" to a shared experience. For some, this will be uncomfortable in a way that inhibits rather than enhances their chances of benefitting from the coaching; other approaches might therefore be preferable.

Ten useful question for Gestalt coaches

1. What's going on for you in this moment?

    This can be asked repeatedly, gently bringing the client's focus back to the *now*. It encourages them to remain curious, acknowledging distractions, sensations and emotions as they arise.

2. Where in your body are you experiencing that?

    The body knows us well. When the client pays mindful attention to what their body is putting into the field, the body is given a voice: "My stomach is churning"; "I feel a tightening in my throat"; "my face just relaxed".

3. How do you know that's what you're feeling?

    The client recognises and labels a feeling they are having now based on how they have experienced it before. That history can serve the present, revealing relevant connections, habits and patterns that, once brought into awareness, can be usefully explored.

4. What would it be like to say out loud what you are not saying now?

    The prospect of speaking the seemingly unspeakable presents a paradox that can be a stubborn barrier to change. Such a question embraces the paradox, drawing attention less to *what* is unsaid, more to the client's resistance to saying it.

5. Would you like to try saying it?

    The client is invited to harness their courage, take a deep breath and experiment. Their reply might be "No", "I don't know how", silence or a powerful emotion: The value is in the insight that comes from the impact of the invitation.

6. If your anger/fear/resentment could speak, what would it want to say?

    When emotion is allowed to speak, the client's truth is spoken from a new place. Giving an autonomous voice to a tricky emotion gives the client some distance from it, releasing them to get it off their chest, clearing the "ground" of emotional rubble and giving their "figure" a revised definition.

7. What do you need from them?

   The client is never in this alone, yet in the moment they might experience the challenge as an isolating burden. Such a question loosens the constraints of a world view that says "it's all down to me", "I'm responsible", "I have to …", freeing them to acknowledge their needs and others' part in them: "I need them to listen … to share the load … to trust me".

8. How do things look from here?

   A change of position supports a change in perspective. Guiding the client to a different viewpoint – physically in a space, in their imagination or on a sketch or table top constellation – creates a new aperture through which to view the scene: "I hadn't seen it quite like that before"; "from here that just doesn't make sense"; "ahh, now I see".

9. Where would be a good place to view this from?

   This hands the map to the client, leaving him to choose a vantage point. It can be useful to explore what they notice as they make meaning of "a good place" and how that paradoxically defines a "not good place". Once there, the coach might introduce the previous question.

10. Now sitting in this chair opposite your own, sitting as your manager, what would they say to you?

    This draws on the principles of the Empty Chair approach. We cannot fully experience ourselves in the way that others do; we are too busy being us. By adopting the place of the other person in the conversation, the client can connect with what it's like to be on the receiving end of herself, equipping her to have that conversation "for real" with greater insight and empathy.

Conclusion

Gestalt coaching has emerged from a robust field of philosophical pursuit, psychological theory and experimental practice. The apparent simplicity of its guiding principles – being in the moment, working with the here and now, opening up awareness – veils the potency of their effects. The Gestalt "toolkit" *is* the coach: It's something that the coach embodies in their way of being, knowing that their very presence shapes the client's reality.

References

Allan, J. and Whybrow, A. (2019). 'Gestalt coaching'. In S. Palmer and A. Whybrow, eds. *Handbook of coaching psychology: A guide for practitioners*, 2nd edition. Abingdon: Routledge, pp. 180–194.

Beisser, A.R. (1970). 'The paradoxical theory of change'. In J. Fagan and I.L. Shepherd, eds. *Gestalt therapy now*. New York: Harper & Row, pp. 77–80.

Bluckert, P. (2015). *Gestalt coaching: Right here, right now*. London: Open University Press.

Leary Joyce, J. (2014). *The fertile void: Gestalt coaching at work*. St. Albans: AOEC Press.

Maurer, R. (2011). 'The gestalt approach to resistance in coaching'. *The International Journal of Coaching in Organisations*, Issue 32, 8(4), pp. 91–99.

Senge, P.M., Kleiner, A, Roberts, C. et al. (1994). *The fifth discipline fieldbook: Strategies and tools for building a learning organization*. London: Nicholas Brealey.

Whittington, J. (2016) *Systemic coaching and constellations*, 2nd edition. London: Kogan Page.

22 Systems-Psychodynamic coaching

Karen Izod

Introduction

Coaching from a psychodynamic perspective draws on the bodies of knowledge concerning themselves with the social, emotional, technical and political aspects of our environments. This is a broader view now than might have been offered in relation to Freud's originating theories of mind, with their emphasis on the unconscious, in the context of 19th/20th century sensibilities (Freud, 1915). Today, the idea of an unconscious, with its capacities to surprise us, keep us in repeating patterns of behaviour, and take us into situations that we would prefer to have more control over, remains central to a psychodynamic approach. It is augmented by knowledge from social psychology and neurosciences (Bowlby, 1969, Fonagy et al., 2004), whether that be in the 'talking cures' of psychotherapy or in the applied practices of coaching, consulting and education.

Systems-psychodynamics is a field of knowledge that brings understanding from the dynamics of social systems within their changing environments (Lewin, 1947), and the behaviour of individuals in groups (Bion, 1961, Izod, 2008) to central tenets of psychodynamic thinking. This is an applied perspective, involving an exploration of how the inner world of thoughts, fantasies and beliefs plays out in the outer world of roles, tasks and interactions.

For a coach and the client, working from this position gives the opportunity to explore the needs and concerns of an individual through identifying the patterns of behaviour we establish over our lifetimes, together with our responses to the dynamics of the workplace. It offers rich opportunity to gain new perspectives about ourselves, how we organise ourselves in relation to others and how we might effect change.

In this chapter I will outline some key elements of coaching from this perspective, with examples from my practice and ideas on scenarios that can particularly benefit from a (systems) psychodynamic approach.

The psychodynamic approach explained

Like any approach to coaching, a psychodynamic approach will hold the coaching task at its core, addressing the usual contractual arrangements: Who is the coaching for, what and whose agenda can be worked with, who needs to know and so on. The primary concern is the coaching participant's capacities to do their work.

A coach working from this perspective will not necessarily have been trained in the application of psychodynamic theories in a clinical setting. Rather, a psychodynamic coach will be interested in the emotional impact that work has on the individual *in the present*, and the individual's resources, both personal and organisational, to manage and sustain their efforts (Sandler, 2011; Beck, 2012; Zagier and Brunning, 2018).

Central to this approach is a curiosity and willingness to explore the thoughts and feelings that emerge between the coach and client, in the context of a coaching relationship, and to jointly attempt to bring some meaning to them. This is a demanding position to take, and the coach will need to invest time in understanding their own emotional repertoire and how it is triggered so as to bring their "self as instrument" to the process (Cheung Judge, 2001, pp. 11–16). Reading widely in the psychodynamic literature and group and organisational processes, as well as the arts, sciences and popular culture are all part of the capacity to bring one's knowledge, imagination and empathy to the role.

Emotional life: The past in the present

Emotional and mental life is complex. From our earliest infancy we are laying down repertoires of emotional and behavioural responses in interactions with our care-givers, built from minute everyday encounters and their sensory experiences. The nature of these interactions, and the extent to which our emotions can be acknowledged, rather than be ignored or shut down, become part of our procedural memory (Crittenden, 2005), an unconscious "default" position of feelings and behaviours that are triggered when faced with a particular threat or loss of security.

Box 22.1: Case study

Farhad, new in role as a project lead, struggled with the time and resources he had available to him, and became increasingly overwhelmed by what felt an impossible work-load. He was reluctant to negotiate for more resources, and easily assumed that he had to prove himself by doing the impossible.

Exploring patterns of response such as these reveals those type of experiences that we embrace and can cope with well enough, and those which we have had to defend against in a variety of ways so as to avoid potentially distressing emotions and protect our sense of self.

This approach attempts to find meaning in behaviours through opening up the possibility for insight and increasing the range of responses that might be possible. Asking for more, in Farhad's case, might well surface earlier feelings of greed or inadequacy, and identifying this enables the setting of a coaching agenda that might explore and rehearse what it feels like in the present to make this kind of request.

A systems-psychodynamic approach offers a means to understand how people behave in social systems, where those systems themselves are constantly evolving in relation to social, economic, technological, environmental and political forces. This approach is concerned with how unconscious processes manifest within and between systems. It places an emphasis on how people take up their roles, undertake tasks, manage themselves at boundaries and handle authority relations (Green and Molenkamp, 2005).

Systems generate their own ways of organising and defending against the anxiety associated with the tasks that they are there to do, or the difficulty of staying connected to those tasks (Menzies Lyth, 1988). Noticing what the strategic debates are within an organisation, who is included and excluded in decision-making activities, will surface power dynamics and help to locate processes that are supportive of, or resistant to, learning and change.

Thinking about Farhad from this perspective would include a consideration of how it is that his team is potentially under-resourced, and what this team might represent for the organisation as a whole. Are those tasks valued or denigrated; it is, for instance, not unusual for one team to always be seen as failing, with the unconscious effect of enabling another team to succeed. Gathering information about how the wider system functions and how the power relations operate between them will give valuable material as to how the unconscious might play out at a systems level.

Psychodynamic coaching theory and research

Most research in psychodynamic coaching will tend to come from a range of psycho-social research methodologies, with an emphasis on qualitative rather than quantitative research (Cummins and Williams, 2018; Clarke and Hoggett, 2009).

This kind of research tends to rely on individual and comparative case studies (Berg, 1990), which give thick descriptions of interactions between coach and client, and may address practice issues: Aspects of taking up the role of coach, the challenges faced and the development of understanding and skills to meet those challenges. The research task echoes the coaching task in that respect.

There are several excellent compilations of practitioner case studies, including: Coaching young adults and senior women professionals in transition (Brunning, 2006), the develop-ment of reflective practitioners and a focus on generating individual and organisational change (Kets de Vries et al., 2010) and internet-delivered interventions (Dent, 2019).

Qualitative research studies invariably are studying particular cohorts, for whom coach-ing attempts to raise awareness, and may include aspects of evaluation of initiatives: As part of an organisational development initiative to help leaders become self-aware in their leadership roles, coaching enabled an attunement to organisational dynamics and grew the leaders' capacities to develop reflective space, in effect making them become coaches within their own organisations (Bell and Huffington, 2008); the value and benefit of a team model in coaching executives within an organisation led to an improved understand-ing of the strategic pressures facing their clients, and a better alignment of developmental goals for individual executive clients (Nardone et al., 2009); and coaching as a means of improving diversity awareness of a group of executives in state departments illustrated how, from a systems-psychodynamic perspective, it proved a trustworthy intervention in exploring conscious and unconscious diversity dynamics operating within these organisa-tions (Motsoaledi and Cilliers, 2012).

Psychodynamic coaching in practice

The fields of knowledge that can be described as psychodynamic do not stand still and are ever-developing in widely branching pathways of theory and practice. I describe my own coaching as "relational"; it concerns itself with the processes that occur in interaction with others, about which there can be greater or lesser awareness.

With an emphasis on the relationship, the dynamic arising within and between the coaching pair becomes the media through which thoughts, feelings and ideas are expressed and where new behaviours can be practised.

Our coaching clients are often looking for a place to express their concerns without being subject to unhelpful assumptions and judgement, and the capacity for both client and coach to build a safe and sufficiently secure and containing base for the work (Bowlby, 1988) is central.

Containment

The concept of containment refers to the usually unconscious process of communication between infant and care-giver, which can acknowledge and respond to the earliest emotional states in the infant. Holding an infant in mind as a thinking, feeling and separate being is the basis for development as a reflective individual (Fonagy et al., 2005). It supports the tolerance for and management of anxiety, and frees the capacity to be curious and explore the world.

Developmental work, such as coaching, depends upon establishing such a containing relationship. Logistically, it can be established through the coaching contract; its agreement on purpose, time-frames, venues, confidentiality together with mechanisms providing for some sense of orientation, exploring who are we and what we are here for (Grueneisen and Izod, 2014).

Containment in the relationship relies on a careful paying of attention: To what is said, how it is said, what is not said that we might expect to hear and an attuning of our own emotional register to the client's mood. Recognising the client in this way in itself can provide a developmental opportunity, capable of bringing about change in the way the client relates to others and expects others to relate to them.

The importance of role

Containment provides the developmental context for coaching, but is in itself not enough. Enabling new understanding can usually provide the impetus for change, but pushing those thoughts into action, feeling sufficiently empowered to bring about change and sustaining it within the workplace requires an interaction with the individual and their environment, and this is often achieved through an exploration of organisational role.

Role can be thought of as the interface between what the individual brings to their work and their identities, their personality, their patterns of behaviour and what the organisation requires of them. It is a construction in the mind between:

What I imagine I am here to do (and how to do it);
What organisational players (and external stakeholders);
imagine that I am here to do (and how to do it).

Role consultation as a coaching intervention attempts to help an individual (and the organisation) align well with each other, bringing a close attention to the way that boundaries and tasks are negotiated, allocated or imposed. These are often not explicit but exist in the "organisation-in-the-mind" (Armstrong, 2005), and in the way that they are expressed through the culture, artefacts and processes of the organisation.

Identifying assumptions about the working space that is available, or made available for an individual role, can shed light on where and how change might be possible.

Box 22.2: Case study

Miranda was newly appointed to a senior HR role, accountable to the Head of Service, her line manager. This was an international appointment and she had relocated with great optimism to the UK. It wasn't long before she found herself thwarted at every turn by her line manager. She had been accustomed to much higher levels of authority and decision-making, as well as the ability to take initiative and act without consultation in her previous position. At the same time, she felt that her manager was treading on her toes and undermining her in each of her projects. The difficulty on referral, was viewed as interpersonal, with a tendency between the two managers to each view the other as hostile and bullyish.

Very often, the space that is made available to an individual to take up a role, or roles, can be over-prescribed or limited, and the intention of coaching in this situation will be to open up that space to greater possibilities – to make elbow-room (Izod, 2014). Conversely, roles can be poorly defined, too vague or overlap too closely with others, as is the case with Miranda, and the coach will work to define and clarify quite what the role's purpose is, locating her within the wider context of stakeholder expectations and what might unconsciously be held in the dynamics of that team. This work will usually involve others so as to bring greater systemic awareness to the role, and to renegotiate the allocation of tasks and responsibilities where needed. In Miranda's case, the nature of competition that emerged between her and her line manager had specific meaning in the context of the industry and its stakeholders, and had become located in these high-achieving, high-autonomy individuals.

Tools and techniques

Using ourselves as sources of data

Working from a psychodynamic perspective will involve us in developing a capacity to use ourselves as an instrument (Cheung Judge, 2001). Our thoughts, feelings and behaviours, when we are with a client, and when we are reflecting on them, give us access to what might be going on for the client through transference phenomena. This unconscious carrying of experience from "there and then", to "here and now", is indicative of the client's world as it interacts with my own. Here I need to be open to my own ideas, images and fantasies that the work evokes in me, alongside an awareness of how I identify with various aspects of the client's experience in my own separate and subjective inner world.

Experiences that we might encounter in the coaching session can range from boredom and tiredness, a feeling of being overwhelmed and flooded with detail, an irritability or frustration with the individual. This is data that can very often tell us about what the client is going through. It can be tempting to offer these experiences as feedback to the client, "I feel very angry/frustrated/tired"; however, we as the coach have to manage ourselves at the boundary of our own inner worlds and the coaching role, to hold onto the experience and try to gain a sense of its meaning.

The formulating of a hypothesis

Developing a hypothesis from the experience of the coaching session is a key skill for the psychodynamically oriented coach. It offers the possibility for furthering understanding and is crafted from the emotional experience and content of what is being talked about. Differing from an interpretation, it is provisional, temporary, a "what might be" rather than a "what is", and is helpful only in so far as it has resonance for the client. Here is such an example crafted from the content material in a session, which brings in my own emotional resonances.

"I'm noticing that you seem frustrated in this conversation, and I wonder if it might be that you somehow expect to constantly make progress with your project, and not have to face these set-backs".

Formulated in this way, the client might well have an insight into their wish for change to be constant, and allow for the revision of expectations. But, equally, the client might say "No – I don't think that's it". But it is nonetheless a stake in the ground, and can usually be revisited or come to have another meaning over time.

Presentation and re-presentation

The organisation-in-the-mind (Armstrong, 2005) is a much-used concept in coaching and role consultation. It refers to the set of images, beliefs and behaviours that make up the culture of an organisation, which unconsciously influence how we relate to the workplace and our own place within it.

Asking an individual to draw a picture of themselves in their organisation is one way of eliciting thoughts that may not yet have been formulated, and sometimes creates surprises and, in these circumstances, the coach is as much interested in what is absent as in what is present.

> I hadn't realised I was so far from the centre of things, how much out on a limb I am, there are no other people in my drawing.
> I can see now how cluttered my workplace is, there is literally no space to think or to spread out with ideas.

In team coaching, asking people to work in pairs or in the whole group to associate to the drawings and bring their own imagination to each other's work gives data as to how and where there are degrees of divergence and coherence, in addition to how such diverse and coherent thinking can be used constructively. Asking the client to draw again, further into the coaching contract, may well illustrate where there have been shifts in perception or act as reminders to one's earlier emotional state.

The psycho-social field of enquiry has developed a range of these kinds of interventions with the intention of revealing under-the-surface experiences. See Long (2013) for examples of working with photo-matrices, visual matrices and social dreaming as forms of enquiry.

Narrative techniques

A conversational approach will involve our clients in telling a story, and we might invite questions such as:

How did you come to apply for this job?
How do you think your team came to rebel in this way?
How is it that you are facing such criticism over this decision?

A story is a narrative that involves self and other, the teller and the listener and, in the co-construction of a coaching session, both the client and the coach interact in relation to the storyline, its characters and its turning points or dilemmas. A story compels – what is going to happen now, who will chose to do what, who is holding the knowledge and who is ignorant of what is going on (Boje, 2001; Brown et al., 2009).

Whittle (2014) describes three main storylines that she uses in her consultancy: The heroic, the tragic and the comedic, and invites her clients to consider how they typically tell their stories. Do you invariable put a spin on your experiences so as to end up the hero, might you often be the one who is left out in the cold, struggling to overcome adversity? We each have our own preferred roles and storylines that we fill with meaning, increase or decrease in complexity and include or exclude others.

Working with narrative structures provides opportunities to interrupt the story and how it is being constructed in a number of ways. Take these questions for the client:

"Who I am in the story? If I am never the central character but a side-lined player, how might I shift that? How can I present myself differently so as to prevent myself from being excluded?".

"How am I dealing with the challenges thrown up at me? If I am always the one to stand up for the group and confront management, how might I let others do that?"

"How does the plot typically develop around me: Do I offer a single narrative thread, from one perspective alone, or can I bring in a greater complexity?". Perhaps there are too many voices and some need to be kept out for the moment.

Systemic questioning to ask, "How might your boss tell this story?" or "How might the customer tell this story?" will often allow for a playful re-presenting of a storyline. Working at one step removed from the client's own experience very often provides an imaginative, or transitional, space (Winnicott, 1953; Whittle, 2014) to attempt change.

Box 22.3: Case study

George, a lawyer, described himself as a ship's navigator, always in the map room, watching their course. He wanted to access something more adventurous in himself, a pirate perhaps. In the telling of his own story, he was able to see the tension in his role, recognising that he was needed to keep the company on track, yet feeling the need to take more risks and knowing that this was needed at times.

When does a psychodynamic approach work best?

People coming for coaching from this perspective are helped by already being curious about themselves and the nature of their work. They will be interested in ideas, thoughts and feelings, happy to work with metaphors and willing to explore the detail of their interaction with themselves and others. Generally clients will wish to invest in a process through which new thoughts can emerge, leading to new possibilities; it is not a place for finding ready-made solutions. Psychodynamic coaching requires a capacity to not rush, though this does not mean to imply that coaching is necessarily a lengthy business and individuals can reach points of greater certainty often within one or two two-hour sessions.

Here are some scenarios from my own practice where psychodynamic coaching has worked well:

Individuals who are concerned about themselves in their role

They may be in complex roles, in situations of uncertainty and ambiguity and having to create ways of working as they go along. Often these individuals are somewhat isolated within the organisation and may be carrying high levels of anxiety in relation to the enterprise.

Typically this is a stressed client (or someone who others perceive as being stressed), unsure about their direction and sometimes of their own competence to do the job. These are situations where examining the nature of the task that is being undertaken, and the feelings that it evokes, individually and with stakeholders, will be valuable at placing a boundary around what can be achieved. It is easy for us to become stressed when we are unable to bring our competence to bear, and understanding what might be getting in the way of that, either individually or within the system as a whole, will be valuable.

Individuals who wish to access or generate greater authority

Very often this will be the case for people who are new in their role, working in temporary systems, or perhaps working across organisational or national boundaries, where the authority lines are ambiguous. Organisational cues about how to behave, who to relate to and the power differentials between different systems may be hard to read and can easily undermine authority. Coaching here can help a client to identify where they are diffident about accessing their own authority, and use those insights to engage in the complexities of power-based relations.

Individuals who find themselves in conflict with others

Sometimes referred to as the "remedial" client, and referred by their managers, patterns of encountering conflict in one's self and others lend themselves well to a systems-psychodynamic approach. The coach will be interested in the way in which an individual is mobilised, in specific situations, to behave in particular ways. Group and organisational dynamics can easily locate unwanted feelings, particularly those of anger, antagonism and resistance, in a receptive individual for whom those emotions are familiar and liable to be acted out. This is not to find excuse, but rather more to look at the mobilising factors that an individual might be drawn to. Taking a role biography (Long, 2006) can be helpful here, highlighting how others who have taken the role before have managed with similar circumstances and dynamics.

Ten useful questions for psychodynamic coaches

1. "How is it that these issues are coming up for you/for your team now?"

    A "here and now" question that focuses on the immediacy of the situation. It invites the telling of a story, with its capacity to consider what is changing in the client's working environment, or in their ability to tolerate or manage these issues;

2. "What do you think might be contributing factors?"

    Locates the client in a broader system of people and agendas that may be impacting, knowingly and unknowingly, and start to focus an agenda for exploration and potential change;

3. "What does your role require you to do?"

The basis for understanding what preoccupations the client carries with them about the work they are contracted to do and their competence to do it. Are there aspects of the tasks that provoke anxiety or are unpalatable?;

4. "Have you been in this situation before?"

Gives an idea of whether the client needs to shift something in their individual narrative or whether the concerns are more organisationally based. It is always helpful to know whether the scenarios being described are being carried forward from the past. Exploring the experiences of previous role holders will start to identify the dynamics that the role carries, and how and where they might be challenged;

5. "What resources do you have that can help you work on these issues?"

Starts to elicit the networks of support available to the client, the extent to which they might be isolated or excluded in the organisation, as well as beginning the process of identifying one's own resources and resourcefulness;

6. "What might be getting in the way of …"

A question both about internal worlds of thoughts, assumptions and fears of change, together with external world realities. Is the opportunity right for this change, now? Bringing about change in one's self, or working practices is a complex process of learning and regression and never a linear process;

7. "Do you recognise the way you are behaving here? Now?"

We bring many different aspects of ourselves to work and, at an unconscious level, we can be mobilised by others to behave in ways that serve a purpose for the role or the organisation but don't yet feel right to us. Noticing these dynamics is a first step to working on one's presence and identity;

8. "What do you think you are known for in your team/organisation?"

Raises the nature of representation and how we become aligned with identity groups (i.e. managers/workers/academics) or specific areas of knowledge and skill. It opens up the opportunity to think about where we may find ourselves being shut down, or unhelpfully demanded upon in specific debates;

9. "How authorised do you feel to do your work?"

Very often there can be a tension between the formal authority that is given with a role and the amount of authority that we feel we can take (Krantz and Maltz, 1997). This question can open up scenarios of where authority is compromised, and where strategies are needed to access one's own authority or to negotiate it with others;

10. "Am I paying attention to myself?"

This is a question for the coach: How much am I listening to the content, how much am I paying attention to the process? Am I in touch with my own thoughts and feelings and, if it is difficult to access them, what might be going on in this encounter? Try to formulate a hypothesis.

Conclusions

This chapter has given an outline of what it entails for both coach and client to work together from a psychodynamic perspective. Coaching is primarily developmental; it gives opportunities to explore patterns of behaviour that have established themselves since infancy, and may be keeping the client in fixed positions, unable to make the most of their abilities.

Systems-psychodynamics, additionally, looks at the dynamics of organisational life within its societal context so that change can be considered as emergent, supported and limited by unconscious processes, particularly as they emerge at interfaces between individuals and systems, and between systems.

Coaching from this perspective will generate insights, and enable the client to shed an unhelpful repertoire of behaviour. Sustaining change, though, will require the coach to draw on broader theoretical perspectives, in particular those coming from organisation theory, change and from group dynamics.

References

Armstrong, D. (2005). *Organisation in the mind: Psychoanalysis, group relations, and organizational consultancy*. London: Karnac Books.

Beck, U.C. (2012). *Psychodynamic Coaching: Focus and depth*. Oxon: Routledge.

Bell, J., and Huffington, C. (2008). 'Coaching for leadership development: A systems psychodynamic approach'. In K. Turnbull James, and J. Collins, eds., *Leadership learning: Knowledge into action*. London: Palgrave Macmillan, pp. 93–11.

Berg, D. (1990). 'A case in print'. *The Journal of Applied Behavioral Science*, 26(1), pp. 65–68.

Bion, W. (1961). *Experiences in groups and other papers*. London: Tavistock.

Boje, D. (2001). *Narrative methods for organizational and communication research*. Sage: London.

Bowlby, J. (1969). *Attachment and loss. Volume 1: Attachment*. London: Hogarth.

Bowlby, J. (1988). *A secure base, clinical applications of attachment theory*. London: Routledge.

Brown, A., Gabriel, Y. and Gherardi, S. (2009). 'Storytelling and change: An unfolding story'. *Organization*, 16(3), pp. 323–333.

Brunning, H., ed. (2006). *Executive coaching: Systems-psychodynamic perspective*. London: Karnac Books.

Cheung-Judge, M. (2001). 'The self as an instrument, a cornerstone for the future of OD'. *OD Practitioner*, 33(3), pp. 11–16.

Clarke, S. and Hoggett, P. (2009). *Researching beneath the surface*. London: Karnac Books.

Crittenden, P.M. (2005). 'Internal representational models of attachment relationships'. *Infant Mental Health Journal*, 11(3), pp. 259–277.

Cummins, A.M. and Williams, N. (2018). 'Further researching beneath the surface: Psycho-social research methods in practice – volume 2'. Oxon: Routledge.

Dent, N. (2019). *'A reflexive Account' Group consultation via Video Conference in Theory and practice of online therapy: internet-delivered interventions for individuals, groups, families, and organizations*, Eds. Weinberg, Haim, & Rolnick, Arnon, New York: Routledge, pp 244–257

Fonagy, P., Gergely, G., Jurist, E. L. and Target, M. (2004). *Affect regulation, mentalization, and the development of the self*. London: Karnac.

Freud, S. (1915). 'The Unconscious. The standard edition of the complete psychological works of sigmund freud, volume XIV (1914–1916)'. *On the history of the psycho-analytic movement, papers on metapsychology and other works*, pp. 116–150.

Green, Z.G., and Molenkamp, T.J. (2005). 'The BART system of group and organizational analysis: Boundary, authority, role and task'. (online). Retrieved on 10 April 20 from www.it.uu.se/edu/course/homepage/projektDV/ht09/BART_Green_Molenkamp.pdf.

Izod, K. (2008). 'How does a turn towards relational thinking influence consulting practice in organizations and groups?' In: S. Clarke, H. Hahn and P. Hoggett, eds., *Object relations and social relations: the implications of the relational turn in psychoanalysis*. London: Karnac, pp. 163–184.

Izod K. (2014). 'Role space'. In K. Izod and S.R. Whittle, eds., *Resourceful consulting*. London: Karnac Books, pp. 53–61.

Kets-de-Vries, M. F., Guillen, L., Korotov, K. and Florent-Treacy, E. (2010). *The coaching kaleidoscope; insights from the inside*. New York: Palgrave Macmillan.

Krantz, J. and Maltz, M. (1997). 'A framework for consulting to organizational role'. *Consulting Psychology Journal: Practice and Research*, 49(2), pp. 137–158.

Lewin, K (1947). 'Frontiers in group dynamics: Concept, method and reality in social sciences; social equilibria and social change'. *Human Relations*, 1, pp. 5–41.

Long S. (2006). 'Role biography'. In J. Newton, S. Long and B. Sievers, eds., *Coaching in depth. The organisational role analysis approach*. London: Karnac Books, pp. 127–144.

Menzies Lyth, I.E.P. (1988). *Containing anxiety in institutions. Selected essays*, Vol. 1. London: Free Association Books.

Motsoaledi, L., and Cilliers, F. (2012). 'Executive coaching in diversity from the systems psychodynamic perspective'. *SA Journal of Industrial Psychology/SA Tydskrif vir Bedryfsielkunde*, 38(2), pp 52–62.

Nardone, M.J., Johnson, N.D. and Vitulano L.A (2008). 'Executive coaching as an organizational intervention: Benefits and challenges of a team of coaches working with multiple executives in a client system'. In S.R. Whittle and K. Izod, eds., *Mind-ful consulting*. London: Karnac Books.

Sandler, C. (2011). *Executive coaching: A psychodynamic approach*. Maidenhead: Open University Press.

Whittle, S.R. (2014). 'Potential Space. pp. 1–10, and Future Developments, pp. 119–128'. In K. Izod and S.R. Whittle, eds., *Resource-ful consulting*. London: Karnac Books.

Winnicott, D. W. (1953). 'Transitional objects and transitional phenomena'. *International Journal of Psychoanalysis*, 34, pp. 89–97.

Zagier Roberts, V. and Brunning H. (2018). 'Psychodynamic and systems-psychodynamic coaching'. In S. Palmer and A. Whybrow, eds., *Handbook of coaching psychology*. Oxon: Routledge.

Further Resources

ISPSO; International Society for the Psychoanalytic Study of Organizations www.ispso.org, and its member's publications written from a systems-psychodynamic or psychoanalytic perspective.

Opus: An organization for promoting understanding of society. www.opus.org.uk.

23 Neuroscience coaching

Patricia Riddell

Introduction

Sometimes we are surprised by our own behaviour. We find ourselves acting in ways that appear illogical, irrational or even way beyond our own expectations. Better understanding of what drives our behaviour is therefore likely to be able to put us at more choice in how we behave. Since the brain and the nervous system are responsible for every thought, emotion and behaviour that we produce, understanding the ways in which these work is likely to give us insight into how our behaviour emerges and therefore provide us with greater choice in what we choose to do. This is the basis of neuroscience coaching. In this chapter, I will outline what differentiates a neuroscience coaching approach from other, more traditional methods. I will then describe some of the techniques that are more unique to neuroscience coaching.

The neuroscience coaching approach explained

In essence, coaching is a process that is used to help individuals to create and fulfil goals. We might, therefore, be able to improve this process by viewing it through the lens of neuroscience both to determine how coaching works and, potentially, to add to the effectiveness of the process. For instance, the GROW model of coaching (Whitmore, 2009) has proved useful for helping clients to set goals, but it has not always been the most effective strategy to ensure that these goals are met (Aarts, et al., 2007). Deconstructing the GROW model from a neuroscience perspective can help us to improve the goal-setting process. In addition, research in health behaviour change has uncovered ways to improve the likelihood of behaviour change (Michie, et al., 2011; Schwarzer, 2008). By considering these models through a neuroscience lens, we can make important additions to the GROW model in order to increase its effectiveness.

Beyond the coaching process, however, neuroscience coaching is also able to introduce individuals to some of the more surprising ways that our brains can work against us. For instance, one of the most important ways that neuroscience has contributed is by providing solid evidence that we are able to change our behaviour at any age. Research in both epigenetics and neuroplasticity has demonstrated clearly that we have tended to underestimate this ability (Kempermann and Gage, 1999; Van Praag, et al., 2000). Not only are we able to change aspects of our brain throughout the lifespan, but this is fundamental to the way that our brains work. Knowing that the processes that create change in the brain are lifelong can change beliefs, and therefore dispels excuses – we can teach old dogs new tricks.

Neuroscience coaching can also draw on research into how we regulate our emotions (Begley and Davidson, 2013; Feldman Barratt, 2017). One of the common challenges brought to coaching is how to deal with difficult people to whom we have negative emotional responses. Being able to control or change our own emotional response can be a stepping stone to creating behaviours that improve the situation. By understanding both how our emotional response is generated and how it is controlled, we can provide tools and techniques to help change unwanted emotional reactions.

Making substantial changes in our lives can sometimes seem daunting. We can become attached to ways of being that are difficult to give up. Neuroscience research has considered what happens in the brain when we are required to make change (Cohen, et al., 2007). By understanding this, we can provide insight into what needs to happen for change to become easier, and be better prepared to direct clients through the change process. This involves understanding both the benefits of the current situation and the benefits of change so that clients can create potential solutions that combine both.

Neuroscience research has also given us some surprising insights into our inner critic and why we can sometimes lack self-compassion (Young, et al., 2010). By understanding both the mechanisms for empathising with others and how these relate to our ability to empathise with ourselves, we can help clients to address their inner critic in ways that increase self-empathy. There has been significant neuroscience research into this relationship, which has provided important insights into how we can become kinder and more compassionate with ourselves (Englander, et al., 2009).

These are only a small selection of the tools that neuroscience coaching can offer (Bossons, et al., 2015). As more coaches become familiar with neuroscience research and the insights that this can bring to the sometimes unintuitive ways in which the brain works, the number and range of neuroscience coaching tools will expand. This is a discipline that is certainly in its infancy, and has a long road to travel before it becomes fully integrated into the range of coaching methodologies.

Neuroscience coaching theory and research

When we consider the evidence base for a particular branch of coaching, it is important to differentiate between evidence-based and evidence-supported practices (Stober, et al., 2006). The best research into the practice of coaching is evidence-based. This uses research methods including the gold standard double-blind, randomised control trial to determine whether a particular tool or technique is more effective than, for instance, paying more attention to an individual.

Unfortunately, very little research of this nature is available for coaching in general and neuroscience coaching in particular. Techniques used in neuroscience coaching are therefore mostly evidence-supported, or based on our understanding of how the brain works. In this approach, research that provides credible evidence for how our brains work is used to create techniques that help us to work better with our brains. This is particularly useful for areas in which the brain works in surprising ways, where we have to develop coaching techniques that work with, not against, the way that our brains work. While some people find ways to do this simply through experience, providing clients with a better understanding of how their brain works can help them, consciously, to create solutions that work better for them.

With respect to evidence-based neuroscience coaching, Panchal and Riddell (2020) have investigated the benefit of extending the GROW model with models of behaviour change from health psychology and neuroscience. Their GROWS model was designed to help clients consider not just whether they were motivated to act, but also to consciously consider what actions they might take, the potential obstacles they might face and what they would do in order to get back on track if they failed. Research has demonstrated that imagining actions make it more likely that these will be taken in the future (Neroni, et al., 2014).

Additional questions in the GROWS model were framed in relation to self-efficacy – beliefs about the ability to cope. Research has related self-efficacy with parts of the basal ganglia (putamen and globus pallidus), which are associated both with movement and reward (Nakagawa et al., 2017). This suggests that we are rewarded by imagining the successful completion of an action.

In the GROWS model, self-efficacy is divided into three stages. The first, action or task self-efficacy, is the ability to anticipate and imagine the outcomes of successful change. Individuals low in action self-efficacy are more likely to imagine failure, obstacles to success or to have doubt in their own abilities. High action self-efficacy predicts intention to act.

Maintenance or coping self-efficacy is a belief that obstacles that stand in the way of maintaining change will be overcome. This requires that a long-term goal (e.g. having a healthy old age by drinking in moderation, eating healthily and staying active) is maintained even when competing goals with higher short-term rewards are present (alcohol, high-calorie foods and sedentary activities). High self-efficacy has been found to be predicted by the size of the lateral prefrontal cortex, which is important in working memory and ability to execute planned actions (Duckworth and Gross, 2014). Thus, when our brains have been wired by experience to imagine successfully completing future actions, we have greater self-efficacy.

Recovery self-efficacy is the ability to recover after a lapse and not to assume that a particular behaviour change is impossible. High recovery self-efficacy requires the ability to attribute the lapse to an external situation and to find ways to limit the damage and to get back on track. This has been defined by Duckworth and Gross (2014) as grit. The volume of the nucleus accumbens (part of the dopamine reward system) has been found to predict grit (Nemmi, et al., 2016). This suggests that focussing on the end reward, regardless of delay or obstacles, can maintain motivation when pursuing long-term goals.

In their small-scale study, Panchal and Riddell (2020) compared the GROW and the GROWS models with 4 coaching clients. Results demonstrated that clients found benefit in the additional GROWS questions as these led to the proactive development of strategies to overcome potential obstacles and to recover from setbacks. This led to more successful initiation and completion of goals (Panchal and Riddell, 2020).

Neuroscience coaching practice

A neuroscience coaching session is similar in structure to other coaching sessions. The purpose is to provide a space and structure for the client to address a challenge of their choosing within a given time-frame. The structure of the GROW model is suitable for neuroscience coaching since the different stages are underpinned by neuroscience.

Goals

The session starts by defining an overall goal, and a goal achievable within the session. When we plan goals, the dorsolateral prefrontal cortex (dlPFC) is active (MacDonald, et al., 2000).

More specifically, different parts of the dlPFC are active when we are pursuing goals that we believe will bring reward (approach goals: Left dlPFC) versus goals which we believe will prevent punishment (avoid goals: Right dlPFC) (Spielberger, et al., 2011).

There are two ways in which this information is used in neuroscience coaching: When we focus our coaching clients away from problems and onto solutions, we are effectively increasing activation in the left dlPFC and decreasing activity in the right dlPFC. Additionally, not every client will benefit from creating approach goals. Asking questions like: "What would happen if you fail to take action?", "What is the worst possible outcome for you?" or "What do you most not want to happen?" will be effective questions for clients who form avoid goals.

Reality

The reality phase of the GROW model encourages clients to use all the available evidence. A client that has more of an approach focus when creating goals (left dlPFC) will be more optimistic and willing to take risks. It is likely that this client will predominantly look for reasons to believe their plan will work.

In comparison, a client that is more avoid focussed when creating goals (right dlPFC) is more aware of reasons that their actions will not be successful. Avoid focus naturally occurs in people who are more pessimistic and averse to risks.

It is important to help the client assess the full reality of their plan in a non-judgemental manner. If your client has an approach focus, check that they have thought about potential obstacles and how these might be overcome. If your client is avoid focussed, encourage them to attend to positive evidence of success when assessing risk.

Options

We use divergent thinking to generate novel solutions for problems that do not have a right or wrong answer. There are three processes involved in divergent thinking. We need to:

1. Make associations across different domains of knowledge or concepts, which result in the generation of possibilities. This is known as "conceptual expansion";
2. Conceive of an object in a manner different from its customary or habitual use (functional fixedness); therefore, we need *to inhibit habitual responses*;
3. Explore possibilities and interpret these to determine if they are appropriate. Only those that meet the requirements are selected for consideration. Testing out possible ideas requires *creative imagery*.

Since there are a number of different processes involved in divergent thinking, it is unsurprising that this involves a complex network of brain areas. There are three major networks in the brain that are active during divergent thinking (Beaty, et al., 2015). These are:

The Salience Network (anterior cingulate cortex, insula): This identifies important aspects of the environment and directs attention to these. This network also is important in switching between the other two networks.

The Cognitive Control Network (dorsolateral prefrontal cortex, medial temporal gyrus): This network controls our thinking processes, including access to long-term memory, working memory, inhibition and self-regulation. It helps us plan actions to complete our goals.

The Default Mode Network (posterior cingulate cortex, inferior parietal lobe, temporo-parietal junction): This network controls our ability to think imaginatively, partly by turning attention inwards rather than outwards. This helps in the production of creative solutions.

To encourage creativity in others it is necessary to help them to eliminate typical learned responses in order to encourage new thinking. One way that coaches can do this is to insist that clients list a large number of options. The first options are likely to be typical while later options will be more creative.

Will

The next stage is to create an action plan that the client is motivated to follow. To move from an abstract goal to action, we have to be able to imagine the action, which requires both the hippocampus (address book for memory) and the ventromedial prefrontal cortex, where our personal goals are represented (Medea, et al., 2016). When individuals are given time to consider their goals, they think about what this would mean for them, especially when their mind is allowed to wander. Thus, the process of day dreaming allows time to consider how the plan might turn out. Thus, in coaching, the effect of giving a client space to imagine a future plan can help increase the likelihood that the plan will be implemented.

It is clear from this short description of the neuroscience behind the GROW model that this creates a useful structure to develop the intention to change. But experienced coaches know that it is not always sufficient to ensure action. The Health Action Process Approach (HAPA) model of behavioural change considers both motivational (intention) and volitional (action) components of change (Schwarzer, 2008).

The volitional phase requires action. Intention is more likely to be converted into action if the behaviour change is imagined. This activates the medial prefrontal which primes new behaviours to occur faster and more automatically (Rosenberg-Katz et al., 2012). See Figure 23.1.

One thing that is not explicit in the GROW model is the reference to our beliefs about our ability to act – or self-efficacy. In the HAPA model, self-efficacy has three components. Action self-efficacy is the ability to visualise and anticipate the outcomes of successful change. High action self-efficacy predicts intention to act. Individuals who are low in self-efficacy are more likely to imagine failure, obstacles to success or to have doubt in their own abilities.

Maintenance or coping self-efficacy is the belief that obstacles will be overcome. This requires that the long-term goal is maintained even when competing goals with higher short-term rewards are present. High self-efficacy has been associated with conscientiousness (Duckworth and Gross, 2014) or the ability to constrain impulses.

Recovery self-efficacy is the ability to recover after a lapse. High recovery self-efficacy or grit (Duckworth and Gross, 2014) requires the ability to attribute the lapse to an external situation and to find ways to limit the damage and get back on track. Grit has been found to be associated with the volume of the dopamine reward system (Nemmi, et al., 2016). Thus, seeking reward regardless of delay or obstacles can help us to keep motivated when pursuing long-term goals.

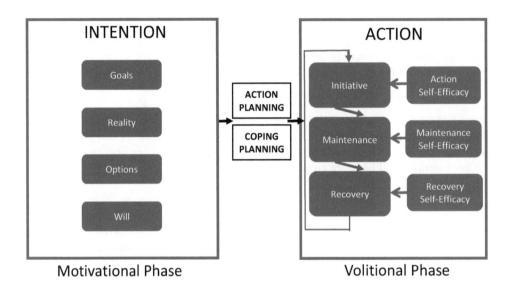

Figure 23.1 Model of behavioural change incorporating both the GROW model and aspects of the Health Action Process Approach (HAPA) model of behavioural change (adapted from Schwarzer, 2008).

Self-efficacy

What is self-efficacy, and how does it improve the chances of behaviour change? Michie, et al. (2011) suggest that, in order to reduce the friction that obstructs behaviour change, we should examine three factors:

1. Capability or individual psychological and physical capacity to engage in the behaviour, including necessary knowledge and skills;
2. Opportunity to perform the behaviour, including all the factors that lie outside the individual that prompt the behaviour and make it possible, including the physical properties of the environment and the social culture;
3. Motivation to change, including all the brain processes that energise and direct behaviour, including habitual or automatic processes, emotional responding and reflective or analytic decision-making.

These factors will be different for any behaviour that we choose to change, and so coaching a client to change behaviour should start by specifically defining the behaviours that are to change – both those that are to be reduced or eliminated and those to be increased or developed. Only then is it possible to determine whether the client has sufficient self-efficacy to make these changes and how this can be supported despite potential obstacles.

When does neuroscience coaching work best?

Typically providing clients with new knowledge is not considered part of the role of a coach. In some situations, however, it can be appropriate for coaches to bring expert knowledge to a coaching situation when the knowledge of the coach is greater than that of the client and the knowledge base is relevant to the client's goals (Stober and Grant, 2006). This might therefore include knowledge about how the brain works (see, for example, the special issue of The Coaching Psychologist: Enhancing the dialogue between the fields of neuroscience and coaching, volume 11, June 2015).

If neuroscience has something to offer in a particular coaching context, it is important to consider *how much* neuroscience should be shared. There is a cost to consider here, since coaching is designed to be a process that the coach holds so that the client can explore their own thoughts, beliefs and goals. In order to share neuroscience knowledge, it is necessary to break the coaching process by introducing an element of mentoring or consulting. This can require a break in rapport and so should be used circumspectly. Not all clients want to know how their brains work; they are happy to be guided by the coaching process. In this case, asking questions that direct their thinking in new ways can be sufficient. For others, however, the neuroscience can add scientific credibility to processes or techniques that might otherwise seem unsubstantiated. For these clients, adding a bite-sized chunk of neuroscience can often work wonders.

Asking permission to share a neuroscience fact and providing a rationale for doing this is a necessary step to ensure that rapport can be, first, broken ("I would like to share a fact about your brain that you might find useful. Would that be helpful to you?") and then recovered ("What might you do with this new information?").

Tools and techniques

There are many ways in which neuroscience can be used in coaching. In this section, five examples are provided (see Bossons, et al., 2015 for further examples).

Neuroplasticity and growth mindset

Change is not only possible – it is inevitable. The human brain has evolved to adapt to changes in our world. Neuroplasticity refers to the structures in the brain (neuro-) that can change (-plasticity) to adapt to changes in our environment. The brain changes by creating new neurones (the active, information-processing cells in our brains) to store new information in the parts of the brain that process memory. For example, the hippocampus (an area of the brain vital to memory) is larger in London taxi drivers who have learned "The Knowledge" – a map of the streets of London and what times of day, for instance, these are busy (Maguire, et al., 1997). New connections between neurones (synapses) can also be created in any area of the brain that is required to process new information. Indeed, we create and lose as many as 10% of the synapses in our brains on a daily basis whether we do anything different or not (Purves, et al., 1987; Umeda and Okabe, 2001). By constantly renewing synapses, the structures in the brain are able to adapt immediately to any changes in the environment. Indeed, if we do the same today as we did yesterday, the energy required to make these changes goes to waste. Coaches can help their clients to understand the potential of the brain to learn (at any age).

Since our brains are adapted for change, this cannot be the reason that we sometimes find learning or change difficult. Rather, this can be the result of our beliefs. If we believe that our intelligence, personality or skills are aspects of our self that we are born with and therefore cannot be changed – then this can become a self-fulfilling prophesy or fixed mindset (Dweck, 2006). There is no point in trying new ways if things cannot be changed. We will be more willing to change if we understand that our brains are designed for change and, therefore, with perseverance and the right strategy – or a growth mindset, we

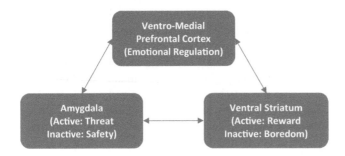

Figure 23.2 The triadic brain. This model demonstrates the parts of the brain that interact when we consider what we consider as threats and rewards, and how we regulate our emotional response in the workplace (adapted from Ernst et al., 2006).

can become better at new skills or learn new concepts. Providing clients with information that changes their beliefs about their ability to learn and change can help to increase willingness to try new strategies.

Calibrating emotions

Our emotions evolved on the savannah when we might have needed to respond to life-threatening challenges (sabre-tooth tigers, lack of food or water, etc.). See Figure 23.2, the triadic brain (Ernst, et al., 2006).

Our current day-to-day existence is a lot less threatening, and yet we have the same emotional range at our disposal. It is therefore possible that we might express our strongest emotional responses for events that are far from life-threatening. This raises the question – how do we calibrate our emotional range? Do we over-react in some situations? Or have we learnt, through our culture, to suppress emotions in some situations? And, if so, can this be changed?

Emotions can be changed, and the first step is to believe that this is possible. One of the major functions of the brain is to identify situations we should avoid (threat: Amygdala) and those we should approach (reward: Ventral striatum). The combined activity in these two areas of the brain determine both our behaviour and our emotional response – more reward than threat causes approach behaviour and is associated with (mostly) positive emotional responses, while more threat than reward will cause avoidance and is associated with negative emotions.

The unconscious, habitual responses of the amygdala and ventral striatum and the emotions that these create, however, can be overcome. Consciously activating the ventro-medial prefrontal cortex (vmPFC) reduces the activity in the amygdala and ventral striatum. Thus, by showing clients how to increase this activity, coaches can help to re-calibrate their emotional response. Techniques for doing this include naming the emotion (Lieberman, et al., 2007), noticing whether an emotion is appropriately calibrated and reframing the event by interpreting it differently (McCrae, et al., 2009).

Empathy for others

Our brains have adapted to be able to understand our own and others' emotional reactions to events. The ability to empathise develops over the lifespan and consists of

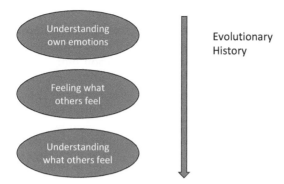

Figure 23.3 The evolutionary development of empathy showing the different mechanisms available for empathy (adapted from Dececty and Svetlova, 2012).

several interacting components. The first stage of acquiring empathy is to be able define and understand our own emotional signals – both those that signal approach (positive emotions, e.g. joy, happiness, fulfilment, compassion; negative emotions, e.g. anger) and those that signal avoidance (negative emotions, e.g. disgust, fear, sadness, guilt, embarrassment). This ability develops at, or soon after, birth (Decety and Svetlova, 2012). See Figure 23.3.

The next system to develop is the nurturance system, which allows us to feel how others feel. This evolved for parenting behaviours that support the extended development of the infant brain. Parents respond appropriately to their children's emotions through emotional contagion when the vocal, facial and gestural cues of the child generate a similar state in the parent. The hormone, oxytocin, has been found to both promote care-giving and decrease fear and anxiety in the cared-for person (decrease in activity in the amygdala). However, in a situation where others consistently express negative emotions, feeling how others feel can lead to increased levels of stress, resulting in poor health, burn-out and social withdrawal.

Understanding what others feel depends on the development of self-awareness. This increases the capacity for empathy through adherence to social norms based on feedback from others. Self-awareness activates the medial prefrontal cortex (mPFC) and requires differentiation of self from other (right temporo-parietal junction: rTPJ). This allows us to notice others' thoughts, intentions and emotions, thus increasing our ability to hypothesise about their potential actions. Compassion for others, which requires self-awareness, can induce positive feelings in response to the negative emotional response of others (Engen and Singer, 2015). Responding to negative emotions with compassion drives good health. Coaches can therefore help their clients to respond better in emotionally draining situations by eliciting conscious compassion for others rather than unconscious emotional contagion.

Empathy for self

Another rather strange aspect of our empathic processing is our ability to empathise with ourselves. We are often more critical of our own behaviour than the behaviour of others. There is more than one reason why this might be true.

The first is level of detail: When we do something embarrassing, we judge ourselves not only on that event, but on previous similar events and therefore believe that people will be more critical of our behaviour than they really are. In fact, we are more correct about another's judgement of us when we reflect on how we might view this in ten years' time. This strips away some of the detail, making our interpretation more similar to that of someone who knows less about our past behaviour (Powers, and LaBar, 2019).

The second reason that this might be true is that the temporo-parietal junction (TPJ) is highly activated in empathising behaviour. However, the TPJ is not active when we think about our own behaviour – therefore, we do not seem to have the ability to empathise with ourselves (Young, et al., 2010). Since empathy developed in order to help social cohesion it is an important aspect of interacting in groups, but not when thinking about your own behaviour.

Coaches can assist their clients in being more empathetic with themselves by pointing out that this requires some effort and then by encouraging them to, for instance, consider what they might say to a good friend in their situation.

Explore and exploit

Some people are impatient when they perceive that there are better ways to do something, and want to try out new ideas. Other people are more likely to be concerned about what they might lose if things change. They like the status quo. Individuals, therefore, can hold very different beliefs about change. Some people can't live with it and some can't live without it.

When a particular situation is going well, we *exploit* it. We *refine* it to our needs, we *choose* how to manage it, we can *select* elements from the role that we enjoy, we can *implement* and *execute* our ideas and we *complete* projects (Cohen, et al., 2007).

By comparison, when a situation is working less well we *explore*. We might feel the need to *search* for alternatives, to *vary* our routine, to *pursue novelty* and *take risks*. We might *play* more, be more *flexible* and *innovate*. We are more likely to explore when we feel that our talents are under-utilised or under-rewarded or when we become bored and want more novelty (Cohen, et al., 2007).

Only exploiting or only exploring is limiting. While, in the short term, exploiting provides certainty and security, only exploiting can fail to create better opportunities through lack of flexibility and willingness to take risk. Only exploring can be exciting but can also lead to undeveloped ideas, inability to develop competence in any area and failure to complete projects.

Recently, neuroscientists have identified a part of the brain in the cingulate cortex (part of the brain used to calculate risk) that is active when we move from exploiting to exploring (or back again). When one part of this area is active, we exploit and when another part is active, we explore (Cohen, et al., 2007).

Understanding how and when individuals switch from exploit to explore enables coaches to help their clients to exploit or explore more. If a client wants to exploit more, then help them to create an environment that contains a sufficient level of challenge and choice which prevents boredom and rewards them for using their talents to the full. Or, if they want to explore more, then notice ways in which the current situation lacks novelty and under-uses abilities in order to feel that it is worth the risk of changing. Identifying increased reward or purpose will also encourage more exploring.

Ten useful questions for neuroscience coaches

The neuroscience techniques described here suggest some questions that might be useful to use with coaching clients. For instance, a coach might ask a client with a fixed mindset:

1. "What do you have to believe about yourself to choose the easy course of action and what would you have to believe to choose a harder course of action?"

    This might help the client to uncover the limiting beliefs that are preventing them from accepting a higher level of challenge.

    Another question that is useful for a client with a fixed mindset, or who reacts badly to feedback, is:

2. "What would you do differently if your only goal was to learn something from this situation?"

    In this case, the coach can help the client to treat feedback as an opportunity to learn and improve rather than as implied criticism.

    Clients that have an unwanted emotional response can be helped to consider whether the response is appropriate by asking them to:

3. "Consider your emotional response to this situation: On a scale of 0 (no emotional response) to 10 (the strongest emotional response to the most serious situation) where would you place this response? What level would be an appropriate response for this situation?"

    This can help a client to put their emotions in perspective and might allow them to choose a more appropriate response to the situation.

    If you have a coaching client that is considering a substantive change, which requires them to explore new opportunities, you might ask them:

4. "What are you currently exploiting that you would not want to lose?"

    Sometimes, what holds us back from new opportunities is fear of loss. Consciously identifying what it is that is important to retain can help your client to consider ways of creating change without losing this.

    Similarly, a client that is a more natural exploiter might be less aware of the benefits that change might bring. In this case, you might choose to ask them:

5. "What would be the benefits of exploring something new? What change is easily accessible and what is beyond the horizon?"

    This can help them to imagine new futures, both by exploring the easier next steps and those that might take more planning.

    A client that is overly focussed on a negative experience and is having trouble putting this in perspective might be helped by asking:

6. "What would this look like from five or ten years in the future?"

    This might help them to reduce the detail in their memory of the event and take a more realistic perspective on how they might be judged by others in the present and themselves in the future.

    Similarly, a client that appears to be judging themselves overly critically and therefore failing to show empathy or compassion for themselves might be asked:

7. "What would a good friend advise you in this situation? And what would you tell a good friend who had your challenge?"

    By saying aloud what they would advise a friend for whom they have empathy and compassion, it is possible that they will be more aware of the difference in compassion they display to others in comparison to themselves. This might help them to learn greater self-empathy.

For a client that has created a negative interpretation of a potentially ambiguous event, a coach might choose to ask them:

8. "What other story would account for the facts of the situation? And what other story?"

Creating multiple interpretations of the same event can be helpful in demonstrating that we construct our perceptions from sparse data and often over-interpret what we know. Sharing a number of different perspectives helps to make this explicit and can therefore reduce the impact of the initial, negative interpretation of events.

At the end of a GROW session, it can be useful to give the client an opportunity to consider both potential obstacles and how they might overcome these. A good question for this is:

9. "What might prevent you from reaching your goal and what steps could you put in place to circumvent this?"

Explicitly surfacing obstacles during a coaching session can help clients either to address these appropriately if they arise, or to prevent them from interfering with the plan at all.

Similarly, at the end of a GROW session, it can be useful to put in place a Plan B so that clients continue to act even if their first plan is not successful. A good question for this is:

10. *What will you do if you find that you do not follow your plan? What steps can you take to re-assess the situation and refocus on your goal?*

By having a Plan B, and even a Plan Z (worst-case scenario), clients can be more proactive in continuing towards their goals in the event of unexpected interruptions.

Conclusion

An understanding of neuroscience has the potential to increase the effectiveness of coaching through a greater understanding of how our brains operate. Already, a number of different techniques have been developed to take advantage of this understanding, and this will no doubt be expanded by the avalanche of research that is emerging from neuroscience laboratories worldwide. It is an exciting time to be a neuroscience coach.

References

Aarts, H. Custers, R. and Holland, R.W. (2007). 'The nonconscious cessation of goal pursuit: When goals and negative affect are coactivated'. *Journal of Personality and Social Psychology*, 92, pp. 165–178.

Beaty, R., Benedek, M., Kaufman, S. and Silvia, P. (2015). 'Default and executive network coupling supports creative idea production'. *Scientific Reports*, 5, p. 10964.

Begley, S. and Davidson, R.J. (2013). *The emotional life of your brain*. London: Hodder Press.

Bossons, P., Riddell, P. and Sartain, D. (2015). *The neuroscience of leadership coaching*. London: Bloomsbury Press.

Cohen, J.D., McClure, S.M. and Yu, A.J. (2007). 'Should I stay or should I go? How the human brain manages the trade-off between exploitation and exploration'. *Philosophical Transactions of the Royal Society, B*, 362, pp. 933–942.

Decety, J. and Svetlova, M. (2011). 'Putting together phylogenetic and ontogenetic perspectives on empathy'. *Developmental Cognitive Neuroscience*, 2, pp. 1–24.

Duckworth, A. and Gross, J. (2014) Self-control and grit: related but separable determinants of success. *Current Directions in Psychological Science,* 23, pp. 319–325.

Dweck, C. (2006). *Mindset: The new psychology of success*. New York: Random House.

Engen, H.G. and Singer, T. (2015). 'Compassion-based emotion regulation up-regulates experienced positive affect and associated neural networks'. *Social, Cognitive and Affective Neuroscience*. doi:10.1093/scan/nsv008.

Englander, Z., Haidt, J. and Morris, J. (2012). 'Neural basis of moral elevation demonstrated through inter-subject synchronization of cortical activity during free-viewing'. *PLoS One*, 7, pp. e39384.

Ernst, M., Pine, D. and Hardin, M. (2006). 'Triadic model of the neurobiology of motivated behaviour in adolescence'. *Psychological Medicine*, 36, pp. 299–312.

Feldman Barratt, L. (2017). *How emotions are made: The secret life of the brain*. New York: Houghton Mifflin Harcourt.

Kempermann, G. and Gage, F. (1999). 'Experience-dependent regulation of adult hippocampal neurogenesis: Effects of long-term stimulation and stimulus withdrawal'. *Hippocampus*, 9, pp. 321–332.

Lieberman, M., Eisenberger, N., Crockett, M., Tom, S., Pfeifer, J. and Way, B. (2007). 'Putting feelings into words: Affect labelling disrupts amygdala activity to affective stimuli'. *Psychological Science*, 18, pp. 421–428.

MacDonald, A., Cohen, J., Stenger, V.A. and Carter, C. (2000). 'Dissociating the role of the dorsolateral prefrontal and anterior cingulate cortex in cognitive control'. *Science*, 288, pp. 1835–1838.

Maguire, E., Frackkowiak, R. and Frith, C. (1997). 'Recalling routes around London: Activation of the right hipocampus in taxi drivers'. *Journal of Neuroscience*, 17, pp. 103–110.

McCrae, K., Hughes, B., Chopra, S., Gabrieli, J., Gross, J. and Ochsner, K. (2009) 'The neural bases of distraction and reappraisal'. *Journal of Cognitive Neuroscience*, 22, pp. 248–262.

Medea, B., Karapanagiotidis, T., Konishi, M., Ottaviani, C., Marguiles, D. et al. (2016). 'How do we decide what to do? Resting-state connectivity patterns and components of self-generated thought linked to the development of more concrete personal goals'. *Experimental Brain Research*, 236, pp. 2469–2481.

Michie, S., van Stralen, M. and West, R. (2011). 'The behaviour change wheel: A new method for characterising and designing behaviour change interventions'. *Implementation Science*, 6, p. 42.

Nemmi, F., Nymberg, C., Helander, E. and Klingberg, T. (2016) Grit is associated with structure of the Nucleus Accumbens and gains in cognitive training. *Journal of Cognitive Neuroscience,* 28, pp. 1688–1699.

Neroni, M., Gamboz, N. and Brandimonte, M. (2014). 'Does episodic future thinking improve prospective remembering?' *Consciousness and Cognition*, 23, pp. 53–62.

Panchal and Riddell (2020). 'The GROWS model: Extending the GROW coaching model to support behavioural change'. *The Coaching Psychologist*, In Press.

Powers, J. and LaBar, K. (2019). 'Regulating emotion through distancing: A taxonomy, neurocognitive model and supporting meta-analysis'. *Neuroscience and Biobehavioral Reviews*, 96, pp. 155–173.

Purves, D., Voyvodic, J., Magrassi, L. and Yawo, H. (1987). 'Nerve terminal remodelling visualized in living mice by repeated examination of the same neuron'. *Science*, 20, pp. 1122–1126.

Schwarzer, R. (2008) Modeling health behavior change: how to predict and modify the adoption and maintenance of health behaviors. *Applied Psychology*, 57, pp. 1–29.

Special issue of The Coaching Psychologist. (2015). *Enhancing the dialogue between the fields of neuroscience and coaching*, Vol. 11, June. London: The British Psychological Society.

Spielberger, J., Miller, G., Engels, A., Herrington, J., Sutton, B., Banich, M. and Heller, W. (2011). 'Trait approach and avoid motivation: Lateralized neural activity associated with executive function'. *NeuroImage*, 54, pp. 661–670.

Stober, D.R. and Grant, A.M. (2006). *Evidence based coaching handbook: Putting best practices to work for your clients*. Hoboken, NJ: John Wiley & Sons, Inc.

Stober, D.R., Wildflower, L. and Drake, D. (2006). 'Evidence-based practice: A potential approach for effective coaching'. *International Journal of Evidence Based Coaching and Mentoring*, 4, pp. 1–8.

Rosenberg-Katz, K., Jamshy, S., Singer, N., Podlipsky, I., Kervasser, S., Andelman, F. et al. (2012) Enhanced functional synchronization of medial and lateral PFC underlies internally-guided action planning. *Frontiers in Human Neuroscience*, Article 79.

Umeda, T. and Okabe, S. (2001). 'Visualizing synapse formation and remodelling: Recent advances in real-time imaging of CNS synapses'. *Neuroscience Research*, 40, pp. 291–300.

Van Praag, H., Kempermann, G. and Gage, F. (2000). 'Neural consequences of environmental enrichment'. *Nature Reviews: Neuroscience*, 1, pp. 191–198.

Whitmore, J. (2009) *Coaching for performance: Growing human potential and purpose*, 4th edition. London: Nicholas Brealey Publishing.

Young, L., Dodell-Feder, D. and Saxe, R. (2010). 'What gets the attention of the temporo-parietal junction? An fMRI investigation of attention and theory of mind'. *Neuropsychologia*, 48, pp. 2658–2664.

24 Narrative coaching

David Drake

Introduction

Narrative coaching was born out of a doctoral study on the liminal spaces between identity and story where growth happens (Drake, 2003). As the author explored what to do with his research, he found himself at a workshop on group dreaming. Narrative coaching emerged from a question that came to him that night: *What if the stories we tell in the daytime serve the same function as the dreams we have at night?* What if, in both cases, the characters are parts of ourselves, projected onto familiar forms as a means to work through our developmental issues in order to grow? This called for a very different approach to coaching in which the process: (1) focuses on the "field" in which it occurs less than the method; (2) engages in praxis as a dialectical process that starts with people's stories, creates a liberating dialogue and fosters a new level of consciousness and action (Freire, 1970); (3) invites clients to stay in their stories as they unfold in the present moment rather than set goals for later; and (4) helps clients explore and reformulate the connections between their stories believed, stories told, stories lived and stories desired (McAdams, 1993; White and Epston, 1990). In this chapter I will explain the nature of narrative coaching, review the developing evidence, and offer ways coaches can apply this approach in their practice through tools, techniques and useful questions.

Narrative coaching explained

Narrative coaching is a mindful, experiential and holistic approach to helping people to shift their stories in order to generate new options and new results. The narrative coaching model (see below) is a window through which coaches observe their clients and their narration, not a series of linear steps. We are coming alongside our clients and the change process they are in, and using the model to help them notice what their stories (and their telling) are revealing about where they are now and what they need in order to move forward. The stories people tell about their lives are of considerable importance in coaching because there is an intimate connection between the ways in which people narrate their identities and live their lives.

Stories provide powerful openings to explore these connections because they bring to the surface how people construct and navigate their world and can be used to guide them in making any shifts (Drake, 2018a; Schank, 1990). Narrative coaching draws extensively on narrative structure, narrative practices and narrative psychology to offer an integrative approach to coaching. These three sources reflect the three parallel processes that are woven into the model: (1) The four acts of a story; (2) the four phases of transitions and (3) the four elements of adult development. As a result, a virtuous cycle forms as people formulate a new story while they move through their change and transition, developing themselves in the process in terms of their identity and agency as someone who can enact it.

The narrative coaching model and approach are designed as a rite of passage, in large part to account for the larger narratives at play in and around clients' lives and work. Anthropologist Arthur van Gennep (1960) defined these rites as cultural practices for guiding people through important and/or cyclical transitions in their personal or communal lives using ritualised processes and resources. In a narrative coaching context, a rite of passage is seen as a movement through four phases (see below):

1. A separation from the outer world to embark on a journey into the inner world to undergo a transformation in one's identity and narrative;
2. An individuation as one overcomes obstacles to transit the inner world in search of what will bring restoration and maturation;
3. A reincorporation as one leaves the inner world to return to the outer world with what has been gained through exploration and experimentation;
4. An integration of the transformation into a new identity and narrative in the outer world, often with subsequent changes relating to the environment. See Figure 24.1.

The narrative coaching model has four phases:

1. SITUATE: Notice how the person is situated (in the moment, the session, the story). Be a non-judgmental *witness* to them as the *narrator*, and build rapport and the crucible for the conversation. The focus is on "*what is*"[1] and *what is being said*.[2] It is about being here now – not setting goals, gathering lots of information or trying to get somewhere. The threshold they must cross to get to the next phase is *Separation* (T1).

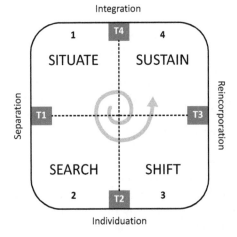

Figure 24.1 Narrative coaching model

2. SEARCH: Help the person discover what they are truly searching for by exploring key elements in their stories, experiencing new perspectives and getting to the crux of the issue. Be an *advocate* for the whole *story* and its reason for being in the conversation. The focus is on "*what if*" and *what is not being said (yet)*. The threshold they must cross is *Individuation* (T2).
3. SHIFT: Help the person identify what needs to shift in order to enact what was discovered in Search. Be a *guardian* of the space and the characters in their story who have an important role to play. Engage in serious play and invite the person to experiment with new ways of being in service of their aspiration. The focus is on "*what matters*" and *what wants to be said*. The threshold they must cross is *Reincorporation* (T3).
4. SUSTAIN: Support the person to create structures for success so they can sustain what they have gained when they "go home". Be a *steward* of the process of closure so the person feels complete and is prepared. The focus is on "*what works*" and using what was significant and effective for the person in the session to inform the scaffolding they will take with them to be successful. The threshold they must cross is *Integration* (T4).

Narrative coaching theory and research

In narrative coaching, evidence is seen as a co-constructed and dynamic process that informs the decisions made in coaching as it unfolds, emerges from what is generated in the conversation, gleans meaning from the results and enriches the broader professional base. It transcends the positivistic discourse on evidence in favour of a more integrative approach to evidence that is more closely tied to and useful for practice. Narrative coaching puts stock in personal reflexivity, valid and relevant research, professional experience and contextual awareness on behalf of clients and the environments in which they live and work (Drake and Stelter, 2014). In part, this is based on the observation that masterful narrative coaches are informed less by academic studies and more by their wisdom, their experience, their mastery and their dedication to generative outcomes.

This stance reflects the commitment in narrative coaching to: (1) The direct experience of human phenomena; (2) the advocacy for alternate discourses, (3) the recognition of collective and non-conscious forces affecting our narration; (4) the value of embodied wisdom and mastery; (5) the commitment to Integrative Development; and (6) the narrative bill of rights for clients. It is not surprising, then, that most narrative research is descriptive and qualitative in nature and aligns with the philosophy and pedagogy in narrative coaching. Much of the research that has informed this work to date has been drawn from narrative analysis and research efforts in the social sciences, as well as from five domains: Anthropology; identity and transformative learning; Jungian psychology; neuroscience and spiritual development; and narrative studies.

Narrative coaching moves beyond the individualistic and psychological orientation used in most approaches to coaching to incorporate systemic perspectives which reflect its commitment to a more integrative approach (Drake, 2018b). Stelter (2014) positions narrative coaching as a "third-generation practice" in which

> the coach's ambition of remaining neutral is toned down, and the main focus is on collaborative and co-creative dialogues. The coach and the client (or group of clients) are dialogue partners and have a mutual relationship as reflective fellow human beings in a relationship that is characterized by varying degrees of symmetry over time.
>
> (pp. 118–119)

In recent years, narrative coaching has been further enriched through the incorporation of non-dualist paradigms such as Buddhism to balance the Western frames that are dominant in coaching.

The extensive academic foundation for narrative coaching was both chronicled and extended through Drake's doctoral work (Drake, 2003). It has been deepened in subsequent years through his over 60 publications in coaching-related journals and books as well as the definitive guide to this work (Drake, 2018b). This includes numerous case studies on the use of narrative coaching (Drake, 2018b), as well as the seminal paper introducing the research on attachment theory into the coaching literature (Drake, 2009). It provides a framework for working with clients' preverbal and somatic patterns as they arise in coaching sessions in support of greater attachment security as the foundation for maturation.

Narrative coaching in practice

Narrative coaches provide both an *interpersonal structure* and a *narrative structure* for their clients. The former is about creating a safe space for the client as a storyteller to bring the whole story into the room and to do the developmental work that arises from doing so. The latter is about offering a process for a client to deeply engage with the stories themselves and to do the instrumental work to bring their new story to life. Together, they illustrate the centrality of the "field" in narrative coaching as a generative time and space for clients, and coaches are committed to radical presence and working in the moment with what is present. To be able to work this way, there is a strong focus in narrative coaching on the psycho-spiritual development of the practitioner to be able to deeply hold that space and freely work in it.

Narrative coaching practitioners are guided by the following six principles:

- Trust that everything you need is right in front of you;
- Be fully present to what *is* without judgment;
- Speak only when you can improve on silence;
- Focus on generating experiences not explanations;
- Work directly with the narrative elements in the field;
- Stand at the threshold when a new story is emerging.

(Drake, 2018b, p. 18)

These principles align with Gallwey's (1981) view that, if you want to change something, first increase your awareness of the way it is. This opens up more space to discover, explore and potentially reframe their habitual narrative patterns and open up new possibilities for their development and outcomes. Often this level of presence leads to an evaporation of initial goals that makes room for a deeper level of truth. Narrative coaches work in the moment with the unfolding narration and *what is* rather than prematurely move to *what could be*, as is common in many other approaches. In this sense, we see narrative coaches in "maieutic" terms (Kenyon and Randall, 1997), as midwives who help people to birth new stories and facilitate their transformation at key junctures.

Narrative coaches track how people organise their stories, e.g., which events are included, which themes they organise around, which characters are portrayed as significant, which voices are privileged in the telling (Botella and Herrero, 2000) and which stories about reality contribute to their suffering. This is best done experientially rather than just discursively, e.g., inviting them to become aware of their experience in telling their story or experimenting with telling it in a new way. The aim is to get to the crux of issues and the thresholds where clients' "*emplotment*" strategies (how they make sense and meaning of events) have broken down or are no longer working. These gaps in narration can be seen as "breaches" (Bruner, 1986) and the stories people tell us as attempts to resolve the discrepancy between what they expected and what has transpired. These gaps are an opportune time to help clients to formulate a different story and outcome because it is in these liminal, in-between spaces, where growth most often occurs.

This is important because, if you want clients to adopt new behaviours or attain new results, you must help them access new aspects of their identity and new narratives that support them. At the same time, to sustain the new identity, people need to enact new behaviours – and the stories that go with them (Markus and Nurius, 1986). Narrative coaches also know that the stories told in coaching sessions, even if they have served as a transformational vehicle in that setting, must survive the "retellings" if people are to sustain the changes they have begun. As a result, there is a greater than usual attention paid to the fourth phase (Sustain) in the narrative coaching model so that they can, with increasing consistency, apply what they have experienced and learned (Drake, 2018a).

The following case story is about a coaching client whose presenting issue was her frustration with and judgment about her boss. A key step in the process was getting her to own and be accountable for the story as hers.

1. SITUATE: I am feeling very frustrated. I'm upset because the leader in charge of this project regularly points out small mistakes in our team's reports, but he doesn't acknowledge what we are doing well or how hard we are working.
2. SEARCH: When I hear myself talk about what it is like to put together these reports every two weeks, I realise that I am not putting in as much effort as I used to and, on top of that, I frankly don't like working at this level of detail anymore.
3. SHIFT: When I look at my situation from the perspective of the reports, they feel like a heavy burden. I was thinking I wanted coaching to help move on, but I see now that this was just a reactive response. What I really want is to figure out how to talk to my boss about communicating with us in a very different way.
4. SUSTAIN: I am noticing a shift in myself from blaming and reacting to my leader to a deeper appreciation for the real issue and how I want to move forward. This has helped me realise that I actually enjoy most of my current job. I'm excited to stretch myself by presenting this request to my boss and working on a solution with him.

Tools and Techniques

A narrative coaching session is like a lab in which clients work with the elements in their stories in real time. Coaches are seen as alchemists, not architects. In coaching this way, narrative coaches often literally and figuratively move between centred and de-centred positions relative to their clients. This may include facing clients at the start to build sufficient rapport and trust, then de-centring themselves by shifting their position to be more at an angle to explore the narrative material with the client, and then re-centring themselves when a stronger relational connection is needed (e.g., due to increased vulnerability) or a new experience seems called for in the moment.

The focus here is on the story as it is being told in the here and now. Gallwey's work on the inner game (see Gallwey, 1981/2009) and Kramer's (2007) work on relational meditation are both helpful here. Narrative coaches continually bring people back into their present experience in order to connect the proverbial "dots" and provide a more solid basis for change. This is important in coaching because, as David J. Wallin (2007) notes, "It is largely through activating bodily and sensory experience in the session and linking such experience to images and words that can be reflected upon that we facilitate the integration that is the basis of therapeutic change" (p. 294). In the process, trust that clients will begin at the level at which they are ready and the critical themes will be forthcoming regardless of which stories they share first. Any story or set of stories can be a portal into the larger issues at play for them and the path to reaching their resolution or aspiration.

A key role for coaches then is to invite people to see their stories from different perspectives, to notice how they are constructed (or even that they are constructed), to note their limits and influences and to discover other possibilities (Freedman and Combs, 1996). It is about helping people to notice the differences between the stories they are telling and the stories they are living, as well as to identify narrative "data" from their lives that would support an alternate view of who they are and/or how they want to be in the world. Narrative coaching draws on Drake's work in Integrative Development see (Drake, 2019) and the iBEAM framework (identity, Behaviour, Environment, Aspiration and Mindset) in particular, to help clients create structures for success as they move back out into the world with what they have learned and gained from coaching. These variables were drawn from the author's analysis of the research on factors for improving performance.

One of the core narrative coaching tools is the Narrative Pivot, and it is often formed in the Shift phase. It is a simple binary choice between two storylines – defined using clients' own words (as short, parallel and memorable phrases) – they can make in the moment. It is about asking themselves, "Is what I am about to do or say move me in the direction of my new story I am moving toward or my old story which I am leaving behind?". They are activated when a client encounters a cue (e.g., just got home from work) or a trigger (e.g., partner did not do the dishes again as promised). Pausing at those points and having a Pivot handy makes it easier for clients to take the first step in a new direction. Pivots work well because they provide a simple focus that can be practised throughout the day and allow for more adaptive responses. Clients can use their Pivots to help them better self-regulate and choose well rather than lapse into reactive defaults. See Figure 24.2.

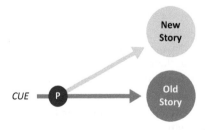

Figure 24.2 Narrative Pivot

A frequently used narrative coaching tool is the Narrative Rewind Process. It is used to help clients notice, own and shift the narrative patterns that impede their ability to achieve the outcomes they are seeking:

1. Reflect on a conversation or situation you found challenging. Answer each of the questions in order, recalling the situation. Notice where you end up and the impact of your story on your outcome.
   - What did you observe? *Experience*;
   - What were you telling yourself at the time? *Story*;
   - What does this say about how you see yourself? *Identity*;
   - What did you do as a result? *Behaviour*;
   - What happened in the end? *Outcome*.

2. Rewind the process, starting with the outcome you wanted instead. Notice where you end up and how this new story would yield a better outcome.
   - What would you like to have had happen in the end? *Outcome*;
   - What could you have done differently as a result? *Behaviour*;
   - What would need to shift in how you see yourself? *Identity*;
   - What could you tell yourself next time this happens? *Story*;
   - What would you observe if "this" were the case? *Experience*.

When does narrative coaching work best?

Narrative coaching has been applied in any number of individual and group settings. It paradoxically feels slow to those who are in it or are observing it, but can often lead to significant breakthroughs more quickly than more traditional methods. This is because we are working directly and experientially at the crux of issues – and can laser in when the moment is right for accelerated development. Even so, it works best when both parties are willing to work in a deeply human and collaborative manner. Narrative coaching clients often report great relief to be able to work in a more natural way that they can continue with on their own after sessions. Coaches appreciate it because they get to bring their whole self to their practice, travel lighter and with greater agility and feel confident knowing that the research is embedded in the process.

Narrative coaching often works best with coaches and clients who have: (1) A comfort with silence and self-reflection; (2) a willingness to work openly at somatic, metaphorical and non-conscious levels; (3) an astute awareness of and ability to articulate their emotional and sensory experience; (4) the necessary ego strength to engage in "moments of meeting" (Drake, 2009) where they are willing to be transformed; and (5) sufficient comfort and capability to work within what Drake calls "structured emergence". Obviously, this is more challenging if any of these four conditions are not present in the coach and/or client.

Narrative coaching works well as a framework for embedding coaching skills in an organisation because it uses natural human language and is built on the human process of change, not an artificial structure for a conversation. It has been integrated into dozens of initiatives, functions and applications to enable clients to shift cultures, develop teams, upgrade conversations and transform how work is done. The most successful uses of it have led organisations to translate and embed coaching in (most) every aspect of how work gets done. A narrative approach to coaching works exceptionally well across cultures as it is less tied to Western epistemologies and more easily tuned to local dynamics. It is quite useful in giving voice to non-dominant groups as part of a larger evolution in the systems in which they work and live, e.g., in organisations embarking on culture change.

Ten commonly used questions for the narrative coach

Questions narrative coaches ask themselves

1. *What am I noticing?*
   This question is designed to help coaches to track their inner and outer experience to ensure they are staying present to what is unfolding in the session more than their own formulation. This keeps coaches aware and alert to what is actually happening.
2. *What is being activated in me as I am coaching?*
   This question is designed to help coaches to notice what is being triggered in them by clients and their stories so they can self-regulate and return to centre as needed. It is essential in keeping coaches true to their professional and narrative ethics.
3. *What do they need most right now?*
   This question is designed to help coaches to assess where clients are in their own change process and what is the work to be done now in order to move forward. It is often more productive for clients to address one issue at a time.
4. *What does this story want us to pay attention to?*
   This question is designed to help coaches to discern the crux of clients' issues through what is being said and not said (yet) in their stories. It is often easier for clients to start by working with their stories in the room before looking within themselves.
5. *What story am I in? What role am I being "asked" to play? Want to play?*
   This question is designed to help coaches to observe the conversation while remaining radically present in order to sense the larger patterns in play. It is about noticing how you show up in clients' stories and what needs to shift in your role to facilitate change.

Questions narrative coaches commonly ask their clients

6. *What are you noticing right now?*
   This question is designed to help clients become more aware of the "field" in sessions, what stories they are choosing to tell and the impact of those choices in the session (and their life). It helps the coach and the client enhance what they can sense.
7. *What comes up for you when you say that? What is important to you about that?*
   This question is designed to help clients become more aware of their internal state as they are recalling, forming and telling their story. It deepens their understanding of what their stories are trying to say and builds their capacity to do so on their own.
8. *Where does that story live in you?*
   This question is designed to help clients to increase their sensory awareness of their body and how/where their stories have informed their way of being in the world. It is also about engaging their whole self in developing and embodying new stories.
9. *What does the story need in order to feel complete?*
   This question is designed to help clients to see their stories as messengers which seek to make visible something that is invisible (to themselves and/or others) so it can be addressed. It is about becoming present to and discerning the longing that is unfulfilled.
10.   *What other perspectives could you take? What keeps you from considering them?*
   This question is designed to help clients to look at their situation in new ways so they can see more of the whole picture and imagine new options. It is about releasing their attachments to old stories so they can make space for new stories.

Conclusion

One of the questions the author has been asked most often, particularly in the beginning, is: "How is this different than therapy?". When asked, his answer remains the same: "Done well, narrative coaching is inherently therapeutic for people. Otherwise, why bother". Narrative coaching uses some of the same techniques as psychotherapy, such as cathartic insight, emotional healing and issue resolution, to create a foundation for new actions. However, there is more emphasis in narrative coaching on direct experience and taking new actions towards the future than you would find in most therapeutic methodologies. The bottom line is that coaches should work at the deepest level for which they are qualified and invited, and at the appropriate level for a client's readiness and the issue at hand.

This human-centred approach to coaching moves beyond modernist assumptions, linear development models, extroverted goal-orientation and lingering biases towards behaviourism to create a truly post-professional and integrative approach to developing people. It shifts the emphasis from the coach and coaching methodologies to the coaching relationship and the stories that emerge there. As William Bridges notes, the main thing to do is not to hurry up and figure things out, but just to centre yourself and wait watchfully. It is a methodology that was made for this time as a pandemic grips the globe and many are raising important questions about the future of communities, economies and the eco-systems in which we live. Perhaps it is time for a collective rite of passage in imagining new ways of living and working on the other side. For all the coaches and clients who are ready for this work and these conversations, narrative coaching will be an invaluable resource.

Notes

1 Acknowledging the parallels between narrative coaching and design thinking.
2 From Drake's Narrative Diamond model (2018b).

References

Botella, L. and Herrero, L. (2000). 'A relational constructivist approach to narrative therapy'. *European Journal of Psychotherapy, Counselling & Health*, 3(3), pp. 407–418.

Bruner, Jerome. (1986). *Actual minds, possible worlds*. Cambridge, MA: Harvard University Press.

Drake, D.B. (2003). *How stories change: A narrative analysis of liminal experiences and transitions in identity* (Dissertation). Santa Barbara: Fielding Graduate Institute.

Drake, D.B. (2009). 'Using attachment theory in coaching leaders: The search for a coherent narrative'. *International Coaching Psychology Review*, 4(1), pp. 49–58.

Drake, D.B. (2018a). 'Narrative coaching'. In Elaine Cox, Tatiana Bachkirova and David A. Clutterbuck, eds., *The complete handbook of coaching*. London, UK: Sage Publications, pp. 109–123.

Drake, D.B. (2018b). *Narrative coaching: The definitive guide to bringing new stories to life*, 2nd ed. Petaluma: CNC Press.

Drake, David B. (2019). Using integrative development to create a coaching culture in a professional services firm. In Robert G. Hamlin, Andrea D. Ellinger, ans Jenni Jones (Eds.), *Evidence-based initiatives for organizational change and development* (pp. 506–514). Hershey, PA: IGI Global.

Drake, D.B. and Stelter, R. (2014). Narrative coaching. In Jonathan Passmore, ed., *Mastery in coaching: A complete psychological toolkit for advanced coaching*. London: Kogan Page, pp. 65–96.

Freedman, J. and Combs, G. (1996). *Narrative therapy: The social construction of preferred realities*. New York: W.W. Norton.

Freire, P. (1970). *Pedagogy of the oppressed*. New York: Seabury Press.

Gallwey, T. (1981/2009). *The inner game of golf*. New York: Random House.

Kenyon, G.M. and Randall, W.L. (1997). *Restorying our lives: Personal growth through autobiographical reflection.* Westport: Praeger.

Kramer, G. (2007). *Insight dialogue: The interpersonal path to freedom.* Boston: Shambhala.

Markus, H. and Nurius, P. (1986). Possible selves. *American Psychologist*, 41(9), pp. 954–969.

McAdams, D.P. (1993). *The stories we live by: Personal myths and the making of the self.* New York: The Guilford Press.

Schank, R. (1990). *Tell me a story: A new look at real and artificial memory.* New York: Scribner.

Stelter, R. (2014). *A guide to third generation coaching: Narrative-collaborative theory and practice.* New York: Springer.

van Gennep, A. (1960). *The rites of passage* (Monika B. Vizedom and Gabrielle L. Caffee, Trans.). Chicago: The University of Chicago Press.

Wallin, David J. (2007). *Attachment in psychotherapy.* New York: The Guilford Press.

White, M. and Epston, D. (1990). *Narrative means to therapeutic ends.* New York: W.W. Norton.

25 Systemic team coaching

Lucy Widdowson and Paul J. Barbour

Introduction

How people work together, are each connected and are part of a wider system, has always been an important aspect of the human experience. During our careers as leaders and team coaches, we have both witnessed the importance of top-performing teams and their positive impact on organisational success. It has been suggested that during the late 19th and early 20th centuries work consisted of a collection of individual jobs. However, more recently, to work with speed and flexibility in an uncertain and global market, organisations have had to embrace the power of teams (Kozlowski and Ilgen, 2006).

In this chapter, we will describe how systemic team coaching is helping teams across the globe become attuned to their deeper purpose and the work only they can do together. We will explain what systemic team coaching is and introduce the "Creating the Team Edge" framework and the research that underpins it. Importantly, we will discuss what it takes to develop as a systemic team coach. Also, we will introduce some practical tools and techniques that we have found useful in our work with teams. The chapter will conclude with ten useful questions for team coaches.

Systemic team coaching explained

There is almost universal agreement that team coaching is a relatively new concept that lacks the consistency of definition, practice and empirical evidence (Jones et al., 2019; O'Connor and Cavanagh, 2016; Clutterbuck, 2014). The 'Ridler Report' (2016) noted that, while team coaching accounted for 9% of total coaching, some 76% of the organisations surveyed expected to increase their use of team coaching over the next two years. This growth in team coaching is being supported by an increasing number of practitioner-led textbooks (see Widdowson and Barbour, 2021; Hawkins, 2017; Thornton, 2016), as well as increased interest from both the professional coaching bodies and academic institutions.

Before considering a definition of team coaching, it is important to understand what we mean by "team". The word is widely yet oftentimes loosely used. Indeed, many teams are teams in name only. Katzenback and Smith suggest a team is: "a small number of people with complementary skills who are committed to a common purpose, performance goals, and approach for which they hold themselves mutually accountable" (Katzenback and Smith, 1993, p. 45).

Team coaching definitions have highlighted the importance of a common goal, individual performance, group collaboration and performance (Thornton, 2016), as well as increasing the collective capability (Clutterbuck, 2014; Jones et al., 2019) of a team. However, team coaching is about much more than the team itself. It's about how the team, consciously and

Table 25.1 Comparison of different forms of coaching

Intervention	Definition
Individual coaching	Coaching is partnering with clients in a thought-provoking and creative process, that inspires them to maximise their personal and professional potential (ICF, 2020).
Team coaching	Team coaching helps teams work together, with others and within their wider environment, to create lasting change by developing safe and trusting relationships, better ways of working and new thinking, so that they maximise their collective potential, purpose and performance goals (Widdowson and Barbour, 2019, p. 2).
Group coaching	Hawkins has differentiated group coaching, as "the coaching of individuals within a group context", from team coaching, where "the primary client is the whole team" (2017, p. 71).
Team building	Team building tends to focus on improving interpersonal relationships, productivity and alignment, with an organisation's goals. It typically consists of short, often one-day interventions (Kriek and Venter, 2009).
Team facilitation	While a coach may at times use facilitation skills, facilitation can be considered a way of helping a team manage their dialogue, compared to team coaching, which aims to empower a team to take ownership for their own dialogue (Clutterbuck, 2007).

unconsciously, works with other teams in their organisation and other organisations. Also, it's about how the team engages with its wider environment. Hawkins (2017) has used the term "ecosystemic team coaching" to describe a team operating dynamically with other connected teams, external partners and wider stakeholder networks.

When developing our definition of team coaching, we have consciously attempted to use terminology that is understandable to as wide an audience as possible. Therefore, we define systemic team coaching as follows: Team coaching helps teams work together, with others and within their wider environment, to create lasting change by developing safe and trusting relationships, better ways of working and new thinking, so that they maximise their collective potential, purpose and performance goals. (Widdowson and Barbour, 2019, p. 2)

Despite our own and others' efforts to define team coaching, confusion still exists. To help increase clarity, it is helpful to draw comparisons to some other major types of team intervention, which we have summarised in Table 25.1.

Despite the limited evidenced-based literature on the impact and results from team coaching, our experience and research has shown that team coaching can have a lasting positive change, both on the performance of a team and the teams interfacing with the team itself. This is supported by numerous studies, including Wageman et al. (2008), with their research of 120 teams and, more recently, Peters and Carr (2013), with their study of 2 Canadian leadership teams. The next step is for the development of a comprehensive theory of team coaching and its effectiveness (Jones et al., 2019).

Team coaching theory and research

The "Creating the Team Edge" approach to team coaching was developed by Lucy Widdowson at Performance Edge. The approach is the culmination of over 25 years experience leading and working with teams and research into the characteristics of high-performing teams. This work has been further developed in collaboration with Paul J. Barbour (Widdowson and Barbour, 2021).

Figure 25.1 "Creating the Team Edge" (Widdowson, 2017; © Performance Edge, 2015)

Our book emphasises the importance of the team coach firstly, building connection with the team and creating a feeling of psychological safety and trust. Nevertheless, models and tools of team effectiveness are also helpful in supporting and guiding the team coach in both the design and delivery of a team coaching intervention.

The "Creating the Team Edge" framework (see Figure 25.1) consists of seven characteristics that can be used by team coaches when coaching a team. The seven characteristics are each described in Table 25.2.

A study conducted in a leading UK retailer (Widdowson, 2018), reported that all seven characteristics were perceived to contribute to improvements in both individual and team development, team effectiveness and team performance. Among other findings, three important themes included:

1. **Alignment of purpose**: The teams became aligned in their purpose, values and beliefs, identity and collective team goals.
2. **Psychological safety** (part of the relatedness characteristic in the framework): The teams developed an increased level of psychological safety, meaning they could be more open and honest, could show vulnerability and give robust feedback.
3. **Team learning** (part of the transformation characteristic in the framework): The teams shared knowledge and best practice with each other.

The study concluded that "the framework was viewed as providing a useful and simple model to support practitioners, leaders and teams to become more effective". It also highlighted the need to provide more tools and techniques to help guide team coaches when designing and developing team coaching programmes (Widdowson, 2018).

Systemic team coaching in practice

We are often asked, "how can I develop as a team coach?". While much focus has been given to competencies for one-to-one coaching, unsurprisingly given its relative newness, less focus has been given to the competencies of a team coach. Nevertheless, we would

Table 25.2 Creating the Team Edge: The seven characteristics and descriptions (Widdowson, 2017)

Characteristic	Description
Purpose	A statement of why the team exists, which captures the spirit of what it is the team is trying to do by working together. It should also include what the team uniquely contributes to both its own organisation, its stakeholders and the wider system. The purpose statement only has weight when accompanied by collective performance goals.
Identity	The team works on developing their unique identity. The identity binds them together and constantly reinforces the team's positive mindset, energy and motivation. The team identity will be recognised and admired by both those inside and outside the team.
Values and beliefs	Values and beliefs in teams provide a sense of what is right and wrong. The team explores and agrees on the culture it desires and considers the values, standards and behaviours that will underpin the team's efforts. Belief in the team's purpose, identity and values are essential for the team to fully perform.
Awareness	Teams increase their awareness and consciousness of each other's strengths and personal preferences and how to leverage them for the benefit of the team as a whole. The team also develops an awareness of how it interacts with its wider stakeholders and system.
Relatedness	Teams develop their sense of unity and build mutual trust, support and understanding. Teams invest time in open and honest conversations to work more closely together and build strong relationships within the wider organisation.
Ways of working	The team invests time in setting up the best systems and processes to enable them to make confident and effective decisions. The team works on improving the structure of their meetings and how they engage with others in order to deliver concrete outcomes.
Transformation	Teams explore ways to challenge their performance and look for opportunities to test their abilities. The team rigorously reviews their plans, applies innovative ways to think differently and ensure they are always improving, learning and supporting each other's development.

agree with the view of Clutterbuck et al. (2019, p. 2), that team coaching is "gradually assuming distinct professional characteristics". A key part of this journey is the development of team coaching competencies, a topic that has attracted the interest of the different professional coaching bodies (e.g. ICF, AC, EMCC). Team coaching competencies help the team coach consider what and how to develop.

Based on our experience and research we have proposed the "Being, Doing and Knowing" model of team coaching competencies. At the core of the model, is the "Being" element (see Figure 25.2). The model has been inspired by the importance of "Being", highlighted by Rogers (1995), Renshaw and Alexander (2005) and, more recently, Van Nieuwerburgh (2017). We will discuss "Doing" and "Knowing" first.

The "Doing" of a team coach

The "Doing" element of team coaching competencies builds upon the core competencies of the professional coaching bodies (ICF, 2019; AC, 2012; EMCC, 2015), which we have identified under eight headings, as follows:

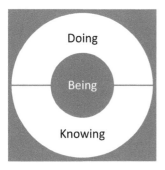

Figure 25.2 The "Being, Doing and Knowing" model of team coaching competency (Widdowson and Barbour, 2021)

- Developing a trusting relationship (psychological safety)
- Ethical practice
- Coaching mindset and presence
- CPD (Continued Professional Development)
- Contracting
- Creating awareness and insight
- Effective communication
- Client growth and momentum

It is our view that, because coaching activities are at the heart of team coaching, a team coach should be competent in coaching individuals. Therefore, the core competencies as presented by the professional coaching bodies, offer a strong starting platform for a developing team coach. However, team coaching is not one-to-one coaching. For each of the eight headings, additional aspects need to be considered for team coaching. For example, when "developing a trusting relationship", the team coach needs to be able to develop a safe relationship with the team collectively, while at the same time attending to individual relationships. Another example is, "effective communication". When working at a systemic level, the team coach needs to be able to listen and ask questions that engage at the level of the team, its individuals, the organisation and the wider environment.

The "Knowing" of a team coach

While there is some overlap with the "Doing" competencies of a team coach, we believe there are several "Knowing" competencies that are essential for team coaches. These include:

- Systemic practice
- Group dynamics
- Facilitation skills
- Physical and virtual learning design
- Team leadership and development

- Organisational development
- Team coaching literature and frameworks
- Organisational and team context
- Team diagnostics

Three key areas we would highlight include the importance of "systemic practice", as discussed earlier in the chapter, "group dynamics" and "physical and virtual learning design".

A team coach needs to be acutely aware of the "group dynamics" that are both visible and invisible (see Thornton, 2016). While the competency of learning design has always been an important area for team coaches, the ability to work both physically and virtually is also important. Working in the virtual environment requires the team coach to be extremely attuned to how they will develop trust and how they read and manage group dynamics.

The "Being" of a team coach

At the centre of our model and, in our view, the most important competency, is a team coach's "way of being". To explain the "Being" competency of a team coach we have proposed "The 4 C's of Being" that include, connection, confidence, continuing and courage (Widdowson and Barbour, 2021).

Connection. The team coach must be able to connect deeply with the team as a whole and its individuals. Rogers (1995) in his book, *A Way of Being*, when discussing the therapeutic relationship has highlighted the importance of being empathic, genuine and non-judging. We believe each of these areas is essential for a team coach to connect deeply.

Confidence. A team coach must have confidence in who they are. They are likely to be presented with difficult situations, that will require them to be secure and confident in their work as a team coach.

Continuing. The team coach needs to accept they will never be the finished article and that is ok. What is important is a commitment to self-reflection and self-discovery. Also, a team coach should be committed to supervision by an experienced team coach or a supervisor with experience in group dynamics and systemic practice.

Courage. A team coach should consider themselves as an instrument, who is aware of their feelings and has thoughts "in the moment" that, with courage, they explore with the team. Also, a team coach needs to plan professionally, but be willing to "let go" and take risks, calling upon all their experience and wisdom.

Tools and techniques

Another common question is: What does a team coaching intervention look like? Whilst there is no exact science, from our experience, a team coaching programme will usually involve a multi-dimensional and integrated approach. An example is shown in Figure 25.3.

The team coaching programme is likely to include a series of module-style workshops either face to face, using a virtual platform or a blend of both. During the workshops, often the work of the team will just emerge. A point supported by Hastings and Pennington

Stage 1 Pre team coaching	Stage 2 Interviews and team diagnostic	Stage 3 Co design team coaching	Stage 4 Workshop1	Stage 5 Workshop 2	Stage 6 Workshop 3 +	Stage 7 Evaluation
Establish team coaching need Establish team coaching readiness Initial contracting with key stakeholders and team leader	1-2-1 with each team member and selected stakeholders Team members and selected stakeholders complete team diagnostic Issue pre reading and links to online resources	Co design and agree team coaching journey using feedback from interviews and team diagnostic	*Example areas:* building relationships, team purpose, identity, values and beliefs	*Example areas:* team awareness, relatedness and ways of working	*Example areas:* Team transformation and additional workshops as per re-contracting	Review (can repeat diagnostic) Evaluation Return on Investment

Intervention format: mixture of face to face and virtual workshops, sharing of materials, 1-2-1 coaching, peer coaching, re-contracting meetings.

1-2-1 coaching: ideally for each team member and at a minimum the team leader and selected team members based on identified team development needs.

Team observation: as per agreement. Can take place at any agreed point during the team coaching intervention.

Figure 25.3 An example of a "Creating the Team Edge" programme (Widdowson and Barbour, 2021)

(2019) who stated, "team coaches should be open to using whatever the emerging situation requires, in a real, live environment" (p. 183). In addition, the team coach may also use tools and techniques to help the team explore, reflect and develop the characteristics of high-performing teams.

Two examples of tools and techniques that teams we have worked with have found very impactful are outlined below. The team coach must build psychological safety and connection first. The tools should be used as a guide that, when used, feel natural and emergent rather than a step-by-step process.

Technique 1: The team shield – developing team purpose and values

In a dynamic world where jobs for life are a thing of the past, individuals and teams want to be clearer about why their job exists, what is important about what they do and how it adds value to the organisation and the wider community.

Teams, therefore, also want to be clearer about why and how they work together as a team – a key question to ask is what can the team deliver that team members on their own cannot? This tool can help teams become clearer on their collective answer to these questions. It can be used for teams of any size or composition and is probably best used at the beginning of a team coaching programme.

This technique helps teams: Develop a compelling purpose; a strapline or team motto; agree on the values that are important to them; and articulate and recognise what they are good at and how they will work with stakeholders within their organisational system.

Exercise 1: Team shield

Here is what you do:

- Create a blank team shield on the wall using flipchart sheets or on a virtual whiteboard.

Example of a blank team shield

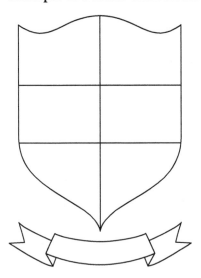

- Agree five or six headings for the team to work on, e.g. purpose, vision, goals, values, team charter, strengths, qualities, behaviours, how the team will work with stakeholders, team strapline/motto.

Example of a team shield with selected headings for populating

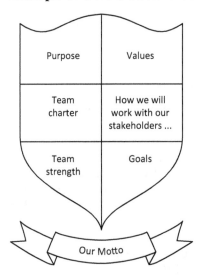

- Split the team into sub-teams depending on the number of headings.
- Each team works on their part of the team shield for around 30 minutes. If using a virtual platform break out rooms can be used.
- During the agreed amount of time, team members from each team have the opportunity to collaborate with other sub-teams to gain further insights and check team

alignment across the different sections of the team shield. Sub-teams can send scouts out to different sub-teams to share and build on each other's ideas.

- At the end of the allotted time, all parts of the shield are displayed together.
- The entire team shares their outputs with the sub-teams, asking each other questions.
- The team then agrees on any amends, resulting in their final team shield content.
- Finally, the team discusses and agrees on next steps and how they will apply the team shield.

Top tip: Teams can find it challenging to work on purpose, therefore they may want to capture phrases and ideas first, gain insight from other groups and then try to craft a purpose statement.

Technique 2: Feedback goldfish bowl – developing relatedness

Teams often shy away from having "real" open and honest conversations. However, teams and team members need to have robust conversations to work more closely together, build strong relationships and ultimately improve their individual and team performance. Teams who lack trust can often avoid debating ideas and engaging in difficult conversations. This, in turn, leads to hidden discussions and team members not openly sharing their views (Lencioni, 2002). This technique enables teams to address these issues.

This technique helps team members: Increase awareness of their strengths and areas to work on; to give and receive feedback from one another; and improve individual and team performance.

Exercise 2: Feedback goldfish bowl

This exercise can be very impactful and enlightening for teams. It can also be very challenging if team members haven't provided feedback for each other previously. It is therefore important to help the team build connection and rapport with each other beforehand and also for the team coach to create a feeling of psychological safety and trust.

Here is what you do:

- Discuss with the team important aspects of giving and receiving feedback, for example, feedback should be given with positive intention, feedback is received with the mindset of "feedback is a gift", feedback should be specific and where possible explain the impact of the behaviour.
- Brief the exercise – everyone in the team will consider each team member and answer the following questions:
  - In what ways does the team member contribute to this being a high-performing team?
  - In what ways does the team member hinder this being a high-performing team?
- Give everyone around 15 minutes to consider and capture their feedback for each team member.
- All the team then comes together in a circle, either sitting or standing. If using a virtual platform you can use a gallery setting on a video call.
- Each team member takes it in turn to receive feedback from every other team member.

- For each team member receiving feedback, another team member volunteers to capture the feedback for their colleague, to allow the person receiving the feedback to be able to listen. It is important to rotate this responsibility.
- The team member receiving the feedback doesn't enter into dialogue around the feedback but just says "thank you".
- The team member who has captured the feedback in writing gives the written notes or sends them on to the team member who has just received the feedback.
- Once all feedback has been offered and received, it can be helpful to leave some time for personal reflection and team members to note down any actions.
- After the exercise, it is important to ask the team to consider how they will continue to give and receive feedback, once back at work.

Top tip: In most cases, this proves to be an extremely powerful, insightful and, in many instances, a transforming exercise for team members. It is important that the team coach makes a judgement call on the readiness or otherwise of the team members to give each other feedback using this technique. It is also vital that the team coach takes time at the start of the exercise, to contract clearly with the team's members, regarding how the technique works and the spirit in which the feedback should be given.

When does systemic team coaching work best?

It is our view that team coaching can be valuable for any team. Nevertheless, there are some important areas to consider regarding readiness and appropriateness of team coaching before embarking on a programme. Some of the key considerations include, establishing if the team is a team or a group, team context, roles that are adopted and, finally, the type of intervention that is appropriate.

When exploring the opportunity for team coaching with a client, it is first essential to explore whether the team is actually a team or in fact a group. A team will have a common purpose, goals and interdependencies compared with a group, who will have individual goals. It is an important distinction to make in order to decide whether team coaching or group coaching is the most appropriate intervention.

Understanding the team context is also key, questions around this area might include: Is the team ready for team coaching?; how committed are they?; how committed is the organisation?; what is the organisational context and does the team have the right composition before starting a programme?

Another important area is to contract around the role of the team leader, for example, will they be part of the team or be the team coach. Research has suggested that team coaching is more effective when the coach is from outside of the team (Mathieu et al., 2008).

Lastly, the team coach needs to discuss and agree with the client, the content and type of interventions. As discussed earlier, team coaching involves a series of interventions rather than a one-off session, more common with team building. The intervention can be a mix of ongoing contracting with all the stakeholders and the team leader, use of team diagnostics, a series of workshops either in person, virtual or a mix of both, one-to-one coaching, observing the team in their day-to-day work, followed by review and evaluation.

When team coaching virtually, the team coach must be creative in how they approach their work. In particular, we have found it useful to use the gallery setting to work with the team as a whole, break out rooms to split the team into sub-groups, virtual whiteboards to increase interaction and chat boxes, as well as polls to capture responses. To help read group dynamics and manage the team coaching environment, we would always advocate, when possible, working with another team coach, both when team coaching in person or virtually.

Systemic team coaching works best when applied to multiple teams within an organisation or across organisations, in order to build collaboration and break down silos. This has been referred to by McChrystal et al. (2015) as a "Team of Teams" approach. Taking this approach, we believe that team coaching can have an even greater impact in helping teams to collaborate more effectively, in working together to make lasting positive change.

Ten useful questions for team coaches

Some of our favourite questions to ask when team coaching include:

1. **What can only this team uniquely do together that it could not do apart?**
   This question gets to the heart of what the team does and does not do. It allows the team to discuss what would happen if they are not successful and hence what real value they add and for whom. It is also useful for helping a team explore their collective team purpose, goals and strategies.
2. **How does this team want to be known or described?**
   A key part of the "Creating the Team Edge" framework is team identity. If a team does not proactively manage their identity, it will be left for others to create their own perception. This question allows a team to discuss how it wants to be known by its various stakeholders and agree on actions that will allow it to proactively develop their identity.
3. **What does this team need to value or believe to achieve its purpose?**
   By the team collectively discussing and agreeing their values and beliefs, they can then define behaviours to hold each other to account.
4. **How aware is the team of how it is engaging with the key stakeholders in its system (actual versus perceived), both internal and external?**
   This question is excellent for allowing a team to step back and interrogate the entire system in which it operates. Once the team has identified its stakeholders, the question can act as a "call to action", that encourages the team to explore how effectively it is engaging with its multiple stakeholders. It is important that a team explores its relationship with aspects of the system that are less obvious, such as the team's history and what future stakeholders may require of them.
5. **What is the level of trust within this team?**
   The paradox of this question is that, for it to be answered honestly, it requires team members to feel psychologically safe enough, to reveal what they are thinking. The more a team can develop and build trust, the more likely the team will have open and honest conversations and give each other useful feedback.
6. **How effective is the team's decision-making process?**
   Our experience has shown that many teams struggle with decision-making. Either one or a few individuals dominate, or the team's members are too obliging to each other. In our experience, allowing team members to reflect individually on the information available, followed by each member sharing their perspective, before starting a team discussion, usually results in a better decision.

7. **What are the team doing to keep transforming themselves?**
   This question allows the team to explore their attitude and mindset towards being agile, creativity and innovation, continual learning and developing team resilience.

8. **How can this team develop its diversity?**
   A team must be encouraged to consider diversity it all its fullness, including areas such as diversity of thought, neurodiversity, age, gender, background, etc.

9. **What does the future require of this team?**
   We love asking this question. It allows the team to focus quickly on what matters rather than the day-to-day issues that commonly attract the team's attention.

10. **What is the one question this team needs to ask itself that nobody is asking?**
    This question allows for the unexpected. It permits the team to explore areas that potentially nobody is willing to talk about. For example, what happens if our new product, despite our best efforts, does not work?

Conclusion

As a society, we will increasingly need to rely on collaboration, a team mentality and a "Team of Teams" approach. Team coaching can play a vital role.

For team coaching to rise to the challenge, it needs to educate organisations about what it is and how it can benefit them. The professional bodies and training providers will also need to develop and accredit team coaches. Alongside this, there is a requirement for more practitioner-led publications, evidence-based literature and studies to show the impact of team coaching. Finally, in our view, while the "Doing" and "Knowing" of team coaching is important, it is essential that a team coach continually grows their "way of being".

Hopefully this chapter can help aspiring team coaches to consider their first steps into team coaching. We believe this meaningful type of work can make a positive difference and look forward to more team coaches joining this journey.

References

AC. (2012). 'AC coaching competency framework revised June 2012'. [online] Retrieved on 28 December 2019 from https://cdn.ymaws.com/www.associationforcoaching.com/resource/resmgr/Accreditation/Accred_General/Coaching_Competency_Framewor.pdf.

Clutterbuck, D. (2007). *Coaching the team at work*. London: Nicholas Brealey Publishing

Clutterbuck, D. (2014). 'Team coaching'. In E. Cox, T. Bachkirova and D. Clutterbuck, eds., *The complete handbook of coaching*, 2nd edition, London: Sage, pp. 271–284.

Clutterbuck, D., Gannon, J., Hayes, S., Iordanou, I., Lowe, K. and MacKie, D. (2019). 'Introduction'. In D. Clutterbuck, eds., *The practitioner's handbook of team coaching*. London and New York, Routledge.

EMCC. (2015). 'EMCC competence framework V2 September 2015'. [online]. Retrieved on 28 December 2019 from https://emcc1.app.box.com/s/4aj8x6tmbt75ndn13sg3dauk8n6wxfxq.

Hastings, R. and Pennington, W. (2019). 'Team coaching: A thematic analysis of methods used by external coaches in a work domain'. *International Journal of Evidence Based Coaching and Mentoring*, 17(2), pp. 174–188.

Hawkins, P. (2017). *Leadership team coaching: Developing collective transformational leadership*, 3rd edition. London: Kogan Page.

ICF. (2019). 'Updated ICF core competency model October 2019'. [online] Retrieved on 28 December 2019, from https://coachfederation.org/app/uploads/2019/11/ICFCompetencyModel_Oct2019.pdf.

ICF. (2020). ICF definition of coaching. [online] Retrieved on 10 April 2020 from https://coachfederation.org/about.

Jones, R.J., Napiersky, U. and Lyubovnikova, J. (2019). 'Conceptualizing the distinctiveness of team coaching'. *Journal of Managerial Psychology*, 34(2), pp. 62–78.

Katzenbach, J.R. and Smith, D.K. (1993). *The wisdom of teams: Creating the high-performance organization*. Boston: Harvard Business School Press, McGraw-Hill Inc.

Kozlowski, S.W. and Ilgen, D.R. (2006). 'Enhancing the effectiveness of work groups and teams'. *Psychological science in the public interest*, 7(3), pp. 77–124.

Kriek, H.S. and Venter, P. (2009). 'The perceived success of teambuilding interventions in South African organisations'. *Southern African Business Review*, 13(1), pp. 112–128.

Lencioni, P. (2002). *Five dysfunctions of a team: A leadership Fable*. San Francisco: Jossey-Bass.

Mathieu, J., Maynard, M.T., Rapp, T. and Gilson, L. (2008). 'Team effectiveness 1997–2007: A review of recent advancements and a glimpse into the future'. *Journal of Management*, 34(3), pp. 410–476.

McChrystal, G.S., Collins, T., Silverman, D. and Fussell, C. (2015). *Team of teams: New rules of engagement for a complex world*. London, Penguin Random House.

O'Connor, S. and Cavanagh, M. (2016). 'Group and team coaching'. In T. Bachkirova, G. Spence and D. Drake, eds., *The SAGE handbook of coaching*. Los Angeles: SAGE Reference, pp. 485–504

Peters, J. and Carr, C. (2013). *High performance team coaching*. Victoria: Friesen Press.

Renshaw, B. and Alexander, G. (2005). *Supercoaching: The missing ingredient for high performance*. London: Random House Business

Ridler & Co. (2016). *Ridler report*. London: Ridler & Co.

Rogers, C.R. (1995). *A way of being*. Boston and New York, Houghton Mifflin Harcourt.

Thornton, C. (2016). *Group and team coaching: The secret life of groups*. London: Routledge.

Van Nieuwerburgh, C. (2017). *An introduction to coaching skills: A practical guide*, 2nd edition. London: Sage Publications Ltd.

Wageman, R., Nunes, D.A., Burruss, J.A. and Hackman, J.R. (2008). *Senior leadership teams. What it takes to make them great*. Boston: Harvard Business School Press

Widdowson, L.J. (2017). *Creating the team edge, Henley Centre for Coaching members' website*. Henley: Henley Business School.

Widdowson, L.J. (2018). *Understanding team leaders' and team coaches' perceptions of the effectiveness of the 'Creating the Team Edge' framework*, M.Sc. Unpublished Dissertation. Henley: Henley Business School.

Widdowson, L.J. and Barbour, P.J. (2019). *Team coaching: Coaching in action guide*. Henley: The Henley Centre for Coaching, Henley Business School.

Widdowson, L.J. and Barbour, P.J. (2021) *Building top performing teams: A practical guide to team coaching to improve collaboration and drive organizational success*. London: Kogan Page.

26 Career coaching

Julia Yates

Introduction

Identifying the ideal route to a successful and fulfilling career has never been an easy task, and careers are more complicated now than ever. The first major challenge facing those trying to pinpoint and pursue their career goals is that there are simply too many career options to choose from. For example, the UK government now recognises 36,000 different job titles (Office of National Statistics, 2019), an impossible number to imagine, let alone research. The second issue concerns the trajectory of career paths, which are more fluid and less predictable than before, with job changes, redundancies, career breaks and self-employment more frequent and less socially stigmatised than they have been in the past. It is a challenging landscape to negotiate and it is no wonder so many people seek out career coaching to help make sure they are capitalising on the opportunities available and making the most of their skills and abilities.

Many coaching sessions, whether under the banner of life coaching, or executive and workplace coaching, will touch on career choice and career development. Our careers are influenced by and impact on almost all aspects of life: Leisure, family, performance, motivation, well-being and mental health, so career experiences and career decisions will be germane to many kinds of coaching conversations. Unfortunately, for the most part, the research into career choice and development lies outside the mainstream coaching literature, meaning that it is not always tailored to the needs of coaches and sometimes can be difficult to access. Career coaches are of course not expected to have an encyclopaedic knowledge of the current labour market, but for coaches who are regularly discussing career issues with their clients, it may be useful to understand a little more about the way that people make their career choices and the processes of career change.

Career coaching explained

Career coaching is generally focused on making choices or facilitating transitions from one job to another. Clients who are looking for support with their choices might be choosing which path to take, or could need help deciding whether or not to stay in their current position or industry. Those looking for support facilitating transitions are generally clearer about what they want to do, but need some help getting there – working out how to look or apply for jobs, or how to excel at interviews. In practice, of course, the distinction between these two aspects of career development is not clear cut: People's choice of career path is influenced by their strategies and chances of success, and the process of job searching can lead people to question or review their plans.

Historically, career support has been something that people called on only once. We were expected to make our career choices early on, and anticipated seeing out our working days in the same field, or even the same organisation that we started in after school or university. Changes in the employment market, accompanied by a more sophisticated awareness of decision-making and the search for fulfilment, mean that career support is now seen as something that people may need to draw on throughout their working lives and beyond.

The first career decision is generally taken whilst people are still in full-time education, whether at school or university. Traditionally, the career support given at this stage has been publicly funded, provided by the education institution and is generally described as careers advice or career guidance. This kind of support, in theory at least, is almost synonymous with career coaching, delivered through one-to-one interventions, which are structured around a GROW-like model and underpinned by a non-directive, non-judgemental, person-centred Rogerian philosophy (Ali and Graham, 1996). But the context in which this advice or guidance occurs means that, in practice, it can look a little different from the kind of career coaching we might recognise. These career sessions are usually one-off, very time-limited (often just 15 minutes long) and, in practice, more directive than the practitioners might want. The public funding for this kind of support has been dramatically cut over the last decades, opening up an interesting gap in the market for career coaches.

More often, career coaches deal with mid-career changes, working either with clients who are voluntarily changing career, or with people who have lost their jobs. This kind of work can sometimes be straightforward support for clients looking for a new similar position, but more often will involve helping people think about a new direction, as people either choose, or find themselves compelled, to consider alternative career paths.

Some clients seek out career coaching to help them back into the workplace after a career break. One client group who often seek the support of career coaches are parents (usually mothers) who have taken time out to raise their children; career coaches also commonly work with people whose illnesses have led to time out of work, or those who are trying to get back into the workforce after a period of unemployment.

One growing area of career coaching work is retirement coaching. Cliff-edge retirement that takes people from full-time work to full-time leisure on their 60th birthday is becoming increasingly rare, and older workers are now more likely to cut down their hours gradually, continue with the same job under another kind of contract, or might retire and embark on a whole new lease of life, reinventing themselves and finding a new direction for their third age. This is the first generation to anticipate so many years of active life after retirement age, so these career paths are inevitably ill-defined, and this group of clients can find it useful to get support with thinking creatively about options and approaches to their next stage. Older workers can also need some support with securing a job or negotiating with employers; despite the changes in legislation, demographics and the pensions crisis which are combing forces to keep people in work longer, social attitudes are lagging behind and older workers have to contend with discriminatory attitudes and practices which exacerbate the challenges of job hunting.

Career coaching theory and research

Career coaching draws on two distinct sets of literature. First there is career development literature. This field is wide-ranging, covering the career paths people take, job hunting and career success, and the experiences of groups of people of different ages, races and nationalities with a particular focus on social justice. Perhaps most relevant to career coaching is the career development research which examines the process of career choice.

The prevailing messages about career choice within the academic literature have shifted dramatically over the last fifty years. The 20th century advice was to follow a clear three-stage plan: Find out about yourself, find out about jobs and make a rational decision about which option is going to suit best (Holland, 1987; Parsons, 1909). This approach continues to dominate in much career practice because it is so intuitive and so accessible, but our understanding of career decision-making has moved on apace since these first theories were devised, and we now understand that this is just not how people make choices. More recently, the academic research has explored using identity as a starting point for career exploration (Ibarra and Barbulescu, 2010; Meijers and Lengelle, 2012), the importance of finding meaning through work (Simonet and Castille, 2020) and a more holistic approach to choices, acknowledging that boundaries between work and life are blurred (Savickas et al., 2009). The research community is also beginning to draw from decision-making literature to understand that people do not always approach career decision-making with a conscious and rational mind (Reddekopp, 2017).

The second relevant body of literature examines the effectiveness of interventions. Career coaches looking to understand the empirical evidence base behind their work can draw from the evidence underpinning coaching (for example, Jones, Woods and Guillaume, 2016 or Theeboom, Beerma and van Vianen, 2014) and career guidance (see Everitt et al., 2018 a review), both of which attest to the positive impact that one-to-one support can have. Evidence that explores career coaching specifically is less bountiful, but the last few years have offered some examples of studies that show the positive impact of career coaching. Career coaching has been shown to lead to higher psychological capital (Archer and Yates, 2017); more effective reconciling of work and life roles with values and needs (Brown and Yates, 2018); reduced career ambivalence (Klonek Wunderlich, Spurk and Kauffeld., 2016); enhanced career optimism, career security and career goals (Ebner, 2019); and career optimism and career planning (Spurk, Kauffeld, Barthauer and Heinemann, 2015). Some studies have also looked at career coaching within organisations, finding that the career coaching itself improves staff retention (Dugas, 2018) and job satisfaction (Fassiotto, Sandborg, Valantine and Raymond, 2018) and that even the very existence of a policy that includes an offer of career coaching is linked to improved institutional satisfaction (Ling, Ning, Change and Zhang, 2018). These papers provide an important starting point, but a more concerted focus on research in this area is much needed.

Career coaching in practice

The boundaries between work life and home life, and career and family are increasingly blurred, and the two parts of life inevitably influence and impact on each other. Conversations about career will touch on other facets of a client's life, and career issues will often crop up in discussions which centre on other topics. There are, however, some specific issues which will be particularly familiar to coaches specialising in careers work.

Initial career choice

In much of the developed world, young people usually face the need to make choices about the career path to pursue, or the job to take, with very limited understanding of the workplace and often a fairly limited understanding of themselves. They can feel that they are making their choices in the dark, and relying heavily on guesswork and luck. For many of them, this can lead to some degree of anxiety which sometimes needs to be addressed during coaching, in parallel with their specific career dilemmas. One reassuring thing to emphasise with the younger clients is that their first job will not be their last. Thorough research to minimise the risks is without doubt important, but it can be comforting for the young people to conceptualise their first job as an experiment – they should enter with all good intentions, but feel comfortable to withdraw and change direction if they can see that it is not making them happy.

Compounding the challenge of limited work experience for younger clients is that of their limited experience of making decisions. It is not unusual to find that a client, emerging from full-time education, does not feel that they have made any significant life decisions for themselves, as schools, families and social norms have steered them quite firmly in one particular direction. Working with a career coach who is expecting them to set the agenda and identify their own solutions can be a new experience for some young people and might be one that is uncomfortable and daunting. A useful strategy to help with this is investing extra time in agreeing a contract before the coaching starts. Time spent ensuring that the client really understands what coaching is, and why they will be encouraged to take control, is often time well spent. And whilst these clients sometimes need a bit of extra handholding throughout the process, don't be tempted to rush things or offer solutions too readily. These are capable clients, they just need to adjust to a new kind of working relationship.

Career change

When working with career changers the focus of the conversations is more often on thinking about the logistical challenges. After 10 or 20 years in the workplace, people have often developed a degree of expertise and a reasonably salary, as well as having other practical commitments such as a mortgage, children to support or ties to a particular loca-tion. A new direction, mid-career, can sometimes be a sideways move to a role in which an individual can capitalise on their experience and expertise, but often a new direction will involve some costly re-training, or starting back at the bottom of the career ladder. This may require considerable sacrifices for the client and perhaps their family, so clients may need to work with their coach to find a way to reconcile their work and life goals and priorities.

Alongside these logistical challenges, people who are facing redundancy or job loss may also be coping with a feeling of rejection and struggling with a lack of control. Psychological issues including denial, anger and depression can emerge and take hold fol-lowing job loss (Blau, 2007) and career coaches need to anticipate, recognise and support their clients throughout. People facing redundancy tend to fall broadly into two camps: Those who were perfectly happy in their roles, and are looking for support in their quest to find something else along the very same lines, and those who were actually not all that happy in their existing jobs, but were perhaps not quite ready to make a change. This latter group can fairly soon grow to see the redundancy as a positive – the spur that they needed to make the change they wanted, and the evidence is generally very encouraging, suggest-ing that most people who are made redundant end up feeling more satisfied in their career paths than they were before (Water and Strauss, 2016).

Return to work

The group who most often seek career coaching to help with a return to work are parents (mostly but not exclusively mothers) who have taken a career break. Here again, logistics are often the biggest challenge. Family dynamics tend to be quite entrenched by this point, which often means that the stay-at-home parent expects to be the children's primary carer, even after their return to work. As such, they might be looking for a job that is part-time, close to home or allows them to work flexibly. Career conversations with returning parents often revolve around priorities and working out what kinds of compromises might be acceptable to all parties. Alongside the practical constraints, there are often issues of confidence to address. Time out of the workplace almost always leads to a significant loss of confidence, and as we know that self-efficacy boosts one's chances of both choosing a career (Ballout, 2009) and securing a position (Saks, 2006), the psychological issues are important to address and highly relevant to the conversations.

Retirement

This generation is the first to have an opportunity for a substantial post-retirement career and, as such, older clients do not have a raft of tried and tested career paths, examples and role models to learn from. Career coaching with this client group can often involve a lot of collaborative creative thinking, as clients design their own futures from scratch. At retirement age, people find themselves in very different financial situations. Some are financially secure, but want to find a way to reinvent themselves, pursue a long-held dream or maintain a positive sense of identity despite their changed work situation. Others will be struggling financially, and need some help working out how to combat discrimination in the workplace.

Tools and techniques

Good career coaching makes use of a non-judgemental, non-directive approach, a structured conversation, as well as listening, questioning and challenging where appropriate. These characteristics of coaching will be familiar to all practitioners but, over and above those guiding principles, there are numerous techniques and tools which have been shown to be particularly useful in career conversations.

Initial career choice

Strengths. I mentioned above that clients making initial career choices can be held back by their limited experience of the world of work, and their limited understanding of themselves within a work context. When faced with a list of skills needed in a job, or the person specification of an interesting-sounding position, it may be very difficult for these clients to work out whether they have what is needed. Working with strengths can be an accessible way for young people to start to understand themselves better and to begin to link their own characteristics with specific jobs.

Put simply, strengths are things that an individual is good at and enjoys. The use of strengths at work is linked to a range of positive outcomes, including work engagement and job satisfaction (Lavy and Littman-Ovadia, 2016), and this makes them a particularly useful technique to use in career coaching. Strengths are not directly work-related, but allow clients to think about their personal characteristics in any context; the power of the approach is thus not limited by the extent of the client's time in the workplace, as they can draw from their experiences within education, at home, or during sport and other leisure activities.

Career genogram. A second technique that works well for young people is the career genogram. We know that values and aspirations are heavily influence by parents (Taylor, Harris and Taylor, 2004) and young people can often find it hard to establish their own identity, struggling to unpick the facets or versions of the self that they have chosen, or feel are authentic and the aspects that are products of their family. A career genogram is a powerful visual tool to help clients reflect on the impact their family has had on their personal development and worldview. With this technique, the client is invited to draw a family tree, which includes their parents', grandparents' and siblings' jobs, and then uses this to help reflect on the influences that have come from their family – the jobs and sectors they are familiar with, the values that are manifest and the family's conceptualisation of career success. This reflection can help clients to think about how their desires and goals have been shaped by their experiences, allowing them to examine them more objectively.

Career changers

Job-crafting. Capitalising on the fluid nature of contemporary career paths, one useful approach to share with people who are finding their current jobs unfulfilling is job-crafting (Berg, Dutton and Wrzesniewski, 2013). The idea behind this concept is that jobs are malleable, and the job a person might actually end up doing can bear very little resemblance to the job description originally given. To some degree, individuals can be in control of shaping these changes, crafting or developing their roles to make them more palatable, satisfying or better suited to their skills. Organisations and teams are dynamic, and there will often be opportunities to shift things around a little bit – people can take on new projects and expand their skills, or divest themselves of elements of work that they find less stimulating. Good managers will always be keen to keep their staff motivated and generally appreciate a proactive attitude, which means they can often respond positively to suggestions for incremental changes. It can be liberating for career coaching clients to explore tactics for making their position more agreeable, even if they feel compelled to stay in their current position, and crafting a new set of daily duties can constitute the first stage of a longer-term exit strategy as they develop new skills and broaden their experience.

The Kaleidoscope Model. The Kaleidoscope Model (Mainiero and Sullivan, 2005, Mainiero and Gibson, 2018) was developed to illustrate the career paths of women. The authors were frustrated that the career development literature from the 20th century had predominately been developed by, and modelled and tested on, men. The assumption in these early theories had been that there was one default way to have a good career – the way that men did it. Mainiero and Sullivan decided to track the career paths of women, and found some consistent patterns. They saw that women's careers could often be divided into three distinct phases; see Table 26.1.

Women often come to career coaching when they are juggling motherhood and career, and this can coincide with the transition from early to mid-career, when they are considering shifting to a more family friendly position, or the transition from mid to late-career, when they are looking for a route back into work. Sharing the Kaleidoscope Model with these clients can stimulate insightful discussions about their values and conflicts. It can also

Table 26.1 Three phases of women's careers

Early career:
The need for
  challenge
	Women are looking to be challenged, focused on learning, development and
	  growth. During this stage, women's career development tends to mirror that of
	  their male counterparts.

Mid-career:
The desire for
  balance
	Women become less interested in traditional markers of success such as
	  promotion and salary and instead look for jobs that allow them to reconcile
	  multiple identities. Most often they are looking for jobs that allow them to be
	  the mothers they want to be, which might include a career break, part-time
	  hours, or a new less intense job.
	It is at this stage that women's career paths tend to diverge from men's.

Late-career:
The search for
  authenticity
	Women in the last part of their career are generally looking for roles which are
	  aligned to their values-system, which they feel are meaningful and in which
	  they can be themselves.

be validating for women to see that their own dilemmas are widely shared and their career paths are well-trodden, and this can offer reassurance and boost their confidence.

Older workers

Possible selves. I noted earlier that older workers can sometimes need to be particularly creative in the way that they carve out a role (or multiple roles) for themselves post-retirement. One approach that can help to stimulate their creative thinking is possible selves (Markus and Nurius, 1986). Possible selves are hypothetical versions of ourselves in the future. We can all have multiple possible selves as we imagine ourselves in all sorts of different possible scenarios. Possible selves interventions have been shown to help clients to identify career goals, as well as helping with motivation and resilience (Strauss, Griffin and Parker, 2013).

In a possible selves career coaching conversation, the coach will invite the client first to identify a number of different possible futures. These hypothetical versions of their futures can be realistic, hoped-for or even feared possible selves and the client can be encouraged to come up with a wide range of possible versions of themselves. The coach then asks the client to pick one of the possible futures to focus on and encourages the client to visualise their future in elaborate detail. The focus during this part of the conversation will be on the visual image, the narrative and the feelings, and the coach should help the client to describe their picture of the future, tell the story of their future and experience the feelings associated. Once the client has explored this possible self in depth, the coach and client can have a conversation about what this process has highlighted about their goals for the future, and discuss possible action steps.

When does career coaching work best?

Career coaching clients will often sign up to see a career coach when they have become dissatisfied by their current work situation and are ready to consider new avenues. These clients have chosen to look for a new path and have decided that it is the right time to think about alternatives. Whilst there may be many challenges for the client to overcome, the coaching sessions are likely to be productive and the coaching relationship is likely to be collaborative, because both parties are engaged with the process and trying to move forward to the same goal. But not all career coaching sessions are like this. Many clients are prompted to seek career coaching because they are facing redundancy, they are needing to make changes simply because of their age (younger clients leaving university, or older workers being pushed to retire) or they are forced to make a change for other personal reasons – perhaps as a result of ill heath, financial or family situations.

When clients come to career coaching because external forces are compelling them to make a change, it can be challenging to develop a collaborating and productive partnership. The transtheoretical model of change offers a useful framework to help illustrate this. This model sets out five different stages of change, which people progress through when making significant changes. The model was developed in a health context, examining the steps people go through when stopping smoking or losing weight, but the model has been shown to apply to change in a range of different contexts, including career change (Barclay, Stoltz and Chang, 2010); see Table 26.2.

Career coaching is most effective when the client has moved beyond the precontemplation stage and is consciously aware that they want to make a change, are motivated to work towards identifying a new direction and prepared to engage positively with the work that is needed. Expecting or encouraging clients to engage with career planning before they are ready is rarely effective, and can prove detrimental to the coaching relationship. One of the most useful approaches to working with clients who appear to be in the precontemplation stage is Motivational Interviewing (Miller and Rollnick, 2012), which can help clients to see the benefits of making a change.

Ten useful questions for career coaches

A host of questions are available to careers coaches to help clients explore what is important to them. These questions explore values, identify the resources and strengths the client

Table 26.2 Transtheoretical Model of Change

Precontemplation	During this stage people are not aware that they are dissatisfied, and have no conscious desire to make any changes.
Contemplation	In this stage, people become aware that they are dissatisfied with their current situation and start to think seriously about their options. They may not be quite ready to make a commitment to a new path, but are open to finding out about possible avenues and reflecting on both what has led to their dissatisfaction and what future possibilities could lead to greater fulfilment.
Preparation	During the preparation stage, the individual is preparing for action, narrowing down their options to a realistic shortlist and clarifying their career goals. Once the goal is identified, the individual can begin to work out what action is needed.
Action	During this stage, the individual starts to implement plans, reflecting and reviewing them as necessary.
Maintenance	The individual has made the change, and now needs to become accustomed to their new environment and their new identity.

(adapted from Prochaska, DiClementi and Norcross, 1992)

can draw upon and also generate ideas about what types of roles might make a good fit based on their interests, values, resources and strengths. In this section I have clustered the questions into three groups: Values exploration; resources review; and ideas generation.

Questions to explore values:

1. Who are your role models? What do you admire in them, in what ways are you like them, and what advice would they give you now?
2. What does "career success" mean to you?
3. What was the best job you ever had? What was so good about it?
4. What is the best day at work you have ever had? What made it so good?
5. Think of someone you know whose job sounds interesting. Why do you like the sound of it?

Questions to help identify personal resources:

6. Tell me about a time when you did something really well. What was it about you that made this successful?
7. What are the characteristics that are really particular to you? What makes you, you?

Questions to generate job ideas:

8. If you knew you couldn't fail, what would you do?
9. If all jobs paid the same, what would you do?
10. If you could wave a magic wand and choose any job you wanted, what would you pick?

Conclusion

Career coaching is growing as a specialist strand of coaching and, as career paths become more fluid, and technology accelerates the pace of change in the workplace, the role of career coaches will continue to become more useful and more prevalent. This chapter has offered an overview of some of the key challenges as well as the most useful techniques within career coaching, and has identified some of the specialism's distinctive features. Describing career coaching as a distinct branch of coaching is, however, arguably somewhat spurious. Career and family, work life and home life are intertwined, and work and home identities are increasingly blurred. Career-related issues will creep into many discussions which ostensibly focus on other aspects of life or work, and so an engagement with the research and coaching tools that are most pertinent to career development could be useful for a wide range of coaches.

References

Ali, L. and Graham, B. (1996). *The counselling approach to careers guidance.* London: Routledge.

Archer, S. and Yates, J. (2017). 'Understanding potential career changers' experience of career confidence following a positive psychology based coaching programme'. *Coaching: An International Journal of Theory, Research and Practice*, 10(2), pp. 157–175.

Ballout, H. (2009). 'Career commitment and career success: Moderating role of self-efficacy'. *Career Development International*, 14(7), pp. 655–670.

Barclay, S.R., Stoltz, K.B. and Chung, Y.B. (2011). 'Voluntary midlife career change: Integrating the transtheoretical model and the life-span, life-space approach'. *The Career Development Quarterly*, 59(5), pp. 386–399.

Berg, J.M., Dutton, J.E. and Wrzesniewski, A. (2013). 'Job crafting and meaningful work'. In B.J. Dik, Z.S. Byrne and M.F. Steger, eds., *Purpose and meaning in the workplace.* American Psychological Association, pp. 81–104.

Blau, G. (2007). 'Partially testing a process model for understanding victim responses to an anticipated worksite closure'. *Journal of Vocational Behavior*, 71(3), 401–428.

Brown, C. and Yates, J. (2018). 'Understanding the experience of midlife women taking part in a work-life balance career coaching programme: An interpretative phenomenological analysis'. *International Journal of Evidence Based Coaching and Mentoring*, 16(1), 110–125.

Dugas, J. (2018). *Career coaching: A study of veterans health administration (VHA) leaders*. Dissertations. 210. Irvine: Brandman University.

Ebner, K. (2019). 'Promoting career optimism and career security during career coaching: Development and test of a model'. *Coaching: An International Journal of Theory, Research and Practice*. online first 1–19.

Everitt, J., Neary, S., Delagardo, M.A. and Clark, L. (2019) *Personal guidance what works?* London: The Careers Enterprise Company.

Fassiotto, M., Simard, C., Sandborg, C., Valantine, H. and Raymond, J. (2018). 'An integrated career coaching and time-banking system promoting flexibility, wellness, and success: A pilot program at stanford university school of medicine'. *Academic Medicine (Ovid)*, 93(6), pp. 881–887.

Holland, J.L. (1987). 'Current status of Holland's theory of careers: Another perspective'. *The Career Development Quarterly*, 36(1), pp. 24–30. doi:10.1002/j.2161-0045.1987.tb00478.x.

Ibarra, H. and Barbulescu, R. (2010). 'Identity as narrative: Prevalence, effectiveness, and consequences of narrative identity work in macro work role transitions'. *Academy of Management Review*, 35(1), pp. 135–154. doi:10.5465/amr.35.1.zok135.

Jones, R.J., Woods, S.A. and Guillaume, Y.R. (2016). 'The effectiveness of workplace coaching: A meta-analysis of learning and performance outcomes from coaching'. *Journal of Occupational and Organizational Psychology*, 89(2), pp. 249–277. doi:10.1111/joop.12119.

Jordan, S., Gessnitzer, S. and Kauffeld, S. (2016). 'Effects of a group coaching for the vocational orientation of secondary school pupils'. *Coaching: An International Journal of Theory, Research and Practice*, 9(2), pp. 143–157. doi:10.1080/17521882.2016.1210185.

Klonek, F.E., Wunderlich, E., Spurk, D. and Kauffeld, S. (2016). 'Career counseling meets motivational interviewing: A sequential analysis of dynamic counselor–client interactions'. *Journal of Vocational Behavior*, 94, pp. 28–38.

Lavy, S. and Littman-Ovadia, H. (2016). 'My better self: Using strengths at work and work productivity, organizational citizenship behavior and satisfaction'. *Journal of Career Development*, 44(2), pp. 95–106.

Ling, F.Y.Y., Ning, Y., Chang, Y.H. and Zhang, Z. (2018). 'Human resource management practices to improve project managers' job satisfaction'. *Engineering Construction & Architectural Management*, 25(5), pp. 654–669.

Mainiero, L.A. and Gibson, D.E. (2018). 'The Kaleidoscope Career Model revisited: How midcareer men and women diverge on authenticity, balance, and challenge'. *Journal of Career Development*, 45(4), pp. 361–377.

Mainiero, L.A. and Sullivan, S.E. (2005). 'Kaleidoscope careers: An alternate explanation for the "opt-out" "revolution'. *Academy of Management Perspectives*, 19(1), pp. 106–123.

Markus, H. and Nurius, P. (1986). 'Possible selves'. *American Psychologist*, 41(9), pp. 954–969.

Meijers, F. and Lengelle, R. (2012). 'Narratives at work: The development of career identity'. *British Journal of Guidance & Counselling*, 40(2), pp. 157–176.

Miller, W.R. and Rollnick, S. (2012). *Motivational interviewing: Helping people change*. New York: Guilford press.

Murtagh, N., Lopes, P.N. and Lyons, E. (2011). 'Decision making in voluntary career change: An other-than-rational perspective'. *The Career Development Quarterly*, 59(3), 249–263.

Office of National Statistics. (2019) *SOC codes*. London: ONS.

Parsons, F. (1909). *Choosing a vocation*. Boston: Houghton Mifflin.

Prochaska, J.O., DiClemente, C.C. and Norcross, J.C. (1992). 'In search of how people change: Applications to addictive behaviors'. *American Psychologist*, 47, pp. 1102–1114.

Redekopp, D.E. (2017). 'Irrational career decision-making: Connecting behavioural economics and career development'. *British Journal of Guidance & Counselling*, 45(4), pp. 441–450.

Saka, N., Gati, I. and Kelly, K.R. (2008). 'Emotional and personality-related aspects of career-decision-making difficulties'. *Journal of Career Assessment*, 16(4), pp. 403–424.

Saks, A.M. (2006). 'Multiple predictors and criteria of job search success'. *Journal of Vocational Behavior*, 68(3), pp. 400–415.

Sampson, J.P., Jr., Peterson, G.W., Lenz, J.G., Reardon, R.C. and Saunders, D.E. (1998). 'The design and use of a measure of dysfunctional career thoughts among adults, college students, and high school students: The career thoughts Inventory'. *Journal of Career Assessment*, 6(2), pp. 115–134.

Savickas, M.L., Nota, L., Rossier, J., Dauwalder, J.P., Duarte, M.E., Guichard, J. and Van Vianen, A.E. (2009). 'Life designing: A paradigm for career construction in the 21st century'. *Journal of vocational behavior*, 75(3), pp. 239–250.

Simonet, D.V. and Castille, C.M. (2020). 'The search for meaningful work: A network analysis of personality and the job characteristics model'. *Personality and Individual Differences*, 152(1), pp. 1–9.

Spurk, D., Kauffeld, S., Barthauer, L. and Heinemann, N.S.R. (2015). 'Fostering networking behavior, career planning and optimism, and subjective career success: An intervention study'. *Journal of Vocational Behavior*, 87(1), pp. 134–144.

Strauss, K, Griffin, M.A. and Parker, S.K. (2013). 'Future Work Selves: How salient hoped-for identities motivate proactive career behaviours'. *Journal of Applied Psychology*, 97(3), pp. 580–598.

Taylor, J. Harris, M.B. and Taylor, S. (2004, Winter). 'Parents have their say ... about their college-age children's career decisions'. *NACE Journal*, 64(2), pp. 15–20.

Theeboom, T., Beersma, B. and van Vianen, A.E. (2014). 'Does coaching work? A meta-analysis on the effects of coaching on individual level outcomes in an organizational context'. *The Journal of Positive Psychology*, 9(1), pp. 1–18.

Van Nieuwerburgh, C. (2017). *An introduction to coaching skills: A practical guide*. London: Sage.

27 Outdoor eco-coaching

Alex Burn and Anna-Marie Watson

Introduction

Coaching has been a predominantly indoor activity since it emerged as a method for personal development and growth in the 1970s. More recently, eco-coaching has appeared as a branch of coaching that takes these coaching conversations outdoors. Coaches who offer this as part of their practice, and clients who have experienced it, report many wide-ranging benefits to both mental and physical wellbeing.

In this chapter we note that there is currently very little empirical research into the benefits of outdoor coaching, but the benefits of contact with nature and natural environments offer significant research. We will look at Attention Restoration Theory (ART), and the parallels we can draw between the benefits of natural environments proposed in ART and the benefits of eco-coaching reported by coaches and clients, and review the tools and techniques used in eco-coaching. Finally, we will suggest ten questions that can be utilised in outdoor coaching sessions and discuss the practicalities of taking coaching conversations outdoors.

Eco-coaching explained

Eco-coaching is a relatively new approach to business coaching which takes coaching conversations outside. Other forms of business coaching that have emerged since the 1970s have taken place indoors, often with the coach and client sat across from each other with a table or desk between them.

However, eco-coaching has evolved from "walking and talking", a form of psychotherapy that links the benefits of movement (walking) with therapeutic techniques (talking). It highlights the critical link between the coaching conversation and ecology – the connection between living things and their environment, and draws parallels with a number of coaching techniques such as Systems Thinking (Whittington, 2016), Gestalt (Leary-Joyce, 2014) and Mindfulness (Howell et al., 2011), which help the client to view themselves as part of a much wider system and to reflect on their challenges in a non-judgemental way.

There are two primary perceived benefits to outdoor coaching, although the potential benefits are many and wide-ranging. One is the benefit of being out in nature, connecting with the "greenspace" of trees and plants, the "bluespace" of water and with the natural world of animal life. Breathing fresh air deep into the lungs, hearing birdsong and feeling the warm sun on the skin are aspects that are hard to replicate indoors.

The other primary benefit, from both a physical and mental perspective, is movement. Walking alongside another person or amongst a group creates synchronicity and a shared experience in a way sitting across from someone in a more traditional coaching session might not achieve. Clients report that side-by-side walking feels less judgmental compared to sitting opposite a coach, and more supportive, with a feeling that they are on both a literal and metaphorical journey with their coach.

These two primary benefits can be combined, hence the link to walking and talking therapy, but for those who are less mobile, the benefits can still be found in sitting outdoors. It does not have to be a trek, or even a walk around a park. The simple act of being outside whilst having a coaching conversation can have beneficial impacts on coaching outcomes.

Multiple research studies have looked at how much time people in the developed world now spend indoors and the statistics are eye-opening. This of course varies widely between countries. In the UK the National Human Activity Pattern Survey (NHAPS) (Klepeis et al., 2001) found that 86.9% of our total time was spent indoors. A UK YouGov report in 2014 found that people thought they spent about 66% of their time indoors, suggesting a significant under-estimation. This can have far-ranging effects on our mental and physical wellbeing, from vitamin D deficiency to lower productivity, lack of sleep to increased risk of asthma and obesity, as well as a reduction in physical activity and mobility.

Eco-coaching theory and research

Evidence-based research on eco-coaching is in its infancy, with few empirical studies conducted to date. However, practitioners have been taking coaching conversations outdoors and experimenting with the effects.

One study by Palmer and O'Riordan (2019) does tentatively show a link specifically between the nature-based activity of walking and coaching, and is one of only a few published studies that does. They conducted two studies and found that a short coaching conversation whilst walking along Regent's Canal in London and Swansea seafront increased self-reported wellbeing scores for the clients. They also found that the weather did not impact on the positive self-reported scores. Whilst this research used very short, 15- and 20-minute conversations (respectively) and no control group, it does provide support to the view that clients taking part in eco-coaching can benefit from the advantages that the outdoors, nature and movement bring.

Research from other fields can help demonstrate why this is. Studies have shown improved cognitive functioning after connecting with natural environments (Berman et al., 2009; Kaplan and Berman, 2010; Bratman et al., 2015), improved mood and wellbeing (Korpela and Hartig, 1996; Palmer, 2015; Howell et al., 2011) and quicker recovery from stressful events (Ulrich et al., 1991). Berman et al. (2012) also found that a significant increase in memory and mood was experienced by adults suffering from Major Depressive Disorder (MDD) following interactions with nature.

As there is little direct evidence yet to explain the benefits of coaching outdoors, we can consider its impact through the lens of other, more widely researched theories. One example is ART (Kaplan and Talbot, 1983; Kaplan and Kaplan, 1989; Kaplan, 1995). ART proposes that being in contact with natural environments increases our ability to recover from mental fatigue and stress. Directed attention is an invaluable executive function

(Kaplan and Berman, 2010), which enables us to process information, make decisions, solve problems and focus our attention (Kaplan, 1995). It can, however, become exhausted over time, affecting cognitive capabilities such as attention, memory, mood and emotion. Nature provides a restorative environment which can help us recover from this fatigue (Berto, 2014). See Table 27.1.

Eco-coaching in Practice

In practice, ART can explain many of the self-reported benefits of eco-coaching. It provides a framework to explain how natural environments can help with coaching conversations. Often people come to coaching because they have a challenge they need to find a creative solution for. They are frequently suffering from mental fatigue and their directed attention capacity may be reduced as they are not giving themselves time to restore and recover. This mental fatigue impacts mood, often increasing frustration, sadness and lethargy. Providing a coaching environment that can restore mental fatigue, improve directed attention and positively affect mood can improve coaching outcomes significantly.

The ART concept of soft fascination is very applicable to taking coaching conversations outdoors. Nature provides unlimited soft fascinations, such as the sun's rays peeking through clouds, the patterns of bark on a tree, the swirl of water on a lake as a leaf lands on it, the sound of birdsong or the rustle of leaves in a windy wood. The human brain can attend to these things with relative ease, letting it recover from mental and attentional fatigue. Advocates of outdoor coaching often describe it as enabling them to see things more clearly and eliciting sudden "ah-ha" moments. These moments of realisation often come after taking time to reflect on a specific coaching question or topic whilst walking, and allowing their minds to drift and be attracted to the soft fascinations of the nature around them. However, some may find that nature provides hard fascination too, and this may become quite distracting. Those who are very excited by seeing animals, for example, may focus more on them than on the coaching session itself, while others may be distracted by approaching inclement

Table 27.1 ART's Four Restorative Functions

a) *Being away*:	from typical, everyday locations. It does not have to be a great distance; only provide the feeling of "getting away", or disconnecting from daily life.
b) *Extent*:	providing a feeling of size. The outdoors elicits the feeling of a wider connection to the expanse of nature.
c) *Fascination*:	everything holds a hard or soft degree of fascination for us, with natural environments providing large amounts of soft fascination. Soft fascination enables us to restore our mental capacity and recover from stress and fatigue, because it requires much less directed attention. Hard fascination requires focus and directed attention, using up mental capacity and causing cognitive fatigue.
d) *Compatibility*:	there is a high level of compatibility between us and natural environments. The concept of biophilia (Kellert and Wilson, 1993) describes this as a human being's genetic predisposition to the natural world; our innate yearning for connection with nature.

weather or, for example, the sounds of particular bird noises that are more irritating than restorative (Ratcliffe et al., 2013). The initial contracting stage and first session with a new client should help to identify if this is the case. Adapting the location to provide less hard fascination may be helpful, or it may be that eco-coaching is not the best approach for these clients.

Many clients get inspiration from the outdoor environment. Clients may experience awe when they see a rainbow, or find a metaphor in the resilience of a little plant shoot poking out from beneath snow. The weather can also provide compatibility, reflecting someone's mood and providing perspective and context – for example, the realisation that the weather cannot be controlled. There will be cold and storms, just as there will be sunlight and warmth. Reflecting on this can help a client to understand circles of control and put things into perspective.

Planning and preparation

Eco-coaching necessitates preparation and planning where the following should be considered:

Dynamic Environment: Stepping outdoors involves an element of risk, from physical safety to more discrete psychological safety and emotional containment. The multi-sensory environment might involve unforeseeable situations that trigger emotional responses, disrupt rapport or raise negative thoughts. Be prepared to embrace an organic and fluid mindset into your practice and to work with a supervisor who has experience within this coaching niche.

Health and Safety: A risk assessment is a systematic method of analysing factors which influence eco-coaching, consider possible challenges and identify suitable control measures. The criteria listed below is a starting point. The information should be recorded in a generic or location-specific document. See Table 27.2. Make sure the necessary first aid, public liability, professional insurance, outdoor qualifications and land access are covered. Clarify any physical or psychological medical conditions relevant to walking outdoors that might not usually arise. Consider your personal safety, especially meeting a new client for the first time; for example, inform a friend of the route and expected time of return, and ensure the client knows in advance you will do this. Carry a suitable first aid kit for the location.

Client Comfort: Some clients are content to walk in wet weather, others may prefer a more comfortable dry option. Co-create the entire outdoor element with your client during contracting.

Location, Location, Location: Think about the venue (near nature versus wilderness), environment (urban park, forest, mountains or beach, etc.) and route in relation to terrain, distance, accessibility, session timings, fitness levels, confidentiality and medical issues.

Experiment: Trial the concept in advance with willing clients, like any new coaching approach. Select an accessible local park or open space to test, and then adjust and learn from the experience.

Table 27.2 Health and safety planning

Ser	Criteria	Think about:
1	Accessibility	• Distance and time from your and your client's workplaces; • Parking availability; • Impact of peak times on congestion, e.g. rush hour or holidays; • Public transport links.
2	Route	• Ease of navigation; • Out and back, circular or meandering; • Width of footpath to enable walking side by side; • Distance with options to cut short/extend if necessary; • Obstacles along the route, e.g. road crossings, stairs, stiles; • Legal access rights for business activities; • Environmental noise levels.
3	Terrain	• Link to fitness levels, client comfort and mobility or medical considerations; • Nearby bodies of water, e.g. ponds, rivers, canals; • Impact of inclement weather, e.g. rain on additional slip hazards.
4	Other users	• Number of other users. Note: Possible challenge of isolated working, particularly during initial chemistry session; • Other users, e.g. walkers, cyclists, prams, drivers, forestry workers; • Areas of congestion; • Impact on confidentiality; • Contact with non-human users, e.g. dogs, cows, wasps.
5	Local amenities	• Address, distance and route to the nearest medical facility; • Local cafes/hotels to break up session or for indoors coaching in line with Plan B; • Access to toilets.

Tools and techniques

A variety of tools and techniques can be drawn from your existing methodologies and integrated into your eco-coaching practice. Themes such as resilience, change, growth, acceptance, letting go, balance and sustainability often emerge during eco-coaching sessions.

1. **Ecological Self**. Drawn from the school of deep ecology, self-actualisation transpires when an individual transcends the "egoic" to "ecological" self. This idea focuses on ethical and moral responsibilities to ourselves, others and the environment (see Box 27.1).

Box 27.1: Case study

The majority of photographs from my childhood are taken outdoors; at school I'd stare out the window waiting for the bell to ring so I was able to escape, and I joined the British Army partly to avoid working in an office. This thread continued during my coach training, where I'd consistently ask my peers to head outdoors for practice sessions. I experience an innate sense of freedom, creativity and deeper connection to a larger entity whilst outdoors; these remain strong drivers that have shaped my career choices, defined my coaching niche and will continue to mould my future.

– Anna-Marie

Eco-coaching also raises the opportunity to connect our work with wider environmental issues and can lead to discussions about a more sustainable future for our work, life and planet.

2. **Systemic Approach**. The ecosystem offers a framework to view the world based on a client's connection to the wider system; organisational, social or systems nested within systems. Networks of relationships and perceptions of gestalts can be explored to encourage self-reflection and self-confrontation of personal responsibilities to the wider system.
3. **Evolution**. Evolution theory explains how living things change over time. These themes regularly emerge in coaching interactions, and the nature versus nurture debate could be introduced as a metaphor to explore fixed versus growth mindset.
4. **Metaphors**. The natural environment is rich with metaphors (see Box 27.2). During a coaching session, attention can be drawn through questions towards a specific or collective parts of the surrounding environment
   a) **Visual Metaphors**. The natural environment offers rich visual metaphors where distinctive parts of the environment can be identified and then used to externalise and explore ideas, e.g. path junctions, weather or seasonal cycles (see Box 27.2).

Box 27.2: Case study

Standing on the Ridgeway near West Kennet, Wiltshire, a dark bank of clouds rolled towards us. The temperature plummeted and snow started to fall. We shivered, wrapped our jackets closer and adopted a slightly brisker pace as we walked back towards our parked cars, our coaching session nearly at its conclusion for the day. Suddenly the clouds ahead parted to reveal an oasis of clear blue sky set against the ominous banks of gloomy grey. This moment of calm held within the storm aligned deeper themes within our dialogue; change, transition and fear. The conversation then shifted to open a window of new possibilities, with hope and possibility moving forwards. This immersive visual experience offered a powerful metaphor to reference in the future.

---

   b) **Linguistic Metaphors**. Specific word choices can refer to parts of nature to express our thoughts and feelings. These expressions can contain rich content to unpack in coaching, e.g. "the black sheep in the family", "the shining star in the business" or "his eyes were ice as he stared".
   c) **Auditory Metaphors**. The natural soundscape is filled with different noises from wildlife, water, wind and other sources. These can range from soothing and gentle to ear-splitting shrieks and can invoke a variety of feelings, physical sensations and cognitive associations. For example, different types of birdsong have been observed to affect physiological and psychological processes. The melodically pleasing sounds of songbirds in comparison to potentially harsh and grating gulls. In contrast, silence found in remote locations can offer a respite to encourage deliberate contemplation and reflection.
   d) **Physical Metaphors**. Touch can be connected to past experiences and support future aspirations; for example, the sensation of wind blowing across bare skin can inspire feelings of freedom. These physical experiences offer inspiration in the future long after the coaching session has ended. In addition, natural objects such as rocks or shells can be chosen to symbolise a commitment or aspiration.
   e) **Embodied Metaphors**. The awareness of our body encourages observations of the self beyond the mind. Mindfulness practices (see below) can be used to acknowledge these sensations. For example, static "earthing" practices are based on direct contact

with the ground and provide the opportunity to observe subtle shifts in emotional and energetic sensations. In addition, the pace of the walk itself can influence emotional and energetic states; consider the differences between a stroll in comparison to a march. At a designated turning point, the physical change in direction can be utilised to shift the dialogue into a different space.

5. **Seasonal Cycles**. Observations of the seasons can be linked to cyclical themes which emerge during coaching, e.g. life, career, self-development or specific projects. Timelines (or other emergent shapes) can be created to identify interrelated elements, connections, opportunities and possibilities (see also Nature Play below).

6. **Nature Play**. This creative approach uses natural resources (stones, leaves, flowers, etc.) to symbolise and externalise a situation, e.g. timelines, relationships (particularly around "stuck-ness"). The experiential element encourages different perceptions and emotions to emerge and shift.

7. **Mindfulness**. There are different approaches to becoming fully immersed in the present moment when surrounded by nature, e.g. a body scan, loving kindness, observer, etc. The "sit spot" Mindfulness practice can be introduced by identifying a quiet and restorative location near home or work and making the commitment to visit regularly, e.g. 20 minutes, 3 times a week over a 4-month period. The client can record observations in a journal related to changes in the environment and personal thoughts/feelings.

8. **Nature Retreats or Pilgrimages**. These are generally longer than an individual coaching session and a variety of coaching approaches can be integrated. Nature retreats usually focus on a holistic lifestyle approach, whereas pilgrimages are a prolonged journey with a possible moral or spiritual component, often to a specific destination of significance.

9. **Deeper Questions**. These provoke how clients think, feel or understand information within a frame of reference, as opposed to simply eliciting more information. Deeper questions challenge assumptions to generate alternatives and possibilities, and then create change (see below for "ten deeper questions to use outdoors").

Ten useful questions for outdoor-eco coaches

Questions offer our clients the opportunity to examine their current context, challenge their assumptions and limiting beliefs, gain self-awareness and set future intentions. Eco-coaching combines this with the natural environment and facilitates a multi-sensory experience at a conscious or unconscious level. This presents the space to build deeper connections, seek inspiration and create change.

The questions below are designed to deepen conversation and prompt internal reflection by drawing on metaphors in the surrounding environment in relation to the human body and mind. It's important to remain client-led when offering deeper questions, maintaining rapport, being empathetic and asking permission, especially if a level of challenge is needed.

1. **What does the path hold ahead?**
   This question directs attention towards a specific part of the environment and integrates the perception of time. The future is visually depicted as the route in front where conversations around change, transformation and opportunity can emerge. Characteristics of the path itself can be unpacked to represent specific elements of the context; for example, stony ground can illustrate a period of uncertainty.

2. **How do you place yourself in the world?**

   This broader frame encourages a shift in awareness from the individual to a wider ecological system. It opens a more inclusive and networked approach through heightened awareness of self and connections with others and the environment. Answers can reveal a deeper insight into the client's model of their world, relationships and purpose. These responses can lead into further conversations at an intellectual, behavioural, emotional and spiritual level.

3. **Looking back over your shoulder, who are you? Or Looking ahead, how do you see yourself?**

   This question draws attention to two distinct physical directions and connects the past with the future. The concept of time and how it is perceived, valued and used by the client is a rich resource. The majority of coaching dialogue is placed in the future space. However, past beliefs, inner scripts and behavioural patterns shape the present context. The recognition and acceptance of these connections between the past, present and future offers scope to explore ideas around deeper identity and purpose. The question enables the client to acknowledge parts of themselves obstructing future aspirations. The client's past can hold valuable information, though it might be challenging for some individuals to access, acknowledge and share.

4. **What does it feel like being within the boundary of the sea and land? Or night and day (at dusk); day and night (at dawn); edge of city and park?**

   This question draws attention to the natural boundaries or liminal spaces between space or time where change is visually present. Change lies at the centre of all coaching engagements. There is inevitably a period of transition, which can be a positive or negative experience for the client. Emotions can range from feelings of fear towards uncertainty and the unknown to excitement and pleasure.

5. **How can you move from here to there?**

   This question highlights two distinct points in the surrounding environment, the first centred on your physical location and the second upon a distant feature chosen to indicate a gap, e.g. a building, tree, water or high ground. It encourages active engagement to create change through specific actions. It can be helpful to reinforce the question through arm gestures and other body language. The question can be adapted by replacing "here" with "there". The presence of two "theres" shifts the physical association and visual perspective with the environment for the client. This can open a different dialogue around future intentions and actions.

6. **What knowledge, skills and attitudes will you need for your journey?**

   The question builds on the metaphor of items needed to support a journey. The client is invited to consider different knowledge, skills and attitudes needed to achieve goals or encourage change. This exposes your client's awareness of their present abilities and identifies blind spots, limiting beliefs or gaps which need to be filled.

7. **If you could invite anyone in the world to be next to you in this moment, who would that be?**

   This question encourages the client to look beyond their personal resources. Possible supporters may emerge from their existing network; alternatively, they might create an ideal persona with specific skills, knowledge and experience who could provide assistance, or they could seek inspiration from a relevant role model (current or historic). The subtext signals that the client has the power to ask for help and is not alone. It can provide a route to explore deeper themes of trust, vulnerability, conflict and communication. It's important to be inclusive and work with all levels of mobility, though this question can be modified to involve movement by asking, "if you could invite anyone in the world to walk with you in this moment, who would it be?".

8. **Which route will you choose?**

This question is useful after several options have been explored. It infers a number of routes (or metaphorical options) are available, which encourages expansive thinking. By literally standing at a crossroads, the client is physically embedded in their context and, from a visual metaphorical perspective, can access change. Junctions where several different routes intersect offer the chance to explore opportunities, discuss the pros and cons of different ideas and move into future actions.

9. **Where next?**

This question encourages client-led discussion, as well as a reflection on the paths (choices) that the client has to make in their life.

10. **When will you arrive at your destination?**

A destination marks an end point of the metaphorical journey, with the successful completion of a desired outcome(s) and introduces a specific timeframe. This specificity helps to identify milestone tasks, fosters commitment and encourages accountability.

Conclusion

Eco-coaching can help our clients benefit from the wider outdoor environment, as well as add additional dimensions to our coaching practice. The natural environment provides restorative opportunities for recovering from mental fatigue and re-energising our directed attention. In doing so, our executive function is restored and our cognitive capabilities are improved, allowing us to think more creatively, access deeper memories and make effective decisions.

References

Berman, M.G., Jonides, J. and Kaplan, S. (2009). 'The cognitive benefits of interacting with nature'. *Psychological Science*, 19(12), pp. 1207–1212.

Berman, M.G., Kross, E., Krpan, K.M., Askern, M.K., Burson, A., Deldin, P.J., Kaplan, S., Sherdell, L., Gotlib, I.H. and Jonides, J. (2012). 'Interacting with nature improves cognition and affect for individuals with depression'. *Journal of Affective Disorders*, 140, pp. 300–305.

Berto, R. (2014). 'The role of nature in coping with psycho-physiological stress: A literature review on restorativeness'. *Behavioural Science*, 4, pp. 394–409.

Bratman, G.N., Daily, G.C., Levy, B.J. and Gross, J.J. (2015). 'The benefits of nature experience: Improved affect and cognition'. *Landscape and Urban Planning*, 138, pp. 41–50.

Howell, A.J., Dopko, R.L., Passmore, H-A. and Buro, K (2011). 'Nature connectedness: Associations with well-being and mindfulness'. *Personality and Individual Differences*, 51(2), pp. 166–171.

Kaplan, S. (1995). 'The restorative benefits of nature: Towards an integrative framework'. *Journal of Environmental Psychology*, 15, pp. 169–182.

Kaplan, S. and Berman, M.G. (2010). 'Directed attention as a common resource for executive functioning and self-regulation'. *Perspectives on Psychological Science*, 5(1), pp. 43–57.

Kaplan, R. and Kaplan, S. (1989). *The experience of nature: A psychological perspective*. Cambridge: Cambridge University Press.

Kaplan, S. and Talbot, J.F. (1983). 'Psychological benefits of a wilderness experience'. In I. Altman and J.F. Wohlwill, eds., *Human behaviour and environment*. New York: Plenum Press, *Vol 6, Behaviour and the natural environment*, pp. 163–203.

Kellert, S.R. and Wilson, E.O. (1993). *The biophilia hypothesis.* Washington, DC: Island Press.

Klepeis, N.E., Nelson, W.C., Ott, W.R., Robinson, J.P., Tsang, A.M., Switzer, P., Behar, J.V., Hern, S.S. and Engelmann, W.H. (2001). 'The National Human Activity Pattern Survey (NHAPS): A resource for assessing exposure to environmental pollutants'. *Journal of Exposure Analysis and Environmental Epidemiology*, 11, pp. 231–252.

Korpela, K. and Hartig, T. (1996). 'Restorative qualities of favourite places'. *Journal of Environmental Psychology*, 16, pp. 221–233.

Leary-Joyce, J. (2014). *The fertile void: Gestalt coaching at work.* St Albans: AOEC Press.

Palmer, S. (2015). 'Can ecopsychology research inform coaching and positive psychology practice?' *Coaching Psychology International*, 8 (1), pp. 11–15.

Palmer, S. and O'Riordan, S. (2019). 'Ecopsychology informed coaching psychology practice: Beyond the coaching room into the blue space'. *The Danish Journal of Coaching Psychology*, 8(1), pp. 21–30.

Ratcliffe, E., Gatersleben, B. and Sowden, P.T. (2013). 'Bird sounds and their contributions to perceived attention restoration and stress recovery'. *Journal of Environmental Psychology*, 36, pp. 221–228.

Ulrich, R.S., Simons, R.F., Losito, B.D., Fiorito, E., Miles, M.A. and Zelson, M. (1991). 'Stress recovery during exposure to natural and urban environments'. *Journal of Environmental Psychology*, 11, pp. 201–230.

White, M.P., Pahl, S., Ashbullby, K., Herbert, S. and Depledge, M.H. (2013). 'Feelings of restoration from recent nature visits'. *Journal of Environmental Psychology*, 35, pp. 40–51.

Whittington, J. (2016). *Systemic coaching & constellations: The principles, practices and application for individuals, teams and groups*, 2nd edition. London: Kogan Page.

YouGov. (2014). *The effects of modern indoor living on health, wellbeing and productivity.* Retrieved on 28 March 2020 from www.velux.nn/indoorgeneration.

28 Acceptance and Commitment Coaching

Tim Anstiss

Introduction

Acceptance and Commitment-Based Coaching (known as AC Coaching) is a theory-driven, research-informed coaching approach to help people live their best possible lives, take committed action in line with their values and better manage the unwanted, uncomfortable and even painful thoughts and feelings which inevitable show up along the way.

It is a form of behavioral coaching which works with a variety of presenting client issues (procrastination, relationship difficulties, anger and anxiety problems, sports and work performance, etc.) and can also be used by coaches in their own lives to help them become better coaches and grow and develop as human beings.

In this chapter I will provide an overview of the Acceptance and Commitment-based approach and look at some of the supporting research, before looking at how the approach is delivered in practice and some of the associated tools and techniques to help bring about client change.

Acceptance and Commitment Coaching explained

Many clients fail to live their best possible lives as a result of not living in harmony with what really matters to them – their values. The reasons for this may include: Not having clarity about what their values are; not having the skills to behave in a values consistent way when pulled and pushed in different directions by their thoughts, emotions, urges, sensations and memories; and not being sufficiently motivated.

AC-based coaching helps with all three reasons. The AC-based coach helps the client to: i) Clarify and act or behave in line with their values, the things which matter to them; ii) Develop and apply four different Mindfulness skills to the challenge of living their best lives; and iii) Strengthen their motivation to take steps towards a more engaged, vital, meaningful values-based life.

AC-based coaching uses a different psychological model from many other coaching approaches. Like other approaches, AC-based coaching recognises that all human beings struggle and suffer – sometimes a huge amount – but places an unusual emphasis on the role of language, attempts to control one's internal world and poorly applied problem-solving in this struggle and suffering. It emphasises that many of the things people do to cope with and manage their internal experiences – their thoughts, feelings, urges and sensations – often end up making things worse. People commonly run into problems when they try to control their thoughts and feelings (the control agenda) and often make better progress towards living their best lives when they step away from the struggle to control this internal experience. The AC-based coach does not try to change the content of a person's mind or their feelings, but rather helps the client change their relationship with their thoughts and feelings, so that they don't get pushed or pulled around by them so much. The coach helps the client take steps towards a more values-based, engaged and flourishing life, whilst carrying their thoughts and feelings lightly. The aim is behaviour change towards a better life, not inner peace or a quietened mind. If some clients experience more inner peace as a result of AC Coaching that is considered a nice side-effect, but it is not the aim and should not be relied upon.

Core concepts

Core concepts in AC-based coaching include: Private experience; the control agenda; experiential avoidance; and psychological flexibility.

Private experience

Private experience is what is happening inside a person which is not available for other people to experience. This can include thoughts (which are commonly words and images), feelings, sensations, urges, memories, etc.

The control agenda

The control agenda describes the common coping strategy of trying to control one's private, internal experiences

Experiential avoidance

Experiential avoidance includes the things people do to get rid of, stop, not have, block out or suppress unwanted thoughts, feelings and sensations – even when doing so creates harm in the long run. Experiential avoidance might include excessive drinking, over-eating, procrastinating, spending too much time on social media or watching TV, having sex, not having sex, staying in bed all day, not going out to a party, not speaking up at a meeting, self-harm, excessive exercising or not taking exercise, etc. From the above list, you can see that it's not the behaviour itself which determines whether or not a behaviour is a form of experiential avoidance – it's the function of the behaviour in the client's life. For instance, the behaviour of having two large glasses of wine may serve different purposes according to the context. Compare a teacher drinking two glasses of wine before work with the same person drinking two glasses of wine at a wedding. The first is more likely to be experiential avoidance and, over time, make the person's life worse. That is why AB Coaching is informed by functional contextualism – the view that the function of a behaviour performs is determined by the context in which it appears.

Psychological flexibility

Psychological flexibility is the dynamic state the AB coach helps their client develop (even if they never use that term with the client). It has been defined as:

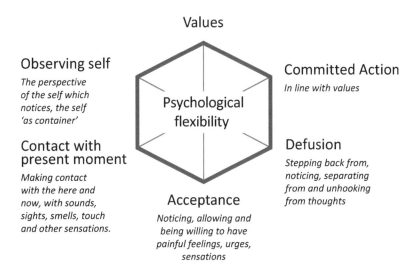

Figure 28.1 The six elements, processes or aspects of psychological flexibility

> the ability to be fully present and open to our experiences to that we can take action guided by our values.
>
> (Stoddard et al., 2012)

And:

> the ability to be present, open up, and do what matters.
>
> (Harris, 2009)

Figure 28.1 illustrates the six elements, processes or aspects of psychological flexibility.

The six processes, aspects or elements of psychological flexibility

To help clients develop more psychological flexibility, have less experiential avoidance and live their best lives, the AC-based coach helps their client with the following six things: 1) Clarify and live a life informed by their values, 2) Take committed actions in line with these values, 3) Learn to defuse from some thoughts, get unhooked from them, see them more as objects which come and go; 4) Be willing and able to accept and allow unwanted or even painful feelings, sensations and urges; 5) Be able to repeatedly bring themselves back to the present moment when their minds wander unhelpfully; and 6) Spend more time viewing life from the perspective of the observing self rather than the narrative self, or "self-as-content" perspective.

AC Coaching theory and research

There are over 300 randomised controlled trials (RCTs) of ACT published (see https://contextualscience.org/state_of_the_act_evidence for a list of these studies). Whilst most studies have examined the effectiveness of the approach on physical and mental health status (e.g. Anxiety, Pain, Depression, Stress, Substance Abuse, Weight loss, Cancer, Smoking, Gambling, etc.), there have been many studies examining the impact of the approach on issues more commonly addressed in coaching, including: Quality of Life; Parenting; Couple/Marital Relations; Training; Sleep; Anger Management; Confidence; Attention; and Skills Coaching.

In addition to individual studies, the approach has been the subject of several systematic reviews and meta-analyses, including in: Weight management (Lawlor et al., 2018); Depression (Howell, et al., 2019a); Student well-being (Howell, A. et al., 2019b); Substance use disorders (Li et al., 2019); Health behaviour change (Roche, et al., 2019); Anxiety (Kelson, J. et al., 2019) (Swain et al., 2013); Health and well-being of carers (Kishita et al., 2018); Burnout (Reeve et al., 2018); Pain (Schütze et al., 2018; Veehof et al., 2016); Eating disorders (Linardon, et al., 2018); Stress (Rudaz, et al., 2017); Sports Performance (Noetel et al., 2017); Mental health and well-being (Brown et al., 2016); Chronic disease and long-term conditions (Graham et al., 2016).

Research also supports the ACT contention that trying to change the frequency or content of particular thoughts may be less helpful than helping people cope better with them (e.g. Wells, 1994), and that helping clients contact the present moment may help to alter the function of a thought without changing its form or content (Borkovec and Roemer, 1994, Teasdale et al., 2002). In addition, many studies have also demonstrated an association between how much a person "fuses" with their thoughts, avoids certain feelings and struggles to act in the presence of difficult private events with psychological disturbance, reduced quality of life, perceived physical health, well-being at work, job-induced tension and depression symptoms (e.g. Bond and Bunce, 2000); performance, negativity and job satisfaction (Bond and Bunce, 2003); and symptoms of depression and anxiety (Strosahl et al., 1998; Tull et al., 2004; Forsyth et al., 2003)

AC Coaching in practice

There is no set or agreed way to get started with AC-based coaching with clients. The coach could, for instance, start coaching using the GROW model and then talk during the options phase about helping the client reduce their avoidance behaviours, live a more values-based life or develop more psychological flexibility. Or they might just invite the client to explore their values and what matters most to them in life early on in the coaching conversation, then agree on actions that help them live a more engaged, values-based life and then explore the skills they may need to help them take these actions when their thoughts, feelings and urges get in the way. Alternatively, they might start delivering coaching using a non-AC-based approach, and if the progress isn't what they or the client hoped for, ask the client if they would be interested in exploring an alternative approach to making progress in life. And if they say yes, talk about and start doing AC Coaching.

Regardless of how one gets started, here are some things the coach may wish to do, and why.

Values-based living

Often clients are not really in touch with their values, what really matters to them in life. And even if they once were, values can change over time, so it is often very worthwhile to help your client clarify and reflect on their values.

This can be done formally – using perhaps a deck of value cards which the client sorts into piles of different importance, or having them rate values from a list – or informally, perhaps by asking them to look forward a few years and describe what would be happening if they were living their best lives: What would they be doing, planning and thinking about? Who would they be spending time with? And why? Or just asking them some open questions such as: What really matters to you, deep in your heart? What do you want your life to be about? What sort of person do you wish to become? What do you want to do with your time on this planet? What personal qualities do you wish to develop?

Things which may emerge might include: Family, success, learning, caring and compassion, making a difference, wealth, power, creativity, sustainability, friendship, God, fairness, etc.

Once a client has given some thought to and clarified what matters to them, the coach might then explore with them how these values currently show up in their lives, or may have shown up in the last few months and how they might live more in harmony with some of these values in the coming weeks, months or years. (One interesting point – your client's pain may help you discover where their values lie.)

It is important to note that values are different from goals. Goals are things that can be achieved or failed at. Values are not like that. Values remain intact to guide and shape a person's life even if they fail to reach their goals. Indeed, without knowing what matters in life, what is important in life, how can person-centred goals even be set? Values are more like a direction on a map, a direction of travel and goals are more like places on the route which a person may or may not visit. The kinds of things that people do with values is to live in harmony with them, embrace them or move in the direction of them. The question "Am I done yet?" can be asked of goals, but not of values (Hayes and Smith, 2005).

Committed action

Committed action involves purposeful and deliberate behaviour change in the service of chosen values, with a willingness to experience thoughts, feelings and reactions that show up in the process of moving forward. This is what AC Coaching considers will actually deliver a better quality of life for the client – holding their difficult thoughts and feelings lightly whilst taking steps in a valued life direction. Taking these actions even when their brain is telling them, for example: "you cant"; "you're a fraud"; "you will fail"; "you're useless"; "what's the point?"; "do it next week"; or "she will laugh at you". And taking these actions even when they may be experiencing anxiety, anger, guilt, shame or sadness.

Defusion

Clients often experience problems and fail to live their best life when they listen to, or pay too much attention to and believe, what their mind tells them. They get "hooked" by the content of their mind and allow their behaviour and actions to be excessively influenced by their transient thoughts rather than their enduring values.

The AB coach helps the client look *at* their thoughts, rather than *through* them. This helps provide the client with some "wiggle room" to take action guided by their values. The unhelpful or unwelcome thoughts won't disappear, of course, but the client's behaviour will become less under their control and the client will be more free to move in their chosen life direction. Some of the things the client may become more aware of as they learn to defuse might be the fact that their mind is almost constantly judging, predicting, evaluating, planning, problem-solving, comparing, labelling, travelling to the future, travelling to the past, providing a running commentary and criticising. That is what normal minds do! It does not make the client faulty or damaged or different – it's just the nature of the mind, and they share this nature with millions of other people on the planet. AC-based coaching holds that it's only when the client "buys into" some of these thoughts and beliefs that hold them back from taking helpful action, or which disconnect them from what is actually happening around them, that all this internal content and mental chatter becomes problematic.

Some of the exercises and activities the AC-based coach might share, do with and encourage their clients to practise, include Mindfulness exercises to help them see their thoughts as things which come and go; visualisation techniques – for instance, placing thoughts on leaves in a stream and watching them float away – or verbal techniques, which help to change words to just sounds rather then symbols full or meaning, such as saying a word like "failure" 30 times rapidly out loud, or singing, e.g. "There's something the matter with me" to the tune of happy birthday (known as deliteralisation techniques).

Acceptance

Acceptance is the psychological skill or process of being willing to have unwanted, painful feelings and sensations, of making space for them, of "expanding around them" or of allowing them to be – rather than trying to get rid of them. The AC-based coach helps clients become curious about their feelings, urges and sensations, really paying attention to them as if they were having them for the first time, noticing them as they actually are – and not as their mind tells them they are (or will be).

It's important to note that the acceptance aspect of psychological flexibility is an active choice and not just passive resignation. And it is not about "wanting" to have unwanted thoughts and feelings, urges and sensations – it is just being willing to have them, to be open to them, in the service of something more important – living their best lives. In the words of Jon Kabat-Zinn:

> You can't stop the waves … but you can learn to surf.

Present-moment awareness

We all know that the mind can be a bit of a time machine – transporting us to and showing us futures that may never happen, and forcing us to rewatch and even relive pleasant and painful events from our past. None of this is problematic in and of itself, but this tendency for the mind to travel forwards and backwards in time can be associated with worry, rumination, anxiety, feelings of dread and hopelessness (when looking forward), and feelings of guilt, shame, regret, anger, bitterness, hate, sadness and loss (when looking backwards).

To help develop the skill of presence, the AC coach teaches and guides the client to bring their attention and focus back to the present moment, time and time again. Noticing when they get "lost" in thought, and then helping them get into contact with their immediate sensory experience – e.g. breathing sensations, sounds, pressure on the skin, things they can see, smells, etc. Here is perhaps the world's greatest ever rugby player on how his team, the New Zealand All Blacks, used present-moment awareness skills to help them perform at their best:

Breathe slowly and deliberately, nose or mouth, with a two second pause … then shift your attention to something external – the ground or your feet, or the ball in your hand, or even alternating big toes, or the grandstand. Get your eyes up, looking out … use deep breaths to help get out of your own head, find an external focus, get yourself back in the present, regain your situational awareness.

(McCaw, 2005)

The observing self

There are different perspectives we can hold about "the self", different "positions", so to speak, from which we can view the world. We all have, for instance, a "biographical self" (also known as the narrative self, thinking self, or self-as-content) – a self full of stories and memories, rules, beliefs and labels we place on ourselves (e.g. intelligent, funny, stupid, ugly, caring, creative, worthless, sporty, a failure, etc.). But there is another part of ourselves, a witness to all this content, a container, as it were, of all this content, a part of us which notices all the change going on inside of us but which remains unchanged by it. It is the subject for which all other things are object. It was present during all the good and bad things that happened in our past, and it is a "self-part" or "perspective" which has been emphasised in many different spiritual traditions throughout recorded history. In AC Coaching we call this perspective or aspect the observing self, and we help our clients access this perspective from time to time to help them make better progress in their journeys towards their best possible lives.

A metaphor may help. Imagine a schoolteacher in the playground being jostled by kids, immersed in all the noise and excitement, being pulled around perhaps, and not being able to see all of what is happening. That may be how some clients feel or experience their lives. The AC-based coach helps their client become more like the teacher on an upstairs balcony, looking down and watching what is happening in the playground below but not caught up in things. Noticing what is happening but not being affected by it.

Getting started using AC Coaching

The coach wishing to make progress with an AC Coaching approach might consider: Learning about and doing several of the exercises and activities found in books about ACT (Acceptance and Commitment Therapy) and ACT-related websites, so as to both develop their own psychological flexibility and gain first-hand experience of how these skills, activities and exercises work; introducing some elements of the AC Coaching approach without referring to them as such – e.g. values clarification, present-moment awareness; practising talking about the different aspects of AC Coaching, including using several of the metaphors (Stoddard, 2014) used to help the client better "get" what is being talked about – e.g. hands as thoughts, passengers on the bus, the self as the chessboard rather than the battle happening on top of it, etc.; practising elements of the AB Coaching approach with colleagues and other coaching students and practitioners, reflecting on how the practice goes and becoming aware of the inner critic, unwanted thoughts, uncomfortable emotions, etc. that arise as you, the coach, step out of your comfort zone into a different coaching approach; and starting AC Coaching with a new client, but explaining to them, perhaps, that you will be offering them a new style of coaching, which the evidence suggests can be very effective.

Tools and techniques

The AC coach will use a range of tools and techniques to help the client develop psychological flexibility, experience reduced experiential avoidance and take steps towards a more values-based life. Some have been mentioned or alluded to in the above section. And, of course, many of the tools and techniques an AC-based coach will use will not be specific to AC-based coaching – including agreeing the agenda, Sardonic questioning, sharing information, collaborative planning, goal-setting, signposting to additional resources, Mindfulness exercises, values clarification, etc.

Two quite specific AC-based coaching tools and techniques are the choice point and the ACT matrix.

Most clearly articulated by Russ Harris (2018), the choice point model is a simple, flexible and comprehensive tool which helps coaches and clients rapidly get to grips with the AC model. Typically drawn by hand, the model starts with a choice point and then has one arrow pointing away from the choice point labelled "towards" and another arrow pointing away from the choice point labelled "away". See Figure 28.2.

Once this has been drawn, the coach might add the words "situations, thoughts and feelings" to one side of the choice point, and "unhooked" and "hooked" onto or over the two arrows. This simple (and in my opinion brilliant) model can be used for explaining to the client how AC-based coaching can help, whilst introducing the client ideas around moving towards their values and best lives, making "away moves" that take them away from what matters (as a result of experiential avoidance), as well as the how the skill of defusion and getting unhooked from thoughts and feelings can help the client make better progress. In addition to an educational framework, the choice point model can be used for taking a history, case formulation and analysis and work on one or more specific issues with which the client is struggling with – e.g. procrastination, poor diet, anger management, problems delegating, dealing with debt, relationship difficulties, etc.

A second helpful model or technique for "doing" AC-based coaching, the ACT matrix (Polk et al., 2016) is another visual framework. More complex than the choice point model, the ACT matrix fulfils many of the same functions – client education, analysis of a client's problem or issue, case conceptualisation, clarifying who and what matters to the client, how unwanted thoughts and feelings can lead to experiential avoidance and "away" moves, thinking about which behaviours and actions would more the client towards what matters, explaining that the things they have been doing to try to control and get rid of unwanted thoughts and feeling may not have helped (at least in the long term) and that

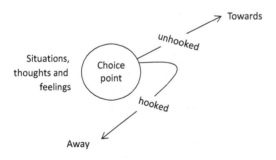

Figure 28.2 The Choice Point model

you, the coach, can share with them another way which involves changing their relationship with their thoughts and feelings and carrying them lightly as they move towards what matters. See Figure 28.3.

Similarly to the choice point model, the matrix may be best drawn by hand with the client, and once the framework has been created and described, the client guided through a series of steps including: (1) talking about who and what matters to them; (2) talking about the thoughts and feeling which show up and get in the way of what matters; (3) the behaviours they do when unwanted thoughts, feelings and urges show up; and (4) what actions and behaviours would result in them moving towards what matters to them in life. Additional things you can do with the ACT matrix include 1) illustrating worsening spirals of unhelpful behaviours and unwanted thoughts and feelings (e.g. client feels bad, eats or binges, feels self-disgust, eats more or self-harms, feels shame, etc.) as well 2) trigger and increase feelings of hope as you indicate to the client that there is another approach which they may not have tried before, a new way forward, a scientific approach which seems to work for many people struggling with different issues. The Matrix can also be used to keep a record of the session, agree practice tasks and inform the agenda of future sessions.

When does AC Coaching work best?

Research shows that Acceptance and Commitment Therapy helps clients and patients with a variety of issues in a wide range of settings. There is no reason to believe that the coaching version – AC-based coaching – isn't equally as effective and flexible as its therapy-focused cousin, and just as able to help a wide range of different clients with a wide range of different coaching agendas, issues and goals.

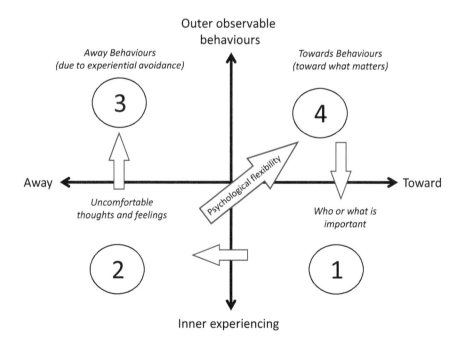

Figure 28.3 The ACT Matrix

But perhaps AC Coaching might work best with clients who are not sure about the direction their lives should take, or who have been struggling with making progress with their lives for several years or whose problem or issue is quite clearly related to experiential avoidance – e.g. procrastination, lack of assertiveness, smoking, drinking, lack of exercise, poor diet, social anxiety or failure to take steps outside their comfort zone.

Ten useful question for AC coaches

1. *What is it you would like to work on with me?*
   Nice open question to get the conversation started and begin to focus on what matters to the client.
2. *Looking forward and imagining your life has got better, what would be different? What would people notice?*
   Two questions to get the client talking more about their desired future, from which the coach might be able to infer the client's values and what matters to the client. Note also that the first question may draw out desired changes in the client's private experience (e.g. I'd like to feel more confident), whilst the second focuses more on behaviour changes which can be observed.
3. *What have you tried so far?*
   Continues to let the client tell their story, helps the coach deepen their understanding (remember, don't just ask questions – use those reflections and affirmations, too) and may also begin to increase client readiness for a different approach to what they have tried.
4. *And how did that go/and how has that been going?*
   A challenging question, helping the client realise that perhaps what has been tried so far (which may include different forms of counselling or coaching) has not delivered the changes they would like to see in their lives, at least in a sustainable way.
5. *Would you be willing to learn about and perhaps try a different approach?*
   Just as a personal trainer may educate their client about how the body works, so too the AC-based coach educates the client about how the mind works and the rationale for the AC-based approach – and how it can help them to live a more vital, values-based life – with the client bringing their unwanted thoughts and feelings along with them.
6. *What do you make of what I've just said?*
   After an explanation of an aspect of the AC-based approach – perhaps defusion, acceptance, avoidance or values, preferably with some metaphors to better help the client "get" the concept – it's important to check what they make of things, how much they understand of what you've said.
7. *Would you be interested in us getting started with the approach, giving it a go and seeing what happens?*
   A closed question, but a respectful, person-centred one – emphasising personal autonomy, agency, choice and collaboration – and seeking permission to continue.
8. *What did you notice?*
   A nice question to use after a small piece of in-session experiential practice. Perhaps you helped them bring their minds back to the present moment, or perhaps helped them to make space for, allow and be curious about unwanted feelings, or helped them defuse from one or more thoughts or helped them contact the observing self.

9. *How might getting better at (defusion, acceptance, contacting the present moment, taking the perspective of the observing self, using your values) help you make progress with* [issue] *or* [living your best life]?

It doesn't matter how many reasons we have for our clients to develop their psychological flexibility, what matters is how many reasons they have. So a question like this might strengthen their motivation as they hear their own reasons. It can also help the coach to check a client's understanding of the underlying model and assumptions – i.e. that the approach and processes can help reduce experiential avoidance and help the client make better progress towards a values-based life

10. *What do you think you might do between now and the next time I see you? What would be helpful?*

It is better to evoke or draw out from the client what they plan to do to make progress, rather than you coming up with a plan yourself – at least in the first instance. Once they have said what they think might be helpful, you can always make one or two gentle suggestions:

> *I'm wondering also if you might be prepared to spend a few minutes each day practising the defusion technique we practised in the session today. Many of my clients notice if they practise when it is easy, they have access to the skills when things are more difficult.*

Conclusion

AC-based coaching is a theory-driven, behavioural coaching approach, supported by an impressive body of research and accompanied by lots of helpful and often free resources. The aim of AB Coaching it to help clients live their best possible lives, develop psychological flexibility and reduce unhelpful experiential avoidance. You can use AC-based coaching as a complete and holistic system of coaching, or you can dip in and out of the approach as you coach clients towards their best possible lives.

AC-based coaching makes extensive use of metaphors to help the client better grasp what the approach is about, as well as experiential learning in the session – e.g. present-moment awareness exercises, practising the skills of defusion or acceptance. The AC coach may let the client know that they too struggle with experiential avoidance, getting hooked by thoughts and unwanted feelings, sensations and urges and use the same techniques and strategies they are sharing with and offering the client.

Two useful visual, multi-purpose tools or frameworks for delivering AC-based coaching are the choice point model and the ACT matrix. Once the coach has practised these with themselves, colleagues and clients they will find them useful approaches for helping clients live their best possible lives.

Applying AC-based coaching principles, techniques and processes in our own lives may not just help us to become better coaches, but may also help us become better human beings.

References

Bond, F. and Bunce, D. (2000). 'Mediators of change in problem-focused and emotion-focused worksite stress management interventions'. *Journal of Occupational Health Psychology*, 5(1), pp. 156–163.

Bond, F.W. and Bunce, D. (2003). 'The role of acceptance and job control in mental health, job satisfaction, and work performance'. *Journal of Applied Psychology*, 88, pp. 1057–1067.

Borkovec, T.D. and Roemer, L. (1994). 'Generalized anxiety disorder'. In R. T. Ammerman and M. Hersen, eds., *Handbook of prescriptive treatments for adults*. New York: Plenum, pp. 261–281.

Brown, M., Glendenning, A., Hoon, A.E. and John, A. (2016). 'Effectiveness of web-delivered acceptance and commitment therapy in relation to mental health and well-being: A systematic review and meta-analysis'. *Journal of Medical Internet Research*, 18(8), e221.

Forsyth, J.P., Parker, J.D. and Finlay, C.G. (2003). 'Anxiety sensitivity, controllability, and experiential avoidance and their relation to drug of choice and addiction severity in a residential sample of substance abusing veterans'. *Addictive Behaviors*, 28, pp. 851–870.

Graham, C.D., Gouick, J., Krahé, C. and Gillanders, D. (2016). 'A systematic review of the use of Acceptance and Commitment Therapy (ACT) in chronic disease and long-term conditions'. *Clinical Psychology Review*, 46, pp. 46–58.

Harris, R. (2009). *ACT made simple. An easy to read primer on acceptance and commitment therapy*. Oakland, CA: New Harbinger.

Harris, R. (2018). *ACT questions and answers: A practitioner's guide to 50 common sticking points in acceptance and commitment therapy*. New Harbinger Press. Oakland, California.

Hayes, S. and Smith, S. (2005). *Get out of your mind and into your life. The new acceptance and commitment therapy*. Oakland, CA: New Harbinger.

Hayes, S.C., Strosahl, K.D., Wilson, K.G. et al. (2004). 'Measuring experiential avoidance: A preliminary test of a working model'. *The Psychological Record,* 54, pp. 553–578.

Howell, A.J. and Passmore, H. (2019a). 'Acceptance and commitment therapy (ACT) to reduce depression: A systematic review and meta-analysis'. *Journal of Affective Disorders*, 260(1), pp. 728–737. London: Heinemann.

Howell, A.J. and Passmore, H. (2019b). 'Acceptance and commitment training (ACT) as a positive psychological intervention: A systematic review and initial meta-analysis regarding ACT's role in well-being promotion among university students'. *Journal of Happiness Studies*, 20, pp. 1995–2010.

Kelson, J., Rollin, A., Ridout, B. and Campbell, A. (2019). 'Internet-delivered Acceptance and Commitment Therapy for anxiety treatment: Systematic review'. *Journal of Medical Internet Research*, 21(1), pp. e12530.

Kishita, N., Hammond, L., Dietrich, C. and Mioshi, E. (2018). 'Which interventions work for dementia family carers?: An updated systematic review of randomized controlled trials of carer interventions'. *International Psychogeriatrics*, 30(11), pp. 1679–1696.

Lawlor, E.R., Islam, N., Bates, S. et al. (2018). 'Third-wave cognitive behaviour therapies for weight management: A systematic review and network meta-analysis'. *Obesity Reviews*, 8(7), e023425..

Li, I., Sato, H., Watanabe, N., Kondo, M., Masuda, A., Hayes, S.C. and Akechi, T. (2019). 'Psychological flexibility-based interventions versus first-line psychosocial interventions for substance use disorders: Systematic review and meta-analyses of randomized controlled trials'. *Journal of Contextual Behavioral Science*, 13, pp. 109–120.

Linardon, J., Gleeson, J., Yap, K., Murphy, K. and Brennan, L. (2018). 'Meta-analysis of the effects of third-wave behavioural interventions on disordered eating and body image concerns: Implications for eating disorder prevention'. *Cognitive Behaviour Therapy*, 48(1), pp. 15–38.

McCaw, R. (2005). *The real McCaw: The autobiography*. London: Aurum Press.

Noetel, M., Ciarrochi, J., Van Zanden, B. and Lonsdale, C. (2017). 'Mindfulness and acceptance approaches to sporting performance enhancement: A systematic review'. *International Review of Sport and Exercise Psychology*, pp. 1-37.

Oldfather, W.A. (1925). *Epictetus: Discourses*. Loeb Classical Library. Boston, MA: Harvard University Press.

Reeve, A., Tickle, A. and Moghaddam, N. (2018). 'Are acceptance and commitment therapy-based interventions effective for reducing burnout in direct-care staff? A systematic review and meta-analysis'. *Mental Health Review Journal*, 23 (3), pp. 131–155.

Roche, A.I., Kroska, E.B. and Denburg, N.L. (2019). 'Acceptance- and mindfulness-based interventions for health behavior change: Systematic reviews and meta-analyses'. *Journal of Contextual Behavioral Science*, 13, pp. 74–93.

Rudaz, M., Twohig, M.P., Ong, C.W. and Levin, M.E. (2017). 'Mindfulness and acceptance-based trainings for fostering self-care and reducing stress in mental health professionals: A systematic review'. *Journal of Contextual Behavioral Science*, 6, pp. 380–390.

Schütze, R. Rees, C., Smith, A., Alater, H., Campbell, J.M. and O'Sullivan, P. (2018). 'How can we best reduce pain catastrophizing in adults with chronic noncancer pain? A systematic review and meta-analysis'. *The Journal of Pain*, 19, pp. 233–256.

Stoddard, J and Afari, N. (2014). *The big book of ACT metaphors, a practitioners guide to experiential exercises and metaphors in acceptance and commitment therapy*. Oakland, CA: New Harbinger Publications.

Strosahl, K.D., Hayes, S.C., Bergan, J. and Romano, P. (1998). 'Does field based training in behavior therapy improve clinical effectiveness? Evidence from the acceptance and commitment therapy training project'. *Behavior Therapy*, 29, pp. 35–64.

Swain, J., Hancock, K., Hainsworth, C. and Bowman, J. (2013). 'Acceptance and commitment therapy in the treatment of anxiety: a systematic review'. *Clinical Psychology Review*, 33, pp. 965–978.

Teasdale, J.D., Moore, R.G., Hayhurst, H., Pope, M., Williams, S. and Segal, Z.V. (2002). 'Metacognitive awareness and prevention of relapse in depression: Empirical evidence'. *Journal of Consulting and Clinical Psychology*, 70, pp. 275–287.

Tull, M.T., Gratz, K.L., Salters, K. and Roemer, L. (2004). 'The role of experiential avoidance in posttraumatic stress symptoms and symptoms of depression, anxiety, and somatization'. *Journal of Nervous & Mental Disease*, 192, pp. 754–761.

Veehof, M.M., Trompetter, H.R., Bohlmeijer, E.T. and Schreurs, K.M.G. (2016). 'Acceptance- and mindfulness-based interventions for the treatment of chronic pain: A meta-analytic review'. *Cognitive Behaviour Therapy*, 45, pp. 5–31.

Wells, A. (1994). 'Attention and the control of worry'. In G.C.L. Davey and F. Tallis, eds., *Worrying: Perspectives on theory, assessment and treatment*. Oxford, England: Wiley, 91–114.

29 Positive psychology approaches to coaching

Christian van Nieuwerburgh and Robert Biswas-Diener

Introduction

"Positive psychology" (PP) refers to the scientific study of "what makes individuals and communities flourish, rather than languish" (Boniwell and Tunariu, 2019, p. 2). While it may be a relatively young field, it has attracted widespread global attention and is now being applied in a wide range of contexts. PP is, in part, a response to a perceived tendency in psychology to focus on deficits and mental disorders. Its purpose is to "develop sound theories of optimal functioning and to find empirically supported ways to improve the lives of ordinary and extraordinary people" (Kauffman, 2006, p. 219). This entails the study of concepts such as wellbeing, strengths, happiness, creativity and hope. It is also an applied science, with research informing practical interventions for use with individuals, groups, organisations and societies.

In this chapter, we will be presenting ways in which coaches, managers and leaders can integrate PP concepts and interventions into their practice. First, we will define the emerging discipline of "positive psychology coaching" (PPC). Then we will present relevant theories and provide a snapshot of some of the most recent research on the use of PPC, before sharing practical ideas that can be used during coaching and management conversations. Finally, we will consider the most appropriate situations for using a PP approach and discuss some questions that could be useful to coaches, managers and leaders.

Positive psychology coaching explained

Although modern coaching was being practised in the 1980s and 1990s, the academic field of "coaching psychology" (CP) was launched in the year 2000. This means that both CP and PP are relatively young fields. Initially, each had its own specific focus: CP focused on psychological theories and techniques to support individuals to reach personal and work-related goals; PP focused on researching the factors that allow individuals and groups to thrive. In other words, coaching psychology was interested in individual flourishing while positive psychology aimed to support flourishing and wellbeing more generally.

It soon became clear that there was a natural alignment between the two fields. Both CP and PP have a shared focus on unlocking potential, building on existing resources, enhancing subjective wellbeing and supporting people to perform at their best. According to Boniwell and Tunariu (2019), "coaching and positive psychology are natural allies in sharing an explicit concern with the enhancement of optimal functioning and well-being, arguing for performance improvement, finding what is right with the person and working on enhancing it" (p. 244). It has also been recognised that there is a vast corpus of psychological theories, evidence-bases, and applied practices – developed across psychology and other allied disciplines – that belong neither to PP nor CP, but can be harnessed by both … Each has its own particular concerns, practices and applications, but there is also a significant area of overlap.

(van Nieuwerburgh, Lomas and Burke, 2018, p. 99)

This has led to the development of a distinct coaching methodology called positive psychology coaching (PPC) in the early 2000s. Subsequently, PPC has been defined as "a scientifically-rooted approach to helping clients increase well-being, enhance and apply strengths, improve performance, and achieve valued goals" (Kauffman, Boniwell and Silberman, 2009, p. 158) and has developed recognised processes and structures (Passmore and Oades, 2014; Green and Palmer, 2019). For us, PPC is simply a managed conversational process that supports people to achieve meaningful goals in a way that enhances their wellbeing. There are a number of theories that are relevant to coaches wishing to adopt a positive psychology approach. We have listed these, along with specific topics and some of the key researchers, in Table 29.1.

Positive psychology coaching theory and research

Whilst there have been great strides taken in the academic study of each of the two fields (CP and PP), there is currently little research about the integration itself. Although practitioner-led initiatives generally outpace research, early studies are promising.

An early study explored the perceived value of positive psychology coaching on women working in the financial services sector. Elston and Boniwell (2011) proposed that using coaching to identify strengths and apply them in the workplace could lead to benefits for the recipients and their organisations. In the same year, Spence and Oades argued that integrating knowledge of self-determination theory (SDT) into coaching conversations would enhance "evidence-based" coaching practice (Spence and Oades, 2011). More recently, Grant and O'Connor (2018) have shown that integrative approaches such as PPC can be more effective than using PP or CP independently. In a qualitative study, Fouracres and van Nieuwerburgh (2020) investigated the experience of clients who had received a PPC intervention. Participants in this study reported that self-identifying strengths during

Table 29.1 Positive psychology theories and topics that are relevant for coaches

Area of focus	Specific topics	Key researchers
Wellbeing theories	Happiness, subjective wellbeing, psychological wellbeing	Ed Diener, Carol Ryff, Sonja Lyubomirsky
Strengths theories	VIA character strengths, Clifton strengths finder, strengths profile	Donald Clifton, Chris Peterson, Alex Linley
Emotion theories	Positive emotions, mood as information, broaden and build theory, "negative" emotions	Barbara Fredrickson, Ed Diener, Lisa Feldman-Barrett
Theories of future focus	Hope, optimism, solution-focused, appreciative inquiry	C.R. Snyder, Michael Scheier, Charles Carver, Steve de Shazer, Insoo Kim Berg, David Cooperrider

a coaching conversation was a positive, multifaceted experience that seemed instinctive. In another qualitative study, Lucey and van Nieuwerburgh (2020) explored the experiences of early career teachers facing challenging circumstances who receive PPC. In this study, participants reported that PPC was a positive experience, one that validated their feelings and helped them to make sense of their situations.

Positive psychology approach in practice

Perhaps the easiest way to understand the PP approach to working with clients and supervisees is to recognise that it is a *philosophy* that guides professional attention, discussion, and outcomes. We argue that there are three primary emphases that are native to the PP mindset:

1. *A focus on the positive.* The PP mindset is one that – as its name implies – emphasises the positive. It is well documented that people have a natural tendency to focus on problems and to experience setbacks more strongly than they do progress (Rozin and Royzman, 2011). The PP mindset attempts to counter this tendency by adding attention to strengths, resources and other positive aspects of life. More broadly, the PP mindset focuses on wellbeing as opposed to illbeing. While acknowledging the reality of hardships and struggles, those working with positive psychology seek to build people's capacities and help them flourish.

   In this way, PP approaches bear more than a passing similarity to solutions-focused approaches. Those working with a solutions focus often work by the adage, "it's okay to listen to problem talk, just don't invite problem talk". Solutions-focused coaching uses a number of specific tools to validate difficult client experiences and then shift the conversation toward positive, practical and future-focused planning. PP approaches differ from those used in solutions-focused coaching, however, in that they might focus more explicitly on client wellbeing and use a research-based vocabulary to identify and discuss strengths, values and other positive topics.

   Specifically, those working with a PP approach would likely establish the foundation of the working relationship by explicitly discussing this positive focus. They would reassure clients and supervisees that struggles are inevitable but that they will not be the exclusive focus of the working relationship. Instead, the practitioner creates the expectation that there will be ample opportunity to explore positive aspects of life and work.

2. *An acknowledgment of the benefits of positive emotions.* The benefits of positive emotion are one of the most exciting findings to emerge from positive psychology research. To date, scientists have explored the consequences of experiencing frequent (but not intense) positive feelings and found that they include social, healthy and work benefits (Kansky and Diener, 2017). The relevance of this research to coaching and positive leadership is twofold: First, it suggests an implicit agenda for the professional relationship – to create goals and plans that will minimise (not eliminate) negative emotions and maximise positive ones. We do not mean to suggest here that coaching with a positive psychology orientation is license for the coach to usurp client agendas with an emphasis on feeling good. Rather, we are suggesting that emotional experience will be a natural part of almost any client agenda. Second, positive emotions can be harnessed during coaching and management conversations themselves. For example, surprising a client with an unusual question might disrupt their myopic focus on a complaint. Similarly,

celebrating a client success might boost their joy and enthusiasm for tackling new challenges.

At first blush, boosting positive emotions in coaching and one-to-one management sessions may not seem unique to positive psychology. Indeed, popular approaches to coaching such as the "Co-Active Model" explicitly encourage coaches to accept, validate and explore emotions (Whitworth, Kinsey-House and Sandhal, 1998). While we agree that mood is an important channel of information, we argue that it is negative emotions that provide more distinct units of information. The exploration of negative feelings can yield important insights, but the PP approach attempts to harness the *in vivo* experience of positive emotion. It should also be noted that many coaches and managers are uneasy with doing so because A) they believe that emotions are the domain of psychologists, B) are, themselves, uncomfortable with emotions, or C) do not know enough about emotions to strategically induce or explore them.

3. *An alignment with science as a way of knowing.* A central concern of coaching and management is improved knowledge (often self-knowledge). There are, of course, many ways of knowing, including faith, intuition, personal experience and common wisdom. The PP philosophy prioritises science as a unique and powerful method of knowing. The empirical method is unique as a system of knowing in that it can establish causality, generalise results with great accuracy and revise knowledge as new results emerge. PP science, therefore, provides a large repository of theory, frameworks and specific results that might help guide PP practitioners in their work.

A caveat: Experienced coaches might express concern with the idea that coaches know about the client or their circumstances even before a session. Indeed, most approaches to coaching favour a "client as expert" perspective and we are no different. We advocate an approach similar to the "local clinical scientist model" (Stricker and Trierweiler, 1995). Although their model is specific to the practice of psychotherapy, we agree with their general argument that knowledge of general psychological processes and phenomena can help professionals. Practitioners, including those aligning with PP, can use this knowledge to form loose impressions about client issues that they then explore, test and revise with information from the client.

Tools and techniques

As an applied science, PP has been able to inform coaching in many ways. Here, we discuss assessments, activities and frameworks that can be used in PP approaches to coaching and management.

Positive Assessment: Coaching has long relied on personality and similar types of assessments to yield new insights and spark fruitful conversations with clients. Because PP is a branch of science, researchers have spent decades creating psychometrically valid assessments that can help us understand a wide range of positive phenomena. Many of these assessments are relevant to coaching and are short, non-invasive and free to use. Formal assessments also have the advantage of efficiency: They ask dozens of questions in a short span of time (Biswas-Diener, 2011).

We encourage those people using a PP approach to be strategic in their use of positive assessments. Rather than giving all assessments to every client, practitioners should offer an assessment when it appears relevant to the client agenda and circumstances. For instance, a client wrestling with emotional stress caused by a work–life imbalance might be an appropriate candidate for an assessment that tracks emotional experience (e.g. The SPANE; Diener, et al., 2009) or the Purposeful Work Scale (Linley and Biswas-Diener, 2009).

The results of positive assessments should be discussed in the coaching or management session. Rather than positioning the coach as an expert who is interpreting the results for the client, this conversation is an opportunity for the coach to ask questions about the assessment. For example, a coach might ask "what was your initial reaction to the results of this assessment?", "how accurately do you feel the results of this assessment describe you?" or "what will you do with the knowledge gained from this assessment?". In each case, the assessment is a springboard to personal insight and action.

Activities: Many coaching sessions are marked by structured and semi-structured activities. These include visioning exercises, card sorts, thought showers and similar activities to augment self-knowledge, planning and goal-setting. As an applied science, PP has yielded a number of such activities that may be successful in boosting client mood and creating a positive frame of mind (Heekerens and Eid, 2020).

One example of such an activity is a short, free-writing exercise known as the "best possible self" exercise (Heekerens and Eid, 2020). Despite the name, this activity is not about the perfect self but an opportunity for clients to imagine a near future in which things have gone well and to describe this life and what has happened. This activity can be modified in many ways to make it more relevant to the client agenda. For example, you might have the client focus on various spans of time such as imagining "the next year" or "the next five years". Similarly, you might focus the client's writing on her life in general or encourage her to confine the writing to her work life.

Another example of a commonly used activity is the so-called "3 blessings" activity, in which research participants have been asked to list aspects of their lives for which they are appreciative (Heintzelman, et al., 2019). We do not recommend using this activity as an off-the-shelf exercise but, rather, using it to guide a more naturalistic coaching conversation. For example, coaches might use questions to direct client attention to resources and solutions by asking "what is going well in your life?", "what are you appreciative of?" or "how does taking time to appreciate the positives affect you?".

Frameworks: Because PP research offers so many insights into such diverse, positive topics, the results of these studies can be used as frames to guide and inform coaching conversations. These frameworks are too numerous to list here, but examples include distinct curiosity profiles (Kashdan, et al., 2018), optimal levels of happiness (Biswas-Diener and Wiese, 2019) and an entire continuum of motivation (Sheldon, 2017).

Using the continuum of motivation as a single example, this framework can provide a specific vocabulary for identifying various types of motivation such as "identified" and "introjected". Coaches can listen for hallmark features of these distinct motives to gain a clearer and better-articulated understanding of the client. In addition, coaching questions can be informed by this framework to produce questions such as "to what extent would you do this if there were no external pressure to do so?" or "how much does this feel like it is *your* goal?". We argue that familiarity with frameworks for emotion, wellbeing, optimism, motivation and strengths can help coaches develop and ask better questions.

When do positive psychology approaches work best?

It can be helpful to integrate PP tools and approaches into coaching and management conversations to support the achievement of meaningful goals, the improvement of performance and the experience of wellbeing. Adopting a PP approach can be helpful in a number of specific situations:

(i)   When it is necessary to increase engagement with the coaching process:
         the coach can introduce a exercise to help the client identify their strengths which can increase engagement.
(ii) When the client feels "stuck" and starts to doubt their ability to achieve the goal:
         the coach can ask questions that increase hope (for example, those that direct attention to personal influence, past successes and relevant resources).
(iii) When greater alignment between values and actions is needed:
         the coach can encourage the client to explore their deeper meaning and purpose.
(iv) When the goal does not seem to motivate the client:
         the coach can listen and encourage the client to talk about goals which are aligned with their values.
(v)   When the pursuit of the goal is affecting the wellbeing of the client:
         the coach can raise awareness of the apparent conflict between goal and the client's wellbeing.

In general, a positive psychology approach is appropriate for most coaching conversations. It is characterised by a heightened interest in the subjective wellbeing of the client and reference to the factors that lead to unlocking human potential, thriving and flourishing. Below we consider some possible questions that can be used to bring a positive psychology approach to a coaching conversation.

Ten useful questions for positive psychology coaches

1. **How can you use your strengths in this situation?**
      This question invites clients to consider how they can draw on their best selves, think about past successes and use similar approaches to the challenges they face in the present moment;
2. **How do people react when you use this strength?**
      Like question one, this question is helpful when discussing efficacy. Simply asking this question will remind the client that they have existing strengths (and related resources) that can be brought in to address challenges. Be careful not to subtly suggest that using strengths will guarantee success. We recommend treating strengths use as an experiment that the client can try to see how it works and then modify as appropriate. Focusing on the reactions of others will support the client to calibrate her strengths to match the context;
3. **What motivates you?**
4. **How do you recover your motivation?**
      Questions 4 and 5 bring motivation into the conversation. Making changes requires effort, so it is important for the client to be aware of their own level of motivation. This can lead to discussion about whether they are driven by intrinsic or extrinsic motivators. We recommend that you do not fall into the trap of believing (and then communicating to the client) that intrinsic motivation is "good" and extrinsic motivation is "bad". Instead, validate the client's current motivation and explore their motivational preferences;

5. **What do you most appreciate about the current situation?**
6. **Who supports you in this situation?**

   Questions 5 and 6 encourage clients to explore the positives within their current situation, as opposed to defaulting to focusing on problems. Although problems, obstacles and setbacks are urgent, it can also be helpful to appreciate the elements that are working well (for example, drawing attention to the client's existing support networks). These factors can be lynchpins to feeling motivated and creating new, more flexible plans to achieve goals;

7. **What are you curious about?**
8. **What most surprises you?**

   If coaching is largely about engaging clients in self-directed learning, there is – perhaps – no greater vehicle for doing so than curiosity. By asking about interest, surprise, confusion and curiosity you can create the space for the client to guide the coaching conversation in a personally satisfying way;

9. **How are you feeling?**
10. **If this feeling had a voice, what would it be encouraging you to do?**

    Emotion is an important channel of information and is worth listening to. When asking about feelings, we would recommend checking to ensure that the client's response is an emotion, rather than a thought. Coaches can ask a number of variations of these questions, such as "how would you prefer to feel?" and "what might you need to do to accomplish that?".

Conclusion

The PP approach is exciting for many reasons. First, because of its emphasis on the positive, many clients and supervisees prefer it. They generally enjoy being recognised for authentic strengths and focusing on progress in addition to problems. Second, the empirical nature of PP means that many of the tools used in this approach have been tested widely. That said, practitioners using a PP approach must always work with clients to determine the appropriateness of PP results to the local situation. Third, because it is grounded in science, the knowledge base is dynamic. This can be particularly exciting for practitioners because it gives them the opportunity (and responsibility) to evolve their own knowledge and skill. Finally, there are thousands of researchers investigating hundreds of positive psychological phenomena. This means that there is a huge sweep of insights and tools emerging from PP that are relevant to many aspects of coaching and management.

References

Biswas-Diener, R. (2010). *Practicing positive psychology coaching: Assessment, activities, and strategies for success.* New York: John Wiley.

Biswas-Diener, R. and Dean, B. (2007). *Positive psychology coaching: Putting the science of happiness to work for your clients.* New York: John Wiley.

Biswas-Diener, R. (2011). *Positive psychology as social change.* New York: Springer.

Biswas-Diener, R., & Wiese, C. W. (2018). Optimal levels of happiness. In E. Diener, S. Oishi, & L. Tay (Eds.), *Handbook of well-being.* Salt Lake City, UT: DEF Publishers.

Boniwell, I. and Tunariu, A. (2019). *Positive psychology: Theory, research and applications*, 2nd editon. London: Open University Press.

Diener, E., Wirtz, D., Tov, W., Kim-Prieto, C., Choi, D., Oishi, S. and Biswas-Diener, R. (2009). 'New measures of well-being: Flourishing and positive and negative feelings'. *Social Indicators Research*, 39, pp. 247–266.

Elliot, A.J. and Friedman, R. (2007). 'Approach-avoidance: A central characteristic of personal goals'. In B.R. Little, K. Salmela-Aro and S.D. Phillips, eds., *Personal project pursuit: Goals, actions, and human flourishing*. Mahwah: Lawrence Erlbaum, pp. 97–118.

Elston, F. and Boniwell, I. (2011). 'A grounded theory study of the value derived by women in financial services through a coaching intervention to help them identify their strengths and practice using them in the workplace'. *International Coaching Psychology Review*, 6(1), pp. 16–32.

Fouracres, A. and van Nieuwerburgh, C. (2020). 'The lived experience of self-identifying character strengths through coaching: An interpretative phenomenological analysis'. *International Journal of Evidence Based Coaching and Mentoring*, 18(1), pp. 43–56.

Grant, A.M. and O'Connor, S.A. (2018). 'Broadening and building solution-focused coaching: Feeling good is not enough'. *Coaching: An International Journal of Theory, Research and Practice*, 11(2), pp. 165–185.

Green, S. and Palmer, S. (2019). *Positive psychology coaching in practice*. Abingdon: Routledge.

Heekerens, J. B., and Eid, M. (2020). 'Inducing positive affect and positive future expectations using the best-possible-self intervention: A systematic review and meta-analysis'. *Journal of Positive Psychology*. Advance online publication. doi: 10.1080/17439760.2020.1716052.

Heintzelman, S.J., Kushlev, K., Lutes, L.D., Wirtz, D., Kanippayoor, J.M., Leitner, D., Oishi, S. and Diener, E. (2019). 'Enhance: Evidence for the efficacy of a comprehensive intervention program to promote subjective well-being'. *Journal of Experimental Psychology: Applied*, 26(2), pp. 360-383. doi: 10.1037/xap0000254.

Kansky, J. and Diener, E. (2017). 'Benefits of well-being: Health, social relationships, work, and resilience'. *Journal of Positive Psychology and Wellbeing*, 1(2), pp. 129–169.

Kashdan, T., Sticksma, M., Disabato, D., McKnight, P., Bekier, J., Kaji, J. and Lazarus, R. (2018). 'The five-dimensional curiosity scale: Capturing the bandwidth of curiosity and identifying four unique subgroups of curious people'. *Journal of Research in Personality*, 73, pp. 130–149.

Kauffman, C. (2006). 'Positive psychology: The science at the heart of coaching'. In D.R. Stober and A.M. Grant, eds., *Evidence based coaching handbook: Putting best practices to work for your clients*. Hoboken: Wiley, pp. 219–253.

Kauffman, C., Boniwell, I. and Silberman, J. (2009). 'The positive psychology approach to coaching'. In E. Cox, T. Bachkirova and D. Clutterbuck, eds., *The complete handbook of coaching*, London: Sage, pp. 158–171.

Lucey, C. and van Nieuwerburgh, C. (2020). 'More willing to carry on in the face of adversity: How beginner teachers facing challenging circumstances experience positive psychology coaching'. *Coaching: An International Journal of Theory, Research and Practice,* 13(2), pp. 1-16. https://doi.org/10.1080/17521882.2020.1753791.

Passmore, J. and Oades, L.G. (2014). 'Positive psychology coaching – A model for coaching practice'. *The Coaching Psychologist*, 10(2), pp. 68–70.

Rozin, P. and Royzman, E. (2001). 'Negativity bias, negativity dominance, and contagion'. *Personality and Social Psychology Review*, 5, pp. 296–320.

Sheldon, K., Osin, E.N., Gordeeva, T.O., Suchkov, D.D. and Sychev, O. (2017). 'Evaluating the dimensionality of self-determination theory's relative autonomy continuum'. *Personality and Social Psychology Bulletin*, 43, pp. 1215–1238.

Spence, G.B. and Oades, L.G. (2011). 'Coaching with self-determination in mind: Using theory to advance evidence-based coaching practice'. *International Journal of Evidence Based Coaching and Mentoring*, 9(2), pp. 37–55.

Stricker, G. and Treirweiler, S.J. (1995). 'The local clinical scientist model: A bridge between science and practice'. *American Psychologist*, 50, pp. 995–1001.

Van Nieuwerburgh, C. Lomas T. and Burke, J. (2018). Integrating coaching and positive psychology: Concepts and practice. Coaching: *An International Journal of Theory Research and Practice*, 11(2), pp. 99-101.

30 Developing an integrated approach to coaching

Jonathan Passmore

Introduction

In this chapter we will be exploring the idea of integration. Integration involves drawing together, in a formal way, the different coaching approaches you use in your practice to form a single holistic model. I have argued elsewhere in this book that coaches should seek to move beyond a single model or framework, to blend different approaches, flexing their approach to meet the needs of the individual client and the specific presenting issue, as well as working with models and approaches which fit their personal values, beliefs and strengths. The chapter starts by exploring what is meant by integration, before arguing the case for integration. Thirdly, I will examine one example of an integrated model and how this can be applied with clients. The chapter closes by noting that there is no one best model for integration. Instead, each coach should, through practice, reflection and training seek to formulate their own approach, which synthesises their knowledge and is appropriate for their clients and the cultural context in which they work.

What is integration in coaching?

Integration involves bringing together the different approaches and models we use, in a considered and planned way, which allows the coach to be able to describe their framework, including what assumptions it is based on and how they make choices about which approach they use and when.

An integrated model is more than a collection of different approaches, it describes why the coaches have brought them together in this way and how they use the model with clients and presenting issues. As an analogy, it's the difference between musicians playing their music by themselves in different rooms and an orchestra playing a symphony together, with each instrument having a specific function, coming in and out as the score demands. Each individual instrument is lost, and what the listener hears is the music.

The benefits of integration

Research into the practices of experienced coaches has suggested that experienced coaches often use a specific label to describe what they did; for example "cognitive-behavioural coaching" or "psychodynamic coaching". But a detailed examination of their reported behaviours suggested that experienced coaches use a wide range of behaviours which are drawn from a diverse range of different approaches. Thus, experienced coaches might maintain a distinct identity, while their actual practice suggests integration from diverse perspectives (Passmore, 2006).

Some writers in coaching (Kilburg, 2004) have argued that there is no difference between different approaches and that, in the end we will find, like the Caucus Race in Alice in Wonderland, where the competitors can run in any direction, that all will have prizes. However, the evidence from therapy suggests this is not always the case (see Cooper, 2008). When all presenting issues are combined, there is a similarity between different approaches, but when presenting issues are categorised; for example, into anxiety, drug addiction or bereavement, some types of presenting problem may be better tackled by specific approaches.

Apart from adjusting to meet the challenges of a specific type of presenting problem, it may also be beneficial if the coach adapts to meet specific client needs. Every client has their own biases and personal preferences, and by adjusting our approach as the coach, we can work in ways which meet our clients' world view or personal preferences.

In the following section I will describe one way of drawing together different approaches.

Integrative coaching explained

In this section of the book we have offered a range of different approaches, from GROW and psychodynamic coaching to person-centred and beyond. But how can a coach draw on each of these and create an integrative approach, allowing them to flex and adapt to individual clients and individual situations?

The integrative model described below is one way of doing this, consisting of six streams that flow together. The first two streams are concerned with relationship. The next four streams focus on behaviours, emotions, cognitions and physiological sensations. The seventh stream focuses on the system in which the client, and the coach, are working. An overview of the model is provided in Figure 28.1.

Streams 1 and 2: The coaching partnership

Before any coaching to enhance performance or develop personal insights can begin, the coach needs to build a working relationship with the client. The coach–client relationship is the foundation stone of effective coaching. Without a firm foundation, progress cannot be achieved, as the coach is less likely to be open, trusting or willing to take the cognitive risks that enable coaching to be the effective intervention (see Chapter 2 of this book: The business case for coaching).

It is this work in building the relationship that I have called Stream 1 (developing the relationship). To create this relationship, the coach needs to actively engage with the client, providing a space where the client feels heard and understood (see Chapter 7 of this book: The Coaching relationship. However, once established, this work on the relationship cannot stop, although less effort may be needed.

What are the key ingredients to create an effective working relationship? This question has in part already been answered by writers within the counselling tradition, such as Carl Rogers (1961). Rogers suggested that a series of elements need to be in place for a successful "therapeutic alliance" to be formed. These relationship elements are of importance to any work with individuals in the consulting world. However, the creation of an intimate and trusting relationship in coaching demands a stronger investment in the relationship by the coach than in a relationship to deliver training or consulting.

During the early part of the coaching relationship, the client evaluates the coach: Do I trust him or her? Do I like him or her? Do I value what he or she is offering me? If the client reaches a conclusion that he or she does trust, like and value the coach, the real work can start. However, if the client reaches the conclusion that they do not trust or value the coach, it is unlikely any real progress will be made.

Carl Rogers' provided an excellent starting point to help in the formation of a coaching partnership through necessary and sufficient conditions. These may be summarised as:

- Positive self-regard;
- Unconditional positive;
- Empathy;
- Non-judgemental mind;
- Congruence;
- Non-possessive warmth.

Once a relationship has been formed, the role of the coach is to maintain this relationship. The maintenance of the relationship is the second stream, and flows on directly from the work of building the relationship. To maintain the relationship, an effective coach needs to pay attention to three further aspects: His or her own emotions and behaviours, the emotions and behaviours of the client and adapting his or her own behavioural responses appropriately to remain professionally detached while offering personal intimacy. These components make up the building blocks of emotional intelligence (Caruso and Salovey, 2004; Stein and Book, 2000).

In addition to emotional intelligence, the highly effective coach also needs to consider and manage transference and counter-transference issues. These aspects are of particular importance in the executive boardroom where power and role modelling are key features. However, these aspects can be relevant to the close working relationship between any coach and client. These two aspects, building and maintaining the relationship, form a ring around the four remaining streams. Without this coaching partnership, the coach is unable to begin to work in the three streams that will facilitate change and enable the development of fresh insights.

Stream 3: Behavioural focus

Having formed a working relationship, and while continuing to manage and maintain this relationship, the coach and their client can turn their attention to the coaching task. This involves working in one of five streams: Behavioural, conscious cognitions, unconscious cognitions physiological sensations and systemic.

The first of these involves behavioural coaching. Whatever the coach's theoretical orientation, a focus on external behaviour and how this is developed is a central feature of almost all coaching relationships. The focus here is on developing enhanced behavioural responses. The most popular example is the ubiquitous GROW model. The model initially developed by John Whitmore, Graham Alexander and Alan Fine (Whitmore, 2017; Alexander and Renshaw, 2005) has been developed and adapted by many coaching writers (Skiffington and Zeus, 2003).

GROW is a four-step coaching model (see Chapter 17 of this book: Behavioural coaching), and has traditionally been viewed as a non-psychological problem-solving model. The first of the steps is the identification of a goal. The second is a review of the current reality, the third a consideration of options and the fourth a conclusion and the agreement on a way forward. There is considerable debate about the nature of goals, and this is covered in more detail elsewhere in this book.

The behavioural approach is of greatest value when the client brings a skills-based problem, or where there is a direct relationship between cause and effect (Snowden and Boone, 2007). Examples might involve: "How can I improve my skills in presenting to an audience?" or "How should I prepare for a job interview next week?"

However, using a single approach limits the coach's ability to facilitate change, where the problem is chaotic or involves emotions and cognitions. In reality, most problems involve a cognitive element, although the client may not recognise this or want to work in that stream. The coach in these cases thus needs to draw on other approaches.

Stream 4: Conscious cognition

The effective coach, having established the relationship and explored behaviours, is able to explore the cognitive patterns that sit behind the visible behaviours. In this stream, the coach will typically draw upon cognitive behavioural techniques, initially developed by Beck (1991) and Ellis (1998) but adapted by coaches (see Chapter 20 of this book: Cognitive-behavioural coaching) to make them more suitable for the work of the coach than the counsellor.

Cognitive-based coaching has become one of the most popular coaching approaches (see Passmore, Brown and Csigas, 2017) and forms an integral part of this integrated model.

The coach might typically begin to explore thought patterns when they judged that the client was displaying or holding irrational thoughts that might inhibit successful performance, or they have already explored behaviourally based solutions. Such irrational thoughts might be harsh judgements about themselves or judgements of their current or future abilities. The key feature is that the judgement is irrational, that is, it is not substantiated by facts. One danger is that "irrational" is confused with "negative". As a result, the coach seeks to help the client challenge all negative views or perspectives. This is not cognitive-behavioural coaching and is unlikely to be an effective intervention.

This stream shares many of the principles that are applied to the other four streams: A dynamic, collaborative process between the coach and client, a focus on the future and on moving towards solutions and a focus on an agreed goal. Each of these principles is important to maintaining the working relationship and using coaching in a way that builds the client's ability to become a self-sustaining learner, rather than increasing his or her dependence on the coach. The central concept within this stream is encouraging the client to identify the irrational beliefs and then helping to challenge them. This two-stage process is supported through the diverse range of cognitive-behavioural and rational emotive behavioural techniques used within counselling. However, these need to be grounded within the appropriate context or focus of the coaching relationship.

Stream 5: Unconscious cognition

Some are less aware of their thoughts and emotions and how these may be influencing their lives and those around them. The coach may need to work with these "unconscious" cognitions. They may be deeply hidden and require work within the psychodynamic tradition (see Chapter 22 of this book: Psychodynamic coaching), they may be related to past traumas and the coach may need to draw upon approaches such as EMDR (Eye Movement Desensitisation and Reprocessing), which can be a valuable intervention (Foster and Lendl, 1996). Or they may be motivational in nature, where the coach's role is to help clients connect with their values and through these to generate the intrinsic motivation to act, using a motivational interviewing approach (Miller and Rollnick, 2002; Passmore, 2014).

Streams 6 and 7: Physiological sensations and systemic

The last two streams that the coach and client work within are with the body and the wider system web of the client. This web is partly obvious, and is reflected in role, team, organisational and sector cultures. It is also less obvious and expressed by the national cultural context and its expression in this moment in history.

While few clients give adequate consideration to their cultural context or how those factors shape their behaviour and how others judge them, it is important to bring them to light and consider which parts of the web can be controlled (few), which parts can be influenced (some) and which parts need to be accepted (most).

The body too can provide a fruitful element for exploration, helping in our exploration of feelings, as well as supporting the client's development their personal impact.

When does integrative coaching work best?

It can be argued that the integrative model has almost universal application within the coaching environment, as it is a blend of different approaches which the coach is selecting. The choice of each approach is based on their client, the presenting issues and what the coach believes is going to be of most help at this stage of the coaching assignment.

However, I believe what is also important is that each coach, taking account of the research evidence of effective interventions, develops their own coach model of integration. What may be most effective for an coach working in a careers or educational context, may work less well in leadership or team coaching. What may work well in a Nordic or Northern European sales organisation culture, may be less well suited to a Middle Eastern public sector organisation culture.

Finally, integrative coaching may seem like a silver bullet. However, coaching is not the solution for all individual or organisational issues. Some clients may need consulting advice, others may benefit from therapy, while others still may simply need to attend a training course.

The reality is that an integrated approach is simply a series of evidence-based approaches that have been blended together. Arguably, most experienced coaches probably do this already, and integrated coaching simply describes what they are doing.

This specific integrative model has its areas of weakness, reflecting its development within the executive coaching arena. The first of these weaknesses is that the model lacks a spiritual element. The desire to deepen one's spiritual self is a healthy and arguably central aspect of life. Where this is an explicit goal of the client, the coach would be better advised to work with models such as the transpersonal model (Einzig and Whitmore, 2016), the Islamic Ershad model (van Nieuwerburgh and Allaho, 2017) or a Christian framework (Collins, 2010). A second weakness of the model is that it assumes that coaching is goal focused. Again, this is an outcome of its executive coaching focus. However, if the client is seeking a more general exploration of his or her experience of life and the future, a different framework may be better suited to achieve this objective.

Tools and techniques

The integrated approach blends together a range of different approaches and employs the tools and techniques which are commonly used in each of these approaches. In behavioural coaching this includes goal-setting and creative approaches to generating alternative options. In cognitive issues, it uses tools such as visualisation, disputation and self-compassion. In the unconscious stream it may use transference and counter transference, as well as tools drawn from MI such as the decisional balance sheet and encouraging-change talk. Finally, at the systemic level, it may encourage the client to consider alternative stakeholders, as well as individuals who may be forgotten but can have a significant negative impact.

Ten useful questions for integrated coaches

In using the integrated model described in this chapter, readers can turn to questions from each of the relevant chapters, but we have included 10 possible questions here.

1. **What do you want to achieve?**
   This is a typical question for use within the behavioural GROW model. The aim of the question is to help the client to explicitly state their goal. Frequently, less experienced coaches take at face value the first statement and move on. It is worth the coach spending some time unpicking both the longer-term aim, as well as considering what would be a successful outcome for the session.
2. **What is happening?**
   This question aims to help the client reflect on their current situation. How close or far are they from their goal? What have they tried? What might be holding them back? In exploring the reality, the less experienced coach can be tempted to accept at face value what the client first describes. It can be helpful for the coach to challenge and probe, encouraging the client to think more deeply about the situation and develop new insights about their current reality.
3. **What options do you think there are?**
   Exploring options is a valuable process in all coaching. As coaches we believe the client already has the answers to help them move closer to the outcome they want. But to do this the coach can help in providing both permission and space for the client to think in fresh and new ways. Sometimes the coach simply needs to get out of the way while the client thinks. On other occasions, they need to inject the chemicals for a creative reaction, to allow new insights to emerge.
4. **Can you summarise what you are going to do and by when?**
   This question is concerned with action planning. The question encourages clients to take responsibility for reviewing their process, summarising what has been discussed and to formally state what they intend to do. In listening, the coach can also encourage the client to consider what barriers they anticipate, as well as which allies and supporters they can call upon and who they would like to hold them to account. Having an 'A-team' of such supporters outside of the coach–client relationship can be an important factor in helping clients to make progress (McKenna and Davis, 2009).

5. **How would your boss, mentor or colleague see this situation?**

This question encourages the client to begin to explore the issue or challenge that he or she faces from a number of different perspectives. Often an issue looks to be an insurmountable problem to us, but when considered from the perspective of another person, either solutions can be found or a deeper understanding of the issue can be gained. A parallel type of question is asking the client to consider the challenge as if he or she were a famous person. For a management issue, the coach may ask the client to consider how Sheryl Sandberg would deal with the problem, followed by a question on how Ronald Reagan would deal with the challenge. For a relationship issue, the coach might select two different characters offering different perspectives: Margaret Thatcher and Nelson Mandela. Initially, the client may laugh, or provide a flippant remark, but the coach needs to encourage the client to consider the issue fully from this perspective for insight to be gained.

6. **I would like you to close your eyes and describe to me what would happen if the event went perfectly?**

This visualisation technique gets clients to engage with a visualisation, explore what they see and, with follow-up questions, what they feel, smell and think. Evidence has shown in the sports psychology arena that visualisation not only builds self-confidence but also creates physical changes in the brain structure that aid subsequent muscle movement and thus enhances performance.

7. **Can you describe for me a typical day?**

The question encourages the client to describe (in detail) their day, and through this process identify triggers that can lead to unhelpful behaviours, thoughts or feelings. The links between such triggers and the behaviours are often outside of the client's immediate awareness and, in this sense, the question (drawn from motivational interviewing) is part of working with unconscious cognitions.

8. **Tell me more about how making the change will help you with your dream to become X?**

This question forms part of encouraging-change talk (drawn from motivational interviewing). The belief being that, once the client has talked about their beliefs and values, the coach can encourage both the motivation and a belief in making the change by encouraging the client to talk more about the positive aspects of the change in addition to the negative aspects of staying as they are. However, in doing so, the coach needs to be respectful that the client will have good reasons for staying as they are and sees risks in making the change. If the coach does not acknowledge these, the client can feel as if they have not been heard, thus a balance needs to be struck, but one which is in favour of change, if this is what the client has expressed as their goal.

9. **How would others, such as your partner or family, be affected?**

This question, also from motivational interviewing, using the balance sheet technique. The coach may be exploring with clients the costs and benefits of their behaviour. Clients can underestimate the effect of their behaviour on others, and thus fail to include this in the calculation. The coach can focus the client's attention on this through the question and often build up the costs side of the equation for the client.

10. **What would the 13th Fairy have to say about your plan?**

This question is drawn from systemic thinking. The 13th Fairy is a character in "Sleeping Beauty" who is forgotten and, when they arrive at the celebration, they case a spell to send everyone to sleep as they are so angry at having been forgotten in the haste of the invitations. Who is the stakeholder, character or agent that the client has neglected, but whose opinion (or actions) could derail the plans? In a multiple stakeholder, inter-connected world, connections are not always easy to see, and thus careful thought about the 13th Fairy can ensure the wider system is brought into the room and unintended consequences can be included in scenario planning.

Conclusion

In this chapter I have explored the idea of integration, synthesising different approaches to create a whole. I have argued that having a range of different models, approaches and frameworks will mean the coach is better able to serve their client as they can change and adapt. However, the model presented here is just one way of integrating different approaches. I would encourage each coach to develop their own model or philosophy of coaching, which is evidence-based, reflects their values and beliefs and is also consistent with the organisational and national cultural context in which they work.

References

Alexander, G. and Renshaw, B. (2005). *Super coaching: The missing ingredient for high performance*. London: Random House Business Books.

Beck, A. (1991). *Cognitive therapy of depression*. New York: Guilford Press.

Caruso, D. and Salovey, P. (2004). *The emotionally intelligent manager: How to develop and use the four key emotional skills of leadership*. San Francisco: Jossey-Bass.

Collins, G. (2010). *Christian coaching*. Colorado Springs: NavPress.

Cooper, M. (2008). *Essential research findings in counselling and psychotherapy*. London: Sage.

Ellis, A. (1998). *The practice of rational emotive behavioural therapy*. London: Free Association Books.

Einzig, H. and Whitmore, J. (2016). 'Transpersonal coaching'. In J. Passmore, ed., *Excellence in coaching*, 3rd edition. London: Kogan Page.

Foster, S. and Lendl, J. (1996). 'Eye movement desensitization and reprocessing: Four case studies of a new tool for executive coaching and restoring employee performance after setbacks'. *Consulting Psychology Journal: Practice & Research*, 48(3), pp. 155–161.

Kilburg, R.R. (2004). 'Trudging toward Dodoville conceptual approaches in executive coaching'. *Consulting Psychology Journal: Practice and Research*, 56(4), pp. 203–213.

Locke, E. and Latham, G. (1990). *A theory of goal setting and task performance*, Englewood Cliffs: Prentice Hall.

McKenna, D. and Davis, S. (2009). 'Hidden in plain sight: The active ingredients of executive coaching.' *Industrial and Organizational Psychology*, 2, pp. 244–260.

Miller, W.R. and Rollnick, S. (2002). *Motivational interviewing: Preparing people for change*, 2nd edition, New York: Guilford Press.

Passmore, J. (2006). 'Coaching psychology: Applying an integrated approach in education'. *The Journal of Leadership in Public Services*, 2(2), pp. 27–33.

Passmore, J. (2014). Motivational interviewing, pp. 283–311. In J. Passmore (ed) *Mastery in coaching: A complete psychological toolkit for advanced coaching*. London: Kogan Page.

Passmore, J., Brown, H. and Csigas, Z. (2017). *The state of play in European coaching and mentoring: Executive report*. Henley: EMCC and Henley Business School.

Rogers, C. (1961). *On becoming a person*. Boston: Houghton Mifflin.

Skiffington, S. and Zeus, P. (2003). *Behavioural coaching: How to build sustainable personal and organizational strength*. New York: McGraw-Hill.

Snowden, D. and Boone, M.E. (2007). 'A leader's framework for decision making'. *Harvard Business Review*. Retrieved on 30 March 2020 from https://hbr.org/2007/11/a-leaders-framework-for-deci sion-making.

Stein, S. and Book, H. (2000). *The EQ edge: Emotional intelligence and your success.* Toronto: MHS.

Whitmore, J. (2017). *Coaching for performance: The principles and practice of coaching and leadership*, 5th edition. London: Nicholas Brealey Publishing.

van Nieuwerburgh, C. and Allaho, R. (2017). *Coaching in Islamic culture: The principles and practice of Ershad*. London: Karnac.

Section 5

Coaching issues

31 Ethics in coaching

Ioanna Iordanou and Rachel Hawley

Introduction

Coaching is a developmental intervention based on conversations that foster curiosity and courage, through mutual respect, to lead to new understandings and the opportunity to flourish. Done well, it offers individuals a safe space to think, reflect and take responsibility for the actions that will help them develop and achieve their intended goals. In this developmental process, the coach's role is pivotal. Indeed, it is the coach's ability to listen attentively, to ask good, reflection-provoking questions and facilitate a structured discussion, which enables the client to fully consider their options, to find curiosity, courage and responsibility for their ensuing actions. An effective coach, however, is not only a skilled practitioner but an ethical practitioner; someone who consciously places their values and ethics to the forefront – rather than the background – of their professional practice, in their effort to constantly develop and maintain a consciously active ethical mind-set for the benefit of their practice, their clients and the coaching profession as a whole. In this chapter we will explore the nature of ethics, the role of ethics in coaching and how coaches can enhance their ethical practice.

The nature of ethics in coaching

During the course of their coaching practice, from novice to expert, every coach is required to make decisions that hold ethical implications. Such decisions involve issues on what is morally right or wrong, ranging from the mundane to the gravely serious. Accepting a dinner invitation from a client with whom we have developed a cordial and trusting relationship, or breaking confidentiality when a client shows symptoms of self-harm, are just two examples of such ethical considerations that can test one's convictions of what actions are morally justifiable, or unjustifiable. Ethics, therefore, is an integral aspect of coaching, since it determines a coach's decisions and actions, as dictated by their values and beliefs. As Allard de Jong (2010) aptly put it, ethics is the practice that determines what is good or bad, right or wrong. Accordingly, ethics dictate "actual rules, codes, and principles of conduct" (Beckett, Maynard and Jordan, 2017, p. 16).

Historically, the concept and practice of ethics can be traced back to ancient Greek philosophers such as Socrates (c. 470–399 BC), Plato (c. 428–c. 348 BC) and Aristotle (384–322 BC). For Socrates, moderation was a key determinant of ethical behaviour, while Plato prioritised the denial of bodily pleasure, advocating that happiness (eudemonia) could be achieved by living a life of virtue (arete). Aristotle also advocated pursuing a life of virtue but, contrary to Plato, who considered knowing what is good (i.e. wisdom) to be sufficient to achieve happiness, he claimed that knowing what is good is inadequate without practising good (Crisp, 2013). These early scholastic views on what is morally right or wrong paved the way for the development of moral philosophy, with three prevailing branches: Deontological ethics, stemming from the doctrines of Immanuel Kant (1724–1804), who situated reason at the core of morality, placing emphasis on one's sense of duty and obligation; utilitarian ethics, premised in the writings of David Hume (1711–1776), Jeremy Bentham (1748–1832) and John Stuart Milll (1806–1873), who emphasised the maximisation of utility for the benefit of society; and virtue ethics, which dictate that the "rightness" or "wrongness" of an action is determined by the virtues that enable an individual to grow and develop (see, for instance, Hursthouse, 1999). We have summarised in Table 31.1 some of the common ethical perspectives which have been developed over the past 2,000 years.

An important aspect of moral philosophy is professional ethics. Professional ethics is a rapidly developing discipline informed by several strands of social sciences and the law. Ethical practice is manifest in a set of values that prioritise an ethical professional conduct, constituting "an integral part of professional identity" (Bond, 2015, p. 47). The most elaborately developed type of professional ethics are medical ethics, primarily due to the long history and ethos of the discipline of medicine that necessitated the combination of ethical and technical issues in the training and practice of physicians (Dunn, 2018). Medical ethics have significantly influenced the development of ethical standards in other relevant "helping" professions, such as counselling and psychotherapy (Bond, 2015), creating a consensus of morally acceptable behaviour that transcends professional activities and encompasses all aspects of human interactions (Brennan and Wildflower, 2018).

From a practical perspective, in coaching, ethical principles determine the virtue of helping clients, focusing on their needs and interests, honouring trust and confidentiality and promoting individual autonomy (de Jong, 2006). Yet, unlike other relevant "helping" professions, such as counselling and psychotherapy, social work, nursing and even medicine, which are subjected to intense regulatory scrutiny, coaching continues to remain largely unregulated. As a result, ethical standards of professional practice are primarily self-imposed and no coach is obliged to comply with any specific code of ethics, unless they wish to do so. Accordingly, as Jonathan Passmore (2009, p. 8) aptly explained:

Table 31.1 Summary of the essence of coaching ethics

Ethical decisions involve what is morally right or wrong.

Values are a set of personal principles that guide our behaviour and, more often than not, they clash.

Ethics are moral principles that determine whether our actions are "good" or "bad", "right" or "wrong".

In coaching, ethical standards of professional practice are self-imposed and no coach is obliged to comply with any specific code of ethics.

Several professional coaching associations have produced their own codes of ethics that have both similarities and differences in their ethical priorities.

Codes of ethics do not ensure best practice in coaching, as they cannot guarantee a solution to every ethical problem a coach is faced with in practice.

Constant exposure to ethical issues in practice and conscious reflection on them will help you develop your ethical maturity.

(adapted from Iordanou et al., 2017: 26)

Most coaches, in most cases, are ethical pluralists, who hold to a few solid principles, but for most of what they do they consider the circumstances of the situation and consider the motives and situations of the characters involved to help them reach a decision about the course of action to follow.

To be sure of building an ethical coaching practice, "a few solid principles" are inadequate to safeguard ethical standards, especially considering the widely unregulated landscape in coaching. It is due to lack of regulation that codes of ethics have been deemed crucial for the discipline of coaching (Iordanou et al., 2017; Brennan and Wildflower, 2018). Generally speaking, codes of ethics provide a widely acknowledged set of guidelines against which coaches and clients can measure a coach's performance and evaluate their practice for continuous development and improvement. Moreover, as coaching is still not universally recognised as a legitimate, stand-alone profession, codes of ethics allow it to move away from "pseudo-credentialising mills" (Grant and Cavanagh, 2004, p. 2) (Table 31.2).

It is important to note that while the various professional coaching bodies operate independently from each other, their "codes of ethics" or "codes of conduct" bear several similarities. A useful list of the primary ethical priorities and responsibilities of the three major professional coaching associations (the International Coaching Federation [ICF], the European Mentoring and Coaching Council [EMCC] and the Association for Coaching [AC]) has been compiled by Ives and Cox (2014). Nevertheless, some caution needs to be exercised when using professional associations' codes of ethics to base our ethical decisions on. This is because, while codes of ethics can provide some excellent guidance on building an ethical coaching practice, they lack the flexibility to allow for the complexity and ambiguity of real-world dilemmas.

Why do ethics matter in coaching?

In coaching, it is important to develop our understanding of how we make choices and take decisions in our practice (Law et al., 2007, p. 196). We describe this as a moral compass

Table 31.2 Why are ethics important in coaching?

Ethical moments can enhance our personal and professional development – they alert us to what is morally right or wrong.

Coaching takes place across diverse professional contexts. Coaching ethically draws on many fields of knowledge, which are reflected in different genres/models, which provide a rich pallet from which coaches can draw according to the coaching context.

Our coaching practice is governed by understanding of our personal and professional values – understanding our personal and professional values is a purposeful process that can be viewed as a continuum, from reflection to reflexivity. Beyond this, external factors – institutional, social and political – can interfere with our personal values and influence our coaching decisions and actions.

A stance for enquiry can help pave the way towards the professionalisation of coaching. This requires us to understand how we view and construct knowledge as there are different perspectives for doing so; we call these research paradigms.

Ethical moments are always present. Thus, ethical coaching is not about finding solutions, but rather creating the conditions, through coaching conversations, that permeate the coaching relationship and bring underlying ethical issues to the surface.

Ongoing reflection on ethical issues that arise in the coaching practice helps build ethical maturity.

Reflection, critical thinking, supervision and continuous professional development are some of the ways that can fine-tune our ethical maturity.

to guide us (Iordanou et al., 2017). Our values, our technical knowledge and our coaching experience can take the form of such a compass to guide our coaching practice. However, such characteristics are rarely challenged and questioned (Bolton, 2014, p. 22). We share the perspective held by David Clutterbuck that "unethical and illegal behaviour in organisations rarely happens because people, as individuals or a group of people, set out to do wrong. Rather it starts with small breeches and gradually grows in scope and scale" (Clutterbuck, 2013). Therefore, to become truly ethical as a coach, it is first necessary for us to step outside of our selves; to be prepared to share our experiences with others and to challenge our assumptions and beliefs (Iordanou et al., 2017). Against this backdrop, we suggest that engaging in the development of an ethical coaching practice stimulates a kind of critical self-dialogue, which is necessary to understand our personal and professional values within our coaching context with greater awareness.

Words such as "good", "bad", "right" and "wrong", which are often used when we discuss one's coaching practice, frame our understanding of coaching ethics (Iordanou et al., 2017). A variety of terms are used interchangeably, sometimes with little or no agreement, often concerning values and ethics. We view ethical coaching practice as a "way of being" (van Nieuwerburgh, 2014, p. 150), a term "which" was first introduced by the influential humanist psychologist Carl Rogers, who was the founder of the person-centred approach. His approach was premised on two fundamental beliefs: that people are their own best excerpts; and that people have the ability to realise their full potential (Rogers, 1980). Many coaches consider Rogers' writing on person-centred approaches, the cornerstone of the coaching practice (Thomson, 2009, pp. 139, 151–60). Despite the passing of time, this still influences the way coaches see and work with clients across professional coaching contexts.

The investment of time to develop understanding of our personal and professional values can help to both identify and address ethical issues and moments of choices. Consistent with Christian Van Nieuwerburgh (2014), our focus is on making the "right" decisions during coaching conversations. As a coach, whether new or seasoned, it is inevitable that you will be faced with "ethical moments of choice". It is important to be able to recognise these moments by developing the kind of critical consciousness that grows from understanding "self" and our personal values. Just as Christian Van Nieuwerburg (2014) and Allard de Jong (2010), we are drawn to the term "ethical choice" as an alternative term to that of "ethical dilemma". We use this because "dilemma" may bring a negative feeling to critically important moments in the coaching conversation. In contrast, the term "ethical moment" shifts this perspective. By virtue, framing ethical moments in this way, helps us to focus on those moments in the conversation when the coach is faced with an ethical issue or question and needs to make the best choices in order to respond appropriately and ethically.

Understanding our values requires curiosity, courage and commitment. It is an ongoing journey of discovery and learning. So often we think we know our story well, yet as we explore our personal and professional values more closely, we tend to discover new insights, gaining greater awareness of how our values influence our coaching practice (Iordanou et al., 2017). Indeed, the way in which coaching practice is premised on conversation and discourse in order to construct meaning (Alred et al., 1998) is the cornerstone for the insights and learning that is cultivated within the coaching practice. This approach to learning is a stark contrast to the dominant linear learning that has been imposed by the intellectual movements of the last 200 years (Garvey and Williamson, 2002). We consider the learning that is generated in coaching to be the product of interaction with

Table 31.3 Common ethical perspectives

Ethical Perspective and thinkers	What does it mean in practice
Utilitarianism (Jeremy Bentham)	This involves comparing the good and bad consequences of each option and selecting the course of action that produces the greatest utility, or usefulness, for society.
Deontology (Immanuel Kant)	Ethical action arises from doing one's duty and duties are defined by rational thought, recognising that all humans are of equal worth.
Social Contract Theory (Thomas Hobbes)	This involves the creation of governments and bodies to establish rules in the wider public (social) interest. These are implemented through an agreement with the public.
Virtue Theory (Aristotle)	This involves basing our decisions on a set of virtues or values, which guide decision-making. The highest virtue may be the pursuit of happiness.

others; thus non-linear. Against this backdrop, our learning about our values can be seen as "socially constructed, so that we create rather than discover ourselves" (Alred et al., 1998, p. 14). Understanding our values moves beyond our personal values, to consider our professional values as a coach. Each have a part to play. As we have observed, values are the bedrock of ethical decision-making. They shape everything we do, not only in the coaching relationship but beyond, in our day-to-day lives. Indeed, they underpin human agency. Similarly, in our coaching practice, every decision we make is influenced – if not dictated – by our values and beliefs. Critically, the question is are we consciously aware of them, or not? When we enter a coaching session as the coach, we bring a particular attitude – our attitudes are premised on our beliefs. In essence, our attitude is the "mental filter through which we experience the world" (Keller, 2007, pp. 12), and it is bound to influence the coaching relationship and the ethical issues that emerge within it. Values and attitudes sit hand-in-hand. See Table 31.3.

Ethical coaches need to have great insight into their own thinking processes in relation to their values and beliefs as well as the context of the coaching interactions. We encourage the view that understanding personal and professional values is "a creative adventure, right through the glass to the other side of the silvering" (Bolton 2014, p. 116). There is no single theory that accounts for the entire journey of values and ethics in coaching. Rather, this is a complex artistry (Iordanou et al., 2017). Practising coaching reflectively and reflexively leads to new insights; of self, of others and of the coaching context. The continuum for reflective–reflexive coaching harnesses the potential for ethical practice (Iordanou et al., 2017).

Navigating ethical issues across professional contexts

Coaching ethically across diverse contexts is complex. So, what do we mean by "context"? The term context refers primarily to the professional settings in which coaching takes place, such as healthcare, education, sports and business. To explore ethical issues across professional contexts more closely, it is important to extend this view to include what Cox et al. (2014) call applied contexts or genres. Applied contexts or genres of coaching, are particular styles of coaching that can be used in a variety of professional settings, such as performance coaching, career coaching, life coaching, etc. Despite the historical narrative in the coaching literature, the context in which the coach works informs their perception(s) of the coaching practice; the values and beliefs they bring to coaching, and the ethical issues that may arise in their coaching assignments. Therefore, in order to understand values and ethics in coaching, it is first essential that we seek to appreciate the context in which coaching is undertaken (Iordanou et al., 2017).

In the following sections we will ask three important questions that carry ethical implications: Who are you when you coach? Where are you when you coach? And how do you coach? (Iordanou et al., 2017) Our hope is to illuminate that, while coaches often navigate from one specific role or context to another, it is important to be aware of the nuances of these variations. Being aware of such differences makes us more able to identify and deal with the diversity in ethical issues that arise in our day-to-day practice.

Developing curiosity about types and varieties of coaching identity can enrich our understanding of our own professional identity as a coach. Importantly, we become more aware of the influences on our identity, and thus of how our coaching identity is constructed and sustained. When we each enter our coaching practice, bringing our earlier lived experiences is inevitable. Each lived experience has the power to impact on how we understand, construct and sustain our coaching identity and consequently frames our stance on ethics in our practice. We use our own experiences as an example here to explain this further. As authors, we began the shared experience of writing from our unique perspectives and diverse professional backgrounds; Rachel with a background in UK healthcare and Ioanna as an academic. It is our shared commitment to coaching, which fosters an ongoing connection. We recognise that our professional backgrounds influence our perspectives on our writing and our coaching practice in important ways we cannot ignore (Iordanou et al., 2017).

Navigating ethical issues across professional contexts is dependent on addressing the boundaries of where coaching starts and stops. So how might we consider the ethical issues that arise in relation to working across professional contexts and, therefore, managing professional boundaries? If, for example, you are a practising coach with a background in counselling or nursing, are these roles competing or complementary? Are there any ethical issues that may arise from practising coaching with a distinct professional background?

The three key principles, which we introduced earlier in this chapter, are the foundation for enabling a more ethical practice for coaching across professional contexts. Iordanou et al. (2017) encourage that the following steps leads us to greater critical consciousness in a number of ways; firstly, "who" we are in the relationship (understanding self, personal and professional values) and secondly "where" we coach (understanding professional contexts and the nuances of ethical issues) means we become more able to navigate ethical issues across professional contexts with competence and confidence (Iordanou et al., 2017, pp. 209–215). As we become more able to align these three dimensions of ethical practice, we see values and ethics in our coaching more clearly. Engaging in a critical self-dialogue around the questions of who we are when we coach; where we are when we coach; and how we coach, we hope, illuminates the implications for ethical practice. The questions we pose around – "who", "where" and "how" we coach enable important reflections that help to raise our awareness about ethical coaching. Once we are clear about the nuances, we will become able to be more ethical.

The very nature of coaching across diverse professional contexts is complex. The complexity of coaching contexts will always hold with it ethical implications. Navigating ethical issues requires us to select the best combination of tools according to the coaching context; theories, knowledge, models and our learning from experience. When we ask these questions of ourselves – who we are in the relationship; where we coach; and how we coach – we cultivate understanding and move on from the blurriness of ethical issues that we first described at the beginning of this chapter. Instead, we become more akin to holding a kaleidoscope, where boundaries are clearly demarcated with distinct, vivid colours (Iordanou et al., 2017). To be able to see clearly it is therefore important to understand our personal and professional values. The questions of "who", "where" and "how" are central to our practice. Ethical issues will always be present in coaching practice. The art of navigating ethical issues across professional contexts rests in developing and maintaining an ethical coaching practice; you are not putting together a puzzle you already know; you're constructing a picture that takes a shape as you collect and examine the parts (Bogdan and Biklen, 2006, p. 6).

These ideas have been developed further into ethical decision-making models, such as the APPEAR framework (Passmore and Turner, 2018), which aims to provide a map to guide coaches through the challenges and turbulence of ethical dilemmas by enhancing sensitivity (Awareness), incorporating regular supervision, reflection, contracting and use of ethical codes in day-to-day practice (Practice), considering options when ethical issues arise (Possibilities), engaging with the network of insurers, professional bodies, clients and supervisors (Extending the field), before moving to implement a decision (Acting on Reflections) and reviewing the outcomes (Reflecting on learning). See Figure 31.1.

Developing and maintaining an ethical coaching practice

"A strong coach, in our view, is one 'who knows what he or she doesn't know' and has a strong enough ego to admit it". This is the apt view expressed by Beverly Brookes (2001, p. 99), who went on to argue that an ethical coach is not only conscious of their knowledge and expertise but, importantly, is also acutely aware of the limits of their knowledge, skills and competence and, thus, the need to refer their clients to a different authority if they deem their competence insufficient to support their clients' needs (Brooks, 2001).

Competence features prominently in the codes of ethics of all major professional coaching bodies. The Global Code of Ethics, initially developed by the AC and EMCC, states that:

> Members will have the qualifications, skills and experience appropriate to meet the needs of the client and will operate within the limits of their competence. Members should refer the client to a more experienced or suitably qualified practising member where appropriate.

Being reflexive of one's competence as a coach is an important step to developing and maintaining an ethical coaching practice. This includes evaluating one's knowledge and expertise in order to identify any intellectual and practical gaps that call for further training and development. Accordingly, some of the key steps coaches can take to ensure they develop and maintain an ethical coaching practice are education and training, continuing professional development and regular supervision (Iordanou et al., 2017, pp. 70–77).

Coach education and training: Currently there are no specific guidelines as to what constitutes appropriate coach education and training and, accordingly, coaches enter the profession with a great diversity of educational and professional backgrounds. This ranges

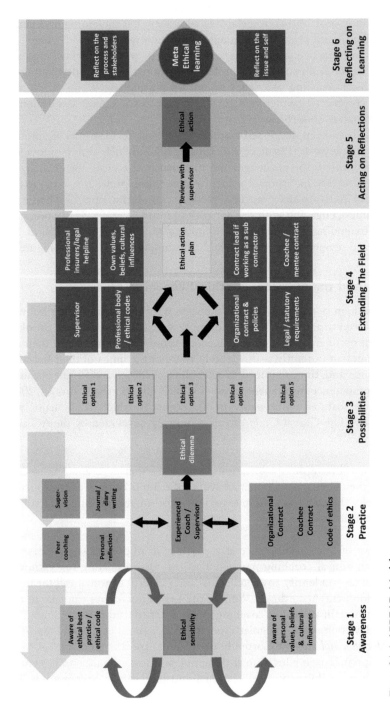

Figure 31.1 APPEAR Model

from education and management to counselling and psychotherapy, to name just a few (Bluckert, 2004; Bachkirova et al., 2018). Moreover, while professional or university-based coaching programmes are proliferating, their evaluation is lagging behind (Devine, Meyers and Houssemand, 2013). While it is important to celebrate the variety and diversity of knowledge and expertise that coaches bring into the discipline of coaching, it is also prudent to be aware of the significance of being reflexive about our constantly increasing training and development needs in order to practise consciously in a discipline that has a gradually developing body of knowledge (Iordanou et al., 2017). Accordingly, and as coaching as a discipline is in constant need of a shared body of applied knowledge (Grant and Cavanagh, 2004), the starting point should be addressing the question of what constitutes reliable and effective coach training and education that can enable an ethical coaching practice (Bachkirova et al. 2017; Iordanou et al., 2017).

Continuing Professional Development (CPD): Following from the above, developing and maintaining an ethical coaching practice entails engaging with a range of learning activities, on a regular basis, with the purpose of constantly updating one's professional knowledge base and, by extension, expertise. Within the discipline of coaching, such activities include reading empirically and theoretically grounded research published in specialist coaching journals; participating in or conducting relevant research; attending and participating in workshops, conferences and other relevant scientific meetings related to coaching; pursuing further coaching qualifications; attending peer-coaching and/or peer-mentoring initiatives; and, of course, pursuing regular supervision (Iordanou et al., 2017).

Regular Supervision: As people actively engaged in what is termed a helping profession, aside from relevant knowledge and expertise, coaches need to be equipped with the resilience to support their clients in their developmental needs and endeavours. While at times this can be a straightforward process, at other times emotionally challenging ethical dilemmas can lead to considerable amounts of stress and even burnout. Consequently, the coaches have a moral responsibility to themselves, their clients and the coaching profession as a whole to protect their wellbeing and, by extension, that of their clients and the wider system in which they operate. Hence the significance of regular coaching supervision.

Within the sphere of coaching, supervision is defined as:

> the process by which a coach with the help of a supervisor can attend to understanding better both the client system and themselves as part of the client–coach system and, by so doing, transform their work and develop their craft.
>
> (Hawkins and Smith, 2006, p. 12)

According to relevant literature, the three most prominent functions of supervision are: Developmental, that is, to develop and enhance coaching skills and capabilities; resourcing, in order to safeguard the wellbeing of the coach and, by extension, the discipline of coaching; and qualitative, with an emphasis on maintaining the quality of coaching, as well as adhering to ethical standards (Hawkins and Smith, 2006). In other words, supervision provides a safe space for the coach to reflect on their practice and relationship with their clients and everyone directly or indirectly involved with the coaching process. Importantly, this understanding allows coaches to articulate and communicate these attributes more effectively to clients, sponsors and any relevant stakeholders (Hawkins, 2014, Iordanou et al., 2017).

While supervision is mandatory in neighbouring helping processions, such as counselling and psychotherapy (Bond, 2015), within the sphere of coaching it is still optional.

It is, to be sure, positive that the debate over the significance of compulsory supervision has been steadily picking up steam over the past decade (Hawkins and Smith 2006; Bachkirova, Jackson and Clutterbuck, 2011; Passmore 2011; de Haan, 2012; Hawkins, 2018). Still, regular supervision is an indispensable aspect of developing and maintaining an ethical coaching practice and, in consequence, this raises the question of why coaching supervision has not been made compulsory as yet. In the final analysis, considering the complexity of the coach's work, involving working through individual, interpersonal and organisational issues, the fundamentality of supervision lies in its instrumental role in supporting the wellbeing of the coach which, in consequence, benefits and safeguards the client (Pelham, 2016, p. 124).

Establishing a commitment to reflective and reflexive practices enables us to critically assess our reaction to ethical moments, words and actions. It enables us to gain a richer understanding of our personal and professional values. We begin with reflection. When we start to critically reflect back on our reactions in the coaching relationship – rather than simply consciously acknowledging such reaction – we reach a tipping point. This is where the process of reflexivity begins: Reflecting on our own reflection (Iordanou, et al., 2017, p. 97). This is not a linear process; the act of reflection and reflexive practice ebbs and flows.

Conclusion

A good coach is an ethical coach. This does not imply that there are bad coaches lacking in moral principles; it means that it takes constant and conscious effort to hold values and ethics at the forefront of the coaching practice continuously. The best coaches operate with their ethical antenna switched on and with an appreciation of the difficulties and challenges of working in complex, multi-stakeholder environments, where there are few perfect answers.

Ultimately, ethical coaching entails fostering a professional coaching culture that prioritises a shared understanding of ethical standards, regardless of prescribed recipes for best practice. Developing and maintaining a common ethical mind-set that is geared towards social and collective requirements is vital (Iordanou et al., 2017). In practice, this means capitalising on the ethical strategies we already have in place: Clear contracting; conscious reflection and reflexivity through critical enquiry; regular supervision; continuing professional development; and, importantly, open and shared communication between colleagues and relevant shareholders, even inviting the input of clients. These are just some of the strategies that enable us to develop and maintain a conscious (rather than idealistic) ethical coaching practice – creating a positive professional culture that is driven by integrity and commitment to embrace the complexities of contemporary life in an era of ongoing change (Iordanou et al., 2017). Being an effective coach is a journey of discovery; understanding our values and ethics holds the key to navigating this complex landscape.

References

Alred, G., Garvey, B. and Smith, R. (1998). 'Pas de deux – Learning in conversation'. *Career Development International*, 3(7), pp. 308–13.

Bachkirova, T., Cox, E. and Clutterbuck, D. (2018). 'Introduction'. In E. Cox, T. Bachkirova and D. Clutterbuck, eds., *The complete handbook of coaching*, 3rd ed. London: SAGE Publishing, pp. xxix–xlviii.

Bachkirova, T., Jackson, P., Gannon, J., Iordanou, I., and Myers, A. (2017). 'Re-conceptualising coach education from the perspectives of pragmatism and constructivism'. *Philosophy of Coaching: An International Journal*, 2(2), pp. 29–50.

Bachkirova, T., Jackson, P. and Clutterbuck, D. (2011). *Coaching and mentoring supervision: Theory and practice.* Maidenhead: Open University Press.

Beckett, C., Maynard, A. and Jordan, P. (2017). *Values and ethics in social work*, 3rd ed. London: Sage.

Bluckert, P. (2004). 'The state of play in corporate coaching: Current and future trends'. *Industrial and Commercial Training*, 32(2), pp. 53–56.

Bogdan, R.C. and Biklen, S.K. (2006). *Qualitative research for education: An introduction to theories and methods*, 5th ed. New York: Pearson Education.

Bolton, G. (2014). *Reflective practice: Writing and professional development*, 4th edn. London: SAGE Publishing.

Bond, T. (2015). *Standards and ethics for counselling in action*, 4th ed. London: Sage.

Brennan, D. and Wildflower, L. (2018). 'Ethics in coaching'. In E. Cox, T. Bachkirova, and D. Clutterbuck, eds., *The complete handbook of coaching*, 3rd ed. London: Sage, pp. 500–517.

Brooks, B. (2001). 'Ethics and standards in coaching'. In L. West and M. Milan, eds., *The reflecting glass: Professional coaching for leadership development*. Basingstoke: Palgrave, pp. 95–101.

Clutterbuck, D. (2013). 'Step forward the ethical mentor'. Retrieved from www.davidclutterbuckpartn ership.com/step-forward-the-ethical-mentor/ (accessed 25 March 2020).

Crisp, R., ed. (2013). *The Oxford handbook of the history of ethics*. Oxford: Oxford University Press.

Devine, M., Meyers, R. and Houssemand, C. (2013). 'How can coaching make a positive impact within educational settings?' *Procedia – Social and Behavioral Sciences*, 93, pp. 1382–1389.

De Haan, E. (2102). *Supervision in action: A relational approach to coaching and consulting supervision.* Maidenhead: Open University Press.

De Jong, A. (2010). 'Coaching ethics: Integrity in the moment of choice'. In J. Passmore, ed., *Excellence in coaching*. London: Association for Coaching, pp. 204–14.

Dunn, M. (2018). *Medical ethics: A very short introduction*, 2nd ed. Oxford: Oxford University Press.

Garvey, D. and Williamson, B. (2002). *Beyond knowledge management: Dialogue, creativity and the corporate curriculum*. Harlow: Pearson.

'Global code of ethics'. (2018). https://app.box.com/s/8s3tsveqieq6vr6n2itb0p9mpsxgcncd (accessed 8 March 2020).

Grant, A.M. and Cavanagh, M.J. (2004). 'Toward a profession of coaching: Sixty-five years of progress and challenges for the future'. *International Journal of Evidence Based Coaching and Mentoring*, 2(1), pp. 1–16.

Hawkins, P. (2018). 'Coaching supervision'. In E. Cox, T. Bachkirova, and D. Clutterbuck, eds., *The complete Handbook of coaching*, 3rd ed. London: Sage, pp. 434–450.

Hawkins, P. and Smith, N. (2006). *Coaching, mentoring and organizational consultancy: Supervision and development*. Maidenhead: Open University Press.

Hursthouse, R. (1999). *On virtue ethics*. Oxford: Oxford University Press.

Iordanou, I., Hawley, R., and Iordanou, C. (2017). *Values and ethics in coaching*. London: Sage.

Ives, I. and Cox, E. (2014). *Relationship coaching: The theory and practice of coaching with singles, couples, and parents*. London: Routledge.

Keller, J. (2007). *Attitude is everything: Change your attitude and you change your life*. Tampa, FL: Tampa International Publishing and Resource Books Inc.

Law, H., Ireland, S. and Hussain, Z. (2007). *The psychology of coaching, mentoring and learning*. Chichester: John Wiley & Sons.

Passmore, J. (2009). 'Coaching ethics: Making ethical decisions – novices and experts'. *Coaching Psychologist* 5(1), pp. 6–10.

Passmore, J., ed. (2011). *Supervision in coaching: Supervision, ethics and continuous professional development.* London: Kogan Page.

Passmore, J., and Turner, E. (2018). 'Reflections on integrity – the *APPEAR* model'. *Coaching at Work*, 13(2), pp. 42–46.

Pelham, G. (2016). *The coaching relationship in practice*. London: Sage.

Rogers, C. (1980). *A way of being*. Boston, MA: Houghton Mifflin.

Thomson, B. (2009). *Don't just do something, sit there: An introduction to non-directive coaching*. Oxford: Chandos.

Van Nieuwerburgh, C. (2014). *An introduction to coaching skills: A practical guide*. London: SAGE Publishing.

32 Contracting in coaching

Karen Foy

Introduction

As we each hear the word "contracting" we will each have our own unique response. My own response has been varied throughout my coaching career, from being turned off by the idea of detailed legal documents to an absolute commitment to building an alliance of trust for transformational coaching work and lots of developmental stages in between. In this chapter, I will explore practical approaches to contracting with individuals or multi-stakeholders and help you turn a legalistic concept into a safe vessel for a voyage of discovery with your clients.

My contract, or promise, to you is to share my experience and thinking around contracting as a coach still on this journey and I ask you to open yourself enough to come along for the ride rather than skipping to the more obviously exciting chapters.

From contract to designed alliance

Stephen Covey urges us to "begin with the end in mind" (1989) and that is exactly what we are aiming to do in contracting with our coaching clients. David Dotlich and Peter Cairo (1999) mirrors this principle in their Action Coaching Model with three steps to reach agreement. Coaches should, they suggest: Determine what needs to happen and in what context, establish trust and a set of mutual expectations and *contract for results*. In these three simple steps is hidden the very heart of our commitments with our clients. A contract suggests the first and last of these steps and the designed alliance (Kimsey-House et al., 2018) invokes the power of the relationship adding the third element into the contract. So how do we maintain the formality of a contract with the human elements of building trust and why is that important?

What I have discovered in my coaching experience is that the more I concentrate on developing a robust, compassionate and safe relationship with my clients the more we can explore their life and work with curiosity, clarity and challenge. The clearer we are at the beginning of the relationship and each individual session, about what the work is that we need to do and how we will do that together, the more quickly and deeply we get to the heart of the matter, as Alison Hardingham suggests "well begun is half done" (Hardingham et al., 2004, p. 98). Mentoring and supervising hundreds of coaches I have observed that time spent exploring and building a shared approach to the coaching relationship saves time and reduces the angst created when a coach realises they have hit an ethical dilemma they failed to consider at the outset.

Co-active Coaching (Kimsey-House et al., 2018) introduces the idea of the "designed alliance", where a contract is developed with the client and their agenda at the centre and where the power resides in the relationship, not resting with the coach. Approaching contracting in this way means coaching is beginning and ending in partnership where clients can explore their work and life in a safe alliance built around the way they think, learn and work. So, we may start from the position of agreeing with our clients on our "terms of engagement", the more usual contractual agreements and then begin to build our designed alliance for our way of working together. Let's walk through these different elements systematically: First thinking about the terms of engagement, or contract, for the relationship, moving on to working through building an alliance for the relationship, bringing in ideas about multi-stakeholders in the arrangement and then considering contracting for each session. Throughout I will offer some ideas for a practical approach.

Terms of engagement, contracting, for the relationship

This is what we more typically think of when we consider contracting in coaching. Agreeing the terms of engagement can be in the form of a written contract or a more verbal agreement and, as Alain Cardon (2008) states, this is the most explicit agreement with legal overtones. Essentially, this is an explicit agreement between coach and client about what each can expect from the other (Block, 2000) but, as John Bennet (2008) suggests, contracting is far more than a formality.

The purpose of contracting in coaching at this stage is to agree together on the basis for your work together. The intention is to ensure everyone connected to the process knows what is expected of them, as these are the terms that will form the basis of the commission.

Contracting for the relationship with individuals

Coaching clients come to coaches in all sorts of ways, on personal recommendations, via websites through marketing campaigns or various other routes. In whatever way they present to a particular coach, the client and coach will want to establish some basis for working together. It has been suggested that possibly up to 30 per cent of the success of the coaching (Lambert, 1992; McKenna and Davis, 2009) will rely on the relationship. Given the importance of these relational factors, it is in the interests of both coach and client to be sure there is a good fit. The most usual approach to the first stage of contracting is to have a conversation; some coaches refer to this as a "chemistry meeting". Katherine Tulpa (2012, p. 38) suggests that taking a coaching approach to that discussion helps both parties to gain greater understanding of each other and the relationship required to meet the goals of the client.

In some ways, the easiest part of contracting as a coach is the contracting for the logistical elements, such as how much, when, where, for how long, payment terms and cancellation policies, etc. As John Fielder and Larry Starr (2008) suggest, focusing on the "what" of coaching is insufficient because coaching is more than "the sum of its parts" (Fielder and Starr, 2008, p. 25) and they argue it is naïve for coaches to simply contract for the exchange of payment for services. They suggest the contract should also acknowledge the "complex systemic and qualitative aspects of coaching" (p. 25). So, of course we will want to discuss the logistics of the coaching relationship, but we also need to make sure we have explored lots of "what ifs", which are more related to the "how" it will be done.

As coaches, many of us are drawn to the profession because we recognise the potential to support people to transform their lives and businesses, but we also need to recognise coaching also has the potential to cause harm. William Rothwell and Roland Sullivan (2005) identify contracting as a "complex, human-interactive process requiring sensitivity, skill and flexibility". When contracting for the coaching relationship, we need to be able to balance the need for clarity around protecting the client and ourselves as coaches with the need for building a trusting, intimate relationship and safe space for shared discovery.

In my experience, I have found the best way to do this is by co-creating a working relationship based on deciding together with my clients how we will manage "what if" situations. For example, what will we do if we find the coaching is no longer working for one of us? What will we do if we uncover something in our work together that raises concern? We can't cover every possible eventuality, but there are a few key areas we can use as a foundation for this safe space.

Contracting as a designed alliance

> This is your relationship: own it, put a human face on it, bring your whole self to it, and make it a shining example of your coaching presence.
>
> (Blakey and Day, 2012, p. 48)

John Blakey and Ian Day (2012) argue that, without strong contracts, coaches have no "personal legitimacy"; they suggest there is no basis to build upon and no boundary to maintain (p. 48). They refer to the coaching contract as a "covenant" [or "sacred promise"]. This term begins to draw our thoughts away from the legalistic and into the more intimate relationship and the co-creation of a sanctuary for honesty, exploration and discovery that provides a safe space to confront sometimes difficult truths.

In a meaningful coaching session, we are encouraging our clients to be at their learning edge and adopt a growth mindset (Dweck, 2007). The conditions to allow this exploration and learning need to be created in partnership; this is where we build the legitimacy and identify the boundaries we will maintain. If we step back as coaches and consider what it takes for us to share some of the less attractive parts of ourselves, we get a glimpse into the needs of our clients. Imagine working with a leader in an organisation, whose very survival in their role is about being decisive, confident and resilient, who commits to coaching to allow them to survive and thrive in work and life. Very often, the coaching conversations are the only opportunity for that person to discuss their concerns or show the slightest vulnerability. What would you imagine they need from you as a coach? What would you need as a coachee?

If we agree with Sir John Whitmore that "building awareness and responsibility is the essence of good coaching" (Whitmore, 2015, p. 33) we have to be brave enough to be alongside our clients whilst they build their awareness through facing the times when they are potentially not so decisive, when their confidence is less robust or when their resilience wobbles. In our contracting, we want to discuss how we can best serve our clients (our legitimacy) to stay with sometimes uncomfortable feelings in the service of self-discovery and understand where our boundaries lie. Our purpose in supporting our clients to re-connect with all parts of themselves is to tap into their greatness, which John Blakey and Ian Day (2012) argue cannot be liberated if we keep the conversation in a cocoon. Perhaps you can recall a time when you felt less than your best, empathise with the vulnerable feelings and sometimes shame in sharing those experiences with another. When we are contracting, we need to be working on an alliance, which means a relationship free from the fear of judgement, where our explorations are held in trust and we are accepted as a perfectly flawed human being by another perfectly flawed human being. In a relationship without power imbalances, clients can be free to speak their shame rather than allowing it to become an inhibitor to learning.

How do we bring this rather esoteric approach into the practical realm of contracting for a coaching partnership with our clients?

A practical approach with individuals

The International Coaching Federation's core competencies suggest one way for coaches to contract. The guidelines follow the spirit of a designed alliance, reflected in the heading *Co-creating the relationship*, and provide behavioural indicators for a coach to establish and maintain agreements (ICF, 2019). The competency covers the relationship from beginning to end of both the relationship and each session. The 11-point definition can seem like overload and formulaically following it by going through it point by point is probably not the best approach to winning business.

Many of the more logistical points, such as cost, cancellation policy and organisational issues, can be consigned to a written agreement for ease. To co-create a relationship the verbal emphasis can be focused on building or designing the alliance that means the client and coach can work together in a trusting space. Bennet (2008) suggests that the less formal approach to contracting could lead to higher degrees of trust and therefore a more effective relationship. There is no empirical evidence to support this assumption, but if we think about the commitments we make in meaningful relationships in our lives, I wonder just how many are held strong because we have signed a document? Any written contract needs to be supported by a conversation to build the alliance.

To contract for the relationship, it is useful to find a way to have a conversation before the coaching starts. This can be a telephone call or a face-to-face meeting. The prospective client will want to know you are the right coach. I have found the most beneficial way for me to conduct these meetings is from the basis that I am not looking to win business but to establish who would be the right coach for what the person seeks. This may seem counter-intuitive when, as new coaches, we are all wanting to accept whatever business comes our way, but if we trust the research that 30 per cent of the success of the coaching is dependent on the relationship, why would we risk our reputations as coaches?

We may not have the appropriate style, skills or personality that meets the need of the client, but we may know other coaches who do. Before this truth became real for me, I would work with anyone who asked me, only to find I was working hard, struggling to connect and not really enjoying working with some clients. Once I committed to having a conversation to really understand the client and be honest with them about my approach, I have increased my client list with great people I love working with.

There are so many things you will want to cover in a contracting conversation before you start the coaching journey together, and the key here is to weave this into a conversation rather than run through a checklist. If we approach the conversation, as Katherine Tulpa suggests, using our key coaching skills of listening and curiously asking questions, we begin to build our alliance. We can check out how someone likes to work, what they need from us and we can gently discuss the nuances between different interventions by discussion rather than rules and weave in the boundaries around confidentiality and exceptions to it.

For example, one person I was having this conversation with said they wanted to learn leadership strategies from our coaching. It would be easy to jump in and begin a lecture on the difference between teaching or mentoring and coaching; but think about what that would do for our relationship-building. What I did was get curious to find out what led them to think they needed that, which uncovered all the great skills and experience they had in leadership and it also uncovered the real issue at the heart of the reason for the coaching, which was related to having lost their motivation for leadership because it took them away from the real job they loved.

The key elements we need to cover in this conversation are: The purpose of the coaching, what brought the person to coaching and what they hoped to achieve, what they expect from a coach and what can be expected from them. We might want to use this time to gain an understanding of how the person best thinks and learns and we can share our way of coaching. We need to discuss confidentiality and exceptions that may require you to take action. This can feel a difficult subject to raise when we are really saying if there is a concern, but none of us know what might be uncovered in a coaching conversation and we need to have discussed what we will do in the event of something being shared that could suggest harm to others or potential illegality. We are not setting ourselves up as judge and jury, but we need to be honest upfront that we may need to take advice. These are conversations best had whilst they are still an academic possibility, not an in-the-moment fact.

It is worth noting that contracting is not a one-off event but something that is revisited regularly as the relationship grows; we also need to invest in good contracting at the start of each session, which we will explore later and note that there are many similarities.

Below is a checklist for you to consider all of the elements in preparation for your first conversation. Using the acronym PROMISES it offers a reminder for the key elements of your relationship contracting. See Table 32.1.

Multi-stakeholder considerations

For many of us as executive coaches there is an added dimension to our contracting: We may be commissioned to coach someone by a sponsor, sometimes a line manager or, quite often, a HR professional in an organisation. This brings at least three people into the contracting arena, maybe more. Internal coaches are also impacted by this extra dimension when asked to coach colleagues in the business. The same areas need to be addressed as for the individual: Purpose, relationship, outcome, boundaries of coaching and logistics and then some specific agreements need to be made to ensure clarity and safety.

A practical approach for multi-stakeholder contracting

The initial pre-coaching meeting is even more important in a multi-stakeholder coaching engagement and I would go so far as to suggest that, without this discussion, it would be advisable not to go ahead with the coaching. One area to pay particular attention to when discussing the coaching with the potential coaching client and the sponsor (usually the person paying for the coaching) is how confidentiality will be managed. I have found it is essential to remind sponsors that, although they are paying for and requesting the coaching, my focus will be the needs of the individual client and I am not prepared to share information without the knowledge and agreement of the coaching client (except in cases of serious criminality or where there is a serious risk of harm). If I undertake

Table 32.1 Promises in the Coaching Relationship

Purpose	What brought the person to coaching? What is the work that needs to be done? Often people present with a long-standing issue or concern, but something will have triggered them to take action and seek coaching now. How do they feel coaching will help them?
Relationship	How will you build a partnership for the work to be done? Has the person had coaching before? If so, what worked well and what worked not so well; if not, what do they need to know about you and you about them to build a trusting and effective partnership?
Outcome	What needs to be different at the end of the coaching relationship; how will success be defined? This needs to be highly specific and measurable.
Margins	What are the margins or boundaries you are working within? What is up for discussion and what is not? Particularly if this work is being sponsored and paid for by a third party. Is there clarity about the boundaries between coaching and other interventions?
In case	This is your opportunity to explore how you will deal, in partnership, with emerging issues or dilemmas. A discussion more easily held in the abstract in advance rather than an embarrassed bargaining discussion when you hit a roadblock. This element of the conversation might start with a "what will we do if …"
Strategy	What strategy will you agree for the relationship. This should cover logistics such as: When, where and how often you will get together and for how long, cost, cancellations, review process and any reporting requirements, payment terms and cancellation policies.
Expectations	In order to avoid entering unknowingly into obligations and commitments, we need to have a discussion where we can surface some of our own and our client's expectations for the coaching relationship.
Safety	How can we create a safe working relationship where the client feels supported by their coach and thinking partner to express themselves fully? Confidentiality will be key but where are the parameters? What does the person need to build trust and intimacy? Have you considered the duty of care to your client and others? In short, how do you intend to honour their information and well-being?

any psychometric assessments or 360-degree feedback questionnaires, for example, the information belongs to the individual client (sometimes called the coachee) and it is up to them to share it. Of course, different sponsors and individual clients may request different arrangements, and this is up to the coach to agree with both parties before embarking on the coaching journey.

It is also important to get an understanding of what can and what cannot be the topics of coaching conversations; for example, what happens if the individual client wants to discuss a plan for leaving the organisation that is paying for the coaching? Some organisations may be fine with this, others may not, but we need to be sure we work ethically by being clear on the parameters.

Again, your coaching skills will be key in this conversation to gain clarity on any vague aspirations and goals the sponsor has for the coaching. As coaches we can be drawn into performance managing by proxy for managers evading their responsibility. In coaching, we should never be stepping into this performance management role and instead remain focused on coaching.

Surfacing hidden agendas and unexpressed expectations can ensure you keep out of the minefield of managing by proxy. Insisting on a pre-coaching conversation with the

Figure 32.1 Three stage multi-stakeholder process

sponsor or manager brings all of the expectations into the open, and it also helps you discourage "off the record" discussions where managers want to discuss your coaching client without their knowledge. Contracting with all stakeholders and agreeing a way forward will keep you working ethically and with integrity. This is another of those points where you will be grateful you took the time to explore the "what ifs" before they happen. One coach I know always includes in their "what ifs" a question to be sure what will happen if because of our coaching your employee decides to leave?

Essentially, whether you are contracting for a one-to-one relationship or there are three or more people in the relationship, you need to think about how you can set the foundations for a safe, productive and rewarding journey of discovery in partnership; how you might review progress at the mid-point in the coaching journey (maybe after session three or four), which allows you to check in with the sponsor and invite them to provide feedback on how they perceive the coaching is progressing; finally, a closing review meeting, offering the opportunity for both parties to provide their closing feedback to the coach and each other. See Figure 32.1.

Contracting for the session

Contracting is a continual process, even in the relational aspects of the contract there may be adjustments over time. An important aspect of the continuum is contracting at the beginning of each session. Coaching sessions can stand or fall on the attention given to the "bookends" or beginning and ending of each session. In the same way as we partner for a coaching relationship, we need to partner for the success of each session.

It is the same basis we are working from: What is the work we need to do together and how will we do it? Often when a coaching session doesn't seem to go as well as we would like we can trace the issue back to a less well-defined beginning. The noticeable differentiator between a novice coach and a more experienced practitioner is the length of time they spend getting a clear objective for the coaching, clarifying success for the session and deciding on how the partnership will work.

Coaches face a number of challenges at the inset of a coaching session: Sometimes it is that it's difficult to get a clear start for the session, when there has been some small talk in the greeting that then blends into the subject area for the client, and the coach struggles to get back to a clear goal setting. There is the challenge of a client bringing a number of different topics for discussion, which may or may not be related, or they bring a topic for discussion that changes part way through the session, or is just such a wide or deep issue that there would never be the time available to cover it in one session.

The beginning of a coaching session can be seen as a place where, like Ariadne, we are gathering up the thread that will allow the individual client to explore the labyrinth of their topic. Once we have the guiding thread, we can explore the topic of discussion and always find our way back to the thread that is leading us to the goal. As we get to the end of the session we can check in: Did we get where we needed to get to? It takes time and exploration at the beginning to be sure we have the right thread. This element of the conversation is a crucial part of coaching, not a process to get through in order to get to the real business of coaching. The key areas we need to get clear on are: What does the person want to discuss in the session; what would make the time spent looking at the issue worthwhile; what makes the subject important at this time; how will coach and coachee work in partnership to achieve the goal, whilst working within the boundaries and confidentiality discussed in the relationship contract.

A practical approach for session contracting

Claire Pedrick (2020) provides a process for coaches to use at the beginning of every coaching session that sets a clear foundation for the work to be done and I offer it here, with permission and a slight adaptation to support the first of the bookends of coaching. It is offered with some ideas about possible questions, but this is not a script. Used as a script it will fail to build the intimate relationship you seek to deepen the exploration and discovery in the conversation; used as a prompt it will allow that deep dive.

As some many know, the stoker is the person on the back of a tandem, offering extra peddle power to get started or climb hills. The term is also used to describe someone who lights and *builds* a fire by adding wood or coal. It's this later definition we use, as we will use a parallel analogy as we draw the relationship to a close. See Table 32.2.

You will notice confidentiality and ethics are not explicit in this model and, of course, you will have explored it in depth at your pre-coaching discussion, but it is worth noting that we need to re-visit our commitment to privacy, with its exceptions at the start of every session. These exceptions are likely to include where there is serious criminality (for example, if the reporting of our "crime" to the police would lead to a visit by a police officer within the following 48 hours and a possible arrest of the individual). Secondly, where there is a serious risk of harm to the client or another individual. The most obvious example is maybe where the client's emotional state means there is a serious risk of suicide or self-harm. In such cases the coach may need to act (hopefully jointly with the client), contacting the appropriate services to ensure the client is safely in the care of others.

Table 32.2 STOKERS – Starting the session

Subject	"What would you like to focus on?"
	"What is the work you would like to consider today?"
Timing	"Given we have 30 minutes today, what would be a good use of that time?"
	"In the time we have, what part of that would you like to focus on"
Outcome	"What would you like to have at the end of that time?" "What would make our time together successful?"
Knowledge	"How would you know you have that outcome?"
	"What would be different at the end of this session?
Essence	"What makes this important?"
Role	"How can we best work together on this?"
	"What would you like from me as your coach?"
Start	"Where would you like to start?"

Once that element is added I find this really useful in my coaching and a great introduction to the work beyond the welcoming chat, a coach can signal a move to the coaching by asking, "so what would you like to focus on today?". Given that often people have wide-ranging topics or maybe multiple topics, the time element allows the client to consider the most relevant aspects, or when there are two or three issues a coach can prompt a focus by asking how the topics link together, a great way for clients to get thinking from the onset.

In the coaching partnership we need a clear objective we are working towards and the client needs to know exactly what success would look like. Checking on outcome and how they will know they have it brings clarity to the conversation. Even if your client says they want to explore a subject and they don't really want action plans at the end you can still help them clarify what they want to know by the end of the session.

A key element in this process, and one that has the power to transform the coaching from transactional to transformative, is checking in on the importance or meaning for the client in this topic; why this subject and why now? This can be viewed as the goal behind the goal. To take a facetious example, if someone's goal was to be a millionaire, we could accept that at face value and work with them on how they might achieve that. But, if we check in on the goal beneath that, there may be much more to discover, so we can ask questions like "and what would being a millionaire give you?", the answer to which could open up the real goal and motivator.

The role element in this process is really an opportunity to uncover those psychological contracts (Carroll, 2005) we discussed earlier. What is the individual client expecting from you, what are you expecting from them? How will you work together to achieve the desired outcome? In early sessions, you might use this opportunity to talk about your particular approach or perhaps to remind your client that coaching is not like regular conversations and that there may be silences and that is OK, they can use the time as they want to. It is also your opportunity to gain permission; for example, to call out incongruence, share observations, challenge unhelpful filters, mindsets or beliefs and bring known history and behaviour patterns into the session when it is in service of the client moving forward.

The final section, the *start*, may seem simple, but this really demonstrates to your client that they are in charge, they are leading the content of this conversation. You are starting to gather the thread of this conversation through this in-depth exploration and you are holding that thread whilst they explore the labyrinth and they choose which tunnels. Using this process means you have a clear picture of where you need to get to and how you will do that together, and you can always check in with your explorer if the conversation seems to go too far from the guiding thread.

Closing an individual session in partnership

We began this chapter thinking about Stephen Covey and "starting with the end in mind" and I would like to conclude with a thought to the other bookend, the ending. Whilst we could explore a full chapter on the ending of a coaching conversation it is beyond the scope of this one, but I would like to offer a glimpse at how you can conclude your contracting by checking in and partnering to close the session.

I mentioned above that we could think about STOKERS as a fire stoker on a steam train or a boiler room on a ship. If we think about it in that sense, we can link our

Table 32.3 DOUSE – Ending the session

Double check the contract/goal against the proposed actions	"Where are we in relation to our contract/the goal for the session?" "What will you do now?"
Obstacles	"What might get in the way?" "How will you be accountable to yourself?"
Uncovered	"What have you uncovered/learnt about yourself that will support your continued progress?"
Support	"What support do you need?" "How can you get that?"
Ending	"How would you like to close the session?" (Acknowledge the work done during the session.)

beginning to our ending by *dousing* that fire. As coaches we need to put as much energy into ending well as we did beginning.

It's not unusual for novice coaches to notice they are running out of time and start to panic. This can be avoided by planning the session structure from the start, keeping a clock in sight through the session and managing the session in a series of chunks, each with its allotted time.

DOUSE offers a parallel process to STOKERS, helping the coach as they move into closing the session, helping them draw the session to an end in partnership with their client. See Table 32.3.

Following this process means you are partnering at the end of the session, so your clients are leaving the session with a well-formed outcome, you are handing the thread back to them for them to continue their self-discovery. As we know, it's estimated that maybe up to 40 per cent of the success of coaching is down to factors outside of the coaching conversation (Assay and Lambert, 1999; McKenna and Davis, 2009). This includes not only the personality and readiness of the client, their context and situation, but also the support they receive from the boss, family and friends. As coaches we want to help clients leverage their network as a mechanism for support, resources and accountability.

Conclusions

The aim of this chapter was to inspire you to consider contracting in your coaching from a perspective of building a safe and productive space for your clients and yourself to learn and grow together. Hopefully it has given you some practical approaches to help you do that. In conclusion, I want to share with you a mnemonic, the ABC of coaching: **A**lways **B**e **C**ontracting. I hope what is implicit here is that contracting is not a one-off event, either for the relationship or the session; we are always checking in and adjusting where necessary.

Another takeaway I hope for your coaching is that time spent in contracting is not something to get through to get to the real work, contracting is the real work and it requires time and commitment. Think of it as a short internal flight from one region to another. The whole flight may take 1 hour but 10 or 15 minutes are spent on the climb to flying altitude and the same coming in to land. If you follow a similar pattern, you will have the bookends for a great journey of discovery.

References

Bennet, J.L. (2008). 'Contracting for success'. *The International Journal of Coaching Organisations*, 6(8), pp. 7-14.

Blakey, J. and Day, I. (2012). *Challenging coaching: going beyond traditional coaching to face the FACTS.* p. 48, London: Nicholas Brealey Publishing.

Block, P. (2000). *Flawless consulting: a guide to getting your expertise used*, 2nd edition. San Francisco: Pfeiffer.

Cardon, A. (2008). 'Coaching contracts and agreements, *how contracts and agreements keep coaching clients in the driver's seat*'. http://metasysteme-coaching.fr/english/-coaching-contracts-et-agreements/ (accessed 15/3/20).

Carroll M. (2005). 'Psychological contracts with and within organisations'. In Tribe, R. and Morrissey, J., eds., *Handbook of professional and ethical practice, for psychologists, counsellors and psychotherapists*. UK: Brunner-Routledge, 34.

Covey, S. (1989). *The seven habits of highly effective people*, 15th edition. London: Simon & Schuster.

Dotlich, D.L. and Cairo, P.C. (1999). *Action coaching: how to leverage individual performance for company success.* San Francisco: Jossey-Bass.

Dweck, C. (2007). *Mindset, changing the way you think to fulfil your potential.* York: Random House Publishing.

Fielder, J.H. and Starr, L.M. (2008). 'What's the big deal about coaching contracts'. *The International Journal of Coaching in Organisations*, 6(4), pp. 15-27.

Hardingham, A., Brearley, M., Moorhouse, A. and Venter, B. (2004). *The coaches coach, personal development for personal developers.* London: CIPD.

Kimsey House, H., Kimsey House, K., Sandahl, P. and Whitworth, L. (2018). *Co-active coaching: the proven framework for transformative conversations at work and in life* - 4th edition. London: Aladdin.

Lambert, M. (1992). 'Implications of outcome research for psychotherapy integration'. In Norcross, J.C. and Goldstein, M.R., eds., *Handbook of psychotherapy integration.* New York: Basic Books, pp. 94–129.

McKenna, D. and Davis, S. (2009). 'Hidden in plain sight'. *Industrial & Organisational Psychology*, 2(3), pp. 244–260.

Pedrick, C. (2020). *Simplifying coaching.* Maidenhead: McGraw-Hill-Open University Press.

Rothwell, W. and Sullivan, R.L., eds. (2005). *Practicing organization development: a guide for consultants.* New Jersey: John Wiley & Sons.

Tulpa, K. (2012). 'Coaching within organisations'. In Passmore, J., ed., *Excellence in coaching the industry guide.* London: Kogan Page, pp. 19-40.

Whitmore, J. (2015). *Coaching for performance: GROWing human potential and purpose*, 4th edition. London: Nicholas Brealey.

33 Feedback and evaluation in coaching

Jonathan Passmore and David Tee

Introduction

Briner (2012) wrote a provocatively titled article (*'Does coaching work and does anyone really care?'*), which challenged practitioners to incorporate evidence-gathering into their coaching practice. Whilst the evidence for the effectiveness of coaching has advanced in subsequent years (see Bozer & Jones, 2018), it is still important for us as individual coaches to evaluate the effect our work with clients has produced. It may be that the evaluation is being called for by a third party, such as organisations that hire external executive coaches. Coaching researchers, too, are calling for greater evaluation of the benefits that coaching produces (see Athanasopoulou & Dopson, 2018; Grover & Furnham, 2016). In this chapter, we will provide an insight into different forms of evaluation and feedback, covering a range of useful theories that can inform coaching evaluation, before offering some practical steps on evaluation.

What is feedback?

Although there may be some approaches to coaching where the coach sees it as permissible to give feedback to their client, other approaches argue the coach should avoid it (Lancer, Clutterbuck & Megginson, 2016). However, many of the models of evaluation in this chapter do require the coach to be able to elicit and work with feedback, be it from the client or other stakeholders. It is in this sense that we shall be exploring the role of feedback here.

McDowall and Kurz (2008) define feedback as a process where a 'sender' relays a 'message' – which is some information – to a recipient. As such, most forms of communication, be they oral, written or other, can be treated as feedback. This chapter features models and techniques that often ringfence certain forms of data, at certain times from certain sources, as feedback. However, all information encountered by the coach when coaching, from a fleeting facial expression made by a client during a session through to a formal written audit of performance, has the potential to be treated as useful feedback.

What is evaluation?

Evaluation is typically defined in dictionaries as judging the worth, value or quality of something. At this simplistic level, for us it would mean answering the question 'How good was this coaching?'. If you pause for a moment to consider any coaching with which you have been involved, you will immediately realise that this question raises many, many more. What does 'good' mean? Good for whom? How will we know? At what time during or after the coaching can we reach a sensible determination of its 'goodness'? and so on.

The research on coaching typically seeks to generate evidence, rather than to evaluate. Of course, these two practices are connected, but 'evidence' to a researcher might be limited only to what we know about coaching when conducted under strict, controlled conditions, such as in a double-blind, randomised controlled trial. It would be highly unusual for us to coach in such artificial circumstances, so we need to look for other means of generating evidence (Grant & Stober, 2006).

Matthewman (2009) suggests a range of approaches that are more suited to the practicalities of evaluating coaching in the real world:

- **Cost**: What were the inputs required to produce the achieved output? These may include your fees, the room hire or the opportunity costs associated with your client's time in coaching;
- **Effectiveness**: To what extent did the client achieve their intended outcome? Has individual or organisational performance changed in a desired manner?
- **Cost-effectiveness**: Could the same outputs have been achieved more effectively using a different intervention? Perhaps the client could have read a book rather than paid an executive coach for eight sessions;
- **Cost–benefit analysis**: Assigning financial values – often problematic – to all the inputs and outputs to determine whether there was a net financial benefit;
- **Value**: To what extent do the outcomes of your coaching contribute to the client's organisational objectives?

Any of these approaches, in isolation or combination, will generate useful information for us, but the last point is critical. Not every organisation that makes use of coaching does so to generate quantifiable performance changes. For example, an organisation may have a strategy of being seen to invest in and develop its staff. For them, the mere act of coaching taking place may mean something they value has already occurred, regardless of the outputs of that coaching. Therefore, as coaches, we do need to think more broadly than just bottom-line impact when evaluating our work.

It is also worth distinguishing between iterative (repeated, ongoing) evaluation and summative (outcome) evaluation. Adopting both strategies allows us to identify issues, opportunities and change possibilities in how we are working with a client *as* the relationship unfolds, rather than solely drawing conclusions once our work is complete.

Theories of feedback in personal development

Theories concerning the importance of feedback are often linked to work by researchers such as Locke and Latham whose work focused on goal setting (1991). You may have the goal of providing consistently world-class coaching, but the goal itself is not enough. Unless you are receiving feedback – ideally specific, real-time, objective feedback – it will be hard for you to evaluate the extent to which your goal is being realised. It is therefore helpful to consider how you will purposefully incorporate feedback into your coaching evaluation strategy.

Feedback Intervention theory (FIT)

Kluger and DeNisi (1996) integrated goal-setting theory, control theory and other models into FIT in an attempt to capture the effect feedback has on performance. It encourages you to take into account cognitive interference from factors such as high anxiety or low self-efficacy, as these may enhance or derail the effectiveness of your coaching in any given single instance.

FIT also encourages you to set clear objectives for what you intend your coaching to generate. Over and above any organisational- or client-level goals, you will also have desired outcomes: by articulating these, you can then purposefully plan for how you can realistically achieve them. In addition, FIT makes you aware of what it calls 'meta task processes' that may explain the feedback you are receiving. For example, you may set yourself very high, demanding standards of perfection in much of what you do. Feedback from one client after a session may indicate that your coaching was not 100% perfect and you may consequently feel despondent. However, through the meta task process of conducting a general comparison with peers (e.g. other coaches), this may result in a more realistic conclusion that no coach is permanently perfect and that your performance goal may need to be adjusted.

Feedback orientation theory

How receptive are you to purposefully seeking out, mindfully considering and then making constructive use of feedback? London and Smither (2002) conceptualise feedback orientation as a range of factors that combine together to determine your typical receptivity to feedback.

There may be cultural or organisational norms around the importance of feedback that have influenced you, in addition to a range of individual-level factors, such as your belief in the value of the feedback or whether you are accountable to use that feedback.

By consciously considering your own feedback orientation, you can determine how likely you are to constructively respond to the information generated as you evaluate the effectiveness of your coaching, and develop a plan on how you are going to respond.

360-degree feedback

Whilst traditional workplace feedback may have been obtained from a single source – typically one's line manager – 360-degree feedback uses multiple raters (Fletcher, 2015). Feedback from any single individual may be shaped by personal bias and their limited experience (i.e. maybe only one coaching session), but by adding together feedback from multiple sources this should, in theory, introduce greater objectivity into the evaluation.

For coaches whose feedback orientation needs them to believe in the accuracy and merit of the data, bringing in a 360-degree feedback system should increase their buy-in to attending to and making changes as a result of evaluations. As we shall detail in the SOAP-M model (below), getting the judgements of multiple sources pre- and post-intervention makes it increasingly likely that we can more accurately assess the impact of coaching in an individual.

Theories of evaluation in personal development

Kirkpatrick's Four Levels of Evaluation

Arguably the most widely used of the evaluation models, Kirkpatrick originally published his four steps in the 1950s (Kirkpatrick, 1959). Intended for workplace training evaluation, each of the four levels becomes increasingly complicated to execute, but the information revealed is considered to be of greater value. Nonetheless, Kirkpatrick stated that all four levels were of importance and that it would be a mistake to skip Levels 1 and 2 to just focus on the latter steps (Reio, Rocco, Smith & Chang, 2017).

Level 1: Reaction

How does your client react to your coaching? You may seek information about the content of the session, your style as a coach or even the location in which your coaching took place. Reaction is important, as it may determine how likely your client is to engage with future coaching or to recommend coaching to others in their work, team or organisation.

Level 2: Learning

In a training context, the learning outcomes may be predetermined, so this would be an opportunity to test whether the trainee has acquired the desired knowledge or skills. Coaching is less prescribed, with some learning possibly being unpredicted, emergent and serendipitous. Nonetheless, we may iteratively (session-by-session) and summatively seek to evaluate what learning or unlearning the client has experienced whilst working with us.

Level 3: Behaviour

This level concerns transfer of learning from the safe, liminal coaching space to the client's place of work. Any manner of 'Eureka!' moments of insight may have occurred during your client's coaching sessions, but this is an opportunity to evaluate how these have manifested themselves in the client's day-to-day conduct in their working role.

Level 4: Results

Similar to Matthewman's 'value' and 'cost–benefit analysis' strategies, Kirkpatrick's fourth level concerns the business results generated by the coaching, ideally with a financial value attached. This should be anticipated when first meeting and contracting with your client: How is what they wish to achieve through coaching aligned to outcomes of genuine value to their organisation?

Reio et al. (2017) point to criticisms raised concerning the Kirkpatrick model. One key criticism is the assumption that the four levels are causally linked. If so, this would mean that, for example, a coaching client would need to positively react (Level 1) to your coaching in order for learning (Level 2) to take place. However, coaching should arguably be a safe but constructively challenging experience: Many clients might not react favourably to having their assumptions and opinions challenged, but it may generate a significant amount of learning for them.

Phillips's ROI Model of Evaluation

Building on the Kirkpatrick model, Phillips and Phillips (2007) acknowledge that value for organisations may take many forms but should ultimately be converted into financial data. Whilst their evaluation framework is intended to identify the return on investment (ROI) of a project or intervention, it is relatively easy to convert this process to capture return on expectations (ROE) instead, where financial benefit genuinely is not the core consideration.

One advantage of this ROI evaluation model is that it provides the coach with a process to follow from initiating the relationship through to post-intervention. Whether it is in conversation with the individual client or an organisational stakeholder, the coach would clarify at the very start what are the payoff (or expectation) benefits for the organisation, align those to the organisation's needs, then align these to the client's job performance needs and learning needs. Finally, the coach and client can negotiate around the client's preferences for how they best learn or work with a coach.

These map, in reverse order, to the four Kirkpatrick evaluation levels. Therefore, as the coaching progresses, the coach can track 'reaction' against the client's stated preferences, 'learning' against the client's stated learning needs and so on, moving back up the Kirkpatrick levels and, ultimately, making a calculation against the ROI metric identified at the very start of the process.

There are certain assumptions and flaws in this approach. Firstly, it assumes that the client and the organisational stakeholder have thought about and can clearly articulate each of these needs and, in addition, that the needs of the client are in direct alignment with the needs of their host organisation. The example of a key senior leader who is contemplating early retirement or a career move would challenge this latter point.

Furthermore, as with any intervention in a real-world setting, it is hard to confidently attribute every gain realised by a client whilst they worked with a coach to the effect of that coaching alone. At best, we can point to a correlation, but the client would also have been gaining more experience and role maturity all the time the coaching was taking place. In addition, the coach may have only had a direct relationship with the individual client, whereas the successful outcome was probably influenced by the efforts of many internal and external suppliers and customers to that client.

Nevertheless, particularly in private sector settings, an increased ability for you as a coach, or for coaching as a profession, to be able to plausibly point to ROI evidence would, as Phillips and Phillips (2007) assert, help organisations buy into and value the benefits that coaching can create.

Kaufman's Model of Learning Evaluation

Although commonly referred to as Kaufman's model, this evaluation framework was devised by Kaufman and Keller (1994). As with the Phillips model, this was purposefully positioned as building upon Kirkpatrick: Kaufman and Keller describe this as 'Kirkpatrick plus', viewing the source model as important but incomplete. The Kaufman model was also designed with training in mind, rather than coaching, but is easy to apply to our context. The five Kaufman levels are summarised in Table 33.1 and Table 33.2.

The key alterations here are:

(a) splitting Kirkpatrick's 'Reaction' into two sub-levels. This may make more sense in a training context, where a well-delivered workshop may be let down by poorly produced resource material, meaning Level 1b: 'Reaction' would be evaluated more favourably than Level 1a: 'Enabling'. With the much more facilitative, non-directive nature of coaching, the coach's way of being with their client is often the main resource or catalyst, so one would expect 'Enabling' and 'Reaction' to be much more closely linked.

Table 33.1 Sample feedback form. Please rate today's session using the scale 1–10, where 10 is high and 1 is low.

Criteria	Rating 1–10	Comments
Building our working relationship		
Helping you feel safe		
Being fully present throughout the conversation		
Listening to you		
Helping develop your awareness		
Facilitating your learning		
Overall		

What did you find most helpful in today's session?

What one aspect could we do different next time to make this an even better session?

Table 33.2 Kaufman 5 levels

Level	What
Level 1: Enabling	What were all the resource inputs (materials, human, financial, etc.) required for the coaching to happen?
Level 2: Acquisition	The equivalent to Kirkpatrick's learning. What mastery and skills or knowledge acquisition has occurred as a result of the coaching?
Level 3: Application	Equivalent to "transfer". How has this learning actually been applied within the organisation?
Level 4: Organisational outputs	This may take the form of identifying organisational performance or strategic gains, or it may be a cost–benefit analysis or ROI calculation.
Level 5: Societal outcomes	The impact and consequences in and for the society in which the client's organisation is situated.

(b)   Bringing in societal considerations. Kaufman had been arguing this point since the 1970s, stating that no organisation was a means unto itself and that it needed to look beyond its own self-serving goals. With HR taking an increasing role in corporate responsibility, it becomes more likely that we, as coaches, should be asking questions about how outcomes have a positive impact upon the immediate community, society more widely and the environment.

Passmore's SOAP-M model

The SOAP-M model aimed to blend four levels of analysis which could be used for HR interventions, with a further level available for academic researchers (Passmore & Velez, 2012; 2015). The model is summarised in Table 33.3. In the following section we describe in detail the levels included in the model, emphasising their objectives, as well as their relevance.

Table 33.3 SOAP-M 5 level evaluation model

Levels	Focus of evaluation
Level 1: Self	Assessment undertake by the client/participant of the impact on them.
Level 2: Others	Assessment undertake by Line manager, peers, direct reports and stakeholders (Others) of the impact on the client/individual.
Level 3: Achievements	Assessment based on an assessment of the individual's achievement of goals or objectives.
Level 4: Potential	Assessment based on the development of potential.
Level 5: Meta-analysis	Researcher review of research studies – combining data from multiple studies to produce an overall effect measure (effect size).

Level 1: Self

In a similar way to Kirkpatrick's model (Kirkpatrick, 1959: 1979), Level 1 is based on evaluation of the intervention by the individual. Data would be collected by a questionnaire; the more specific the questions, the more helpful the evaluation will be to the coach.

Level 1-type evaluation offers benefits to the participant and the organisation. Collection of data is low-cost. It provides the opportunity for learners to have a voice and reflect on their own learning. It provides quick, almost instant feedback for the coach at the end of the session and allows for adaption for the next encounter.

This level might include:

- Experiential feedback at the end of a coaching session from client;
- Experiential feedback at the end of a coaching assignment from the client;
- Competency ratings by the client.

Where possible, the completion of an anonymous experiential feedback form is likely to reduce bias, such as socially desirable answers, and thus enhance the quality of the data. However, in many situations this is not possible. Secondly, providing the form at the end of the session can increase response rates and specificity of the feedback.

It could also include the completion of a self-rating competency questionnaire; for example, one which has been designed specifically for the organisation or sector. This could be completed as a pre- and post-intervention questionnaire to measure the individual's development during the coaching. It could include the completion of a self-rating psychometric questionnaire, such as the MSCEIT (an emotional intelligence questionnaire) or MTQ48 (a resilience questionnaire). Such instruments allow the self-assessment results to be compared with a norm group as well as the potential to undertake a pre- and post-coaching intervention assessment.

Level 2: Others

The evaluation at Level 2 is completed not by the individual themselves but by others. In this case, their line manager, peers, direct reporters and stakeholders. The evaluation could use either a predesigned internal or sector-specific questionnaire, a generic competency-leadership questionnaire like ILM72 or a psychometric, which allows 360 ratings such as

Saville Wave. As with self-rating, the evaluation could use a pre- and post-assessment by others to evaluate the impact of the coaching on the individual.

A number of weaknesses exist at the 'individual' and 'other' level. Firstly, personal factors such as divorce, or the impact of other interventions, such as attending a leadership programme or engaging with an informal mentor, may account for the change, or lack of change, over the time period of the intervention. Secondly, the use of individual evaluation does not allow for the use of a control group.

Level 3: Achievements

While Levels 1 and 2 are concerned with behaviour, personality or attitude, Level 3 shifts the focus to the impact of these newly-acquired behaviours on the achievement of key personal tasks. This may include performance against targets set at the annual appraisal or monthly/quarterly goals – such as sales targets. This type of assessment requires measurable goals and some form of comparison with previous attainment levels and/or comparison with colleagues in an attempt to isolate factors such as changing economic conditions or personal circumstances. The impact of a pandemic can have widely differing impacts, from significant increases in the sales of face masks and a depression in holiday sales for the same period. Level 3 can also be used to assess organisational-level goals such as profit, growth in turnover, market share or stock value/share price, where the responsibility for these rests with the individual, such as a chief executive or sales director.

The higher one moves up the organisation, away from individual performance, the harder it is to identify any single intervention which has had an impact, which is one of the challenges facing the use of ROI as a mechanism. Other variables, such as economic conditions, competitor behaviour and technology change, may all play a role.

Level 4: Potential

Level 4 of the SOAP-M model looks at potential. Recently developed psychometrics claim to assess an individual's potential as well as their actual performance. Coaching may help individuals develop their ability to self-reflect and to be more self-aware, thus growing future potential. Over time this may show itself in enhanced relationships and more effective management of crisis situations, which may not be present over the period of the coaching intervention. Such aspects are harder to measure through a competence framework and, as we note, may not be immediately evident in individual achievements.

As with previous levels, the assessment could take place as pre- and post-assessment, with completion of the questionnaire at T1 (prior to the intervention) and at T2 (a few weeks or months after the intervention).

SOAP overview

We believe the first four SOAP levels are all practical methods which most HR professionals could use to evaluate coaching's impact on individuals and groups. As we have identified, this works best when there is pre- and post-assessment and when there is an ability to compare an individual's results with others.

Level 5: Meta-analysis

Meta-analysis is a more sophisticated data analysis and we believe this is a useful tool for wider reviews of interventions, such as coaching. The approach combines individual studies to assess the overall effectiveness of the intervention. By grouping studies together, the significance of local factors can be reduced and a greater focus be placed on assessing the intervention.

However, while meta-analysis has been used extensively in health interventions, the number of meta-studies of organisation interventions, such as coaching, is more limited. Some studies have been conducted but more research is needed to better understand coaching effectiveness in different situations and as a tool with different presenting issues.

Practice of coaching evaluation

Stakeholder needs

In the previous section we offered a number of alternative evaluation models, each providing ways in which coaching's impact can be evaluated. At a practice level, most coaching assignments have multiple stakeholders, each with their own needs. At a sponsor level, the sponsor is interested to assess the impact of coaching on organisational performance. The line manager may be more concerned about an individual's work performance, while the individual client's concern may be toward a mix of short-term performance and longer-term personal development. The coach too seeks feedback for learning and development, as well as to track the value they are providing to clients. We have summarised the perspectives of different stakeholders and their needs in Table 33.4.

Feedback/evaluation for coaches

The coach may be seeking data for a number of purposes: to provide evidence that their coaching works, as well as feedback that can help their development and enable them to adjust their coaching approach with this specific client. The coach may use informal methods to achieve these outcomes, such as inviting feedback at the end of the session or issuing a questionnaire.

Table 33.4 Stakeholder needs

Stakeholder	Evaluation needs
Coach	• Learning and development; • Impact of coaching on their client.
Individual client	• Skills/performance development; • Personal growth.
Line manager	• Impact of coaching on their team member against the specific areas of development.
Sponsor	• Impact of coaching individual performance; • Development of potential.
Board	• Long-term impact of investment in coaching.

In our experience, asking specific questions can be more helpful in eliciting constructive feedback. Asking the question, 'How was the session for you?' often leads to vague statements such as 'That was great' from clients. Instead, the coach may be better having follow up questions to the general starter question: 'What specifically did you find most helpful?' and, 'If there as one thing we could do differently next time to make the session even better, what would that be?'

We would also suggest that coaches not only seek feedback at the end of a session, certainly after the first or second session, but that they also invite a review conversation at the end of the assignment. This offers an opportunity to gather data about how the client both experienced the coaching assignment and how it has impacted on their work. The opportunity exists at this stage to return to the original goals, and to consider whether or which of these have been achieved and where further work is needed.

Evaluation for clients

From our experience, individual clients tend to be more focused on their experience of coaching than on measurable data. Intangible facts play a large part, including the coaching relationship. Rather than draw on performance data, the client may take a wider perspective and consider how they have grown and developed through the coaching relationship. Of course, this is not universally true: some clients may be interested in their development against specific competences or performance data.

Evaluation for sponsors and line managers

In some assignments the sponsor may be the same person as the client. In other assignments, this role is separated, with the coaching co-ordinator, HR manager or chief executive-chairperson acting as the sponsor who commissions the coaching. In our view, the role of the sponsor is one which needs to be managed, with the sponsor's voice brought into the contracting, goal-setting and evaluation. This can be achieved through tripartite contracting at the start, between coach, client and sponsor, a review meeting at the mid-point of the assignment to review progress and revise (if needed) the goal or objectives and a final review meeting to evaluate the impact of the coaching from the perspective of both the client and the sponsor.

Evaluation for commissioning managers

In addition to individual sponsors, many organisations have a programme or commissioning manager who may be responsible for evaluating the coaching programme and reporting this to a project board. At this level, a more quantitative approach is required which extends beyond the number of people coached and hours of coaching delivered (input data) towards a greater focus on outputs and outcomes. However, as we noted above, such data can be tricky to collect and susceptible to contaminating factors. While much attention has been paid to ROI as a model, results from that model rely so heavily on estimates of the benefits that its value as a tool has been robustly challenged (Grant, 2012).

Evaluation timing

We have suggested above that evaluation should be a regular practice that takes place across the coaching assignment. This can happen at the end of each session by the coach, at the mid-point of an assignment with the client and the sponsor or at the end of an assignment with the client and the sponsor. It can also happen at an organisational programme level through an annual review or a periodic programme evaluation; for example, at the end of a contract period with a provider (see Table 33.4).

Feedback has many uses for coaches, helping their ongoing development, as well as enabling them to flex and adapt to meet the needs of specific clients. These feedback data can be useful not only for self-reflection, but as material to explore in supervision.

For sponsors, too, seeing evaluation as an integral part of the process is important, and one which runs from beginning to end, moving from a focus on the individual over time to a focus on the impact of the coaching programme on organisational objectives and performance.

Conclusion

In this chapter we have explored the issue of evaluation and feedback. Evaluation has been an often-neglected aspect of coaching, with the methods employed tending to be more informal than formal and more experiential than quantitative. However, this is beginning to change, with more organisations adopting a strategic view of coaching and more coaches adopting more formal feedback systems into their process.

References

Athanasopoulou, A. and Dopson, S. (2018). 'A systematic review of executive coaching outcomes: is it the journey or the destination that matter the most?' *The Leadership Quarterly*, 29(1), pp. 70–88. doi:10.1016/j.leaqua.2017.11.004.

Bozer, G. and Jones, R.J. (2018). 'Understanding the factors that determine workplace coaching effectiveness: A systematic literature review'. *European Journal of Work and Organizational Psychology*, 27(3), pp. 342–361. doi:10.1080/1359432X.2018.1446946.

Briner, R.B. (2012). 'Does coaching work and does anyone really care?' *OP Matters*, 16, pp. 4–11.

Fletcher, C. (2015). 'Feedback development as a development tool'. In K. Kraiger, J. Passmore, N. dos Santos and S. Malvezzi, eds., *The Wiley Blackwell handbook of the psychology of training, development and performance improvement*. Chichester, UK: Wiley Blackwell, pp. 486–502.

Grant, A.M. (2012). 'ROI is a poor measure of coaching success: towards a more holistic approach using a well-being and engagement framework'. *Coaching: An International Journal of Theory, Practice and Research*, 5(2), 74–85. doi:10.1080/17521882.2012.672438.

Grant, A.M. and Stober, D.R. (2006). 'Introduction'. In D.R. Stober and A.M. Grant, eds., *Evidence based coaching handbook*. Hoboken, NJ: John Wiley & Sons, Ltd., pp. 1–14.

Grover, S. and Furnham, A. (2016). 'Coaching as a developmental intervention in organisations: A systematic review of its effectiveness and the mechanisms underlying it'. *PLoS ONE*, 11(7), pp. e0159137. doi:10.1371/journal.pone.0159137.

Kaufman, R. and Keller, J. (1994). 'Levels of evaluation; beyond Kirkpatrick'. *Human Resource Development Quarterly*, 5(4), pp. 371–380. doi:10.1002/hrdq.3920050408.

Kirkpatrick, D. (1979). 'Techniques for evaluating training programs'. *Training and Development Journal*, 33(6), pp. 78–92.

Kirkpatrick, D.L. (1959). 'Techniques for evaluating training programs: Reaction'. *American Society for Training and Development Journal*, 18, pp. 3–9.

Kluger, A. and DeNisi, A. (1996). 'The effects of feedback interventions on performance: A historical review, a meta-analysis, and a preliminary feedback intervention theory'. *Psychological Bulletin*, 119(2), pp. 254–84.

Lancer, N., Clutterbuck, D. and Megginson, D. (2016). *Techniques for coaching and mentoring*, 2nd ed. Abingdon, UK: Routledge.

Latham, G. and Locke, E. (1991). 'Self-regulation through goal setting'. *Organizational Behaviour and Human Decision Processes*, 50, pp. 212–247.

London, M. and Smither, J.W. (2002). 'Feedback orientation, feedback culture, and the longitudinal performance management process'. *Human Resource Management Review*, 12(1), pp. 81–100. doi:10.1016/s1053-4822(01)00043-2.

Matthewman, L. (2009). 'Evaluating coaching effectiveness'. *Coaching Psychology International*, 2(1), pp. 21–22.

McDowell, A. and Kurz, R. (2008). 'Effective integration of 360 degree feedback into the coaching process'. *The Coaching Psychologist*, 4(1), pp. 7–19.

Passmore, J. and Velez, M. (2015). 'Training evaluation'. In K. Kraiger, J. Passmore, N. dos Santos and S. Malvezzi, eds., *The Wiley Blackwell handbook of the psychology of training, development and performance improvement*. Chichester, UK: Wiley Blackwell, pp. 136–153.

Passmore, J. and Velez, M.J. (2012). 'SOAP-M: A training evaluation model for HR'. *Industrial and Commercial Training*, 44(6), pp. 315–325. doi:10.1108/00197851211254743.

Philips, J.J. (2007). 'Measuring the ROI of a coaching intervention'. *Performance Improvement*, 46(10), pp. 10–23. doi:10.1002pfi.167.

Phillips, J.J. and Phillips, P.P. (2007). 'Show me the money: The use of ROI in performance improvement, part 1'. *Performance Improvement*, 46(9), pp. 8–22. doi:10.1002/pfi.160.

Phillips, P.P., Phillips, J.J. and Edwards, L. (2012). *Measuring the success of coaching: A Stes-by-step guide for measuring impact and calculating ROI*. Alexandria, VA: Association for Talent Development.

Reio, T.G., Rocco, T.S., Smith, D.H. and Chang, E. (2017). 'A critique of Kirkpatrick's evaluation model'. *New Horizons in Adult Education and Human Resource Development*, 29(2), pp. 35–53. doi:10.1002/nha3.20178.

34 AI and digital technology in coaching

Edith Coron

Introduction

Coaching, like many industries, is increasingly drawing on technology to augment or replace functions previously carried out by humans, or to support the delivery of services. The pace of change and the use of these technologies are likely to increase over the coming decade, with implications for coaches, as well as for those who use coaching services. In this chapter I discuss how the technology is developing, what digital does, what artificial intelligence offers and the implications for the coaching profession.

Hall of mirrors

Exploring the impact that digital technologies already have, and that artificial intelligence can have, on the world of coaching is like entering a hall of mirrors with a maze of reflections. The mirror – a threshold between reality and fantasy in Alice in Wonderland – is confusing for most people when it comes to AI and digital technologies, and blurry for many in the context of coaching. To orientate ourselves in this haze, some definitions are needed.

Definitions

Digital technologies is an umbrella term for computer-based products and solutions that, through programs, combine simple algorithms with limited amounts of data.

An *algorithm* is a suite of mathematical instructions that are programmed by a human, which are to be followed in calculations or other problem-solving operations. Algorithms pre-existed the computer era and can be traced to Euclid in 300 BC. Digital coding and microprocessors gave birth to *digital algorithms* and have penetrated our lives through everything from online shopping, social networks and global positioning systems or GPS, to head-hunting and even university entrance applications.

Data are either a mass of information collected to be examined, considered and used to help decision-making or information in an electronic form that can be stored and used by a computer. The term *big data* refers to extremely large data sets that may be analysed computationally to reveal patterns, trends and associations, especially those related to human behaviour and interactions.[1]

Artificial intelligence incorporates into computer programs complex algorithms applied to a vast quantity of information.

Machine learning is a branch of artificial intelligence wherein a computer generates rules that underlie or are based on raw data that have been fed into the computer.[2]

Deep learning is a subset of machine learning and comprises algorithms that permit software to train itself to perform tasks such as speech and image recognition by exposing multi-layered neural networks to vast amounts of data.

Neural networks are computer programs that simulate the interconnections between neurons in a human brain and are able to learn by a process of trial and error.

Chatbot is a computer programme that simulates human conversation through voice commands, text chats or both and uses Natural Language Processing or NLP.

Natural Language Processing (NLP) is the understanding, analysis and generation of human natural language.

When discussing AI specialists often refer to three types of artificial intelligence:

Artificial Narrow Intelligence (ANI) mimics human intelligence and/or behaviour within a narrow range of parameters and contexts. So far, all existing AIs are "narrow". This includes even AlphaGo, which beat a professional Go player in 2015, and AIs that can now do a better job of detecting cancer than doctors. They perform in one specific area in which they have been programmed.

Artificial General Intelligence (AGI) mimics human intelligence and/or behaviour to be indistinguishable from that of a human and capable of handling any intellectual task. We are not there yet.

Artificial Super Intelligence (ASI) mimics human intelligence and/or behaviour and surpasses it. ASI has long inspired science fiction and there is much speculation about the moment when, if ever, it will come into existence. That moment is known as the "point of singularity".

AI applications to coaching

One could argue that the ancestor of the "digital coach" was ELIZA, the first ever chatbot, which was designed in 1966 by a Massachusetts Institute of Technology professor, Joseph Weizenbaum MIT. This text-based programme identified a relatively small number of key words and simulated the conversation a therapist might have with a patient (Standford, 1966). These exchanges would sound familiar to many coaches.

Box 33.1: Sample ELIZA conversation

A sample conversation was as follows:

Young woman: It's true. I'm unhappy.
Eliza: Do you think coming here will help you not to be unhappy?
Young woman: I need some help, that much seems certain.
Eliza: What would it mean to you if you got some help?
Young woman: Perhaps I could learn to get along with my mother.
Eliza: Tell me more about your family.

Some 50 years later, technology has made some significant inroads into the coaching profession. These include:

Communication technology (video conferencing), enables virtual individual or team/group coaching, while technologically supported facilitation tools can be used for brainstorming, surveys and questionnaires.

Admin digital tools cover booking appointments, logging in coaching hours, sending reminders to clients, accounting and legal contracting.

Feedback questionnaires filled in by the client and/or the coach help to measure client satisfaction and coaching effectiveness.

Sourcing platforms offer coaches on demand. These may be either B2B (subcontracted coaches) or B2C (coaches connecting directly with clients) such as the International Coaching Federation's "Find a Coach" platform. Clients choose from a list of coaches in explicit, predetermined categories (coaching qualifications, gender, professional background, location, languages, etc.).

Matching seeks to go further and put coaches and clients in contact with one another using questionnaires to gather both objective information to create profiling categories, as in the sourcing platforms, and subjective information based on values, communication styles and preferences and personality profiles (either self-declared or through the questionnaires), among others. Answers are correlated by similarities in pools of coaches and clients on the assumption that these similarities will create an affinity or the right "fit".

Numerous *digital coaching platforms* incorporate sourcing and sometimes matching. They offer distance coaching, either by prior appointment or on demand. The coaching is carried out live or through voice or text messages.

Online self-awareness tools such as self-evaluation psychometric tests (MBTI, Hogan, Process Communication Model, etc.) or 360-feedback profiles are now common features in the coach's toolbox. A qualified coach may then play a complementary role, debriefing after the tests and following up with additional coaching sessions.

Online tools and coach services can be incorporated into *e-learning* platforms that often offer digital resource libraries (videos, TedEx talks, articles, blogs) with or without teaching modules.

Metaphoric associative cards are drawn from psychotherapy and commonly used in coaching. They, along with numerous other coaching support tools or models, can be found online and are included in virtual coaching sessions.

All the above are digital adaptations of resources that coaches have long used in their original, non-technological forms. MBTI Step I was a handwritten test that used carbon paper to calculate scores!

The frameworks, categories, criteria and contents are all defined by humans. Digitalisation allows different stages of the coaching processes to be automated and systematised and has already profoundly changed the profession.

Virtual exchanges also are taking the place of face-to-face sessions. Coaching, indeed, has become ubiquitous, adapting to the exigencies of time zones and remote connections. Building and sustaining a meaningful relationship through electronic communications can be a challenge for coaches. It tests their capacity (and that of the client) to be fully present when much useful information can be lost and to develop new "listening" skills.

Many business clients are experienced in remote professional interactions with teams spread around the world, struggling with the shortcomings of long distance and digital exchanges. They know how hard it is to sustain effective communications, build trust and maintain a relationship. We can learn from them.

"Coach on demand" is also a slippery concept that could question the very principle of ownership by the client of the coaching itself. The risks of the coach being a crutch and of the coaching session being a quick fix are real. The commoditisation of coaching is a growing trend with implications for all coaches.

Artificial intelligence at the heart of coaching

It is at the very heart of coaching – that is, the coaching relationship and the coaching conversation – that artificial intelligence, as it is developing, has the potential to play an even more significant role.

Automatic coaching chatbots are question-and-answer exchanges between a human being and a programme. They use tree-diagram formats based on pre-established scenarios, where an AI can understand speech or text delivered in natural language. In our daily lives, we are familiar with Alexa or Siri. Several similar programs that are adapted to coaching are available, with some of these operating only as telephone applications (apps).

Asynchronous data analysis: Some digital platforms are applying machine learning to recorded coaching sessions. Using Net Promoter Scoring (a marketing indicator), and Natural Language Processing, they analyse what they define as "anonymised data" from their users by monitoring an array of criteria.

Coaches have long been recording their sessions for the purpose of certification by their professional organisations. The recordings and their transcripts are analysed by assessors who evaluate the coach's professional competencies based on an explicit set of criteria. Recordings of sessions are also used in the mentoring and supervision of coaches.

Synchronous Data Analysis: Introducing AI in real time into the coaching conversation implies, in the words of David Clutterbuck, a "coach–AI partnership" (2018), and potentially puts a wealth of information, literally, at the fingertips of the coach. The AI could be an observer of the session, a source of additional information, a sounding board and a mirror – in short, a "third party" resource. This resource, which must be made accessible in full transparency to the client, would also dramatically impact the coach-client relationship. A new alliance needs to be built in which coach and client jointly define the role they want to assign to the tools and without which their mutual trust could be threatened by an excessive reliance on the AI.

Monitoring the client, the coach and the exchanges between them, the AI could identify silence, body language and various patterns, among them linguistic (repeated words), narrative (limiting assumptions) and conversational (flow and tracks) (Clutterbuck, 2018).

Some physical trackers, already widely used in sports apps that are marketed as "digital coaches", could be added (e.g. body temperature, heartbeat, etc.) to gain insights into the emotional state of the client and perhaps even of the coach. Big players like Google and Facebook are working on voice and facial emotion recognition through deep learning with neural networks.

Crossing the threshold

By stepping into the world of emotions, AI-supported tools could cross the threshold separating "machine intelligence" from what has been, until now, the preserve of human intelligence. Moreover, and because they are designed by humans, AIs have suffered since their inception from a strong dose of anthropomorphism; it is almost AI's birthmark.

When computer pioneer Alan Turing designed his now-famous test – the Turing test – (1950), the machine was deemed to have succeeded if it fooled the judge into thinking it was human. Regarding his own test, Professor Weizenbaum was reportedly so annoyed that people confused the early chatbot, ELIZA, with a real psychiatrist that he abandoned all research on AI. The "ELIZA effect" has now entered our vocabulary.

By moving into the heart of coaching and seeking to decipher human emotions, the AIs are seen by their critics as crossing a point of no return, one that ultimately threatens the very humanity of coaching and carrying the risk that coaching becomes a mere commodity.

Their supporters argue that digital technologies and AIs are instead an opportunity that the coaching profession should embrace and that they merely reflect what coaching is, with all its shortcomings and achievements.

AIs are permeating coaching, much as they have permeated and will continue to permeate many other human endeavours. They are the Janus, the two-faced Roman god, of our time or, as the astrophysicist Stephen Hawkins once warned, "either the best, or the worst thing, ever to happen to humanity".

Developing literacy

This binary proposition calls on our profession to develop literacy around AI in order to influence AI development and applications in a way that reinforces the ethical tenets and raison d'être of coaching.

The International Coaching Federation defines coaching as "partnering with clients in a thought-provoking and creative process that inspires them to maximize their personal and professional potential" (ICF, 2019).

How then might this new "three-way partnership" (client–coach–AI) best serve this definition? While it appears paradoxical, could so-called "cobots" (collaborative robots) actually enhance the unique human contribution that coaching brings to the world by relying on what only human coaches so far have the capacity to do – that is, not merely identifying emotions but connecting with them, tapping into their intuition, nourishing a relationship and holistically blending thoughts, perception and experience?

Digital and AI applications are, and will be for the foreseeable future, tools that we humans define and design. In coaching, we must choose how they are used with transparent intentionality and mature ethical responsibility. We can apply the same mindful care and professional standards that we bring to a coaching conversation, where we define the intention and the objectives, to "Coaching 5.0", starting with our profession itself. What do we want coaching to be and to become and to what purpose?

From its humanistic roots to the role it plays in the prevailing performance culture, coaching has become a kaleidoscope that confuses many. The transformation coaching is experiencing could prove to be an additional opportunity to clean up and strengthen our profession.

For instance, the various monitoring tools discussed above could be used to further define, implement and guarantee the standards of a profession that is not regulated and is often seen as lacking clear metrics. To accomplish this, the various professional organisations that set those standards (International Coaching Federation, European Mentoring and Coaching Council, International Association of Coaching, etc.) must co-operate more and proactively engage in the design of AI-supported measurement tools. The introduction of AI, some argue, could minimise the subjectivity inherent in human judgment and further standardise the assessment process in the credentialing of coaches and potentially in measuring the return on investment of coaching.

With asynchronous recordings as data, AI could allow for more precise monitoring of the coach's professional development needs. It could create opportunities for in-depth review of each coaching session. The coaches themselves could use AI-supported analysis of their work to self-monitor and to gain additional insights on their coaching sessions.

Coaching suffers from the confusion, in the public eye, over what it really is and does, in light of the frequent crossover between coaching, counselling, mentoring, training and consulting. Many coaches too often cross the lines, and several online coaching platforms reinforce this confusion by offering "blended solutions" to people's development. Professional organisations still have an important role to play to reduce this confusion.

Data and coaching

Indeed, looming over technology-supported coaching is the crucial question of the data.

Artificial intelligence requires algorithms, computing power, storage capacity and data.

When it comes to coaching, the topic of data is highly sensitive since the cornerstone of the coaching relationship is confidentiality.

Many questions arise:

- What databases could be built and used in coaching?
- Who has access to them and for what purpose?
- How might they be modelled?
- What kind of ethical rules should govern them?
- Who sets those boundaries?

As noted earlier, coaching and technology have remained worlds apart for a very long time. The relationship remains tarnished by mutual suspicion stemming from ignorance on each side about the other's world, a suspicion that is also fuelled by the general brouhaha that surrounds AI and the firm conviction that human complexity – the realm of coaches – cannot be left to mere algorithms.

Some coaching startups are bridging the gap, working hand in hand with AI developers to test and implement prototypes with tools for linguistic/semantic analysis in coaching platforms and apps, as well as others in the matching process. Some of these are highly mindful of setting ethical boundaries, particularly when it comes to the use of the data they access and build.

Some online coaching platforms pride themselves on being able to offer HR professionals the data they need to monitor motivation, performance and well-being by feeding back to the client company what are known as "rich data", which can be broken down by clusters such as gender, age, geography, etc. But where does the anonymity they pledge start and confidentiality end?

One constraint is the lack of universal rules regarding data protection. In the European Union the General Data Protection Regulation (GDPR) governs the use and management of personal data. Different territories have different requirements. Overall, coaching professionals must engage with these standards along with AI developers and decision-makers. This implies that coaches need to familiarise themselves and keep up to date with the digital environment in which they operate.

Coach training schools have a crucial role to play in educating future coaches in the use of technologically supported tools. Newcomers to the profession have a digital fluency and appetite that can put them in a good position to contribute to the coaching of the future. There is also a need for established coaches who are less dependent on market demand and less likely to be lured by the hipness of these tools, to offer their professional maturity.

AI literacy is also needed to better serve those of our clients whose jobs are increasingly impacted by AI. Concern about job loss, the risk that their skills become obsolete and the need to learn how to work with "cobots" are all issues that could arise in coaching conversations. Most coaches take their professional development to heart, and our accrediting bodies require that we do so. By broadening our skills and strengthening our credibility, AI literacy could be an additional string to our bow.

Finally, AI literacy would allow coaches do what they do best, at their best: Coach. It enables them to tap into their best coaching tool, themselves, and thus to embrace what coaching, at heart, is all about; that is, developing and nourishing a reflective approach that sustains informed and intentional choices.

In machine learning, AIs need to be trained. The machines are fed and annotate tens of thousands of data points. AI trainers verify, validate or, in the event of errors, re-annotate the data points. Coaches have the skills to undertake this task as AI trainers.

A much talked-about issue regarding AI concerns biases. Which data points based on which criteria are fed into the machines? How are they refined? Humans bring their own biases to this process and the programs and, in turn, risk magnifying those biases. Professional coaches who are aware of the recurring pitfall of the coach setting the agenda, and are also familiar with the models that can be applied and the tools that can be used, would act as safeguards.

Coaching and AI: A picture in the picture

Coaching is but a microcosm of the broader picture. The issues raised about data and the introduction of AI in coaching echo familiar questions about AI in general.

In this debate, philosophers have taken centre stage, because the term "artificial intelligence" itself brings up philosophical questions. Does intelligent behaviour imply or require the existence of a mind, and to what extent is consciousness replicable as computation? AIs act intelligently. Does that make them intelligent? The "narrow" artificial intelligences, the only type of AIs existing, likely to exist for quite some time, that we have been referring to all along, are computer-based systems that exhibit intelligent behaviour. To step into the fictional world of Artificial Super Intelligences (ASI), those would need to be self-aware and to make independent choices.

Philosophers, as well as leading figures in the scientific and business worlds, have been calling for an "ethics of action" for machines and humans alike when it comes to AI developments. Tellingly, the Institute on Artificial Intelligence at MIAI@Grenoble Alpes, has established an Ethics Committee headed by a philosopher, Thierry Ménissier. The Institute is one of the four AI hubs in France that bring together public and private sectors.

Coaches are well placed to engage in support of the "ethics of action". Ethics are the backbone of coaching and we are directly plugged into these changes, at an individual and collective level, as coaching professionals – through our clients, whether they be organisations and/or individuals – and as members of society at large..

A cognitive co-revolution of the machines and the humans is underway, and it is accelerating, observes Olivier Malafronte (2019). In line with these changes, and when AI brings "new models of society", coaches have the potential to support the development of specifically human competencies: Cognitive and emotional, favouring "being" rather than "doing".

Coaches as role models

Interestingly, some of the very players who are changing our world are encouraging coaches to step up and assume this role. David Peterson (2019), Global Director of Leadership and Coaching at Google, has offered a list of actions for coaches in the digital world:

- Do transformational, not transactional, development;
- See the really big picture;
- Get better at understanding art and science;
- Embrace and leverage new technologies;
- Be role models in adaptability.

Virtual coaching

As for anything technology-supported, the first requirement for virtual coaching is that the coach be fully comfortable with the technology used. Coaches can do this by:

- Becoming familiar and at ease with handling remote communication tools so all the available interfaces and features of the tools are used seamlessly;
- Being mindful of the type of communication tool that their clients can access in the client's specific geographical location;
- Having the ability to troubleshoot technical problems the clients might encounter (image, speakers and microphones) and, when needed, having a mutually understood, communicated back-up plan (phone instead of video).

When receiving clients in our office, we are mindful of the space we offer. The same applies to remote coaching. How does the virtual room look? What background is displayed for the client to see and what does it convey? Is the virtual room quiet and private? Can the coach's face and upper half of their body be clearly seen? The coach can encourage their client to follow their lead.

The coach has the responsibility to be as present in a virtual coaching session as they would be in a physical one. This involves being mindful of the state of their body, maybe using a Mindfulness meditation to prepare and having a glass of water at hand. It may also involve being aware of and managing the pitch and volume of their voice, speaking slowly and articulately, while also allowing for silence and maintaining eye contact through the camera. Thought thus has to be given to both the positioning of the camera and the screen, allowing sufficient distance between the person and the camera, to allow not just their face to appear and for the camera to be at eye level.

It is equally important to check the client's level of comfort; e.g. whether their space is suitable for the meeting, encouraging them to reframe the camera to allow more of themselves to be visible and checking whether they have what they may need to hand, such as a glass of water. It is equally important to review these aspects at the end of the session, checking what has worked well and what may need to be adjusted in technological terms for the next meeting.

Thought also needs to be given to the length of each session. It may work better to plan for shorter sessions than in face-to-face coaching, such as one hour instead of two, or to allow for a break if a longer session is planned. The coach also needs to pace the virtual coaching engagements to allow time for note-taking and meta reflection on the session, as well as ensuring there is enough time between sessions for the coach to resource, refresh and refocus.

Thought also needs to be given to which tools might be used in the session. Different tools may be needed to suit the digital environment, or familiar ones may need to be used in different ways. In the case of psychometric tools, 360-degree feedback and other types of data, it is essential that the coach be qualified to use them and is proficient in their debriefings.

If working through a blended coaching platform, the coach must be knowledgeable about the resources offered by the online library as well as the content of the learning modules.

The coach needs to explicitly define the boundaries of the confidentiality of all the data. One specific issue is the recording of sessions. Who owns the data, who has access to it and when will it be deleted are all worth discussing as part of the contracting process.

Conclusion

In our journey through the hall of mirrors charted in this chapter, we must remain focused on our humanity. Coaching, the intimate relationship between two people, is a uniquely human process. While digitisation can enhance this relationship, such as through accessibility, AI may reshape it. Coaches need to be part of this transformation and steer it, making AI coaching a tool for clients which democratises coaching for all.

Notes

1 www.lexico.com/en/definition/big_data
2 www.collinsdictionary.com/dictionary/english/machine-learning

References

Braddick, C. (2019). 'Democratization coaching platforms, products and personalization'. Blog IOC, Retrieved on 3 April 2020 from https://instituteofcoaching.org/blogs/democratization-coaching-platforms-products-and-personalization.

Clutterbuck, D. (2018). 'The coach–AI partnership'. Retrieved on 3 April 2020 from www.coachingandmentoringinternational.org/the-coach-ai-partnership/.

ICF. (2019). 'Definition of coaching'. Retrieved on 3 April 2020 from https://coachfederation.org.

Turing, A. (1950). 'The turing test'. Retrieved on 8 April 2020 from https://plato.stanford.edu/entries/turing-test/.

Peterson, D. (2019). 'The digital coach', Conference paper, Sydney, Australia shared with the author by The Leadership Group.

Stanford. (1966). 'ELIZA'. Retrieved on 3 April 2020 from https://web.stanford.edu/group/SHR/4-2/text/dialogues.html.

Cezon, M. and Ménissier, T. (2020). 'IA et coaching, une réflexion éthique et prospective sur leurs apports réciproques'. Retrieved on 8 April 2020 from https://revue-europeenne-coaching.com/numeros/numero-10-04-2020/ia-et-coaching-une-reflexion-ethique-et-prospective-sur-leurs-apports-reciproques.

Malafronte, O. (2019). Founder of Pocket Confident AI, interview with the author.

Section 6

Continuing coach development

35 Supervision in coaching

Suzanne Lines

Introduction

Coach supervision is now an established practice. Each of the coaching bodies recognises the importance of coach supervision, the Global Code of Ethics for Coaches, Mentors and Supervisors (GCMA) requires all signatories to engage in supervision and many organisations today expect coaches to be actively engaged in coaching supervision. To make the most of supervision and recognise the importance for our continued professional development, we need to understand what it covers and how best to prepare for it. In this chapter, we will look at the core functions and purposes of supervision, in addition to how the focus of supervision has changed to meet the needs of coaches today. We will offer a framework for supervision and the multiple lenses we need to develop as coaches. We will look at some of the key relationship dynamics which benefit from a supervisory lens (for example parallel process, transference and counter transference). We will also offer a framework for choosing your supervisor, what to consider in creating an effective supervision relationship and the benefits to you, your clients and the client's organisation.

The development of supervision

Supervision is still a relatively new activity. Coach supervision emerged in the early 2000s, as practitioners looked to therapeutic practice to enhance their coaching (Hawkins and Smith, 2006). Since then, a small body of evidence has emerged to demonstrate the value of supervision (Bachkirova et al., 2020; Hawkins, Turner and Passmore, 2019). Many coaches work in organisational settings and therefore need to manage multi-cornered contracts and a range of stakeholders. Balancing this range of needs is very different to 1:1 contracting.

Michael Carroll noted how supervision has changed in the last 40 years. From therapy the focus was on the supervisor, then the focus on the supervisee to our profession's current focus: The work itself: "centred on practice; the actual work done with a view to using that work to improve future work" (Carroll, 1996, 2014, p. 124). More specifically he suggested:

1. Supervision is no longer only an inward-looking process to help supervisees do their work better. It also helps them look outwards and take a systemic approach;
2. Supervision should be supervisee not supervisor-led, with a focus on learning not teaching;
3. Critical reflection is a central method for generating learning;
4. The supervisor has a dual role of facilitating learning and promoting high quality work by their supervisees (Carroll, 1996, 2014).

The purpose of coach supervision

The primary purpose of supervision is to provide a reflective space to ensure we as coaches provide the best service we can to our clients. Our clients are at the heart of all that we do and that requires us to apply a rigour to our practice, reflecting on our work, how we have been with our clients and what we are learning so that we can work as cleanly as possible in service of the multiple systems to which they belong. That rigour requires that we also continue to grow vertically and horizontally and that we take care of ourselves as professionals.

Peter Hawkins and Nick Smith (2006) suggested that coach supervision has three main functions:

- Developmental:
    - Developing the coach's skills and understanding of their processes, their interventions and their impact;
- Resourcing:
    - Attending to the emotions triggered in the coach from the work. Examples include feeling competent, potential over-identification with clients or being well defended against some emotions which we therefore don't see or work with and therefore miss key elements of the work;
- Qualitative:
    - Attending to the quality of the work, working ethically, looking out for blind spots, our biases and our own areas of vulnerability. Working with ethical dilemmas where there is no clear right or wrong.

Other writers have provided alternative views on the purpose of supervision. These are summarised in Table 35.1.

What is coaching supervision?

As with coaching, there is currently no single definition of coach supervision. Given the continued debate about the precise nature of coaching itself, it seems unlikely that we will come to a single definition on coaching supervision, and yet there are important unifying key elements.

Let's look at some of the definitions of supervision:

> Coaching supervision is a co-created learning relationship that supports the supervisee in their development, both personally and professionally, and seeks to support them in providing best practice to their client. Through the process of reflecting on their own work in supervision, the supervisees can review and develop their practice and re-energize themselves. It offers a forum to attend to their emotional and professional wellbeing and growth. Through the relationship and dialogue in this alliance, coaches can receive feedback broaden their perspectives, generate new ideas and maintain standards of effective practice.

> (Hodge, 2016, pp. 87–106)

> Coaching Supervision is a collaborative learning practice to continually build the capacity of the coach through reflective dialogue for the benefit of both coaches and

Table 35.1 The purpose of supervision

Writer			Kadushin (1976)	Proctor (2000)	Hawkins (2006)	Carroll and Gilbert (2005–2011)	Newton (2012)
Field			Social work	Counselling		Coach-specific supervision	
Focus of supervision			Supervisor →	Supervisee →		The work	
The 3 core functions	1		Administrative/Managerial	Normative	Qualitative	Accountability	Accounting for all parties, taking a meta perspective.
	2		Supportive	Restorative	Resourcing	Reflection	Nurturative, offering recognition, encouragement, support.
	3		Educative	Formative	Developmental	Experiential Learning	Transformative New ways of thinking, feeling and behaving.

(Adapted from Newton 2012, p. 104)

clients. Coaching Supervision focuses on the development of the coach's capacity through offering a richer and broader opportunity for support and development. Coaching Supervision creates a safe environment for the coach to share their successes and failures in becoming masterful in the way they work with their clients.

(ICF, 2020)

Coaching Supervision is a formal and protected time for facilitating a coach's in-depth reflection on their practice with a Coaching Supervisor. Supervision offers a confidential framework within a collaborative working relationship in which the practice, tasks, process and challenges of the coaching work can be explored. The primary aim of Supervision is to enable the coach to gain in ethical competency, confidence and creativity so as to ensure best possible service to the coaching clients, both clients and coaching sponsors. Supervision is not a "policing" role, but rather a trusting and collegial professional relationship.

(Association for Coaching, 2019)

Supervision is the interaction that occurs when a mentor or coach brings their coaching or mentoring work experiences to a supervisor in order to be supported and to engage in reflective dialogue and collaborative learning for the development and benefit of the mentor or coach, their clients and their organisations.

(EMCC, 2020)

In reviewing these definitions, five key principles emerge:

- Clients: At the heart of the process;
- Regular: Creating protected time;
- Relationship: Safe and trusting;
- Process: Reflexive and collaborative; developing mastery;
- Ethics: Ensuring ethical practice.

Michael Carroll and Maria Gilbert offer a definition of a supervisee: "anyone, of any profession, who brings his/her work experience to another in order to learn from it" (Carroll and Gilbert, 2005, p. 11). This for me simplifies something that is complex, rich, rewarding, challenging and testing, and reminds me as a coach, supervisee and coach supervisor, that the primary purpose of supervision is to continue learning and expanding our frame of reference so that we become ever more effective in service of our clients and their systems.

Increasingly, many issues brought to supervision have an ethical dilemma that offers an opportunity to develop "the ethical maturity of the client, coach, supervisor and the wider systems" as well as finding a resolution to the issue (Hawkins, Turner and Passmore, 2019, p. 26). Ethics, as we know, are not a simple case of "right or wrong"; they invite us to reflect and take responsibility for developing our own "moral map" (Malik, 2014, p. 344) and are core to effective supervision.

Our coach training will have given us great tools, models and techniques: The next stage of that learning is the live ongoing application and reflection on our practice to develop the skilful capability of when and how to use that knowledge and skills to best effect.

Peter Hawkins and Nick Smith (2006) talk about three C's: Competencies, Capabilities and Capacities. See Table 35.2.

Table 35.2 Three C's of supervision

Competencies	Capabilities	Capacities
Both are about doing and know-how.		Being.
Content and Process: Skills/models/ frameworks.	Context appropriate use of Skills / models/frameworks.	Personal qualities.
Can be learned – in the classroom.	Can be learned – only live and on the job.	The human qualities that can be nurtured and refined.

They describe supervision as having "a vital role to play in helping the supervisee turn their competencies into capabilities and to ensure that the capabilities are held within an ever-increasing capacity to work with others with fearless compassion". To do this well, we need to know ourselves well. The best medium to achieve this is through critical reflection. A reflection that goes beyond content and explores, unpacks and reframes assumptions underpinning our map of the world: Beliefs, behaviours and theories (Carroll, 1996–2014). Supervision at its best is "transformative rather than transmissive" (Carroll, 1996–2014).

David Kolb's experiential learning model (1984) is at the heart of this critical reflection and that mindset shift. Reflecting on our experience, learning from and through the testing of that new learning, we can then transform the way we think, feel and behave. See Figure 35.1.

There are of course other ways to critically reflect and you will come across terms such as Coach Mentoring and Peer Supervision, in addition to group or 1:1 supervision. A brief summary is provided in Table 35.3.

A framework for supervision

The 7-Eyed Supervision Model offers 7 different lenses or perspectives to support critical reflection (Hawkins and Smith, 2006). See Figure 35.2.

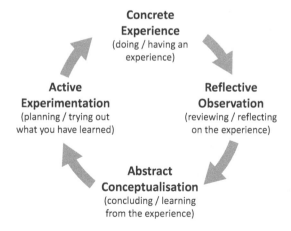

Figure 35.1 Kolb's Learning Model

Table 35.3 Methods to engage in reflective practice

Critical Reflection includes	Coverage of the 3 core functions of supervision	Elements covered from the 7-Eyed Model for Supervision (a framework for supervision overleaf)
Coach Mentoring	A term specific to the ICF. Focussed on coaching skills relevant to the core competency credential level. The focus is on the Developmental function. The Resourcing and Qualitative elements are excluded.	Eye 2 – the coach's interventions.
1:1 Supervision	Expect to include all 3 core functions of supervision. More likely to have time for a personal deep dive. If contracted for, can include coaching credential preparation.	All 7 eyes.
Group Supervision	Expect to include all 3 core functions of supervision. Opportunity to learn from others, may have less time on personal issue. Supervisor has responsibility for group process. If contracted for, can include coaching credential preparation.	All 7 eyes.
Peer Supervision	Opportunity for shared learning, vulnerability, deep reflection and productive challenge in both parties (David Clutterbuck, 2018). Needs greater commitment as no one person has responsibility for group process therefore greater need for structure. Quality dependent upon the rigor of individuals involved. Potential risk of psychological (out of awareness) game playing, collusion, competition, playing safe. Less likely to be acceptable for accreditation.	Eyes covered will be dependent on the individuals involved. Works best for those experienced in psychological contracting and managing group process For a comprehensive guide, have a look at '*Peer Supervision in Coaching and Mentoring*' by Tuner, Lucas and Whitaker and '*Group Supervision*' by Proctor

Any time one person meets another, we are not only meeting that individual but coming into contact with their whole system: We are meeting their values, beliefs and their behaviours shaped by their life experiences, and we also bring in our own values and beliefs, and our behaviours that have been shaped by our life experiences. Some of these experiences will be openly shared: Things that would appear comfortably on a CV perhaps. Other elements that have shaped us as individuals are not always so visible: Some we will be aware of and some will be out of conscious awareness. So there is a lot to take account of in any relationship. We then overlay the organisational culture and the key stakeholders within that (our client's organisation, their key stakeholders, our own organisation or the associate company we work for) and you can see there is a lot that comes into the coaching space. When we contract with our client, we become part of their system and can then not always see other relational dynamics at play. The 7-Eyed Supervision Model can help us see and work with those complexities more clearly. See Table 35.4.

Cochrane and Newton (2018) add an 8th eye: "the contact, awareness, connectedness, overall values and philosophy that the supervisor" brings. When this is working well, it can constructively impact the quality of the supervisory relationship whatever issues and challenges arise and therefore has a constructive impact on the work. See The Eyes, the Focus and Skills of the 7 Eyed Model in Table 35.4.

Figure 35.2 The 7 Eyes from the 7-Eyed Model for Supervision (Hawkins & Smith, 2006)

Key dynamics occur in any relationship and not just between clients, coaches or supervisors. Supervision provides a lens for us to catch these and work through them in a way that our own biases, vulnerabilities or blind spots often mean we can't see as clearly on our own. As a helping profession, we can be at risk of wanting to be helpful to our clients, when looking to be useful will be more effective and more sustainable. In order to be of use to the organisation as well as the individual, we need to hold the balance of needs in our contracting, which requires an appropriate psychological distance between all parties so that "parties are perceived as equal" (Micholt, 1992) and we don't fall into the drama triangle (Karpman, 1968) with "organisation as persecutor, client as victim and coach as rescuer" (Hawkins and Smith, 2006). See Table 35.5.

Choosing your supervisor

Stephen Palmer (2017) in a survey exploring the supervisor–supervisee relationship, suggested "trust" was a key feature of the coaching supervision relationship. This may seem obvious, but as coach supervision is a place to which we bring the things from our client work that may result in us feeling vulnerable, a trusting relationship with your supervisor is vital. The relationship needs to be one in which you are supportively stretched and challenged with no element of shame or judgement. That safety enables you to bring your vulnerabilities: "uncertainty, risk, and emotional exposure" Brenee Brown (2012). She describes vulnerability as "the birthplace of love, belonging, joy, courage, empathy, and creativity. It is the source of hope, empathy, accountability and authenticity". Whilst the word love is a word not often used in an organisational setting, these are essential qualities to bring to our work as coaches, supervisees and supervisors.

In addition to the quality of relationship with your supervisor, think too about mutual social power:

Table 35.4 The 7-Eyed Model: Eyes, Focus and Skills

The Eyes	The Focus	The Skills
1 The Client The Client's system	The client's issue The client's values, beliefs, culture, their organisational context. What they brought, how they presented, impact they are have.	Separating data from any preconceptions/assumptions/interpretations.
2 The Coach's interventions	Strategies employed. How, why and what. Often the coach will bring an impasse, where they are stuck.	Exploring new options. What else might we have done?
3 Relationship between Coach and Client	Relationship, rapport, dynamic between the 2 and how that relates to the client's system.	Developing an observer's perspective by standing outside the relationship, what does this meta perspective tell us about the work to be done?
4 The Coach	The Coach's experience How are they affected? What resources do they have, what more may be required?	Working through anything that was stimulated in the coach and explore how this might provide useful data for what else is going on in the client's system.
5 The supervisory relationship	Quality of relationship and being alert to parallel process.	Attending to the dynamic of this relationship and how it might illustrate the dynamics in the coach–client relationship (parallel process).
6 The supervisor's process	The supervisor's inner response.	Using the unconscious data (feelings, thoughts, hunches) from the supervisor's own internal process and using that as a reflection of what the coach might be picking up from their client.
7 The wider context	Key stakeholders: Organisational context and need; cultural, political, economic, social, technological, legal, ethical and environmental context.	Attending to context and the "whole-systems perspective" Requires a high level of transcultural competence (Hawkins and Smith, 2013) both organisational and geographical to understand the organisational patterns and how these show up in the client's challenges.

Table 35.5 Common dynamics processes in supervision

Parallel Process	The process which reflects what is going on between coach and client mirroring what is going on between client and the organisation. It can be seen in the supervisor and supervisee relationship too.
Psychodynamics	The dynamic interplay between our conscious and unconscious mind with the more positive emotions in our conscious awareness and those more negatively charged in our unconscious mind or "out of conscious awareness". How we deal with emotions, our hopes and fears and how those ensuing behaviours might relate to early life experiences and the sense we made of them. Denial and anxiety being central defence mechanisms in this framework (Murdoch and Arnold, 2013).
Transference or projection	"When clients shift across the characteristics of someone else onto the coach" (Hay, 2007). As examples looking to be rewarded, punished, parented etc. You can also see this when we project onto others, feelings or behaviours that belong in the past and/or belong to someone else.
Counter transference	Our own emotional reaction to a client or their issues: An emotional reaction which arises from our own past experience. This could show up in potential blind spots as we can mirror or get caught up in patterns that match our own and potentially collude (Murdoch and Arnold, 2013).

A strong supervisory relationship is based on mutual social power. The supervisor needs to be seen by the practitioner as having sufficient reward, coercive, expert, legitimate and referent power to carry out their responsibilities. In particular, they need "referent" power (reference point or role model of shared world view and values.) It doesn't matter how expert you see someone; if their values and approach don't fit with yours then you will dismiss their input. Practitioners also need social power in the eyes of their supervisor. The practitioner is not a blank slate that the supervisor writes on. They have experience and expertise that needs to be recognised. They have a legitimate right to have their own ideas and to be an active participant in supervision, rather than a submissive follower. Most importantly, they need to have their values and worldview recognised and appreciated. If the supervisor doesn't appreciate the practitioner's value position, then they can't provide supportive and congruent supervision.

(Hewson, 2016, pp. 1–2)

As you think about choosing your supervisor, you may find Julie Hay's C5 cluster a useful framework: Context, contact, contract, content, contrast (Hay, 2007). See Table 35.6.

Supervision works best when it is ongoing as a key part of your ethical practice and for those unplanned for challenging situations or issues that need to be unpacked in a timely manner. Regular supervision enables you to develop your own internal supervisor and, for most of us, helps develop that internal muscle quicker than we could on our own. Our supervisor will notice our patterns and help create a greater awareness of those patterns that resource us and get us stuck. They provide a helicopter view, and will make links across time with progress we are making and areas for growth. As coaches, we look to support our clients in developing greater autonomous behaviour:

- Thinking, feeling and choice of actions which is based on present centred awareness rather than being driven by archaic responses to triggers from the past;

Table 35.6 Hay's C5 cluster

Context	Contact	Contract	Content	Contrasts
Their professional context and organisational experience. Their coach and supervision training, code of ethics, commitment to CPD, psychological underpinning.	Quality of relationship as described above.	**Practically**: the administrative part: how often, how many, length of sessions, length of contract, cancellation, location, how long for, where, when how much. **Professionally**: purpose and outcomes. **Psychologically**: our hopes and fears for the working relationship; how could these get in the way, how will they be addressed? How do you best learn? How do you respond to feedback, challenge, support? What will stop you from bringing the things you most want to explore?	What you most want from your supervision, your supervisor. What is the focus of supervision and your learning edge? What do you not want them to bring?	How are you alike, how are you different? How might that impact your work together?

And we look to contribute to organisational cohesion and growth;

- Looking at the health of the organisational system and accounting for stakeholders.

An ongoing supervision relationship creates safety and context for those challenging situations where we need support right away. Someone who knows us and the context of our work can tune in really quickly to our patterns and unpack unexpected issues that arise more deeply and in a more timely fashion.

Preparing for supervision

As with any meeting, thinking about your purpose and desired outcome in advance will help you shape the session with your supervisor. As you prepare, you will have begun the process of self-supervision, enabling you to have a richer discussion with your supervisor.

1. Put some quiet time aside;
2. Reflect on your recent client work:
3. Create an agenda for what you'd like to cover;
4. Identify what you would most like from the session;
5. Identify what you most want from your supervisor.

In that reflective preparation, include your helicopter thinking:

- Remind yourself of your contract with your supervisor and the overall goals you have to develop your practice; as well as
- The detail of the specific issues arising from your client work.

As you reflect on your client work (you might refer back to your notes, your learning journal if you keep one or review any recordings of the work) include both task: The interventions you chose and how you used them; and relationship: The relationship with your client, you in relationship to yourself and your supervisor). It can be useful to include:

- Progress update: Your objectives and your client's;
- What's working well, what could be working better (and balance the two!);
- Things you might be wrestling with (an intervention, reactions, emotions, getting stuck or the contract);
- The additional skills and competencies you want to develop;
- What niggles and stresses are you noticing? Either in your system or your client's system?
- What personal patterns in you are you noticing and how are these affecting your work?
- What patterns are you noticing across your client base? What do these tell you about your signature strengths and areas for growth?

You may find the Henley Eight useful. See Table 35.7.

Notice any areas you'd rather not bring to supervision, any patterns you see.

Use the 7-Eyed Supervision Model and see if there are any relevant perspectives that shed new light on your enquiry or that you might have missed and have a look at the three core functions of supervision.

Imagine an equilateral triangle in which a balance of all three core functions need to be addressed for us to be effective with our clients. Too much time on the qualitative aspect and the risk is that the supervision is too structured; too much on resourcing and it will be too comfortable; too much on transformative and it will be too challenging. See Figure 35.3.

David Clutterbuck believes "that over 90% of what is brought to supervision is not solely about the coach and clients but involves the complex interfaces with the sponsoring client organisation" (Hawkins et al., 2019), with current research "suggesting that supervisors believe half of the issues brought to them by executive/business coaches are related in some way to the original contracting between clients and their organisations" (Turner and Clutterbuck, 2019).

You will notice the emphasis on the contract in this piece: Going back to the contract gives you a clear container to evaluate progress and aid your critical reflection.

Table 35.7 Henley Eight

---

1. What did I notice?
2. How did I respond – behaviourally, emotionally, physiologically and cognitively?
3. What does this tell me about myself as a person?
4. What does this tell me about myself as a coach?
5. What strengths does that offer?
6. What pitfalls should I watch out for?
7. What did I learn from this observation/reflection?
8. What might I do differently next time?

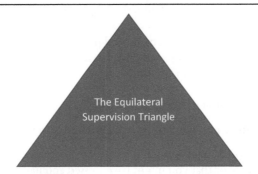

Qualitative / Accounting

Practising Competently & Ethically

Quality of the work. Contracts, ethics, organisation, context
Boundaries & responsibilities
Competencies, standards, criteria
Focussed on thinking; learning philosophy; behaviour and
technique

Risk – too structured

The Equilateral
Supervision Triangle

Resourcing / Nurturing

Support & Confront

Attending to the emotional responses to
the work personally and professionally
Transference and counter transference
Philosophy: humanistic
Reflection, supervision of supervision

Risk – too comfortable

Developmental / Transformative

Development & Growth

Reflect on content, process and skills
Action, research
Learning cycle; experiencing, reflecting,
analysing, doing, exploring methods, models and
philosophy. Exploring self as instrument
Developing competency, narrative

Risk – too challenging

Figure 35.3 The Supervision Triangle (adapted from Newton, 2012)

Notice any patterns and where you feel most comfortable. Consider how you might use those three corners to really stretch and support your practice.

Benefits of supervision

Supervision is a critical part of our CPD and it evidences to our clients that we take our professional responsibilities seriously. It offers:

- Protection to clients (cases are reviewed);
- Reflective space for practitioners (resulting in insights for improvement);
- Help for practitioners to identify their strengths and areas for development;
- Alerts practitioners to ethical and professional issues in their work;
- A forum to consider and explore:
  - ○ tensions that emerge from various stakeholders (the company, the client, the profession);
  - ○ personal impact of the work and how the coach deals with the personal reactions to their professional work;

- A third-person perspective from the supervisor who is outside of the client system and with that separation may see more of the dynamics at play;
- A forum for accountability.

(Carroll, 2008)

It can "accelerate competence, maintain professional and ethical standards and protect the psychological health of the coach" (Cochrane and Newton, 2018).

Peter Hawkins and Nick Smith capture a number of these elements in their definition:

> The process by which a coach/mentor/consultant with the help of a supervisor, who is not working directly with the client, can attend to understanding better both the client and the client system and themselves as part of the client–coach system, and by so doing transform their work and develop their craft. Supervision also does this by attending to the transformation of the relationship between the supervisor and coach and to the wider contexts in which the work is happening.
>
> (Hawkins and Smith, 2013, p. 169)

Not only is the learning accelerated, it is also tailored to you and your client situations. You develop greater awareness of your signature strengths as well as developing your own internal supervisor. It offers you a pause to take a helicopter view and critically reflect on your own patterns and how these are affecting your client work, allowing you to notice deeper systemic patterns for you, your client and their systems. However much work we have done on ourselves, there is always more to learn, and working in supervision is a place where we won't be let off the hook. Expect to be re-energised, leave with greater clarity on next steps far more quickly than if you'd tried to get there on your own, new learning with more choices and more ideas for next time.

Healthy supervision enables us to integrate that learning and develop our ethical maturity as professionals, which Michael Carroll and Elizabeth Shaw define as:

> having the reflective, rational, emotional and intuitive capacity to decide actions are right and wrong or good and better, having the resilience and courage to implement those decisions, being accountable for ethical decisions made (publicly or privately), being able to live with decisions made and integrating the learning into our moral character and future actions.
>
> (Carroll and Shaw, 2013, p. 153)

Conclusion

In this chapter, we have shared an overview of supervision, a range of definitions and how to make it work for you and your clients. Coaches bring their own development to coaching, their discomforts (conflicts of interest, values clash), conversations that have triggered an emotional response, where choices are to be made that affect the client, the organisation, the coach and where there is no right or wrong, as well as when a coach needs a safe space to explore and make sense of their own thinking and feeling. Many coaches report that some of their most useful supervision is when they didn't think they had anything to bring. We invite you to revisit your supervision arrangements and alliance. What will take your coaching to the next level and how might you use your supervision now to support yourself as you continue with your mastery of our craft?

References

Association for Coaching (2019a) Coaching Supervision Guide. [Accessed 25 April 2019] https://cdn.ymaws.com/www.associationforcoaching.com/resource/resmgr/accreditation/coach_accreditation/supporting_documentation/ca_supervision_guide.pdf

Bachkirova, T. et al. (2020). 'Supervision: a systematic literature review'. *International Coaching Psychology Review*, 15(2), in press.

Brown, B. (2012). *Daring greatly. How the courage to be vulnerable transforms how we live Penguin group*, London: Penguin Books Ltd.

Carroll, M. (1996). *Effective supervision for the helping professions*. London: Sage Publications.

Carroll, M. (2008). 'Coaching psychology supervision: Luxury or necessity?'. In S. Palmer and A. Whybrow, eds., *Handbook of coaching psychology, a guide for practitioners*. Hove: Routledge, pp. 431–448.

Carroll, M. and Gilbert, M.C. (2005, 2011). *On being a supervisee: Creating learning partnerships*, 2nd ed. London: Vukani Publishing.

Carroll, M. and Shaw, E. (2013). *Ethical maturity in the helping professions: Making difficult life and work decisions*. London: Jessica Kingsley Publishers.

Cochrane, H. and Newton, T. (2018). *Supervision and coaching, growth and learning in professional practice*. Abingdon: Routledge.

EMCC (2020) Supervision. Retrieved on 23rd April 2020 from https://www.emccouncil.org/quality/supervision/ and https://www.emccouncil.org/quality/supervision/guidelines/

Global Code of Ethics (2019). Retrieved on 23rd April 2020 from https://www.globalcodeofethics.org/

Hawkins, P. (2018). 'Chapter 28.' *Coaching supervision, The complete handbook of coaching*, Third Edition. In E. Cox, T. Bachkirova, and D. Clutterbuck (ed), London: Sage Publications, pp. 434–450.

Hawkins, P. and Smith, N. (2006). *Coaching, mentoring and organizational consulting, supervision and development*. Maidenhead: Open University Press/ McGraw Hill Education.

Hawkins, P., Turner, E. and Passmore, J. (2019). *The manifesto for supervision*. Henley on Thames: Henley Business School. ISBN: 978-1-912473-24-3.

Hay, J. (2007). *Reflective practice and supervision for coaches*. Maidenhead: Open University Press/McGraw Hill Education.

Hewson, D. (2016). 'Social power in supervision'. Retrieved on 26 April 2020 from www.reflectivesupervision.com.

Hewson, D. and Carroll, M. (2016). *Reflective practice in supervision*. Hazelbrook, NSW: MoshPit Publishing.

Hodge, A. (2016). 'The value of coaching supervision as a development process: Contribution to continued professional and personal wellbeing for executive coaches'. *International Journal of Evidence Based Coaching and Mentoring*, (14)2, pp. 87–106.

ICF. (2020). 'Coaching supervision'. Retrieved on 23 April 2020 from: https://coachfederation.org/coaching-supervision.

Karpman, S. (1968). 'Fairy tales and script drama analysis'. *Transactional Analysis Bulletin*, 26(7), pp. 39–43.

Kolb, D. (1984). *Experiential learning*. Englewood Cliffs: Prentice Hall.

Malik, K. (2014). *The Quest for a Moral Compass*. London: Atlantic Books Ltd.

Micholt, N. (1992). 'Psychological distance and group interventions'. *Transactional Analysis Journal*, 22(4), pp. 228–233. doi: 10.1177/036215379202200406.

Murdoch, E., Arnold, J., Hodge, A., Magill Sr, S.P., Patterson, E., Mackenzie, I., Lanz, K. and Prentice K. (2013). *Full spectrum supervision "Who you are is how you supervise"*. St Albans: Panoma Press Ltd.

Palmer, S. and Whybrow, A. (2019). *Handbook of coaching psychology*, 2nd ed. Hove: Routledge.

Passmore, J. (2006). *Excellence in coaching, the industry guide*. London: Kogan Page.

Passmore, J., Peterson, D. and Freire, T. (2013). 'The psychology of coaching and mentoring'. In J. Passmore, D.B. Peterson and T. Freire, eds., *Wiley-Blackwell handbook of the psychology of coaching and mentoring*. Chichester: John Wiley & Sons, pp. 1–11.

Proctor, B. (2008). *Group supervision, a guide to creative practice*, 2nd ed. London: Sage Publications.

Turner, T., Lucas, M., and Whitaker, C. (2018). *Peer Supervision in Coaching and Mentoring: A Versatile Guide for Reflective Practice*. Oxon, Routledge.

36 Manager as coach

Jenny Rogers

Introduction

Coaching is now seen as a key skill for managers, not only as a tool to develop their teams, but as a way of leading and managing. In this chapter, I will explore the concept of coaching for managers and how this can often be seen as a contradiction of previous assumptions about both management and coaching. In the second section, I will explore alternative styles of leadership and argue that coaching is a leadership style which can enhance individual and team performance. Finally, I will offer a questionnaire to aid managers reflection about their style of leadership and advice on how to move closer to a coaching style.

What is managerial coaching?

While most readers will be clear in their minds what is and is not coaching, managerial coaching, or a coaching style, is harder to define. McCarty and Milner (2013, p. 769) offered one definition: "Coaching managers are managers who coach their team members in a work context". Beyond this, most writers refer to the core definitions of coaching from John Whitmore, or professional bodies. At its heart, managerial coaching is when a manager uses a coaching style in the leadership of their team, which encourages their team members to take personal responsibility and develop greater self-awareness as a result of the conversation.

However, where managers are concerned there are common misapprehensions. Many managers will claim that they are already coaching their staff when in fact what they are doing is offering advice but in a terribly nice way. Julia Milner and Trenton Milner's research (2018) reported in the Harvard Business Review confirms the naïve complacency of the 98 managers in their study. Untrained participants were asked to coach each other for five minutes and then to rate their own videoed performance, while experienced coaches rated the same material. The managers thought they had done pretty well, while the experts disagreed, pointing out that mostly what the managers had done was telling not coaching. The good news here is that after only 15 hours of training, the managers' performance as coaches improved enormously.

I have heard many managers claim that coaching is an optional extra rather than a mainstream way of managing staff, or that it is a "technique" that can be switched on and off at will. It would not be at all unusual to find managers who wistfully claim that they would do more coaching if only they had more time, based on the assumption that coaching has to be a tortuously long process rather than something that can include a two-minute conversation in a corridor. Others will tell you that they consider it to be a fad and that if they wait long enough, it will surely pass.

None of this is surprising when you remember that management itself is a relatively young profession and that its origins in the late 19th century have been permanently influenced by the theories of Frederick Taylor at Bethlehem Steel in Pennsylvania and whose ideas about "scientific management" were the forerunner of every later attempt to improve productivity and control through top-down methods involving measurement and scrutiny.

Think about any organisation you know well. Does it set objectives and expect them to cascade downwards? Does it have a performance appraisal system with bonuses? Do people have targets and Key Performance Indicators? Do people work long hours with implicit encouragement to leave their personal lives at home? Are the most senior people permanently exhausted? Do bosses confuse giving orders with being in control? Is there an assumption that leaders can influence everything right down to the last detail on the shop floor and that if any or all of this doesn't seem to be working then you simply have to try the same tactics but harder? The more of these questions are answered with a yes, the more likely it is that some version of scientific management is still firmly planted in the heads of the organisation's bosses.

Mostly these ideas achieve precisely the opposite of their intention. They result in pointless meetings, demotivated staff, frontline staff who "know what's really going on" while those at the top remain in sunny ignorance. These beliefs waste time and energy, creating fear and dependency because people are too risk-averse to make their own decisions, dread punishment and skilfully delegate upwards. This then produces decision-making bottlenecks at the top of the organisation. No wonder that, the more senior you are, the longer the hours you work and the more stressed you are likely to feel.

The other pervasive influence on all of this is the impact of the military. In the 19th and early 20th centuries, armies were one of the few examples of large organisations. Ordinary soldiers, whether conscripts or volunteers, tended to be barely educated men, often with poor health. An army is potentially in a constant state of emergency, so it is essential for orders to be given through a clear hierarchy and to be obeyed without question. In the middle years of the 20th century, war and National Service exposed many thousands more men and women to these ideas. Modern armies are very different, but the principles linger on; for instance, in formal corporate dress where the underlying visual metaphor is still some faint facsimile of military uniform.

There have been plenty of healthy counter-influences. One of the stated aims of Tom Peters' and Robert Waterman's best-selling book (1982) '*In Search of Excellence*' was "to challenge the bean counters". Daniel Goleman's work (1996) on emotional intelligence has filtered into virtually every leadership and management development course, and in '*Coaching for Performance*' (1992) John Whitmore made a coherent and compelling case for coaching as a mainstream way of managing people. Whitmore himself was a product of Essalin and the "Human Potential Movement" of the 1960s and 1970s in California. Here the essential philosophy was that humans have an infinite capacity for resourcefulness, that we are responsible for ourselves, can make choices in all but the most extreme circumstances and can achieve our potential without manipulating or exploiting others. The Essalin legacy, often underrated or forgotten as crucial to the development of modern coaching, thrives as the Landmark Forum even today.

Along with all of this has been a sharp decline in automatic respect for authority. Ordering people about no longer works, if it ever did. This creates the central paradox of a manager's work. The only justification for being a manager is to manage performance, holding people to account. Everything else is secondary. If you press too hard you will get resistance. If you don't press at all because you have too much faith in harmony and in wanting everyone to be happy or to like you, then you will get sloppy performance along with the chances that your own role will become an irrelevance.

Defining coaching in the world of management

In the world of executive coaching there is a wide measure of agreement about what we mean by coaching. In the world of management there is much less. Daniel Goleman (2000) offered six leadership styles, coaching was one of the six and his approach may have unintentionally contributed to this confusion. Goleman claims that each style has its pluses and minuses. His point is that the most effective leaders mix and match at least four of the styles. See Table 36.1.

This article is now 20 years old and it seems to me to be showing its age. The descriptions of coaching suggests it is a soft-belly activity. Goleman accentuates this by compares it with "counselling". He writes, "Coaching focuses primarily on personal development, not on immediate work-related tasks", though he comments that coaching is most probably poorly understood and that managers may lack the essential skills to do it well even if in the longer term it is likely to improve results.

The contemporary approach to managerial coaching is far more ambitious. It emphasises the importance of personal connection, curiosity, open-mindedness and emotional intelligence while linking this firmly with the duty to manage performance. It blends management interest and support for personal goals and career development of your staff with performance standards and holding people to account. As in executive coaching, your aim is to raise self-awareness so that people make better choices, own their choices, learn – and do their best work for the organisation. It is not abdication nor is it a soft option.

This may explain why the holy grail for organisations is now *engagement*: Staff who willingly work hard, are open to learning, will take responsibility without being told and who believe that their jobs add value. It is more than "the learning organisation" and certainly

Table 36.1 Goleman's Six Leadership Styles

Coercive	Do it my way – or else. Can work in an emergency or for severe performance problems but demotivates and creates resistance.
Authoritative	Inspires; sets direction while giving a degree of freedom around how to implement it. Can work where there have been long standing problems; less effective where the leader lacks credibility in technical expertise relevant to the role.
Affiliative	Puts the emphasis on harmony and teamwork but may collude to ignore poor performance.
Democratic	Consults, builds consensus and involvement, but sometimes at the cost of swift decision-making.
Pacesetting	Drives for high performance standards but may alienate people who can't keep up.
Coaching	Concentrates on personal and career development but may not work when less motivated or less competent staff resist change.

much more than "job satisfaction". It is an intensely felt commitment to the organisation and the job – and it is rare. The reason the canny organisation wants to achieve this is because of the clear link between employee engagement and performance. Some of the benefits are described, for instance, in Michael Treacy's book (2003) *Double Digit Growth*: You retain the most talented people, they behave with more care around safety issues, sickness absence is reduced. Research commissioned by the Gallup Organization across 26 countries shows that organisations who score highly on employee engagement perform nearly five times better than those at the bottom.

Linking engagement with managerial coaching

What has this got to do with coaching? A simple questionnaire can help managers reflect on their own levels of engagement. See Table 36.2.

The starred items; that is, 9 out of the 12, are strongly associated with coaching behaviours. Sometimes what participants fill in shows sadly low levels of engagement. One useful question to encourage further reflection is: "What would your boss need to do to engage you more?" Followed by, "How much of this behaviour do you do yourself?".

This research fits beautifully with some classic mid-20th-century thinking based on the work of the social psychologist Kurt Lewin. Lewin set up action research projects with matched groups of boys who were given the same task. The only variable was leadership style. Lewin named the three styles *Autocratic*, *Laissez Faire* and *Democratic*. This ground-breaking work (1939) was followed up in the early 1960s by George Litwin with Harvard MBA students, repeating the experiments with similar results. The groups led in the Autocratic style were initially productive but, soon enough, disputes, protests and sabotage invariably undermined performance. The groups led in a Laissez Faire style had a pleasant time but achieved little. The groups led in the Democratic style, defined as an emphasis on goals and a great deal of good humour and reinforcing feedback, consistently outperformed the other two groups.

Table 36.2 Engagement Questionnaire

	Yes ✓	No ✓
*My boss takes a keen interest in me as a human being.		
*The organisation invests in my learning and development.		
My job is important.		
*I am clear what is expected of me at work.		
*I have helpful conversations about my future with my boss.		
*I get a lot of recognition for my work.		
*I ally myself closely with my colleagues.		
*My ideas about how things can improve in the organisation are taken seriously.		
*I'm fully able to use my skills at work.		
*I am developing in my role all the time.		
I respect what this organisation does.		
I feel well informed about what is going on in the organisation.		
	High ✓	Low ✓
Your overall level of engagement?		

(Tables 36.2 and 36.3 are reproduced by kind permission of McGraw Hill Education Ltd. from '*Manager as Coach*' by Jenny Rogers with Karen Whittleworth and Andrew Gilbert)

Lewin's methods and data have been subjected to some fierce critical scrutiny but it seems to me that the essential message holds true. I have re-lived and reproduced the results of this research myself, running a simulation called The Climate Lab. It was developed by the American consultant John Bray, who had worked with George Litwin – themes that are explored in their book '*Mobilizing the Organization*' (1996). Groups of managers are randomly divided into three. The task is to make paper planes to a tightly defined specification. Unknown to participants, the groups are led by actors briefed to manage the groups in the three styles identified by Lewin. In the many dozens of times I have run this simulation, the results are exactly as Lewin and then Litwin describe. In effect the "Democratic" style is just another word for coaching and effortlessly produces superior results. The democratically led group produces far more paper planes of higher quality and in a far more enjoyable way than is ever achieved by either of the other groups.

In this sense modern line management coaching builds on a hundred years of research into human motivation. Of the many distinguished 20th and 21st century ideas in this territory, the one that I find most persuasive is Richard M. Ryan and Edward L. Deci's Self Determination Theory (2000). It embraces many other similar theories. Their proposition is that for emotional health, human beings have three needs:

Autonomy: being able to make your own decisions, feeling in control of your life;
Relatedness: feeling connected to, respected and liked by others; being able to connect, respect and like in return;
Competence: having skills that you can use and develop.

Any top-down managerial style potentially breaches all three of these needs. The more managers insist, the more people are robbed of autonomy and the more their energy goes into resistance. The less a boss is able to make and encourage genuine relationships that are based on liking and respect, the less connected staff will feel. The less people are able to identify, grow and feel proud of their skills, the less willing they will be to make such skills available to the organisation. At the same time, the organisation needs to create alignment, to develop and insist on technical and behavioural standards. No wonder that being a boss is such hard work and that it takes such high levels of maturity.

Traditional and coaching styles of management compared

One way to make these differences clear is to contrast what we might call the best of the traditional approach to line management with an approach which puts coaching at the centre of the action. See Table 36.3.

The benefits of a coaching style

While most of us can cite examples from our experience of how coaching is a tool which helps employees develop and grow, there has been less research in this area than one might imagine. Taylor Sparks and William Gentry in their research looked at trends in leadership competencies since 2001. They argued that listening and communication skills that involve others, the setting of clear performance expectations and self-awareness had all become vital skills that the millennium leader must master to be effective (Sparks and Gentry 2008).

Table 36.3 Traditional and coaching styles compared

	Traditional manager	*Manager as coach*
Beliefs about my role	Power comes with the job; More seniority means more stress; Decisiveness is important; I add value by giving direction.	I have to earn authority; Sharing responsibility reduces stress; My staff are intrinsically resourceful; I add value by developing my people.
I am good at	Giving instructions; Clarifying and analysing problems; Making decisions quickly; Offering people my solutions; Creating momentum and urgency.	Listening without judging too soon; Facilitating other people's thinking; Challenging people's self-imposed barriers; Offering feedback; Holding people accountable for jointly-made decisions.
I dread	My staff getting something wrong; Expressing uncertainty; Admitting mistakes.	Avoiding opportunities for feedback; Undermining my staff by doing their thinking for them; Showing off how experienced I am.
Enjoyment in my role comes from	Pleasure in my status and its tangible rewards.	Seeing my staff develop.

In a second study by John Larrson and Stig Vinberg (2010) the researchers noted that leaders in successful organisations were more likely to have 1–1 conversations with team members where individual and organisational goals were discussed; they were more likely to give constructive feedback, both positive and negative; and they were more likely to reflect on their own leadership practices.

In this sense, managerial coaching appears to be a response to changing expectations in the world of work. In the modern workplace, team members are more highly educated than two decades ago and have different expectations about the type and level of engagement. Managers ignore this at their peril. Failing to adapt to the new leadership characteristics according to the research is likely to lead to lower levels of performance and a manager who is seen as out of touch.

Coaching skills for line managers

Having coaching skills as a boss starts with having a coaching mindset. This is the big leap that managers find so challenging. Many managers are astonished to find out how often they are doing the opposite of genuine coaching, with behaviours like these:

Giving advice in disguise and using closed questions, which contain a hidden instruction such as "Would it be a good idea if you …?" or "Have you considered …?";

Delving into an interrogation of factual detail around some tricky issue rather than finding out what appetite the other person has to think independently or of asking first what their own ideas are;

Asking "Why?" questions, which make people close down because they feel under attack – and typically get the answer "I don't know" or else a rambling justification;

Failing to ask what people already know about a subject before launching into giving instruction;

Acting on the assumption that the core of a manager's job is to solve other people's problems by taking over their responsibilities;

Finding genuine delegation extremely difficult, secretly believing, "Only I can do this to my own very high standards".

It is still news to many managers that giving instructions, especially if offered curtly, can create biological as well as psychological defences. The amygdala, the brain's alarm signal, may see attack, and responds by sending cortisol to the prefrontal cortex, shutting down our higher levels of thinking. We become preoccupied with defending ourselves, we stop listening, trust is destroyed. The resulting response can be anywhere on a spectrum from frank aggression to the passive resistance of playing dead.

Learning to coach as a boss means working from the basic assumption that everyone is resourceful and that, with the right support, can reach their potential. When managers protest that many of the people they lead seem incapable of acting independently and allegedly want to be babied and directed all day, every day – which can indeed seem to be true – the question to ask is, "How did they learn to be like that?" followed by, "How could they learn that you now expect something different?".

The skills of coaching as a leader

The actual skills involved have a large amount of overlap with the skills that all executive coaches must also have. The five foundation skills are these: Creating rapport; listening and summarising without judgement; questioning that encourages people to think for themselves; goal-setting; challenging. None of these is an everyday skill. Genuine listening is rare. Impatience gets in the way: The belief that you already know the answer or that what the other person is saying differs so much from your own viewpoint that it is not worth paying attention properly, wanting to reform and correct others, talking about yourself and your own amazing experience, psychologising and interpreting. We can all be guilty of every one of these barriers to the genuine listening that forms the heart of coaching, whether as a boss or as an external coach. It is a shock for many managers to find out through training how poor their listening skills are, and then a relief to discover that guided practice can quickly make a positive difference.

Where managers are concerned, the other primary skill is knowing how to give feedback. This skill, crucially, takes coaching as a boss way beyond the territory described by Goleman. Can there be any skill taught on virtually every management development course and which is so underused or misunderstood in practice? Feedback is constantly confused with criticism; the two words are frequently used as synonyms. Genuine feedback is given for the benefit of the receiver, its aim is development, rather than being an excuse for the other person to unload their anger. It is a calm two-way process, descriptive rather than evaluative. When given skilfully, it can dismantle resistance, increase self-confidence and raise self-awareness.

Much of the time feedback at work is not offered at all or is not given skilfully. It may consist of vague compliments such as "Thank you, that was good, you did well". Then there may be hurtful criticism such as "Everyone thinks that you're not a team player" or convoluted statements in which some nugget of real feedback is entombed inside

equivocation and distraction. These common problems explain why so many poor per-
formers can hide successfully in an organisation, often for years, and why the high-fliers
can feel under-appreciated and leave. Neither is good for organisation health. What makes
the difference as a boss is learning how to get over your reluctance to give feedback at
all out of fear of offending or of being misunderstood and then learning how to describe
exactly what you have seen and how it affected you:

> At that meeting, I saw how well you intervened by leaning forward slightly at just the
> critical moment, keeping a smile on your face and insisting on finishing your sentence
> despite the way X tried to interrupt you. I saw how it changed the dynamic of the
> meeting. It landed really well with me, I felt proud to have you in my team. What did
> you feel about it yourself?

This kind of feedback is essential to managing performance in a coaching style. It works
for positive messages as well as negative ones, and when it becomes the default way of
managing people you would expect to see a dramatic effect on bottom line results.

Much of this is new to the managers whom I train. One way to help managers embed
these ideas is the OSCAR framework. OSCAR was developed by Karen Whittleworth
and Andrew Gilbert (for more details, see *Manager as Coach*, 2012). We feel it is far better
suited to the managerial role than the venerable GROW model. This is because it allows
for the manager-coach to disagree or add ideas at the Choices and Consequences phase, it
has an emphasis on action and, unlike GROW, specifically includes a review stage.

OSCAR is easy to remember and emphasises that there is an optimum place for a particular type of question at each phase. See Table 36.4.

Table 36.4 The OSCAR Framework

Outcome	What's the issue?
	What would you like to achieve here?
	What help do you need from me in this conversation today?
Situation	What's going on around this issue right now?
	Tell me who is involved apart from you
	What's the immediate trigger to deciding something needs to change?
	In an ideal world what would be happening?
	What's standing in the way of that ideal?
	What would you say your own contribution is here?
	What happens if you do nothing?
Choices and Consequences	What have you already tried?
	What other options have you considered?
	Might there be some other less obvious things to try?
	Taking each of the main options in turn what are the upsides and downsides of each?
	Which seems to be the best option?
Actions	What immediate action might you take here?
	What longer term plan might be sensible?
	Who else needs to be involved?
	What could sabotage this plan?
Review	What's the best way to review progress here?
	When might we review it together?

When is coaching not the answer?

When you are an enthusiast for coaching as the default management style, it is easy to overlook its limitations. In an emergency, no one needs to be coached: Crisp, direct instructions are what is needed. If you are at the end of a long process of consultation, it is part of a boss's role to call time and say which path will be followed, however unhappy some people are going to be that their own ideas will not be adopted.

Coaching may help to identify the problem, but it is also not the answer if what you see is the persistent, intrusive distress that suggests a long-term mental health problem needing the help of an expert clinician or therapist. Nor is it the solution for the most extreme type of performance problem. The give-away signs here are low levels of technical competence combined with low levels of emotional intelligence in someone who has lost the confidence of their colleagues and who has little motivation and ability to improve. Here, a formal disciplinary process is often the only solution.

I have heard some very senior bosses proudly claim that they have "a coaching culture" when what they mean is that they and their colleagues all have external coaches and, in some cases, that they have, most commendably, invested in training a cohort of internal coaches. This is a long way from having a coaching culture where a coaching style permeates every interaction at every level in the organisation, including Sales and relationships with suppliers. For a discussion about coaching culture, see Chapter 3.

Coaching as a boss is significantly different from being an executive coach, though the overlap is also enormous. As an executive coach you can be clear that the client's agenda is the one that counts, even though it is important to acknowledge that in executive coaching there are always three parties: The client, the coach and the organisation. Even so, it is perfectly legitimate to put personal issues as well as professional ones on the agenda: Clients can allow themselves to be vulnerable here in a way that it may feel unsafe or inappropriate to explore with a boss. The confidentiality boundaries are different. As an executive coach both you and the client can walk away if you wish. When you coach as a boss, it is the organisation's agenda that has to dominate; performance is at the heart of it because the boss's own reputation is intimately connected with the reputation of their staff. As the boss or as the team member, you can't just say, "This relationship isn't working" and terminate it. That makes true objectivity impossible for the manager-coach.

Conclusion

The benefits of becoming a manager-coach are clear. There is the pleasure of seeing people develop and grow, knowing that you have probably had a significant hand in the process. There will be more creativity, higher levels of problem-solving and a greater likelihood that bottom-line performance will improve. Those managers who try it will consistently report greater job satisfaction and reduced stress. Their offices are less likely to be filled with apparently powerless and unhappy people dragging in their heavy load of moans and problems and expecting the boss to magic it all away. Because coaching is based on respect rather than on hierarchical authority, relationships improve and work can become enjoyable, not a chore. Where coaching becomes deeply embedded as a shared set of assumptions about how to manage people, the organisation becomes more nimble, far better able to manage change without trauma.

The benefits can spread to improved ways of dealing with suppliers and customers too. However, these gains do not just happen by chance. Few managers genuinely know how to coach unless they have had training, and this needs the insight to see why it matters, the budget to make it happen and endorsement at the highest levels in the organisation.

References

Gallup engagement surveys (n.d.). www.gallup.com/access/239210/employee-engagement-survey.aspx?g.

Goleman, D. (1996). *Emotional intelligence: Why it can matter more than IQ*. London: Bloomsbury.

Goleman, D. (2000). 'Leadership that gets results'. *Harvard Business Review*, March–April, pp. 79–90.

Larsson, J. and Vinberg, S. (2010). 'Leadership behaviour on successful organisations: Universal or situational dependent'. *Total Quality Management and Business Excellence*, 21(3), pp. 17–334.

Lewin, K., Lippitt, R. and White, R.K. (1939). 'Patterns of aggressive behaviour in experimentally created social climates'. *Journal of Social Psychology*, 10, pp. 271–301.

Litwin, G., Bray, J. and Lusk Brooke, K. (1996). *Mobilizing the organization*. London/New York: Prentice Hall.

McCarthy, G. and Milner, J. (2013). 'Managerial coaching: Challenges, opportunities and training'. *Journal of Management Development*, 32(7), pp. 768–779.

Milner, J. and Milner, T. (2018). 'Most managers don't know how to coach people. But they can learn'. HBR, August 2018. https://hbr.org/2018/08/most-managers-dont-know-how-to-coach-people-but-they-can-learn.

Peters, T. and Waterman, R. (1982). *In search of excellence*. New York: Harper and Row.

Rogers, J. with Whittleworth, K. and Gilbert, A. (2012). *Manager as coach*. Maidenhead: McGraw Hill Education.

Ryan, R.M. and Deci, E.L. (2000). 'Self-determination theory and the facilitation of intrinsic motivation, social development and well-being'. *American Psychologist*, 55(1), pp. 68–76.

Sparks, T. and Gentry, W. (2008). 'Leadership competencies: An exploration study of what is important now and what has changed since the terrorist attacks of 9/11'. *Journal of Leadership Studies*, 2(2), pp. 22–35.

Treacy, M. (2003). *Double digit growth: How great companies achieve it – no matter what*. New York: Penguin.

Whitmore, J. (1992). *Coaching for performance*, 25th Anniversary edition. London: Nicholas Brealey Publishing.

37 Reflective practice in coaching

Ann James

Introduction

The concept of "reflection" will mean something to most of us; we are invited, in all sorts of situations and contexts, to reflect on our actions, our ideas, our behaviour, on events. Taking time to reflect provides a means for the coach to examine the evidence available about themselves, their presence and the quality of their coaching. For coaches, reflective acuity is an asset. It can be applied deliberately to enhance their propensity for self-awareness, and enrich the experience of those with whom they work. In short, it's a skill worth having. In this chapter I will examine the place for reflection in coaching, drawing upon a range of theories and models and go on to present some hands-on, practical techniques for making reflection a natural part of the coach's toolkit.

Why reflection matters

Reflection gives coaches a way of examining what they do, who they are when they are doing it and how they can do it better. In an unregulated field, every coach has a responsibility and duty of care to protect themselves, their clients, stakeholders and the wider profession. Through reflection – and in conjunction with supervision – they can explore their actions and "test" their instincts and insights in the interests of creating and maintaining a coaching environment that is physically, ethically and psychologically safe.

Reflection has a role in a coach's training and qualification as they journey towards accreditation or credentialling. It draws attention to gaps in technical, practical and academic resources that the coach may wish to address. It might also reveal areas which the coach might want to develop or explore further.

Professional bodies will usually expect applicants for membership or accreditation to be able to demonstrate the ability to reflect on their practice – International Coaching Federation (ICF), European Mentoring and Coaching Council (EMCC), Association for Coaching (AC), to name but a few, all encourage reflection as part of the coach's period of training and development.

It is through reflection that we all can become aware of our otherwise out-of-awareness patterns. These patterns show up in the behaviour, thinking, attitudes and beliefs of coaches, just as they do in everyone, whatever their context. Bringing these patterns into awareness can help coaches to identify their natural strengths: What comes most instinctively to them and how they can leverage that; what approaches they are drawn to and, conversely, what they might be resistant to trying.

Regular engagement with reflection can therefore help to crystallise one's identity as a coach, bringing a useful clarity not only to the coach's self-perception but also to their capacity to differentiate themselves in a competitive coaching marketplace.

Later in this chapter, we'll be dipping into some practical activities that coaches can use to aid reflection; there are also some examples taken from practice to illustrate how some of these can be applied. First, let's consider some of the theories that underpin the approaches we'll be illustrating.

Theories of reflective

Donald Schön (1991) was a leading MIT social scientist and consultant. He examined five professions – engineering, architecture, management, psychotherapy and town planning – to understand how professionals in practice solved work day problems. He described an attentive process of experimentation, of "probing, playful activity by which we get a feel for things. It succeeds when it leads to the discovery of something there" (Schön, 1991, p. 145).

He distinguished between two kinds of reflection: Reflection-*in*-action and reflection-*on*-action.

Reflection-*in*-action is the kind that takes place during the "doing" stage. For the coach, that would suggest bringing reflective awareness to the coaching conversation as it is happening and, in doing so, making it possible to adapt his interventions, demeanour and decisions there and then, in service of the desired outcomes.

Reflection-*on*-action takes place later. The coach will look back at the conversation and seek insights that serve his wider learning.

Schön advocates that we develop our professional competence as much through reflecting on our actions as we do through gaining knowledge; it's a process of systemic feedback, review and adapting how we do things which is ongoing and cyclical, not linear or transactional.

Cassidy, Jones and Potrac (2004) were interested principally in sports and athletics coaching. They identify three levels of reflection – technical, practical and critical – which transfer elegantly to the world of coaching.

Technical reflection could be described as the "entry level" and demonstrates what many coaches would recognise as something they do already. It involves the application and effective use of knowledge in order to establish *whether* stated objectives were achieved: Was the session successful? did the coaching "work"?

The Practical stage involves a closer examination of *how* and *why* the objectives were met or not met, and the impact of the individual coach's contribution to the outcome: What precisely was done? What drove the coach's decisions to do it that way?

Equipped with these, the coach can move on to the Critical stage of their enquiry. This is the most considered level of reflection, opening up insights into the effects of the perceived meanings, biases and understanding of applied knowledge that the coach brings to their work. Beyond this level lies the deep learning that can be drawn upon for future benefit.

Jones (2018a; 2018b) similarly looks to sports coaching as a useful source, identifying three questions to prompt reflective learning: What? So What? What Now?

In asking *What?* the coach is invited to describe what has happened factually, in terms of observable evidence. This is a purely descriptive process. Moving to *So What?* helps to establish why it is important to examine what has been observed. It overlays the descriptive with a more theoretical approach, prompting insights into what has been described. *What Now?* suggests time for action, focusing the coach's attention on how those insights can influence and inform what they do next time. There are clear similarities here with the Action Learning model (Revans, 1998). This is expanded on later in the section on Supervision.

Whilst some frameworks we use in reflective practice are sequential in nature, reflection itself is a non-linear and cyclical process.

Kolb (1984) defines learning as "the process whereby knowledge is created through the transformation of experience" (Kolb, 1984, p. 38). His theory of experiential learning and the Reflective Learning Cycle gives us a useful frame of reference for reflective practice, suggesting that learning happens when knowledge is expanded through the reflective examination of actual experience. Kolb identified four stages in the cycle:

The first is *Concrete Experience*: That's when something happens for the first time, or a previous event is experienced in a new way. When it has happened, the reflector moves on to *Reflective Observation*, which flags up any inconsistencies between the experience itself and their prior understanding or expectation of how it would be. The scene is then set for some *Abstract Conceptualising*, noting any new ideas and insights that are emerging from the reflective observation. Energised and equipped with these, the reflector – the coach - can get busy with *Active Experimentation*, generating and committing to ways they can apply those new ideas and insights to their future coaching to see what happens. Then it all starts again.

The coach in the coaching

Reflection sits at the heart of coaching: Coaches guide their clients through an essentially reflective activity, whilst simultaneously drawing upon their own "inner voice" to do it as best they can. The coach is not an outlier in the coaching setting; they are an intrinsic part of the dynamic and, as such, contribute to what plays out in the coaching interaction. The coach is *a part* of what happens, not *apart* from it. Whatever one's chosen model or preferred approach to reflection, one's practice of it is likely to be enhanced by recognising and working through certain identifiable stages.

Jackson's Four Cornered Model (2004) is a reliable "catch all". It gives us a useful checklist when choosing resources for reflection: Balance, Objectivity, Perspective and Capability. The model is applicable to all of the approaches explored and illustrated in the rest of this chapter.

Reflection encourages us to become aware of our preferences and biases by challenging our "default" ways of experiencing and interpreting events. We are then better placed to engage. It's a bit like working those muscles that have become a bit lazy or underdeveloped because we tend to rely on the ones that have already strengthened without thought. In learning about how we learn, we extend the range of options available to us and create *Balance*.

Reflection allows us to review events with a degree of emotional and temporal distance. In the immediacy of the moment, events can have an impact that drive – and can then be driven by – our emotional responses and reactions. For example, an encounter, a conversation or any other stimulus that leads us to feel threatened, unsure of ourselves or defensive can set off physiological processes in the body that inhibit our capacity to be at our best. From a position of reflection, the event and its consequences can be considered with *Objectivity*, affording opportunity for measured insight and learning.

Perspective becomes possible through this objectivity. In stepping back from the confines of immediacy, we can take a bigger view of the matter in hand. We are more able to extract the learning from the experience, and to take that learning into future events, meaning that when we encounter similar challenges, we can engage with them in a different way.

The more we reflect, the better we become at reflecting; the better we become at reflecting, the more *Capability* we have for doing it in the moment, in real time, even as we are in the midst of events.

Developing reflective practice

Whilst reflecting is something everyone can do, some may have a greater predisposition for it than others. For those with a natural leaning toward introspection, the invitation to reflect takes one to a familiar and comfortable place. Time spent journaling or working quietly through some of the other approaches set out here is something to relish. Others might regard these as potentially isolated and lonesome endeavours, and prefer to use more physical, interactive approaches, reflecting for shorter periods or in company.

It's important that every coach identifies what works for them. This isn't the same as sticking with what comes most easily. It might help to settle on at least one or two techniques that they can engage with readily and regularly; then to experiment with some that feel less intuitive and reflect on the learning from the experimentation itself.

Developing reflective capability and supervision

The more a coach becomes used to reflecting, the more able they are to adopt a "reflexive" stance. The distinction is an important one, captured by Bolton (2014, p. 7):

> Reflection is in-depth review of events, either alone … or with critical support of a supervisor or group … Reflexivity is finding strategies to question our own attitudes, theories-in-use, values, assumptions, prejudices and habitual actions; to understand our complex roles in relation to others.

The *reflective* coach will typically engage in a coaching session, then go away and mull over that session using any number of approaches or frameworks that allow them to think deeply about it. The *reflexive* coach has the ability to elevate their application of those reflective skills, noticing and working with their unique imprint on the coaching session as it happens, and so informing their choices in real time, coaching with greater agility and awareness.

The International Coaching Federation (ICF) advocates reflective practice through supervision as a vehicle for "illuminating the corners and rooms that we are not paying attention to".

Supervision is a powerful medium for reflection in the company of another or others, bringing an important extra dimension to the – also valuable – solo reflective activities that the coach will be engaging in independently.

Supervision provides a framework and guided environment, facilitated by a trained supervisor, where the coach can bring and extend their reflections on their work. It's an opportunity to engage in a two-way exploration which can shed light on otherwise uni-dentified blind spots, biases and gaps.

The supervisor can prompt new thinking and insight in the coach by encouraging him to adopt a "fly on the wall" view of himself in the context of the coaching relationship: For example, how do his values and personal qualities show up? Does he want to "be helpful"? Offer solutions or advice? Share his stories and experiences with the client?

What information can the coach get from their feelings and responses in the coaching relationship? If the coach doesn't recognise them as "mine", where might they belong? Is the coach picking up feelings that could be a clue to what is going on in the client's world?

What experiences might the coach have had elsewhere that are present in the coaching in a way that might hinder the work?

Group supervision is conducted in a variety of ways, informed by the skills and prefer-ences of the supervisor and the needs of the group members. Group supervision some-times draws on the Action Learning Set model (Revans, 1998), which was designed to examine complex, real-world challenges and problems with a diverse group of peers. The "Set" follows a structured reflective process, encouraging curiosity, creative insight and a commitment to turn words into possible future actions and commitments. The group reconvenes to explore the outcomes and to consolidate learning.

Techniques for reflective practice

In this section, we'll consider some hands-on reflection tools and set out some step-by-step suggestions for giving them a try. The "Stories" are those of coaches who have shared their experiences in supervision.

Metaphor and visualising

Both these approaches engage the imagination, creating the possibility of distancing one-self from the immediacy of a perplexing or emotive scenario, making it easier to engage with, rather than retreat from it. Metaphor gives us a way of making sense of something by seeing it in terms of something else with similar qualities or dynamics that we already know; visualising is an implicit aspect of working with metaphor, "seeing" differently with the mind's eye.

Box 37.1: Story

My supervisor invited me to speak for a few minutes about what was on my mind. I offloaded some wor-ries about a recent coaching session where I had introduced a coaching technique and lost my way part way through. I thought I looked incompetent, I was anxious and felt I never really got back on track. My confidence had been hit; I was due to meet the client again the following week and I felt embarrassed.

My supervisor asked me to pause, close my eyes and notice any images that came to mind.

I saw a twisty, bumpy road with lay-bys and tracks off to the left and right.

My supervisor then suggested we take a few minutes break. Then he asked me to talk about my image: "What do you notice?"; "What stands out?";

The words came easily, if slowly:

the road looks rough and bumpy … those lay-bys make me feel anxious, like I'm hesitating, stalling; it's where you pull over with a puncture … I feel my hands gripping as I look at those bends … I wonder where the exits go? … my road doesn't have a clear end, it just fades into the distance.

My supervisor's final question took me deeper into reflection:

"What does your image have to say to you about the coaching session you described?"

After a pause, I remember feeling my face relax and smiling softly. The insights started to come:

the road has texture; coaching is all about light and shade, nuance … the lay-bys are places to pull over and to pause; I can slow down, draw breath and think … the bumpy moments will hurt less if taken at low speed … go easy on those bends, loosen up, be curious about what's around the corner … I wonder where the exits go? there's always an alternative route.. like my road, the session didn't have a clear destination … how can I address that in setting goals and outcomes?

I left feeling settled, fired up and with ideas for things to try. And I'd completely forgotten that I had felt incompetent!

In a group, one coach can talk freely about their enquiry for a few minutes whilst others notice and capture in sketch form the images or scenes that come to them. They then simply hand the sketches to the coach with no verbal description or requirement to explain. What do they prompt in the coach's thinking?

Working with pictures and space

Mind mapping, drawing or working with spatial representations (for example, as with constellations work) are all ways of bringing visible order to arbitrary elements of an event.

Such approaches help us to see connections and relationships that might be inaccessible by just thinking or talking. Sketching out an image, setting to work with some coloured pens and a blank page, arranging a handful of pebbles on a table top, for instance, all are ways of creating a scene for reflection. As with the story told above, what does the scene have to say about the coach's enquiry? What are the emergent insights and learning?

Keeping a reflective learning log or journal

Keeping a private log of events, thoughts, ponderings, niggles and experiences is a way of building a rich and diverse treasure trove of raw material for reflection. The treasures may be collected in written form, be recorded either as audio or audio/video, or be sketched, photographed or captured in any number of other ways.

Newby (2018) suggests a series of questions and activities to keep in mind when building a log:

What to ask:

- What happened in the session?
- What techniques and tools were used and were they effective?
- What did you learn about the client?
- What issues remain?
- What were the action points agreed?
- What did you learn about your coaching?

What to do:

- Gather information and evidence by describing the incident and explaining the context;
- Reflect by teasing out what you were trying to achieve and noticing what were the consequences of your actions;
- Identify the learning by analysing how you feel now, whether you could have acted differently, what you have learned and how that learning will influence your future practice.

Hay (2007) offers six steps for working deeply and reflectively with log material, which may be applied and interpreted as follows:

1. *Capture* events as they occur: By taking written notes, mentally "logging" what's happening, perhaps supported by an audio/video recording of the session (being diligent about confidentiality and contracting);
2. *Review* those events: Alone or with others, using a reflective model such as those discussed here to gain insight into what was going on in the session;
3. *Review* a series of sessions to look for patterns, paying attention to any themes that may be showing up in the coach's beliefs, behaviours or emotions. For example, offering advice, paying disproportionate attention to "favoured" elements of the conversation, feeling anxious about competence. Useful tools might be a learning journal, log or a map, highlighting words and phrases that draw attention;
4. *Plan* ahead to implement the learning points that have emerged, with the intention of applying these to deliver better coaching. These may be specific, small changes and experiments that can then be reflected upon further once tried;
5. *Plan* for intentional application of that learning to specific events, deciding exactly when, how and with whom to introduce something different. This helps to keep the change manageable, and ensures it is introduced in a deliberate and ethical way;
6. *Do* it, stick with the plan and capture what happens – this creates a new "event" to work with, effectively starting the entire cycle again.

The act of writing is something that most of us are able to do; drawing upon writing as a tool guides us towards reflection via a familiar path. We all write; reflective writing requires us to think about how we write differently, moving to a more reflective stance.

Rosinski (2003) advocates journaling as a means of engaging with reflective practice, suggesting "a coaching journal is a valuable tool to help you reflect on your own personal journey, to aid your thinking about what is truly important to you … where you can capture insights and learn from experience" (p. 16).

Moon (2004; 2007) is particularly interested in the activity of reflective writing. She acknowledges that reflection is tricky to define and to demonstrate with any degree of consensus, evidenced by just some of the approaches and models explored in this chapter. It can therefore be tricky to communicate and to grasp quite what is required in stepping into "reflective practice".

She provides what she calls a "map" for reflective writing, identifying four levels which I have characterised with the following titles (i) description writing, (ii) shallow reflective writing, (iii) reflective writing and (iv) deep reflective writing.

Box 37.2: Levels of reflective writing

Level 1: Description or reporting of what happened: Typically this is written as a blow-by-blow account of observable events;

Level 2: Shallow reflective writing: This includes an acknowledgement of the raw materials for reflection, perhaps by noting the impact of the events described, but without taking it any further into the reflective space;

Level 3: Reflective writing: This includes evidence of self-awareness and some attention to one's own and others' motives and impact on events;

Level 4: Deep reflective writing: This exhibits clear evidence of the writer taking a more objective view of events, being curious about what they notice, learning from their observations and considering how they might apply the learning in future.

For most people moving straight to deep reflective writing is a step too far. Instead those new to reflective writing need to undertake a journey of development, which starts by recognising they probably use a descriptive style in most of their current writing tasks and aiming to add some reflection to their work. The next stage is to move to Level 3, with a consistent use of a reflective voice and finally over time to develop a deep reflective stance.

Box 37.3: Story

A coach came to supervision with a concern about an ethical dilemma. She had made these notes, which she brought with her:

Tough session today and I'm on the train home feeling sick. He (the client) said he wants me to help him prepare to go for a promotion. He looked and sounded like he didn't really mean it. There's a baby on the way and his partner wants to take time out. I know from 'a reliable source' he's not in the running – on the contrary, he's probably going to be let go. Stupid me … I heard myself blabbering, congratulating him on the baby and saying I was right behind him. What was I thinking? Help!

The coach had captured her narrative in mainly descriptive terms (Level 1), with some evidence of Level 2, noticing the impact of events ("Feeling sick", "Stupid me", "What was I thinking?", "Help!").

Using Moon's approach, this coach was able to take the reflection further and deeper, first to Level 3:

I'm noticing how agitated I feel, cross at myself for taking the easy option and actually a bit angry with him for springing that one on me. I notice I'm feeling responsible for protecting his family; I wonder why that might be? I feel I've been put in a difficult position by the company sharing their reservations about him with me.

Then into Level 4: I'm curious about that feeling of having this sprung on me; I rarely get taken by surprise. I wonder if that feeling's relevant for him? where's the anger coming from? and the feeling of responsibility? Next time, I'll share my feelings with him – lightly and in the spirit of curiosity – and be fine if he brushes me off. I also need to speak to the sponsor to clarify boundaries and encourage my client to have a conversation with his boss about his aspirations.

With further reflection and by following through on her commitment to action, the coach discovered in the next session that her client and his partner had been taken by surprise by the pregnancy; he was feeling a weight of responsibility for his family and was worried that he might lose his job. The coach focused her attention on supporting him to prepare for a conversation with his boss. That opened up the possibility of a sideways move with longer-term prospects if he committed to further training.

In her seminal book, *The Artist's Way*, Julia Cameron (1994) advocates a daily, private writing exercise, *The Morning Pages*, as a discipline for capturing one's apparently random thoughts.

> These daily morning meanderings are not meant to be *art*. Or even *writing* … Pages are meant to be, simply, the act of moving the hand across the page and writing down *whatever* comes to mind. Nothing is too petty, too silly, too stupid or too weird to be included.
>
> (Cameron, 1994, p. 10)

The idea is that the writer sets aside time first thing in the morning, even before getting up, to fill three pages with continuous writing. In adopting a judgement-free, stream of consciousness approach to capturing deliberately unorganised thoughts on paper, one can clear the mental clutter and re-connect with a more centred state. These pages have no need to "make sense"; no-one else will read them. In fact, Cameron suggests that even the writer doesn't re-read them for at least several weeks.

As a doorway to reflective insight, the combined act of emptying out, leaving be, then returning later is a powerful one, whatever one then chooses to do with the results.

Working with feedback

Feedback is rich source of material for reflection. Skiffington and Zeus (2003) identify three important components of feedback: Data gathering, measurement and evaluation. Coaches can elicit feedback in each of these areas from several sources: For example, their individual clients, their corporate sponsors and their peers. The client might be asked to offer their thoughts on what happened in a coaching session (the data), perhaps using some form of scaling to quantify their responses (the measurement) and then to share how effective or otherwise the coaching session was in relation to their desired outcomes (the evaluation). A series of sessions undertaken as a coaching package could be reviewed in this way, too, inviting feedback from the sponsor and other stakeholders.

The Henley Eight

Henley Business School (Passmore and Sinclair, 2020) has developed a resource for its coach training programmes; "The Henley Eight". This framework supports reflective thinking and writing through the application of eight questions, designed to bring the coach's attention to the responses they have, in the moment, when events occur. More significantly, they keep the focus on what the coach can learn about themselves from those responses.

It can be very easy to attribute one's responses to the other person or the event, locating the reasons for one's responses somewhere "out there": "He annoys me", rather than "when he does that, I feel annoyance"; "she's too much", rather than "in her company I can feel overwhelmed".

Behind our feelings and thoughts are deeply held personal beliefs and values that can lead us to interpret or judge other people and their motives. Once we can recognise those beliefs and values as ours, rather than allowing them to be at the mercy of external events, we are better able to take ownership of our responses and to learn from them.

The Henley Eight offers a pathway, one question at a time:

- What did I *observe*? (noting visual and auditory evidence that could be picked up by a video camera;
- What was my *response*? (noting emotions, physical sensations or physiological indicators evoked by what just happened);
- What does this tell me *about me*? (rather than what do I interpret this response to mean or tell me about them);
- What does this tell me about myself *as a coach*? (based on what I have just learned about myself);
- What *strengths* does this offer? (how what I have just learned about me as a coach might serve my coaching practice);
- What are the potential *pitfalls*? (how what I have just learned about me as a coach might hinder my coaching practice);
- What did I *learn*? (noting what I can take forward into my practice);
- What might I *do differently* next time? (committing to applying the learning).

Box 37.4: Story

A coach used The Henley Eight framework to reflect alone on a couple of minutes of a coaching session. The client had come to the session very excited and with "great news for you". At the last session, she had asked for her coach's help in preparing for a presentation to an important potential client. She had just heard that the pitch had been successful and she wanted to thank the coach for "making it happen". When the excitement settled, the coach felt he had got a bit carried away and shared his reflections with his supervisor:

What I noticed was: She bounded into the room, smiling, hugged me, said "I've got great news for you" and "I couldn't have done it without you";

My response is/was: I felt flattered, a bit superior, hugged her back, "caught" her excitement and was a bit over the top;

What that tells me about me is: I enjoy praise and like being told I was responsible for someone's success;

What that tells me about me as a coach is: I want to be seen as an expert helper;

What this says about my strengths as a coach is: I will be driven towards achieving successful outcomes;

What this says about my potential pitfalls as a coach is: I might lead my client to my version of their success so that I can share or claim the glory;

My learning/reflection is: Flattery, appreciation and success can be very enticing to me; I can now recognise the emotional and physical signs that I'm being drawn in;

I will apply this new insight/learning by: Focusing on acknowledging my clients' successes and place the credit for their achievements with them. My role is to support the coaching process that enables their success.

Conclusion

In many professions and educational settings, reflective approaches are becoming increasingly commonplace as ways of supporting development and a culture of lifelong learning. In times of constant and rapid change, learning cannot be confined to organised training and education alone. Perhaps more than ever before, our experiences are our main educators. Some experiences will be planned, leading to intended learning; others will be unplanned and unpredictable and the learning therefore emergent. Reflective practice gives us a means of engaging with our experiences productively: That is, having ways of recognising what we know *after* having an experience that we didn't know *before* having it, then being able to articulate how we intend to *apply* that new knowledge to future experience. Coaching is by nature reflective; it's about asking the client to pause and spend time examining their thoughts, feelings and behaviours as a means of bringing about desirable change. It follows that the reflective coach who examines themselves in such a way will be better placed to bring about desirable change in how they work.

There are many different ways to reflect; some of them have been introduced in this chapter. What they all broadly have in common is pausing the action, asking critical questions, being receptive to answers and insights outside of one's typical range, being willing to apply those, to experiment and to take measured risks in the interest of growing capability and expanding future resourcefulness. Importantly; enjoy it. Without the "feelgood" factor, reflection is unlikely to be sustained (Chivers, 2003). Find what works, nurture variety, work through the tough bits and then do it all again.

References

Bolton, G. (2014). *Reflective practice writing and professional development*, 4th edition. London: Sage Publications.

Cameron, J. (1994). *The artist's way, a course in discovering and recovering your creative self*. London: Souvenir Press.

Cassidy, T., Jones, R. and Potrac, P. (2004). *Understanding sports coaching, the social, cultural and pedagogical foundations of coaching practice*. London: Routledge.

Chivers, G. (2003). 'Utilising reflective practice interviews in professional development'. *Journal of European Industrial Training*, 27, pp. 5–15.

Hay, J. (2007). *Reflective practice and supervision for coaches*. London: McGraw Hill, Open University Press.

Jackson, P. (2004). 'Understanding the experience of experience: A practical model of reflective practice for coaching'. *International Journal of Evidence Based Coaching and Mentoring*, 2(1), pp. 57–67.

Jones, G. (2018a). What is reflective practice, Spielverlagerung, Retrieved on 18 June 2020 from https://spielverlagerung.com/2018/03/07/what-is-reflective-practice/

Jones, G. (2018b). 'Good reasons to become a reflective coach'. Available at https://newbycoachlive.wordpress.com/2018/02/05/5.

Kolb, D.A. (1984). *Experiential learning: Experience at the source of learning and development*. London: Prentice-Hall.

Moon, J. (2004). *The handbook of reflective and experiential learning*. London: Routledge Falmer.

Moon, J. (2007). 'Getting the measure of reflection: Considering matters of definition and depth'. *Journal of Radiotherapy in Practice*, 6, pp. 191–200.

Newby, A. (2018). 'Good reasons to become a reflective coach'. Available at https://newbycoachlive.wordpress.com/2018/02/05/5.

Passmore, J. and Sinclair, T. (2020). *Becoming a coach: the definitive ICF guide*. London: Pavilion Publishing.

Revans, R.W. (1998). *ABC of action learning*. London: Lemos and Crane.

Rosinsky, P. (2003). *Coaching across cultures*. London: Nicholas Brealey.

Schön, D.A. (1991). *The reflective practitioner, how professionals think in action*. Aldershot: Avebury.

Skiffington, S. and Zeus, P. (2003). *Behavioural coaching*. Sydney: McGraw-Hill.

38 Establishing your coaching business

Michael Beale

Introduction

Running a successful coaching practice can lead to both financial and geographical freedom, together with a tremendous feeling of success and fulfilment when you've helped your clients succeed. However, many coaches struggle to make a commercial success of their coaching practice. This chapter aims to give you some pointers and questions to answer that will significantly increase your chances of developing a successful coaching practice.

In the first section I'll consider the challenge of setting up a coaching business, in the second I'll give a top-level view of the solution, in the third I'll give more detail and, finally, in the fourth section I'll summarise this into ten tips for making your practice a success.

The challenge

A major reason that many coaches struggle to make a commercial success of their practice is that they assume that developing their coaching skills is enough to establish a successful coaching practice. This may be true for a few individuals, but not for the majority. Coaching is, at least in theory, an easy career to enter. Anyone can set themselves up as a coach, and the financial cost to entry is low. Jonathan Passmore (Passmore, 2019) describes these as the "Uber-coaches", reflecting the low barriers to entry and lack of checks required in the coaching profession to establish core knowledge or fitness to practise.

Unfortunately, these low barriers to entry in an unregulated market mean that there is a lot of competition, with widely varying degrees of competence.

At the same time, many potential coaching prospects do not make commercially good clients. They may not understand the value of coaching, how it can help them, or they don't want to pay or, of equal importance, are not prepared to put the work in to get the results they want. So, attracting and contracting with the right clients to make your practice a success is not a trivial pursuit.

In addition, the traditional routes to market are full of "noise" and "confusion", so finding a way to get heard or noticed above the crowd may be a bigger challenge than many new coaches anticipate.

The solution

In my experience, there are four areas that lead to a successful coaching practice:

- Looking after yourself;
- Attracting the right clients;
- Working on the business as well as in it;
- Continually developing your coaching skills.

It's easier to invest our time and energy in what we enjoy most, rather than what we need most for our business to succeed. Curiously, it's often easier to notice this trait in our clients rather than ourselves – it may be worth investing in a coach to help you on this journey, or at least consider how you would coach yourself if you were your own client!

The good news is that, provided you invest enough time and energy into each of these areas, the challenge becomes very doable.

In this chapter I'm going to focus on the first three, with the emphasis on the second, attracting the right clients, which is often the most challenging. The rest of this book focuses on the fourth area, continually developing your coaching skills.

Looking after yourself

This may not seem a challenge when looking out from the comfort of a well-paid job. However, without that job, the regular income and support network that often goes with it, the mortgage payments and school fees can begin to look frightening which, in turn, can make prospecting and coaching even more challenging.

To turn this from a potential challenge to a genuine opportunity:

- Invest in your mental and physical health;
- Be clear about your vision for your business and your purpose, how it helps you, your clients and (assuming it does) the community in general. This will help you maintain your motivation while you establish your business;
- Ensure you have saved enough saved cash, or you have cash flow from other sources, to give your business enough time to succeed. Monitor cash flow carefully;
- Have a plan Z. Know in advance what you'll do if the business isn't successful.

At first the last point may seem counterintuitive; however, hiding from this possibility rarely works and can drain your energy. Very few of my clients that have taken the time to develop a plan Z have needed to use it, and those that have are the ones who have been surprised by how well they've subsequently done.

Unless you've previously worked in a coaching practice, establishing your practice is like going on a hero or heroine's journey. You can plan for many of the challenges you'll face, but some can't be planned for.

You'll need some of the attributes your best clients have as they overcome the challenges they face. A touch of ambition, courage, discipline and openness will be a great help.

Attracting the right clients

Many potential coaches look for the one or two guaranteed magic bullets in setting up their practice. This rarely works on its own. What works is finding out what's current best practice, and then continually testing and building on this to find out what works with your target clients in the environment they work in and with the coaching approach you use.

I've found the following ideas useful both for myself and my clients:

1) The principles of luck;
2) What's next;
3) How will clients benefit?
4) How do clients buy?
5) Who are your ideal clients?
6) How do you qualify out clients you don't want?
7) What's your proposition?
8) How do you reach out to them or get them to reach out to you?
9) Pricing;
10) Case studies, referrals and testimonials.

Let's look at what works in more detail, to give you something to build on. I'm presenting this as a linear list; however, one answer may impact the others, so it's often best to answer all these questions fairly quickly, and then start again, this time starting with "who are your ideal clients?" and then ask and answer the remaining questions in order, tailored to your prospective clients.

1: The principles of luck

When I completed a short modelling project on how coaches attracted clients, I found that many successful coaches exhibited the characteristics that Richard Wiseman identified in his book "The Luck Factor" (Wiseman, 2003).

Wiseman outlines four such factors. Incorporating these behaviours can act as an amplifier for any approach for attracting clients.

- Be proactive. We don't really know what's going to work, until we test it. Being proactive maximises our chance of success.
- Listen to our lucky hunches. We often know more than we think we do. Pay attention to our feelings and intuition. Meditative practices can help.
- Expect good fortune. This can be easier said than done if we're going through a tough patch; however, if we keep a keen look out for what might work, we're much more likely to find it.
- Turn bad luck into good. Often what we think is bad luck isn't. If we've tried something and it hasn't worked yet, we can normally develop it so it will work. Focus on what we can learn and develop, rather than what appears not to have worked.

These principles are a great starting point for any sales and marketing activity.

How are you going to use the principles of luck to establish your business?

2: What's next?

A good next step is to use a feedforward approach, developed by Marshall Goldsmith (Goldsmith, 2008). Start with a list of 6–10 potential clients that you know and create your own version of this script:

"You're someone who whose opinion I respect, I am going to start a coaching business that is going to offer clients exceptional value. I'd like your advice; can I have 10 minutes of your time?" Most people will say yes. Then ask, "If you were me and starting a coaching business, what are the top two ways you would go about attracting clients?". Whatever they say, write it down and then say "Thank you, I really appreciate your input. Is it OK if I come back to you if I have any further questions later?".

You'll end up with some great ideas, and have introduced your business, in a very professional way to several potential clients.

Variations of this approach have significantly improved the career trajectory of many of my clients.

How can you use this approach to help establish your coaching business?

3: How will clients benefit?

Clients contract with us because they perceive they will benefit in some way. We owe it to prospective clients to be clear about how they might benefit from coaching.

In my experience, coaching helps clients:

- Clarify and achieve what's important to them, literally help the client get from A to B.
- Turn learning into results – clients often know what to do, but still don't do it. Coaching can be the catalyst that makes it easier for them to take and maintain the right action.
- Significantly improve their results with respect to areas such as leadership, management and project management, sales and relationships.
- Overcome blocks such as limiting beliefs and procrastination.

Being clear about the value you offer and being able to articulate the value you bring, either in a direct, straightforward way or through case studies and stories, will help you attract clients, you'll come over better and you'll find it easier to reach out to new people.

In addition, if you're also clear about how the practice benefits you, you'll find it much easier to motivate yourself through both the good and the less good times.

Throughout our coaching assignments, and particularly when a programme has finished, it's always worth clarifying the benefit the client has achieved. It helps both our coaching and our marketing. You may find out that clients benefit in ways you hadn't yet thought of.

How will clients benefit from your coaching?

4: How do clients buy?

Something else that will increase your chances of success is if you know the steps your potential clients go through before they buy coaching services. You can then either add value by guiding them through the whole journey or focus your efforts at potential clients who are at one particular stage.

James Muir (Muir, 2016) suggests that buyers go through these stages before they contract:

- Unaware of any problem or opportunity;
- Aware of problem, but not its implication;
- Defined problem or opportunity but not a way of solving it;
- Understand and compare solutions;

- Evaluate best option;
- Justify decision;
- Final decision and contract;
- Implement.

If we want to help guide our clients through these stages, we need different activity and messages for each stage. This explains why selling any service is more complicated than we might have first thought.

- Unaware of any problem or opportunity (not a prospect; however, we can seed the idea of coaching through telling stories about successful coaching);
- Aware of problem, but not its implication (facilitate the client to understand the full implications of a problem or challenge if not addressed);
- Defined problem or opportunity but not a way of solving it (articulate how we can help our potential client solve their problem);
- Understand and compare solutions (we may introduce alternative solutions for comparison purposes);
- Evaluate best option (demonstrate how our approach is best);
- Justify decision (this if often about reducing any risk associated with what we're offering);
- Final decision and contract (contracting);
- Implement (set up for success).

It's much simpler to focus only at the latter stages, when our client has already decided they want coaching. The problem is that there may be significantly more competition at this stage, compared with a coach that can guide them through all of the steps.

How do your ideal clients buy coaching services?

5: Who are your ideal clients?

Attempting to appeal to everyone doesn't work as a marketing approach. As Seth Godin says (Godin, 2018) "begin with the smallest viable market".

Choose the people who are ambitious, are coachable, will pay well, will recommend you, you'll learn from and will enjoy working with. This means you must either reach out to the right potential clients or find a way of attracting them to you. This may mean hard work and learning new skills when you start but will pay off when your clients recommend you to others.

From a marketing perspective, attempting to market to everyone simply doesn't work. So, write out a list of the potential clients that you want to work with.

Ideally, they will have some significant problem or challenge that you can help them solve, you'll know how to reach them, they'll talk to you and either have a budget for coaching or access to one. They also need to be coachable.

Who are your ideal clients?

6: How do you qualify out clients you don't want?

Attracting the right clients can be the biggest predictor of success for your practice. It's not only attracting clients; it's attracting the right clients for you. It's equally important to know who you don't want to coach. This can save a significant amount of time and unnecessary heartache.

I've found that the following criteria works for me. If they have these characteristics, coaching always works; if they don't, it's unlikely to.

- The client has a touch of ambition, courage, determination and openness;
- They are prepared to invest at least a minimum amount of time and emotional energy to the programme;
- We select each other. The client chooses the coach, and the coach chooses the client, we genuinely enjoy working together;
- The client is able and happy to pay, provided I meet or exceed the service I've contracted to provide.

Age and sector aren't important for me, but they may be for you and the market you operate in.

I'll always qualify clients for these characteristics in either the sales process or the discovery phase of any programme. I'm happy to walk away from any client that I don't think will get value from what I do.

How do you qualify the clients that you want to coach?

7: What's your proposition?

It's useful to be able to articulate the value we offer in a couple of short sentences, so our potential clients immediately know that what we offer might be of value to them. While there are several structures, I prefer a three-part approach:

I work with ambitious people of all ages (*description of my ideal clients*)
and coach them (*verb describing what I do*)
to achieve success and fulfilment (*an example of the results I get*).

I've learnt what I say isn't so important provided I'm congruent and catch their interest enough to be able to ask them some questions to talk about what's important to them.

What's your client proposition?

8: How do you reach out to them or get them to reach out to you?

In my experience there are four key ways of attracting or reaching out to potential clients:

Hunting. This is traditional selling; we directly reach out to potential clients with an attractive proposition. While this may not be for everyone, there are many useful lessons to be learnt from good sales practice.

Three approaches that work include asking for advice, asking to take part in a research project or offering a free taster, like a leadership assessment or free discovery phase.

Attraction. This encompasses content creation and new media. The idea is to create and distribute content which appeals to potential clients so they follow you and contract with you when they have a real need for your services. This includes books, articles, podcasts and websites.

You need to be able to create content and either know about or know people that know about the latest changes in media technology and apps. While the principles may be the same as they always were, the technology is changing very quickly.

Nurturing. This is where we build very strong relationships with influencers and buyers of coaching services, so that when they have a need, they contact you first.

Existing clients are a great starting point. Developing case studies is useful, as is the offer of a small number of free coaching sessions, to help them better understand the process and what they can achieve.

Outsourcing. We pay others to market for us. This may be through paying people to sell for us, paying a commission on sales or through advertising such as LinkedIn, Google or Facebook ads.

Warning, just like gambling in a casino, this can be a sure way of losing significant amounts of money unless we test with seed investment first. In all cases we want to keep our investment as small as possible until we've achieved a positive ROI from what we're doing. We can then scale our activity.

In my experience each can be made to work, however each requires a certain skill level and therefore an investment in time to master. It's therefore recommended to choose one and master it before spreading yourself too much between all of them. Choose the best balance between how your target clients buy, and what you'll enjoy doing.

It's also worth thinking about your brand. Your brand is the sum of all the touchpoints with your clients. It is the "personality" your clients and potential clients perceive and is made up of several factors including your marketing, the price you charge, the service you give and what people say about you. If your brand is unique you have the potential of charging significantly more for the service you offer.

How will you attract the clients you want?

9: Pricing

Knowing what to charge is a key part of establishing your coaching business. Coaching fees range from free or pro-bono assignments to £250K+ for coaching top international CEOs. There are four different approaches to pricing. Free, by time, by brand and by value. Each has advantages and disadvantages, and each creates a different impression on your potential clients.

Free can be both very good and very bad. Good free clients can teach you to help them solve interesting challenges, recommend you, help you with case studies and pay you later, when they are in a situation to do so. Bad free clients don't get better, don't recommend us, complain and we don't learn anything (other than we should have qualified them out earlier.)

My recommendation is that we have stricter qualification for free clients than for clients who pay. We can, of course, choose to coach for free to give back to the community, but make it a conscious choice.

Time – Most coaches charge by time. This has the advantage that most buyers of coaching understand paying for time. The disadvantage is that we're likely to coach to fill the time available, which may not be in the best interest of the client. In addition, it's easy to compare the prices between coaches, which can push down prices.

Brand – If, for example, a CEO or celebrity asks for a coach by name or reputation, then (within reason) the coach can charge what he or she likes as they haven't any competition. It's the return on your investment for establishing a unique brand.

Value – This is where you and the client establish what you expect the client to achieve at the end of the programme, and agree a fee based on the client achieving or beating whatever criteria is set. This requires establishing realistic measurement criteria and a high level of trust between the client and coach. The benefits are the client and coach are working to totally aligned objectives, the coach is focused on helping the client achieve value and the coach has the opportunity of earning significant fees.

My recommendation is that whichever pricing approach you choose, invest in finding more about value pricing, as this method of charging is likely to lead to you improving your coaching skills on a continual basis.

How will you approach pricing?

10: Case studies, referrals and testimonials

Case studies, referrals and testimonials improve our coaching (we know what value we've helped our client achieve), the process helps our clients articulate the value we bring to others and gives us material for our marketing.

The art is to seed the idea as part of the contacting phase, rather than ask at the end of the programme. Ask a version of "If I do a really good job of helping you achieve what's important, would you be happy to contribute to a case study? (or referral, or testimonial)". Then later remind them that they agreed earlier.

How will you approach getting case studies, referrals and testimonials?

Working on the business as well as in it

It's worth taking a step back from time to time and consider all the elements that will lead to the success of your practice. We've already considered you looking after yourself and attracting clients.

In addition, you will be choosing the people you work with, you will have to keep track of your finances, particularly cash flow, which we'll discuss shortly. In addition, you'll need processes to keep all the areas of your business working effectively and efficiently. You'll need to follow all the legal and statutory rules of running a business.

Invariably you'll make mistakes, often it's the only way to learn. As Ray Dalio (Dalio, 2017, p. 352) notes, "Mistakes are a natural part of the evolutionary process. Without them we don't evolve". In marketing and establishing a successful practice we're likely to make more mistakes than we do in most endeavours.

Who will you get to help you? What will you want them to do?

Before we sum up, there are two key areas that I've found make a significant positive difference to my clients. Developing the right support network and managing cash flow.

Develop the right support network

There at least four reasons to develop the right network to support you.

1) You can share experiences, resources and ideas;
2) Some will become clients and/or introduce you to potential clients;
3) Some will be role models with significant in-depth experience in key aspects of the business;
4) We're social creatures. Starting a practice can be lonely, so having people who will genuinely help us that we're not selling to, and are not selling to us, is empowering.

Who do already have in your network? What are you doing now to grow your network? What else could you do in the future?

Managing cash flow

Building on the previous section, Alan Weiss commented (Weiss, 2008, p. 3), "Fees are actually dependent on only two things: Is there a perceived value for the services provided that justify the fee, and do both parties possess the intent of acting ethically?"

Fees, the amount you charge, are one of the most important aspects of cash flow. Others include the number of paying clients you have and how quickly they pay. On the debit side you have your marketing expenses, bad debts, how much you need to draw out of the practice and any other costs your practice incurs.

A 12-month cash flow plan is an essential part of establishing your practice. Many potential coaches use this as part of the decision whether to leave their current job and spend 100% of their time on their practice or start more slowly and start their business as a side project to their current employment.

If you run out of cash and can't borrow, your business fails.

How much cash, or additional income will you need before you start your business?

Ten points to consider for your business

To conclude, here is a checklist of actions and questions to help you succeed:

1) Imagine you were your own client; how would you coach yourself to establish your coaching business? This can be a surprisingly effective approach at improving both your coaching skills and your ability to establish your business.
2) Commit how much time you'll invest every week in 1) working with clients 2) developing and marketing the business 3) developing yourself.
3) Do you know what you will do if your business fails? At first glance this appears a very negative question. However, very few of my clients who have asked and answered it have needed to follow it through.
4) Make a list of all the people you can ask for feedback and feedforward. Confirm with them that they will help you if asked. Assuming the answer is yes, ask them what they would focus on (one or two key areas only) if they were you and starting a successful coaching business. Write down their answers. Depending on their answers, feel free to modify the following questions.
5) Write out a list of potential ideal clients: What are the characteristics of the clients that you want to work with? How might they benefit from working with you? How might you contact them or how might you attract them? What would you say first? How might you engage with them? What's the first small step in the engagement process? How would you contract with them? How would you measure the success of the engagement? Write out the characteristics of clients who you would NOT work with. How would you say "no" to them politely?

6) Write out who else you need to help you with your business. This may include an accountant, PA, coaching supervisor, copywriter, social media support. What will you want from them? How are you going to contract with them?
7) Write out 2–3 milestones to achieve each quarter for the next 12 months. What are your key 2–3 focus areas for the next quarter; what additional 1–2 skills do you need to develop over the next 12 months? How are you going to measure progress?
8) Write out your cash flow forecast for the next 12 months. How many months can you work without bringing in any revenue?
9) How are you going to publicise your achievements? How are you going to celebrate every step forward?
10) Write out the long-term vision for the business. How are you planning to exit the business when the time is right?

Conclusion

Almost all the successful coaches I work with say that setting up their coaching practices turned out to be much more of an adventure and a challenge than they initially expected. However, all are grateful that they persevered. Their coaching practice has been an enabler for them to achieve financial and geographical freedom, together with a significant amount of personal satisfaction. Answering the questions posed in this chapter will significantly help you make your adventure easier and more satisfying.

References

Dalio, R. (2017). *Principles: Life and work*. New York: Simon & Schuster.
Goldsmith, G. (2008). *What got you here won't get you there*. London: Profile Books Ltd.
Godin, S. (2018). *This is marketing: You can't be seen until you learn to see*. London: Portfolio Penguin.
Muir, J. (2016). *The perfect close: The secret to closing sales*. Herriman, UT: Best Practice International.
Passmore, J. (2019). 'How to develop a coaching culture in your organization – a 10-step plan for every organization'. *17th March Serbian Coaching Conference*, Belgrade, Serbia.
Weiss, A. (2008). *Value-based fees: How to charge – and get – what you're worth*. Chichester: John Wiley & Sons.
Wiseman, R. (2003). *The luck factor: Four simple principles that will change your luck – and your life*. London: Arrow Books/Penguin Random House.

Section 7

Tools and techniques for coaches

39 Fifteen tools and techniques for coaches

Julie Flower

Introduction

During coach training, and as you progress through your career, you are likely to draw on a range of theoretical approaches and pick up a sometimes-dizzying array of tools and techniques. It may seem that each new CPD module or learning workshop you attend presents yet more handy diagrams, acronyms and models. This can sometimes seem overwhelming. A tool is only a tool and can never replace a strong client relationship, a sound theoretical base or core coaching skills. However, coaching tools can provide clients with new and helpful ways of exploring situations, reflecting and structuring their thoughts, as well as gaining commitment to act. They can also provide a refreshing change in energy and a different way of working, for both client and coach.

This chapter offers 15 tools and techniques that are drawn from areas as diverse as leadership and management theory, creative problem-solving and improvised comedy. They are deliberately described in a practical, rather than theoretical, way and are likely to suit the eclectically trained practitioner. They are intended to be used, adapted and integrated into your wider coaching practice, within the bounds of your own professional competence, preference and curiosity. You will amplify the use of the tools through the quality of your questions, your presence and your knowledge of underpinning coaching theory and the evidence around behavioural change. Many of the tools can be used equally well in individual and group or team coaching settings. It is hoped that you will find something in here to add to your existing repertoire of tools and techniques, in order to best support your clients.

Technique 1: Visual metaphors

What is the tool?

Visual metaphors are a useful tool to help clients access and explore a situation. They can be expressed in multiple ways; for example, inviting the client to draw or to cut pictures out of magazines during the session, or by using imagery/picture coaching cards from which the client can choose.

Metaphor can be a very powerful way to explore situations (past, present and future), especially where they may be complex, sensitive or difficult to express in words. Often a metaphor can more effectively capture the emotions and nuances of a situation and provide parallels that are helpful to a client in identifying and effecting change.

How is it used?

- The coach asks the client to select (or draw) an image with which they specifically identify as a metaphor, given their current situation or their goal for the future.
- The client is then asked to briefly explain why they selected the metaphor and how the metaphor relates to them.
- The coach uses the language and imagery used by the client to explore the metaphor to encourage insight and learning.
- Areas of focus might include: Their role, and the role and perspective of others in the metaphor; the benefits and pitfalls – present and future; emotions; what needs to change; learning.

When does it work best?

Visual metaphors can be very effective with clients who clearly have a preference for images and stories. However, they can also work well in bringing a fresh approach to those who usually express themselves in words. Visual metaphors are versatile and can be used to explore almost any kind of coaching scenario, including handling difficult relationships, developing new strategy or goals; and decision-making. They can provide a relatively quick route in to a complex situation and can provide a less challenging way to articulate sensitive situations, making them very useful in a team coaching context.

Technique 2: Expert Interviewer

What is the tool?

The Expert Interviewer is an exercise from improvised comedy in which a client is endowed with being an "Expert" in a specific (usually nonsensical) field and is required to answer questions on the topic. It is designed to build confidence in clients, increasing their spontaneity and flexibility of thinking, enabling them to feel more comfortable thinking on their feet and reacting "in the moment". Through practising with a "nonsense" subject, the client may observe patterns, frameworks and approaches that can help when it comes to exploring "real" subjects. The approach also generates humour in a situation that many people would naturally find terrifying.

How is it used?

- The coach endows the client with a "specialism".
- It should be a subject that appears to defy logic or is something that no one would normally be an expert in (such as teaching mice to tap dance or manufacturing edible cars).
- The coach sits or stands across from the client and asks them questions, as if they were being interviewed on a chat show or as part of a conference Q&A session.
- The questions should be open and encourage the exploration of themes that have parallels with the client's real situation (such as how they came up with such an innovative idea; how they dealt with detractors; what their dreams are for the future of the project; or what are the secrets of their commercial success) but are always specifically related to the nonsensical subject.

- In the debrief, explore how it felt for the client (emotions, physical sensations) and the techniques/resources they used to respond as the "Expert".
- Encourage the client to draw out the learning. It may then be helpful to repeat the exercise with a "real" subject.

When does it work best?

It is of most benefit to clients who are struggling with their confidence and spontaneity when speaking in public or who want to develop their style. Clients who are open to new ideas and have a sense of playfulness and fun are likely to enjoy it more, but the most learning will come for those who find public speaking and thinking on their feet uncomfortable. The coach is well-placed in this exercise to reflect back observations with respect to body language, facial expression and voice.

Technique 3: Hypothesis trees

What is the tool?

A hypothesis tree is a way to logically explore and test assumptions, recommendations or decisions. It is problem-solving tool that invites individuals to consider how much evidence is required to make a convincing case. The tool is used extensively in management consulting; it can be an efficient way to get to the heart of an issue and a compelling way to construct an argument. The tool enables the grouping of similar ideas and helps clients structure their thinking, particularly in the case of complex, multi-faceted decisions and promotes critical thinking.

It starts with an assumption and then groups arguments and evidence beneath it in a logical and ordered way. See Figure 39.1.

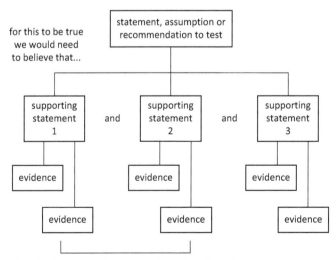

Figure 39.1 Hypothesis tree

How is it used?

- The coach asks the client to identify a hypothesis (in the form of a statement) that they would like to test. The coach invites the client to writes this on a Post-It note.
- The coach then asks the client "what would need to be true?" in order for the hypothesis to stand.
- These ideas should be captured on Post-Its and then grouped to form three or four themes (statements again) at the second level of the tree, e.g. issues relating to capacity, resources and timing might fall naturally under a theme of "It is feasible".
- The coach then explores each branch with the client by asking what evidence would be needed to make each thematic statement true and where that would be found, as well as what evidence would undermine the statement.
- Exploration is likely to lead to action-planning around collection and review of evidence; refinement or complete rewriting of the hypothesis; and an improved awareness of the most important factors for the client in their decision-making.

When does it work best?

Hypothesis trees work well when clients have a potential way forward that they would like to test or when they are faced with a complex problem and limited time and resources in which to address it. The hypothesis tree can also be a useful way to bring an evidence-based perspective and challenge to a topic. The coach helps to shine a light on potential gaps and shortcomings in the evidence. The main pitfall of hypothesis trees is the risk of confirmation bias – the selection of evidence to support the argument. Challenge from the coach and an encouragement to consider alternative hypotheses can guard against this.

Technique 4: The "Yes, and ..." exercise

What is the tool?

The concept of "yes, and" comes from improvised comedy. It is a way of thinking and interacting which focuses on accepting and building on "offers" made by others ("yes, and") rather than blocking suggestions ("yes, but"). It intends to heighten self-awareness of accepting and blocking behaviours and enable clients to practise and develop new skills. It is associated with improved collaboration, communication and creativity.

The principle of "yes, and" can be illustrated and explored through a range of exercises, either in a 1:1 or group situation. A simple approach is outlined below.

How is it used?

- The coach asks the client to imagine that they are planning a day out together.
- The coach explains that the only rules are that they will alternately make suggestions and each sentence must begin with the words "yes, and ...", trying to build on the previous idea. It is important to say that ideas don't need to be considered "rational" or "feasible".
- One will begin with an "offer", such as "let's go to the beach".
- The other will then respond with "yes, and ..." then adds something to the previous idea, such as "yes, and let's build a sandcastle".

- This should continue, alternating between coach and client for a couple of minutes, trying to keep the energy up and avoiding too many delays thinking about responses.
- Encourage the client to genuinely seek to build on the last suggestion (such as "yes, and let's make the sandcastle resemble the Eiffel Tower") rather than purely building on the general theme (such as making lots of different suggestions for things to do at the beach).
- In the debrief, encourage the client to reflect on how it felt to have to respond in the moment: When did they (feel they wanted to) block? What skills did they need? How might this be relevant to their current situation?
- A development of this exercise is then to repeat with a "real" topic (the coach may want to step aside and the client can "yes, and" themselves).

When does it work best?

"Yes, and …" works well when clients feel that they would like to be more spontaneous with their thinking and more supportive of others' ideas. A "yes, and" approach can help leaders to create more collaborative climates and more powerful individual conversations. If a client tends to jump to the negative aspects of a new idea, "yes, and" can be a powerful way of encouraging flexibility of thinking.

Clients often find "yes, and …" revelatory in its simplicity and breadth of application. A helpful homework activity is to ask the client to deliberately take a "yes, and" approach (saying it to themselves in their heads) with different types of interaction, including with family, friends and at work, and to note their reflections on the impact on themselves and others.

Technique 5: Paired comparison analysis

What is the tool?

Paired comparison analysis is a simple analytical tool which can help clients to weigh-up options and make decisions. Using a simple grid, clients are asked to compare specific pairs of options, choosing the preferred option in each pair. All the options are compared with each other in this way, with the most frequently chosen emerging as the preferred option, either to be taken forward or to prompt further research or analysis.

Where clients have a small number of options or ideas to consider but the criteria may be relatively subjective or the ideas quite different from each other, this tool provides the basis of a focused and structured conversation. See Figure 39.2.

How is it used?

- Ask the client to identify all the relevant options/ideas that they are considering, listing them with a short name (up to three words).
- Ask them to think about what is most important to them in making their decision, so they start to explore their decision-making criteria.
- The client should list the options vertically down the left-hand side of a simple grid, each denoted by a letter (A, B, C, etc.), if helpful.
- The same options should be listed across the top to produce a grid.
- Work through the grid systematically, comparing each pair of options in turn (i.e. beginning with options A and B).

	A	B	C	D	E	Total for each option
Option A		B	A	A	E	2
Option B			C	D	B	2
Option C				C	E	2
Option D					E	1
Option E						3

Figure 39.2 Paired comparison analysis

- The client should write the letter denoting the preferred option of each pair in each of the relevant squares in the grid.
- When completed, total up the choices in order to identify a preferred choice or choices.
- Throughout the exercise, encourage the client to consider why they have made the choices they have and to explore pairs of options that they find more difficult to compare in greater depth.
- The outcome of this exercise may be surprising to clients and may provoke further discussion around what is most important for clients and their next steps in researching an option or implementing a decision.

When does it work best?

Paired comparison analysis works best when there is a relatively limited number of options (no more than 8–10), and the criteria may be somewhat subjective for the client. Having to choose one option over another in each pair helps to drive insight and awareness for the client about what is most important and why.

As a decision-making tool it works well in a range of client situations, including changes in career direction, prioritisation of new product/service ideas and purchasing decisions.

Technique 6: Lifeline

What is the tool?

Lifeline is a visual tool that involves a client reflecting on key moments in their life to identify common themes and consider events and transitions in context. By drawing peaks, troughs and plateaus with respect to the level of positive, neutral or negative impact each event has had on their life, valuable insight can be gained which may help with managing life transitions, making career choices, identifying values and raising self-awareness more generally.

How is it used?

- Ask the client to draw a line across the middle of a piece of paper (or, ideally, a flip-chart) to represent their life.
- The line should include peaks, plateaus and troughs to represent the impact that each event has had on the client's life. Intensity of positivity or negativity may be represented by the height of the peak or depth of the trough.
- Encourage the client to select and represent events/moments that are meaningful to them, rather than necessarily those that others would choose.
- Use the lifeline as the basis for an in-depth discussion in relation to the client's goals.
- Areas of exploration might include:
  - What patterns do you notice with respect to the highs and lows?
  - What surprises you about the lifeline?
  - What does your choice of events tell you?
  - Which aspects of this are relevant to the present/future/your goal?
  - What insights does this give about you as a person? (Exploring values, sources of meaning, strengths.)
- The lifeline can be embellished by the client with symbols, drawings or further words as the conversation develops.

When does it work best?

Lifeline works well with clients who are keen to make some kind of significant change in their lives but are unsure where to begin. By taking a longitudinal approach, patterns and insights may be brought into a client's conscious awareness. Lifeline can also help those who are facing transitions in their life and would like to draw on learning from the past to build resilience and inform their future approach.

It can also be a helpful and relatively rapid way of accessing and exploring a complex client story at the beginning of a relationship, building a foundation for further work.

If a client has experienced a particularly difficult childhood or past, lifeline may not be a helpful choice of exercise within a coaching context or within the boundaries of an individual coach's professional competencies. Sharing the approach with the client and offering a choice of whether or not to proceed is particularly important with this tool.

Technique 7: Sculpt

What is the tool?

A sculpt is an experiential tool that involves a client "embodying" an action, idea or concept. It is a flexible tool that can be used to help a client or client group physically explore a feeling, a change or an idea, both in themselves and in relation to other people or parts of a system. The role of the coach is to help the client explore their experience during the sculpt in order to develop insight and learning in relation their area of focus or goal.

Sculpts are used in a number of coaching approaches, including as emergent creative experiments in Gestalt, constellations and in systemic team coaching. They also have origins in psychodrama and can be powerfully phenomenological. A sculpt may be static or involve movement. It may be emergent or more structured, such as exploring a metaphor or a timeline.

How is it used?

- For an *individual*, an application is to ask the client to physically embody the change they would like to make.
- After they have done that, encourage them to experiment with the embodiment to experience how (different) it feels. Prompts could be to experiment with status, physicality, emotion or positioning with respect to "others".
- You may wish to share how you are experiencing the client's embodiment. You may also invite the client to embody other stakeholders to explore their potential reactions.
- In a *group or team setting*, a potential application is in the embodiment and exploration of a situation as a metaphor. A good example is a swimming baths, with deep and shallow ends, lifeguards, changing rooms, sun loungers and any number of other details.
- Ask the group members to take up a position in the metaphorical swimming bath space that represents how they feel in relation to a relevant issue, such as the team's new strategy.
- Once everyone is in place, ask each person in turn to explain their position and their choice. Encourage members to reflect on their position in relation to others. Ask participants to articulate where they would like to be and what they might need from themselves or others to get there.
- During this exercise, people may decide to move and explore different positions in relation to each other. Ensure you give time for participants to explore the physicality of being in the space, including what that looks and feels like.

When does it work best?

Sculpts work well when clients are "stuck" in their heads and may benefit from a change in perspective. Sculpts can also help clients who want to develop the confidence to do something different and may benefit from embodying the change in the safety of the coaching session.

They can also help to explore complex and potentially challenging group dynamics in a way that focuses on the system and relationships within it, rather than individuals.

Technique 8: Ladder of Abstraction

What is the tool?

The Ladder of Abstraction is a tool used in creative problem-solving to help frame a problem or question at the most useful level and to drive the generation and exploration of options and ideas. The Ladder is based on the principle that a problem needs to be asked at the right "level" in order to come up with the most useful solutions. Using the analogy of a ladder, when you are on the higher rungs you are likely to be able to see the bigger picture and, when you are lower down, you will have greater detail. Both those perspectives are needed in order to address many complex issues.

The Ladder uses the questions "why?" (moving up the ladder) and "how?" (moving down) to help a client explore what is driving a problem, determine how best to frame it and generate ideas at the most helpful "level" to address it. See Figure 39.3.

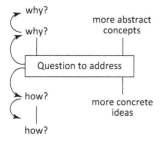

Figure 39.3 Ladder of Abstraction

How is it used?

- The Ladder of Abstraction can be used in a 1:1 or team coaching situation.
- Identify a problem question beginning with "how to …?", write it on a sticky note and put it on the wall or on a large piece of paper.
- Ask the client to identify all the reasons they can think of for why this question should be addressed. These should be listed on separate sticky notes and added to the level above the original question.
- It may be useful to continue up another "rung" or two, asking "why?" each time, to determine the root causes of the problem/question.
- Throughout this exercise, encourage the client to reflect on what "level" it would be most useful to address the problem.
- Use "how?" questions to prompt the client to generate ideas for how specific problems identified in the "why?" levels can be addressed, again, going down a number of "rungs" if it makes sense to do so.
- The client should be encouraged to generate "how?" ideas freely and creatively before considering the different options in greater detail.
- Encourage the client to identify where they would like to focus their next efforts in addressing the problem question, at the level they have framed it.

When does it work best?

The Ladder of Abstraction works well when a client is working on a complex problem that they are finding difficult to define (for instance, it may have multiple root causes and many possible solutions). It is a visual tool and enables clients to see links between issues and gain insight on how the framing of a problem can impact on how fully and appropriately it is ultimately addressed.

By encouraging the creative generation of ideas and exploration of root causes, the Ladder can work very well as a group problem-solving tool. It enables exploration at both a strategic and more operational level. A tool called a strategy map uses similar principles.

Technique 9: 2×2 matrix

What is the tool?

A 2×2 matrix is a simple grid that enables a client to map and potentially prioritise different options and ideas based on two variables determined by the client. The process of

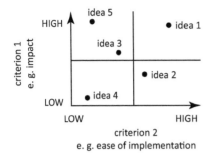

Figure 39.4 2×2 matrix

selecting the position of each option relative to the selected variables/criteria and to each other can lead to helpful insights for the client about what is most important to them and how to move forward with any decision. Popular with management consultants, the 2×2 matrix is simple, adaptable and accessible as an individual or collaborative technique to aid prioritisation, decision-making and problem-solving.

Also known as the Ansoff Matrix, it was originally developed as a strategic planning tool. However, any pair of variables can be used and the applications are very wide. Common variables include, for service improvement ideas, impact vs. ease of implementation, or for stakeholder mapping, influence vs. interest. See Figure 39.4.

How is it used?

- Ask the client if they are familiar with a 2×2 matrix and explain the basic concept.
- Draw out or ask the client to draw a grid (ideally on a flipchart) and to identify what should be on each axis (this can promote an interesting discussion about what is most meaningful for them).
- Once the axes are labelled, an optional stage is to ask the client to name each quadrant as this sometimes helps them to gain a greater understanding of their analytical process and to bring the quadrants to life.
- Using sticky notes, identify the ideas or options and ask your clients to work through placing each of them on the grid. Ask questions to help them challenge and clarify their thinking, noticing any contradictions, incongruency and times of hesitation or emphatic behaviour.
- Invite the client to step back from the grid and consider:
  ○ Is anything missing?
  ○ Does anything need to be moved in relation to each other?
  ○ Are there any placements that you are unsure about? What do you need to gain clarity?
  ○ What is this telling you about your next steps?
- Work with the client to action plan and build commitment based on their analysis and reflection. This may mean a decision to do one specific thing, to find further information and test with others, or to prioritise certain activities over others.

When does it work best?

A 2×2 matrix works best when a client has identified a number of options or ideas that they would like to weigh up against each other, in order to choose one or prioritise their course of action. It helps if a client has a reasonable amount of information about each idea or option. However, the use of the matrix can be helpful way of exposing and exploring gaps in knowledge.

It also works well as a facilitated team activity, providing a framework for exploring and agreeing what is most important and how to progress, with a strong visual reference.

Technique 10: Letter from the future

What is the tool?

This is a very simple yet powerful tool to help clients explore, articulate and build commitment towards a goal or future vision. By imagining a specific point in the future and engaging in the physical act of writing, clients can connect not only with the activities but also the emotions and thoughts of that future state. This can help build confidence and motivation, as well as a much clearer sense of what they would like the future to look and feel like. It is a playful and powerful way for a client to hold themselves to account.

How is it used?

- The technique can be used within the session or as a "homework" activity.
- Ask the client to choose a timeframe for their letter from their future self. Depending on what they would like to achieve, they may want to write more than one letter, based on different stages of their plan.
- Encourage the client to use letter paper or a card, which they can then place in an envelope.
- This is a free-form exercise but, if the client would like prompts, ask them to consider:
  - What will be happening in the future state, once the vision or change has been realised?
  - How will it feel?
  - Who else will be involved?
  - What will have been some of the high points along the way?
  - And what were the setbacks?
  - What have you learned in getting there?
  - What might be next for you?
- The letter should be placed in an envelope and kept by the client.
- At the next session, ask them to reflect on what they learned from writing the letter. They may want to share the letter but there is no obligation to do so.
- Ask them how they would like to refer to and use the letter in the future.

When does it work best?

Clients who enjoy writing are likely to enjoy this exercise, but others may derive benefit and could be encouraged to begin with a postcard if a letter seems too challenging.

The approach works well with clients who would like to instigate significant change in their life or career and may have doubts about the feasibility of the plan or their own motivation to get there.

Technique 11: Crazy Eights

What is the tool?

Crazy Eights is a flexible and creative tool to rapidly enable a client to gain different perspectives on an issue or to develop new ideas for a product, service or change in their lives. Originating in the design industry, it puts clients on the spot to respond creatively and spontaneously in the moment to question prompts related to the goal or theme of the coaching.

Using one sheet of paper, a client generates eight images or responses in eight minutes before taking a step back to explore certain ideas or wider themes in more detail. The technique helps to free-up the mind and encourage flexible and playful engagement with a topic, which often leads to new insights and ideas.

How is it used?

- Give the client a piece of paper (A3 or A4) and ask them to fold it into eighths and then reopen it again so the folds are visible. Place the sheet vertically so the client has four pairs of horizontal boxes in front of them. Ideally, give them a felt tip pen.
- Explain that they will be asked to fill one box each minute in response to a question. This is likely to be an image but can contain text and they should try and withhold judgement about the quality of their work.
- Ensuring that you are clear about the goal they would like to work on, set a timer for one minute, ask the first question and press "start".
- After one minute, instruct them to stop, immediately ask the next question and start the timer again. Repeat until all eight boxes are filled.
- You have free rein to invent your own questions and have chance to do so in the one-minute gaps. Or you can simply ask them to come up with an idea a minute in response to a design question or problem.
- Here are some potential questions to prompt the generation of "Crazy Eights", using an example of a client wishing to improve cross-organisation working within their work system:
  - What is the first thing that comes to mind when I mention the system?
  - What does happiness look like in the system?
  - How would your grandmother view/have viewed the system?
  - If there were no divisions within the system, what would it be like?
  - A computer programme is being made to help clients navigate the system. What does the homepage look like?
  - A film is being made about the story of your system. What's on the poster?
  - The system has had a great day. What does that look like for you?
  - Money is no object and anything is possible! What does that look like in the system?

- Once the boxes have all been filled, ask them to reflect on the Crazy Eights and identify:
  - Which boxes stand out for them and why;
  - Any wider themes or insights.
- At this point you can then continue the coaching conversation, supporting the client in their development of a specific idea or approach towards achieving their goal.

When does it work best?

Crazy Eights is a very adaptable tool which may help clients who feel they overthink things and would like to develop their flexibility. It is also useful for clients who feel "stuck" for new ideas or perspectives as the rapid nature of the exercise encourages creativity and provides a choice of ways to access ideas.

Technique 12: Connecting with what is important

What is the tool?

This simple approach is the use of an object, book or piece of music of the client's choosing to help gain greater insight on what is important and meaningful for a client. The items or sounds provide a powerful reflective tool for the client, offering emotional connections and access to new insights in a way that may sometimes be difficult with words alone.

How is it used?

- Ask your client in advance to bring along an object, book or piece of music (or all three) that means something to them to your next coaching session.
- Discuss and clarify your client's goal for the session before beginning the activity.
- Give the client time to explain why they have chosen the item(s) to you in their own words.
- Use the client's share as an opportunity to ask reflective questions to encourage further insight in relation to their goal.
- If you find that this sort of exercise would be useful during a session, but you haven't had chance to prepare, you can adapt it by asking the client to find something in their bag or the room that is meaningful to them or giving them a moment to search for a piece of music on their phone.

When does it work best?

This approach works well when a client is keen to reflect on what is most important to them or to reconnect with their values and sense of self. This can be particularly helpful when clients are facing change or transition in their life or career. It may also be useful for clients who are experiencing stress, feel overwhelmed at work and would like to find new ways to connect with important themes in their lives.

Technique 13: CIA technique – Control, Influence, Accept

What is the tool?

The CIA model is a simple way of gaining perspective and commitment to act in a complex situation where a number of external strategic factors are at play. By encouraging clients to consider what is directly within their control, what falls under their influence and what is a wider issue that they may wish to influence in the future but, currently, probably simply needs to be accepted, new insight and motivation can be found. This is particularly useful where the size and complexity of the challenge has led to overwhelm and stasis.

Problem-solving can feel overwhelming, particularly when the issues concerned appear "wicked" or very "messy". This approach begins by focusing on what a client does have agency over, rather than what they do not, building up their confidence and resources for wider influence in the future.

How is it used?

- This tool works well if you use a flipchart and draw three large concentric circles, with the inner one marked "control", the next one "influence" and the outer one "accept".
- Using sticky notes, ask the client to work through and identify some of the things that they can control about the situation or problem they are facing (this might include their own attitude, behaviours or emotional responses).
- Do the same process for factors that are within their realistic sphere of influence, such as the design of new rotas.
- And, finally, do the same for factors that are causing them concern and are relevant to the context but over which they have little or no influence, and which they probably need to accept in order to address their current goal.
- Once these are mapped out, ask the client to reflect on the choices they have made and anything they feel uncomfortable about. Challenge them on assumptions and "thinking errors", where relevant.
- Continue the coaching conversation by working with the client to identify how they could make changes within the themes under their direct control and how they could influence them. Encourage them to identify a plan of action, monitor progress and report back at the next session.
- Encourage the client to keep a copy of their diagram so that they can review it at points in the future.

When does it work best?

CIA works well when clients have become frustrated or overwhelmed about the strategic context in their organisation or industry (such as national policy or consumer trends) to such an extent that they feel unable to make any change or improvement. By focusing on what is within the client's ability to control or influence, momentum and confidence can be gained so that, in the future, influence can potentially be exerted on factors that initially fell into the "accept" circle.

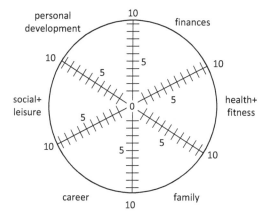

Figure 39.5 Wheel of Life

Technique 14: The Wheel of Life

What is the tool?

This Wheel of Life is a simple yet powerful tool to enable a client to look holistically at the integration of different aspects of their life and identify where they would like to make changes. By identifying the factors that are most important to them, clients engage with those areas and consider them in relation to each other and their lives as a whole. Using simple scaling, the tool can be used to establish a baseline and measure change over time, providing a useful opportunity for reflection and evaluation. See Figure 39.5.

How is it used?

- Ask the client to draw a large circle on a piece of paper and to draw lines on it to split it into a number of equal "slices" – usually between six and eight.
- The client should add a scale on each section, where zero is in the middle and 10 is on the outer rim of the circle.
- Ask the client to identify the most important and relevant factors that they would like to cover. Depending on your client's goal and area of focus, these may be obvious. If a client is looking holistically, highlight if they have made clear "omissions", such as health, work or relationships, explore the reasons for their choices to ensure the most useful and appropriate selections are made.
- Ask the client to write a factor in each section of the circle. Work through with them where they currently are in terms of satisfaction with each aspect on a scale of 0–10.
- Once this is completed, as them to reflect on the whole and to identify the areas they would like to focus in on. These may not always be the factors with the lowest scores as they may be content with a lower score in some areas of their lives, relative to others.
- Continue the coaching conversation, incorporating a solution-focused approach, where helpful, to identify where on the scale they would like to get to and how they will do it.

When does it work best?

The Wheel of Life is very helpful for clients who are finding it difficult to find balance in their lives or have a sense of being "off kilter". Often, clients who have significant responsibilities (such as caring responsibilities) or have been through a major change (such as a redundancy) may benefit from looking across different aspects of their lives in a more holistic way. By using simple scaling, clients can gain insight into where they need to focus their attention and can gain a sense of progress and impact.

Technique 15: The Story Spine

What is the tool?

The Story Spine uses a series of simple prompts to help a client develop a compelling story, building on techniques used within theatre, literature and film-making. It is a simple and versatile tool with a number of applications, including: Promoting client creativity; exploring a client's vision and developing a commitment to act; putting together personal stories for use in presentations or articles; exploring past decisions and pathways leading to the present moment.

How is it used?

- Share the basic story structure with the client:
    - Once upon a time there was …
    - Every day …
    - One day …
    - Because of that …
    - Because of that …
    - Because of that … (repeat as many times as needed);
    - Until finally …
    - And ever since that day …
- Encourage the client to experiment with completing the sentences, writing them down where possible. This will often lead to the revisiting of themes, exploration of different endings and reflection on the "because of" statements.
- Ask the client to stand back from the stories and reflect on where that leaves them with respect to their goal.

When does it work best?

The Story Spine is an adaptable tool that works well with clients who are interested in, or would benefit from, harnessing the power of storytelling. This can be very powerful for those wanting to make presentations and speeches more personal, emotionally resonant and compelling. The story spine is also an excellent way for clients to engage in a creative and insightful way with their own past, present or future "stories".

Index

Page numbers in *italics* indicate figures. Page numbers in **bold** indicate tables.